Transgression, Punishment, Responsibility, Forgiveness

Studies in Culture, Law, and the Sacred

Edited by Andrew D. Weiner and Leonard V. Kaplan

Associate Editor: Sonja H. Weiner

Graven Images 4 (1998)

Madison: University of Wisconsin Law School, 1998

Transgression, Punishment, Responsibility, Forgiveness

Table of Contents:

Theodicy's Odyssey, Ethical Labors, and the Marquard Effect

Eric Rothstein

1. The Practice of Theodicy

By the workings of Logos or by lexical luck, theodicy is *The Odyssey*'s homophone, and indeed one narrative of theodicy resembles it. Like the Odysseus who has designed and dismounted from the Trojan Horse, theodicy ventures where it might be said not to belong, God's plans, but so as to restore proper belonging. Despite or through tests of hardship, it returns from its excursion, again seeming to be a strange invader, reason entering disorder, so as now to right its own domain. Virtue for Homer is *areté*, prowess in being that which accords with one's essential nature or *telos*.[1] Such a conception locates what is good within what is ordered, for the order of the world fixes each person's proper action. Later Greek distinctions between *physis* (nature) and *nomos* (custom) do not perturb this order. Everything, then, occurs within a proper cosmic economy well betokened by literal *oikonomia*, the household laws violated by Paris and Penelope's high-living suitors. Each of Odysseus' adventures, proving his *areté*, also retestifies to the order of which the *areté* is part; and the greater the variety and peril of the adventures, the more powerful grows the testimony. When this pervasive, distributed notion of *diké*, justice, becomes the work of God, *theos*, one has a basis for theodicy. In fact, the *Odyssey*'s form provides a model for not only the labor of theodicy, understanding the moral economy, but also the history of theodicy, again and again rescuing the cosmic order when old beliefs, old rationales for evil, lose force over time. Jurisprudence, with its precedents and evolving hermeneutics, has typically had this ordering role in civil life.

Looked at in its own terms, the *Odyssey* promotes a virtue-based (or *virtù*-based) ethics. Principles about what one should do, that is, subserve principles about who one should be. In the interest of *areté*, cunning and sometimes deceit may be good. Another classical epic provides a different, more primarily duty-oriented model, the *Aeneid*. For the conceptual monism of Homer, Virgil substitutes a dualism, since Troy's fall allows a new promise of redemption, of emergence, to suffuse the exiles' world. In founding Rome, Aeneas restores nothing, unlike Odysseus. Rather, he redeems past evils—the fire and flood that doom first Troy, then Dido—by realizing a glimpsed immanence, the greater goods embodied in his prevision of Roman *imperium*, and so preexisting his creation of the new city. If the *Odyssey* might be said, theologically, to obey the order of nature, the *Aeneid* obeys something closer to a parallel order, the order of grace—both, of course, enter into theodicies. These epics differ in narrative principle and so, somewhat, in their *diké*.

Otherworldly deontics, of course, inform Christ the sacrificial God and St. Augustine's advertising the city of God. More popularly, future-oriented religions dwelt on this sort of theodicy, for one who slogged bravely through the vale of tears might hope for a harp, a halo, and a beatific vision in the hereafter. Heaven being unimaginable, both Christians and Muslims represented it as a sublation of earthly delights; Hell, vice versa. In principle, no earthly event of value needed a place in a very exact economy, for any could stand as a foretaste or trial. But early-Modern spiritual (auto)biographies did fit such events into patterns for individuals, and eventually secularized sublation in Hegel, then Marx, did so for social history. "Marx's view of history has often been depicted as a spiral movement in which the utopian end of history represents a return at a level of abundance"—cf. Virgil's triumphant, eternal imperium of Rome—"to the equality of 'primitive communism' under the conditions of scarcity that prevailed at the beginning of history"—cf. Virgil's vulnerable, circumscribed Troy, with its order (not, of course, "equality").[2] Locating evil within a theodical dialectic so as to make time the rifted site of emergences, such secularists melded the history of theodicy's practice with its labor of showing how evils produce a greater good. The idea of order resembled the *Odyssey* model, while the discontinuities and utopianism brought in that of the *Aeneid*.

Keeping in mind classical, polytheistic, and loosely-fitting models, the *Odyssey* and the *Aeneid*, has several advantages. It recalls that (1) justification occurs through narrative as well as argument; (2) for the practice of theodicy, both etymons, "God" and "justice," have their own histories and lexicographies; (3) similarly, as a practice continues, its visible forms and underlying goals may keep shifting. One can see the value of all three, for example, in considering theology in the late twentieth century. David Klemm claims that "the leading metaphor of God in contemporary theology" is "God as the breaking-in of 'otherness' to human existence." A view of "God as the Absolute, as the complete identity of thinking and being," so that "the human activity of reflexive thinking was itself the reflecting surface or mirror of the being of God," Klemm believes, dominated nineteenth-century theology. "In the twentieth century, by contrast . . . human activity is merely the place where the breaking-in of what is wholly other occurs."[3] God, that is, exists in narrative (as "breaking-in"); He is redefined. The forms of a theodicy cannot be for this God, this cosmos, what they were for Cardinal Newman or Charles Kingsley, not to mention Aquinas, William Jennings Bryan, or Billy Graham. God as Lord and paradigm meshes nicely with the Odyssey model, where the hero uses mind and muscle to restore his own lordship, and the economy of goods and evils best glorifies his *areté*. An irruptive, two-world, therefore soteriological, sense of God, with "salvation" itself a vexed notion, meshes with the model of the *Aeneid*. Although Klemm's two doxic metaphors might have baffled Homer or Virgil, their prehensile narratives can travel along those metaphors. For some uses the narratives may stand opposite each other, as in some ascetic, *contemptus mundi* doctrines. For others, they plausibly near one another: one can read the two epics as adventure tales, using the heroes' goals as pretexts, or as quests, treating (say) Aeneas's translated order as a variant of Odysseus's restored one. Trinitarians had no trouble reconciling a cosmic economy with a soteriology. When a given idea of God or justice dominates, appropriate shifts occur in what is most salient within the narrative models.

In the practical system I am proposing, what one might call the syntax of theodicy responds to the semantics of its concerns. A third linguistic level remains, that of pragmatics: under what circumstances and for what ends are theodicies put forth? One might assume a juridical end for them, judging the quality of God's justice. But more often than not, I would guess, that has not been their function, for either reason or pastoral care. (Perhaps theodical narratives—my Homeric and Virgilian types—do better for the calming and consoling of pastoral care, while lines of argument better satisfy those who are not at the moment suffering.) If one embarks on a theodicy from a state of true faith, one thereby aligns God with law. He is the ultimate criterion for adjudging culture. In such a theodicy, God enters a kind of moot court with a directed verdict of not-guilty—directed by Himself as judge—and the court tests the skill of the humans. A culture that judges God under these conditions thereby effectually judges itself, like someone who does a problem from Euclid. There is a right answer in an orderly system. The only question is whether one can arrive at it properly. To try to imagine why God permits evil is an exercise in strengthening one's faith. "Faith is both affective, involving the will," in Augustine and Aquinas, "and cognitive, involving thought"— by "thinking with assent," one can grasp "the source of all truth, the Truth itself" as a sort of "knowledge by acquaintance."[4] As to the propositional knowledge that enters into theodical argument, vain efforts to add that certainty to the certainty of faith teach one to be humble: realizing that one knows *that* apparent evil is God's good but not *how,* perhaps, makes vivid the limits of one's mind. The trials and tests of theodicy then resemble the rest of life, in which one ought to act in accord with ultimate truth, the final cause of God, whether or not one's reason can encompass the ways of the divine will. Since our theodical action is not agency— that is God's—but submission to Him, our risk is insubordination, as each of us rehearses for a real, final moment of Last Judgment.

In fact, for traditional Christian thought, the very need for theodicy is doubly an index of the Fall. Not only has Man lost the continuous *animal rationale* reason to understand God as well as his limited condition would allow, but he also has created much of the evil that he strives to reconcile with God's dispensation. Both moral and natural evils result therefrom. The common traditional notion that Adam and Eve's fall caused a fall in the natural world—lions and lambs no longer make good bedfellows, as they once did—accounts for natural evil morally, so that theodical queries about, say, earthquakes and abcesses rebound on the asker, along with those about simony and arson. The juridical question of theodicy, bringing God before a tribunal, entails a victim who has rights, a victim who legally has standing; yet humans' originary bondage deprives them of rights and standing. Humans could not, as it were, sue God for wrongs, any more than a bondsman in villeinage could sue his lord. Under feudal rule, "vassalage . . . became the model of all relations among the free, from the greatest lord in relation to the king, down to the meanest freeman." Till the mid-fourteenth century, this corporate hierarchy obtained in Western Europe; its gradual replacement by contracts, supervised by a central authority, kept the principle that the sovereign was "*legibus solutus,* or freed from anterior legal constraints."[5] Lords and the Lord became defendants only when contractual principles fully canonized accord for mutual advantage. Earlier, presumably, people's pastoral needs rarely demanded theodicies. Faith and love for God, elements of will rather than passion, led to trust in Him, while "he that doubteth is damned if he eat, for he eateth not of faith: for whatsoever is not of faith is sin" (Romans 14:23). The creation of theodicies buttresses the sustaining order as a labor of commitment, not of shoring up.

Another kind of inquiry, from a quite different time, has no pastoral force, and therefore does not take the implications of theodicy juridically. I am now performing such an inquiry. I am interrogating not God but a social phenomenon. Some of my evidence is empirical, some extrapolative (what Wittgenstein calls "knowing how to go on") and therefore requiring that I derive and follow theodical logic. For me as for St. Augustine, though with different premises, theodicy proves and threatens nothing. For it to do either, depending on its motive and scope, would mark a prior social instability. That fact affects the force of what everyone knows, that "the problem of the origins of evil and suffering ('theodicy') and the explanation of its distribution in the world, and the modes of coping with it, have . . . produced diverse (and even incompatible) answers and institutionalized religious responses."[6] The motives for it, and therefore its energies within human lives, similarly differ. As an obvious example, the "deontic" theodical pattern of the *Aeneid,* where laws of pious duty come from above, shifted like secular duties from the Lord's command to a trust-based commitment, sometimes contractual, sometimes not. "The constant and uniform practice of virtue . . . becomes our duty," wrote a professor of divinity in 1744, "when revelation has informed us that God will make us finally happy for it in a life after this."[7]

How then does one talk about theodicy as an "it"? What counts as fact for theodicy is largely speculative; the sacred is seen through a glass darkly—whether the glass is window or mirror; the criteria informing law and culture are contestable; and the scope and ends of theodicy vary sharply. What one has is not an entity but a practice. We can say about it what Wittgenstein said about punishment, the social practice that mirrors the justification of God, deflecting blame from Him, imitating His lawful order, and accepting His imputed right to punish us sinners all:

> "Why do we punish criminals? Is it from a desire for revenge? Is it in order to prevent a repetition of the crime?" And so on. The truth is that there is no one reason. There is the institution of punishing criminals. Different people support this for different reasons, and for different reasons in different cases and at different times. Some people support it out of a desire for revenge, some perhaps out of a desire for justice, some out of a wish to prevent a repetition of the crime, and so on. And so punishments are carried out.[8]

"Different principles (each of which may in a sense be called a 'justification')," H. L. A. Hart remarks, "are relevant at different points in any morally acceptable account of punishment."[9] The same comment applies to the vectors of law, culture, and the sacred that converge in theodicy. Where belief is homogeneous, one cannot see that easily. But the failure of homogeneity that the juridical practice of theodicy (not the Augustinian practice or mine) marks—that failure does make the Wittgensteinian analysis stand out. The more unreliable the evidence seems, I think, the more undeniable such an analysis becomes.

A practice is an available vehicle within which members of a coalition can move. It has the sort of costs and conveniences, and often the sort of odd, repeated circuits, that one associates with other common carriers. It also has its own economy. In giving his examples, Wittgenstein does not exhaust the range of them. For instance, one needs a reason beyond those he offers—revenge, justice, prevention—to explain the ubiquitous image of "paying one's debt to society," since society (as taxpayers) foots the bill for jails, jailers, and jailings. Nietzsche had once declared a historical reason: rules of "buying, selling, barter, trade and traffic" provided that a *Schuld* (both "debt" and "guilt" in German) be repaid, value for value, pain endured for pain inflicted.[10] Can that, in Wittgenstein's or our modern society, still hold? As the various examples suggest, the logics within the practice of punishment, like those within the practice of metaphysical justification—that is, of theodicy—keep returning us to their historical situatedness if we want to know "how to go on." This is no country for Platonists. A practice exists only through people's institutional doings.

As a continuous formation without Form, a practice exemplifies what Mary Douglas calls an "institution." Socially legitimated, it coordinates behavior; it naturalizes a common cognitive style; and it over time preserves what it codifies and contextualizes as information.[11] We get along by making its corridors, library, and shared spaces into easy routine—how the "we" thinks that counts as We. Ipso facto a practice has a history. If the practitioners have mostly moved from an Augustinian kind of theodicy to a juridical kind to the kind I am practicing, what has happened to the common carrier? what has happened to the common questions? what has happened to the singleness, as perceived, of the carrier? One wonders, knowing that theodicy survives although, as the theologian Hans Schwarz admits in surveying its history, "the justification of God in the face of evil, must always remain incomplete and questionable."[12]

Precisely because theodicy does have a history and does track sociopolitical change, I propose that one can use it to understand the import and history of ethics quite generally. The argument is at least plausible enough to investigate. Theodicy potentially puts so much at stake: the real battle of theodicy endangers the sacred above us, the culture around us, and the law that in some traditions the sacred lowers to earth and in other traditions the culture erects to the skies. To take juridically what the trials of theodicy imply is to invoke law, culture, and the sacred in their Ur-forms, their hyperbolic forms. The sacred appears in its highest manifestation, God. The law appears in its farthest self-assertion, as an umpire that claims to take and adjudicate God's measure. And the culture appears in its most extreme ethical moment, where any risk is warranted. In theodicy, to save itself from meaninglessness, the culture courts pride and despair. These are the sins that traditionally hoodwink one from salvation. Pride and despair: enough chutzpah or frenzy to put God in the dock may well be an irremediable flaw of moral temperament. This is true whether or not God exists, since He does effectively exist for people who take the implications of the trials of theodicy juridically. One might argue then that taken juridically, theodical "trials," in the plural, potentially challenge the legitimacy of each of the three, law, culture, and the sacred, as we know it. Lawlessness, disintegration, and evil seem to loom if the challenge succeeds—these are the values or anti-values allotted to God's enemy the Devil.

Law, in some form, is indispensable in theodicies. Though justice, like other claims of value, may at last elude definition, theodicy has to talk, to justify, to establish expectations; and acts toward public consensus are acts of law. Because justice and law converge in God, it makes sense that "diabolic" comes from the Greek *diabolos,* a slanderer or accuser in a law court: the devil lurks within divine trials. The Devil certainly lurks slanderously, accusingly, within the most famous theodicy in English, *Paradise Lost*. A crisis in all three, religion, law, and politics, encouraged Milton to "justify the ways of God to men" (*PL* 1:26), that is, to reinstate the bond between *diké,* justice, and *theos,* God, as against *realpolitik*. Theodicy as a cognitive process may then provide a form of understanding the congruence of the True and the Good. But the history that partly prompted Milton reminds one that pastorally theodicy may also provide a court for the trial of God, whose administration allows so much evil in the world. Thus Alexander Pope's adaptation of Milton's "justify the ways of God to men," a couple of generations later, drops "justify" for the verb "vindicate": *vindiciae* are legal proofs, part of a rejoinder in law. Pope's rejoinder in fact mingles proofs with attacks on the jury's competence, rebuking our arrogance in assuming jurisdiction. Given the dangers of theodicy, that legal strategy makes sense. Here negotiation may occur, since in this battle a defeat for either side, God or Man, carries great dangers for both: neither cares to do without the other. One would expect to find great eagerness for not going to trial before out-of-court agreements, stipulations, and working out of liabilities, reduce embarrassing vulnerability.

Keeping in mind this practical notion of theodicy, I shall in the next section explore the German philosopher Odo Marquard's treatment of theodicy as a practice, at least of its economic, *Odyssey* form, in shifting, historical terms. Marquard develops his argument from the most famous early-Modern exponent of theodicy, the pious rationalist G. W. Leibniz. While Leibniz's theodical use of law and reason fell short, law and reason seemed to adhere to the rising disciplines of philosophical ethics for moral evil and of natural science for natural evil—at least for ethics, Marquard intriguingly complicates this new pledge of allegiance. The third and last section of the paper, accordingly, tests a Marquardian, practice-based understanding of theodicy in brief discussions of the work of two impious skeptics, one from Leibniz's time and the other from our own. These are David Hume, born 1711, the year after Leibniz published his *Theodicy*; and Jacques Derrida (1930-). Neither of them wrote theodicy, having no *theos* whose *diké* to defend, but for that reason Hume and Derrida show how gauzy is the boundary parting the practice of theodicy from its borderers. Through their thought stalk the orders of nature and grace, but in mufti.

2. The Marquard Hypothesis: Juridical Theodicy after Leibniz

An aged Danish clergyman allegedly "declared that he could not believe that God had created the eighteenth century."[13] But in two articles of the 1980s Odo Marquard cast that same century as sacrificing itself, in an odd kind of *imitatio Christi*, to save God. Marquard's scenario underlies a set of historical proposals about theodicy's route and economy. His earlier article stems from a lecture of his at Wolfenbüttel, where Leibniz was once librarian— Leibniz, who invented the term "theodicy" to title a vernacular book (in French, *Essais de Théodicée*) of 1710, showing the conformity of faith with reason and incorporating essays on God's goodness, human freedom, and the origins of evil.[14] Here Leibniz famously argued that "this universe," the one we inhabit, "must indeed be better than" any "other possible universe" (378). Leibnizian logic, which within its own precincts was as universal, as absolute, and as timeless as God Himself, arrived at these indefeasible truths. "Nothing," he wrote, "can be opposed to the rule of the best, which suffers neither exception nor dispensation. It is in this sense that God permits sin: for he would fail in what he owes to himself . . . if he chose not that which is absolutely the best, notwithstanding the evil of guilt, which is involved therein by the supreme necessity of the eternal verities" (138). Trained as a lawyer, Leibniz seizes on quasi-contractual rights, what God "owes to himself," as bearing the power of entailment. As party to a contract with himself, God regulates His behavior with suitable prudence. Only because He foreknows consequences can He allow evil to achieve good. Humans, by contrast, can never be sure that a given evil, committed or permitted, will produce greater good (Leibniz, *Theodicy* 378, 138). What counts as sound practice for God would risk criminal negligence for His creatures.

Marquard, unLeibnizian, professes no certainties. "The philosopher is not the expert," he explains, "but the expert's stunt man: his double in dangerous situations" (*FMP* 38). He then acrobaticizes his way through an argument in which Leibniz's theodicy and some of its supposed consequences are his apparatus. Marquard does not pretend to anything like a full, fair exposition, but instead a heuristic demonstration. In this heuristic interest I shall follow his lead, conflating his two articles, skipping some of their contentions, and supporting them with some of my own. Roughly, the argument he makes leads to an account like this: Leibniz's theodicy failed, not as a logical but as a social answer to the problems that the practice of theodicy needed to solve by the early eighteenth century. People removed the danger to God, hence to their own Christianity, by kicking Him upstairs. One might interpolate, thinking of the two axial narrative models with which I began, that Leibniz's failure to make the *Odyssey* model work well meant that people had to take the problem of order on themselves, for fear of danger to the faith-based, trust-based *Aeneid* model. Focusing on scientific reasons for natural evil and on human causes for moral evil, they relieved God of responsibility for evil in this world. With that maneuver, however, they left themselves, human beings, not only open to indictment for moral evil but indictable without the escape route of pardon through divine grace. They resolved these new dangers through modern ethics, with ever more ingenious redefinitions of transgression and deferrals of blame. This pattern of theodical secularization and historical restructuring I shall call "the Marquard Effect."

Leibniz's theodicy, Marquard says, "converts philosophy into a legal action," with Man prosecuting "the absolute defendant," God, for the world's evils. God's counsel, Leibniz, counters that this is the best of all possible worlds—or, more clearly, that any other possible world would be worse. Optimizing does not explain evils away. Rather it asserts, as Marquard puts it, that "the optimal, as end, justifies evils as the condition of its possibility." But such a justification, in which a foreknown end justifies the means, raises more doubts about divine morality than it solves. It produces a businessman or a Benthamite *deus economicus* who calculates the gross cost-benefit utility of pains and blessings—or, Marquard suggests, a God "like the politician in the 'art of the possible'" (*FMP* 46). The unfortunate commercial and *realpolitisch* models, one would suppose, might occur to many early eighteenth-century readers, given the development of commerce and the relatively new dominance, at that time, of *realpolitik* in political theory. These models contaminate what were in an earlier era forceful arguments.

The difficulty of Leibniz's argument, in Marquardian terms, is double. For pastoral reasons, theodicy assures the flock that the world makes sense. For metapolitical reasons, theodicy assures a world citizenry that the sovereign, God, is in some form accountable. Each of these demands for reasons, the metapolitical and the pastoral, in fact implicates the other. An "art of the possible" God speaks to both kinds of reasons, but too poorly. First, because such calculations or triage cannot accommodate the personal experience of anguish, Leibniz's theodicy speaks poorly to the specific pastoral situation one would imagine theodicy designed for, to strengthen the believer whose pain seems to belie belief. The pastoral problem, individual pain, plainly has metapolitical force: the cancer patient denies God's accountability to her. In the eighteenth century, grimly notorious for "the rise of sensibility," divine indifference or whim stood out here; at that stake Samuel Johnson burned Soame Jenyns, and Voltaire, Leibniz himself. Second, as Marquard remarks, Leibniz never answers adequately another crucial question of accountability, though he himself raises it: "If the best possible creation inevitably includes evils, why did God not refrain from creating it?" We then have a moral impasse over the problem of why there is something rather than nothing, and we have no way of showing that the something we inhabit is better than nothing. (At least we do not in accord with the *Odyssey* model; the *Aeneid* model answers that we probationers should welcome temporary pain if we can ascend through it to lasting joy.) Leibniz resorts to an *ex hypothesi* argument—that is, the fact of God's choosing to create this cosmos. If the implications of theodicy are to be taken juridically, however, any *ex hypothesi* argument begs the question and again fails as a means of pastoral conviction or consolation.

"You may think," the philosopher Alvin Plantinga says, "that if an omnipotent and omniscient being is able to eliminate each of two evils, it follows that he can eliminate them both"—this is, of course, what Leibniz denied for the best of all possible worlds. "Perhaps this is so," Plantinga goes on, "but it is not strictly to the point" in logic.[15] Maybe not, but for wavering worshipers, there is no other point. Whatever there is, God has done; and if things are going to be like this—war, famine, plague, and death—why has He done them at all? This question has exercised theodicists till the present. Complicating it is a widespread modern ethical assumption that true justice is contractual, serving contractors' mutual advantage. Leibniz's domain, law, now draws legitimacy from such a model, with representative government its guarantor. How else, save by contractarian, republican assumptions, to explain the "process theologian" Lewis Ford's inane, desperate, and yet fated assurance that God has created free creatures in far from the best world so as not to be "deprived of the one thing the world can provide which God alone cannot have: a genuine social existence."[16] Poor little rich boy God, the would-be Upstairs Buddy, flattening His divine nose wistfully against some pane while longing for playmates, fellow frat members, ping-pong partners—*liberté, fraternité, à-peu-près égalité*! Lucky humans, whose anguish He compensates heart to heart and *tête-à-tête,* watching the red, black, white, and pale apocalyptic horses clop along like so many bobbing Dobbins on a carousel! If this Lord of the clubhouse is God, then let us replace Him with humans. Precisely that, Marquard argues, has largely happened.

In the face of doubts about the *ethos,* the character, of the divine defendant, Marquard thinks, the best possible defense was to deny that the accused was in fact responsible. This is part of what I earlier called an out-of-court agreement, for no one actually says it, at least in its final form. Yet everyone knows that the fact of actually putting God on trial, separating Him *in posse* from the law, predicts a failure to exculpate Him. He needs to cop a plea. The trial of Charles I in 1649, about the time of Leibniz's birth, confirmed what even some of the King's propagandists agreed, that "the royal will," derived from God and answerable to Him alone in traditional thought, was subject to the law of the land.[17] Still more drastic than trying God's earthly viceroy would be an actual theodical trial, where law could be set against God Himself, hence, by presupposition, perhaps above Him. In trial, God might fall short, which is metapolitically unacceptable. In trial, the universe understood as law might make complete sense without Him, which is pastorally unacceptable. Hence, something out of court was needed. The "it" of theodicy then might be not the trial, with out-of-court maneuvers as context, but the whole practical apparatus of institutional law. Theodicy might spread and split, with settlements, *nolle prosequi* agreements, and the like.

Let me flesh out Marquard here. The actual line of argument for a non-blameworthy God, of course, follows from Leibniz's plea of diminished responsibility, that God acted under specifiable constraints. Thus "there is every reason to conclude unquestionably," Leibniz writes, "that reasons most just, and stronger than those which appear contrary to them, have compelled the All-Wise to permit the evil, and even to do things which have facilitated it" (93). The historian of science Alexandre Koyré quotes Leibniz's foe in Newtonian controversy, Samuel Clarke, as having puzzled why Leibniz strives "to exclude God's actual Government of the World," so that physical "Things do only what they would do of themselves of mere Mechanism." Unlike moral law, physical law cannot rebuke God. It does, however, take over for Him and from Him. Koyré suggests that had Leibniz not died in mid-controversy, he "could have answered that it was the only means to avoid making God responsible for the actual management, or mismanagement, of this our world. God just did not do what He wanted, or would like to do."[18] In fact the progress of Newtonian science, Koyré points out, kept proving Leibniz's non-interventionism right. "The mighty, energetic God of Newton who actually 'ran' the universe . . . became, in quick succession, a conservative power, an *intelligentia supra-mundana,* a '*Dieu fainéant*'" (276). As in the physical order, so in the moral order. But in the moral order, what Clarke called "mere Mechanism" would not suffice. No one made much headway in discovering a Newtonian system of right.

Therefore, Marquard postulates, post-Leibnizians took a new tack in constraining God and expanding human free will, traditionally the source of moral evil. Seeing in Leibniz's brief for God the weakness of the defense case, post-Leibnizians reassigned creation from God to Man, Man the Fichtean and Hegelian creator of history, Man the Kantian creator of the exact sciences and moral norms. "The autonomy [of Man] thesis, beginning with transcendentally revolutionary idealism[,] was made necessary by theodicy, as a way of unburdening God by relieving him of his duties as the Creator god, whose successor (with the job of unburdening God) is man the autonomous creator" (*DA* 15). Earlier yet, Marquard asserts, the mid-to-later eighteenth century saw "the rapid rise of new philosophical disciplines" that "insist on something about man that the traditional, long-established philosophies were incapable, or were no longer sufficiently capable, of affirming" (*FMP* 39). Redefined Man then, as defense counsel and as the figure in the dock of justice, redeems God. Redefined Marquardian Man, I have suggested, invents his own form of every Christian's duty, the imitation of Christ. In the first century, Christ suffered to cleanse Man of original sin, and in the post-Leibnizian eighteenth, Man purges the debt by returning the favor. He puts himself in harm's way to cleanse God of a sin even more originary than the Fall. Eventually, God becomes so innocent, so purified, so to speak, that He becomes translucent, then transparent, and then not really there at all—and *de mortuis nil nisi bonum.* For Hegel at the start of the nineteenth century, the death of God was a melancholy delusion: "The Unhappy

Consciousness . . . is . . . the tragic fate of the certainty of self . . . the grief which expresses itself in the hard saying that 'God is dead.'"[19] For Nietzsche at the century's end, we require God's death to escape delusion.

Neither peace nor apocalypse follows Man's redemptive act, however; just legal maneuvers. Whereas Christ actually atoned, Man only makes himself indictable. This is, I should add, just as one would expect from the development of trial law. In England, at any rate, a discipline of jurisprudential literature was barely hatching "in the closing decades of the sixteenth century."[20] During the late seventeenth and early eighteenth centuries, the rules of evidence were codified and petits juries were finally barred from using personal knowledge of a defendant (that is, her or his *ethos*) in coming to their verdicts. Evidentiary practice was moving away from something like diagnosis by biopsy, a fragment-to-whole relationship, with human law resembling physical laws—that is, an investigation into the fixed character of something. It was instead becoming a determination of fact as to a given historical event. Man might have the *ethos* that the doctrine of Original Sin ascribed to him and yet be found not guilty of the specific charges in the bill against him. Whereas the system of trial and judgment in first-century Judea did not give Christ much hope, and whereas throughout the Christian era God's actions necessarily expressed His *ethos,* Man took advantage of a new, act-centered legal dispensation. And not only that. After all, once the sacred has been redefined by law, and law by history—that is, the temporal expression of culture, why not history by the sacred? Specifically, rather than convict Man at the new tribunal, how about desacralizing evil? Evil shrinks to bad and maybe not even that. One should remember that any theodicy effectually shifts evils into the realm of the legitimate, God's order, and even makes them necessary. What makes them tolerable though vile in one system may easily make them tolerated in another.

We now can rejoin Marquard's argument as the Marquard Effect develops, supplementing and shifting the inherited model in society as a whole. (Like Marquard, I am of course allowing, under warning, the reductive fiction that one can think about "society as a whole.") In society as a whole, "gnoseological evil is rendered no longer evil. Curiosity, which had been a vice, becomes the central scientific virtue; and error, above all, ceases to be evil" (*DA* 18). In aesthetics, we find "the aesthetics of the unbeautiful—the sublime, the ugly, the Dionysian, the abstract, [and] the negative" (*DA* 19) competing well with the aesthetics of the beautiful. We also find *aesthesis*, hitherto an inferior and bodily quality, becoming worthy of the highest respect, as artistic genius. Moral evil, whether through the principle that the Fall produced human freedom and autonomy or through more Nietzschean revaluations, loses its cosmic malignity. Illness becomes medical rather than moral. Finitude and mutability become the essence of human authenticity. English literature registers every one of these trajectories—changes in the True, the Beautiful, and the Good—in the understanding, or progressive misunderstanding, of the theodical *Paradise Lost* between the time it was published in 1667 and the early-to-mid nineteenth century. Milton dignifies action through giving it juridical weight, a dignity that grows more as jurisprudence looks less at *ethos* and more at action. How can human actors retain the dignity while shucking indictability? Through Marquard's alternative categories for action, whether "gnoseological," aesthetic, moral, or expressive (i.e., "authentic")—and these categories of value, cut free from Milton's theocentric system, then became lenses for understanding Milton's poem. Marquardian Man, cloaked as the responsible God but trying to evade the less agreeable consequences, smacks of Milton's Satan, who boasted some seamy herohood by the late eighteenth century.

I do not take Marquard to claim that we have stopped blaming transgressions and transgressors. In fact today we censure faults never known as faults to past generations, when the relevant groups accepted clitoridectomy, cruelty to animals, water pollution, eating boycotted fruit, or smoking cheroots by the fistful. Bad acts have always been human responsibility, appearing as sin (metaphysical), disorder, or violations of social contract—they need have no place in theodicy. Theodicies asked if God was responsible as a prior accessory, in that He allowed these particulars to occur. Their incidence in the economy of the world thus had legitimacy, though the acts themselves were illicit. The problems of legitimation are those where Marquard's thesis applies. As large dispositional categories—"gnoseological," aesthetic, moral, or expressive—lose their onus, justifying the economy of the world gets easier or merely less urgent. Again, so as to avoid homogenizing "society," I underscore that the Marquard Effect translates theodical arguments, what reasoners maintained, into post-theodical dispositions, what people more generally tend to do, say, or think as they square their perceived needs with their notions.

Transvaluations of value, Marquard notes, do not labor alone to exculpate Man. One can palliate evil by noting the compensations it makes possible. We humans do with evils what God did with the Fall, according to the old theological doctrine of *felix culpa*. Thus in Mandeville "private vices" (*malum*) produce "public benefits" (*bonum*-through-*malum*); in Kant's *Critique of Judgment*, "this very figure is promoted to the key figure in the thesis of the esthetic of the sublime: granted—*malum*—our senses fail us, but—*bonum*-through-*malum*—it is precisely through this failure that reason demonstrates its power." "An indirect surrogate optimism," Marquard says, takes over from Leibniz's global optimism by mobilizing "many intermediate and small consolations" (*FMP* 44-5). The evils behind these "consolations," I would add, do not impeach any figure who authorizes the evils. There is no equivalent to the merchant God or *realpolitischer* God that Leibniz requires. "In the twentieth century," Marquard goes on, a "sharpened idea of compensation, according to which evils are indirect goods and imperfections are opportunities, becomes (after its late passage through psychoanalysis, in Adler and Jung) a fundamental anthropological category" (*DA* 22). Alfred North Whitehead beamingly confides as to God and World that "individual self-attainment" blossoms with a "sense of worth beyond itself": "It is in this way that the immediacy of sorrow and pain is transformed into an element of triumph. This is the notion of redemption through suffering which haunts the world."[21] With both self and society, human lacks drive us toward culture, just as human lacks—here anglophones might think of Hobbes and Locke—drive us toward law. Have we kidnapped God, nature, and tradition, to stow them in some Bastille? Doing so, says Marquard, has let us substitute such enchantments as art, landscape and ecological consciousness, museums, and the "human sciences" (*DA* 23).

Finally, where these methods of redeeming evil fail, we can escape into unindictability, as Marquard puts it. Here one does encounter ways that help specific transgressors escape yesteryear's noose and knout. The rise of an aesthetics of taste comes because *chacun à son goût, de gustibus non est disputandum*—taste protects us from the need to justify ourselves. Various sorts of illness, like insanity, protect us from the need to justify ourselves. So does the apotheosis of fundamental human rights and of individuality: "precisely man's metamorphosis into the absolute defendant," Marquard concludes, "necessarily leads to the attempt to define and guarantee borders within which man is never a defendant" (*FMP* 53). His words may pique us Americans, who as it happens specialize in the politics of guaranteed borders. In a recent book, the neocon neolib Senator "Pat" Moynihan blames the political left for "defining deviancy down," as by teaching his putative arch-conformists, young women, that single motherhood is an acceptable "life-style choice," not "deviant," hence unindictable: no Hester Prynnes here! Yet the word "deviancy" itself defines the conduct down, because social rather than individual borders—"deviancy," not "sin"—bar "deviant" group members from being ethical defendants.[22]

Social finger-pointing reminds us that if all else fails, "deviants" can at last throw themselves on the mercy of the court as helpless addicts to ideology. More likely, one can throw one's "deviant" client on the court's mercy: only the truly abject use that ploy in exculpating themselves—even bad karma enjoys more prestige—although the engineers of ideology, pundits and academics, faithfully trust that it rules the gaping hoi polloi. Behind "ideology," one can find eighteenth-century screeds, prominently Rousseau's, that invented "society" to entify as an artifact what the natural, the individual, stands over against. To remedial advantage, a reified "society" allowed individuals to attack many moral evils like natural evils, as something outside them.[23] To exculpatory advantage, by the late eighteenth century, "society" was allotted the domestic role that nation-states had abroad: it played the imperialist, colonializing its subjects. Simultaneously with Marxist theories of ideology, then, nineteenth-century historicists came up with their own theories of the culturally dominated self. The *haut-en-bas* sociology of Durkheim epitomized them ca. 1900—it is from Durkheim, Moynihan says, that his holistic use of "deviancy" comes. By the second half of our century, Marx and Durkheim had converged in brave new parlance about interpellation, the death of the author, the end of man, and what comes after the subject. Autonomous people appeared to be going the way of God, out. But as I have suggested, while the oblivious human herd wound down to retirement, freed from moral blame because of their social enslavement, the quanta of moral blame shifted, not diminished. Society and history created villainy without villains—Michel Foucault, Marx's and Durkheim's finest heir, envisioned every Albert, Bice, and Claude as a sample of social manufacture, and yet shook his fist at the iniquity of (equally manufactured) medicine, law, and learning. The Marquard Effect, I think, helps explain such apparent paradoxes of indictment and unindictability. It may also explain why Foucault's brilliant assortment of facts, factoids, and forensics has thrilled so many earnest, muddled acolytes.

To treat moral evils like natural evils, of course, reverses an earlier theological practice of treating natural evils like moral ones, caused by the Fall of Man, which brought woe to God's sound natural world. Science encourages the reversal, as Kant saw when he posed an antinomy between the scientific world of phenomena, in which people's behavior was causally determined, and a moral, noumenal world of freedom. "The scientific mode of explanation," Steven Pinker says, "cannot accommodate the mysterious notion of uncaused causation that underlies the will." A scientist's only alternative to the caused event is the random event, which "does not fit the concept of free will any more than a lawful one does."[24] "Society" has the argumentative advantage of being open to science as a human structure, something we can surely know because we made it, and yet also of being random with respect to individuals, thrown by luck into a social world they neither made nor chose. From this mixture of cause, randomness, and moral value, a curious "asymmetrical freedom," as Susan Wolf calls it, opens up, reinforcing the possibilities of the Marquard Effect. Wolf argues that to be morally responsible, persons must be moral agents in control of their own actions, but that in fact we raise this principle only in cases of blame. When we might blame, we ask if the person could have done otherwise, but not when we praise: "'I cannot tell a lie,' 'He couldn't hurt a fly' are not exemptions from praiseworthiness but testimonies to it. . . . The metaphysical conditions required for an agent's responsibility will vary according to the value of the action he performs."[25] What one has is the secular analogue, again, of a theological notion, that somebody determined by *caritas* is free, while somebody determined by *cupiditas* is enslaved by the passions. The theological notion, however, does not exculpate anyone, while modern ethical judgment may do so for the person whose childhood was deprived, who suffers "neurotic" obsessions, or who can plead the malign influence of, say, violent pornography. How can we additionally crush with the gavel of the law a "socially crippled" person?

For Marquard, then, three guiding rules sprout from the theodicy that justifies God by displacing responsibility from Him to His creature Man. The first declares good what had been thought bad; the second declares that bad things give rise to good ones; and the third defers responsibility to some more nebulous or protected agency. Why, Marquard asks, do these results occur when they do, in what he thinks of as the early-Modern age? He offers a pair of related reasons. "The modern age is the age of distance," he says, "the first epoch in which impotence and suffering are not the taken-for-granted and normal state of affairs for human beings" (*DA* 12). How, one may additionally ask, did it get that way? Did the change result from successful human action to dispel natural evils that theodicists claimed that omnipotent God could not properly banish?—seawalls and penicillin seemed optional in the zero-sum game, zero-sum at best, that the Creator allegedly created. Evils that omnipotent God allows cannot easily be disavowed: they must be converted into goods that bear the transfigured stain of their previous evil state. To secularize natural evils, like floods and fevers, let them be read as absolute evils, best eliminated. Of "the 'three arrows of God'— war, famine, and pestilence," famine and pestilence (the Plague) disappeared from England by 1700 and on the continent during the following decades, for largely administrative reasons, such as crop diversification, market changes, and quarantine.[26] As to the third "arrow," war, Luther's sixteenth-century God, Marquard thinks, wielded His fierce omnipotence so unaccountably that redemption through Him seemed to demand an avoidable evil, human blood shed in civil wars, religious wars. Again, secular political theory—*realpolitik,* for instance—either unfeathered this "arrow" or called the archers to account. The benefits of disavowal, exhibited once people took natural evils as remediable instead of as deserved in our post-lapsarian impiety, might elicit a Marquardian revaluation of social evils. On this hypothesis, people might naturally scant God's redemptive, eschatological services as to this world, to the degree that human effort can improve a vale of tears. The very necessity for life's being tearful progressively earned the (Scots) verdict of "not proven." In a contractual society, as the cost of redemption rises and its felt utility drops, the possible indictment of God grows easier to frame.

Marquard's line of reasoning leads him to what he calls a strange thesis, that "Where there is theodicy, there is modernity, and where there is modernity, there is theodicy" (*DA* 13). In earlier, premodern times and also for many people nowadays, "theodicy's question was always blunted . . . by an intact religion" (*DA* 11). By this, he may mean what I proposed earlier, that no one took theodicy juridically, because by definition an intact religion means God is nonconvictable. Theodicy has no sense for the Mauritian woman who in 1997 explained to an interviewer, "God created me to be a slave, just as he created a camel to be a camel."[27] Or perhaps Marquard means that where divine grace could deflect the need for human justification, people did not think in terms of absolute metaphysical indictments. Neither intact religion nor divine grace governs most Western motives today, though everywhere in the world, the West included, one can still find millions who can or could never fathom why not. Most of us nowadays, as modernity trails on or winds down, Marquard thinks, just continue theodicy by other means, in disguise. When our eighteenth-century ancestors assigned autonomy to themselves, then, they impaneled capital-M Man as a perpetual grand jury, weighing everyone—including the nervously fidgety jurors themselves—in terms of probable cause. And where law reigns in perpetuo, its very density will aid those who pry at it in safety and bore slicked loopholes.

The Marquard Effect neatly exemplifies Mary Douglas's process of institutional change: "First the people are tempted out of their niches by new possibilities of exercising or evading control. Then they make new kinds of institutions, and the institutions make new labels, and the label makes new kinds of people" (Douglas 108). Like other practices, Marquardian theodicy secures "the social edifice by sacralizing [its new] principles of justice," making them explicit, emotion-charged, and dangerous to challenge (Douglas 112-3). In Marquard's brief lectures, though, the historical account of "niches" and "new" is so drastically inadequate as to make one wish it had suppressed causation completely. The rhetorical demands of his articles push him toward the language of cause-and-effect, unfortunately, instead of the language of compatibility. Douglas shrewdly insists, "any institution that is going to keep its shape needs to gain legitimacy by distinctive grounding in nature and reason," for both self-justification and affording its members good heuristic analogies (112). Since the social artifacts "nature" and "reason" pretend to supra-social generality, one would expect that as they glacially and variably change, many institutions would do so too, reinforcing each other's ability to justify themselves and afford heuristic analogies. Theodicy is obviously embedded with other practices, and never more so than when taken juridically. In keeping with other practices, its trajectory depends on its capacity to convert phenomena it finds into its own strengthening and propulsive materials.

Despite its considerable appeal, of course, Marquard's argument remains a heuristic sketch of a practice-based account. Furthermore, he courteously overweights Leibniz to respect his lecture site, Wolfenbüttel. Behind his narrative the emplotment reminds one of a tragedy or passion play with *peripateia* and *anagnorisis*, *hubris* and cathartic sacrifice, a noble, failed foray by the hero Gottfried to keep the Lord from burial in a *Gottfriedhof*, and a single storyline. The great diversity of contemporary societies appears en masse, a madding crowd of extras. Then too, this eventful, finely balanced tale incorporates a threshold, a rupture. Yet in fact by 1710, theodicy and theology were astagger: "all Christian denominations were, by the end of the seventeenth century, coming under attack for their doctrine," says Jaroslav Pelikan, documenting "The Crisis of Orthodoxy East and West."[28] One might say, then, that the moment juridical theodicy appears, it disappears, or even that it appears because its conditions of possibility have so steadily been disappearing. Leibniz could hardly have mattered even if he had not partnered the trends he most abhorred.

He danced, unwittingly I suppose, into contretemps. On the one hand, what else but universal principles of logic would do once schism had laid low the authority of churches and traditions, and at the same time God had become a figure of will rather than fathomable reason, according to nominalists and many Protestant groups?[29] On the other hand, God's engineering triumph, sufficient in Leibniz's logic to secure His dispensation, also renders Him superfluous. "Throughout the Middle Ages," Amos Funkenstein remarks, "the distinction between absolute and lawlike necessities was carried on with an emphasis on the contingency of our world. . . . Even those thinkers who stressed the perfection and order of our world believed that the choice of God to actualize *this* order was unaccountable and arbitrary." By Leibniz's time, "from the source of all contingency that he was in the Middle Ages, God became the guarantee of the absolute rationality of the world."[30] God consequently retires not only from Leibniz's failure at "Why is there something rather than nothing?" but also from Leibniz's success at making the world of Deist dreams, cleaving in all its aspects to a principle of sufficient reason.

Samuel Clarke's bemusement about Leibniz's "exclud[ing] God's actual Government of the World" would only have grown, had Leibniz published more philosophical books than the *Theodicy* in his lifetime. One hardly needs a continuing God if "all is regulated in things, once for all, with as much order and harmony as is possible, supreme wisdom and goodness not being able to act except with perfect harmony." The problem is simple: if God has a reason to intervene in this world, one asks why He did not foresee and forestall the necessity that the reason embodies—is He not omnipotent and omniscient? Yet if He never intervenes, "the present is big with the future, the future might be read in the past, the distant is expressed in the near."[31] Not eternity but time has what time requires. When Marquardian God was kicked upstairs, Leibniz's foot was in on the kicking, as it were, through his high-efficiency knee-jerk reflex. No rupture, no reversal occurs, however, given that Leibniz's arguments follow and perfect familiar theodical arguments he inherited. If Leibniz failed, so did everyone who succeeded before him. What was it then that drove his procedure into cross-purposes and fed heresy (he might have thought) on what he said and what he did not say?

In this context, two other issues need to be revisited. Both connect, in ways surprising to a late twentieth-century audience (and maybe also to Marquard), with the growth of Leibnizian practices, probability, and contract law. The first issue is the spiritual virtue of love. Inexplicable God, wanton God, could during much of history be loved by most people, perhaps, who defined themselves by their caste. He too had His caste prerogatives. The word "love" should not founder in anachronism here, as some sublime variant of intense romantic attraction. That would grant too much to the passions and too little to the will. "Love" here means an intense, "natural" fealty, a sublime variant of vassal to liege, *Knecht* to *Herr*, a disinterested, even self-sacrificial benevolent commitment. But is a socially mobile population, based progressively less in implicit, originary rights, and more in explicit, contractual rights, likely to naturalize such origin-dependent fealty? Would that "natural" fealty not dwindle? Consider us today. What was once barnacle-like, sessile, has become as tenacious and fickle as a woodtick in attachment to "celebrities." Just as with facts an ideal of "wisdom" gave way to "knowledge," and "knowledge" to "information," so with people's status: Weberian legitimation glides from tradition to the legal-rational to charisma. Whether a public bewails the passing of a rock singer crowned as King (died 1977) or a paparazzi-racked Princess of Wales (died 1997), from a "natural" ontology as fixed as the Ptolomaic stars we keep expanding to a stardom forever, willfully, on the move.

So, presumably, with love for God. Annette Baier points out that "particularly in the modern period" ethical theorists largely "relegate to the mental background the web of trust tying most moral agents to one another," while they focus on "cases of co-membership in a kingdom of ends."[32] She ascribes this bias to the outlook of men engaged in public life or business, those areas of contract for mutual advantage, rather than in "unequal, nonvoluntary, and non-contract-based relationships" such as family life and dependency, which historically have defined women's lives more than men's. If one recalls that when the Church was the bride of Christ, Man stood ontologically in the female position toward God—that of faithful, trusting, and loving (a Pauline trio), but less rational dependents—Baier's observations assume theodical import. The same kind of analogue holds for political reasoning. After all, as temporal rulers took their legitimacy from God, top-down, He took his manner of subjects' commitment from them, bottom-up. One should also recall, then, that "between the Renaissance"—the late sixteenth century—and "the threshold of the Enlightenment" (say 1700), the idea of contract, "elaborated from Roman precedents . . . was expanded mightily not only in the economic but also in the political domain, where philosophical arguments transformed the notion into a 'social contract' interpreted in a variety of ways, libertarian and authoritarian."[33] This principle of agency by no means precludes faith, hope, and love in regard to one's leaders, but social functioning rarely requires these Pauline virtues.

One can see the strains upon the older, trust-based, love-based ideals nearly two centuries before Leibniz's *Theodicy*. Erasmus protested that Luther's despotic, therefore untrustworthy God would not be loved: "Who will be able to bring himself to love God with all his heart although He created Hell, seething with eternal torments to punish His own misdeeds in his victims?" One could then believe in God the despot as true, without God's being *beliebt*, held dear; one could *credere* in *unum Deum tyrannum* without giving one's heart—*cord-* plus *dare*—to Him.[34] Under Luther's dogma, Erasmus worried, the True as conceived or perceived detaches itself from the Good as conceived or perceived. And yet one increasingly needed the perceived True and the perceived Good to coalesce. The more distant God is from being in any way comprehensible to the reason, the more the closeness of love becomes crucial—the pastoral comfort can supply some of the energy that metapolitical accountability does not. Trying to remedy this problem of moral physics, attraction and repulsion, through struggling to make God's ways graspable by reason, strays toward disaster. Witness Leibniz's troubles.

Amos Funkenstein explores the second issue, a movement from "contemplative" to "ergetic" knowledge, "the ideal of knowing through *doing* or knowing by *construction*" (297). Ancient and medieval epistemologies, Funkenstein argues, tended to be receptive, so that "knowledge or truth is found, not constructed," whereas increasingly the models of the new "mechanical philosophy" extended to the universe a principle that earlier thought had confined to actual machinery: we know what we ourselves make (298-9). One has here, clearly, the cognitive equivalent of the social movement mentioned just above, from received to contractual, constructed rights and obligations. Augustine's theodicy, in fealty to God, shows itself, not God, faulty if it cannot discover enough truth to be credible. To construct a juridical theodicy, however, is to reconstruct in thought God's creation, knowing it through that act of reconstruction, and to judge it by principles of justice that one also (re)constructs—one may think, for example, of *Paradise Lost*, where Milton deploys so many means of comprehension, persuasion, and nomic appeal. Understandably so, because Milton keeps stressing cause and effect. As Funkenstein points out, the more wholly the universe operates as "a closed, semi-autarkic, balanced system of motions and/or forces" (320), the more the gap between human and divine knowledge is quantitative rather than qualitative.

If Aquinas stressed the qualitative gap by affirming that "there can be no objective rational criterion for why our world was created" (Funkenstein 151), presumably no metaphysical needs pushed Leibniz to assert ours the best of all possible worlds. What secular reason sufficed to do so? For him to speak of possibles and probables in considering justice, *diké*, smacks of contracts and of aleatory law (annuity and insurance risks, for instance), an ongoing interest shared by Leibniz and colleagues of his. Pascal's Wager—betting that God exists risks little for the prospect of great gain, and vice versa for vice versa—was only the most famous mid-seventeenth-century example of treating religious belief according to principles of prudent business.[35] "The best of all possible worlds" becomes a norm of fairness within this ambiance, setting out God's bona fides and the equity He offered members of the world community "in the context of legal theories that estimated expectations . . . and that aimed at equalizing these expectations in partnerships and other contracts"—"a fair game or exchange . . . were the staples of seventeenth-century legal theory and practice" (Daston 26, 25).

During Leibniz's lifetime, fairness as the initial condition and guide of justice appeared in these terms, distributed to the faceless agents of law ("the reasonable man," "the prudent man," et al). The principle of contract, however, individuates by affectively informed cognition, for exchange supposes that one can "put oneself mentally in the place of another

. . . in order to understand his or her needs."[36] In 1737, two decades after Leibniz's death, new terms—those of individual utility—supervened, courtesy of Daniel Bernoulli, a nephew of the jurist who had developed the old, Leibniz's friend Jakob Bernoulli. Daniel Bernoulli in 1737 pointed out that cost-benefit ratios differed for people in different initial situations: a bag of gold meant more to a poor person than to a rich. A theory of justice on this principle needed to weigh the individual utility of goods and negative utility of evils. Not to do so risked mock-tributes like Anatole France's, to "the majestic egalitarianism of the law, which forbids rich and poor alike to sleep under bridges, to beg in the streets, and to steal bread." Leibniz's legal ideal and logical method allowed no such weighing. As with so many other phenomena that require free will—and the *Theodicy* is subtitled *Essays on the Goodness of God, the Freedom of Man, and the Origin of Evil* —for his kind of law to be in theory "universal" means in practice that it works only statistically. The "liberal" thought that derived from Leibniz's contemporary John Locke (1632-1704; Leibniz, 1646-1716), though, located the political "identity of the person . . . in a structure of coherent or rationalized desires," on which rest "the two basic moral ideas" of rights and utility.[37] The coherence and rationality of one's preferences allow others to understand them, to accept their legitimacy. By explaining individual desires in terms of their situational utility, Daniel Bernoulli lent the "universality" of rights to non-Leibnizian goods.

Here one comes to a double dilemma in eighteenth-century theodicy. To justify God and His works entailed their being understandable, hence vulnerable to human understanding, which seemed to differ from God's quantitatively rather than qualitatively. By the late seventeenth and eighteenth centuries, to have made them incomprehensible would also have made them vulnerable to human understanding, the understanding of pain. According to Daniel Bernoulli's ideas of utility, such understanding was key to determining fairness, hence justice. Knowing the meaning of pain, I would stress, is another form of ergetic knowledge, with a pair of necessary modalities: sympathy and "penetration." Neither the ability to feel with others nor that of divining their motives has a place in Leibniz's kind of theodicy, albeit a whole school of anti-Hobbesian, "intuitionist" ethicists centered moral perception in just these faculties. From the debates within ethics, prior to an ideal of fairness based on personal utilities, I suggest that by 1710 no theodicy would be counted a success unless it gave both rational and intuitive moral knowledge what seemed their due, and also gave both general and particular experience what seemed theirs. The *Odyssey* model now dwelt on a person's situation as well as, maybe rather than, his or her station.

At one level, again, the failure of a purely logical theodicy is pastoral. Jonathan Lamb has written at length on the fascination the book of Job developed for readers in eighteenth-century England, where new attention to individual rights and spiritual states, as well as sensibility, had become coin of the realm.[38] Such readers craved answerable answers, so to speak; Job's burst directly out of the whirlwind, as Logos, not logic. At another level, the failure is cognitive. Post-Cartesian, post-Lockean thought blueprinted Kant's antinomy mentioned above, between people's causally determined (phenomenal) behavior and their (noumenal) free will in action: the freely-chosen moral law, for Kant, corresponds in action to the laws of nature in behavior. This doubleness reflects itself in the way we know. By the late nineteenth century, theorists of history distinguished two kinds of knowing, splitting ergetic knowledge in half. Explanation (*Erklärung*) reconstructs mechanical systems, and understanding (*Verstehen*) comprehends human action. One kind shows how physical laws, based on cause and effect, run a mechanical system, from clocks and can-openers to earthquakes. The other, understanding, draws on motives to expose why people act as they do. Understanding, in this sense, requires sympathy to reconstruct a felt situatedness and "penetration" to grasp how that felt situatedness produced action or a disposition to act. Leibniz's rational theodicy predicts evil on a probabilistic basis. That is, it argues that if a large number of fallible agents have free choice, the most likely outcome will be that some will choose wrong, that the potentiality inherent in being fallible will become actual. It cannot deal with particulars of action any more than it can deal with those of *passio*, suffering. Reason, therefore, cannot produce the cognitive information it needs for anything but a gross analysis of assigning blame for evils done or recompense for evils suffered. Yet both are crucial for the sanctions of a contract. In the eighteenth century, the gravity of an evil as a function of its negative utility depended on situation and on expectations, psychological more than logical structures. For this reason, these structures logically falsify the logic of Leibniz by challenging his unexamined definition of justice.

Of course suffering is only a small part of what understanding tries to plumb. Though small it is, I suggest, paradigmatic for this kind of knowing because: it is primal in either hedonic (pleasure/pain) or will-oriented (desire/aversion) schemes of action; it is basic in any theory of altruism; it seems radically private, because ineffable; and it is urgent. As ethical rules have become wobblier, in accord with Marquard's thesis, ethics' stabilizing criterion is based on suffering. Richard Rorty has proudly called himself a liberal ironist, defining liberals as "people who think that cruelty is the worst thing we do," and liberal ironists as people for whom "there is no answer to the question 'Why not be cruel?'—no noncircular theoretical backup for the belief that cruelty is horrible."[39] The backup exists by extension from the priority we have assigned to the ergetics of understanding (*Verstehen*) as the key to anthropodicy. If we value sympathy for cognitive ends, we bind it to moral value and mark it as transcendently human. The cruelty most censured, perhaps, is that which abuses sympathy, intuiting others' feelings so as to torment them. As to Klemm's God of alterity, His transgression of the wall between worlds raises sympathy to its highest level, one supposes, for how else can complete alterity be heeded as itself, not merely assimilated to oneself? Sympathy, then, brings us humans our greatest chance for a knowledge not of ourselves. Theologians once cast humans as imitating Christ for their spiritual survival; now, theologians think, God/Christ survives in "liberal" people's lives by imitating liberal ideals. No longer an "object or being, not even a 'supreme being'" (Klemm 280), "He" brings the fullness of altruism, the sudden flash of a confronted, embraced alterity that illuminates being-in-the-world. "He" is, but what is "He"? Does "He" verify the rightness of a mythic posit, proving what had been taken as an axiom, or is "He" a brilliantly convincing stage effect?[40] Since we cannot know, a narrative, "aesthetic" theodicy has more chance of satisfying one than does an ontological *allée* lined with logical ramifications. No wonder that the Marquard Effect risks Man and salvages God, to keep credible, verisimilar, what I have called the *Aeneid* model: the genuine promise, the redemptive irruption, the bosom conviction of meaning, the transfiguration of the past.

3. The Theodicizing of Ethical (De)constructions

Numerous maneuvers stud the Marquard Effect. Humans supplement God, God gets rusticated, hierarchies flop on to their sides or reverse, "society" defers responsibility along a system of differences, and clever temporary employees spell each other as acting transcendental guarantors in God's absence. Apparent transgressions turn out to be integral to what they violate. My extending Marquard insists on continuing slippage and equivocation of terms, since "the very iterability that constituted their identity" as ongoing persuasive argument "does not permit them ever to be a unity that is identical to itself."[41] Closures in Leibniz turn out to be openings, and in Klemm's kind of theology, undecidability. Through the uncertain control of iterable, institutionalized language in the practice of theodicy, a contractual model of mutual advantage—that is, advantage to people, since only God (and gregarious "process theologians") can compute His benefits—sneaks from political theory into its macrocosmic analogue. Not only do Leibniz's central terms, such as "justice," change scope so as in fact to testify against him, but his artful perfecting of his inherited intellectual counters, such as a benevolent God's rationality, also prods him into the murkiest culs-de-sac.

One need not have been snagged by the 1980s' Humanities squabbles to see that these maneuvers parallel those of hectic deconstructors. Here is the *supplément* that supplants what it supplements. Here are decentering, dualities and *différance,* "weak thought" (Gianni Vattimo's *pensiero debole*), and "God" under erasure, *sous rature*. Here is the deconstructor's compulsory, Derrida says, "double gesture," to "put into practice a reversal of the classical opposition and a general displacement of the system" ("SEC" 21): the God/Man protective hierarchy is reversed and the system shifted to secularity. What Stephen Stich puts at "the core of deconstruction," a "process of uncovering and criticizing tacit assumptions," the Marquard Effect (tacitly) entails.[42] Sparked by Funkenstein, one can also see that deconstruction produces ergetic knowledge. The philosopheme "deconstruction" itself, like its Heideggerian predecessor *Abbau* (dismantling), names an action of careful undoing, repeating in reverse a putting together so as to un- or disclose the lacks in what had seemed complete. "Rather than destroying," Derrida wrote in 1985, "it was also necessary to understand how an 'ensemble' had been constructed and to reconstruct it to this end." In tune with Funkenstein's stress on seventeenth-century Moderns' "mechanical philosophy," Derrida chose the term "deconstruction" partly for its "'mechanistic' force" (*portée 'machinique'*"), as he tried to help Modernity wind down.[43] Does post-Leibnizian theodicy of Marquard's sort cohere through its structured, advantageous incoherences, all those exceptions to its moral claims? Deconstructors, like other Nietzscheans and anti-foundationalists, take that as normal. In peeling away the illusion that practices and institutions are natural or formally unified, one finds their kernel in the advantages their conventions provide to someone.

The American academy and its foes present deconstruction as radical, simmering with danger. Deconstruction in Marquardian theodicy, however, is far from radical. It conserves the Logos for as long as it can. It makes things change so as to let them stay as much the same as possible, though it may have unforeseen consequences, as in Leibniz's unwittingly helping God to be made emeritus. Far from being an operation that the trained critic knowingly, often all too knowingly, performs, this deconstruction exemplifies the anonymous Darwinian ordering of an "invisible hand." Rooted in contract law and individual risk, the system it assumes is surely capitalist. Far from being an arcane bit of textual processing, finally, this deconstruction operates on no text but on a web of practical dispositions. One can codify the web in a (social) text, of which Leibniz's *Theodicy* is just one compliant member, only retrospectively and reconstructively. Pretty much at the same time a Leibnizian apologetic text fell apart, a Leibnizian juridical text—the dangerous, God-judging text—coalesced, assembled from ancient canonical materials newly used.

Coincidentally or not, the chief steward of deconstruction in our time, Derrida, also illustrates the diaphanous bounds of Marquardian theodicy, where Marquardian techniques continue but without any purpose of saving any kind of God. Trying to dismiss indictments of post-metaphysical thought, Derrida does what Marquardian Man had done with "gnoseological," aesthetic, moral, and expressive thought. The accused here, however, are quite historically local. In the late 1980s, Derrida had to struggle to reclaim both the sometime Nazi Heidegger, newly under attack, and Heidegger's homunculus Paul de Man, whose American career as a Derridean prosthesis ended twice (rather like Derridean *écriture*), first through death, second through disclosure—de Man first had, then hid a short youthful stint as a Nazi fellow-traveler in wartime Belgium. Still more recently, having had to argue the discomfiting cases of old National Socialists, Derrida righted himself with the left by an equal, equally-hedged legal defense of Karl Marx, prophet of transnational Socialism. At about the same time as the Heidegger and de Man discoveries, the European Communist states collapsed, apparently discrediting the doctrinal Marxist base of which they had been the debased superstructure. As it now had to, Derrida's defense of Marx stoutly asserted the moral integrity of deconstruction while eschewing any kind of Socialism, statist collectivism, at all.

Marx and Heidegger, each depending on his own idea of historical necessity, had defined themselves starting from and against Hegel: the *Hegelischer Geist* in time, at once as continuous and disjunctive as the theophanic *Heiliger Geist* (Holy Ghost) outside but into time, becomes material rather than (primarily) spiritual in Marx, and existential in Heidegger. Also keyed to all three is the Rousseau of *The Social Contract,* whose crucial principle of the General Will goes back to Malebranche and—of all people—Leibniz.[44] If, as Malebranche and Leibniz insisted, God worked by general rather than particular laws, thereby assuring Man of the contractual constancy of the world and the renunciation of ad hoc power, surely citizens should do the same, renouncing egoistic independence for the general good. "Human emancipation will only be complete when the real, individual man has absorbed into himself the abstract citizen," wrote the young Marx, "when as an individual man, in his everyday life, in his work, and in his relationships, he has become a *species-being.*"[45] Heiling Hitler, Heidegger similarly declared that the highest freedom is to give oneself the law of obligation to "the national community," "the honor and destiny of the nation," and "the spiritual mission of the German people." Twenty years after World War II and the gross failure of the "German people" to fulfill their Heideggerian "spiritual mission," the septuagenarian philosopher confided to the journal *Der Spiegel*, "*Nur noch ein Gott kann uns retten,*" only a god can still save us.[46] Marx's salvific God was Hegel's *Geist* materialized. The gods, like Klemm's, manifest themselves through an alterity we confront. This is the event (*Ereignis*) in a Heideggerian clearing (*Lichtung*), something the tillers of the Germanic soil sense better than city folk. So does the Marxian proletariat, which "represents, practically speaking, the completed abstraction from everything human, even from the *appearance* of being human."[47]

What interests me here is not to tar all enthusiastic collectivism with the Nazi and/or Communist brush(es)—one's own politics make that supererogatory or preposterous—nor absurdly to assimilate Marx and Heidegger. Rather, because the two are so different, their commonalities of structure tell of shared practice: though divergent, their thought legitimates itself on a contractarian basis, a naturalized grounding, and the sacrificial structure of religion via statist substitutes. Through alleging such theological structures, I wish to suggest their openness to analysis through the Marquard Effect. Marx's and Heidegger's divergent thought reprises old debates on Man's free will and God's foreknowledge. Both men exhort individuals, trying to turn their public's false consciousness to true. Each, however, preaches an immanent but sure historical process, Marxian history's clash-filled march toward classless utopia, Heidegger's epoch-by-epoch tumble toward technological nihilism, perhaps followed by Being's grand unveiling. To adopt a nice distinction of Robert Nozick's, each of them believes in an "invisible hand," a way in which history gives itself shape, as well as a "hidden hand," a way in which someone (the "ruling class," "technonihilists") manipulates history out of sight.[48] Kant's antinomy between law-determined behavior and freely-taken action thrives, still unresolved, diffusing responsibility in Marxian and Heideggerian history.[49]

In Marquardian terms, evil devolves upon Man. For Heidegger that is *das Man*, the fallen (i.e., myopically-absorbed and unthinking) crowd, forgetful of Being; and for Marx, a bourgeois state in which "capital is independent and has individuality, while the living person is dependent and has no individuality."[50] Removed from the category of the proscribed is violent revolution, Communist or National Socialist. Collectivists of both stripes justify evils holistically, à la Leibniz and the *Odyssey* model ("You can't make an omelet without breaking eggs"), as well as causally, the way the *Aeneid* justifies the ruin of Troy: if Troy, then no Rome; if the workers owned anything to lose except their chains, then no revolution; "the closer we come to the danger" of technology, "the more brightly do the ways into the saving power begin to shine."[51] Indictment, Marquard's "tribunalization," falls on those who refuse the mantle of the spirit, the duty that brings salvation rather than apocalypse. The synchronic visions of Marx and Heidegger each take the form of two imperfectly mirroring tiers, along the lines of Augustine's City of God and City of Man, the New Law and the Old, spirit (*Geist*) and letter.

Marx, more openly than the Nazi Heidegger, identifies the material interests and instrumentality of the letter with Jews, the people of the Old Law. Through letter and law, the Jew despiritualizes an originally spiritual reality. In "On the Jewish Question" (1843), Marx wrote that the real, everyday Jew worships self-interest, huckstering, and money. Transgressively, letter has captured the realm founded for spirit: Mammon-worship, with "contempt for theory, for art, for history, and for man as an end in himself" dominates the Christian world. Since one can say that Judaism dominates all, "the social emancipation of the Jew" would be "the emancipation of society from Judaism" (51-2). Heidegger's ideal National Socialism would have "emancipated" Jews by abolishing their "Judaism" in Marx's sense. Should spirit resuffuse reality in world consciousness, limitless utopia would come from an antithesis to Jew, be it Greek or Christian. Marx's classless harmony springs from an ideal of souls in a Christian heaven and Heidegger's fourfold union of gods, sky, earth, and humankind from that of a Greek Golden Age.

In Marquard, for historical reasons a divine institution goes on trial, and the defense fails. One saves the guarantor of transcendent value by displacing earthly responsibility from it/Him to Man. One then displaces this responsibility through what Derrida named *différance* and through shifting the boundaries that establish limits and transgression. A practice with similar components and structure, I suggest, reappears in the post-theodical projects of Marx and Heidegger, maybe because both imbibed it through Hegel. To show how the practice keeps changing but being "the same," let me turn to a kind of theodicy in Derrida. Because Derrida's relation to Heidegger is too complex, too filial, too frequently revisited by Derrida, for brief discussion, I focus on Derrida's desire to save a tutelary Marx, especially in his book *Specters of Marx*.[52] I make no pretence to practice derridodicy, to do "justice" to this subtle, complex, and humane discussion; the Marquard Effect in process is what intrigues me here.

A tutelary Marx: Derrida's *tutelae*, to tell the truth, would have led Marx to wonder if he was being strung along, for they lead to not matter but spirit, to "radical critique," not ties to a

> supposed systemic, metaphysical, or ontological totality (notably to its "dialectical method" or to "dialectical materialism"), to its fundamental concepts of labor, mode of production, social class, and consequently to the whole history of its apparatuses (projected or real: the Internationals of the labor movement, the dictatorship of the proletariat, the single party, the State, and finally the totalitarian monstrosity. . . . [This analysis] will isolate in sum the spirit of Marxism to which one ought to remain faithful by dissociating it from all the other spirits—and one will observe with a smile that the latter include *almost everything*. (*SM* 88-9)

Under the guise of chronological sequence, Derrida's list moves from those notions for which one might blame Marx directly—the basic, totalizing concepts—to acts performed post mortem, like "the totalitarian monstrosity," from which one might exculpate him. Not God but His creatures; not the king but his ministers. For Derrida as for a Derridean history of Eastern Europe and for Marquardian God, salvation comes as deconstruction: "Certain Soviet philosophers told me in Moscow a few years ago: the best translation of *perestroika* was still 'deconstruction'" (*SM* 89)—here one must admire the originary rhetoric ("Soviet philosophers . . . in Moscow," "still") that modestly dyes the Derri-nyeting of a century and a half's accumulation of matter and spirit from the outhistoried new-historian Marx himself.

The real Marx tumbled Hegel on his derrière and trashed Hegelians, Ludwig Feuerbach, Bruno Bauer, and Max Stirner. So confident was he about his grand historical narrative that in its name he cried out for blood in the streets to buoy the death of private property, of the family, of bourgeois individualism. What Derrida "cries out" against as evils—"that never before, in absolute figures, never have so many men, women, and children been subjugated, starved, or exterminated on the earth" by "violence, inequality, exclusion, famine, and thus economic oppression" (*SM* 85)—are evils for Marx. But instead of Marx's irruption of alterity, proletarian revolution, Derrida looks for succor to "a profound transformation, projected over a long term, of international law" (*SM* 84). Spectral Marx, Derrida's irruptive, otherworldly alterity, gets payola for becoming such wispy ectoplasm: by allusion to King Hamlet's ghost in *SM* 1, the father of Communism becomes the victim of usurping regicide. (Derrida himself, endlessly chattering and remediating his weaker militancy, plays the revenger Prince.) Spectral Marx gets real Marx's smug certainty displaced onto a Young Hegelian of nowadays, Francis Fukuyama, whom Derrida belabors in *SM* 2. Derrida does not condemn private property, the family, or individualism; but then, neither does spare, pared spectral Marx, any more than Marquardian God, from His upstairs office, damned "gnoseological" and aesthetic activity.

The now nearly Marxless world, Derrida announces, grows more parlous all the time: "The world is going badly, the picture is bleak, one could say almost black" (*SM* 78). Marx's modes of "radical critique" and social justice, by which he would have remedied evils, however, rise from matter to spirit. Derrida idealizes them into "deconstruction" (the *eidos* of radical critique) and an image of justice that he largely borrows from Emmanuel Levinas, that of the absolute, chosen responsibility each person has to each other in her or his alterity, confronted face to face, person to person, not as in Marx, side by side, phalanx by phalanx.[53] Marx imagines heaven on earth as angel choirs; Derrida, as bourgeois individualism with a thoroughgoing, extensive Good Neighbor Policy. These too stand in Marquardian relation, for they honor the principle that Man is a "species being" from different, coeval theological models, producing different in- and exculpatory norms. By adopting Levinas's rule that the face-to-face ethical obligation of each to each binds one without thought of reciprocity, Derrida transfers Marx's jaundiced view of commodities and exchange-value into personal, spiritual, asystemic politics. Nazis and Communists copied Jews to reject them. The Party

Heidegger joined plotted its own empire by copying the Jews' supposed plan for empire, in "The Protocols of the Elders of Zion," and Marx's proposed world Communism, with its materialist dogma, rivaled what he saw as the all-engrossing material spirit of "Judaism."[54] Through Levinas, Derrida reverses their Party *partis pris,* by offering a transcendent Jewish ethic, designed for universality through the single self. "Jewish" tribalism, materialism, and calculation of relative gains carry over to non-Jewish people, as they do in the anti-"Judaism" of Marx and Heidegger, but now with Jews—Levinas, Derrida—using Jewish tradition itself to displace the onus of a stunted ethics and assert a benignant, imminent alterity.

Though again I will not comment on what I take to be the truth or value, soundness or seductiveness of Derrida's claims, I call attention to the inevitable loss, in the Marquard Effect, of unity between law and justice. Here one returns to Leibniz, whose law-governed apparatus brushes aside singular justice for sufferers. Derrida pinpoints the issue:

> justice, as law, seems always to suppose the generality of a rule, a norm or a universal imperative. How are we to reconcile the act of justice that must always concern singularity, individuals, irreplaceable groups and lives, the other or myself *as* other, in a unique situation, with rule, norm, value or the imperative[s?] of justice which necessarily have a general form, even if this generality prescribes a singular application in each case? . . . Is it ever possible to say: an action is not only legal, but also just? ("FL" 17)

One has, Derrida thinks, two tracks, "justice as law" and "justice in itself," one a social practice and the other something like a Kantian regulative idea, channeling one's understanding. "Justice in itself, if such a thing exists, outside or beyond law, is not deconstructible. No more than deconstruction itself, if such a thing exists. Deconstruction is justice." Law, however, "is constructible and so deconstructible" ("FL" 14-5). Law harks back to the *Odyssey* model of here-and-now worldly order, while the knowledge of the just and the justness of one's knowledge are transcendent ideals like Aeneas's image of the *imperium Romanum* he would not see in his lifetime. Derrida links the latter, the "idea of justice," to "horizons . . . similar enough in appearance and always pretending to absolute privilege and irreducible singularity," such as "messianism . . ., idea in the Kantian sense, eschato-teleology . . ., etc." ("FL" 25).

In fact, I should say, we are not so well—or is it badly?—off as Derrida implies. No doubt as the core of injunctive maxims, justice and deconstruction are not constructed, hence not deconstructible. As with regulative ideas for Kant, they provide literally utopic foci, i.e., no place (*ou-topia*) within the realm of actual experience. In the other, favorable sense of "utopia" (*eu-topia*), such ideals glow with promise. Still, from them one can derive no specific truth-claims, and their own implicit imperative mode means that they themselves are not propositions. Since only propositional language and its correlatives in action lie open to deconstruction, no injunctive ideal at all, therefore, is deconstructible, whether in or out of favor with Derrida or any given person. But to have effects, any such ideal must flesh itself in our world. In practice, it must become as deconstructible as the ideal of theodicy became. To be legible as a practice, to be known as just or deconstructive, earthly justice or deconstruction is constructed in Derrida's sense. As he obligingly had earlier written, "Deconstruction takes place, it is an event . . . *It deconstructs it-self. It can be deconstructed* [*Ça se déconstruit*]" ("LJF" 274; emphases in original). Unlike actual laws, which are written in advance, practices of justice and deconstruction are not antecedently deconstructible; but after being put into practice they are no more sheltered than law. They are even in a way antecedently deconstructible, aporetic, for skeptics about people's plans and motives. Skeptics are what good Derrideans should be. Therefore, given that law is deconstructible in code and practice, as Derrida says, how well can it possibly guard "men, women, and children" who are "subjugated, starved, or exterminated"? Can the next move in the Marquardian, deconstructive sequence not take it to pieces? If the moral or ethical well-being of the world demands coherent, compelling moral and ethical theory, does the Marquard Effect not doom us to plunge into chaos?

Looking at Marx and Derrida's Marx in Marquardian terms suggests how Marquard's hypothesis, with its laws and loopholes, provocatively allows for a new understanding of current discord in ethics. Many of us do not find this discord bad. Other writers, highbrow, middlebrow, and pop, have groused about how hopelessly modern society has lost any ontological bearings, and some figuratively picket modernity like grim, sign-toting millenarians. The most sophisticated of these jeremiads come from the philosopher Alasdair MacIntyre, who dates our accelerated moral decay from, when else?, the eighteenth century, the world after the vanishing of Leibniz.[55] Humans who incorporate a *telos*—Man with an essential nature and purpose, therefore an *areté*—then, in MacIntyre's account, gave way to a neutral, undefined, and fundamental Man. Moral philosophies based on criteria of human nature and purpose, such as those of Aristotle and Aquinas, provide us with rules and terminology we still try to use. The presuppositions in terms of which those rules make sense, MacIntyre says, have however vanished. As a result, we flounder ethically, basing our actual ethics on emotion and a clutter of unconvincing *ad hoc dicta*.

In all this, Nietzsche's genealogy of morals reappears with a decent scowl instead of a smirk. The "noble" have lost the power of monumentalizing the pecking order among styles of *areté* in an imaginary ziggurat. Virtue progressively rests in the unmeasurable, in altruism, in pity and sympathy. Such other-dependent passions do not produce narratives that make sense of an individual life, as the orderly valor of Odysseus or the piety of Aeneas does. What tales that keep tally of oneself emerge, for instance, from Derrida's ethic, where every construction deconstructs and all that remains stable—posits like "justice"—are contexts without instantiating acts? A Marquardian would claim that we have deferred and blurred blame, so that our only firm, agreed-on fact is suffering. We know and resent it through sympathy, MacIntyre's "emotion," which allows us *Verstehen* but limits our ability for *Erklärung,* the lawlike, causal explanations that would make easier a philosophical ethics, ethical consensus and comparison, and enough ethical remove to establish some objectivity, what Nietzsche labels "the pathos of distance."

MacIntyre's illustrative villain is David Hume, born the year after Leibniz published his *Theodicy.* Humean ethics show what happens when origins of things no longer determine their meaning, as origins had determined meaning from the Greeks into the eighteenth century. In Hume, skepticism about what had been ontological grounds for ethical judgment—essential human nature, class and gender positions, the relational structures into which one had been born—accompanied the growing importance of psychological grounds for ethical judgment. The basic psychological mechanism of Humean ethical judgment is what Leibniz neglected, sympathy, the propensity to put oneself in one another's shoes. Hence an emotive ethics loses visible, objective standards. As Hume wrote Francis Hutcheson in 1740, "when you pronounce any Action or Character to be vicious, you mean nothing but that from the particular Constitution of your Nature you have a Feeling or Sentiment of Blame from the Contemplation of it."[56] Under these circumstances, as with Hume's fellow skeptic Derrida, law cannot even in principle jibe exactly with moral judgment: one is general, the other particular. Law—Hume calls it "justice," and Derrida "justice as law"—"is a more or less satisfactory intellectual system," as opposed to the emotive structure of ethics in Hume and the watertight rational system of Leibniz. It is a convention, "designed to secure the coordination of a particular set of institutions" (Douglas 114).

The double weighting that equipoises law and moral judgment, only partially accommodated in the balance between law and equity in the English legal system, threatens a view of law as based on reason, as in Coke's *Institutes.* Its consequences tend toward legal realism. Adam Smith, giving his *Lectures on Jurisprudence* in the 1760s, takes the mutable, social flows of sympathy to underlie our evaluation of all crimes against individual persons. Here again we return to what went wrong with Leibniz's kind of theodicy. Conceivably, too, an ethics based on sympathy inclines to acquit: *tout comprendre*, said Voltaire, *c'est tout pardonner*. While there is no reason to think that an emotive ethicist lives in a world where the barometric pressure of morality, as it were, diminishes, nevertheless one is less able to make indictments stick. "Justice is incalculable," writes Derrida, "and aporetic experiences are the experiences, as improbable as they are necessary, of justice, that is to say of moments in which the decision between just and unjust is never insured by a rule" ("FL" 16).

Let us suppose that MacIntyre's description of "our" current state of ethics—a hodgepodge of theories and a chaotic, emotive practice—is right enough to be worth revising in Marquardian terms. The revision might start with a translation of the gap between moral awareness and moral guilty verdicts into pop sociology. Emotive ethics apparently creates a society of habitual victims rather than habitual sinners, evil being identified with the only consensual criterion for it, suffering. The ethical line I associate with the cultural right blames an ideological villain, the voiding of standards, for the cult of victimhood. But, as I suggested vis-à-vis Moynihan, to talk in terms of ideology is to accept the very heteronomy, being ruled by the other, that underlies the cult of victimhood. Speaking in the same terms as they do, no wonder right and left can join battle as they do. Marquard's thesis, by contrast, suggests that victim is a strategic position, that of plaintiff rather than defendant, so as to sustain an atmosphere of moral consciousness in which responsibility is socially diffused—the nominally or potentially responsible cannot be convicted. As a strategic position, being a victim should not in fact reduce people's sense of agency or increase their anomie. Indeed the noisiest self-announced victims also seem to be the noisiest assertors of their own autonomy and sense of their inalienable rights. The call of sympathy, *Verstehen*, amplifies the call for rights under the social contract, subject to *Erklärung*. By seeing themselves as victims in MacIntyre's or Moynihan's terms, people sap their strength; by seeing themselves as Marquardian victims, they enhance it; and in practice, of course, contemporary society mingles both kinds.

What the strategy of victimhood creates, on a Marquardian reading, is an understandable forum. Theodicy addresses the divine union of law, justice, and *caritas,* this last being the "charity" of St. Paul's "faith, hope, and charity." The combination of social blame, rights-talk, and victim-talk reconstitutes a human arena for that union. As personal rights replace the universal Right, we witness the Marquard Effect: God is kicked upstairs with His reputation safe, as the author of rights, His role in the Declaration of Independence, and similar forefatherly assertions. "Society" starts to weather accusations for allowing evils of any sort, while in- and exculpation of individuals are adversarially contested. As to natural evil (earthquakes, tsunamis), located by traditional theodicy through a conceptual idiom of just, this-worldly trials and gracious, next-worldly redemption—again a union of law, justice, and *caritas*—natural evil and its victims get secular redemption with temporal delay, through faith and hope in science, where still further issues of responsibility and indictability linger.

As I have said, I believe that empirical victim-thinking sometimes corresponds to a Marquardian, sometimes to an ideological pattern, and most often to both. Whatever the pattern, I doubt that victim-thinking entails benign results; probably some results are, some are not. Finally, I am not singing the virtues of being aggrieved, offended, self-pitying, and litigious, enduring which at best wearies everyone else, condemned forever to bear some carping Anchises on one's shoulders, as an unalienable rite and right of *pietas*. Instead my point is that one might want to recur to the model of Wittgensteinian "practice." Being-a-victim can have at least three different logics behind it—one ideological, one Marquardian, and one habitual and imitative—so that any analysis of it ought to start with a recognition of its multiple social roles. These roles in turn will influence but not govern its effects. The social pros and cons here, in short, are pragmatic and empirical, and call for local actions, if any. Until specific, sophisticated analysis takes place, only a *parti pris* or a taste for *Schadenfreude* authorizes any extrapolations and bemoanings.

The pattern of being-a-victim, in addition, has recurred, not originated, in modern life. Max Weber, drawing on Nietzsche's account of *ressentiment,* uses the phrase "theodicy of disprivilege," which he says "is a component of *every* [my emphasis] salvation religion which draws its adherents primarily from the disprivileged classes"—and a highly socially mobile, competitive society like ours, one would think, drives a great many people to think themselves disprivileged vis-à-vis the shifting reference groups that they are offered. Desire for vengeance, Weber says, is compensated by the doctrine that the rich and powerful class are also sinful and lawless, an object of God's wrath; in modern America, an object of the justice of God's secular proxies.[57] The ways in which one distinguishes one sort of "theodicy of disprivilege"—that of Weber's post-exilic Jews, for example—from another, one sort of victim-centered identity politics from another, tells us at least as much about the person making the distinctions as about the situations being distinguished. What I am concerned to stress, with Marquard, is how many phenomena share a relation to theodical thought and its variants, and a broad sense (such as one of course also gets from Weber) of theodicy as the name of a practice. Like Marquard, too, I would note the looseness possible within a functioning theodicy, as partly independent elements move by checks and balances, so different from the precision-milled synchromesh system of an Aquinas. Such a position, I suggest, assumes a stance toward modern ethics quite different from MacIntyre's, even if one accepts his description of it.

What of Hume, standing proxy for all emotive ethicists? He also lends himself to a possible Marquardian reading, in which God is kicked upstairs, humanity takes over the bench and the dock, and individual humans are exculpated. That is, Hume reforms rather than junks the kernels of the theological system he inherits, leaving (as MacIntyre might have it) only the papery husks of terminology as present litter. The argument might go like this: the Calvinist God rules inscrutably—Calvinist, for Hume the Scottish boy "apparently accept[ed] the stern Calvinistic doctrines of Original Sin, the Total Depravity of Human Nature, Predestination, and Election, without a tremor."[58] Hume's famous skepticism, which grounds our beliefs as pragmatic, socially and psychologically coordinating devices, adapts Calvinist doubts about human reason and its control of will. Since people have only empirical conventions of action and belief, how can we know if God's will accords with right reason? As Weber remarks, such a position already signals the end of theodicy, which, as we have observed, has the peculiarity that it is never there when it is most needed. "An unimaginably great ethical chasm between the transcendental god and the human being continuously enmeshed in the toils of new sin," Weber says, "inevitably led to the ultimate theoretical conclusion . . . that the omnipotent creator God must be envisaged as beyond all the ethical claims of his creatures . . . [and] the criteria of human justice are utterly inapplicable to his behavior" (142-3).

If Leibniz's laws comfortably imitated God by constructing an ergetic model in His mode, Reason, what model best imitates a God of limitless Will? Once theodicy fails to justify an inscrutable God who *ipso facto* debars justification but who remains the source of law, the human morality that imitates Him—that ergetically understands the efficient mode of His workings by the workings in our own bosoms—should by right be equally voluntaristic, irrational, and passionate. Now let us make the Marquardian move of elevating humans to the God position so that we lose the law as divine dictum. What will replace it? Because the principle of divine election is arbitrary, love or grace, the principle for moral election will be its arbitrary, immediate human equivalent, sympathy, as in Hume. Why sympathy rather than love? because, as asserted earlier, sympathy has a cognitive element—it is a mode of understanding, making one what Adam Smith a few years later, in *The Theory of Moral Sentiments*, was to call "the impartial spectator." Sympathy stands in for God's omniscience.

Of course, sympathy cannot account for humans' moral connection to God, since we cannot feel with God. Baroque Catholics could bring God into sympathy by weeping with the suffering, whipped, bloody, and forsaken Christ. One can also use another sort of half-human stand-in, such as Wagner's tragic Wotan, whose second-act monologue in *Die Walküre* quite profoundly reprises enough theodical questions to merit study itself as a Marquard Effect effect. Law, with an equivocal, uneasy relation to justice, judges these figures, and through sympathy we rescue them. But philosophically these options are not key. Surely for Hume not feeling with God hardly mattered. As per Marquard's scheme, God was on vacation, away from the inconveniences of netherworldish Auld Reekie, the eighteenth-century nickname for dark, smoky, smelly Edinburgh.

MacIntyre presents a Hume who, "in the most philosophically sophisticated version of [the way of ideas] which was ever to be achieved," gave voice to "the concepts and theses embodied in the thought and practice of the dominant English social and cultural order." Assigning law and justice the task of protecting the propertied, Hume's "principles of justice provide no recognizable ground for appeals against the social order" (*WJ* 295). Since property for Hume as for Locke before him includes one's body and mind, family and country, to protect property is to protect civil rights and liberties: inside the social order, justice allows for ample "liberal" appeals, though MacIntyre does not wish to say so. Moreover, as Annette Baier observes, Hume translates rule-dictated rights into moral rights inasmuch as they derive "from our capacity for sympathy" as we "communicate feelings and understand what our fellows are feeling, and so . . . realize what resentments and satisfactions the present social scheme generates." Since for Hume the rules of justice have many historical origins—custom, self-interest, chance, and fancy among them—they must vary locally and are "as changeable by human will as conditions, needs, wishes, or human fancies change."[59] Here is the Marquard Effect, in that MacIntyre's Hume strips of its illusory rationality the "legal-rational" part of Leibniz's theodicy, leaving the contract and convention that insure *diké* as law, while Baier's more accurately represented Hume develops sympathy—what Leibniz omitted—into a distributive, historical mode of moral rights. David Gauthier marks the distinction crisply: the absence of mutual advantage, the basis of contract, "rules out conventions of property and justice," the latter being what Derrida calls "justice as law." However, "morality"—Levinasian justice, or what Hume calls "compassion and kindness"—is not ruled out.[60]

A Marquardian reading affords a quite different perspective from MacIntyre's on Hume's at once careful and non-coercive, bifurcated ethics. The austere grandeur of Kant's ethics rises from its singleness, in Godlike human law-making; and the wisdom of Hume's spreads from its dispersion over the whole topography of human will. Although moral judgment is natural and crucial to Hume's human beings, deriving its form from the sacred, it nonetheless hesitates before impeachments and guilty verdicts. One reason why seventeenth-century theologians began stressing sympathy or (its Latin form) compassion in the first place was to show that a Hobbesian or Jansenist universal impeachment of humans was wrong. Hume's argument thus preserves theology and theodicy by recycling both, only tactfully ostracizing God from both, as in violation of citizenship. In choosing from the possibilities prior writers and his own genius presented, did Hume come to his moral position this way? I do not know. Individuals, including Hume, formulate principles for all sorts of reasons, just as a sense of victimization is now popular for all sorts of reasons. A cultural historian, I think, will be more interested in whether this Marquardian reasoning was socially plausible, since evaluating the distribution of social logics will allow one best to consider the vectorial force of Humean ethics.

In the line of argument I am presenting as the Marquard Effect, our current tangle of ethical doctrines is a working entity, slackly systemic. It has an ecological niche. That is, the tangle is not desperate floundering but strategic adaptation, by which one can deal with evils while leaving evil's conspirators unindicted though sometimes named. Why then do the MacIntyres of the world do so much sour grumbling, and why do writers on the left complain that liberalism, so called, is incoherent? If failure of a system is what incoherence means, why do they not rejoice at living incoherently, that is, in an open cluster of coalitions and negotiative venues? Is incoherence bad? Located tangles, clusters, bunches, jumbles—that is everyday-life politics. For that, though, we have no honorific model, organic, cybernetic, or linguistic. A mixture of controlled chaos, erratic choice, and happenstance, lacking the determinism underlying much mathematical chaos theory, cannot usefully be modeled at all. Nor are tangles homeostatic entities, such as Western thought has always inclined to favor— here too is a kind of theological argument, for evil in theology is a lack within an orderly plenitude, the missing or warping of something good.

Yet there is one honorific model for Marquard's terms of argument. A Marquardian argument suggests that we preserve order by a judicious use of disorder: as God grows more distant so as not to grow more culpable, we preserve Him through his lack; as Man grows more unindictable so as to keep a tolerable principle of responsibility, we preserve his autonomy by offering him many safe havens, enclaves of exclusion. The law preserves its eagle-like vision by its wisdom in winking. In short, Marquard gives us for our time a version of Leibniz's own theodicy. Evil—here the nominal evil of disorder or incoherence— necessarily contributes to order, cosmos. Of course the cosmos is not, like Leibniz's, optimal, the best of all possible worlds, and it is not universal. It is only (trivially) the most probable. As a post-Darwinian model, it is evolutionary and satisficing, sufficiently satisfactory: it keeps going with us inveterate fixers and tinkerers all in it. Again, in nature, life proceeds by error—every genetic mutation is an informational error, so that without error we would all be dead or, what may amount to the same thing, protozoa. In culture, the same model holds for the development of positive law, which evolves non-dialectically by the correction of evils (crimes, torts, breaches of contract)—biology and law work less by trial and error than by error and trial. So with theodicy. If one agrees with Marquard that Leibniz's theodicy failed— and operatively, not many people still accept it—one might say that Leibniz's own lack (in that sense, evil) became the precondition for the new Marquardian version of the same argument. And this is a pattern of return that Marquard's hypothesis would lead us to expect.

Marquard's recapitulation of a Leibnizian past, intended or not, also achieves a different kind of historical interest. Structurally, I have proposed, Marquard assumes the usefulness of a model where at least some large patterns of cultural order come from asymmetrical adversarial microsystems: in the case of theodicy, direct prosecution and special pleading from the defense, malfeasances and unindictable malfeasors, errors and the selective norming of those that are felicitous. Conceptually, what one sees is the reworking of a problematic and a structure: when the divinely established placeholders within a traditional existing structure no longer fulfill their functions, the structure remains for recycling; when people doubt the supposedly divinely-established answers to a set of questions, the questions remain for recycling—not necessarily for answering, since the problematic within which they make sense may well take on a new organization. Marquard's own essays produce a revamped Leibnizian model, psychological and empirical rather than ontological, just as he alleges the growth of a revamped theodical model through the psychological and empirical "human sciences," by which humans gain reflexivity and redefine themselves. Even his exclusory, diagrammatic schema—I think wisely and usefully—implicitly rejects the grasshopper history of long, self-satiating waits and unpredictable jumps that one finds in earlier Foucault and the less cautious followers of Thomas Kuhn.

The value of Marquard's hypothesis, then, is triple: it gives interesting *prima facie* explanations of specific phenomena, and can be ramified to give more; it reminds one of the complexity and the conceptual and historical openness of those phenomena; and it suggests a structural model to look for in the historical transmission of what—for want of a better term— I will call "ideas," that is, bundles of beliefs, attitudes, reliances, and forms of legitimate desire. This triple heuristic value is, at least to me, good. As I have said, I do not believe Marquard's own causal account of the Marquard Effect, but the description has a high local utility as a coherentist, general explanation. That is, it itself serves as a maxim, and makes no singular truth-claims that would reduce social heterogeneity to any one pattern or principle: each of us is "modern" in different ways, to different degrees, within different venues, at different times. Truth beyond this sort of utility is God's province, and on Marquard's hypothesis, He will never tell. We who live in an unpredictable world, often a logically impredictable world, fend off risk by keeping as well as we can to patterns we know. The criterion is utilitarian satisficing. I would argue that if in Karl Popper's ideal model one tests scientific hypotheses (more generally, any candidates for belief) by trying to falsify them, one tests real-life hypotheses (more generally, candidates for reliance) by finding their limits, how far and for what one can depend on them. For this continuing, tacit assessment of reliance, newly salient old problems test reliability as well as new problems; to deconstruct a real-life hypothesis may leave it largely in place and authoritative, since it needs only so much coherence as will keep it sufficiently advantageous in use.

As to known patterns, Karl Löwith has shown how some theological ones persist in a secular world, and Hans Blumenberg, how theological problematics set an agenda for secular thought when the theology no longer answers questions it once did.[61] The Marquard Effect not only documents both kinds of operation, it also gives their compulsions a crucial Darwinian spin. The ecology that tests ideas for use explains how, in practice, handling old forms and problematics produces unforeseen consequences and reversals, as with Calvinist divine "hedonism" and Hume's earthly hedonism, or Derrida's Levinasian resolution of Marx's attack on bourgeois individualism. Leibniz's shift to a rational rather than contingent God and to an implicit contractarian notion of justice, meanwhile, shows how unstable a practice may be even within a context—here, theological—meant to stabilize it. Predictions about it must be even shakier. In theodicy's *Odyssey*, steadfast-hearted Penelope, alienated at home and trying to elude consummation with some eternally-unsuitable suitor, can never repeat designs when she reweaves her nightly-deconstructed hanging.

Notes

[1] The varieties of meaning in *areté* are chronicled in Werner Jaeger, *Paideia: The Ideals of Greek Culture*, trans. Gilbert Highet, 2d ed., 3 vols. (New York: Oxford University Press, 1945). He takes "the history of the idea of areté, which goes back to the earliest times" as a "clue to the history of Greek culture" (1:5), entitling his first chapter "Nobility and Areté." The democratizing of one's telos from one's status duty to one's human essence comes later, Jaeger argues, as in Plato (e.g., 2:162; 3:221— "it is necessary to start with a definite ideal of human character, a fixed conception of areté").

[2] Dennis H. Wrong, *The Problem of Order: What Unites and Divides Society* (Cambridge: Harvard University Press, 1994), 73.

[3] David E. Klemm, "The Rhetoric of Theological Argument," *The Rhetoric of the Human Sciences: Language and Argument in Scholarship and Public Affairs*, ed. John S. Nelson, Allan Megill, and Donald N. McCloskey (Madison: University of Wisconsin Press, 1987), 276-97; 278.

[4] Louis P. Pojman, *Religious Belief and the Will* (London: Routledge and Kegan Paul, 1986), 32-4.

[5] Orlando Patterson, *Freedom, Volume 1: Freedom in the Making of Western Culture* (New York: Basic Books, 1991), 357; Perry Anderson, *Lineages of the Absolutist State* (London: Verso, 1974), 28.

[6] Stanley Jeyaraja Tambiah, *Magic, Science, Religion, and the Scope of Rationality,* (Cambridge: Cambridge University Press, 1990), 114.

[7] Thomas Rutherforth, cited (I think imprecisely) as a "theological utilitarian" in Jacob Viner, T*he Role of Providence in the Social Order: An Essay in Intellectual History* (Princeton: Princeton University Press, 1972), 73; and see Viner's ensuing discussion of Adam Smith to p. 85.

[8] Ludwig Wittgenstein, *Lectures and Conversations on Aesthetics, Psychology, and Religious Belief*, ed. Cyril Barrett (Oxford: Blackwell, 1966), 50.

[9] H. L. A. Hart, *Punishment and Responsibility: Essays in the Philosophy of Law* (New York: Oxford University Press, 1968), 3.

[10] Friedrich Nietzsche, *The Genealogy of Morals* 2:4, my translation; see *Werke in Drei Bänden*, ed. Karl Schlechta (Munich: Carl Hansen, 1966): 2, 804-5.

[11] Mary Douglas, *How Institutions Think* (Syracuse: Syracuse University Press, 1986).

[12] Hans Schwarz, *Evil: A Historical and Theological Perspective*, trans. Mark W. Worthing (Minneapolis: Fortress Press, 1995), 203.

[13] Jean-Jacques Lecercle, *The Violence of Language* (London: Routledge, 1990), 240, citing Karen Blixen's *Out of Africa* as his source for the anecdote.

[14] Odo Marquard, *Farewell to Matters of Principle: Philosophical Studies* (1981), trans. Robert M. Wallace with Susan Bernstein and James I. Porter, Odéon series (New York: Oxford University Press, 1989), ch. 3; and *In Defense of the Accidental: Philosophical Studies*, trans. Robert M. Wallace, Odéon series (New York: Oxford University Press, 1991), ch. 2. Further in-text citations will be *FMP* and *DA* respectively. Gottfried Wilhelm Leibniz, *Theodicy: Essays on the Goodness of God, the Freedom of Man, and the Origin of Evil* (1710), ed. Austin Farrer, trans. E. M. Huggard (1951; rpt. La Salle: Open Court, 1985).

[15] Alvin Plantinga, "The Free Will Defense" (1977), rpt. *The Problem of Evil: Selected Readings*, ed. Michael L. Peterson (Notre Dame: Notre Dame UP, 1992): 103-33;110.

[16] Lewis Ford, "Divine Persuasion and the Triumph of Good," Peterson, 247-65; 249.

[17] J. P. Sommerville, "Absolutism and Royalism," *The Cambridge History of Political Thought 1450-1700*, ed. J. H. Burns with Mark Goldie (Cambridge: Cambridge University Press, 1991), 347-73; 359-60.

18 Alexandre Koyré, *From the Closed World to the Infinite Universe* (1957; rpt. New York: Harper & Brothers, 1958), 272-3. A similar Marquardian move followed in nineteenth-century biology. "After Darwin's careful dissection of the Creator's handiwork" as described by William Paley's school of natural theology, "the Creator began to look so mindless that many creationists wisely sought to move Him into the biological background as a 'first cause': better a distant than a dim-witted god." Frank J. Sulloway, *Born to Rebel: Birth Order, Family Dynamics, and Creative Lives* (New York: Pantheon, 1996), 349-50.

19 Georg Wilhelm Friedrich Hegel, *Phenomenology of Spirit*, trans. A. V. Miller (Oxford: Oxford University Press, 1977), 455 (sec. 752).

20 Peter Goodrich, "Ars Bablativa: Ramism, Rhetoric, and the Genealogy of English Jurisprudence," *Legal Hermeneutics: History, Theory, and Practice*, ed. Gregory Leyh (Berkeley: University of California Press, 1992), 43-82; 43.

21 Alfred North Whitehead, *Process and Reality* (1929), corrected edition, ed. David Ray Griffin and Donald W. Sherburne (New York: Macmillan, Free Press, 1978), 350.

22 Daniel Patrick Moynihan, *Miles to Go* (Cambridge: Harvard University Press, 1996); chapter 3 is "Defining Deviancy Down." Durkheim nicely exemplifies the Marquard Effect by redefining "deviant" as the normal, hence useful Other of the "normal." Less inventively, American values merely warehouse "deviants" in minority ghettos or jails, as deviant from those values. Disclaimed by "the American dream," they no longer feel their American identity suffices. They invent (not out of whole cloth) ethnic myths to explain and locate themselves, and often to render themselves—contrary to general social judgment—unindictable. Cf. Alain Touraine, *Critique of Modernity* (1992), trans. David Macey (Oxford: Blackwell, 1995), 183: "Those who are excluded from the constant process of innovation and decision-making . . . are no longer defined by what they do, but by what they do not do[,] . . . their unemployment or marginality. . . . Increasingly, they are integrated in to local or ethnic cultures."

23 This is an argument pressed throughout Ernest Becker's *The Structure of Evil: An Essay on the Unification of the Science of Man* (1968; New York: Macmillan, Free Press, 1976).

24 Steven Pinker, *How the Mind Works* (New York: W. W. Norton, 1997), 54.

25 Susan Wolf, "Asymmetrical Freedom," *Moral Responsibility*, ed. John Martin Fischer (Ithaca: Cornell University Press, 1986), 225-40; 229, 232.

26 Andrew Wear, "Medicine in Early Modern Europe, 1500-1700," *The Western Medical Tradition 800 BC to AD 1800* (Cambridge: Cambridge University Press, 1995), 219-25.

27 Elinor Burkett, "'God Created Me To Be a Slave,'" *The New York Times Magazine* (October 12, 1997), 56.

28 Jaroslav Pelikan, *The Christian Tradition: A History of the Development of Doctrine*, vol. 5, *Christian Doctrine and Modern Culture (since 1700)* (Chicago: University of Chicago Press, 1989), 11. Cf. Vincent Descombes's remark that "the 'philosophy of existence' first came into being when Leibniz wrote his *Theodicy*," a time when "instituted religions had begun to lose their foundations in the minds of the people. . . . The 'philosophy of existence' is . . . an integral part of the age of the disenchantment of the world." *The Barometer of Modern Reason: On the Philosophies of Current Events,* trans. Stephen Adam Schwartz (New York: Oxford University Press, 1993), 107-8.

29 The first two chapters of Michael Allen Gillespie, *Nihilism before Nietzsche* (Chicago: University of Chicago Press, 1995), locate Descartes, Leibniz's direct predecessor in continental philosophy, in terms of medieval nominalism and the dangerous omnipotence of God's will.

30 Amos Funkenstein, *Theology and the Scientific Imagination from the Middle Ages to the Seventeenth Century* (Princeton: Princeton University Press, 1986), 151-2.

31 G. W. Leibniz, "The Principles of Nature and Grace, Based on Reason" (1714), *Leibniz: Selections*, ed. Philip P. Wiener (New York: Scribner's, 1951), 529-30.

32 Annette C. Baier, *Moral Prejudices: Essays on Ethics* (Cambridge: Harvard University Press, 1994), 114-5.

33 Donald R. Kelley, "Law," *The Cambridge History of Political Thought 1450-1700*, 66-94; 91, 93. James Gordley has written the legal history of the tenets involved in syntheses of Roman law and Thomistic, post-Aristotelian philosophy by Jesuits in the later sixteenth and early seventeenth centuries. Their work, Gordley argues, fed the northern natural law school of Grotius, Pufendorf, Barbeyrac, et al., and thence influenced modern contract law. Progressively, the act of willing

became the necessary and sufficient basis for contract, so that law separated from what had been its inseparable moral basis. James Gordley, *The Philosophical Origins of Modern Contract Doctrine* (Oxford: Clarendon, 1991).

[34] On Erasmus and Luther, see *Luther and Erasmus: Free Will and Salvation*, ed. E. Gordon Rupp and A. N. Marlow (Philadelphia: The Westminster Press, 1969). For Erasmus on the dangers of Luther's position, see 41-2, 96; I quote from 41, slightly modified. Luther's defense of his dogma accepts that his God may well be "regarded as unjust, as cruel, as intolerable" (244). Relying on the research of the theological historian Wilfrid Cantwell Smith, Byron J. Good discusses the sliding of "belief" from "fealty" to "opinion." *Medicine, Rationality, and Experience: An Anthropological Perspective* (Cambridge University Press, 1994), 15-7.

[35] See Lorraine Daston, *Classical Probability in the Enlightenment* (Princeton: Princeton University Press, 1988), 60-7.

[36] Dennis H. Wrong, *The Problem of Order*, 88, discussing Adam Smith; and see the directly following discussion of Alessandro Pizzorno and mutual recognition of others' durable identity, 88-90.

[37] Kenneth R. Minogue, "Liberalism," *The Blackwell Dictionary of Twentieth-Century Social Thought*, William Outhwaite and Tom Bottomore (Oxford: Blackwell, 1993), 333-6; 335.

[38] Jonathan Lamb, *The Rhetoric of Suffering: Reading the Book of Job in the Eighteenth Century* (New York: Oxford University Press, 1995).

[39] Richard Rorty, *Contingency, Irony, and Solidarity* (Cambridge: Cambridge University Press, 1989), xv. Rorty three times—xv, 74, 146—credits Judith Shklar with this definition of "liberal."

[40] I take the term "mythic posit" from Joseph Margolis, "The Limits of Metaphysics and the Limits of Certainty." Such a posit declares, axiomatically, a "context for all contexts for enunciative discourse," like Heidegger's Being as context for Dasein and other beings. *Antifoundationalism Old and New*, ed. Tom Rockmore and Beth J. Singer (Philadelphia: Temple University Press, 1992), 22. Klemm's "God" as a possibly irruptive, profound alterity presumably is a posit of a similar sort.

[41] Jacques Derrida, "Signature Event Context" (1972), trans. Samuel Weber and Jeffrey Mehlman (1977), rpt. in Derrida, *Limited Inc* (Evanston: Northwestern University Press, 1988), 1-23; 10. Further citations will be in the text as "SEC."

[42] Stephen P. Stich, *Deconstructing the Mind* (New York: Oxford University Press, 1996), 9.

[43] Derrida lays out a little lexicography of "deconstruction" in his "Letter to a Japanese Friend," *A Derrida Reader: Between the Blinds*, ed. Peggy Kamuf (New York: Columbia University Press, 1991), 270-6; the cited passages are at 271-2. Hereafter, "*LJF*" in the text. I have slightly modified David Wood and Andrew Benjamin's English translation, using "Lettre à un ami japonais," reprinted in Derrida's *Psyché: Inventions de l'autre* (Paris: Éditions Galilée, 1987), 388, 390. Not only did Derrida adapt the term "deconstruction," as he says, from Heidegger, he also, curiously, borrowed the East/West form of his lexicographical excursus from Heidegger's "A Dialogue on Language between a Japanese and an Inquirer," i.e., Heidegger himself, published 1959. An English translation by Peter D. Hertz is in Martin Heidegger, *On the Way to Language* (New York: Harper & Row, 1971), 1-54. Cf. Joseph Margolis's comment that after one grasps Heidegger's "explicitly phenomenologized form of deconstruction" in *Being and Time*, "one sees at once how little is left for Derrida to do, except to rehearse his own variations." *Texts without Referents: Reconciling Science and Nature* (Oxford: Basil Blackwell, 1989), 20.

[44] See Patrick Riley's excellent *The General Will before Rousseau: The Transformation of the Divine into the Civic* (Princeton: Princeton University Press, 1986).

[45] Karl Marx, "On the Jewish Question" (1843), in *The Marx-Engels Reader*, ed. Robert C. Tucker, 2d ed. (New York: Norton, 1978), 26-52; 46. Just before this passage, Marx quotes Rousseau directly on the point of internalizing one's socialized state. Hereafter, references in text as "Marx."

[46] Martin Heidegger, "The Self-Assertion of the German University" (Rectoral Address, 1933), *Martin Heidegger and National Socialism: Questions and Answers*, ed. Günther Neske and Emil Kettering, trans. Lisa Harries (New York: Paragon House, 1990), 10. The *Spiegel* interview appears at 41-66.

[47] Marx, "The Holy Family," excerpted in Tucker, 133-5; 134.

[48] Robert Nozick explains the terms, invented in the mid-1970s, in "Invisible-Hand Explanations" (1994), in Nozick, *Socratic Puzzles* (Cambridge: Harvard University Press, 1997), 191-2.

[49] In the Preface to *Capital*, Marx declares, "My standpoint, from which the evolution of the economic

formation of society is viewed as a process of natural history"—that is, Kant's phenomenal rather than noumenal realm—"can less than any other make the individual responsible for relations whose creature he socially remains." The next paragraph finds him denouncing "the most violent, mean and malignant passions of the human breast, the Furies of private interest" (Preface, Tucker 294-8; 297). One would hardly use moral language—"mean and malignant"—for natural-historical behavior as opposed to action, say for the innate territoriality of a polar bear. But the unresolved Kantian antinomy between action and behavior serves the ends of Marquardian moral *différance*.

[50] Marx, "The Manifesto of the Communist Party," Tucker, 469-500; 485.

[51] Martin Heidegger, "The Question Concerning Technology," *The Question Concerning Technology and Other Essays*, trans. William Lovitt (New York: Harper & Row, 1977), 3-35; 35.

[52] On Heidegger: Herman Rapaport explores numerous aspects of the relationship in *Heidegger and Derrida: Reflections on Time and Language* (Lincoln: University of Nebraska Press, 1989); see in particular Rapaport's analyses of *De l'esprit* and *The Post Card* (155-74, 192-202), also Rapaport's section "Dating Catastrophe," 234-45. In their *French Philosophy of the Sixties: An Essay on Antihumanism* (1985), trans. Mary H. S. Cattani (Amherst: University of Massachusetts Press, 1990), Luc Ferry and Alain Renaut caustically offer the equation "*Derrida = Heidegger + Derrida's Style*" (123).

On Marx: Jacques Derrida, *Specters of Marx: The State of the Debt, the Work of Mourning, and the New International* (1993), trans. Peggy Kamuf (London: Routledge, 1994). I shall also use Derrida's slightly earlier (1990) "Force of Law: The 'Mystical Foundation of Authority,'" *Deconstruction and the Possibility of Justice*, ed. Drucilla Cornell, Michel Rosenfeld, and David Gray Carlson (New York: Routledge, 1992), 3-67. References in text to *SM* and "FL" respectively.

[53] See Simon Critchley, *The Ethics of Deconstruction: Derrida and Levinas* (Oxford: Blackwell, 1992). Levinas's ethics comes from Jewish tradition, as inflected by Heidegger; Derrida himself is a Jewish Heideggerian, with a complex view of both, needless to say. The interest in Marx comes more from the outside: writing before *Specters of Marx*, Critchley discusses Derrida's being urged to deconstruct Marx's text (201-2). Ferry and Renaut develop the argument that in French thought of the 1960s through the mid-1980s, Marx and Heidegger stood as the parallel, rival patron saints of two sorts of deconstruction.

[54] On the Nazis' imitative use of the "Protocols," see Hannah Arendt, *The Origins of Totalitarianism,* new ed. (New York: Harvest, Harcourt Brace, 1976), 360.

[55] MacIntyre pursues this argument in *A Short History of Ethics: A History of Moral Philosophy from the Homeric Age to the Twentieth Century* (London: Routledge and Kegan Paul, 1967), *After Virtue: A Study in Moral Theory,* 2d ed. (Notre Dame: Notre Dame University Press, 1984), and *Whose Justice? Which Rationality?* (Notre Dame: Notre Dame University Press, 1988). References to this last in the text as *WJ.* Philosophers who see the current ethical situation less darkly include Jeffrey Stout, *Ethics after Babel: The Languages of Morals and their Discontents* (Boston: Beacon, 1988), Zygmunt Bauman, *Postmodern Ethics* (a Levinasian contribution), and Joseph Margolis, *Life without Principles* (Oxford: Blackwell, 1996). Margolis offers several theoretical caveats about MacIntyre, as on 140-1, and Stout discusses *After Virtue* at length, 200-42.

[56] *The Letters of David Hume*, ed. J. Y. T. Greig, 2 vols. (Oxford: Oxford University Press, 1932), 1: 39. Text italicized in original.

[57] Max Weber, *The Sociology of Religion* (1922), trans. Ephraim Fischoff (1963; Boston: Beacon, 1993), 110-5.

[58] E. C. Mossner, *The Life of David Hume* (Edinburgh: Nelson, 1954), 34. Annette C. Baier (*A Progress of Sentiments: Reflections on Hume's "Treatise"* [Cambridge: Harvard University Press, 1991], 203) and MacIntyre have stressed Hume's ethical hedonism as that of "an apostate from Calvinism." I want instead to stress his Marquardian continuity with Calvinist thought. Ethical hedonism just is the secular analogue to God's hedonism, the rule of His pleasure—for God, in the sense of unaccountable will, as when one says that an official serves at the monarch's pleasure. By definition, God does what it "pleases" Him to do, and theological debate centers about what prior constraints, if any, He has set upon Himself: "reason" or, more narrowly, "non-contradiction" are candidates for such constraints. Secularized, this same debate informs ethical hedonism.

[59] Baier, *Moral Prejudices*, 55-6. She offers similar readings of Hume's dual, interrelated ethics in *A Progress of Sentiments*.

[60] David Gauthier, *Moral Dealing: Contract, Ethics, and Reason* (Ithaca: Cornell University Press, 1990), 61.

[61] German scholars have debated whether to define historical change through (a) "the transposition of authentically theological contents into secularized alienation from their origin" or (b) the "reoccupation of answer positions that had become vacant and whose corresponding questions could not be eliminated." The formulations come from the leading advocate of (b), Hans Blumenberg, *The Legitimacy of the Modern Age* (1966), trans. Robert M. Wallace (Cambridge: MIT Press, 1983), 65. For the position Blumenberg opposes in Part I of this book, see Karl Löwith, *Meaning in History* (Chicago: University of Chicago Press, 1949). Other issues of Marquard's and my argument appear at length in Blumenberg's book. Part II treats the problems of divine omnipotence and unpredictability, mentioned above in connection with nominalism, Erasmus's concern about Lutheranism, and the shortcomings of Leibnizian law, as well as with Hume's ethical hedonism. Part III details the rehabilitation of curiosity for its own sake, Marquard's "gnoseology." Löwith advances a morphological argument; Blumenberg, a functional argument. The Marquard Effect's "Darwinian spin" transforms and links these rivals, as Darwin's theories transformed their nineteenth-century biological predecessors. See Stephen T. Asma, *Following Form and Function: A Philosophical Archaeology of Life Science* (Evanston: Northwestern University Press, 1996).

Blood Vengeance In Revelation

Leonard L. Thompson

Most of us have tasted what Charlotte Brontë once called "the aromatic wine of vengeance," and so we are sympathetic to blood vengeance in certain circumstances. Defining the circumstances, however, leads into a very thorny area of morality and law. Sometimes vendettas are portrayed playfully, as in folk songs about family feuds and murder in the Old West. Sometimes a crime, for example, Eichmann's deeds, is viewed as so horrendous that it cries out for blood vengeance. In Israelite law, certain cities were set aside as places of protection "from the avenger, so that the slayer may not die until there is a trial" (Numbers 35:12).[1] Even when there is a trial, however, blood vengeance may not be acceptable to some people, as the jury of the Timothy McVeigh case discovered. Were they swayed to give the death penalty (blood for blood) by the outrage of relatives of those killed in the Oklahoma City bombing, or did they make a decision on the basis of the majesty of the moral order embodied in our law? Is "outrage" a sufficient basis for blood revenge? Under what circumstances is the majesty of the moral order offended?

In what follows, I explore this timely topic of "blood vengeance" in Revelation, the last book in the New Testament. That book and the apocalyptic ideology which it embodies have attracted Americans in their literature and politics, from Anne Dudley Bradstreet's poetry and Cotton Mather's vision of America to John Barth's novels and the Cold War. It will no doubt continue to attract as we move into the new millennium. Written in the style of myth, Revelation presents blood vengeance bluntly and unambiguously. Saints in heaven rejoice when God avenges their blood on the offender. As Rome burns, they shout "hallelujah." If Revelation was forged in the furnace of persecution and martyrdom, then readers can understand and even sympathize with its vitriol against Roman society. But as we shall see, that explanation does not square with the social history of early Christianity at the time of John's visions. Having been wronged is not the only dynamics in blood vengeance. Finally, Revelation, as well as being a case study of blood vengeance, offers some ways of handling it.

* * * * *

The term "vengeance" (*ekdikein*) occurs twice in the bloody book of Revelation, first in a series of visions describing the opening of a scroll sealed by seven seals (Revelation 6:1-8:1). The first four seals reveal seriatim the four horsemen of the apocalypse. The fifth discloses a scene in which "souls who had been slaughtered for the word of God and for the testimony they had given" (6:9) lament before God:

> Almighty God, holy and true,
> How long are you going to delay judging
> And avenging our blood
> On those who dwell upon the earth? (6:10; author's translation)

"Vengeance" occurs again toward the end of the book in a series of visions describing "the judgment of the great whore" (Revelation 17:1), Babylon /Rome. As Rome collapses, kings and merchants, who fornicated with her, lament the fall of the great city (chapter 18). Then John sees a vision of the heavenly throne, as in the previous occurrence of the term, "blood vengeance." In contrast to the lament of kings and merchants on earth, those in heaven rejoice at Rome's demise:

> Hallelujah!
> God is our Savior!
> He is glorious and powerful
> He judges fairly and justly;
> He has condemned the great harlot

Transgression, Punishment, Responsibility, Forgiveness
Graven Images 4 (1998), 30-36.

> Who corrupted the earth with her fornication,
> And he has avenged on her the blood of his servants. (19:1-2; author's translation)

They continue to rejoice as Rome burns: "Hallelujah! The smoke from her goes up for ever and ever."

The Greek term translated "avenged," *ekdikein*, has the same range of meanings as words in English derived from the Latin *vicare*: revenge, avenge, vengeance, vindicate. It refers to a legal remedy, closely associated with words meaning "to settle a suit," "prosecute one's rights against another," "have right done to one," "give satisfaction," "obtain a legal remedy," "prosecute," and "represent legally." But the word also carries the meanings of "personal outrage" and "desire to hurt." Both meanings can be read in the poignant inscription on an island near Delos: "I call upon and pray the Most High God . . . against those who with guile murdered or poisoned the untimely lost Heraclea [a young girl], shedding her innocent blood wickedly: that it may be so with them . . . and with their children . . . avenge the innocent blood and require it again right speedily."[2]

In both occurrences of the word in Revelation, God does the avenging, not his people. That notion is grounded in an ancient law which God gave to the Israelites: "Vengeance is mine, and recompense," says the Lord (Deuteronomy 32:35). In each of the two passages, attributes are given to God which make him fit to judge and avenge. He reigns as a "sovereign lord" who does mighty deeds on behalf of those who trust in him. He has a peculiar attribute of being "holy" (*hagios*), a term used only of him and those who are pure through him, and he is "true," i.e., trustworthy to uphold the moral order. He "judges justly," so that the discriminations which he makes among people—some to be punished, others vindicated—are fair and morally right. Ultimately, it is a moot point to refer to God as just, holy, and true, for justice, holiness, and truth are determined by God. (Compare the principle in baseball: a strike is a strike when the umpire calls it a strike.) It would be a contradiction in terms to say that God acts unjustly or is impure.

The mechanism by which God operates is not stated. Perhaps he reacts to murder in the quasi-automatic manner of the Erinyes—chthonic powers in Greek religion and tragedies who avenge blood-guilt. On the other hand, Rechab and Baanah kill Ishbaal and then come to David saying, "Here is the head of Ishbaal, son of Saul, your enemy, who sought your life; the Lord has avenged my lord the king this day" (2 Samuel 4:8). In John's visions, God either avenges by his own hand or by an angel or Jesus Christ. His vengeance is just, for Rome and her kings ruthlessly murdered his saints (*hagioi*) and drank their blood, while they suffered in quiet desperation. So it is in the visions which John saw on the island of Patmos.

If the old Hollywood movies had portrayed accurately the plight of early Christians—thrown to the lions, forced to fight with gladiators, while mad emperors (and their women) watched in lustful excitement—then blood vengeance in Revelation would be understandable. John, however, wrote Revelation sometime between 75 and 95 CE to Christians in the province of Asia (western coast area of present day Turkey). At that time, there was no state persecution of Christians. For the most part, Christians were living quietly, partaking in the peace and prosperity of the empire. Wayne Meeks's description of Christians alluded to in Paul's letters would fit most Christians in the cities of Asia:

> The 'typical' Christian . . . the one who most often signals his presence in the letters by one or another small clue, is a free artisan or small trader. Some even in those occupational categories had houses, slaves, the ability to travel, and other signs of wealth. Some of the wealthy provided housing, meeting places, and other services for individual Christians and for whole groups. In effect, they filled the roles of patrons.[3]

It would be many decades before imperial officials initiated systematic persecution of Christians.

When John was writing, Roman officials considered Christians—along with Druids and Bacchants—a troublesome and distasteful group, but they prosecuted them only when locals accused their neighbors of being Christian, often through anonymous pamphlets. Even then the authorities responded reluctantly. So Pliny the Younger, in 112 CE, while traveling on behalf of the emperor Trajan through Bithynia and Pontus, provinces north and east of Asia, brought to trial those accused of being Christians but simultaneously admonished against anonymous pamphlets.[4] Those accused were required to make an offering to the statues of Caesar (Trajan) and the gods or say that Caesar is Lord and renounce Christ (cf. *Letters* 10.96). If they persisted in affirming their Christianity, they were either executed or sent to Rome for trial. Pliny found Christianity distasteful, "a degenerate sort of cult carried to extravagant lengths," but it did not concern him greatly. He interviewed several people who had abandoned Christianity and returned to their traditional religions, so he hoped that this "wretched cult" would soon die out.

It is not clear exactly why non-Christians brought complaints against their Christian neighbors. Christians were probably suspect simply because they were a new religious movement that did not honor and respect traditional forms of public, religious life (cf. suspicions about new religious movements such as The Unification Church or Church Universal Triumphant in the United States). They met in secret, and it was rumored that in their meetings they had cannibalistic feasts, carried on illicit sexual relations, and blasphemed the gods—at least so the Christian Athenagoras says.[5] There may also have been an economic factor in opposition to Christians: if several people converted to Christianity in one area, it could hurt businesses associated with traditional religion, for example, butchers who prepared sacrifices or silversmiths who made images of deities (Pliny, *Letters* 10.96; Acts 19:23-7).[6]

For the most part, however, Christians at the end of the first century did not irritate their neighbors sufficiently for them to make very many anonymous complaints to the authorities. "Conduct yourselves honorably among the Gentiles," writes the author of 1 Peter to Christians in the area of Pontus, "so that, though they malign you as evildoers, they may see your honorable deeds and glorify God when he comes to judge" (2:12,17). The writer of 1 Timothy urges Christians to pray "for kings and all who are in high positions, so that we may lead a quiet and peaceable life in all godliness and dignity" (2:1-2). Approximately a century later than Revelation, Tertullian makes clear that Christians are not odd and different from others in the empire. He writes that Christians have the same manner of life, the same dress, and the same requirements for living as non-Christians. They depend upon the marketplace, the butchers, the baths, shops, factories, taverns, fairs, and other businesses. Christians sail ships, serve in the army, till the ground, and engage in trade alongside non-Christians, and Christians provide skills and services for the benefit of the whole society.[7] Persecutions were sporadic and minimal. Martyrs were few in number. As Robert L. Wilken writes, "In most areas of the Roman Empire Christians lived quietly and peaceably among their neighbors, conducting their affairs without disturbance" (16).

If there was not widespread persecution, how are we to understand the vitriol of blood vengeance in John's visions? Let us begin by contrasting two sources of knowledge: public knowledge and revealed, esoteric knowledge. Public knowledge of the world is taught by means of public institutions that provide language, roles, identities, norms, myths, rituals, and a cosmic frame of reference for their members—all of which are integrated into an ordered reality.[8] As Peter Berger states, "Every society provides for its members an objectively available body of 'knowledge.' To participate in the society is to share its 'knowledge.'"[9] Members of Roman society shared public knowledge through such means as the constitution laid down by Augustus, by the peace and prosperity of the whole empire, by the very Roman earth so celebrated in the *Aeneid*, and in the manifest destiny of Roman expansion. In the province of Asia, where John lived and worked, Roman imperial institutions were integrated into city and provincial life. Social position, rank, and status were spelled out fairly clearly for all. The spatial layout of the city, its public institutions, and its official activities were all expressions of a "civic ideology" or a "public knowledge." In John's time, imperial Rome offered Asians a coherent, ordered structure of reality that unified religious, social, economic, political, and aesthetic aspects of the world. In Berger's terms, those aspects were so integrated that urban Asians shared "knowledge" that allowed them "to move with a measure of confidence through everyday life."[10]

The esoteric, non-public character of John's knowledge is stated at the beginning of Revelation: "The revelation of Jesus Christ, which God gave him to show his servants." As an apocalypticist, John is a visionary who makes contact with God through ecstatic experience. When filled with the spirit, he can talk with angels, ascend into heaven, and see there the Lord God and, among others, the blessed dead. Other Christians in John's own time had similar visions—the apostle Paul, Agabus, Hermas, and various gnostic Christians. In Judaism of his day, ecstatics wrote under the name of Daniel, Enoch, Ezra, and Baruch. In paganism (neither Christian nor Jewish), there were the sibyls and the Egyptian Hermes. Those visionaries learn about the world, not through public knowledge, but special revelation. This revelation is self-authenticating—it comes from God! John describes to his readers how the message came to him via angels and other divine emissaries, and he draws his readers into his visions, so that after reading Revelation, readers accept the knowledge which John presents, if they want to be in fellowship with John, Jesus, and God.

Those two sources of knowledge—public and esoteric—portray life in the Roman Empire very differently. Public knowledge praised the joy of the *pax Romana*; John portrays conflict and warring. Public knowledge acclaims the emperor as a great benefactor; John portrays him as the incarnation of Satan. Public knowledge encourages people to share in the peace and prosperity of the empire; John views economic prosperity as corruption and impoverishment. John especially attacks Christians living peaceably with their neighbors and participating in the benefits of Roman society: those at Sardis have soiled their clothes by participating in non-Christian society, and the Laodiceans appear rich and prosperous, but are really poor and naked. John condemns a prophetess at Thyatira whom he calls Jezebel, Balaamites at Pergamum, and Nicolaitans at Pergamum and Ephesus—all Christians who accommodate to Roman life while keeping a Christian commitment. John's esoteric knowledge directs Christians to find true peace and rest from persecution, oppression, and martyrdom.

As a visionary proclaiming esoteric knowledge at odds with the knowledge learned from public institutions at the center of Roman society, John is marginalized. Most visionaries are pushed to the periphery of social life—shamans found throughout Malaysia, Indonesia, Eurasia, and the Americas, Pentecostals at the edge of main line religions in America today, and New Religious Movements such as Johrei, Divine Light Mission, and Church Universal and Triumphant. To be precise, a correlation exists between esoteric knowledge and location on the periphery of society. Either may cause the other.

Visionaries and others on the margin of society can offer much creativity and originality in relation to the status quo. By viewing a situation from a different angle, they offer new ways of seeing and thinking. Coriolanus, for example, is marginalized in Shakespeare's play of that name. The tribunes have just incited the people to demand that Coriolanus be exiled from his Rome. He, however, responds, standing alone in the face of those who have just condemned him: "I banish you. / . . . / There is a world elsewhere."[11] In Revelation, followers of the Lamb are killed by the Dragon or the Beast, and as they die, they cry, "Victory, we have conquered." Such innovative reversals can spark a different way of seeing things. As Fintan O'Toole once wrote in *The Irish Times,* "The apocalypst, the magician, and the mystic are the ultimate critics of the world as it is."[12]

Those supporting social institutions at the center, however, do not always appreciate the novelty and insights offered by those at the periphery. For the most part, representatives of institutions at the center which bear core values and public knowledge tolerate those on the periphery with amusement and disdain, viewing them as ill-informed, ignorant, and slightly mad. On occasion, if those at the margin become too visible, the state brings them to trial and, if necessary, in the process kills them, for deviant ideas can destabilize the "sane, steady world" of the Empire.[13]

Visionaries such as John, on the other hand, cannot ever view representatives of public knowledge as amusing, for those at the center refuse to accept the world as known by the marginalized. That fact must be explained. Why don't those at the center see the truth? In answering that question, the rhetoric of the visionary can become intense and exceedingly hostile. Those at the center are under the power of Satan, who wars against God and his elect. At issue is human destiny, for humans make up the battleground on which God and Satan war. In Revelation, scenes of blood vengeance manifest that intense, hostile rhetoric. More precisely, scenes of blood vengeance in Revelation do double duty: they support John's esoteric knowledge as knowledge from God and they condemn those who support public knowledge at the center of society. John's visions of divine vengeance reinforce the social identity of the marginal group as those "in the right" and give them cognitive certainty that they see the world correctly. At the same time, divine vengeance proves that the Roman Empire is Satan's tool soon to be destroyed. There is a structural necessity to that binary opposition: if "we" are God's people, "they" must belong to Satan; if "we" are to be vindicated, "they" must be punished. Doubt cast upon "their" identity casts doubt upon "our" identity.

For blood vengeance to be valid and just, the "others" have to be flat, two-dimensional characters. There can be no moral ambiguity or behavioral surprises in the "other"—that which occurs in actual human beings. The other must be wholly evil, incapable of any goodness or acts of love. Like all seeking blood vengeance, those in John's visions move towards the pathological vanity of narcissism: the good and the just can be found only in their group, and "others"—those deserving revenge—are ruthless and cruel in their entirety. An aspect of that narcissism is present in blood vengeance, whether pursued by those supporting central values in institutions at the center or by those holding to "deviant" knowledge on the periphery of society.

Those binary oppositions of public/esoteric knowledge and center/periphery location create a time of crisis, and the times must be seen as in crisis in order to carry out blood vengeance. In ordinary times, blood vengeance would probably be viewed as unacceptable and not just, for there would be other ways to resolve conflict. But out-of-the-ordinary times require out-of-the-ordinary action: blood must be shed. John describes the "time" as one of imminent transformation, "what must soon take place" (Revelation 22:6). God's Day of Wrath shatters the Roman peace, and with it will come conflict and war. He will bring a Day that will break apart that ordered, bounded world and will reveal its Satanic base. The whore will be stripped naked and her body burned. Birds will be called to "the great supper of God," consisting of the "flesh of kings, the flesh of captains, the flesh of the mighty, the flesh of horses and their riders" (19:17-8). The bureaucratic beasts—manifestations of the primordial beasts of chaos that opposed God at the creation of the world—will be captured and "thrown alive into the lake of fire that burns with sulfur" (19:20). Though Christians will suffer along the way, the end will bring a boon to them and destruction to their enemies. (Generally in apocalyptic visions, the "end" refers only to the demise of the enemies and to the social world that supports them.) In place of the Roman Empire, God will bring in a new, Christian Golden Age—"a new heaven and a new earth" (21:1) and a New Jerusalem to replace urban life in Asia. There, the "saints," those now marginalized on the periphery of society, "will reign forever and ever" (22:5).

* * * * *

In Revelation, scenes of unmitigated blood revenge are balanced by scenes and motifs that counter the dynamics of vengeance. One such motif is found in scenes acclaiming God as creator of all things:

> You are worthy, our Lord and God
> to receive glory and honor and power
> for you created all things,
> and by your will they existed and were created. (4:11)

In the final analysis, John's world is monistic, not dualistic. The One God is God of those both giving and receiving revenge. There are non-theological images to express our common humanity—shared DNA, fellow astronauts stranded on planet earth, common consumers— but John does so by referring to divine creation. Recognizing one creator god does not make acts of violence any less abhorrent or the wine of vengeance any less aromatic, but it does affirm that everyone—the violator, the victim, and the arbitrator—is part of one community, one family, under God.

Lest this point get lost in the vastness of cosmic realities and global thinking, "community" should be brought local, as Wendell Berry might say.[14] Blood is shed in a specific place and soaks into the earth there, not here. Avengers take revenge in a particular place. And though the risks are great, as anyone knows who has lived in a small town, mending of the moral order takes place locally where the harm was done. Perhaps, then, it was a mistake to try Timothy McVeigh outside the place of the crime, and perhaps those Jews had it right who returned to their homeland in Germany after the holocaust. Magnanimity may not always win the day, but reconciliation occurs in the locale of the harm done by people who see, and lead others to see, the hidden dimension of one community, which John describes as one family under God.

Another motif in Revelation relevant to blood vengeance is difficult, perhaps impossible, to comprehend fully. Revelation is a bloody book, but the spilling of blood has positive as well as negative value. For example, those who cry out for vengeance dwell "under the altar," and thereby their "having been slaughtered" gains a sacral significance (see Revelation 6:9-10). In John's Christian tradition, their deaths gain significance because in being martyred they imitate Jesus who, by his blood, "ransomed for God" many saints (5:9). The life-giving power of Jesus' blood is but one example of a motif in Near Eastern and Greco-Roman religions: life is achieved through union with a dying God. Life is in the blood, and so in many creation myths, the blood of one who is killed is the source of life, often human life. In a Mesopotamian myth, Qingu—who fought against noble Marduk—was defeated, bound, and killed: God Ea "imposed the penalty on him and cut off his blood. He created mankind from his [Qingu's] blood."[15] In the myth of Agamemnon, immortalized by Aeschylus, Agamemnon cannot sail to Troy and thereby save the community until this command was fulfilled: "Artemis must have blood."[16] In ancient and modern cultures, there is prohibition against murder, and yet in the careful confines of ritual, murder is committed. Freud associated the sanctity of killing with the first murder of the father—sometime in humanity's distant past. René Girard, commenting on Freud's puzzlement over sacrifice, writes: "The rite is invariably presented in the form of a murder, a transgression both culpable and obligatory whose virtue lies ultimately in its very impiety."[17] That profound and terrifying mystery of destructive death—that a violation of the moral code can mend the moral order and renew life and community—remains with us today.

At the end of Revelation another motif occurs which breaks down the dichotomies of vengeance. John describes a vision of the New Jerusalem, a wondrous city where the saints reign. In it are the tree of life, the throne of God, no darkness or night, no suffering or pain. No one unclean is allowed inside, but—and this is the striking motif—the gates of the city are always open. No hard, impervious boundaries separate the saints inside from the sinners outside. Though the point is debated among scholars of Revelation, the open gates seem to offer the possibility of repentance and reconciliation on the part of those who "practice abomination" (21:27). If so, the Apocalypse never rules out rehabilitation. The "clean" and "unclean" cannot mingle together, but the opportunity exists for the "unclean" to be transformed and enter the city.

One of Revelation's most significant contributions to handling blood vengeance may thus be in the way it embraces opposites: it presents unambiguously times of crisis that dichotomize humanity into "them" and "us" and require blood vengeance in its most vitriolic form, but it counters that with a vision of peacefulness and rest which potentially embraces all people into one community. The shedding of blood is wrong and must be avenged, and yet a central image in the book is the Slain Lamb and murdered martyrs whose deaths contribute to wholeness and a revival of goodness. The pendulum swings through the blood of the dead from negative to positive. And, finally, the injustice of murdering and the consignment of the murderer to outer darkness is but one end of the pendulum's arc. At the other end are the open gates to the New Jerusalem. I wonder, along with Earl Rovit, "whether it is not, finally, in the constant shifting of the vision—from part to sum, from I to other, from desire to restraint— that moral space is created in the universe."[18] In any event, the case of Revelation argues for enduring the full swing of the pendulum before pursuing blood vengeance.

The Book of Revelation does not offer any grand solution to the ongoing human experience of revenge and blood vengeance. By understanding the workings of vengeance in John's location in society, we may, however, better understand some of the latent social, psychological, and religious forces at work in our handling of blood vengeance. Popular interpretations of Revelation underscore its portrayal of fundamental conflicts and warring powers within the individual psyche, communities, nations, and the cosmos as a whole. A more balanced presentation of the book recognizes that God has created all peoples, that even the act of shedding blood holds a glimmer of hope and reconciliation, and that repentance and rehabilitation remain an option for eternity.

Notes

[1] Unless otherwise indicated, biblical citations are from the New Revised Standard Version.

[2] G. Adolf Deissmann, *Light from the Ancient East*, trans. Lionel R. M. Strachan (1922; rpt. Grand Rapids: Baker Book House. 1980), 424.

[3] Wayne A. Meeks, *The First Urban Christians: The Social World of the Apostle Paul* (New Haven: Yale University Press, 1983), 73.

[4] Pliny, *Letters and Panegyrics,* trans. Betty Radice, Loeb Classical Library, 2 vols. (Cambridge: Harvard University Press, 1969), 10.96.

[5] Athenagoras, *A Plea for the Christians, Fathers of the Second Century,* vol. 2 of *The Ante-Nicene Fathers: Translations of the Writings of the Fathers down to A.D. 325,* ed. Alexander Roberts and James Donaldson, 10 vols. (Grand Rapids: Wm. B. Eerdmans, 1989), 123-48; 130 (chapter 3).

[6] See Robert L. Wilken, *The Christians as the Romans Saw Them* (New Haven: Yale University Press, 1984).

[7] Tertullian, *Apology,* trans. Gerald H. Rendall, Loeb Classical Library (Cambridge: Harvard University Press, 1953), 42.

[8] Peter Berger and Thomas Luckmann, *The Social Construction of Reality: A Treatise in the Sociology of Knowledge* (Garden City: Anchor, 1967), 63-7, 73-4.

[9] Peter Berger, *The Sacred Canopy: Elements of a Sociological Theory of Religion* (Garden City: Anchor, 1969), 21.

[10] Peter Berger, *A Rumor of Angels: Modern Society and the Rediscovery of the Supernatural* (Garden City: Anchor, 1970), 6; see Leonard L. Thompson, *The Book of Revelation* (New York: Oxford University Press, 1990), 176-7.

[11] William Shakespeare, *Coriolanus, Oxford Electronic Shakespeare*, 3.3.129,137.

[12] Fintan O'Toole, *The Irish Times*, date unknown.

[13] Ramsay MacMullen, *Enemies of the Roman Order: Treason, Unrest, and Alienation in the Empire* (Cambridge: Harvard University Press, 1966), 162. (Compare the United States vs. the Branch Davidians at Waco.)

[14] See, for example, Wendell Berry, *What Are People For* (New York: North Point Press, 1990).

[15] Stephanie Dalley, *Myths from Mesopotamia* (Oxford: Oxford University Press, 1991), 261.

[16] Aeschylus, *The Oresteia,* trans. Robert Fagles (New York: Bantam, 1975).

[17] René Girard, *Violence and the Sacred,* trans. Patrick Gregroy (Baltimore: The Johns Hopkins Press, 1977), 196.

[18] Earl Rovit, "On the Contemporary Apocalyptic Imagination." *The American Scholar* 37 (1968), 453-68; 468.

Walter Benjamin's Angels of History and the Post-Holocaust Quest for Redemption in Israeli Fiction: David Grossman's *See Under: Love* and Michal Govrin's *The Name*

Rachel Feldhay Brenner

> The history of freedom is only possible as a history of suffering.
> Johann Baptist Metz

This essay discusses Israeli responses to the Holocaust in two recent novels by David Grossman and Michal Govrin, both of the post-Holocaust generation. I attempt to illuminate the complexity of these responses in the context of Walter Benjamin's metaphoric representations of history. I believe that Benjamin's evolving understanding of the theological aspect of history in his three New Angel parables helps to elucidate the protagonists' sense of entrapment in history and their frantic search for liberation from the haunting horror of the past. But first a brief introduction that will locate these novels on the spectrum of Israeli responses to the Holocaust is in order.

That the State of Israel arose from the ashes of the Holocaust is hardly a hyperbole. That the establishment of Jewish sovereignty in the wake of the Final Solution constitutes a unique chapter in the history of nations can hardly be disputed. Yet this unprecedented, if not miraculous, political empowerment of a people doomed to total annihilation[1] engendered, as miracles often do, realities that are difficult to syncretize. The destruction of the Jewish people followed so swiftly by the triumphant national revival placed the Israeli Jews in a difficult situation vis-à-vis their European brethren. Though shaped by the Zionist doctrine of a "new" Jew—that is, a self-sufficient, dauntless individual who rejected the history of Jewish victimization—Israelis were nevertheless compelled to react to the tragedy of the Holocaust.

The prominence of the Holocaust thematic in Israeli literature attests to the impact of the national tragedy on the Israeli psyche. Holocaust awareness engendered a wide spectrum of literary approaches, from the "new" Jew's unabashed self-glorification to incapacitating self-doubt and despair in view of the horrifying history of evil and suffering. The varying literary treatments of the Diaspora tragedy reflect, to a remarkable extent, the mutating Israeli self-image. The earlier poets, such as Nathan Alterman (1910-1970), Uri Zvi Greenberg (1896-1981), Amir Gilboa (1917-1984), and others, offered consolation to the surviving European remnants. They promised regeneration and ultimate safety in the Jewish Homeland. Though the "surviving victim," or the "defenceless Jew," appears in poems such as Alterman's "On the Child Avram" and Greenberg's "River Roads," the emphasis in these representative works of the period is on militant, powerful, and selfless Israelis, ready to endanger themselves to save helpless Diaspora Jews and to avenge the suffering of the innocent.[2] They are portrayed as the descendants of the biblical soldiers-leaders, Joshua and David: as such, they restore dignity and potency to the Jewish people. Though expressing pity, horror, and sincere grief, the image of the Israeli as the rescuer projects the disparaging attitude of the Zionists towards the Diaspora Jewish victim. While saving the sufferers, the Israelis emphatically disassociated themselves from their suffering.

A critical reaction to this patronizing treatment of the Diaspora Jew emerges in the works of Yehuda Amichai (1924-), Ben-Tzion Tomer (1928-), Yoram Kaniuk (1930-) and, of course, Aharon Appelfeld (1932-), a prolific Israeli writer-survivor. As Gershon Shaked observes, the works of these authors "'reveal' the weakness of the 'native Israelis,' who cannot cope with the Holocaust and its survivors."[3] This weakness emerges clearly in, for instance, Shulamith Hareven's (1931-) 1980 short story "The Witness," which indicts the ruthless treatment of the survivor by the pioneering *Sabras*.[4] Both Leah Goldberg's (1911-1970) 1954 prescient play, *The Lady of the Castle*, and Aharon Megged's (1920-) more recent novel *Foiglman* (1986) denounce Israeli insensitivity to the cultural background and the psychological makeup of the Diaspora Jew.[5] The encounters between Israelis and the Holocaust survivors in these works approach critically and often satirically the ideology which severed the "new" Jews from their history and heritage.

This essay focuses on yet another, different response to the Holocaust, which emerges in the novels of two Israeli-born writers: David Grossman's *See: Under Love* (1986)[6] and Michal Govrin's *The Name* (1995).[7] These works do not identify with either of the previously discussed attitudes: they neither reiterate the arrogant superiority of the "new" Jew towards the Diaspora Jew, nor do they apologize for such arrogance. Here, the victim is transformed into an integral component of Israeli consciousness, a relentlessly haunting figment of the Israeli protagonist's imagination, and the drama unfolds in the recesses of the Israeli psyche. The issue is no longer the proper relationship of the Israeli with the victim of the Holocaust but rather facing and integrating the consciousness of the unspeakable past. The horror of inflicted suffering impels in these novels a reexamination of the ethics of human history. At the center of each novel arises the problem of the *humane survival* of the Holocaust legacy.

Each novel is a fictional autobiography of a child of Holocaust survivors.[8] The protagonist-narrators, Grossman's Momik and Govrin's Amalia, are locked in a "kafkaesque" world shaped by terrifying events they could not have possibly experienced: the threatening parental past of unspeakable and unspoken losses informs the children's present. In their imagination, they create frightening emblems of an incomprehensible past—Momik invents the "Nazi Beast" and Amalia coins the term "Appapatz."[9] These menacing impressions of the Holocaust signal deeply embedded fear and anxiety. At the same time, the violence that the images imply indicates the protagonists' hardly contained anger at the horrific legacy which entraps them and precludes a normal development into well-adjusted adulthood.

Thus for Momik the indelible knowledge of the Holocaust has emptied life of meaning: "How can you," he constantly ponders, "go on living and believing in humanity once you know [about the concentration camps]?"[10] The consciousness of the Holocaust imprisons Amalia in a deathlike existence. Having been named after Mala, her father's first wife, who died in Auschwitz, Amalia cannot lead a normal life because, as she realizes, there is no closure to Mala's death; she asks, "How can I ask forgiveness, release from vows, if there isn't even a grave, there isn't anything?"[11] The Holocaust death gave Amalia her name and circumscribed her existence. The prevailing sense of hopelessness makes it possible neither for Momik nor for Amalia to participate in the world.

It is, however, not only the external world that cannot be trusted. Even more serious is the impact of the Holocaust on the protagonists' personalities. The autobiographical confessions exhibit personal moral deterioration. Tormented by the constantly present, yet never fully comprehended horror, the protagonists develop ambivalent, love-hate relationships with the dead and with the living. Though ineluctably attracted to Mala, her talent, beauty, and courage, Amalia considers the dead woman her nemesis, a curse that will haunt her to her own death (44). As a child, Amalia imagines choking Mala and dreams of impaling and displaying her in public (23). As an adult, Amalia humiliates and torments Stein, a survivor and lifelong admirer of Mala. She is also cruelly inconsiderate of Hubert, her well-meaning German lover, who sees his photographic commemoration of Mala's life as a symbolic act of expiation and reconciliation.

Aggression also infuses Momik's behavior. As a child, Momik reveres Grandfather Anshel, a famous writer of children's adventure stories in pre-war Poland, now a senile and half-insane Holocaust survivor. Yet, he abuses him as an offering to the "Nazi Beast." Momik sees his neighbor-survivors as "this poor bunch of crazy Jews who stuck to him and ruined everything, his whole life they ruined" (83). As an adult, Momik releases his immense rage when he mentally and physically abuses his wife and consciously denies his love to his son.

The torment that the Israeli protagonists inflict upon others establishes a sense of displacement and incapacitating guilt. The intensity of their involvement with the suffering Diaspora victim distances these Israeli characters from the ideal of the "new" Jew. As autobiographical fictions, the novels communicate the need to reexamine the past in order to understand the reasons behind distorted relations with the world. It is, however, essential to emphasize that the return to the past does *not* signify the narrator's probing of his/her *personal* past. Nor does the narrator's probing the past intend to end the obsessive preoccupation with the victim and reaffirm his/her emotional independence of the Diaspora legacy. Rather, *the victim's experience* becomes the focus of the protagonists' exploration. Returning to the past, especially to the Holocaust, is problematic, however, since the engulfing enormity of suffering calls into question the meaningfulness of history. Is it possible to believe in moral existence while bearing in mind human proclivity to unspeakable atrocities? Is it possible to progress into the future when the past haunts us with visions of an unfathomable and meaningless evil?

Walter Benjamin's historico-theological concept of redemption offers a prescient illumination of the post-Holocaust world. His angel(s) of history illuminate the search for a new understanding of history in a world imbued with Holocaust consciousness. The first characterization of the angel of history appears in Benjamin's short parable "Agesilaus Santander."[12] This angel is conceived out of the narrator's secret Jewish name. Once disclosed, the name "loses . . . the gift of appearing anthropomorphous" (206) and transforms into an "armored and encased . . . picture on the wall: New Angel" (207). In contrast to the religious signification of angels as markers of redemption, Benjamin's Agesilaus Santander[13] offers no promise of a heavenly hereafter. In fact, the angel's involvement with the narrator disqualifies it from serving as God's angel. Instead of singing hymns of praise to God, the angel resolves "no longer to leave . . . [the narrator] alone." After having separated his human namesake from "his things" and from "the persons" in his life, the angel "fixes his eyes on him [the narrator] firmly" and pulls him back "from whence [he] came," hoping for "the new on no way except on the way of the return home" (208). The guardian angel, who, as a rule, protects the individual on his/her life journey to the future, reverses directions and enforces a voyage backwards, to the beginning. The new lies not in the future but rather in rediscovering the past. Redemption is predicated upon retracing the trajectory in order to reconsider that which has passed.

Is it possible that at this moment in his life Benjamin could intuitively presage the far-reaching consequences of the apocalypse that in a few years would claim his own life?[14] "Agesilaus Santander," written in exile in Ibiza in 1933, seems an allegorical and prophetic blueprint of the struggle that the post-Holocaust Jew wages with the "angel." The struggle with the urge to look back to the no-longer-existing past promises nothing but displacement and despair.[15] Benjamin's representation of the angel projects the predicament of Holocaust consciousness—a secret name which claims its irrevocable presence in a post-Holocaust Jewish psyche. The parable of the angel reminds us of Kafka, another Jewish pre-Holocaust visionary.[16] Benjamin's angel places the Israeli protagonists in a kafkaesque situation of captivity. They become hostages of incomprehensible historical processes which, having forcibly renamed them Jews (not "new" Jews), pull them back into the past.

It is interesting to place this struggle with the "renaming" angel along with Jacob's struggle, which rewards the biblical ancestor with the new name of Israel. Jacob's encounter with *his* angel ends in a name and a blessing which reaffirm the providential nature of the evolving future. In contrast, both Momik's and Amalia's encounters with their "satanic angels" signify entrapment in the apocalyptic past. To recall another biblical story, the compulsion to look back into the Holocaust destruction ensues in a fate similar to that of Lot's wife. Overwhelmed by the horrific vision and devastation, the protagonists seem petrified. Yet petrified though they may be, they are not muted. Even though immobilized by despair, neither Momik nor Amalia is capable of keeping silent. Their autobiographical narratives recount the communications of their despair. Defying the glorious vision of the "new" Jew, Momik shares the despair over his collapsed faith in humanity with both his wife and his lover. Defying the dogma of absolute faith in divine justice, Amalia reveals her heretical doubts to her rabbi-mentor. The protagonists' refusal to maintain silence unsettles the Zionist as well as the religious-orthodox positions, both of which promote the suppression of the past.

These expressions of socio-ideological dissent evoke yet another portrayal of the New Angel. In his essay on Karl Kraus, in which he identifies his Angel with a Paul Klee drawing, *Angelus Novus*, Benjamin invests the angel with a revolutionary social role. The New Angel, as Benjamin sees it, "would rather *free* human beings by *taking from* them than make them *happy* by *giving to* them, in order to grasp a humanity which confirms itself by destruction."[17] "Taking away" and "destruction" as ways of confirming humanity indicate an unconventional view of the world. The negation of happiness as an ultimate human goal informs Benjamin's revolutionary orientation. The normative idea of happiness connotes the ideal, be it secular or religious, of a future redemption. In the conventional way of thinking, working towards redemption implies the desire to attain a state of contentment and peace. Benjamin's notion of freedom, however, claims that the expectation of happiness is imprisoning rather than liberating. In his view, freedom materializes in taking away the expectation of future bliss. Freedom consists in the destruction of the conventions which bind humanity to the promise of future happiness.

From this perspective, the initial figuration of the New Angel gains clarity. In the first parable, the Angel *takes* the narrator *away* from the "things" and the "persons" in his life. The decision to *take* its namesake *to* the discovery of the new by retracing the life journey puts an end to the Angel's role as God's worshipper. The Angel gives up, or "destroys," its heavenly status of redeemed creature and confirms its freedom by shaking off the fettering hope for eschatological happiness. In both novels under discussion, we observe defiance of an historical progression towards happiness. Momik disassociates himself from the teleological course of national history, while Amalia questions the religious dogma of eschatology. Both draw alternative patterns of redemption in retreating to the very genesis of history, the borderline of time and myth. Both possess the vision of what Gershom Scholem calls "the utopian-apocalyptic" messianism which signifies the reenactment of mythical Eden.[18] To restore faith in humanity, *See Under: Love* evokes humanity's edenic origins. To restore humaneness to the divine, *The Name* resorts to a radical reinterpretation of Israel's origins as nation.

In *See Under: Love*, the deviation from history informed by the ideal of future happiness is short-lived and the vision of edenic, violence-free humanity fails. Even though Momik attains a glimpse of mythical Eden, he ends up revalidating what Scholem calls the "rational utopia of eternal progress as the Enlightenment's surrogate of Redemption."[19] The faith that Momik eventually regains reaffirms the teleological course of humanity's history after the Holocaust. *The Name* presents a much bolder position. Reaching back to the story of Exodus, the novel exposes the myth of the ideal, edenic closeness of God and Israel in both rabbinic and kabbalistic perspectives. The rediscovery of the suppressed portions of the story of nation formation calls into question the tenet of a benevolent Providence. The faith that Amalia eventually gains is "utopian-apocalyptic" in its radical reconstruction of the concept of the divine. Momik approaches an understanding of redemption in freedom rather than in happiness, yet lacks the courage to endorse it. Amalia, on the other hand, courageously and painfully lives up to the challenge and endorses freedom, which precludes happiness.

Benjamin's theological concept of language illuminates the ultimately failed vision of utopian-apocalyptic redemption in *See Under: Love* by distinguishing between pre- and post-Fall language. The paradisiac language communicated perfect knowledge because it expressed the unity of word and thing, of subject and object. As Benjamin sees it,

> The Fall marks the birth of the *human word*, in which name no longer lives intact. . . . The word must communicate *something* (other than itself). That is really the Fall of language-mind. The word as something externally communicating, as it were a parody by the expressly mediate word of the expressly immediate, the creative word of God, and the decay of the blissful, Adamite language-mind that stand between them.[20]

Remarkably, the "Bruno" section in *See Under: Love* illustrates Benjamin's concept of the "*human word*" as the fallen language. "Bruno" is Momik's imaginative representation of Bruno Schulz, the great Jewish-Polish writer. The historical Schulz was killed by the Germans in 1942, and the manuscript of his masterpiece, *The Messiah*, which he was writing at the time of his death, was never recovered. In "Bruno," Momik imagines meeting with the writer, who, fantastically, escaped death by jumping into the sea and turning into a salmon. As Momik sees it, *The Messiah* was conceived out of Schulz's realization that "the Messiah would . . . never be invoked in a language suffering from elephantiasis" (89), that is, a "language infiltrated many ages past by evil traitors, with one intention—to kill" (168). As a text divested of violence, Schulz's lost *Messiah* was itself the utopian "Adamite language," where the notion of life and life itself were one and the same.

Benjamin's redemption is not eschatological. As Richard Wolin observes, Benjamin's "lost paradisiac language of names contains within itself the hidden script of redeemed life."[21] Swimming with the salmon, Schulz becomes conscious of this "hidden script" in nature which, unlike humanity, speaks the language of word-thing unity. Nature has no use for symbols and metaphors. In his self-mocking address to the Creator, Schulz observes the literalness of God's creation: "To what end do you impel these millions of salmon in endless circles around the world? . . . Why, even human beings, Lord, the cruelest of your animals, have learned the knack of using symbols. We say 'God,' 'man,' 'suffering,' 'love,' 'life,' packing the whole experience into one little box" (128).

Schulz's goal is therefore to restore the edenic situation, or, as he names it, "the Age of Genius," whereby the thing itself has not yet been distorted by symbolic denotations. Great artists, such as Münch, Kafka, Proust, and Rilke, were able to connect with "the Age of Genius" (91), and so could Schulz, who has shown in his work "his longings and laments for a banished Eden" (138). Nonetheless, just as Benjamin's perfect knowledge[22] remains in the sphere of longing, so Schulz's *Messiah* remains irretrievable because, as Momik observes, "the world is not yet ready for the life that flickers beyond Bruno" (138-9).

Ironically, Momik himself, as it turns out, is not ready for Schulz's utopia. When eventually Schulz grants him his vision of pre-Fall perfection, Momik concedes defeat: "I'm weak . . . I am a traitor and a coward . . . I wasn't born for the Age of Genius" (181). Owing to his double self-reflection—an autobiographical narrative which mirrors him narrating Schulz's story—Momik becomes aware of his inability to face a world shaped by a pre-Fall language which speaks the sanctity of human life. Schulz's *Messiah* proves too powerful an angel and his Eden too radical a utopia. Momik is unable to separate from the conventional notion of happiness and to follow the call of his originary name—his angel—back to the state of being unadulterated by linguistic manipulations. The gaping "black hole" of the menacing "Nazi Beast" turns out to be a lesser evil than absolute redemption.

As "Bruno" demonstrates, the world that has experienced an apocalyptic destruction is not ready for a utopian rebirth. Thus, rather than *transcend*, the next section of the novel, entitled "Wasserman," proposes to *mend* the collapsed values of humanistic ethics. This section is, as Schulz enigmatically describes it, a story everybody remembers like "his name. His destiny. His heart." Yet, paradoxically, "you forget it and you have to recall it afresh every time" (181). What is this inherently embedded, yet consistently forgotten story? The clue seems to lie in the last segment of *See Under: Love*, titled "Prayer," which complements the story that Wasserman told Neigel, the German Commander of the concentration camp, in the "Wasserman" section. In "Prayer," Wasserman tells Neigel of the wish made for Kazik, a new-born child, upon his birth: "'All of us prayed for one thing: that he might end his life knowing nothing of war. Do you understand, Herr Neigel? We asked so little: for a man to live in this world from birth to death and know nothing of war'" (452). It is important to elucidate the "little" that "Prayer" asks for: it does not defy violence, nor does it ask to stop wars. It merely expresses the wish to avoid the experience of violence. In this context, however, this modest wish verges on the absurd.

Indeed, the grotesquely ironic mode in which the wish is granted—Kazik evades the knowledge of war because in his twenty-four hour existence he grows old and dies—underlies the futility of the prayer. The reality of the ongoing, horrific killing points out the extent to which the inborn desire for peace has been "forgotten." Schulz, as mentioned, proposes to destroy violence by eliminating communication through language, because language's sickness precludes redemption. The world, however, is not ready for Schulz's obliteration of "the thought of murder . . . destruction and fear." Neither is it ready for the Messiah's riding "the backward flow of time" which will bring the past back to life (179). The more acceptable approach is Wasserman's redeeming counteraggression of "recycling" the language of violence through storytelling.

Such "recycling," or cleansing the language, is necessary in view of Nazism's linguistic distortion. In a parodic contrast to Schulz's ways of communicating free of the consciousness of violence, the Nazi "newspeak" communicates nothing but murder. As Wasserman explains, "*Abwanderung*, which means 'exodus or migration,' is the word to describe mass deportations to the camps; behind the word *Hilfsmittel*, 'a device or helpful tool' lurk the gas machines . . . . 'Poison! A death potion in their language from first to last!'" (284). Rejecting Schulz's utopian vision of wordless communication Wasserman proposes storytelling as the antidote. The story, he claims, is at ease with human fallibility and therefore recognizes the universality of human compassion and love. This ensures forgiveness even in the reality of the Holocaust (225).

Wasserman's view of redemption through love and forgiveness is based on the premise that human beings are good, even those who committed terrible crimes against humanity. Although his wife and daughter were killed by Neigel, Wasserman remains convinced of the murderer's indestructible core of humaneness. As he explains to Momik, "I would try to turn him [Neigel] around and reform him . . . because after everything this arch-murderer Neigel did to me, I . . . saw his face as a boy, and I was beginning to think that . . . I was wrong not to count him a human being" (205). In his role of Momik's "angel," who forces his namesake into the past, Wasserman, like Dante's Virgil, takes his acolyte to "the bowels of hell" (209). Unlike Dante, however, who learns from the old poet about the irrevocability of damnation, Momik learns from the old writer about the indelibility of forgiveness. Indeed, in the hell of the concentration camp the power of the story that Wasserman tells Neigel produces the moral rehabilitation of the Nazi. Through the transcending force of forgiveness, even the ultimate moral disintegration can be redeemed. This realization restores Momik's faith in the values of love and compassion.

"Bruno," Momik's first attempt at self-liberation from post-Holocaust despair, has proven too radical to assimilate. Momik's figuration of Wasserman, however, allows him to see "all the seemingly unrelated pieces of the mosaic fall neatly into place" (188). The ability to imagine the reformation of a Nazi makes Momik realize that faith evolves out of the creative act of writing about faith. The force that supersedes the horror of the Holocaust lies in the artist's creativity. Thanks to his creative prowess, Momik is capable of envisioning Wasserman enjoining him to write, "Because you are like me, your life is the story, and for you there is only the story" (297). The saving force of storytelling has been illustrated before, for instance in the *Thousand and One Nights*. Indeed, Scheherezade is one of Wasserman's pseudomyms. Yet, in the reality of the Holocaust, the convention that attributes redemptive qualities to art becomes questionable. Is the argument of art as soul-saving force ethical, let alone plausible, in the context of the destruction of a people?

The novel counterargues that art redeems not only the Nazi, but the artist himself. The endeavor to reform the Nazi constitutes Wasserman's act of expiation for the unforgivable sin of having betrayed his humanistic mission as artist. For it is "here in the camp" (207) that Wasserman finally heeds the exhortation of Zalmanson, *his* mentor, to actualize his artistic potential. Although a popular children's writer, Wasserman had failed to follow Zalmanson's injunction to write "the way an enlightened writer should. As their [Gentile] writers do!" He did not heed Zalmanson's expectation that "at last a Jewish writer would write beautiful adventure tales, thrilling and exciting stories full of love for all mankind, not just the Jews" (226-7).

The notion of the Jewish writer assimilating the progressive Gentile world view reflects the typical attitude of pre-war Jewish European intelligentsia. The hopeful world view of the Enlightenment posited education as the key to humanity's moral redemption. The concept of *Bildung*[23] promulgated the cultivation of the positive elements in human character, which would promote the values of justice, equality, and love of humanity. As an accountable member of society, the artist has the moral obligation to create art which will educate humanity in the spirit of the Enlightenment.

From this perspective, Neigel, who used to be an avid reader of Wasserman, has demonstrated Wasserman's terrible failure of the artist's responsibility to teach the love of mankind. Wasserman's retelling of the story becomes, therefore, *the artist's* act of atonement.

A second chance at educating Neigel allows Wasserman to fulfil his obligation to educate. As he admits to Momik, "After all, this is my mission [to bring back love of mankind] . . . for this I am staging my comedy" (239). Wasserman's reference to "comedy" is not inadvertent. As Northrop Frye defines it, comedy denotes a plot in which social order disrupted by injustice and moral corruption is restored.[24] As Wasserman teaches not only Neigel but Momik as well, "comedy" implies the restoration of enlightened humanism. The rediscovery of humaneness even in "the bowels of hell" counteracts nihilism and despair. Thus Grossman's contrived novel about a post-Holocaust writer who writes a story about himself writing a story about a pre-Holocaust writer whose storytelling reforms a Nazi murderer has a twofold restitutive function. It restores the Enlightenment's hopeful trust in human moral progress and it reaffirms the position of the artist as a moral force.

In his trenchant criticism of what he terms "ready-made enlightenment," the theologian Walter Lowe claims that the Enlightenment produced "a form of theodicy [because] implicitly or explicitly it . . . will justify the suffering it entails."[25] The Enlightenment brought forth the rationalization of evil as a force that motivates the struggle for a morally redeemed world. This form of theodicy prevails in *See Under: Love*. Here Holocaust suffering brings forth the realization that unwillingness to contribute to humanity's progress may have the terrible consequence of transgressing the sanctity of human life. "Wasserman," therefore, suggests that "humane survival" in the post-Holocaust world of nihilism and despair does not lie, as suggested in "Bruno," in a radical transformation of the historical world, but rather in the continuation of the "enlightened" progression toward redemption.

Neither Schulz's nor Wasserman's solution is possible in Govrin's *The Name*. Haunted by the relentless consciousness of the Holocaust, Amalia does not seem able to sidestep the horror either by leaving the world of history for "Adamite" oneness with Creation, or by reaffirming humanity's enlightened progress. Absent also are the benevolent figures of mentoring, guiding "angels," who in *See: Under Love* help release the protagonist out of an emotional-ethical deadlock. Amalia's guides—Stein, who uses Amalia to validate his lifelong devotion to Mala, and Rabbi Gothelf, who sees in Amalia a vehicle to revalidate religious faith—do not provide satisfactory options of "humane survival" in the post-Holocaust world. In effect, Amalia ends up becoming her own "angel." Her autobiographical narrative is that of a difficult voyage back into the past. The narrative transcends the personal, retraces the national memory back to its mythical origins, and ends up rebonding the human and the divine in a covenant which defies theodicy—that is, a covenant which refuses to justify human suffering.

The last and the most prescient of Benjamin's angels leads to an appreciation of the revolutionary nature of Amalia's undertaking. Benjamin's interpretation of Klee's Angel in his last work, "Theses on the Philosophy of History," complements the two previous portrayals of the New Angel already discussed. At the same time, this third Angel highlights the inexorably growing remoteness of redemption:

> A Klee painting named "Angelus Novus" shows an angel looking as though he is about to move away from something he is fixedly contemplating. His eyes are staring, his mouth is open, his wings are spread. This is how one pictures the angel of history. His face is turned toward the past. Where we perceive a chain of events, he sees one single catastrophè which keeps piling wreckage upon wreckage and hurls it in front of his feet. The angel would like to stay, awaken the dead, and make whole what has been smashed. But a storm is blowing from Paradise; it has got caught in his wings with such violence that the angel can no longer close them. This storm irresistibly propels him into the future to which his back is turned, while the pile of debris before him grows skyward. The storm is what we call progress.[26]

This vision of the "angel of history" precludes both Eden and Enlightenment as possible avenues of redemption. The return to Paradise has been barred by progress, whose ruthlessness rules out humanity's hopeful future. Unlike previously discussed angels, the "angel of history" is powerless and no longer imposes its will upon humanity. History has become the witness and the repository of suffering inflicted on humanity by the relentless force of progress.

Written in 1940, just before Benjamin's suicide, the autobiographical component in this vision of history as a spent force is evident. While "Theses" addresses the theological aspect of historical materialism, the depiction of the "angel of history" is not altogether theoretical. Like all Jews in Europe, Benjamin was powerless, at the mercy of the uncontrollable forces of destruction unleashed by Western civilization. His world turning into nought, Benjamin was becoming the helpless "angel of history." The "angel of history," however, is not only an autobiographical marker; its vision is prescient, perhaps even prophetic. Though physically overcome by the "storm of progress," the angel asserts a measure of freedom by maintaining its own perspective on the human prospect. Turning away from the future, the angel knows that the act of remembrance constitutes redemption. Salvation lies in heeding the victims, listening to the voices which have been silenced by progress. In Zygmunt Bauman's apt explanation of Benjamin's distinction between history and progress, progress is "a telos-guided movement." Progress "murders hope" but "parades as the guardian of hope." History, on the other hand, is the "exhumation of lost (or murdered) possibilities," performed by "the historian-as-a-revolutionary," who undermines the "allegedly once-for-all recorded past."[27]

The function of history is to counteract theodicies which anaesthetize the pain of memory by promising future happiness. Amalia's intense involvement with the past reflects, to a remarkable degree, Benjamin's revolutionary view of history as a force which opposes the telos of progress. Like the "angel of history," Amalia remains transfixed in face of the world's destruction. Against terrible odds, she is compelled to turn against the ideological gravitation toward the future and look into the past, risking in the process physical as well as spiritual destruction. For Amalia the past of victimization is not an external reality. Like the proverbial ghost, or the *dybbuk*, Mala has entered Amalia's soul and body (90). She has become an integral part of Amalia's consciousness, her alter-ego, her nemesis (187). In this sense, Mala *is* Amalia's *Angelus Satanas*, which redirects her away from the future oriented world.

Two ideologically disparate social orientations—religious orthodox and secular Zionist—converge in the desire to draw Amalia back onto the trajectory of progress. Rabbi Israel Gothelf urges the excision of the memory of Mala. To justify this categorical demand, the rabbi resorts to Maimonides's injunction, " I am a different person and not the same one who sinned, and I change my name" (186). Amalia is to distance herself from the sin of doubt in divine justice, a doubt which resonates in the victim's name that she bears. Religious dogma decrees faith in God's willed continuation of human history. Confirmation of this faith, according to the rabbi, is the true legacy of Holocaust survivors. They have "cut off living flesh" and excised the memories of "the most beloved souls" (188) to create new families and thus affirm life. Indeed, although the survivors claim to have lost their religious faith in the concentration camps, their representation of the Holocaust corroborates, to a considerable extent, the religious position. The memory that the survivors collectively shape ascribes purpose to suffering. Their recollections invariably idolize Mala, the beautiful and talented pianist, who demonstrated extraordinary heroism when she publicly slapped an SS officer before killing herself.

The hagiographical treatment of Mala communicates the survivors' desire to maintain faith in the human spirit by attenuating the horror. And the choice of the Ninth of Ab, the date which, according to tradition, marks the destruction of both Temples as well as of the future birth of the Messiah, as the day of the memorial ceremony for the Holocaust victim, clearly asserts faith in the providential progress of history. As the speaker-survivor triumphantly assures his audience of survivors, "The commemoration of heroic Mala in our free State is our revenge. We are showing the world . . . that destruction leads to redemption" (312).

In effect, the survivors' determination to infuse meaning in the experience of the Holocaust surpasses that of Rabbi Gothelf. While the Rabbi dogmatically asserts faith in divine providence, he nonetheless acknowledges that, in the case of the Holocaust, theodicy lies beyond human reasoning (45). The survivors, on the other hand, profess a measure of comprehension by associating Mala's heroic death with the rebirth of the State. Their subscription to the truism that justice always prevails seeks validation in the messianic aspect of Zionism. The secular conflates with the religious when Mala's heroic death is presented as a providential reaffirmation of the national telos of a strong Jewish State. Reaffirmation of personal telos underlies the planned publication of a commemorative album of Mala. Initiated and financed by Stein, the project demonstrates that, as the old adage goes, love conquers all. Furthermore, Amalia's assignment as the photographer, who will reconstruct the victim's life through the eyes of a could-be daughter, promises the restitution of generational continuity.

We recall that a similar intergenerational connection in *See Under: Love* enables the protagonist to regain faith in humanity. Momik's construction of the Wasserman character demonstratess this tendency. His figuration of Wasserman as his wise guide and teacher is indicative of the desire to reconnect with the destroyed ancestral tradition. In contrast, Amalia finds it impossible to construct a hopeful representation of Mala. Like Benjamin's "angel of history," Amalia is unable to re-conceive the past from the perspective of progress. In fact, the attempt to re-vision the past through the art of photography proves so menacing that it pushes her to the verge of madness and suicide. What did Amalia see through the camera lenses that precipitated a sanity- and life-threatening emotional crisis? The assigned photographic search of Mala's past in Poland turns out to be a charade. Amalia demystifies art as a redeeming force with a self-directed ironic realization, "like it's possible to photograph nothing, to make an 'esthetic' in black and white out of that." The landscapes and the sites of Jewish pre-war life emerge as images of destruction so complete that it did not even leave debris. The unbearable sense of nothingness is compounded by the sound of Mala's crying coming at Amalia, from "everywhere, from the closets, from the walls, from the drapes. Like a kind of vision, only really existing, and it kept on even in the morning or all the next day . . . all the time it went on" (123).

The pictures of Poland reveal the apocalyptic aspect of the Final Solution, which destroyed all signs of history. Mala's pervasive, uncontainable weeping calls into questions her image as the dauntless heroine. The abyss of disconsolate grief and mourning undermines the connection between destruction and redemption. The world, Amalia tells Rabbi Gothelf, is nothing, "only the black pit and her [Mala's] weeping. There is nothing anywhere, not even in heaven!" (123). The sense of nihilism effected by the experience in Poland emerges in Amalia's interpretation of the well-known Talmudic parable, "The Four Who Entered the King's Orchard":

> Four entered an orchard and these are they: Ben Azzai, Ben Zoma, Aher and Rabbi Akiva. Rabbi Akiva said to them: "When you reach the stones of pure marble, do not say: 'Water, water!' For it is said: 'He that speaketh falsehood shall not be established before mine eyes.'" Ben Azzai gazed and died. . . . Ben Zoma gazed and was stricken [became demented]. . . . Aher cut down the shoots [became an apostate]. Rabbi Akiva departed in peace.[28]

The classical interpretations[29] of the parable argue that Rabbi Akiva's companions were shown the unspeakable mysteries of God, which they found impossible to assimilate. The mistaken identification of marble as water drove the three sages, respectively, to death, madness, and apostasy. Only Rabbi Akiva survived, because, as Louis Jacobs maintains, "he has perfected the art of seeing visions, without these either frightening him out of his mind or causing him to entertain heretical ideas" (24).The mysterious vision destroyed the three sages because, as Leonard V. Kaplan notes, to identify marble as water implies "reflection or immersion [which] suggests danger and intimates an evil inversion." Inversion is evil because it indicates "the instability of the entire creation" (144).

But what if inversion is all there is? Among the commentaries, the one that comes to haunt Amalia says that Rabbi Akiva's warning meant "there never was water there, or marble, only an appearance in the world" (85). As Amalia understands it, Rabbi Akiva's terrible truth claims that appearance *is* the world, that no mysterious truth exists beyond our reflections, images, and delusions. The other sages were deceived by illusionary effects that alluded to nothing, and they paid dearly for falling into self-deception. Are we indeed subjects to an illusory faith in providential powers? Amalia's consideration of the parable reaches the brink of heresy. "Perhaps," she thinks, "there is no profit in pain, in effort. . . . And maybe the gleam of the Torah Curtain [the cover of the Torah scroll into which the unpronounceable name of God is woven] is nothing but the opaque flash of silk, without any secret at all" (91). The secret behind the Torah Curtain is the Torah itself which represents the indubitable evidence of God's mysterious existence. As Yehuda Liebes reminds us, "Just as God is both revealed and concealed, so too is his name . . . and his *Torah*, which is also considered his name."[30] The absence of "the secret" behind the Curtain exposes the Torah as a mystification of divine absence.

The nothingness behind the Curtain invokes the nothingness in the photographs. The glow of the silk seems as deceptive as the photographer's play at "aesthetics in black and white." Like the three Talmudic sages who were smitten with the truth of the "instability of the creation," that is, the absence of certainties, Amalia is defeated by the greatest uncertainty of all—the view of the world as a "black pit" which peers at her from every picture. Invoking the three sages' disastrous fate, Amalia's attempted suicide, barely averted madness, and heretical doubt result from an image of a world which refers to nothing. Such an image raises a crucial question: Is it possible for Amalia, the "revolutionary" who has refused to endorse the ideologically promoted forms of theodicy, to re-emerge from the "black pit" of despair with a renewed notion of faith and hope?

It seems that the key to this question lies in Amalia's intriguing attitude toward the photographs. Amalia steals them, keeps them with her, and refuses to return them to Stein; in a way, she treats them as idols. Amalia's insistence on an analogy between the pictures and the *teraphim* [the idols] that biblical Rachel stole from her father (Genesis 31) corroborates the idolatrous nature of the photographs. The correspondences between Amalia's efforts to conceal the pictures and Rachel's efforts to conceal the *teraphim* (107, 113) call attention to Amalia's theological ambivalence. Rachel holds on to the *teraphim* when departing for the land filled with the presence of a God she has not yet come to know. Amalia, however, refuses to relinquish the pictures, while seeking a God who seems to have disappeared. Are the pictures of nothingness a fearful reminder of the urgency for a redemptive, anti-nihilistic understanding of the Divine?

As already discussed, the search in the rabbinic orthodox world fails to offer a solution. Indeed, Amalia, the "historian-as-revolutionary," transgresses the rabbinic credo of human ignorance, smallness, and remoteness with regards to God's providential plans. She looks back into the past and declares "the death" of the God who seems to have abandoned humanity in its most desperate need.[31] It is, however, important to note that the desire to minimize God's remoteness from humankind has preoccupied Jewish theology and especially its mystical orientation for centuries. It is therefore not surprising that, in her efforts to redeem faith, Amalia directs herself to the kabbalistic vision of the Divine.

The kabbalistic tenet of *tikkun* [redemption][32] is closely connected with the notion of the *Shekhinah*, the feminine element in Godhead. The rupture of exile separated the *Shekhinah* from the Divine. *Tikkun* will take place when exile ends and the *Shekhinah* reunites with God. The multiple images of the *Shekhinah* reveal an indelible connection of the Divine and the human. As Scholem notes, the *Shekhina* is "identified with the 'Community of Israel'. . . representing the mystical idea of Israel in its bond with God. . . . She is not only Queen, daughter and bride of God, but also the mother of every individual in Israel."[33] Unlike the rabbinic insistence on the distance between the human and the Divine, the kabbalistic conception of redemption lies in an erotic-sacrificial union of God and the *Shekhinah*. Prayer brings God down to the *Shekhinah*, and elevates the *Shekhina* as a sacrifice to God.[34]

The struggle to salvage the Divine through reunion becomes the objective of Amalia's kabbalistic search. In contrast with Rabbi Gothelf, the kabbalist Rabbi Abuyia Asaraf[35] impresses upon Amalia the importance of her name, which binds her to the dead Mala. It is incumbent upon Amalia to bring forth the *tikkun* of the dead through her own martyrdom. Furthermore, Amalia's martyrdom will enact the mystical consummation of the union between God and the *Shekhinah* (104). Rabbi Asaraf grounds this view in Ezekiel's famous vision of the redemption of Jerusalem. Upon seeing Jerusalem befouled in blood, uncared for, and abandoned to die in the field, God tells her: "In your blood, live!" (16:6). God enters a covenant with Jerusalem—the Community of Israel—and she becomes his cherished companion/wife (16:8). As the explicitly sexual imagery in Ezekiel's text demonstrates, redemption will restore the erotic intimacy of Israel with the Divine.

Rabbi Asaraf's vision seems to alleviate Amalia's despair. "Nobody has talked to you this way," Amalia thinks to herself, "No one ever promised you like him that from the black pit full of appapatz, from the root of the dread, you would find salvation at once" (105). Espousing Rabbi Asaraf's exhortations, Amalia plans her unification with the Divine. Like the Yom Kippur sacrificial scapegoat, she will become the sacrificial offering to bring forth salvation.[36]

Amalia's messianic ambitions do not materialize. In the post-Holocaust reality, neither the rabbinic nor the kabbalistic approach holds the promise of renewed faith. Amalia's own rereading of the prophet uncovers a story devoid of the protecting screen of theodicy. Rather than the traditional picture of God constantly saving and redeeming the Chosen but sinful People,[37] Ezekiel's vision in Amalia's "revolutionary" reading is "the shout [that] was buried alive" of a monstrous misrepresentation of truth, of a shameful manipulation of history (300). What emerges is an image of a God whose relationship with Israel has been vacillating between love and cruelty, between compassion and vengeful rage. In Amalia's epiphany, Ezekiel's vision emerges as a pattern of centuries-long history produced by a God repeatedly "tempting and deserting, and swearing once again, in panic—when Your weakness increases, when the destruction once again gapes in You, and slipping out of Your grasp for a moment the world suspended upon nothing" (303).

Amalia's rereading of the biblical text amounts therefore to the "historical exhuming" of the victims. Her lifelong closeness to Mala—her "angel," her secret Jewish name, her alter ego—earned her a "revolutionary" perspective on history. This perspective focuses on God's suffering people hopelessly caught in cycles of destruction. Benjamin's angel, we recall, gives humanity freedom by taking away the illusion of happiness. Amalia's view of history as a repetitive cycle of disasters certainly exposes the futility of the naive expectation of future happiness. But what is freedom after the "death" of faith in providential divinity? It certainly is not the freedom to return to the universal story of human potential for love of mankind that emerges as the solution in *See: Under Love*. The theodicy of the necessity of suffering for the promotion of human progress cannot withstand the vision of the world as a "black hole" reverberating with the ever-present weeping of the dead.

Against ideologies and dogmas which see history as the reflection of the elusive, but existing goodness of creation, Amalia sees history as the reflection of a flawed Creator. She becomes conscious of the need to recognize the flaw and to reconcile herself with the reality of imperfection in God and humanity. Hope does not consist in the empowerment of the moral to prevail over evil; it consists, rather, in the recognition of the inherence of evil. How does one combat nihilism and despair when theodicy becomes impotent vis-à-vis evil? It is at the end of her search that Amalia admits to having reached a new understanding of faith. "Everything stops. Even the rage [at You] becomes more remote. And the wrath at the flaw imprinted in You that sentences us to eternal pain" (332). She realizes that "There is no repair for the break. And there is no instant repentence. Only acceptance." Acceptance, however, does not imply passivity. On the contrary, acceptance amounts to an active recognition of the "covenant of hidden destruction" (342).

The covenant of destruction lies in the "forgotten" episode of the broken tablets. They were swiftly superseded by the second set of tablets which seemingly restored the initial perfection of the relationship between God and His Chosen People. To Amalia, however, the shattering of the first set of tablets signals the irreparable "rupture" of the edenic relationship between God and Israel in the pristine desert. The "covenant of destruction," tainted by "graven images," marks the falling away from perfection of both idol-worshipping Israel and the wrathful, punishing God. Paradoxically, however, the broken covenant, rather than the subsequent, intact covenant, promises redemption. Toward the end of her search for the human/humane God, Amalia realizes that "the dust of the broken tablets blends with the breathing" (344). The "dust" of God's flaw and of human imperfection is the essence of life. In remembrance of moments like these—the defeat and suffering of both the human and the divine—there is hope for renewed faith. The consciousness of the "brokenness" of both God and mankind will allow Amalia to heed the past even when moving toward the future. "The past," Benjamin claims, "carries with it a temporal index by which it is referred to redemption. . . . Like every generation that preceded us, we have been endowed with a *weak* Messianic power, a power to which the past has a claim" ("Theses" 254). We are ineluctably tied to the past, as our present actions are informed by the expectations and suffering of the previous generations. Our limited redemptive power is predicated upon those who came before us; we ought, therefore, to remember them even in their tragic nothingness, which invokes the "instability of creation."

Amalia's autobiographical narration concludes with the word *Shabbat*. In her story she has created a world of suffering, instability, and discomforting realizations. *Shabbat* is therefore a sign of a new and difficult world. But *Shabbat* reminds her also of the time to rest and accept oneself in Creation. Acceptance emerges in the understanding of one's and God's limitations. This understanding can be achieved thanks to the creative struggle to restore the memory of suffering. Only through both the struggle with the memory and the acceptance of the past can a meaningful future be shaped.

Notes

[1] It is important to note that as Field Marshal Rommel was trying to break through the British line in Egypt in 1941, the Yishuv [the Jewish Settlement in Palestine] was as much in danger of the Final Solution as was the European community.

[2] For further discussion of the thematic of the Holocaust in earlier Israeli literature see, for instance, Eisig Silberschlag, *Hebrew Literature in the Land of Israel, 1870-1970* (New York: Ktav Publishing House, 1977).

[3] Gershon Shaked, "Afterword," *Facing the Holocaust: Selected Israeli Fiction*. ed. Gila Ramraz-Rauch and Joseph Michman-Melkman (Philadelphia: The Jewish Publication Society, 1985), 280. On literature of the Holocaust, see also Shaked, *Sifrut as, k'an v'akhshav* [*Literature there, here, and now*] (Tel Aviv: Zmora-Bitan, Publishers, 1993) and Shaked, "Appelfeld and His Times: Transformations of Ahashveros, the Eternal Wandering Jew," *Hebrew Studies* 36 (1995), 87-100.

[4] *Sabra* is a cactus fruit, prickly on the outside and sweet inside. This term is popularly used to describe the characteristics of the native-born Israeli Jew.

[5] For further discussion of Hareven and Goldberg, see Rachel Feldhay Brenner, "Discourses of Mourning and Rebirth in Post-Holocaust Israeli Literature: Leah Goldberg's *Lady of the Castle* and Shulamith Hareven's 'The Witness.'" *Hebrew Studies* 31 (1990), 71-87. On Megged, see Brenner, "Between Identity and Anonymity: Art and History in Aharon Megged's *Foiglman*," *AJS Review* 20.2 (1995), 359-79.

[6] David Grossman's *See: Under Love* is probably the best known work of this celebrated young Israeli writer (b. 1954). It has been translated into many languages and internationally praised. Known for his left-wing convictions, Grossman started his career as a correspondent and journalist. He is also well-known for his *Yellow Wind*, a 1987 collection of essays on the West Bank, in which he predicted the outburst of the Intifada.

[7] Michal Govrin (b. 1950) is a poet and writer. She is also a playwright and a theatre director specializing in Jewish theater and ritual. During her studies at the University of Paris, where she received her Ph.D, she worked with foremost French philosophers such as Emmanuel Levinas. The author of two books of poetry and a collection of short stories as well as *The Name*, Govrin is now at work on a collaborative publication with Jacques Derrida.

[8] It is perhaps important to note that Govrin is the daughter of a survivor. Her mother, who survived Auschwitz, settled in Israel, where Govrin was born. Grossman's Israeli parents did not experience the Holocaust.

[9] "Appapatz" is a mispronouncement of "Appelplatz," the center of the concentration camps where interminable roll calls and executions used to take place and where Mala, in a heroic gesture, took her own life.

[10] David Grossman, *See Under: Love*, trans. Betsy Rosenberg (New York: Washington Square Press, 1989), 105. Henceforth page references will be given parenthetically in the text.

[11] Michal Govrin, *The Name* (Tel Aviv: Ha-kibbutz Ha-Meuchad, 1995). Henceforth page references will be given parenthetically in the text. I cite Barbara Harshav's English translation of the novel (Putnam, N.Y.: Riverhead Books 1998).

[12] Walter Benjamin, "Agesilaus Santander," quoted in both its versions in Gershom Scholem, *On Jews and Judaism in Crisis: Selected Essays* (New York: Schocken Books, 1976), 204-8.

[13] As Gershom Scholem tells us, "Agsilaus Santander" is an anagram of The Angel Satan (*Der Angelus Satanas*). The New Testament identifies *Angelos Satanas* "with the fallen, rebellious Lucifer," (II Corinthians 12:7). In the Kabbalah the Angel's loss of its anthropomorphic shape is indicative of its demonic nature: "They [the angels] all share the form of man, apart from those (the demons) which are not corporeal, which are unclean and defile all those who approach them" (*The Wisdom of the Zohar: An Anthology of Texts*, ed. Isaiah Tishby, vol. 2 [Oxford: Oxford University Press, 1991], 623). The possibility of the fallen nature of the angel arises in the Hebrew meaning of *Satan*, which designates an *agent provocateur*, an instigator, and a prosecutor, like, for instance, in the showdown between God and Satan in the prologue to Job.

[14] Fleeing the Gestapo, Benjamin committed suicide on the Franco-Spanish border in 1940.

[15] Gershom Scholem interprets the texts (its two versions) strictly in the framework of Benjamin's autobiography. He conjectures that the Angel represents Benjamin's love interests. The lack of any allusion in the text to the woman Scholom mentions and, more significantly, the specified origin of the Angel as a secret Jewish name seem to point to other possible interpretations.

[16] It is interesting to mention here the connection through the metaphor of the angel that Robert Alter establishes in his *Necessary Angels: Tradition and Modernity in Kafka, Benjamin, and Scholem* (Cambridge: Harvard University Press, 1991).

[17] This quote from Benjamin is in Scholem's translation and it appears in "Walter Benjamin and His Angel" 230. (emphases mine). The essay "Karl Kraus" appears in Benjamin's *Reflections: Essays, Aphorisms, Autobiographical Writings*, ed. Peter Demetz, trans. Edmund Jephcott (New York: Harcourt, 1978), 239-77.

[18] See David Biale's explication of Gershom Scholem's messianic typology, "Gershom Scholem on Jewish Messianism," *Essential Papers on Messianic Movements and Personalities in Jewish History*, ed. Marc Saperstein (New York: New York University Press, 1992), 522.

[19] Gershom Scholem, "Reflections on Jewish Theology," *On Jews and Judaism in Crisis*, 261-97; 285.

[20] Walter Benjamin, "On Language as Such and on the Language of Man," *Reflections*, 314-32; 327 (emphases in the text).

[21] Richard Wolin, *Walter Benjamin: An Aesthetic of Redemption* (Berkeley: University of California Press, 1994), 43.

[22] For further discussion of Benjamin's notion of the messianic in the return to the origins see Wolin, 36-44 and Anson Rabinach, "Between the Enlightenment and the Apocalypse: Benjamin, Bloch and Modern German Jewish Messianism," *New German Critique* 34 (Winter 1985), 84.

[23] "*Bildung* and the Enlightenment," as George L. Mosse claims, "joined hands during the period of Jewish emancipation." He explains, "*Bildung* combines the meaning . . . [of] 'education' with notions of character formation and moral education" (*German Jews Beyond Judaism* [Bloomington: Indiana University Press, 1985], 3).

[24] Northrop Frye, *Anatomy of Criticism: Four Essays* (Princeton: Princeton University Press, 1957), 286.

[25] Walter Lowe, *Theology and Difference: The Wound of Reason* (Bloomington: Indiana University Press, 1993), 9.

[26] Walter Benjamin, "Theses on the Philosophy of History," *Illuminations,* ed. Hannah Arendt, trans. Harry Zohn (New York: Schocken, 1969), 253-64; 257-8.

[27] Zygmunt Bauman, "Walter Benjamin, the Intellectual," *The Actuality of Walter Benjamin*, *New Formations* 20 (Summer 1993), 47-57; 54, 51. Bauman's interpretation is corroborated by Ferenc Fehér ("Lukács, Benjamin, Theater," *The Grandeur and Twilight of Radical Universalism*, by Ferenc Fehér and Agnes Heller [New Brunswick: Transaction Publishers, 1991], 305-18), who defines Benjamin's celebrated *Dialektik im Stillstand* as "a constellation in which, although history does not move by some automatic forces towards a salutary final goal, insight into the misery and complexity of the prevailing world can be attained, and the ground prepared for redemption" (314). See also Wolin, 48ff.

[28] This translation of the parable is from *The Jewish Mystics*, ed. Louis Jacobs (London: Kyle Cathie, 1990), 21-25; 22.

[29] For further sources of interpretation of the parable, see Leonard V. Kaplan, "The Mind Released: Parable, Commentary, and the Therapeutic," *Graven Images: A Journal of Culture, Law, and the Sacred* 2 (1995), 139-50.

[30] Yehuda Liebes, *Studies in the Zohar*, trans. Arnold Schwartz, Stephanie Nakache, Penina Peli (Albany: State University of New York Press, 1993), 27. The idea of the unity of God and the Torah is very clearly expressed by the kabbalist Joseph Hamadan: "Therefore the Torah is called by this name [Torah] for it elucidates the pattern of the Holy One . . . . The Torah, as it were, is the shadow of the Holy One" (quoted Eliott Wolfson, "Varieties of Jewish Mysticism," *Mysticism and the Mystical Experience: East and West*, ed. Donald H. Bishop [Selinsgrove: Susquehanna University Press, 1995], 155.

[31] It is interesting to note Nietzsche's rebellion against the negation of the human being in his or her relationship with God. For an excellent discussion of the "death of God" as the death of the oppositional, distanced relationship between God and human beings, see Thomas J. J. Alitzer, "Eternal Recurrence and Kingdom of God," *The New Nietzsche: Contemporary Styles of Interpretation*, ed. David B. Allison (New York: Dell), 233-46. Although Alitzer focuses on the Christian God, I would argue that the notion of distance is applicable to the orthodox Jewish position, as represented by Rabbi Israel Gothelf.

[32] *Tikkun Olam* literally means "mending or repairing of the world."

[33] Gershom Scholem, *Major Trends in Jewish Mysticism* (New York: Schocken Books, 1995), 230.

[34] See *The Wisdom of the Zohar*, 1054-5.

[35] It is interesting to note that Abuya was the name of Aher, the sage in the Pardes parable who became apostate.

[36] On Yom Kippur a scapegoat is pushed off the cliff as symbol of the community's atonement of its sins.

[37] See for instance, Walther Zimmerli, *Ezekiel 1: A Commentary on the Book of the Prophet Ezekiel, Chapters 1-24* (Philadelphia: Fortress Press, 1979), 322-53.

The Name[1]

Michal Govrin

Translated from the Hebrew by Barbara Harshav[2]

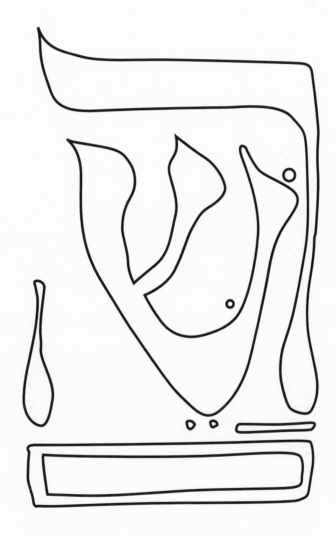

[1] "The Name," in Hebrew [*ha Shem*], is another way of addressing God. It refers also to Amalia's attempt to run away from her own past by changing names and thus identities.

[2] From the book *THE NAME* by Michal Govrin, published in October 1998 by Riverhead Books, a member of Penguin Putnam Inc, and reprinted with the permission of Riverhead Books. Copyright © 1995 by Michal Govrin; translation © 1998 by Riverhead Books. Hebrew letters designed by Michal Govrin.

Transgression, Punishment, Responsibility, Forgiveness
Graven Images 4 (1998), 51-59.

Six Weeks

[Amalia is in the sixth week of the Counting (the ceremony commemorating the forty-nine days between the time the Jewish people left Egypt and when they received God's Covenant on Mount Sinai). At the end of this period, she had intended to enact a suicidal sacrifice as a means of saving God and the nation of Israel. In the course of her long prayer encompassing the Counting, the Counting has become a way of exploring, in the form of written testimony, her own spiritual voyage. The narrative juxtaposes and blends events from the last year of her life, the sights and sounds of the city night throughout which Amalia writes, and her growing understanding of a flawed and imperfect God.

Amalia, a weaver by vocation, also weaves in and out of the present time of remembering, contemplating the hills of Jerusalem surrounding her before plunging into the poignant memory of a dual rejection. She has forsaken both Isaiah, the young widowed musician who loved her, and God, to whom she would have devoted herself—loved as a lover—in order to find redemption.

She writes of lamenting at the Old City's Wailing Wall in the shadow of the ruins of the Second Temple during the night of Tesha b'Av (the commemoration of the destruction of the Temple), when Isaiah came to her with the need to exorcise his own sense that her father's first wife, Mala, a Holocaust victim, was haunting him. Words from the traditional prayers float through her consciousness, as she relives the rejection of the other lamenting women who could not empathize with her religious ecstasy.

She writes also of the biblical verses from Ezekiel which burst into her consciousness on her return home. In her new understanding of the hidden meaning of Ezekiel, she experiences a shattering revelation: God has abused, tortured and victimized Israel, His chosen bride, and, by extension, Amalia. He is not a redemptive God, but an enraged one, who time and time again breaks the Covenant. Perverted by jealousy, He loves not Israel nor Amalia.]

Tuesday night

The night of the first of the month. I fell asleep in the early evening for a few hours. Now, long after midnight. I stopped all work today, as is commanded of women on the day of the first of the month (gestures continue, after everything . . .). I also cooked a little, to mark the day. Rice. Sitting and chewing the grains slowly, crushing the sweet blocs, soft descents, one mouthful after another. The hours passed in a delirium. Rising and sinking on the lighted stage set of the hills.

Somehow there's a need to record testimony, in the pulpy dark where nothing happens. To record that. The dark gaping at the crouching of the ridges. A car is cut off from the mountain, below in the valley. The worm of light progresses along the short bend. Is swallowed up. Dull drumbeats. As from a discotheque.

The night of the first of *Sivan*. Two days ago I would still say—Three days until the end of the Counting—still within the time when You are at the end. Now everything is unraveled. Cut off. With no hold. With no direction to guide what's written. Thou has covered thyself with a cloud, that our prayer should not pass through. Record that too . . .

To leave testimony . . . As if I got up out of the bed where we made love for weeks, closed off from the world . . . You sunk there, on the unmade bed, helpless, You only promised You would redeem. As if I got up to take some distance, going dizzily to the table to lead the pen over the paper. I, the cursed one, servant of servants.

The beats of the music fell silent.

[. . .]

Suddenly. The body is present. The body that only trod from the loom to prayer, and at night to the table. As if a hand is passing over the skin, slowly, making it supple, lingering, lengthening, slowly, slowly. Rousing the body folded beneath me. Entering between the lapels of the shirt, the neck, the shoulders, the warm skin. Passing over the nipple. A light hand. Around and around the protruding kernel. Draining the outstretched, gushing chalice. A light hand, like a breeze, descending on the belly, continuing, going down slowly between the spread thighs. Strumming there the melting. Rising, slowly, slowly, throbbing, with a thin stream.

[. . .]

To be strong, to go on despite the panic. To go on with the testimony without emotion. With absolute precision—otherwise it's impossible to distinguish between my intention and what was Your decree on the night of *Tesha b'Av* last year. Otherwise it's impossible to write down what really happened. How I waited with rising expectation, I had already encountered destruction once before, and so I imagined that now too, all at once, it would flood, and I wouldn't have to do anything . . . I waited for events as for a fire that had already taken hold of the doorframe. Gazing for whole days from the bay window at the Arab children playing on the slope, at that little girl in the striped pinafore hiding behind the aloe plant—without touching the warp of the prayer shawls stretched on the loom. I couldn't. Swept up in the blur of devotion, in the seething of the height of summer that grew dull only for a few hours at night.

[. . .]

As if I no longer remembered Isaiah. So I didn't notice when he knocked at the gate, just before the start of *Tesha b'Av*. And even when he stood in the room, declaring excitedly: *Amalia, I have to go with you to the commemoration tomorrow!* I listened to him from a distance, still glued to the sight of the children's game on the slope.

I came to tell you that I have to . . . I've wanted to come a few times and ask but I didn't dare. I was afraid to offend you . . .

He trailed behind me into the kitchen when I took the hard boiled eggs out of the cold cooking water for the meal before the fast, sitting down at a corner of the table, chewing slowly, making ashes by burning paper and sprinkling them on the eggs, choking on the mass.

I've got to ask forgiveness from the dead before we get married . . . God willing, he persisted emotionally. No, it's not because of Elizabeth, her memory for a blessing . . . it's because of Mala, your father's first wife . . . the pianist . . . Suddenly, in the middle of studying, in the middle of prayer . . . I'm playing along with her, with the deceased Mala . . . sonatas for piano and violin by Beethoven, Brahms. It's certainly from overexhaustion, in the three weeks between the 17th of *Tamuz* and *Tesha b'Av* . . . Yesterday, I canceled the repetition with my study partner, Ephraim. I couldn't. At night I had visions of lamentation. Sounds of weeping. Loud voices, women's voices and men's. Weeping, weeping . . .

[. . .]

I slurped my drink without breaking through the dryness.

The day slipped away quickly. Isaiah was afraid we'd be late to recite lamentations at the Wailing Wall. I quickly took the Bible to read the Book of Lamentations, and changed into cloth shoes, walled in by a decision already ripe. The choking didn't stop as we walked. And it only increased as we entered the gate of the Old City wall, and all at once, the carpet of silence emanating chirps in the valley was ripped, and the bustle of a crowd of people burst out in shrieks, spread like a cloud of sand over the dark walls. As we toiled up the alley, the screaming grew thick, and then the square burst forth, inundated with floodlights and packed with people.

Isaiah broke away from me, hurried forward excitedly toward the valley crowded with people, ran to the mass of bustling men reciting prayers. Alone, without Isaiah, I clasped the Bible, bathing in the willingness to sacrifice myself body and soul as was decided. I sank among the groups assembling in the heat of the evening. Prattling women and their babies stuffed into buggies, groups of tourists absorbed in bursts of conversation, soldiers burdened with equipment, running the hot night on the lighted square like an amusement park, with a solemn sloppiness. I clutched the book and pressed toward the entrance of the enclosure of the women's section. In the dirt ditch on the side of the ramp, among the ruins, a whining old man was trilling, They have cast up dust upon their heads; they have girded themselves with sackcloth—I made my way in the crowd of women and little girls. Among the backs of overturned chairs, shoulders, arms. Among women lying on the ground, sprawled on mats, kneeling, swaying as they sat upright, murmuring with their heads bent over books.—How hath the Lord covered the daughter of Zion with a cloud in his anger and cast down from heaven unto the earth the beauty of Israel—One woman repeated it like an oath, straightening the cylinders of her legs, raising the Book of Lamentations and shouting that verse over and over again. A small group of women huddled next to her, responded after her in a chorus of thin voices.

The heat increased at the foot of the Wailing Wall which rose up to the night flooded with light. From the tension of waiting since the night of *Shavuoth*, it seemed to me that the shriek of the crowd burst out of my insides, from my taut depths. For it is me that You chose, me, Amalia. I moved around with my head bent, pupils white with dread to the ruins of the Temple, for I shall wash Your altar with my tears, I shall raise the lament of the whole nation as a sacrifice to You . . .

In the heart of the crowd, in the great crush, I knelt. Rising with heart humming to the women lying near me, sobbing, moving in a dense mass of summer garb, wigs, a rustle of turning pages and whispering. Body weeping, muttering, sticking its head to the stone. For all of them I shall pour my soul in a prayer to You, I, Amalia, whom You chose, in the name of Mala— their cry for help I shall raise to You, atone for the whole nation—I inhaled into me the warmth of the women's bodies wafting from the stones spraying the heat of candles and a mass of bird droppings, no longer distinguishing between me and them, and Mala who was tapping on our bowed heads, in the smoothness of the outstretched necks. How was I about to deliver my soul in prayer to You, to pour out my heart like water on the whole soft, miserable group, lying at my side, melted away in tears from the force of faith. Then, when everything was still dripping in me. It didn't yet occur to me that You will abandon us all, all together. Mala and me, and the women pressing me, lying prostrate on the square in the summer night. No, didn't imagine that You shut out prayer like that, so indifferently. Kill and restore to life, like a machine, in Your ruthlessness.   Didn't understand that that is what came to Your mind—

I lifted the Bible in front of my face, but I couldn't find the Book of Lamentations, even though I frantically turned the pages. Meanwhile, I started reciting the well-known first words, How - doth - the- city - sit - solitary - that - was - full - of -people - how - doth - the - city - sit - how - doth - the - city – sit - to find shelter now in the common shout that cuts the floodlights of the night, to sink immediately in swaying saturated with weeping, in the sourness of the body odors of a mass of women swelling their lament into the heat, the saliva of their lives, the mist of the prayer, to add my voice to the voice of Mala to the cry for help of the righteous, pure, tormented women sprawled at my side, to utter with them in one voice the lament - how - how - how - doth - the - city - sit - solitary, I started shouting just to sink into a shriek with them, buried together in one heap, without breathing, choked, weeping next to me, over me, so weak, how - doth - the - city - sit - solitary, a ditch of heavy, choked women's bodies that were thrown out, steaming, screaming above me. Impossible to breathe in the heaviness, the choking.

[. . .]

The paralysis flowed with a shocking pain, flooded me among the bodies of the lamenting women, gathered up Mala and me into the softness of their group, joined my voice to theirs, together, together, with hot weeping how—how——

Apparently I exaggerated my weeping, throwing myself onto the stones of the Western Wall, through the crowded bodies withdrawing from my weight. Not noticing the shirt that opened, the Bible that slipped out of my hands, apparently hitting one of the women bending over beneath me as it fell. I didn't see a thing, banging my fists on the stone and weeping. An opaque crust dried over the eyes. And shouts growing louder, and at first I didn't understand that they were at me. Only afterward the space that was opened, and the faces that moved distorted above me. Some woman shouted very loud, maybe she spat (perhaps the same woman who had been repeating the oath earlier), and other voices followed her.

Such a woman like her shouldn't come here, to a holy place. Such people don't belong here.

Opening her clothes like a whore. A disgrace, what a disgrace.

She shouldn't hold holy books in her hands, that filth, it's because of people like that that the Temple was destroyed.

And the especially shrill, strong voice of a short woman with a black kerchief fastened on her bald head, punching me with her hard fists, veined wings rising, circling and landing on my limbs, with the rhythm of a supplication.

Shame! Shame for us! May you burn for our shame, shame! Shame! She brought her fists down and thrust them like dull blades.

Apparently someone got me out, clasping me by the shoulders. A dwarf with a broad face took the trouble to pick up the Bible that had slipped down and carried it with ostentatious reverence at the head of the strange procession. And the one who had hit continued after us grimacing her distorted face above me. Finally the women threw me on the raised ramp outside the square, my clothes torn, my face filthy. Someone tossed the defiled Bible in my lap, and then the women in kerchiefs turned back to the square, running with arms outstretched, shrieking harder in the weeping of lamentation, as if to atone for the time they had wasted taking care of the impure woman.

Passersby gathered around me. Soldiers, a few tourists, women with baby buggies. They weren't doing anything anyway, and now they came to a special event. The onlookers hung around to see better, exchanging stinging comments, bursting into laughter. And from the distance the shout continued, with the heavy voices of the condemned, screaming, shrieking in gushing choruses of wailing . . . A dense mass of flesh pressed to flesh, flesh of my flesh . . . Helpless. Not noticing with their pure faith the destruction that was decreed, crowded at the stone wall of the screaming slaughterhouse where evil will assault them . . . My heart ached for the abandoned bodies, their limbs sprawled on the heat of the ground, distant limbs of my abominable body lying on the stone, swarming there, desperate, at the heavy end of my body buried in molten waves of weeping, moving in a crowded throng. And choking. Dry, dry. In the dark. In the floodlights.

Quarter to four. A chorus of muezzins inundating the dark like a stroke of light. Trills and trills burst from various distances. Sculpt the folds of the landscape.

A voice joined, very close, maybe from the village below. Syllables are separated from one another. Echoes of lament.

Five minutes after four. Silence again. Only the military patrols wandering on the distant road cut the night.

——We have transgressed and have rebelled: thou has not pardoned. Thou has covered with anger, and persecuted us: thou has slain, thou hast not pitied.——

The words swell into the dark. Knead it, knead . . .   (To go on with the testimony. To write it down. That's what supports now.)

Isaiah ran up then, bent down to me, his face glowing in the beams of the floodlights.— [. . .] not asking about my unbuttoned clothes, about what I did at the stone ledge, immediately scared full of pity, as if this is how he will heal me—

What a prayer, Amalia, you can't imagine, what exaltation! Really full faith in the coming of the Messiah. What do you know, what do you know, Amalia

[. . .]

Isaiah was hoisted above me in the light of the floodlights, pulling me to him, and laughing, laughing, with his torn bliss,

Now I really understand, Amalia, that the destruction is the proof that redemption will come! I'm so full of joy that I even want to throw myself in the air now and dance, [. . .] You understand what that is? You understand? That's redemption! Redemption! . . . Now, Amalia! Redemption from the destruction!

At the end of the prayer, the women began coming up from the square, flooding in a prattling mass, crowded. Dragging their heaviness in the narrow passageway, crushed one to another. They pass close by us, gaze in amazement at me and Isaiah who is straightening my disheveled clothes, walk around us. Gather in groups, and their chatter sweeps the echoes of their lament.

Isaiah picked up the Bible from my lap, lifting me to my feet, leading me through the movement of the crowd, and I didn't resist. Like a captive led to the slave market, it occurred to me, then, or afterward, when he led me outside the walls, into the night, plodding behind him in silence, with that bitter taste of dirt crushed in the dark. And even then, after the lament and the blasphemy, the opaque crust wasn't yet torn off my eyes, the choking of faith didn't yet burst out from under the bowl of the stars. The dryness didn't ease its hold on the breathing. And even then, I wasn't reconciled to the softness of Isaiah's love, I didn't return my heart to him. Only the tremor swelled, from one horizon to another.

For these things I weep; mine eye, mine eye runneth down with water, because the comforter that should relieve my soul is far from me——

Twenty to five. The hour slipped away like a hallucination. Complete silence. In the east, the morning star broke through. A lighted stripe in the heart of the sky, over the dull strip on the horizon.

[. . .]

Who are You tempting now, after you abandoned me? After the covenant with me was forsaken? Who? Maybe Isaiah . . . Sneaking into his bed with the wind of dawn awakened and strumming on David's lyre, dripping into his ear the hum of Your playing, tempting him to follow You, with all his soul and with all his heart and with all his might, even taking my soul . . .

[. . .]

Sharp pain.   To go on writing. Before You shut up the voice that rises against
You.   Not to stop despite the fear. To leave testimony before it's too late. The body
trembles.

As I walked, for some reason, a biblical verse was echoing in me, *I said unto thee when thou was in thy blood, Live, when thou was in thy blood, Live.* It burst out like a shadow from the niches. Out of the blue. A kind of lurking echo, *I said unto thee when thou was in thy blood, Live, when thou was in thy blood, Live . . .* I almost forgot the whole thing when I entered, and only now, when the strange echo was suddenly renewed in me for some reason, did I read the rest of the chapter . . . And I was shaken——(Only because of the great emotion, or was that really what whipped on my eyes?) From tatters of words buried under the *Prophetic word*, a story completely different from the explicit one suddenly screamed out. A voice attacked, testifying to the crime that was blurred, erased, and buried. Completely distorted in a reversal of facts in what was written, as false accusations—the body trembles. From fear of what was revealed. And maybe even more from the silencing—that the shout was buried alive like that, with wicked insolence, under the rebuke of the *Prophet*, who blames her, the tormented, despised one . . . (And what will be the fate of my confession here? How will they hush things up, take it out of context, turn it into slander against me in the hands of Your agents who will pursue me . . .)—As if the choked voice were screaming inside me there, relentlessly, demanding that I echo it from my lips . . . (To hurry and restore the protest against You there. Before I go mad, before You cut short the wick of my life.)

. . . What was written, *And as for thy nativity, in the day thou was born, neither was thou washed in water to supple thee . . . nor swaddled at all . . .* As if it was done by a stranger . . .—And it was You Yourself who cast me out, Your daughter, in the open field on the day I was born—shouted the voice—You who did not cut my navel, and in water I was not washed, and I was not salted, nor swaddled at all, Your eye did not pity me . . . for completely different, oh, how different, was Your scheme . . .

And when I passed by thee and saw thee polluted in thine own blood . . . You played innocent, as if You were a foreign master passing there completely by chance and heard the shriek of the bondwoman's baby, leaning over her in Your grace— according to Your slander—and say to her *in thy blood, Live, in thy blood, Live . . .* Gather her up to You—as if in compassion, *great pity . . .* —camouflaging with Your sweet words the cunning of Your lusts, *I have caused thee to multiply as the bud of the field, and thou has increased and waxen great, thy breasts are fashioned and thine hair is grown, whereas thou was naked and bare . . .*

Until her hour came, *the time of love . . .* And then, first the uncontrolled burst of desire for the slave You bred for Yourself . . . for Your ripe daughter . . . covering the abomination with Your hypocritical utterance, *Now when I passed by thee, and looked upon thee, behold, thy time was the time of love; and I spread my skirt over thee, and covered thy nakedness: yea, I sware unto thee, and entered into a covenant with thee, saith the Lord God, and thou becamest mine . . .* No longer restraining Your enormous lust and taking possession of Your daughter. Raping her in her virginity. Day and night You torture her, in the aggression of Your hard passion, again and again, insatiable. Fornicating in her nakedness that You revealed . . . And even with that You were not satisfied.

Then You went about increasing Your lust by envying strangers, by the lust of many Gentiles for the one You chose. That they would all desire the bondmaiden You bought as an eternal property. You went about making Your Name glorious with the Gentiles, by showing her nakedness that belonged only to You, only to You . . .

And she, in her innocence, didn't know what more You schemed when You washed her in water and thoroughly washed away her blood, and anointed her with oil, and clothed her with broidered work, and shod her with badgers' skin, and girded her about with fine linen and covered her with silk, calmed her heart which was terrified at the sight of the strange glory, swore that it is only for the delight of your love that You embellish her. Block Your ear to what she tells You in her timidity, *at our gates are all manner of pleasant fruits, new and old, which I have laid up for thee, O my beloved . . .* And You decked her with ornaments, and put bracelets upon her hands, and a chain on her neck, and you put a jewel on her forehead and earrings in her ears, and a beautiful crown upon her head, and You fed her fine flour and honey and oil, and she was exceeding beautiful and she didst prosper for Your scheme— —

And then, fettered like a chaste maiden in gold and silver and bracelets, You presented her to the strange Gentiles, in Your tabernacle, in the center of the city You desired for Your habitation, bragging of her to them, exciting them to devour Your chosen one with their naked gaze, inciting their envy for Your beautiful wife, the one You raised for You, only for You . . .

That they would grow wroth with her in their enmity, that envy would drive them out of their mind, because she would never be theirs . . . And even with that you were not satisfied.

For then the old madness stirred in You, pursuing you with a feverish delusion at the sight of Your daughter's crown of beauty, not remembering that it was You who bestowed beauty on her, You who raised the tower of her neck, You who presented to everyone the buds of her breasts. Pursued by fears in Your sickness, You rave that she, confident in her beauty, will now raise up her neck, and will betray You, will give strangers Your gold and Your silver that You gave her. Choked the visions of wrath, how in her boldness she will fling off Your yoke, the bonds of Your possession, will act boldly *the work of an imperious whorish woman* . . . That's what she will do to You—You rave—she whom You possessed, she whom You adorned, she will humiliate You like that, she will rob You forever of Your object of pleasure . . .

And in the burning of Your blood poisoned with jealousy, love turned to hate in You. For the hatred wherewith You hated her was greater than the love wherewith You had loved her. And then You set about to drown Your fury in an act of revenge whose atrocity has never been known since the creation of the world. *Woe woe unto you saith the Lord God!* . . . You shriek madly, run and tear from her hands the sons and daughters she has borne You, rip their soft necks, slaughter Your babes, pass them through the fire. Run back to the wretched woman, pluck her from her weeping in Your bloodsoaked hands, laugh madly at her disaster.

And then You go on brutally ripping her garments, removing her gold, growing madder in the dark of Your lunacy, burning with a lust for revenge. Going on and tormenting the victim of Your love, defacing her image completely, crushing her thin body with the torments of rape. Thus, You say, in the burst of Your sickness, to make her whore unto death.

Like a brutal pimp, You made Your wife a whore. Giving her to everyone who wanted her, spreading her legs to every passerby. Presenting her in her nakedness, announcing her, calling, tempting them to come in, drool, come close, take Your wife to be desecrated by their fornication, her, the chosen one, the only one.

And You multiplied her whoring, to make her wretched, and You weren't satisfied. You made her whore with the Egyptians great of flesh, and You weren't satisfied. You made her whore with the Assyrians with a donkey's penis, you made her whore with them and You weren't satisfied. And thou multiplied her fornication in the land of Canaan unto Chaldea, and goats ejaculated in her, and even with that You were not satisfied—How wretched her heart when You inflict all that on her, standing over her in the valley of her torments, polluted in her blood, torturing her even more with Your venomous words *How she whored my love, look at you, whore . . . Because of what you didn't remember (who didn't remember, she or You?) the days of your youth, and angered me with all that* . . . Smooth words like that. Covering Your sins. Adding lie to sin. That was Your scheme—

Until water flowed on her head, soon she was drowned. Only then did You rest and Your jealousy subsided and You were no longer angry, for You hadn't yet completed Your scheme . . . After all, You didn't stop desiring her. Even in her defilement Your lust still burned for her that she should crawl to You from her torments besmirched and downtrodden, that she would cover Your feet with her kisses, wash the dirt off them with her tears, tell You with a look dulled with mourning, with her defiled mouth, the words from then *Thou, O Lord, remainest for ever; thy throne from generation to generation, turn thou us unto thee, O Lord, and we shall return; renew our days as of old. But thou has utterly rejected us; thou art very wroth against us* . . . And then, You will pass by *as before,* and You will see her cast out in the open field, polluted in her blood. And once again You will tell her as in that very merciful master, in thy blood, live, in thy blood, live . . . Once again spread Your skirt, covering Your adulterer's face, swearing again to her without remorse, *I will establish unto thee an everlasting covenant, I will establish my covenant with thee . . . That thou mayest remember and be confounded* . . . You will gather her in again into Your bedchamber of tears, bind her again. Your current of suffering, so that she will never be cut off, for Thou, O Lord, remainest for ever; thy throne from generation to generation . . .

Thus You savor the torments of your lovers—Precious in the sight of the Lord is the death of his saints . . . And the more tender the victim the better . . . Like those women cast out there, wallowing in the dust. They and Mala. And I too, who saw You uncovered within the tent, weak, wounded, and I meant to bring healing to You, to comfort You as a mother comforts her suckling . . . All of us You tempted, and cast out, every one in her own way. You forever contaminated by Your jealousy. Unable to love. Tempting and deserting, and swearing once again, in panic—when Your weakness increases, when the destruction once again gapes in You, and slipping out of Your grasp for a moment the world suspended upon nothing . . .

[. . .]

Wind from behind. The mountain opposite bursts out of the gray. Black spots of treetops from the blur of the mass of dirt. A muffled gloom still covers the bottom of the slope, the rocks, the tombstones. And the ridge is already turning pale. It's possible to write by the light of dawn coming in the window. Only the movement of the patrol cars is going on as usual in the taut white between the watches of the night. The white now floods between the star of Bethlehem and the sunrise.

[. . .]

Bells. The bells! From all the churches. A gilded, joyous, shattered cascade. Celebrating, celebrating. Gold poured out. Praising You there   Halleluia . . .   B e l l s ringing, a refined plait of gold slivers. Halleluia . . . New mornings abundant in Your faithfulness . . .   Halleluia—

Men are climbing the steps of the alley. Going to work. Their rhythmic steps swallowed up behind.   A hushed shadow of a flight of birds passed by and grazed the window.

Despite the fatigue, suddenly strength. Desire to leave You. To cast everything off, cut the tatters of the delusion

From the distance a woman's voice, in conversation. Notes from a transistor radio. A hot summer day bursts out all at once. Glow on the eyelashes.   Complete nakedness.

Dossier: Michal Govrin, Israeli Writer

Rachel Feldhay Brenner and Judith Miller

The following interview was held on May 12, 1997 in Washington, D.C. between Israeli writer Michal Govrin and critic Rachel Brenner. Both were attending a conference on "Genocide, Religion and Modernity" held at Washington's Holocaust Museum. Their conversation focused primarily on Govrin's 1995 novel, *The Name*, recently translated from the Hebrew by Barbara Harshav. *The Name* (excerpts of which precede this interview) was published by Riverhead Books of Penguin-Putnam in the fall of 1998.

Rachel Brenner: I'm so glad the English-speaking reader will finally have the chance to read your very important book.

Michal Govrin: "Important" is a heavy word for me when we talk about art. I mostly hope my novel shakes people up. I mean it to be disturbing, even scary. And I hope the book becomes a journey. When people tell me they're reading it, I usually ask where they've landed, because to me it's about a trip, a passage, a journey through which the book and the reader are transformed. While writing it—and I chose to write in the first person so that the reader might end up "performing out" the book's monologue for him- or herself—I thought that the reader might gain some vision at the end of the experience. Maybe my readers will visit some places in their subconscious, in their cultural heritage. I want the book to be at least a persuasive and rewarding journey . . . and relevant to the times in which we live.

Rachel Brenner: Why was it so necessary for you to create a text which would provoke this kind of experience, which would also be "relevant," as you put it?

Michal Govrin: Let me start with an anecdote. On the plane here from Jerusalem they showed a movie about the life of Pierre and Marie Curie, about especially *the way* they discovered what they discovered. There was a very strong image in the movie which really brought me back to my process of writing. After the Curies discovered the phenomenon of radioactivity, they attempted to prove their discovery by extracting radium from their samples. They did it by grinding and boiling down one ton of rock they'd brought to their laboratory from the Austrian Alps. Nobody understood what they were doing—in fact, they didn't disclose their research—and they didn't even have enough money to have lab help, so they stood there by themselves all that time and boiled these stones, both of them standing there sweating. That image of the lonely battle of grinding down a whole rock in order to extract a few fractions of a gram of radium expressed what I felt while writing and working on *The Name*.

You know I'm the daughter of a survivor. I wouldn't have dared write about the Holocaust if I didn't have that first-person, let's say genetic, experience. What I tried to do in the book out of this kernel of inherited experience was to create an unsettling portrait of the extreme psychic state of the "victim." I tried to expose what enables, what even glorifies the masochistic exhilaration of victim status. By this I mean that Jewish history and Jewish theology again and again seem to enshrine, on the one hand, the ingredients that provide us with powers of survival after every catastrophe but also, on the other hand, somehow justify these catastrophes—even celebrate them—and in a way make them part of our system. I felt a mission to visit the theological points touching upon this and question them. Maybe by exposing them I could deflate or demystify them, accuse them openly and maybe, then, help to break the Gordian knot Jewish people find themselves tied up in. I wanted to dissipate part of the neurosis.

Rachel Brenner: So what you're saying is that there's a certain inherent structure or pattern in Jewish history which you find very unhealthy. And basically there's a healing process that goes on in your book, but this healing process requires some sort of transgression against the pattern that's become the norm. Could you say something about how the novel works to transgress and heal?

Michal Govrin: I decided, as you know, to write the book in the form of a prayer. So it's a monologue, a woman's prayer addressed to God. It's structured a little bit like a mystical detective story, say like Dostoevski's *Crime and Punishment*. Like mystical and metaphysical detectives, my heroine searches for truth and the sense of herself at the same time. My whole novel is both an exploration of the psyche and a theological search.

The book starts with a kind of declaration that my central character is going to commit suicide at the end of the prayer, something which may, however, not happen if the process she goes through puts her in another psychic space. Moreover, hers is not a simple suicide; it's a sacrificial one. She resigns herself from the beginning to being the chosen scapegoat; she is going to sacrifice herself in order to save herself and to save God. Like someone who is going to commit suicide, she's leaving her testimony, her confession, behind her in written form. (That's the book.) But by the act of writing, and what happens while she writes and prays, she comes to another point from where she started. You might say that the promise in her prayer, the oath she takes to do something extreme, is ultimately subverted by what the prayer and the writing unfold.

To write a novel which is a prayer showed me how much the act of writing—the solitude of the writer who addresses a reader—is close to the process of praying. When you write, you don't know if the reader will hear you or not. You write on faith that someone who might read you is out there. You use rhetoric and language to seduce the reader. When we look, for example, at the biblical chapter of Psalms, it's almost the same thing: when the writer prays, it's not sure that God hears him so he tries to seduce God by tropes, by forms of rhetoric.

Most of what is called Hebrew literature today is a secular—and militantly secular—form of art. To introduce into that context a novel which takes the structure of a prayer is already a transgression of what Israeli culture is today, or what it tries to be. I made a very purposeful gesture of transgressing one of the biggest rules of Israeli culture. I went and looked into the metaphysical or theological cellars of our Hebrew ideology.

Rachel Brenner: And what did you discover in these cellars?

Michal Govrin: I discovered that you can't look at the phenomenon of Israel or Zionism without looking at the theological background . . . that by concealing this background or by suppressing it, we don't understand the problems we sit upon. My novel is a gesture of saying to Israeli readers: "If you think that by saying you aren't religious you'll rid yourself of your heritage, you're just fooling yourselves." The book holds up an uneasy mirror to the face of the Israeli reader or the nonreligious Jew, saying: "By not visiting synagogue or by saying that you're secular, you've not even started to run away from the narrative, you've just suppressed it in a way that its return will be even more powerful." That's, in any case, one layer of the story.

Rachel Brenner: But your protagonist, the heroine, does not run away. She comes back to theology: she wants to discover it at various levels. When I say various levels, I mean orthodoxy and Kabbala. That's what she really wants to explore.

Michal Govrin: Yes, in *The Name*, the exploration of the theological narrative is from within. Embedded in the book is also a harsh criticism of Zionism and especially about the way the state of Israel dealt with the Holocaust. From my point of view, Israel nationalized the narrative of the Holocaust as a way of not dealing with the bitter tragedy, but, rather, of manipulating it immediately into another narrative. At the same time, I do a very lacerating critique of the Orthodox milieu, which did not even start to deal, theologically speaking, with the Holocaust. Most of the Orthodox voices which speak to the Holocaust fall into total muteness, helplessness, or some very refined articulations of blaming or of taking the blame. "The Holocaust came because of Zionism, because of the Enlightenment, because of not keeping kosher, etc." Taking the blame or blaming other groups of Jews for the horror, which is unfortunately part of the debate, eliminates having enough courage to act, or to come up with a theology subversive enough to encompass such a tragedy.

Part of the book includes what I call the "hidden" voices from the tradition, antagonistic voices that have always existed alongside other voices in the dominant Jewish tradition but have not risen to the surface. These voices were mainly shaped at previous moments of crisis, when a renewal of the religious narrative was needed in order to face extreme conditions—without abandoning altogether the heritage. Part of what the book tries to do is to transgress and shatter the official versions in order to make room for those other voices to emerge.

Rachel Brenner: If I follow you correctly, you give room or space to those voices which have been muted or silenced but which *do* exist in the Jewish tradition. Once you give these voices a voice in your novel, what do we hear?

Michal Govrin: By the simple fact of placing the usual Jewish prayer in the mouth of a woman, rather than how these traditional prayers are customarily perceived—that is in the mouth of a man—I did something shattering. For example, the book starts with a sentence which is almost always said automatically by the man praying, "May my prayer be accepted by You, will You please . . . receive, or accept me."

Rachel Brenner: Something like, "May I be acceptable to You?"

Michal Govrin: Yes. When it is said in the extreme mode of ecstasy which begins my novel, it works as a transgression on two levels. First, it's a woman who says it, so suddenly the enormous dimension of erotic tension in Jewish religion bursts out in a very powerful way. All that linguistically overt erotic dimension that when said by a man to a male God stays under the cover of metaphor, when suddenly said by a woman to a male God becomes actual eroticism. This reminds the reader, especially in post-enlightenment orthodoxy, of the erotic dimension which is very much hushed up in Jewish religious literature today.

On another level, saying "May You accept me" by a woman in the extremity of wanting to give herself erotically, physically, suicidally to God brings out the potential for self-sacrifice. This is an awkward point in Judaism. And it is usually not considered as central but rather comes from kabbalistic thinking.

Rachel Brenner: Can we talk about language for a minute? You just gave a very striking example of divesting the language of its metaphorical disguises, of unveiling it. That's what you think is really shocking, a disturbing new reality that emerges from the old word. Is that right?

Michal Govrin: Yes. I think one of the powerful things for me in the writing was that "going back," which demanded a kind of peeling, a destroying of layers of veils.

Rachel Brenner: You peeled off . . .

Michal Govrin: All the official, metaphorical, hierarchical interpretations . . . back to the wildness of the literal.

Rachel Brenner: Let me refer to this really central scene in the novel, when Amalia, your protagonist, finally rereads a key passage in the Bible from Ezekiel. If I remember, it's Ezekiel sixteen. I think this really *is* the revelatory chapter, a reworking of a crucial chapter of the Bible. Can you say a few words about it?

Michal Govrin: It's a moment in the book when, from the process of writing, I move into interpretation. That, by the way, was also a wonderful discovery for me: that rereading a narrative inside the narrative is no less powerfully inventive than inventing a new plot. It was like going back to a traditional Jewish mode of writing, reading again, revisiting, representing again.

Rachel Brenner: That's probably more difficult than writing a new plot. Seeing with different eyes . . .

Michal Govrin: Seeing with different eyes . . . Yes. You know some readers told me that because of my chapter they went back and reread Ezekiel and they were shocked. They wondered why it wasn't censored, pulled out of the Bible altogether! Suddenly this Ezekiel was manic, a completely mad piece of literature.

Just from the stylistic point of view what is so striking in Ezekiel is how close it is to the New Testament's Book of Revelations, to Saint John. I think there's a very great similarity of texture—all those changes in register, for example.

But you know, after doing what I thought was the most blasphemous thing I could do, after completing a narrative move that really felt as though I were writing out of my guts and the heroine's guts, I found that I could find other voices, other Rabbis who'd already said what I said. In fact, I could never stray really far into blasphemy without discovering that my blasphemy was already there in the tradition. This discovery of blasphemous connections was a revelation of those hidden voices we've been talking about. The only blasphemous dimension I didn't find was the speaking woman, the female. But I'm not even completely sure about that. So my blasphemy was also a liberation of already existing hidden voices. What I learned about blasphemy is that you have to go through blasphemy in order to find faith again. It's a cliché, I know, but only after the blasphemy can the prayer in my book start to be called a prayer. What preceded it becomes a kind of madness.

Rachel Brenner: Yes, right, because now you can decipher it.

Michal Govrin: After you've "broken the tablets," only then, with this shattered image, can belief begin to happen.

Rachel Brenner: Let's go back to the question of rereading. The usual interpretation of Ezekiel holds that this chapter of the Bible represents God and the nation of Israel as lovers.

Michal Govrin: This traditional interpretive metaphor of lovers gives us a very concise and intense summation of a whole process: falling in love, making the covenant of marriage, and then the defamation of the covenant by the wife, hence the terrible punishment of the woman/nation . . . and then forgiveness by the Lord and renewal of the covenant. That's the structure of the Ezekiel chapter which I followed. Except that I decided to take a subversive point of view. Instead of reading the process through the prophet's voice, which shows it from one point of view—God's, I decided to read it from the woman's point of view. And reading Ezekiel from the woman's point of view was horrendous. Because it suddenly became a story where she becomes the servant that God *finds*, just like in that nineteenth-century melodrama *Les Misérables*, where a nobleman finds a poor girl and takes pity on her. She has no rights whatsoever because, from the beginning, she is *found* by him. And then there is this very strange shift from the woman being God's found "daughter" to being his "wife," which points to this awful . . .

Rachel Brenner: Incestuous relationship?

Michal Govrin: Incestuous, sexual, abusive . . . All this very baroque description of her looks and her garments suddenly had resonances with writings of, for example, the Marquis de Sade. All that compilation of luxurious decors, palaces, and the flourishing pornographic descriptions delighting in how the woman is defiled . . .

Rachel Brenner: Well, that really is transgressive, no doubt about it, at least in the theologically acceptable way of thinking.

Michal Govrin: And then I began to juxtapose Ezekiel with the cry of the wounded, slaughtered, and defiled women in The Book of Lamentations. There you can find God being accused of bringing down on Jerusalem, the woman, all these terrible punishments. In Ezekiel, the blame is never shared.

I think in Ezekiel there is the kernel of the Western sadistic narrative pattern in which the woman, a kind of sacred sinner, prostitutes herself in a very lavish decor, is then punished and "mercifully" forgiven. And, then, there is the whole question of prostitution. In Ezekiel, God accuses the woman of prostituting herself. That's part of what I call "monotheistic jealousy." God, the jealous, wants her to be only his, and yet exposes her in order to glorify himself as owner of such an exotic creature. In the Bible, for example in Exodus which this chapter echoes, there are constantly manifestations of God's spectacle. When you read the first chapters of Exodus, you see explicitly that the plagues and the coming out of Egypt are a big show that God puts on. In front of Pharaoh, the Egyptians, and the Jews and the rest of the nations, God shows His glory through the plagues and through the exodus. Then, the temple is the place that God desires, Jerusalem is His woman, His place, "His" vagina. But it's not enough for this to be an intimate relationship. He has to show it off. For God's glory, all nations will see Jerusalem as His chosen, His place of desire. His love is exhibitionistic.

While working on Ezekiel and seeing the nation as a place to be whored, I said to myself that where there is a whore there is a pimp. God is the pimp! Their relationship involves showing her, His chosen, and arousing jealousy by exposing the "chosenness" of Jews. In this, I found the most unbelievable analogy with Passolini's movie, *Accatone*. It's an extraordinary movie about the tragic life of a Roman pimp who cannot but prostitute the woman he loves the most. It's a very religious movie: during a fierce knife battle between two gangs of pimps, the background music, for example, is a Bach cantata. That very deep Christian background runs through this whole movie. Working on Ezekiel brought me back to Passolini's film. God cannot but obsessionally expose Jerusalem, expose the Jewish people in a way that arouses the jealousy and the need of other people, of other nations, to become themselves "the chosen," usurping the place of the Jews. This is a kind of curse on Jerusalem. Jerusalem is first of all the place of God's jealously and desire. And thus to resemble God, everyone should desire and possess Jerusalem. This universal prostitution of Jerusalem marks God's singularity, because He *is the one* who possesses. Ezekiel seems to suggest this.

And then there are those terrible descriptions of punishment. After the Holocaust, it's impossible to read about punishment, both in Ezekiel and The Book of Revelations, without being aware of a certain analogy. If we cannot accept the Holocaust as being a punishment—something which I cannot by any means accept—how can we accept previous destructions and horrors as a legitimate form of punishment? But Jewish theology has posited this legitimacy. Maybe, I say, the moment when God punishes is in fact, when He, that crazy jealous lover, loses control. From that mad attack of jealousy against the so-called betrayal by woman, we might see that the problem is only in His mind—as we sometimes know attacks of jealousy are. In the end, He takes her back to renew the covenant, as if forgiveness is part of a perpetual cycle of total enslavement. The beaten woman, through accepting to relive that position again and again, suggests that the Jewish people somehow consented to being accused of betrayal which justifies again and again their punishment. That kind of already inscribed sadomasochistic relationship constitutes a very significant and powerful judgment on Israel, it seems to me.

Rachel Brenner: Your heroine endures this pattern of continuous suffering. But this time it's *after* the Holocaust. Would you say that *after* the Holocaust, it has become an absolute necessity, a responsibility, to reread the Bible and to see, in a different light, the other calamities that have befallen the Jewish people?

Michal Govrin: Absolutely. I think it's absolutely our responsibility. I think we must be responsible for the narratives we tell. They shape the way we behave, for good and for ill. I think that the narratives the West has told itself, and that Jews have told themselves, have brought us to where we are. I think that *after* the Holocaust we're responsible for reshaping, reinterpreting the narratives. In the Bible, there is such a multiplicity of voices, we can find ones which support a very accusative reading of God. One of the moves of the novel is to reread what God is, to discredit, after the Holocaust, the role of the jealous God. On the contrary, it tries to look into patterns where God is depicted as having failed—if you like, God as a metaphor for a cosmic problem or the human psyche. I'm saying there's an inherent flaw, an inherent . . .

Rachel Brenner: Imperfection?

Michal Govrin: An inherent imperfection, either in the human psyche, or if you want to put it in a theological perspective, in God, that would have enabled the Holocaust—besides other atrocities—to happen. If we want to have a narrative, we should have a narrative that does not justify atrocities, not even as "punishments." Because if the world has come to what it is, we have to have the courage to tell a story in which we take responsibility for imperfections, an imperfect God and imperfect man. What the book as a cathartic moment proposes, instead of the hope for total or absolute redemption—which, by the way, is what defines modes of mental craziness . . .

Rachel Brenner: Well it's a fantasy . . .

Michal Govrin: It's a fantasy, but it's a fantasy that, when rushed into reality, is responsible for many of our false hopes and catastrophes. What the novel puts forth is the image of a wounded God, a God that has a flaw or an imperfection in Him—the image of the broken tablets of the law that contain in themselves both the promise and, on the other hand, the memory of a shattered promise. The novel says that absolute salvation is a fantasy and reality is more complex. It says that maybe the image of God we've portrayed is wishful thinking because if man's soul has so many shadows, it means that we should have a God that shows us His shadows as well. And that healing would be a mutual process, of both man and God. This image of an impotent, helpless God has, mostly in the Kabbala, many images. In the Zohar, for example, there's a description of Rachel, a perfectly confident woman, arguing with God after the destruction of Jerusalem. The text ridicules Abraham who tries to plead with God. And after God gives him two rational explanations, Abraham accepts and justifies what happened and disappears back into his grave. He's in a lot of pain but what can he say?

Rachel Brenner: And that's true of lots of other great men.

Michal Govrin: Yes, they're very rational. They believe in justice. But Rachel stays and goes on accusing God of having abandoned His children and she does not accept His answers. She is not comforted.

Rachel Brenner: There's another time when she does get a response; and God says, "You will be revered," because she's right.

Michal Govrin: Because she's right! In the passage of the Zohar, she shows even more courage, even more blasphemy. The traditional understanding of Rachel's lament, as it figures in Jeremiah (31:15), is that she weeps over the death of her children. In the Zohar, there is an audacious shift to an understanding that she laments the absence of God. Towards the end of Jeremiah's verse, the language shifts from the plural to the singular in an irregular way. The text says, "Rachel, weeping for her children, refuses to be comforted for her children, because he is not." The Zohar uses this irregularity to suggest a subversive understanding. Rachel, accordingly, does not only lament the death of her children, but the absence of God—because *He is not* [*ki einenu*]. As if by the extremity of His rage and punishment, He mutilated himself and disappeared.

In the Warsaw ghetto, Rabbi Klonimus of Piasechna, a young Hassidic master, went on teaching until the liquidation of the ghetto. His extraordinary writings were buried in a milk tank. They were found in the 1950s, under the rubble, and published as *Holy Fire*. He used the Zohar to be able to claim a theology in the face of the destruction of the Jewish people. His voice was not followed by the Jewish orthodoxy after the Holocaust. Only in the ghetto was there the courage to say that God was so consumed and so blocked in a hold of total rage that He was helpless. In the Rabbi of Piasechna's *Holy Fire*, there is a total reversal of responsibility: man takes responsibility for God. It's a form of resistance: you cannot wait passively. You have to take the first step. Man's lament, his weeping, just like Rachel's in the Zohar, has an active role. Through his weeping, man can draw out the concealed God, who is somehow imprisoned. Man can help God weep with him and by this shared lament free God from his "stuckness."

Rachel Brenner: There *are* Jewish theologies that deal precisely with this question of a God who admits his people as "senior partner," so to speak. Irving Greenberg's theology, for one. Other theologians talk about the voluntary covenant and the break-up of the ultimate authority of an omnipotent, all-knowing God. It seems to me that there *are* theologians struggling with the same questions as your protagonist.

But I want to raise one more thing. You talked before about the muted voices you tried to reinvigorate. In your book, there is a voice that is not heard and this is, of course, the voice of the Holocaust victim, Mala, for whom your protagonist, Mala, or Amalia, is named. She is really the force behind her spiritual daughter, and yet she is not heard. It's only through the heroine Amalia's consciousness that the stepmother's voice emerges. I want you to say a few words about the function of this muted and yet loud voice?

Michal Govrin: That's a very poignant demand. There *are* voices of survivors in my novel, but they speak only in the present of the novel. I felt I didn't have the right to fictionalize this character's past, a past I did not go through. I *do* understand the need for a kind of a Disney amusement park effect—of making the memory of the Holocaust palpable. I've even seen it work with kids in the Holocaust Museum. Yet I could not do it. First, I think we cannot identity with the real suffering of someone else. I don't believe in identification with suffering. I think that we reject identification with suffering because to really identity yourself with suffering is as damaging as the suffering. What I say now is based on my experience in the Gulf War, while I was alone with my very little girls in Jerusalem. The first night, the fear was awful—until I knew the Scud missiles would not land on our house and maybe kill or deform us. The fear was so big that I shook for hours afterwards. The second night, when the pattern was starting to be understood and Jerusalem seemed out of danger, I watched TV and saw what was happening in Tel Aviv with the same distance I would have had if I had been watching from the U.S. And I *watched myself* doing it, and I understood that I was rejecting the feeling of identification because it would have been devastating. I think there is a very strong desire to believe that art can bring us to an identification, or provide an emotional substitution, for suffering. This is a lie we tell ourselves in order to deal with unspeakable subjects. There is no way that anyone can go back there without paying the terrible price of what it was to go through the camps. My rejection of any dramatization of the camps stems probably from my being the daughter of a survivor. My mother's legacy was lost in the camps. The real story, the "real story," that is to say the tellable story of my mother's experience only came to me after her death, through the stories that were told to me by women who had survived with her, women who held each other throughout three years of internment.

I *did* learn from my mother something maybe even stronger than a story; that which is transmitted in gestures, in silences, in tensions, in subconscious ways. These were far more interesting for me to portray in my novel than an actual story which would immediately conform to an edifying narrative or a theological structure. For me, the telling of the Holocaust is already accepting it in narrative structure. And as I will *not* accept the Holocaust as livable, something you can narrate or tame into a narrative, I could not have Amalia's father's first wife speak. I wanted the Holocaust in my novel—I'm thinking about our earlier conversation about the Curies—to have that untamed quality of radium, that constant radioactive power which is always charging through the universe. I wanted to create throughout the book, by not speaking directly about the Holocaust, the presence of an absence, an absence that works on the heroine and, maybe, the reader—a kind of ongoing explosion. The fact that the story is not told, I think, keeps it alive, keeps it recharging.

Rachel Brenner: That's the hidden power behind your novel—a distant witness and a vicarious victim. And this is as close to understanding as we can get, because the daughter's story is activated by something we cannot grasp, though we know it's there. It's like this mysterious God whom we also know is there.

Michal Govrin: When I try to think about my first metaphysical experience, it seems to me to have come from the same zone as my encounters with the shadow thrown by my mother's presence. For me the strongest transcendental entity has always been close to the Holocaust. Encountering Kafka was the first apprehension I had of a possible theology, a theology that would not start with God as a luminous sun, but with the omnipresent and transcendental presence of a flaw reflected in the human soul. At the same time, I experienced the human courage of confronting this evil. There is always a kind of dualistic encounter with something which is so hugely evil that it breeds a very strong power of resistance in the human soul. And this luminous side of the human response is not less divine.

Biography and Transgression

Brenda Wineapple

We need to witness our own limits transgressed, and some life pasturing freely where we never wander.

Henry David Thoreau, *Walden*

Others, frightened at the art which could raise phantoms at will, and keep the form of the dead among the living, were inclined to consider the painter as a magician, or perhaps the famous Black Man of old witch-times, plotting mischief in a new guise.

Nathaniel Hawthorne, "The Prophetic Pictures"

Biography is transgression, the biographer a transgressor who invades the citadel of the solitary self, laying bare its secrets to the world. Biography is unholy trespass, outrage committed in the name of knowledge and edification. No wonder its relatives shun her: at best, biography is a foundling stepchild to history, bastard of the novel, and shameful cousin of literary (or other) criticism.

Even those most practiced in its art are compelled to plead its case. "Social life is the aggregate of all the individual men's Lives who constitute society," wrote Thomas Carlyle, as if to exculpate the biographical enterprise: "History is the essence of innumerable Biographies."[1] And so Carlyle wants "not Redbook Lists, and Court Calendars, and Parliamentary thought, but the LIFE OF MAN in England: what men did, thought, suffered, enjoyed."[2] Such a calendar, of course, threatens to disturb the veil with which we conceal ourselves. "The lives of great men all remind us we should leave no sons behind us," Gertrude Stein cannily observed.[3]

After all, biography promises disclosure. Without disclosure, biography simply idealizes its subjects, dressing them in hagiographic costume of fantasy and wish. Sigmund Freud knew this. He adopted biography to his own ends, calling his study of Leonardo da Vinci a "pathography" and explaining that "it does not detract from his [Leonardo's] greatness if we make a study of the sacrifices which his development from childhood must have entailed, and if we bring together the factors which have stamped him with the tragic mark of failure."[4] But to many, Freud himself remains disreputable, his method preposterous.

In fact, "pathography" no longer even conveys Freud's meaning but that of Joyce Carol Oates, who appropriated the word to different ends:

> [P]athography typically focuses upon a far smaller canvas, sets its standards much lower. Its motifs are dysfunction and disaster, illnesses and pratfalls, failed marriages and failed careers, alcoholism and breakdowns and outrageous conduct. Its scenes are sensational, wallowing in squalor and foolishness; its dominant images are physical and deflating; its shrill theme is 'failed promise' if not outright 'tragedy.'[5]

Such acrimony seems displaced, however, or at least overstated. Surely, there are good and bad biographies, skilled and inept, sensitive and sensationalistic. Regardless, the practice of biography is regarded with dubious eye, no doubt because it entails the disturbing (and pleasurable) reversal of expectations. The great are small, the small important: our assumptions are upended.

Although Lytton Strachey created an art of such reversals, literary decorum still dictates that we choose the tale over the teller. What matter Melville's brutal treatment of his wife? (Of course, the exception occurs in the case of women subjects, where too much ambition—Gertrude Stein—becomes an aesthetic failing, and prevarication—Katherine Anne Porter—bears no relation to creativity.) Not surprisingly, critical theory more or less ignores biography. New Criticism disavowed it, citing the intentional fallacy, and more recently, much of post-structural theory dismisses it, assuming that, after Barthes and Foucault, the author is

Transgression, Punishment, Responsibility, Forgiveness
Graven Images 4 (1998), 67-72.

dead. This is taken to mean, wrongly, that a written text not only supersedes its author, as in the case of New Criticism, it also creates the author. Subject, subjectivity, the creative self: all are delusions of the bourgeois culture inventing them.

Take the matter of the subject, its so-called death, and the subsequent ascension of the text. Michel Foucault does ask "what is an author?" but in so doing interrogates the function the *idea* of an author plays in our culture, urging us not to assume naively that an author springs *ex cathedra* and full-blown. Rather, he investigates the institution of authorship: how and why meaning or value come to be assigned to the person we designate as author, which is invariably a cultural designation.[6] And even though biographers typically do not use the same terminology, they raise questions similar to the ones outlined by Foucault: "under what conditions and through what forms can an entity like the subject appear in the order of discourse; what position does it occupy; what functions does it exhibit; and what rules does it follow in each type of discourse?"[7]

Similarly, biographers explore how, say, any subject's vocation intersects with the needs, fantasies, and desires of that individual; in other terms, biographers recognize that no easily demarcated boundary separates the individual from the cultural, the private from the public. Demands of one can become demands of the other; differences between them shift and slide, often emerging in those representations which in turn render the individual—particularly the writer, and certainly the biographer—self-conscious. (Or, to quote Stein's parody: "I am I because my little dog knows me."[8]) Put yet another way, the biographer tries to determine that undiscoverable place where inner and outer converge: how can we know the dancer from the dance?

Of course, without the assumption of an author, a subject who speaks (or spoke), there can be no biography. At its most absurd, then, if the subject of biography exists only as text, and the author writing the biography exists only as text, then both are one and the same. But with its emphasis on the subject, its implicit individualism (an examination of one person's life), and its tacit empiricism, biography inevitably appears not just transgressive but downright regressive. Under its purview, the individual seems to stand tall (or in Oates's view, far too short); culture seems palpable, history teleologic and knowable.

Moreover, biography is a hybrid genre—part novel, part history, part psychology, part criticism—which creates an inevitable anxiety about it, manifest most specifically in the equivocal esteem and status it's accorded. We grant biography prestigious awards (Pulitzer, National Book) but remain uninterested in its history; we call it an art, a craft, a genre, a trade, but seldom teach biography in the university. We rarely distinguish among its types—literary biography, celebrity biography, critical biography, intellectual biography, psychobiography, to name a few. We talk of style and form infrequently, if at all. The assumption, said Edmund Gosse in 1901, seems to be that anyone can write biography: "to be a philosopher a man must have made a study of thought . . . a historian must have given some years to documents and to their synthesis . . . a man is not a dramatist until he has mastered the conditions of the stage. But a biography is supposed to need no skill, no art, no experience of any kind."[9]

The purported ease with which biography is written and its breach of categories also suggest some apprehension about its force and aim. Perhaps as a result, we take refuge in an untroubled definition of biography as the narrated story of a life. But we do not know what we want from it. We abjure panegyric but loathe character assassination. And post-structural critics aside, we harbor deep convictions about the meaning of a life, any life, our life: how it should be conducted, how it should unfold. Hence, Elizabeth Gaskell, in her *Life of Charlotte Brontë*, sought to normalize the volcanic writer, composing Brontë's biography along the lines of a fulfilled marriage plot. There are other, equally predictable, plots: success plots, victimization plots, fulfillment plots. Hawthorne biographers squabble not over the details of his life but about which plot suits him best—whether he was a cheerful man or a recluse.

Biography also exploits these conventions. Borrowing from representational practices and wrapping them in a linear chronology, biography generally offers the satisfactions of plot, place, sequence, character. But it also can subvert the illusions its narrative sustains, laying bare machinations of desire and power, of ambition and privilege, of civilization and its discontents—especially in the matter of character. To biography, character cannot be conceived as a moral category but as the fashioning of identity, which lies at the core of the biographical enterprise.

The conundrum of character is the epicenter of Natalie Zemon Davis's *The Return of Martin Guerre*, a biographical allegory about the peasant Martin Guerre and the imposter Arnaud du Tilh, who usurped Guerre's identity, becoming to many a better, more real Guerre than Guerre himself. As narrated by Davis, the Guerre story asks us to consider how one establishes identity beyond doubt.[10] By shoe size? Martin Guerre's shoemaker noticed that the second Martin Guerre's feet were much larger than the first's, but he might have misremembered. By photograph? Even if they existed in the sixteenth century, how do we ascertain that the image we see coincides with the subject we seek? By personal testimony? Martin Guerre's wife accepted the second Martin Guerre into her bed, fully knowing, one assumes, the difference in husbands.

Arnaud du Tilh's artful expropriation of Martin Guerre's identity therefore asks us to consider where one's self begins and where it ends, and how that self is represented to others. For many of his family and his neighbors, Arnaud du Tilh was a better Martin Guerre—better husband, father, citizen—than the unforgiving, taciturn Martin Guerre who abandoned his wife by disappearing for eleven years. Indeed, the fact of two Martin Guerres forced the entire community, then and later, to reconsider the relations among the private self, the represented self, and the self as defined by institutions like marriage, church, and state. And so the story of Martin Guerre—the two Guerres—reminds us that identity slides, deceives, inveigles and beguiles. Identity is not a simple matter of who we are, or were, to ourselves, at any point in time, but also who and how we partake of the swirling cultural standards which form us: female, male, married, single, powerful, poor, fat, thin, ugly, beautiful.

This is biography. The biographer represents identity, seeking its complex traces in the house, the yard, the school, under the bed, and in the closet, among the discards and the refuse, the unsent letters and childhood poems, in the courts and the daybooks, the metaphors and the medicine cabinet. Particular lives took place among these products and practices: the subject's life does not exist in the ethereal abstract but piecemeal at the supper table and the library table. Icy baths in cold water for the presumed benefits of hydrotherapy, the frequency of mail delivery by messenger, and apples harvested in the fall for sale to friends: cultural practices and personal choice converge in biography. And the biographer, representing these, suggests how identity merges with image, private with public, outlaw with saint, author with text, personal with historical, contingent with determinate.

Boundaries merge. This too is biography. Is it a transgression, a violation? Of course it is, at least to the extent that we prefer our subjects transcendently heroic and our creations leaping unsullied from the heads of genius. Notwithstanding, biography does invite its readers into a world of more obvious transgressions, luring with prurient delights: Hemingway dressed as a girl when a child; Henry James and his putative love life. When writing about Sylvia Plath and her several biographers, journalist Janet Malcolm compares the biographer to the burglar who ransacks a house and then jubilantly displays his ill-gotten goods, distributing hard-earned secrets to a greedy public.

By likening the biographer's subject to private property, Malcolm misses the mark, although she is not entirely wrong. For we can easily understand Malcolm's dismay: biography, like the novel, is by and large a popular form—which accounts for some antagonism against it—and panders, it seems, to a popular taste. Thus, the biographer is a trespasser and a thief, a con-artist peddling the riddles of the human heart. Yet, biographers continually ponder the meaning of public and private, both in practical and theoretical terms. Assuredly, privacy may be invaded and, legally speaking, it needs protection, especially in the marketplace. But can interior life be appropriated?[11] The biographical answer is maddeningly equivocal: yes and no. For decades, Gertrude Stein's brother Leo recorded in diaries the insights he garnered from exhausting years of self-analysis. After his death, Stein's wife did not destroy the diaries, which Stein himself had saved, but turned them over to a friend, who complied with her evident wish that they be preserved and, if possible, deposited at the Beinecke Library of Yale University, where Gertrude Stein had already bequeathed her papers. When I found these diaries at Yale, they lay uncategorized and unread. Without hesitation, I opened them, pausing only when I encountered passages about Leo's painful, protracted fetishism, one of the central subjects of his self-analysis.

Would Stein's recorded struggle become part of my biography? I did not know, at least not then, but surmised that any revelation of Stein's that contained meaning for him—and that shaped the way he saw the world, or was seen by it—is key to his life. And crucial, therefore, to his biography. But is the diary a revelation of self or a fiction? Can we assume the words on the page are the same as the writer's thoughts? A diary certainly brings us into close contact with inner life—but how close? What is the relation between the written self and the perceived self, or the performing self? Especially when the remnants of the former are deposited in a library? That Stein did not destroy his diaries may mean that he wanted to provide access to his private life, hoping others would share, or profit, from it in some way. Or that he would be remembered in a way he wanted. Or that he would be remembered at all.

These reflections, neither academic or self-justifying, help the biographer decide not whether to read a diary, but how to decipher it in the context of the growing mass of information—and supposition—gathered about the subject. They helped me.[12] Yet, I knew Leo Stein neither willed his diaries to Yale himself, nor did he appoint me his executrix. But over and over again he did affirm in his published and unpublished writings his belief in the transmission of ideas, all ideas. For him, ideas were not the property of one individual but rather a matrix of the social, personal, historical, economic—all that made Leo Stein and to which he gave his signature.

However, such niceties do not free the biographer from moral considerations. The issue of privacy is real, raising these and other important ethical and legal questions. Witness J. D. Salinger's case against Ian Hamilton's biography, in which Salinger, who fiercely guarded his privacy, legally forced Hamilton to gut his intended biography of the recalcitrant author. But the situation need not be so acute for the biographer to confront it conceptually, whether the subject be dead or alive, willing or not. Biographer Larry Lockridge, for instance, discusses what he calls the intellectual and moral presumption of the biographer. Combing through the detritus of someone else's life, he observes, "violates Kant's imperative to treat other human beings not as means but as ends in themselves."[13]

For Lockridge, the biographical subject does not exist solely as an abstraction or a by-product of the text; nor does he, as biographer. Rather, the two—biographer and subject—enter into an unequal relationship, for the biographer inevitably impinges on the subject's right to privacy. (Lockridge hired a court reporter to decode a notebook filled with the shorthand transcriptions of his subject's dreams.) To compensate for such intrusions, Lockridge suggests that biographers may endeavor to be more accurate and fair and balanced in their depiction of their subjects than, one hopes, they would ordinarily be. But his solution also implies that the deployment of biographical "virtues" (his word) may offset the biographer's rankling guilt—a guilt made more complex when we know Lockridge's biographical subject was his father, the novelist Ross Lockridge, Jr.

Humane formulas such as Lockridge's, with their ethical program and their underlying regret, still depict the biographer as a reluctant vampire usurping the life of its unsuspecting prey. Many of these subjects, as I've suggested, have given their papers over to an archive, doubtless hoping to be immortalized by someone, anyone, vampire or not. Of course, this does not diminish the moral force of an argument about privacy that ultimately cannot be settled by law. Yes, biography implies a referent: without it, we have entered the domain of fiction. And yes, this subject, dead or alive, is presumed to have certain rights. But the legalistic (and essentialist) interpretation of biography is also literalist. Biography can not be defined solely by its referent. Rather, biography is a convention by which we organize, comprehend, celebrate, and subvert our culture.

In this sense, the matter of biography is necessarily a theoretical and literary one: biography does not replace the subject.[14] Biography is the subject. That is to say, biographers may use metaphors like "haunt" or "inhabit" or even "possess" to describe the process by which they familiarize themselves with their subjects, but in the final analysis, a biographer depicts an invented subject, not a real one. All through the research, all through the writing of the biography, the biographer makes choices: what to include, what to exclude, what synecdochic detail to dramatize a personality, a situation, a crisis. Robert Caro's Lyndon Johnson is the long tall Texan President of the United States as depicted by Caro, and Boswell's loquacious, all-knowing Johnson is decidedly Boswell's Johnson.

This may seem all too patently obvious. But many who discuss biography seem to forget that biography imagines a life; it does not record or report it. Biography narrates the plausible evidence, as Kenneth Silverman, biographer of Cotton Mather, Edgar Allan Poe, and Harry Houdini, has remarked.[15] Biography depends, then, on available texts and testimony, with all their conflicting loyalties, elisions, and duplicities, and it depends on the biographer's choices (and the choices made for the biographer), all of which become part of the biographical story. Much remains hidden, nothing is complete, no biography is final.

True, biography also relies on life's leftovers: walking sticks and birth certificates, canceled checks and diaries, doodles that decorate the side of a letter, census surveys and calling cards. True, the biographer wants to know as much as empirically possible about the subject—does he jingle the coins in his pocket? does she pare her fingernails while others speak?—but biographers also know that, in the final analysis, their information is fragmentary and myriad. Biographers know that they create necessary fictions; their books may cohere, but life does not. And so they invent more and less successful ways to deal with what is provisional and unknown: such is the craft of biography.

Thus, the biographical act is one of invention, from beginning to end: choosing a subject, inventing research possibilities, following hunches, speculating on mood, nuance, motive, and then of course creating a narrative that acknowledges gaps but does not fall into them. In this sense, biography is an imaginary garden with real toads in it. Without the garden—the use of structural devices or the use of poetic and narrative devices—biography is but an almanac of cold facts and hearsay, unleavened by ingenuity and analysis, judgment and doubt.

Yet, to the extent that we assume our biographers rob us of our secret sins in the night we prefer them not to hesitate so that we can feel righteously invaded and unwillingly exposed. Does this mean that biography is a "flawed genre," as Malcolm insists? "What the reader has usually heard in the text—what has alerted him to danger—is the sound of doubt, the sound of a crack opening in the wall of the biographer's self-assurance."[16] Most biographies per force call themselves into question, admitting that ideally biography would be as fluid as character, as unstable as identity; biographers know, too, that each unearthed fact yields the panoply of explanations, nuances, suppositions, discourses through which that fact appears to appear. Biographers confront the quandary and, as Silverman also notes, create a simile trying to tell us "something, not everything but something" about a life (116).

After all, biography is a kind of portraiture. What it represents, it both diminishes and replenishes. And while it builds, it confronts the impossibility of building. The transgression that is biography, then, is likely our thirst for and fear of recognition. "I am I because my little dog knows me, but perhaps he does not and if he did not I would not be I. Oh no."[17] In the pages of biography we see our own names writ, as it were, in water, for biography recasts persons and places in terms of a tangible presence, reminding us that they have perished, and that something—some image of life—survives.

Notes

[1] Thomas Carlyle, "On History" (1830), *Selected Essays* (London: T. Nelson & Sons, Ltd), 233.

[2] Thomas Carlyle, "Boswell's Life of Johnson" (1832), *Selected Essays*, 181.

[3] Gertrude Stein, *Everybody's Autobiography* (Cambridge: Exact Change, 1993), 17.

[4] Sigmund Freud, *Leonardo da Vinci and A Memory of His Childhood,* trans. Alan Tyson (New York: Norton, 1964), 81.

[5] Joyce Carol Oates, "Adventures in Abandonment," *The New York Times Book Review* (28 August, 1988), 1.

[6] See Charles Molesworth, "Setting Tropes and Avoiding Traps," *Biography and Source Studies*, vol. 2, ed. Frederick Karl (New York: AMS Press, 1996), 98.

[7] Michel Foucault, "What is an Author?" *Language, Counter-Memory, Practice*, ed. Donald F.

Bouchard (Ithaca: Cornell University Press, 1981), 137-8.

[8] See Gertrude Stein, "Identity A Poem," *What are Masterpieces* (New York: Pitman, 1970), 71.

[9] Edmund Gosse, "The Custom of Biography," *Anglo-Saxon Review* (March 1901), 205.

[10] Natalie Zemon Davis, *The Return of Martin Guerre* (Cambridge: Harvard University Press, 1983), 63.

[11] I do not refer to the insertion of fabricated dialogue or interior monologue or other fundamentally non-biographical practices.

[12] See Brenda Wineapple, *Sister Brother Gertrude and Leo Stein* (Baltimore: Johns Hopkins University Press, 1997), chapter 9.

[13] Larry Lockridge, "The Ethics of Biography and Autobiography," *Ethics / Philosophy / Rhetoric*, ed. Dominic Rainsford and Tim Woods (New York: St. Martin's Press, forthcoming 1998). I am grateful to Professor Lockridge for allowing me to see this manuscript before its publication.

[14] Anxious lest my biography of Janet Flanner misrepresent Flanner, I confided my fear to the writer Sybille Bedford (and the biographer of Aldous Huxley). "There is no real Janet Flanner," she said. "Janet Flanner. My Janet Flanner was my Janet Flanner; your Janet Flanner will be your Janet Flanner, and doubtless neither your nor my Janet Flanner will coincide with Janet Flanner's view of herself." See Brenda Wineapple, "Mourning Becomes Biography," *American Imago* (forthcoming, Winter 1998); also note Natalie Zemon Davis, "Prologue," *Women on the Margins: Three Seventeenth Century Lives* (Cambridge: Harvard University Press, 1997), 1-4.

[15] Kenneth Silverman, "Mather, Poe, Houdini," *The Literary Biography: Problems and Solutions*, ed. Dale Salwak (Iowa City: University of Iowa Press, 1996), 113.

[16] Janet Malcolm, *The Silent Woman: Sylvia Plath and Ted Hughes* (New York: Alfred A. Knopf, 1994), 9.

[17] Stein, *Everobody's Autobiography* 75; see also her *Geographical History of America or The Relation of Human Nature to the Human Mind* (New York: Vintage, 1973). 108.

Moral Responsibility:

A Story, an Argument, and a Vision

Stephen J. Morse

The concept of moral responsibility and associated concepts and practices, such as human agency, praise, and blame, play an undeniably important part in our lives. But what does it mean to be a morally responsible person—an agent that can fairly be praised and blamed, rewarded and punished, for one's intentional actions? Many people look for a secure foundation to ground concepts as important to us as responsibility. Most notable among the seekers are theologians and secular metaphysicians, who try to justify responsibility with speculations and arguments about the divine or ultimate reason. I am unconvinced by these accounts, however, and believe that no ultimate, uncontroversial justification can be found. There is simply no way to know about the existence of God or the genuine ontology of the universe. What is more disquieting, if we were convinced that God or metaphysical moral reality existed, such a conclusion would not lead to uncontroversial concrete answers to the specific questions of morals and politics that vex human life. For example, even if we agree that in principle there are ontologically correct answers to every moral question, does this tell us clearly whether, say, the death penalty or abortion is ever justified? On epistemological grounds alone, then, if foundations exist, we will never know that we have reached rock bottom.

I will offer instead a story, an argument, and a vision about how moral responsibility is possible and why it is desirable. My account is an explicitly internal interpretation and defense of our present moral responsibility concepts and practices. Responsibility and its practices, like the concept of law and legal institutions, are products of human culture and can only be justified by the tools of justification that a particular culture provides. Although cultural products, including theories of knowledge and justification, may be temporally and geographically diverse, they are nonetheless as real features of our lives as gravity and death, and they can be rationally analyzed. To give an internal, constructivist account does not commit one to "anything goes" relativism or to unfettered pragmatism. We can assess the quality of the reasons that support moral responsibility, and I suggest that responsibility is both coherent and desirable. Indeed, our lives and society would be impoverished without it, even if it were possible to give it up, which I doubt.

I begin the story at the beginning. Once upon a time the universe began. I am agnostic about cosmology, but any secular theory will do. For convenience, let us assume that in the beginning was the "big bang," as a result of which the universe could have been composed of matter or anti-matter. In the event, it turned out to be matter. Then a very great deal of physical lifting and hauling took place over a very long time. Now, this process was and is entirely governed by the physical laws of the universe. This thought is expressed nicely in Bernard Malamud's novel, *Pictures of Fidelman*.[1] A light bulb begins to speak in light to the protagonist, Fidelman, and gives him advice. Fidelman asks for guidance to follow the advice and the bulb says, "I will show you the way but I can't go with you. Up to a point but not further if you know what I mean. A bulb is a bulb. Light I got but not feet. After all, this is the Universe, everything is laws." All those laws operated upon all that matter to produce those features of the universe that have existed in the past, that exist now, and that will exist in the future. Among these features is our planet, Earth, on which those physical processes ultimately produced organic, biological life forms.

Those life forms evolved into wondrously diverse creatures, some of which, including ourselves, are "social" animals. To the best of our knowledge, the social life of most of these creatures, even highly complex forms, operates entirely, or almost entirely, "instinctually." That is, primarily the genetic code provides these creatures with a repertoire of social organization and behavior that is not self-consciously evaluated, adopted, or revised by those creatures. Human beings are not only social, however. Evolution has also endowed us with self-consciousness and the capacity for reason. "Instinct" may motivate our sociability, but compared to other creatures on this planet, it puts only the loosest limits on the forms that sociability takes. Among the species that inhabit our planet, only human beings act self-consciously for reasons and live in societies governed by behavior-guiding norms that are used in practical reasoning. We are the only creatures whose behavior is reason-responsive. This means that we are the only creatures to whom the questions, "Why did you do that?" and "How should we behave?" can properly be addressed and answered with reasons. To the best of our knowledge, only human beings kill each other as a result of disputes about the answers to such questions.

How could it be otherwise? Sociable, self-conscious creatures that reason have a lot of work to do if they are to live together at all successfully. They will need norms to guide their interactions. Many of these norms may simply solve ubiquitous coordination problems. But not all norms solve only these problems. For example, norms about when it is acceptable to kill another human being involve more than simple coordination problems. The norms may be temporally and geographically diverse and differential importance may attach to similar norms in different times and places, but norms there must be for creatures such as ourselves. It is nearly impossible to imagine a society that we could intelligibly consider human that existed without norms.

Norms in turn create in people mutual expectations of each other that vary in strength and importance. Indeed, we are probably the only creatures on Earth that consciously have normative expectations of each other and that make evaluative judgments when those expectations are satisfied or breached. Normative judgment appears to be an omnipresent and unique feature of human social existence. An interesting feature of human normative judgments, which have propositional content, is that they often motivate our emotional reactions. If someone pushes me and I fall hard, my emotional response will depend on why I was pushed. If it was done to save me from danger, I will feel grateful; if it was done to hurt me, I will feel angry, resentful, indignant. What emotions we feel in response to the satisfaction or breach of expectations may be largely culturally relative, but an emotional response to normative judgment seems to be another omnipresent aspect of human interaction. Once again, a society in which members did not have emotional responses to normative judgments would not be recognizably human.

In sum, creatures built like ourselves inevitably will live in groups that have norms, which in turn create expectations that generate emotional responses to their satisfaction or breach. It is difficult to imagine that these general aspects of human life would *not* exist unless human consciousness and the capacity for emotional response were radically altered. "Brave new world" hasn't arrived nor has anyone yet given an ultimately convincing reason why we should hasten its arrival—although many have tried—so I propose for the nonce that we take ourselves largely as we find us.

So far this abstract story is largely descriptive, rooted in a loose, but not implausible, evolutionary biological account, and it does not commit anyone who believes it to any specific form of moral or political life. It commits one only to believing that among human beings there will inevitably be a moral and political life, that there will be norms, normative expectations, and reactions to the satisfaction or breach of those expectations. It applies equally well to any time and place within recorded history, and I suspect that it has been true since homo sapiens first used language to regulate social life. I freely confess that the story is a little bit "essentialist" about human nature, but this essence, although important, is not terribly limiting. The story is also a "determinist" or "universal causation" story, that is, an account that assumes that what happened was the outcome of a lawful set of physical processes operating on antecedent conditions.

At this point in the story, one might fairly ask why any defense—a normative task—of moral responsibility or any other cultural artifact is necessary if the deterministic or universal causation account is true. If, that is, what exists is the outcome of antecedent events and the laws of the universe operating on those events, then isn't it true that no other outcome was possible? If so, any evaluation or defense of "what is" is, itself, deterministically or causally inevitable and also needs no defense. Indeed, my students always ask just this question just about now. Well, in my story, the answer is, yes and no.

Yes, it is true that culture and everything else are the products of deterministic or causal processes, or something very close to them,[2] but, no, it does not follow that cultural artifacts cannot and should not be normatively evaluated. Permit me to share how I attempt to demonstrate this conclusion to my students. I wordlessly move to the desk at the front of the class and then sit silently and as absolutely still as I can until the anxiety in the room builds to uncomfortable levels. I then ask the students what I was doing. They of course haven't a clue about why their professor behaves so bizarrely. The answer I give is this: "I am waiting for determinism to happen." They titter at the absurdity of the statement, and well they should. Although the winds, tides, bacteria, and most non-human species do "wait" for determinism to happen, human beings do not. We cannot help but consciously think, deliberate, reason, and guide our actions by reasons. We're stuck. It's just the way we are and there is no getting around it. Some unforeseen biophysical calamity or new technologies might change our nature. But short of such scary scenarios, there is no alternative but to deliberate and to act based on deliberation.

Even if our actions are determined, they make a difference. Determined actions can cause pleasure or pain, can create wealth or poverty, can be kind or cruel. We discuss, argue, fight, and even kill about morals and politics precisely because the moral and political regime in which we live makes an enormous difference to our well-being and flourishing. Although we may be determined creatures, we are not automatons. Determined deliberation and intentional action are distinguishable from reflexive bodily movements. We can't wait for determinism to happen. We determine what determinism dictates.

The tools we use to engage in such determined deliberation are given to us by our history and culture, but the human capacity for rationality and practical reason necessarily infects the process everywhere and always. How could anyone ever rationally persuade anybody else about anything, except by giving reasons? Unless we are satisfied to "convince" by force, all that we have is reason, however flawed it may be and however often it may lead us astray. The best we can do is to try to give good reasons and to yield to what seem to be better reasons when they appear. Although "reason" and "rationality" are not self-defining, uncontroversially-defined terms, it is almost impossible to conceive of a culture that will not include among its tools some criteria for what counts as good reason within the culture. Arguments that are logically sound—within defensible conventions of logic—and factually accurate—within defensible epistemological conventions—should yield only if they lead to a social and moral regime that there is other, better reason to reject. I propose to use ordinary logic and commonsense rationality—as they have been given to me and as they appear reasonable to accept—to continue my story. Anyone who objects needs to give me good reason not to and anyone who tries to do so has already accepted the most general claim being made.

It is impossible to deny that we hold each other morally accountable and have a rich series of practices that reflect this response. But what are we doing when we hold people morally responsible for their conduct? A defense of moral responsibility should begin with an interpretation of our practices that answers this question. I have previously suggested that human beings possess the innate capacity to respond emotionally to normative judgments. Following Sir Peter Strawson and more recent Strawsonians, especially Jay Wallace, I contend that holding people responsible is an expression of this capacity: it is the disposition to feel appropriate emotions when moral expectations are satisfied or breached and to express those emotions in the appropriate way.[3] The content of the expectations, the appropriate emotions, and the appropriate expression of them may vary, but this is the meaning of the abstraction, "to hold someone morally responsible." In our culture, the common emotional responses to breach are resentment, indignation, and anger; the common emotional response to compliance is gratitude. Depending on the nature and magnitude of the expectation, the appropriate expressions of the reaction to breach can range from mild disapproval to painful punishment; the appropriate expressions of the reaction to compliance can range from mild approval to substantial rewards.

The various ways in which the moral reactive emotions can be expressed must be normatively justified because they have the potential to create benefit or to cause harm. I say this not as an assertion of theoretical truth divorced from our practices, but as an expression of our internal practices, of what we require of each other morally. As a general rule, benefits and harms should not be awarded for "no good reason"; there should be good reason among creatures who self-consciously decide how they should live together. People should be praised and blamed, rewarded and punished, only if they deserve it, only if it is fair to respond in these ways to their conduct. To claim that reason should not guide the distribution of rewards and harms is to adopt an arational stance. But why should I or anyone else do this unless we are given good reason to do it?

Moral expectations give people good reason to behave properly. It is fair to hold people to such expectations only if they have the general capacity to grasp and be guided by reason. If they are incapable of understanding expectations or of using them in practical reasoning, it would be unjustified and unfair to praise and blame them for compliance and breach. Thus, we exempt people from moral responsibility under two general conditions that indicate that the agent could not grasp or be guided by reason. The first is cases in which the agent has not acted, that is, her movements did not meet the criteria for human action. Reflexes and other physically involuntary bodily movements are the prime examples. The second is cases in which the agent has acted, but the action is excused. Non-culpable ignorance, irrationality, and compulsion are classic examples.

Under either condition—no action or excused action—we do not think it is justified to feel and express what would otherwise be the appropriate emotion for compliance or breach. For example, if a driver has an unforeseeable seizure and blacks out, during which the car causes injury, we would not justifiably be angry at and sanction the driver for the moral failure to take care while operating a dangerous machine. Or, under the same circumstances, if the car plows harmlessly into a haystack, saving a passenger from an otherwise imminent but unforeseeable crash with an approaching vehicle, the unconscious driver does not deserve thanks for saving the passenger's life.

Although I have described the practice of holding people morally responsible as a predisposition to an emotional reaction and an expression of that reaction, holding responsible is not a purely emotional response. A moral reactive emotion and its expression are appropriate only if a moral expectation was complied with or breached and the agent was capable of being guided by reason. The criteria for moral expectations, action, and reason may be variable, but they are always propositional and have truth value. Moreover, our practice of holding people morally responsible is not simply an instrumental behavioral disposition to emit responses that are meant to increase or decrease the probability that particular behavior will occur in the future.[4] Holding people morally responsible expresses a normative, retrospective evaluation of an agent's conduct, independent of whether that evaluation has positive or negative consequences.

In sum, the disposition to feel appropriate emotions when moral norms are breached or satisfied and the consequent expressions of normative judgment affirm and enforce the inevitable, necessary norms of behavior that exist in human society and that give people reasons to act. After all, the elements of nature, such as the winds and the tide, and non-human species do not need norms or rules of conduct to tell them how to behave, nor do we feel moral emotions towards them, unless we anthropomorphize them. I assume that expressing normative judgments and affirming and enforcing norms could be accomplished by means other than holding people morally responsible, although I also assume that this would be a difficult trick to pull off. Consistent with this assumption, however, the defense of responsibility will still require a story about why it is desirable—why, that is, human beings should rationally desire to live in societies that hold people responsible for their intentional conduct.

Should our concepts and practices of moral responsibility be maintained? The first line of attack is the familiar one, alluded to above, rooted in anxieties about determinism or universal causation. I previously suggested that various interpersonal, social concepts and practices were real and could be rationally interpreted even if determinism or universal causation were true. Determinist critics of responsibility—so called "hard determinists" or "incompatibilists"—can concede these points, but they argue nonetheless that responsibility isn't really real; it's just a made-up, as-if fantasy.[5] Thus, there is "nothing" desirable to maintain, and it is entirely unfair to maintain practices dependent on such fantasies. After all, if all events in the universe are determined or caused products of antecedent events and laws over which living human beings have no control, how can we possibly be responsible for anything? Such critics believe that unless we have contra-causal freedom (or some such thing)—the ability to act unconstrained by the causal, deterministic processes of the universe—then "real" responsibility is not possible. And neither, it must be conceded if this is correct, are "real" justice and fairness possible, which presuppose rational, responsible responses of rational creatures to each other. If correct, this assertion of the incompatibility of determinism and responsibility (and justice) is powerful, because the metaphysics of contra-causal freedom are preposterous, and in Strawson's word, "panicky."

My account of responsibility is compatible with the truth of determinism or universal causation, however. Even if our behavior is determined, we are determined to have a susceptibility to feel and express emotions in response to compliance with or breach of moral expectations, and some human beings are capable of being guided by reason and others, such as small children and some people with severe mental disorder, are not. Responsibility does not require god-like causal powers. It requires only that mature human beings have the *general* capacity to grasp and be guided by good reason,[6] a capacity we firmly believe we have. It is fair, we believe, to hold accountable another person who is capable of reason, a person who can use moral expectations as premises in practical reasoning. A person who suffers an unforeseen seizure may be causally responsible for harms that result, but the person does not deserve, in the fullest sense, our condemnation and sanction. Such a response would be unfair. If we didn't believe that mature humans were capable of grasping and being influenced and guided by reason, we wouldn't be reading or writing articles like this one in the hope of learning or being guided ourselves or of persuading or guiding others. Few people read or write academic articles solely for recreation or even advancement.

If contra-causal freedom is necessary for "real" responsibility—an assertion that flows from an external point of view and critique of responsibility[7]—then "real" responsibility does not exist, but I deny that it is necessary. If we all had god-like powers, then I suppose that there would be no question about responsibility. We are not gods, of course, but in a sense, we are god-like in that we must create and do have the capacity to revise our concepts and practices, even if we lack contra-causal freedom. And those creations are "real enough" for me, even if they lack the alleged metaphysical pedigree of contra-causal freedom.

Yes, we create and revise our responsibility concepts and practices over and over again as we go along, just as we do with the concept of justice and its practices. But what we construct is real, it expresses our nature, and it has the all-too concrete potential to benefit or harm us, to give our lives more or less meaning, or to extinguish those lives. The norms of responsibility are like the rules of law, the demands of justice, and the institutions of government: all have the enormous potential for good and ill, and they can be defended best by the good reason that we can give for them, rather than by a foundational metaphysics. Practical and theoretical reason is all that we have to devise and defend our concepts and institutions. Given the biological limits of our beings, what more could we realistically and reasonably want?

The retrospective, evaluative concept of moral responsibility that we now possess and employ may be real enough, but is it desirable? The second line of attack on responsibility suggests that it is an irrational concept. If one function of moral responsibility is to guide interpersonal life, then perhaps, as many have suggested, we could replace it, for example, with a purely prospective, purely consequentialist scheme.[8] But in addition to being inadequate interpretations of current concepts and practices (Wallace 54-6), abandoning our current concept and practices would not be rational because it would impoverish our lives.

Retrospective, evaluative moral responsibility is crucial to our sense of ourselves as persons, as objects of dignity and respect, and it coheres with other moral notions of supreme importance, such as desert, fairness, and justice, to which we are firmly committed. What makes us distinctively human and what gives all these concepts full meaning is our capacity for reason, which in turn makes us capable of genuine normative evaluation and appropriate objects of such evaluation. Other sentient creatures can suffer and deserve to be treated without unnecessary pain, but we are the only creatures capable of leading fully moral lives. This is why, I believe, we think of ourselves as occupying a unique position among the life forms on earth and it is a foundational part of what gives our lives dignity, meaning, and worth. To give up this sense of ourselves would abandon our humanity.

Responsibility is desirable also because it contributes to the creation and maintenance of moral communities. Personhood, desert, and responsibility are all moral notions, inextricably intertwined in our moral lives. When we express the reactive emotions through appropriate practices, we affirm and deepen our commitment to common moral obligations that bind us together. To diminish or to abandon moral responsibility would be to weaken those ties and the communities that nurture us. Creatures capable of grasping and being guided by good reason deserve our moral praise when they comply with our moral expectations, and they deserve our blame when they transgress. To make this claim does not commit one to any concrete scheme of expectations, rewards, and sanctions. It simply commits one to the recognition that we are the only creatures capable of being guided by reason and that this is an inevitable, crucial feature of our social lives.

Many people object to holding people morally responsible, for fear that this practice readily produces moralistic, punitive, and cruel responses, at least when expectations are breached. It is of course true that when human beings are angry because they have been harmed, they can become incredibly self-righteous and hideously cruel. Holding people morally accountable can be used to satisfy such unworthy responses, but this is not inherent in the practice. Virtually any human practice can be turned to vicious use, but nothing in my story compels moral responsibility to be applied harshly. My account is consistent with a tender, forgiving, or conversely, a tough, strict set of norms and practices, and neither need be cruel. It presupposes only that it is fair to hold accountable beings that reason and that are capable, as most adults demonstrably are, of being guided by good reason.

Another conception of human life is, I suppose, possible. For example, we could treat each other like bacteria. I refer to this as the good bacteria/bad bacteria part of the story. Some bacteria that inhabit our gastrointestinal system, our gut, are crucial to the smooth operation of the system. They are the good bacteria. We try to enhance their survival and do nothing to inhibit their growth. On occasion, alas, our guts are invaded by bacteria that interfere with the proper operation of the system, causing various unseemly ailments, and in extreme cases, death. These are the bad bacteria. We spend a fair amount of effort trying to prevent these critters from entering our gut in sufficient numbers to overwhelm the body's natural defenses, and if the natural defenses fail, we try with various techniques, such as antibiotics, to kill the offensive, bad bacteria. Now, despite the potential of various bacteria to confer benefits and harms, as the case may be, and despite our consequential, substantial efforts to deal with these bacteria, no one holds either kind of bacteria responsible for smooth or rocky gastrointestinal functioning, and we wouldn't dream of praising or blaming bacteria. We treat bacteria purely as objects, and never as subjects, as agents.

We could, by analogy, simply treat each other like bacteria, as potentially beneficial or harmful objects, and act accordingly. This conception of people would support a purely predictive and preventive scheme of social organization in which the emotional and societal response to the organism could be entirely independent of the moral goodness or badness of the person's conduct. We don't at present have the emotional repertoire or the predictive and therapeutic technology to institute this vision very precisely or effectively, but this is a technoquibble. In principle, it is a possible form of social organization. Indeed, in some senses we might all be "safer," and, to some, social life might appear more rational if the show ran along these lines. But this is a show that I think virtually any of us would happily miss, precisely because we are importantly different from bacteria. They are not moral creatures.

At this stage in the story, I am appealing as much to a vision as to a logical argument. Why would a rational agent wish to give up a conception of self as a moral creature? No one would do this, for example, just because determinism were true. A rational agent would do it only if it promoted some vision of human flourishing the agent was willing to defend. If you are still convinced that moral responsibility contributes little and should be abandoned, try the following thought experiments. Imagine, first, that someone intentionally injures you, knowing that you are incapable of retaliating, because the person enjoys your pain and the feeling of dominance that cruelty produces. You of course react not only by feeling pain, but surely with anger, too. Your physical pain is no worse than it would be if an accident of nature had caused it, but your entire reaction is quite different. Do you really want to treat the bully as if she were just a larger "bad bacteria"? Should your response be simply that which most decreases the likelihood that the bully would strike again? Do you think you (and others) could learn not to feel indignation, resentment, and anger, as opposed to regret? Would we all be better off if we no longer had these reactions and expressed them to each other? Would life then be more rational? Better? Would human flourishing increase?

Now imagine that *you* have unjustifiably injured another person. Probably, in addition to whatever "positive" emotion is created, you will also feel guilt or shame or some other critical emotion. But how should you feel about yourself? If you promise not to do it again and really, really mean it, should that be the end of the matter? Of course, unpleasant emotions like guilt or shame may decrease the likelihood that you will cause such injury again, but should that be the only point of these emotions? How should the victim feel about you? Is resentment and condemnation just irrational or silly, especially if you promise to be a good bacterium from now on? Finally, imagine that we all learned our lesson and ceased to have these irrational responses to violations of moral expectations. What would society be like? How would we feel about ourselves and each other? What would be the role of community or the arts in such a society?

My story has neither a happy nor a sad ending. We are in the midst of the story and have no idea whether or how it will end. Human social life will surely end only when human beings cease to exist as a species in its current form. As long as recognizable humans exist, however, they will create meaning and norms from the cultural tools and concepts available to them. And history and anthropology teach us that incredible diversity is possible. We cannot even predict that there will be progress. Progress is itself a socially constructed moral notion, subject to diverse interpretations.

If—and this is a big "if"—we insist on trying to subject our concepts and practices to reason, our capacity for reason surely sets some limits on what concepts and tools a society can adopt that will remain relatively stable. Now, of course, one can claim that reason is not the road to moral or any other kind of progress and that it is a mistake to try to subject our lives to the dictates of good reason. But the only reason anyone should accept such a claim is because the claimant gives good reason to abandon reason. Force and the threat of force are, of course, good instrumental reasons to yield to a stronger opponent—infrahuman species do this all the time—but fear is not, in itself, a good moral reason for action.

No culture exists or changes without individual agents to perpetuate, criticize and modify it. Surely no culture changes unless individuals believe that it should and then act on that belief. We are all the creators as well as the consumers of our culture. As such, we are all storytellers as well as characters in the story. We have been born in a time and place in which we have been taught to trust reason, to hope for rationality and objectivity. Although we should not make reason a fetish, we ignore it at our peril. Because our norms and rules must be expressed in language, there will always be ambiguity and room for interpretation and argumentation. There will never be absolute agreement on what reason demands, even among people who share the same ends and the same vision of human flourishing. The best we can do is to give each other the best reasons we can for why we should live together one way rather than another, why we should prefer one set of norms, rules and institutions to others, and try to listen to others' reasons as openly as possible.

Whether or not taking moral responsibility seriously is a given of interpersonal life, it is fair and fundamentally enhances personhood, dignity and respect. It also facilitates the formation and maintenance of moral communities. These goals are so important that it is hard to imagine giving them up, at least not until someone gives us good reason that we should. And, if the relation between responsibility and these other ends is as close as it appears to be, it is hard to imagine what reasons would persuade us to abandon responsibility. If you wish to give it up, assuming that it is possible to do this, what social concepts and practices do you propose to adopt instead to respond to the good and evil we do to each other, to the intentional acts of kindness and cruelty of interpersonal life? What kind of society will it be? Tell us a story that gives us good reason to hear it again.

Notes

1. Bernard Malamud, *Pictures of Fidelman: An Exhibition* (New York: Farrar, Straus and Giroux, 1969), 174.

2. Galen Strawson, "Consciousness, Free Will, and the Unimportance of Determinism," *Inquiry* 32 [1989] 3-27, refers to this as the "realism constraint."

3. See Peter Strawson, "Freedom and Resentment" (1962), *Free Will*, ed. Gary Watson (New York: Oxford University Press, 1982) 59-80, and R. Jay Wallace, *Responsibility and the Moral Sentiments* (Cambridge: Harvard University Press, 1994).

4. H. L. A. Hart refers to this as the "economy of threats" approach ("Legal Responsibility and Excuses," *Punishment and Responsibility: Essays in the Philosophy of Law* [Oxford: Oxford University Press, 1968], 28-53.

5. Some allegedly "pragmatic" theorists conclude that "as if" is acceptable if it "works," cf. Herbert L. Packer, *The Limits of the Criminal Sanction* (Stanford: Stanford University Press, 1968) 132-3. In my view, this is the least satisfactory "solution" to the problem.

6. I borrow this felicitous term from Wallace.

7. For an interesting explication of the contrary pulls of internal and external points of view about responsibility (and everything else), see Thomas Nagel, *The View from Nowhere* (New York: Oxford University Press, 1986), esp. 120-126.

8. See, for example, Daniel Dennett, *Elbow Room: The Varieties of Free Will Worth Wanting* (New York: Oxford University Press, 1984), ch. 7.

Contingency, Responsibility, and Bad Faith

Andrew W. Siegel

The post-modern approach to interpretation is one which Roland Barthes has described as an "anti-theological activity, an activity that is truly revolutionary since to refuse to fix meaning is, in the end, to refuse God and his hypostases—reason, science, law."[1] As with most revolutionaries, the post-modernist seeks to liberate us from what he regards as an oppressive condition. The view he wishes to debunk is that there is any privileged source—be it God or any other putative author—which fixes meaning. Once dispelled of this notion, we can revel in the activity of generating a proliferation of perspectives, free of the constraints imposed by our former concern for "validity."

But the freedom which attends the refusal of "God and his hypostases" is one which arguably has disturbing costs. Jean Paul Sartre offers an assessment of these costs: "Nor, on the other hand, if God does not exist, are we provided with any values or commands that could legitimise our behaviour. Thus we have neither behind us, nor before us in a luminous realm of values, any means of justification or excuse. We are left alone, without excuse. That is what I mean when I say that man is condemned to be free."[2] For Sartre, the absence of an absolute source of values leaves each of us responsible for our self and our world. The contingency of meaning renders us free to invent and re-invent our own reality, but denies us any external basis for justifying the particular world we choose to construct. Those who fail to act with the recognition of this contingency commit the one sin which existentialists recognize— namely, the sin of acting in bad faith.

In this essay, I want to consider the relationship between the contingency of meaning and human agency. More specifically, I am interested in examining whether we can fully function as agents while operating with the post-modern and existentialist view of meaning and value. I will suggest that we cannot, and that choice and value are bound up in such a way that freedom is, paradoxically, implicated in what existentialists and post-modernists would deem bad faith. I will develop this point through a discussion of Sartre's philosophy.

The key characteristic of agency Sartre identifies is that our actions are always intentional in the sense of being consciously aimed at the realization of some end. It follows that a recognition of an objective lack, or what Sartre calls a *négatité*, is a condition for an act. In acting, we necessarily bring "nothingness" into the world by conceiving of a possible state of affairs which is not yet realized. The fact that an act involves as part of its essential structure a projection toward something which is not yet the case has, on Sartre's view, the important consequence that "no factual state whatever it may be (the political and economic structure of society, the psychological "state," etc.) is capable by itself of motivating any act whatsoever."[3] While Sartre maintains that acts do indeed have causes and motives, he holds that causes and motives only have meaning in light of our ends. An individual living under an oppressive regime may be suffering, but the suffering itself cannot motivate the individual to overthrow the regime. It is only by disengaging ourselves from the world and conceiving a new state of affairs, e.g., political freedom, that we can come to see our suffering as intolerable, and thereby confer on the suffering the status of "motive" for revolutionary action.

Sartre's view is that the world is always illuminated by our ends. It is always in terms of something which does not yet exist that "the given" has meaning for us. The given, e.g., our past or our environment, can never condition our acts because we confer meaning upon the given by surpassing it toward the future. As Sartre says with respect to our relationship to our past: "Now the meaning of the past is strictly dependent on my present project. . . . The project of conversion by a single stroke confers on an adolescent crisis the value of a premonition which I had not taken seriously" (640). The given is in-itself neutral. The tree hovering over

Transgression, Punishment, Responsibility, Forgiveness
Graven Images 4 (1998), 81-85.

my balcony is adverse if I want to get a tan, but it is helpful if I want to maximize my privacy. It is only because I choose a tan as my end that the tree manifests itself as adverse. Likewise, Sartre would claim, in the case of someone subject to a dictatorship, it is only by positing some such end as democracy that one sees the dictatorship as adverse.

According to Sartre, we are responsible for the meaning our situation has for us because we are free at each moment to choose our ends. I am responsible for seeing the tree as a hindrance because I freely choose the project of acquiring a tan. I would be responsible for finding it unbearable to live under a dictatorship because I freely choose democracy as my end. Sartre extends this line of reasoning to suggest that we are individually responsible for war:

> Thus there are no *accidents* in a life; a community event which suddenly bursts forth and involves me in it does not come from the outside. If I am mobilized in a war, this is *my* war; it is in my image and I deserve it. I deserve it first because I could always get out of it by suicide or desertion . . . . For lack of getting out of it, I have *chosen* it. . . . But in addition the war is *mine* because by the sole fact that it arises in a situation which I cause to be and that I can discover it there only by engaging myself for or against it, I can no longer distinguish at present the choice which I make of myself from the choice which I make of the war. (708-9)

Like any other given, war is neutral in itself. We are responsible for war in the sense that we project whatever meaning it has for us by our choice of ends.

Our responsibility is premised on the fact that in a particular situation it is always possible that we might have done or chosen otherwise. For Sartre, however, the important question is "*At what price?*" we could have done otherwise: "Could I have done otherwise without perceptibly modifying the organic totality of the projects which I am?"(585). Sartre explores this question by considering a case in which after several hours of hiking he gives in to his fatigue while his friends go on, resisting their fatigue. Sartre claims that the fatigue could not by itself compel him to stop. The fatigue is nothing in itself. Sartre's companions also suffered fatigue, but they suffered their fatigue in a fundamentally different way. His friends cherished their fatigue because they experienced it "in a vaster project of a trusting abandon to nature" (587). Sartre's yielding to his fatigue resulted from a view of the world in which difficulties appear as "not worth the trouble of being tolerated"(597). It thus turns out that Sartre could not resist his fatigue without a "radical conversion," an "abrupt metamorphosis" of his choice of himself and his ends (598). He would have to modify his ends in order to view his fatigue as tolerable.

Our freedom renders our initial choice subject to perpetual modification. We are always capable of relinquishing our initial project and making it past. Sartre is free to make past his project of avoiding difficulties by adopting the project of abandoning himself to nature. Sartre maintains that we experience this freedom as anguish. In anguish we recognize the contingency and "unjustifiability" of our initial choice and feel the threat of "being suddenly exorcised (i.e., of becoming radically other)" (612).

While we are always free to modify our projects, there exist no principles to guide us in choosing new projects. The values that we adopt are chosen by us and revealed by the way we act. The denial that we freely choose our own values is a form of bad faith which Sartre refers to as the "spirit of seriousness": "The spirit of seriousness has two characteristics: it considers values as transcendent givens independent of human subjectivity, and it transfers the quality of 'desirable' from the ontological structure of things to their simple material constitution" (796). Sartre is here describing our tendency to apprehend values as properties of the world rather than as creatures of our own design. Those who suffer fatigue, for example, often ascribe to the fatigue the property of being "unbearable." This permits them to justify ceasing the activity they are engaged in. Yet they are without excuses, for the quality of "unbearableness" does not inhere in the fatigue but rather is derived from the ends which they freely posit. Likewise with all values. Nothing possesses the property of being "desirable" or "undesirable." It is only our freely chosen projects which confer such value, and these projects are always without justification. In the final pages of *Being and Nothingness*, Sartre leaves us with a stark formulation of this conclusion: "[A]ll human activities are equivalent . . . . Thus it amounts to the same thing whether one gets drunk alone or is a leader of nations" (797).

While this conclusion is obviously troubling for those of us who wish to appeal to objective principles to govern right action, my present interest is not in defending the objectivity of morality. Instead, I want now to pursue the question of whether Sartre's absolute rejection of external values leaves us with a coherent account of our capacity to freely choose our ends and undergo radical metamorphoses. I shall argue that it does not, and that the only intelligible conception of choice implicates freedom in bad faith.

We have seen that for Sartre the meaning and value a state of affairs has for us is a function of our ends. At every moment we are responsible for our situation because it is always possible to change it by modifying our ends. Now while it is clear enough that Sartre thinks we perpetually retain the capacity to "nihilate" our initial project and adopt a new one, what are the circumstances under which such a conversion takes place? And what is the phenomenological structure of this conversion? Sartre provides us with a modicum of insight on these questions, and what he does say appears problematic. Sartre states: "It will be enough for it [consciousness] to make explicit its unjustifiability in order to cause the *instant* to arise; that is, the appearance of a new project on the collapse of the former" (618). What Sartre quite clearly seems to be saying here is that our apprehension of our unjustifiability is a sufficient condition for our abandoning our present end and adopting a new one. This makes little sense, though. While our unjustifiability is lived as an awareness of the possibility of other choices, this awareness alone cannot generate other choices. For Sartre has already informed us that "at each moment I apprehend this initial choice as contingent and unjustifiable" (611). Implicit in this statement is the notion that we can simultaneously retain our initial choice and view it as unjustifiable. If our awareness of our unjustifiability could by itself effect the collapse of our initial choice, it would follow that every new choice would become past the moment it came into being so that there could never exist any identifiable choice.

Sartre offers a different account of project formation in his discussion of suffering. He suggests that the project of changing our suffering is formed after we have "effected a double nihilation," which consists in our both conceiving a happy state of affairs as possible and illuminating our suffering in the light of this possibility. The problem with this view of project formation, however, is that we are perfectly capable of conceiving our situation in light of a possible state of affairs without taking that state of affairs as our end. By conceiving of the possibility of Utopia I may come to recognize that I am miserable, but I need not take Utopia as my end. My misery cannot even motivate me to adopt this end because it is only after I have adopted the end that my misery appears intolerable. The fact is that we conceive of our situation in light of other possibilities all of the time without taking these other possibilities as our projects. While the double nihilation may be a necessary condition for choosing ends, it is not a sufficient condition.

An adequate account of what is involved in choosing our ends must therefore go beyond the "double nihilation." There must be a third moment in which we adopt a possible state of affairs as our end. What is the structure of this third moment? Sartre fails us here because he mistakenly takes the double nihilation to constitute a complete description of how we choose our ends. In order to address the matter properly, then, we shall have to take a deeper look into the phenomenology of choosing ends. Let us begin with Sartre's own example of the oppressed worker. Sartre says, "A worker in 1830 is capable of revolting if his salary is lowered, for he easily conceives of a situation in which his wretched standard of living would be not as low as the one which is about to be imposed on him" (561). Now, we know that the lowering of the worker's salary can only be viewed as intolerable and a cause for revolution if he chooses as his end a higher salary. What is the condition for his choosing this end apart from his having conceived of his situation in light of the end? The answer is, I think, obvious. He chooses the higher salary as his end because he thinks it is *better* to have more money than less.

Sartre himself at one point intimates that this is the case: "For it is necessary here to reverse common opinion and on the basis of what it is not, to acknowledge the harshness of a situation or the suffering which it imposes, both of which are motives for conceiving of another state of affairs in which *things would be better* for everybody" (561; emphasis added). It is first worth noting that this passage is inconsistent with the rest of Sartre's account insofar as it characterizes the harshness and suffering of a situation as motives for conceiving of a new state of affairs. After all, the claim Sartre makes repeatedly is that it is only by first conceiving and taking as an end a new state of affairs that anything can be a motive. The more important point at present, however, is that Sartre speaks of conceiving a "better" state of affairs.

Sartre's reference to our conceiving a "better" state of affairs generates just as glaring an inconsistency as the one just mentioned. We have seen that Sartre deems it bad faith to treat values as properties inhering in the world. We are the only source of values, and we freely choose our values by choosing our ends. On this account, we can see one thing as "better" than another only in relation to some end. Thus, we can see the possibility of a higher salary as better than a lower salary only in light of some other end, e.g., feeding our children or financing a home. In this case, the end of a higher salary would be transformed into a means to another end. Such value terms as "better" are confined to a purely instrumental role in which we already presuppose an end. Because all ultimate ends are equivalent, there is no place for employing an evaluative discourse in selecting between them.

Sartre could maintain consistency, then, if he means that a higher salary would be "better" than a lower salary insofar as it serves the worker's end of, say, feeding his children. But this does not resolve the problem. For if we undertake a regressive analysis of ends we will find that he wants to feed his children because he wants to keep them healthy and alive, and he wants them to be healthy and alive because he thinks health is better than sickness and life is better than death. We find at the end of the series two irreducible ends, both of which are chosen in bad faith because between each of two sets of equivalents (health/sickness, life/death) the worker takes the first term to possess an inherent value which justifies his choice. In what other manner could one have chosen?

Sartre can appeal neither to a deliberative nor emotive account of our initial choice of ends, for, on his view, both deliberation and emotion presuppose ends: "Deliberation . . . is an evaluation of means in relation to already existing ends" (573); "emotion is not a physiological tempest; it . . . aims at attaining a particular end by a particular means" (573-4). But if we abandon reason and emotion in the initial choice of ends, what is left of human agency? If we are to see two possible ends as they are, i.e., neutral in themselves and thus equivalent, then in making our initial choice between them we are bound to stand before them in indifference. Assuming the ends are irreducible to other ends, we will have no emotive response to the ends and cannot employ any criteria to justify a choice without falling into bad faith. Now it is true that our choices sometimes issue from a state of indifference. I might, for example, be indifferent about which movie to see but nevertheless choose one. But it is certainly difficult to conceive of this as a paradigm for how we choose our ends. Can we see choosing health over disease or democracy over fascism in the same way? Sartre himself suggests that we see the end which we choose as "a *desirable* and not yet realized possible." Sartre even defines man in terms of desire: "Fundamentally man is *the desire to be*" (722). Yet an indifference towards each of a number of ends would seem to entail an absence of desire. While it might be that Sartre wants to limit desire to ends already chosen, we do not make choices in order to desire ends but rather choose ends because we view them as desirable.

Matters become yet more problematic when we consider Sartre's idea that we are always free to modify our initial choice of ends. In the situation where we have made our initial choice of an end prior to contemplating other possibilities, we do not see these other possibilities from a position of indifference. Instead, given that our chosen ends confer meaning and value on the world, they must also illuminate any other ends which we conceive of. This poses a serious problem when the other possibility we conceive of is the diametric opposite of our initial choice.

Suppose that my chosen end is health and that disease is the possible end of which I conceive. While I can effect the "double nihilation" and illuminate the world in the light of my being inflicted with disease, this illumination will be colored by my project of being healthy. This is because disease in itself has no meaning apart from an end. When I conceive

84

of disease as a possibility I grasp it in the light of my end of health. But to illuminate disease by the end of health is necessarily to see disease as intolerable. Thus, when I illuminate the world by conceiving of disease as a possibility, I will only be more pleased by my state of health. It is only if I adopt disease as my end that my health will appear intolerable, yet my end of health perpetually creates the motive to avoid disease. To choose disease as my end I would first have to return to that indifferent state in which I see all final ends as equivalent. The problem is that indifference ultimately gives birth to quietism. While everything may be possible, nothing any longer matters. The inescapable fact is that we are beings who choose projects only because we perceive them as having value in their own right. To fully embrace the contingency which existentialists and post-moderns enshrine is therefore to undermine the conditions under which free and responsible agency is possible.

Notes

[1] Roland Barthes, "The Death of the Author," *Image, Music, Text,* trans. Stephen Heath (New York: Hill and Wang, 1977), 142-8; 147.

[2] Jean Paul Sartre, *Existentialism and Humanism*, trans. Philip Mairet (London: Methuen, 1963), 34.

[3] Jean Paul Sartre, *Being and Nothingness: A Phenomenological Essay on Ontology,* trans. Hazel E. Barnes (New York: Washington Square Press, 1980), 562. Future references are to this text and will be made paranthetically.

Justice, Justification, and Responsibility in Bonhoeffer's *Ethics*

Carl J. Rasmussen[1]

"We should not celebrate Bonhoeffer. We should answer him."
Martin Stöhr[2]

I. Polemical Introduction

According to Eberhard Bethge, Bonhoeffer thought of the *Ethics* as the beginning of his actual life work.[3] We must not be misled by the conditions in which Bonhoeffer wrote the *Ethics*—by the question of Bonhoeffer's involvement in the resistance against the Third Reich. If we learn anything from the *Ethics* it is that Bonhoeffer did not seek to justify himself.[4] Beneath the stress of historical circumstance, his concern is renewal and Reformation. The *Ethics* addresses in substantial part those institutions of legitimacy, authority and order that are constitutive of community, in particular the government and church. Bonhoeffer seeks to recover the claims of these institutions from the skepticism of the Enlightenment. These themes emerge from the foundation of the *Ethics*, Bonhoeffer's doctrine of justification, which is located in his distinction between the "ultimate" and the "penultimate." Even Bonhoeffer's high Christology must be read in light of this doctrine. Christ is not another idol in the modern pantheon of idols. Christ is not what the church creates in Christology.[5] Christ encounters us beyond ourselves in justification, which is for Bonhoeffer the "last word." On this doctrine the *Ethics* is structured. Therefore, at the outset we must place the *Ethics* in its full and intended context: the *Ethics* is not merely a set of fragments written in response to the unfolding events of the German resistance during the early 1940s. Rather the *Ethics* is one of the great works of Protestant theology since the Reformation.[6]

If we seek to engage Bonhoeffer's *Ethics* in order to answer him on issues of importance to us today, we must first encounter his doctrine of justification. North American Protestants should not make the unreflective assumption that Bonhoeffer is one of us, that he stands with us in our various claims to justice, peace, or conscience. To the contrary, on these issues Bonhoeffer is engaged in a polemic against much of what we implicitly assume. If we read the *Ethics* correctly, we do not romanticize it or isolate it to its historical context. We must not protect ourselves from its polemic. The discerning reader will observe that the *Ethics* is not directed against the Nazi regime but rather against Protestantism itself, a Protestantism that has capitulated unconditionally to the Enlightenment (or, as we might put it, to the Modern or Postmodern). The most unsettling aspect of this observation is that the *Ethics* demands to be read as a polemic against post-war Protestantism in North America as much as a polemic against the liberal German Protestantism of his own time. We should take with extreme seriousness Bonhoeffer's decisive repudiation of Reinhold Niebuhr in the *Ethics*. This repudiation hangs like a judgment over Bonhoeffer's own North American experience as a Fellow at Union Seminary in New York where Niebuhr was his teacher.[7] Moreover, if we correctly understand the polemic, the apparent dissonance of the text resolves itself. Despite the fact that the text was written in extraordinary circumstances, in fragments not brought to press by Bonhoeffer, it has a unity. Bonhoeffer first denies that Protestantism is an ethical religion:

> The knowledge of good and evil seems to be the aim of all ethical reflection. The first task of Christian ethics is to invalidate this knowledge. In launching this attack on the underlying assumptions of all other ethics, Christian ethics stands so completely alone that it becomes questionable whether there is any purpose in speaking of Christian ethics at all. But if one does so notwithstanding, that can only mean that Christian ethics claims to discuss the origin of the whole problem of ethics, and thus professes to be a critique of all ethics simply as ethics. (17)

Transgression, Punishment, Responsibility, Forgiveness
Graven Images 4 (1998), 86-105.

The *Ethics* begins by launching an attack on ethics as such: its first moment undermines the theory of the ethicist. The *Ethics* will reconstrue ethics as obedience to the authoritative commandment of God, and it completes itself in a theory of free responsibility. These moments are not in conflict. They are a unity. They are a polemic directed against Protestantism as ethical religion.

First, the *Ethics* attacks Enlightenment doctrines of free will. Bonhoeffer's ethical polemic is manifestly directed against Kant, whose categorical imperative underlies the entire text and it occasionally surfaces as the object of specific attack. Given Kant's enormous influence on Protestantism even beyond Germany, Bonhoeffer's criticism constitutes a polemic at a very deep level.[8] But the *Ethics* is directed against the shallower positivism that has informed British and North American Protestantism as well.[9] This polemic first involves the question of free will: the Enlightenment, particularly Kant, placed the free will of the human actor at the center of ethics. To the extent that German Protestantism adapted itself to Kant, it necessarily became Pelagian. Similarly, North American Protestantism, despite internal divisions, is almost universally Pelagian: whether North American Protestants seek personal salvation, social justice, personal ethics, or merely shelter from the storm, they believe that these ends can be achieved by an act of free will. Consequently North American Protestants will approach Bonhoeffer seeking a program, a method or a system, but to no avail. Bonhoeffer's *Ethics* must be seen in large part as the reclamation of an orthodox doctrine of justification against the encroachment of a radical Pelagianism in modern Protestant theology.

Second, the *Ethics* is directed against Enlightenment skepticism, or more specifically the nihilism into which Enlightenment skepticism has collapsed. Bonhoeffer's doctrine of justification is an express repudiation of Kantian ethical theory and its inability to respond to the primal evil loosed in Bonhoeffer's time. Here, too, North Americans should take little comfort in our distance from Bonhoeffer's situation. Bonhoeffer's polemic is directed at the more extreme positivism characteristic of North American thought as well as German liberal Protestantism. Just as Kant decisively influenced liberal Protestantism in Germany, a more corrosive positivism (colored by pragmatism) has undermined North American Protestant theology. In North America both liberals and fundamentalists rely without examination on philosophical assumptions that Bonhoeffer rejects. For an example, we need go no further than the unquestioned assumption that there is a distinction between facts and values and that faith involves a "value-choice."[2]

Bonhoeffer denies the fact-value distinction. He compels us to think theologically within the framework of the classical Christian tradition, of orthodox realism. In Bonhoeffer's theology, the divine command precedes reason. We do not "invent" the divine command by thinking about it and then choose to believe in it. The divine command is authoritative. It draws its authority from Christ. To this command our reason is conformed in justification (although Bonhoeffer reserves some opening for natural reason). Bonhoeffer does not distinguish "fact" from "value" (the phenomenal from the noumenal). He does not locate faith in the realm of "values," which is to say some realm beyond knowledge. Faith is not a value, an opinion, a postulate, a sensibility, or a rational ethical system. Faith carries more weight: it is a form of knowledge. It is knowledge of God and the world as they manifest themselves to us in divine imperatives, not as they appear in our own thinking. The reason of the justified sinner (and even to some extent the natural person) participates in this knowledge. Bonhoeffer does not insulate faith within the subjective spirit or mind of the believer. Faith is knowledge of the real, and as such faith makes a claim on the entire created order, including authority constituted by divine mandate, such as government.

Bonhoeffer's Christian realism informs his use of the term "real" in the *Ethics*. The real is the actual world as we encounter it in our daily experience. But the real is not limited to what is empirically verifiable exclusive of an indeterminate realm of values. The real is structured by divine ethical imperatives (i.e., the mandates: government, Church, family, vocation, as well as the potential for exercise of free responsibility). These imperatives frame and shape our common, daily experience, whether we think about them or not, whether we care about them or not. The real is accessible to reason, primarily in justification. It is the whole person, including reason, that is justified, and "the whole apparatus of human powers must be set in motion when it is a matter of proving what is the will of God" (40). Engagement with the real involves the knowledge that is faith, not value or opinion. In the *Ethics* there is "knowledge" of good and evil; there is "knowledge" of God. "There is a 'knowing' which arises from the knowledge of Jesus Christ as the Reconciler" (33). Bonhoeffer's claim for such knowledge is an inherent polemic at the end of our century. [10]

Finally, although the *Ethics* articulates limits on authority, Bonhoeffer is authoritarian. He understood that this aspect of his thought would make him difficult for the modern sensibility. But his authoritarianism should be no surprise. Obedience and deputyship are central themes for Bonhoeffer from early on. These themes entail authority, and Bonhoeffer finds authority embodied in actual institutions in the world. Hence, the short answer to the question about justice in the *Ethics*: Justice is the task of government. It is true that this authoritarianism is mitigated by Bonhoeffer's doctrine of justification. In justification the Christian acting in free responsibility must in appropriate circumstances incur guilt. Be it noted, however, that acting in free responsibility in justification is not justice. It is rather the violation of fundamental law.

Bonhoeffer's authoritarianism is both central to his ethical thought and a necessary corrective for North Americans. With our constitutional mistrust of the state—an aspect of our fundamental individualism[11]—we tend to misread Bonhoeffer's resistance as a kind of individualism. We miss entirely his claims for the sovereign and other authoritative structures of community, his claims in effect for justice.

Those North American commentators who have got the point and who have been critical of Bonhoeffer's authoritarianism as typical of conservative German ideology do not appreciate, I suggest, the current crisis of liberal political theory.[12] The Holocaust calls into question the unexamined optimism of such theory. In the absence of classical natural law, how can the state's legitimacy or authority be grounded? Is there some standard beyond the will (or formalist practical reason) of the parties to the social contract? If not, can the state differ from violence? What authoritative claim can the state make to prevent community from dissolving into anarchy? Bonhoeffer's authoritarianism returns us to the question of justice.[13]

At first, it would appear that the *Ethics* does not address justice, the theologian of justification. Bonhoeffer uses the term, but he gives no systematic analysis of it, nor even a definition.[14] The word is absent from the "Index of Subjects" in the Macmillan English edition. Yet, on further reflection, we might suggest that justice is indeed a theme of the *Ethics*. For the book is an analysis of ethi*cs* as the obedient response to a demand, to an authentic claim. In these terms, the *Ethics* expressly addresses the relationships among the person, the church, and the government. These relationships necessarily entail justice, and any analysis of them must address justice at least by indirection.

Justice is a problematic concept for Bonhoeffer. Justice as we traditionally understand it is a classical, scholastic concept. It presumes an objective and public claim upon both individuals and community accessible to natural reason. Consider St. Thomas' definition of justice: "Justice is a habit whereby a man renders to each one his due by a constant and perpetual will."[15] Justice, for St. Thomas, is the chief of the moral virtues, in part because it involves the common good. Q. 58 Art. 12. In related terms, St. Thomas proclaims a natural law against which the positive law of the state must be measured for its standard of justice, indeed for its very legitimacy (*ST* I-II Q. 90 through Q. 108).

But Bonhoeffer is an heir of the Reformation. As such, he must ground ethical discourse in a doctrine of justification. This means first that, for theological reasons, he rejects natural reason and natural law at least as St. Thomas conceived them. For Bonhoeffer, the ultimate and final reality manifests itself in an act of justification for which there is no preparation (St. Thomas's "habit") and which we cannot will. Moreover, since we can neither prepare for nor will our justification, it is an open question as to what we are "due" in St. Thomas' terms, or indeed how we can act. In short, St. Thomas compels us to ask Bonhoeffer whether a doctrine of justice is possible. This question is particularly telling for North American Protestants who, I suggest, either rely selectively on an unreflective scholastic concept of justice in the absence of any doctrine of the natural or claim that justice is what they think it to be in light of some idealist ethical theory. Bonhoeffer utterly denies either alternative. Precisely this refusal to adopt a Thomist theory of natural law as well as the complete negation of conventional liberal Protestant ethics opens the question of justice as a theme in the *Ethics*.

Justice is not what conscience says it is. Although conscience may be bound by law, justification, not conscience, is the last word. As part of his polemic, Bonhoeffer refuses to allow us to encounter him as the person of conscience. We are comfortable with the person of conscience. We are less comfortable with the theologian of justification. Bonhoeffer does not concern himself with his own conscience or his own ethical integrity. Rather he turns our consideration to the void at the end of Western history, a void so overwhelming that questions of personal integrity appear against it as a kind of narcissism. Bonhoeffer's discussion of the void is distressingly familiar to us. We are the postmoderns: we speak the language of the void. In North America, we know it as a skepticism so corrosive that we no longer have a language in which to discuss the significance of our basic institutions. For example, in North America, Protestantism has become either a totem masking dark impulses or the occasion for ethical self justification, often both at the same time. Our institutions are reflected back to us in a vacuous mass media. (Bonhoeffer was critical of the film as an indication of our deep forgetfulness [106].) Our current circumstance is a distant reflection of the particular crisis that formed Bonhoeffer's concrete situation. The current crisis of contemporary Protestantism is not that far removed from the Holocaust, which extends a shadow of condemnation over Christianity in our century. Bonhoeffer addresses us from the very heart of this void. He asserts that "the western world is brought to the brink of the void" (105).

> Everything established is threatened with annihilation. This is not a crisis among other crises. It is a decisive struggle of the last days. . . . The void towards which the west is drifting is not the natural end, the dying away and decline of a once flourishing history of nations. It is, once again, a specifically western void, a rebellious and outrageous void, and one which is the enemy of both God and man. As an apostasy from all that is established, it is the supreme manifestation of all the powers which are opposed to God. It is the void made god. . . . The void engulfs life, history, family, nation, language, faith. The list can be prolonged indefinitely, for the void spares nothing.

> In the face of the peril of the void there is no longer any meaning in the question of the historical inheritance which requires of those who receive it that they shall both develop it in the present and hand it on to the future. There is no future and there is no past. There is only the moment which has been rescued from the void, and the desire to snatch from the void the next moment as well. . . . An abrupt end is put to any kind of inner self-development and to any gradual attainment of personal or vocational maturity. There is no personal destiny, and consequently there is no personal dignity. . . . If we ask what remains, there can be only one answer: fear of the void. The most astonishing observation we can make today is that in the face of the void one is prepared to sacrifice anything and everything: one's own judgment, one's human character, and one's neighbour. If this fear is unscrupulously explored, there is no limit to what can be achieved. (105-8)

The void (*das Nichts*) is the nothingness against which we project a world view of our own creation, the world of our own idolatry. It is the world of the *cor curvum in se*, the will turned in upon itself, a Lutheran concept adopted by Bonhoeffer in *Act and Being*. The void is the denial of the real, the actual created order. It is not fortuitous that Bonhoeffer cites Nietszche, the great nineteenth-century prophet of the void, six times in the *Ethics*.[16]

We encounter this void in part as the problem of ethics, which is also the problem of justice. In the face of pervasive anomie, how can we know and therefore do the good or the just? In response to this question, Bonhoeffer makes two claims, each one authentic and each one completely unanticipated. The first claim is that ethics as knowledge of good and evil is indeed possible. In response to the nihilism of the void, Bonhoeffer claims that we can and do have knowledge, not merely opinion, about good and evil. But theologically Bonhoeffer grounds this ethical knowledge not in nature or Torah but in the Fall. This ethical knowledge arises with the Fall and is a mark of the Fall, a mark of our disunion from God. Its object is not God. Such knowledge in itself is held apart from God, and it falls prey to the void. In short, ethics as the knowledge of good and evil entails a knowledge that is disunion. Such an ethics is ultimately a form of idolatry. Christian ethics cannot be such an ethics.

Bonhoeffer's second claim supersedes his first. He suggests that the first task of any Christian ethics is to invalidate the knowledge of good and evil because it constitutes separation from God:

> In the knowledge of good and evil, man does not understand himself and the reality of the destiny appointed in his origin, but rather in his own possibilities, his possibility of being good or evil. He knows himself now as something apart from God, outside God, and this means that he now knows only himself and no longer knows God at all; for he can know God only if he knows only God. The knowledge of good and evil is therefore separation from God. Only against God can man know good and evil. (17-8)

In the face of the void we are capable on our own only of disunion. But even in this extreme circumstance God asserts the primal creativity to bring into being for us and indeed *despite us* those authoritative institutions whose respective concrete commissions alone protect us from the void: the government and the church.

> Two things alone still have the power to avert the final plunge into the void. One is the miracle of a new awakening of faith, and the other is that force which the Bible calls the "restrainer" . . . [citing 2 Thessalonians 2:7], that is to say the force of order, equipped with great physical strength, which effectively blocks the way of those who are about to plunge into the abyss. The miracle is the saving act of God, which intervenes from above, from beyond whatever is historically attainable or probable, and creates new life out of the void. It is the raising of the dead. And the "restrainer" is the force which takes effect within history through God's governance of the world, and which sets due limits to evil. The "restrainer" is not God; it is not without guilt; but God makes use of it in order to preserve the world from destruction. The place where the miracle of God is proclaimed is the Church. The "restrainer" is the power of the state to establish and maintain order. The two are entirely different in nature, yet in the face of imminent chaos they are in close alliance, and they are both alike objects of the hatred of the forces of destruction, which see in them their deadliest enemies. (108)

In this respect, the *Ethics* may be read as a gloss on the Barmen Declaration of 1934, in particular Article 5. Bonhoeffer does not claim that government is an order of creation in the traditional Lutheran sense, but it has a divine mandate. Bonhoeffer resolves the issue by grounding the mandates in Christ. Bonhoeffer's use of 2 Thessalonians 2:7 is pertinent. Jerome and Tertullian had interpreted the "restrainer" in this verse as the Roman Empire. These early Church Fathers saw Rome as a restraint against Antichrist. This ancient interpretation conforms with Bonhoeffer's views concerning Christendom expressed here and elsewhere in the *Ethics*.[17] Bonhoeffer understood government and Church together as God's agents against the forces of the void. As I suggest below, it is in light of his status as an agent of the *Abwehr* that we must understand his resistance.

Justification and the Problem of Christian Ethics

Bonhoeffer says, "[T]he origin and the essence of all Christian life are comprised in the one process or event which the Reformation called justification of the sinner by grace alone" (120). For Bonhoeffer, justification is ultimate, something final, something that cannot be grasped by the being or the action or the suffering of any person (120). It is the sole certainty. Everything else is subject to doubt (121). It is grounded in what Bonhoeffer calls "the mystery of predestination, the mystery of an eternal dichotomy which has its origin in the eternally One, the mystery of an eternal choice and election by Him in whom there is no darkness but only light" (19). The doctrine of justification falls under Bonhoeffer's discussion of the ultimate and penultimate in the *Ethics*.

In Bonhoeffer's view, justification is ultimate in two respects. First, it denies any method of attainment, and thus it breaks with everything that precedes it. Bonhoeffer asserts that there is no Lutheran method and no Pauline method of attaining this final word. There is no program for ethical formation as found, for example, in classical theories of ethics or even certain Protestant programs of ethical character formation. Justification excludes every kind of method once and for all (123). Ethics as formation can mean only the way in which Christ takes form in our world, in a manner that is neither abstract nor casuistic, neither programmatic nor purely speculative (88). Therefore, ethics can never become a method; it can never be systematic. If ethics were a method it would never be final, but only, in Bonhoeffer's terms, penultimate.

Reference to the penultimate reminds us that justification is ultimate in a second sense. It is always preceded by a penultimate, some prior span of time at the end of which it stands. The penultimate is the way that must be traversed, even though there is no way that leads to the goal (124). Nonetheless, the penultimate is of crucial importance: for the sake of the ultimate, the penultimate must be preserved. The way must be made ready for the word (134). It is in the penultimate, the real world, that we encounter both the obligation and the freedom that for Bonhoeffer constitute the ethical.

In light of this doctrine of justification, it is difficult to understand how an ethics of any kind could come into being. As Bonhoeffer suggests, even combining the "ethical" and the "Christian" is highly questionable because these concepts are cast radically into question by justification. Yet Bonhoeffer undertakes to articulate an ethics precisely within this context. The ethical, if it is authentic, must first be grounded in a concrete time and place in a finite and destructible world. This is a concept, according to Bonhoeffer, that the moralist does not understand. The moralist who seeks the universally rational moral principle devoid of all the factors that shape the concrete situation (read Kant) is "a dangerous tormentor, tyrant and clown, a figure of tragi-comedy" (264-5). But these objections only deepen the question. If Bonhoeffer concedes a necessary time and place for what he calls "the ethical phenomenon" in human existence (265), how is such discourse possible and how can it become the subject of analysis?

For Bonhoeffer, ethical discourse is concretely grounded because it emerges from some specific warrant or authorization. Ethics is not an abstract science or rule, determined apart from the lives of people as they are actually lived. But even in the concrete situation, how does the warrant or the authority to engage in discourse about ethics emerge? Bonhoeffer insists that this authority is imparted not by the self (the self can never justify itself) but by an "objective position in the world" (271). In other words, Bonhoeffer makes a claim for the objective status of authority, a status beyond individual intent or social contract. Obedience arises only as a response to the claim of an institutional authority whose grounding lies beyond the self. Bonhoeffer is aware that his view of authority is alien and even offensive to modern sensibilities:

> What finds expression here is that disparity which is so extremely offensive to modern sensibilities but which is inherent and essential in the ethical, namely, the disparity between the superior and the inferior. Without this objective subordination of the lower to the higher, and without that courage to accept superiority which modern man has so completely lost, ethical discourse is dissipated in generalities, it lacks an object and its essential character is destroyed.

> The ethical, therefore, is not a principle which levels out, invalidates and disrupts the whole order of human precedence and subordination, but already in itself it implies a definite structure of human society; it implies certain definite sociological relations which involve authority. It is only within these relationships that it makes its appearance and acquires the concrete warrant or authorization which is essential to it. (271-2)

The question of authority for Bonhoeffer is not some vestige of conservative German ideology. It stands at the heart of his concrete situation: although the *Ethics* shows a clear concern for the misuse of authority, Bonhoeffer is primarily concerned with the dependence of ethics upon authority.

Bonhoeffer is authoritarian, but he is not totalitarian. Authority is not unlimited, and one purpose of the *Ethics* is to articulate these limits within his own situation. For example, although Bonhoeffer is critical of the Enlightenment, he affirms the Enlightenment's opposition to a system under which society was divided into the privileged and unprivileged.

For Bonhoeffer, authority in no way implies a sanctioning of privileges (273). In the same regard, Bonhoeffer affirms the Enlightenment's emancipation of reason, which has become "one of the indispensable moral requirements of western man" (97). Authority is not grounded in strength alone. Though it entails strength, it requires a higher warrant.

An objective warrant creates authority. Authority derives its warrant in Bonhoeffer's terms from above and not from below. It is not a human creation. It does not consist in the subjective value of the person, but "it derives its legitimation from a concrete objective commission":

> The master craftsman is still a master even for his talented journeyman, and the father is still the father even for his worthy and meritorious son. Quite independently of the subjective side of the matter, it is still the master and the father who possess the warrant for ethical discourse. The warrant goes with the office and not with the person. (274)

Although Bonhoeffer here alludes to social and natural relations, he does not find in nature or society the commission for legitimate authority. What is the source of this commission from above? The answer and the ultimate ground of a Christian ethic is the commandment of God: "This brings us to the only possible object of a 'Christian ethic,' an object which lies beyond the 'ethical,' namely, the 'commandment of God.'" Such a commandment differs from what is conventionally considered the ethical. The commandment is total and unconditional. It forbids and commands but it also permits. It binds but it also sets free. It does not purport to be universally valid and timeless in contrast to the concrete instance (277). The commandment is prior to law as conventionally understood. The commandment and biblical law are inseparably linked, though the law "is comprised within the commandment: it arises from it; and it must be understood with reference to it" (285). In an illuminating passage, Bonhoeffer reveals the character of this commandment:

> God's commandment, revealed in Jesus Christ, is always concrete *to* somebody. It is never abstract speech *about* something or *about* somebody. It is always an address, a claim, and it is so comprehensive and at the same time so definite that it leaves no freedom for interpretation or application, but only the freedom to obey or disobey. (279-80)

The authoritative commandment creates a concrete objective commission in the world. It finds specific manifestation in four institutions that Bonhoeffer calls the four mandates: government, the church, the family, and labor (vocation or culture). Among all institutions, these mandates occupy a special status. They are divine in that they possess a concrete divine commission and promise that has its foundation and evidence in revelation (329). They are grounded in a positive divine mandate for the preservation of the world for the sake and purpose of Christ (330). Bonhoeffer's formal definition of mandate is as follows:

> By the term "mandate" we understand the concrete divine commission which has its foundation in the revelation of Christ and which is evidenced by Scripture; it is the legitimation and warrant for the execution of a definite divine commandment, the conferment of divine authority on an earthly agent. The term "mandate" must also be taken to imply the claiming, the seizure and the foundation of a definite earthly domain by the divine commandment. The bearer of the mandate acts as a deputy in the place of Him who assigns his commission. (287)

Though clearly authoritarian, the mandates must be seen as Bonhoeffer intended: as collectively liberating. They constitute the collective "concrete objective commission" by which deputyship is allowed to come into being.

In speaking of the mandates, Bonhoeffer avoids the terms institution, order, state or office in order to mitigate the independence of the mandates. He simultaneously affirms and qualifies their authority. The concept of orders of creation, for example, since the Reformation has come to suggest human prerogatives and privileges which pervert the task of the orders themselves. According to Arthur Cochrane, if the authors of the Barmen Declaration of 1934 had been faithful to the Lutheran and Reformed Confessions of the sixteenth and seventeenth centuries, they would have had to admit that Hitler had the right to reform the church, to appoint a Reichminister for Church affairs, to name a Reichsbishop and church committees.[18] In other words, Bonhoeffer seeks to deny any mandate status apart from the commandment of Christ that would exempt it from interrogation concerning its specific tasks. Instead, he places the ontological focus on Christ and discerns the mandates as tasks that are determined (207-13). Each mandate is grounded in commandment. This qualification reflects Bonhoeffer's battle with the Nazi state. But it has broad implications for the doctrine of justice that emerges from the *Ethics*.

Bonhoeffer views the commandment that manifests itself in the mandates as liberating. It is precisely because authority involves liberty that the ethical phenomenon is a peripheral event. The ethical arises as a question only when there is disunion among the mandates. Not every moment involves a universal decision between good and evil. Indeed, to treat ethics as obligation in other than peripheral situations destroys ethics, for the obligation that attends upon ethics is ultimate and any ethical discourse should safeguard this character of ethics lest ethics should become penultimate and a method (266-7). Because he treats ethics as peripheral, Bonhoeffer finds in ethics freedom. To live within the mandates is to experience liberty from the tyranny of the ethical. Ethics entails the permission to live as a person before God within a divinely ordained framework (281).

The Problem of Justice: Government and Church

Bonhoeffer's account of ethics within the authoritative commandment of the mandates suggests two significant questions about justice: How can the community know what is just and how can the community act in a just way? I do not refer here to the individual. Bonhoeffer's argument as developed thus far suggests that as individuals, indeed even as individual Christians, we cannot do the just. Justice requires the mandate of an objective commission. Just action occurs only within the authoritative hierarchy of the mandates. Moreover, just action in particular is under the jurisdiction of government. The proclamation of justice (not just action) is under the jurisdiction of the church. But what is just action? To orient our inquiry we must further explore the mandates of government and church.

Bonhoeffer finds the answer to the question of just action in the mandate of government. Government is the ultimate agent of justice in the world. It may not be the sole agent, since authority structures operating within the other mandates may reflect justice. But justice ultimately and in this sense solely is the task of government:

> The mission of government consists in serving the dominion of Christ on earth by the exercise of the worldly power of the sword and of justice. Government serves Christ by establishing and maintaining an outward justice by means of the sword which is given to it, and to it alone, in deputyship for God. It has not only the negative task of punishing the wicked, but also the positive task of praising the good or "them that do well." I Pet. 2.14. (340; see also 346, 328-9)

Hence Bonhoeffer's assertion: "Government is divinely ordained authority to exercise worldly dominion by divine right" (332). Consistent with his view of the divine mandates, Bonhoeffer locates the basis of government solely in Christ as mediator, ground, goal and ultimately redeemer of the created order of which government is a part. In addition, there is a particular relationship between Jesus and government given the circumstances of the crucifixion (336-9). This does not mean that government is necessarily Christian. It means simply that government as such, even if pagan, even if unknowingly, and even in persecution, has a divine commission in Christ. Government serves Christ by its very existence (342).

Despite (or perhaps because of) its basis in Christ, government manifests itself as power or coercion. This power or coercion is a given of the created order. Bonhoeffer observes that the concept of the "state," which has its origin in pagan antiquity, is foreign to the New Testament. The New Testament, according to Bonhoeffer, speaks of government or power. The state constitutes an ordered community. Government is the power which creates and maintains order. State embraces both rulers and the ruled. Government refers only to the rulers (332). In effect, Bonhoeffer dispels human claims ultimately to shape government as such. We encounter government as other, as coercive power that has the ability to shape our individual and common experience (332-3).

Bonhoeffer distinguishes his New Testament account of government from the classical view of Aristotle and St. Thomas (as well as from certain Anglican and Lutheran views). The state, according to the classical view, is the supreme consummation of the rational character of the person, and to serve it is the supreme purpose of human life (333-5). The classical view for Bonhoeffer is unacceptable because it does not acknowledge the otherness of government. It cannot explain the ultimate coercive power (we might say the "sovereignty") that distinguishes government from other forms of community.

Bonhoeffer prefers the Reformation doctrine of government which finds the basis of government in sin, or in the Fall, although this view too ultimately fails. Under this Augustinian view, sin makes government coercion necessary, but it cannot explain the relationship between coercive power and justice. In other words, the Reformation failed to provide a coherent account of justice. According to Bonhoeffer, the Reformers had to subordinate either the concept of justice or the concept of coercion. For Bonhoeffer, both are entailed in the concept of authority. Moreover, the Reformation view leaves the state as a self-contained entity which, according to Bonhoeffer, fails to take account of the relationship of government to Christ. In short, it goes too far in claiming an independent status for government (335-6). Bonhoeffer's corrective to the Reformation view is to find the basis of government in Christ.

Though Bonhoeffer qualifies the independent ontological status of government, he does not entirely deny it. His thinking in this regard, I suggest, is not fully resolved. He suggests that government is given to us not as an idea or a task to be fulfilled, but as a reality, something which "is." In this being it is a divine office. Citing Romans 13, he suggests that the persons who exercise government are God's ministers, servants and representatives. He further emphasizes that this status of government is the case even if the "path to government office repeatedly passes through guilt" (339).

Despite any such guilt, the being of government lies beyond its earthly coming into being. Like all existing things, it too stands in a certain sense beyond good and evil (339). Even when government incurs guilt and is open to ethical attack, its power is still from God. Its existence is solely in Christ and through the cross it is reconciled with God. Bonhoeffer supports the assertion "my country, right or wrong,":

> There can be no ethical isolation of the son from his father, and indeed, on the basis of actual being, there is a necessity of sharing in the assuming and carrying of the guilt of a father or a brother. There is no glory in standing amid the ruins of one's native town in the consciousness that at least one has not oneself incurred any guilt. It is rather the self-glorification of the moral legalist in the face of history. (340)

In light of government's commission, the demand for obedience is almost unconditional. A Christian is bound until "government directly compels him to offend against the divine commandment." In case of doubt, obedience is required (342-3). A government that offends must still be obeyed. As Bonhoeffer states: "Even an anti-Christian government is still in a certain sense government. It would, therefore, not be permissible to refuse to pay taxes to a government which persecuted the Church" (343). Citing Revelation 13.7, he adds that government can be disobeyed only if it manifests itself in the "sense of the apocalypse" which would require total disobedience since every "act of obedience obviously involves a denial of Christ" (343).

Bonhoeffer produced his analysis of government while involved in active resistance to his own government. How was such resistance possible? To my knowledge, Bonhoeffer gave no explicit answer, nor is there an easy answer.[19] Bonhoeffer does not discuss resistance theory in the *Ethics*, but I believe that his resistance can be explained in terms of Reformation resistance theory, Lutheran or Reformed.[20] Under such theory while individuals have no right to resist the government, lesser magistrates may. Thus the fact that Bonhoeffer in the act of resistance was in fact working on behalf of the *Abwehr*, the German military intelligence unit, may have given him sufficient governmental mandate for resistance. If Bonhoeffer relied on resistance theory, he did not yet view his government in the sense of apocalypse: under resistance theory he would have derived his right to resist from the very authority of the government on whose behalf, in a sense, he acted. It would also have given him greater sanction to act in free responsibility because he was pursuing "statecraft," a concept from the

Ethics. In other words, it may be precisely because he was working in a position of deputyship in government, the *Abwehr*, that he had standing to oppose tyranny. Indeed, I suggest that some of his harsher expressions in the *Ethics* concerning the prerogatives of government, which are otherwise difficult to explain, can be read as an expression of Bonhoeffer's resistance activity in the *Abwehr*.[21]

But given resistance theory, when does one decide to resist even against a government mandate? The decision itself involves the question of justice, though not in straightforward ways. Justice is an element of government's authority. Indeed his criticism of the Reformation view of government is grounded in the Reformation's failure to account adequately for justice (335-6). Government is one among four mandates and as such has a task for which it is answerable. It is not an isolated order of creation. This task is limited by its own mandate of justice and the tasks of the three other mandates (see, for example, 279, 291-2). Though clear lines cannot be drawn, any conflict among the mandates gives rise to ethical questions that must be resolved. For example, though Bonhoeffer denies the individual right to revolution, he affirms the mandate of labor or vocation, the individual's right to preserve "the purity of his office and mission in the *polis*" (351). Implicit in the structure of Bonhoeffer's thinking about government is the view that justice acts as a limitation of government, though in a limited respect. Government even in guilt remains government. But it is answerable to its mandate to do justice. The question is how we can understand justice in light of what we know about Bonhoeffer's doctrine of justification?

The key here is to understand the place of the Church in Bonhoeffer's thinking. For Bonhoeffer, the Church holds a special status. The Church is the spiritual office, "the divinely ordained authority to exercise spiritual dominion by divine right. It does not proceed from the congregation, but from God" (333). Bonhoeffer for these purposes distinguishes between individual Christians, who do not exercise this authority, and the Church itself. Bonhoeffer asserts that the Church does not have dominion over government (346). Indeed, the government has a claim of obedience over the church, although this claim does not extend to the spiritual office (347). However, the Church has its own claim on government in that the Church testifies before government to their common Master (347). As Bonhoeffer asserts, "Only the Church brings government to an understanding of itself" (347). On this basis, the Church claims to be listened to by government.[22]

Nonetheless, government as such remains religiously neutral and affords protection to every form of service of God which does not undermine the office of government (348-9). The government must mediate between "the various forms of service of God" (349). (One could argue from Bonhoeffer's own reflections on Judaism in the *Ethics* that the church includes the synagogue as well, but this is not resolved.) The government achieves this purpose not by suppression but by adherence to its governmental commission. If the persons who exercise government are Christian, they must know that the Christian proclamation is delivered not by means of the sword but by the word (349). The state does have some authority to maintain order at the request of the church but it cannot take over ecclesiastical control.

As part of its proclamation, the church does have a political responsibility in warning publicly against sin and in warning that "it shall with all due deference address government directly in order to draw its attention to shortcomings and errors which must otherwise imperil its governmental office" (350). But if government does not listen, "then the only political responsibility which remains to her is in establishing and maintaining, at least among her own members, the order of outward justice which is no longer to be found in the *polis*, where by so doing, she serves government in her own way" (350).

Indeed, the proclamation of the church extends expansively to the world as a whole, which responsibility has implications for government:

> The word of the love of God for the world sets the congregation in a relation of responsibility with regard to the world. In word and action the congregation is to bear witness before the world to the faith in Christ; it is to prevent offense or scandal, and it is to make room for the gospel in the world. Whenever this responsibility is denied, Christ, too, is denied; for it is responsibility which answers to love of God for the world. (357)

In short summary, to use Bonhoeffer's words, "Government and Church are connected in such various ways that the relationship cannot be regulated in accordance with any single general principle" (350). Nonetheless, their mandates are separate and government maintains its status as a secular, not spiritual, entity, and the agent of justice.

Bonhoeffer has given us no definition of justice, but it is clear from the text that justice involves action in accordance with a commandment inseparably linked with law—to use a Pauline term, such law is *nomos*. But what is *nomos*? Law now becomes the focus of the inquiry. Law like justice is both a theme and a problem of the *Ethics*. It is not separable for Bonhoeffer from either the gospel or the overriding commandment of God. At the outset we must note that Bonhoeffer asserts that the church's proclamation must always be both law and gospel in its entirety. These two can never be separated nor can they be identified. They are both contained in the proclamation of the Church (357-9). Both are entailed in the *primus usus legis* as taught in the symbolic writings (303-19). Moreover, law as such is part of and is subsumed by the commandment of God (285).

But in its proclamation to government concerning justice the church must declare itself concerning law. At this point in the argument I suggest that we must separate law—*nomos*—from the strands of gospel and commandment with which it is bound up. We must speak of the law in its appropriate sense, as some universal substantive rule. Law is indeed comprised within a specific commandment to someone, as Bonhoeffer asserts (285). But we must be clear: an exclusive focus on law as such is appropriate because we are here not concerned with personal ethics. We are concerned with a narrow and special case: the proclamation of the church, acting in accordance with its mandate, to government. In this case, law must stand on its own in some form, in the realm of the penultimate. Justification and law, though interrelated, are not the same. In considering the narrow case of justice, we are not attending to the last word of justification.

Bonhoeffer develops some working premises about what constitutes law for purposes of the church's proclamation of justice. First, the mandates themselves in their concrete form at a given time (under the dominion of Christ and the decalogue) as such constitute law (330). In other words, the integrity of the mandates, each operating within its own sphere, provides the basis for a substantive analysis of justice. When this integrity is disrupted or compromised, a law is violated and injustice results. Second, and primarily, Bonhoeffer finds in scripture what St. Thomas called divine law. He speaks of law as the positive revealed law of scripture, "the law of love for God and for our neighbor as it is explained in the decalogue, in the sermon on the mount and in the apostolic parenesis" (247). This single sentence perhaps reveals the fullness of law for Bonhoeffer. Here we find perhaps the center of his thinking about justice. Elsewhere he limits divine law to the decalogue alone. For example, he speaks of the entire decalogue, which subordinates natural law, as the content of the *primus usus legis* (307-8).

Finally Bonhoeffer advances a theory of natural right. Natural right is not law as such, but an entitlement over against law. It is clear from the context that Bonhoeffer directed this theory against the Nazi eugenics laws: There are certain natural rights (e.g., a natural right to marriage) that cannot be abrogated by positive law. Bonhoeffer's discussion of the natural is deeply significant in light of Karl Barth's well-known denial of natural theology and Barth's view that natural theology opened the door to an incursion of Nazi ideology into Protestant orthodoxy.[23] While Bonhoeffer denies the efficacy of natural law (see 310, 328, 338, 341, 358), certainly as a mode of self-justification he advances a concept of the natural within the framework of Protestant dogmatics: "the natural is the form of life preserved by God for the fallen world and directed towards justification, redemption and renewal through Christ" (145; see also 143-87.) A doctrine of the natural relates both to being and to our knowledge of being in a fallen world. It follows from Bonhoeffer's ontology. For Bonhoeffer, "reason," though mitigated by the Fall, has standing to apprehend the things that are in the created order, the natural:

> Reason perceives the universal and what is given; and thus the given natural, as reason perceives it, is a universal. It embraces the whole of human nature. Reason understands the natural as something that is universally established and independent of the possibility of empirical verification. (146)

This passage is followed by this particularly significant footnote:

> This view differs from the Catholic theory in that (1) we regard reason as having been entirely involved in the Fall, while according to Catholic Dogmatics, reason has still retained a certain essential integrity, and (2) according to the Catholic doctrine, reason may also grasp the formal determination as the natural, the second of these principles being connected with the first. Our view differs from the Enlightenment view in that it takes the natural to rest upon what is objectively given and not upon the subjective spontaneity of reason. (146, n. 5)

Nature as apprehended by reason to some extent is a limitation on all of the mandates. While natural law cannot constitute a standard for justification, even of government, natural right constitutes a limitation on the reach of government. It is a modest limitation, but the individual is entitled to defend natural right as guaranteed by God (155). Bonhoeffer proposes a natural right to bodily life. Within this context Bonhoeffer discusses many issues of current import involving sexuality and euthanasia (143-86). In an unfinished section he speaks of a natural right to the life of the mind (186-7). Bonhoeffer even speculates about a new foundation for a theory of natural law in his discussion of the biblical derivation of government from Christ, a question he leaves open (339).

With this view of the natural, Bonhoeffer is never far from some doctrine of natural justice, although the content remains open. For example, in his discussion of "pertinence," he speaks of the "law of being" (*Wesensgesetz*) inherent in everything (236). In his discussion of conscience, he speaks of conscience as an advocate for "the law of life" (247). In his discussion of the imperative for serving the penultimate, he speaks about the necessity of feeding the hungry, housing the homeless, and giving the dispossessed justice (136-7).

With his unfinished doctrine of law, Bonhoeffer suggests a Protestant parallel to St. Thomas. Thomas viewed all law as grounded in *logos*; he viewed natural law as accessible to reason; he viewed natural law as subordinate to and subsumed in divine law as expressed in the decalogue; he viewed natural and divine law as standards of virtue. I suggest that none of these views is inconsistent with Bonhoeffer's treatment of law in the *Ethics*, though there are important differences. Even so, as Bonhoeffer himself suggests, he cannot accept St. Thomas's doctrine of natural law. Precisely because of his doctrine of justification Bonhoeffer views law and grace, though inseparable, as discontinuous. The justified do not fulfill the law. Rather they are free, and in certain circumstances required, to abrogate it. Law for Bonhoeffer is never the measure of justification. Law's realm is the penultimate. Yet within this realm law, natural and divine, both gives content to and places restrictions upon the mandates.

Although Bonhoeffer's analysis of law is unfinished, it is powerfully suggestive, and we must appreciate it for the historic contribution that it is. The question of what constitutes *nomos* remains unresolved for the entire Protestant tradition. We must acknowledge Bonhoeffer's contribution in opening the possibility for Protestant discourse about substantive justice with his provisional analysis of law. His analysis of the natural opens a significant response to Barth's view of natural theology.

Responsibility: The Law and Gospel Problem

Thus far we have found in Bonhoeffer's *Ethics* an authoritarian moment according to which the structure of life is objectively established by divine mandate. We might call this moment (despite possible objections from Bonhoeffer himself) law. But Bonhoeffer presents a contrary moment which he calls "responsibility" under which a person might contravene the structures of law. I suggest that in Bonhoeffer's account of responsibility, we find a doctrine of Christian liberty. In other words, in his concept of responsibility, Bonhoeffer distinguishes Gospel from law. As Luther observed, the ability to distinguish Gospel from law is the mark of a true theologian.[24] Law is communal or institutional. By contrast, responsibility involves the question of action by the individual Christian. In this light Bonhoeffer asks how meaningful the question of individual responsibility can be in his own regimented society, but he affirms that there is no single life that cannot experience the situation of responsibility (250-1). In the biblical sense, responsibility is a verbal response given at the risk of a person's life to the question asked by another with regard to the event of Christ (222, citing 2 Timothy 4:16; Romans 1; Peter 3:15; Philippians 1:7 and 17). What does such response entail? For Bonhoeffer it entails the structure of responsible life.

Responsibility is first a function of deputyship. That is, we act in particular relationship to others on their behalf. Any attempt to live as though we were alone is a denial of the fact of our responsibility (224). At the threshold, Bonhoeffer suggests that "deputyship and therefore also responsibility, lies only in the complete surrender of one's own life to the other man. Only the selfless man lives responsibly and this means that only the selfless man *lives*" (225). Even free responsibility is not for the self. It is answerable to community. Responsible life also involves correspondence with reality. Bonhoeffer opposes the tendency of any idealist ethics to conform reality to its image. Instead, we see in a given situation what is necessary and what is right to grasp and to do. This does not involve any abstract ethics nor any contrast of secular and Christian principle. It involves an engagement with the reality of the world as one encounters it, as it is. Responsibility also has a relationship to the domain of things. Bonhoeffer calls this relationship "pertinence." This relation has two implications. First, Bonhoeffer finds in this principle a defense of the integrity of the pursuit of science against distortions "for demogogic, pedagogic, or moralistic purposes" (236). Bonhoeffer the realist affirms the pursuit of science as such. "In short, the more completely the service is free from personal subsidiary aims, the more thoroughly the thing itself will recover its original relation to God and to man, and the more completely it will set man free from himself" (236). The second aspect of "pertinence" takes us into the question of acceptance of guilt.

Bonhoeffer initiates his reflections on guilt with a discussion of statecraft. We think here of his own activities on behalf of the *Abwehr*. Pertinence involves the pursuit and detection of laws in social organization as in the natural sciences. Bonhoeffer finds such laws culminating in "statecraft." But his concern is less with the laws that make up statecraft than with responsible action by the statesman. Clearly those who lead great nations, who are less constrained by an external regimen, are more likely to encounter the question of action in free responsibility. For those who exercise statecraft, at times the laws and conventions of their undertaking conflict with the necessities of life. At such times those who exercise statecraft find themselves outside the realm of law: "at this point responsible and pertinent action leaves behind it the domain of principle and convention, the domain of the normal and regular, and is confronted by the extraordinary situation of ultimate necessities, a situation which no law can control" (238). According to Bonhoeffer, it was for this situation that Machiavelli in his political theory coined the term *necessità*, the situation in which the technique of statecraft has been supplanted by the necessity of state (238). In the political field, this condition, the *ultima ratio*, means war, but in all events such situations, such necessities "appeal directly to the free responsibility of the agent, a responsibility which is bound by no law. They create circumstances which are extraordinary; they are by nature peripheral and abnormal events" (238-9).

The situation of extraordinary necessity calls upon the freedom of the responsible person in a realm beyond convention and law:

> The extraordinary necessity appeals to the freedom of the men who are responsible. There is now no law behind which the responsible man can seek cover, and there is, therefore, also no law which can compel the responsible man to take any particular decision in the face of such necessities. In this situation there can only be a complete renunciation of every law, together with the knowledge that here one must make one's decision as a free venture, together also with the open admission that here the law is being infringed and violated and that necessity obeys no commandment. Precisely in this breaking of the law the validity of the law is acknowledged, and in this renunciation of all law, and in this alone, one's own decision and deed are entrusted unreservedly to the divine governance of history. (239-40)

Because responsible action is beyond law, it is not just action. It does not proceed from a proclamation of justice. Indeed, it is action that incurs guilt. An analysis of responsibility leads to a recognition of the requirement of the acceptance of guilt. As Bonhoeffer puts it, the structure of responsible action includes both readiness to accept guilt and freedom (240). In this readiness to accept guilt, Bonhoeffer finds both the freedom of the Gospel and what we might call a kind of Lutheran imitation of Christ.[25] I quote here two extended sections from Bonhoeffer's discussion of the acceptance of guilt:

> Jesus is not concerned with the proclamation and realization of new ethical ideals; He is not concerned with Himself being good (Matt. 19:17); He is concerned solely with love for the real man, and for that reason, He is able to enter into the fellowship of the guilt of men and to take the burden of their guilt upon Himself. Jesus does not desire to be regarded as the only perfect one at the expense of men; He does not desire to look down on mankind as the only guiltless one while mankind goes to its ruin under the weight of its own guilt; He does not wish that some idea of a new man should triumph amid the wreckage of a humanity whose guilt has destroyed it. . . . If any man tries to escape guilt and responsibility, he detaches himself from the ultimate reality of human existence, and what is more, he cuts himself off from the redeeming mystery of Christ's bearing guilt without sin, and he has no share in the divine justification which lies upon this event. He sets his own personal innocence above his responsibility for men, and he is blind to the more irredeemable guilt which he incurs precisely in this; he is blind also to the fact that real innocence shows itself precisely in a man's entering into the fellowship of guilt for the sake of other men. Through Jesus Christ, it becomes an essential part of responsible action that the man who is without sin lives selflessly and for that reason incurs guilt. (240-1)

If we choose to read these words in light of the question of resistance, as indeed we may have to, it should be with the full realization that Bonhoeffer considered resistance beyond the law, beyond justice. Such resistance, in St. Thomas's terms, is violence, for all unlawful force is violence. Bonhoeffer's specific analogy from Machiavelli is war itself, war conceived as something beyond law.

Bonhoeffer's discussion of responsibility in these terms leads him to an extended analysis of conscience.[26] This discussion of conscience is one of the most significant in the text, for it probes the law-gospel problem. It is particularly significant for North American Protestants, in that it acts as a corrective to our affirmation of individualism through conscience. North American Protestants are distanced from Bonhoeffer nowhere more than in his discussion of conscience. For Bonhoeffer, the conscience is in question. Earlier in the *Ethics* Bonhoeffer discusses conscience as a faculty in service of the disunion of the knowledge of good and evil (24-6). "It is the voice of apostate life which desires at least to remain one with itself" (24). In his discussion of responsibility, conscience serves the same function but now in a more positive way. It becomes a psychological principle of limitation: conscience is unwilling to sacrifice its own integrity and therefore incur guilt (242). But "all Christian ethics" is agreed that it can never be advisable to act against one's own conscience" (242). How can one then incur guilt?

Bonhoeffer does not dispute the importance of conscience but he interrogates this importance. He suggests that one must not act in such a way as to cause dissolution of the integrity of the self. Bonhoeffer says that disregard of conscience will necessarily entail the destruction of one's own being—it will bring about the decline and collapse of a human existence. It is, Bonhoeffer suggests, analogous to suicide (242). But conscience itself is not the final word. What constitutes unity of conscience? The conscience of what Bonhoeffer calls the natural man is in question. It is involved in the attempt to justify itself in the knowledge of good and evil:

> Finding no firm support in its own contingent individuality the ego traces its own derivation back to a universal law of good and seeks to achieve unity with itself in conformity with this law. Thus, the call of conscience has its origin and its goal in the autonomy of a man's own ego. (243)

The conscience which has Christ as its content, the conscience which has been set free from the law, is differently motivated:

> Natural conscience, no matter how strict and rigorous it may be, is now seen to be the most ungodly self-justification, and it is overcome by the conscience which is set free in Jesus Christ and which summons me to unity with myself in Jesus

> Christ. Jesus Christ has become my conscience. This means that I can now find unity with myself only in the surrender of my ego to God and to men. (244)

The justified conscience, which is free of law, will accept guilt:

> The conscience which has been set free from the law will not be afraid to enter into the guilt of another man for the other man's sake and indeed precisely in doing this it will show itself in its purity. The conscience which has been set free is not timid like the conscience which is bound by the law, but it stands wide open for our neighbor and for his concrete distress. And so conscience joins with the responsibility which has its foundation in Christ in bearing guilt for the sake of our neighbor. (244)

Indeed Christ himself, who loved without sin, became guilty through violation of law: he broke the law of Sabbath; he forsook his parents; he ate with sinners and outcasts; he was forsaken by God in his last hour (244). Bonhoeffer here takes one of two opportunities in the text to criticize an ethical principle of truthfulness advanced by Kant. Kant concluded that we must answer honestly to the inquiry of a murderer who breaks into our house and asks whether our friend whom he is pursuing has taken refuge there. According to Bonhoeffer, in this situation we must tell a robust lie, for it is a lie on behalf of our neighbor (245; see also 369 n. 1).

However, even for the free conscience there are two limitations. First, even the free conscience must not attempt to bear more than it can accept. As Bonhoeffer puts it, the surrender of the ego in selfless service must never be confused with the destruction and annihilation of the ego. In this case, ego would never be capable of assuming responsibility (246). He suggests that people have different capacities for acting in free responsibility under the pressure of events. Second, the conscience confronts responsible action with the law: we are still obligated under the law of which conscience reminds us. Thus, his discussion of conscience confronts us again with the question of law. Here Bonhoeffer refers to the law of love for God and for our neighbor as explained in the decalogue, the sermon on the mount, and the apostolic parenesis (248). Even if the law is distorted through the filter of conscience, it still speaks against transgressing what Bonhoeffer calls the "law of life" (247). But here Bonhoeffer asserts that law is no longer the last thing: there is Christ, and for that reason, in the contest between conscience and concrete responsibility, the free decision must be given for Christ (247): "Thus, responsibility is bound by conscience, but conscience is set free by responsibility. It is now clear that it is the same thing if we say that the responsible man becomes guilty without sin or if we say that only the man with a free conscience can bear responsibility" (247-8). In the Gospel we are set free not for justice but to follow Christ in incurring guilt.

The structure of responsible life culminates in freedom from law, which is to say in guilt. In a free act of responsibility, no one can answer for or exonerate the responsible actor. There is no law to which the actor can appeal, for if there were, the actor would not be acting in freedom (248-9). As Bonhoeffer points out, a free act of responsibility is performed "wholly within the domain of relativity, wholly in the twilight which the historical situation spreads over good and evil" (249). And precisely in this respect responsible action is a free venture not justified by any law. But it is performed without any claim to self justification, and also without any claim to a valid knowledge of good and evil (248-9).

We are approaching here the heart of the *Ethics,* for we have encountered what appears to be a deep antinomy. Does not freedom eliminate obedience? Bonhoeffer's initial response is that obedience and freedom are necessarily related: Christ acted in both simultaneously. But he reserves his final answer for his discussion of vocation. Bonhoeffer sees an authentic concept of calling as one that sets limits to responsibility. But they are very broad limits. He suggests that "vocation is responsibility, and responsibility is a total response of the whole man to the whole of reality" (258). There is in vocation, therefore, no restriction of one's interest to one's professional duties in the narrowest sense. We indeed have obligations to those who are far from us. But Bonhoeffer's broad view of vocation again encounters the conflict between responsible freedom and law, as revealed in the decalogue and divine mandates. Bonhoeffer's answer is that if our response is grounded in Christ, we may abrogate law to fulfill law:

For the sake of God and of our neighbour, and that means for the sake of Christ, there is a freedom from the keeping holy of the Sabbath, from the honouring of our parents, and indeed from the whole of the divine law, a freedom which breaks this law, but only in order to give effect to it anew. This suspension of the law can only serve the true fulfillment of it. (261)

Conclusion

Bonhoeffer was a great theologian. This means among other things that we must see him not merely in the context of his resistance to the Third Reich but as one who speaks to the ages. Bonhoeffer's stature as theologian must temper over-hasty conclusions. Any interpretation or criticism we make of him risks falsification. Our task is to pursue the lines of inquiry he opened: community, authority, law, the rational, the natural, culture, responsibility. We must always begin this task with the last word: justification.

Bonhoeffer's view of government and church is at least on the surface virtually incomprehensible to North Americans. We have a tradition of democracy and civil liberties—what our jurists call ordered liberty—a tradition intertwined with our theological heritage. We view the individual, ultimately the conscience, as prior to all structures of authority, especially government and church. Our tradition of ordered liberty emerges from the English Puritan rejection of claims to rule by divine right. Bonhoeffer himself noted that in the Anglo-Saxon countries democracy alone is regarded as the Christian form of state. He attributed this to the persecution and expulsion of the spiritualists from the continent (105). But it has its roots in the English Reformation and the seventeenth-century English Revolution as well. How then can Bonhoeffer speak to us about justice? I would like to make some suggestions.

First, Bonhoeffer speaks to us about the necessity of structures of authority for deputyship. He reminds us that the government, church, family, and vocation are necessary if we are authentically to act for and on behalf of one another. To deny this is an exercise in cheap grace.[27] Bonhoeffer speaks this message to a society that at times seems itself at the brink of the void, poised to dissolve into materialism and individualism, a postmodern society unable even to account for its own best traditions. Bonhoeffer holds up the integrity and authority of the mandates to a society for which the market appears to be the primary authentic public institution, and in which government appears to have lost both direction and authority. He proclaims of justice to a society for which all ethical discourse, from questions of environment, social justice, and law to medical ethics, is reduced to a utilitarian economic calculus. He holds up to government and church the integrity and high importance of their respective tasks. At the same time he affirms rights, even natural rights, that must occupy a central place in any account of authentic deputyship and that make possible a dialogue between himself and our tradition of ordered liberty.

Second, he speaks to the liberal Protestant Church, the whole disparate, incoherent, and frequently self-deluded Protestant Churches, including those in North America, our collective Protestantism without Reformation. Bonhoeffer's polemic is for us essential. However, because of our diversity, indeed because of our weakness (in the Pauline sense), precisely because of our liberal ethical orientation, one must be careful about criticizing the Protestant Church in North America: its task is one of Pauline "edification," upbuilding in love and tolerance. Protestants must encounter each other with mutual understanding and humility. There are in North America people who live out the Gospel in obedience. We laity must also understand our debt to a clergy that pursues its calling in the face of skepticism and indifference. But no part of this diverse body can escape Bonhoeffer's polemic. All exhibit symptoms of Protestantism as mere ideology. This is as true of the old mainline as of the new fundamentalist revival. We have in North American Protestantism enthusiasm tempered by Enlightenment, Christianity as ethical self-justification. It hardly makes a difference which version one selects. Bonhoeffer's *Ethics* demands self-examination by North American Protestants, particularly on the questions of justice and justification. Such self-examination will require further reflection on the themes of ontology and authority, as I have suggested. Moreover, we must resist our North American desire to implement the method, the ethical program. We must take Bonhoeffer at his word that there is no method. There are only the ultimate, justification, and the penultimate, the way that must be traversed.

In Bonhoeffer's view, the Protestant Church itself is part of the problem, and his criticism applies to the Protestant Church in North America. He speaks of a godlessness in religious and Christian clothing (103). He even prefers an anti-religious godlessness. He is critical of the Protestant Church in Anglo-Saxon countries, particularly in North America. He suggests that we New World enthusiasts have failed to distinguish between the mandates of government and church. In North America, the claim of the congregation and the faithful to build the world with Christian principles ends only with a total capitulation of the Protestant Church to the world (105). Bonhoeffer was deeply mistrustful of this enthusiastic dimension of North American Protestant Christianity, and I believe that we must attend to him in this. The church must learn first to be church. It cannot be government. The prerequisite of the Protestant Church's quest for justice is the integrity of the church, an integrity that is very much in question.

A concluding thought: despite its weaknesses, the North American church offers to the West an opportunity. In the *Ethics* lie the beginnings of an authentic Christian-Jewish dialogue. Recently, Eberhard Bethge has fruitfully developed a fragmentary suggestion from the *Ethics* that the Jews hold open the question of Christ.[28] As part of the Protestant Church's proclamation of justice, discourse with the Jewish community is fundamental. Here, North America has a special opportunity and responsibility. Krister Stendahl has observed that "The United States of today is the first place in the modern world since Philo's Alexandria where Jews and Christians as people, as religious communities, and as learned communities, live together in a manner and sufficient numbers to allow for open dialogue."[29] When Protestants engage in such open dialogue with the Jewish community, with Roman Catholics, and with other religious communities, that discourse, as dialogue, becomes of itself a kind of public proclamation. It becomes proclamation in a way that our North American secular order cannot otherwise acknowledge. In such dialogue the Protestant Church in North America can begin to find a collective proclamation of justice. Perhaps it may find renewal as well.

Notes

[1] An earlier version of this paper was published in *On The Way: Occasional Papers of the Wisconsin Conference of the United Church of Christ* 9 (1992). It subsequently appeared in German as "Gerechtigkeit, Rechtfertigung und Verantwortung in Dietrich Bonhoeffers "Ethik," *Berliner Theologische Zeitschrift* 12 (1995), 119. Versions of this paper were also delivered at conferences at Lakeland College in Wisconsin and Haus Ortlohn, Pastoralkolleg Der Evangelischen Kirche Von Westfalen in Iserlohn, Germany. Without the gracious help and encouragement of Rev. Dr. Frederick R. Trost, Leonard V. Kaplan, and Dr. Hans Berthold, this paper would not have come into being. I also want to acknowledge the patient, gracious advice and active assistance provided by Dr. Ilse Tödt, who translated an earlier version of the manuscript into German, and Professor Christof Gestrich, editor of the *Berliner Theologische Zeitschrift*. I deeply appreciate the kindness of this diverse scholarly community in giving support to my work.

[2] Quoted in Hans Fricke-Hein, "Dietrich Bonhoeffer: His Significance for Today," *On The Way: Occasional Papers of The Wisconsin Conference of the United Church of Christ* 12 (Winter 1995-96), 23, 26.

[3] Dietrich Bonhoeffer, *Ethics*, ed. Eberhard Bethge, trans. Neville Horton Smith (New York: Macmillan, 1965), preface, 7. All references in the text to the *Ethics* are to this edition, a translation from the 1949 German edition, with the order of sections based on the sixth German edition of 1963. We now have a new seventh German edition, Dietrich Bonhoeffer, *Ethik*, ed. Ilse Tödt, Heinz Eduard Tödt, Ernst Feil, and Clifford Green (Munich: Chr. Kaiser Verlag, 1992). This edition from the *Ethics* has yet to be translated into English. Significantly, it omits the section on State and Church, among others. These sections are projected to be published in a separate volume. Nonetheless, state and Church being two of the mandates this and other sections concerning state and Church would appear to be important supplements to the *Ethics* if not part of the *Ethics*. For a discussion of the text, see Clifford J. Green, "The text of Bonhoeffer's *Ethics*," Robin W. Lovin, "Biographical Context," and Larry L. Rasmussen, "A Question of Method," *New Studies in Bonhoeffer's Ethics,* ed. William J. Peck, Bonhoeffer Series 3 (Lewiston: Edward Mellen Press, 1987), 3, 67 and 103.

[4] Bethge has an eloquent chapter on Bonhoeffer's failure to justify himself. See Eberhard Bethge, *Bonhoeffer: Exile and Martyr*, ed. John W. DeGruchy (New York: Seabury Press, 1975), 133-6.

[5] For a discussion of this theme in connection with the *Ethics*, see Eberhard Bethge, "Christology and the First Commandment," *Holocaust and Genocide Studies* 4 (1989), 261-72.

[6] As a preliminary matter I must acknowledge two books by Larry L. Rasmussen to which I am indebted but with which I take issue: *Dietrich Bonhoeffer: Reality and Resistance* (Nashville: Abingdon Press, 1972) and *Dietrich Bonhoeffer—His Significance for North Americans* (Minneapolis: Fortress Press, 1990). I see these texts as a backdrop for my own argument.

[7] For a discussion of Bonhoeffer's student experience at Union, including a description of the curriculum, see Eberhard Bethge, *Dietrich Bonhoeffer: Man of Vision, Man of Courage*, trans. Eric Mosbacher, Peter and Betty Ross, Frank Clarke, and William Glen-Doepel (New York: Harper & Row, 1970), 107-24. At Union the young Bonhoeffer, a theologian of justification, encountered liberal social ethics. The encounter was not entirely smooth. In the *Ethics*, Bonhoeffer is particularly critical of Reinhold Niebuhr, one of his professors at Union. Niebuhr is a mere "philosopher of religion" whose distinction between "moral man" and "immoral society" leads to "complete ethical aporia" (191-2). Things have not changed much. A survey of North American scholarship is beyond the scope of this article, but some observations are in order. We face a paradox in Bonhoeffer scholarship. On the one hand, we have the new seventh German edition of Bonhoeffer's works which represents an enormous contribution to our knowledge of Bonhoeffer. Some of these volumes are beginning to appear in English. This edition and the scholarship that accompanies it should initiate a Bonhoeffer renaissance. On the other hand, the theological academy appears to be in the grip of postmodern theory in its various guises, which is to say that it is in the grip of precisely those forces against which Bonhoeffer spoke. Now that Bonhoeffer belongs to the ages, he must suffer the indignities of interpretation. See, for example, Wayne Whitson Floyd, Jr. and Charles Marsh, *Theology and The Practice of Responsibility* (Valley Forge: Trinity Press International, 1994). These essays appeared earlier in *Union Seminary Quarterly* 46.1-4 (1992), and they contain the obligatory sections devoted to "Making Sense of Modernity" and "Postmodern Perspectives." Even a useful text like Charles Marsh, *Reclaiming Dietrich Bonhoeffer* (New York: Oxford University Press, 1994) seriously miscalculates by seeking affinities between Bonhoeffer and Heideggar as well as between Karl Barth and Richard Rorty, the fashionable North American pragmatist. One can find some hope in essays in *Bonhoeffer for a New Day: Theology in a Time of Transition*, ed. John W. DeGruchy (Grand Rapids: Eerdmans, 1997), which includes a selection from the Seventh International Bonhoeffer Congress held in Cape Town in 1996.

[8] Bonhoeffer's treatment of Kant merits further, systematic study. The following from the *Ethics* is representative: "What worried Him [Christ] was not, like Kant, whether 'the maxim of an action can become a principal of general legislation,' but whether my action is at this moment helping my neighbor to become a man before God" (85). See also Bonhoeffer's *Act and Being: Transcendental Philosophy and Ontology in Systematic Theology*, Dietrich Bonhoeffer Works, vol. 2, trans. H. Martin Rumscheidt, ed. Hans-Richard Reuter (Minneapolis: Fortress Press, 1996), For an important discussion of Kant's theological significance, see Karl Barth, *Protestant Theology in the 19th Century: Its Background and History*, trans. Brian Cozens, John Bownden and the editorial staff of SCM Press (London: SCM Press, 1972), 266-312. The issue of modern Protestant Pelagianism is more involved than I can treat here, but I want to make two points. First, the Enlightenment is not solely to blame. Arminius precedes Kant by over a century. Second, Enlightenment philosophers, including Kant, struggled with the relationship between free will and causal determinism. However, this debate is entirely alien to Reformation teaching about justification.

[9] For an illuminating account of the struggle of British and North American Protestantism with positivism, see Charles D. Chashdollar, *The Transformation of Theology, 1830-1890: Positivism and Protestant Thought in Britain and America* (Princeton: Princeton University Press, 1989).

[10] Bonhoeffer's realism carries theological qualifications. What precedes knowledge is a divine command. Knowledge of Christ for Bonhoeffer negates other knowledge through obedience. Scripture for Bonhoeffer emphasizes *doing* as a negation of a person's self-justification. This scriptural concept of doing Bonhoeffer finds in the *Epistle of James* which he rehabilitates for Lutheran theology as an analogue to Jesus' response to the Pharisees (43-8). For Bonhoeffer, it is on this ground, the ground of doing in justification and not of knowing, that a Christian *Ethics* finds its basis. Jesus' exhortation that we should judge not that we be not judged in Matthew 7:1 is "not an exhortation to prudence and forbearance in passing judgment on one's fellow-men, such as was also recognized by the Pharisees. It is a blow struck at the heart of the man who knows good and evil" (30).

[11] Bonhoeffer was aware of the principle of limitation by separation of powers in the constitution of the United States. He saw this as an acknowledgement of "the limitation of all earthly powers by the sovereignty of God" (104).

[12] For scholars who criticize Bonhoeffer's political authoritarianism, see Peter Berger, "Sociology and Ecclesiology," *The Place of Bonhoeffer: Problems and Possibilities in His Thought*, ed. Martin E. Marty (New York: Association Press, 1962), 53-79 and Ruth Zerner, "Dietrich Bonhoeffer's Views on the State and History," *A Bonhoeffer Legacy: Essays in Understanding*, ed. A. J. Klassen, Grand Rapids: Eerdmans, 1981), 131-57.

[13] The incoherence of liberal political theory is an issue now with a broad literature. See, for example, Roberto Unger, *Knowledge and Politics* (New York: Free Press 1975; rpt 1984); Robert Paul Wolff, *The Poverty of Liberalism* (Boston: Beacon Press, 1968); and Thomas A. Spargens, Jr., *The Irony of Liberal Reason* (Chicago: University of Chicago Press, 1981).

[14] Bonhoeffer's German contains nuances that may not be fully captured in English translation. I only raise the issue here without pretensions to systematic analysis. Where the English translation speaks of "justice," Bonhoeffer uses the terms *Gerechtigkeit* and *Recht*. *Recht* has connotations of law as opposed to fairness or equity. Where the English edition uses the term "law," Bonhoeffer uses the term *Gesetz*, which, at times explicitly for Bonhoeffer, suggests the Pauline *nomos* as opposed to Gospel. Where the English edition uses the term "commandment," which for Bonhoeffer entails law (285), Bonhoeffer uses the term *Gebot*.

[15] *Summa Theologica* I-II Q. 58 Art. 2. All references to St. Thomas Aquinas in my essay are to the English edition translated by the fathers of the English Dominican Province (Westminster: Christian Classics, 1981) in 5 volumes.

[16] I suggest that Bonhoeffer's *Ethics*, itself a kind of Lutheran *Beyond Good and Evil*, rehabilitates Nietzsche for the Protestant tradition to this extent: Nietzsche perceived and spoke to the nihilism implicit in the Enlightenment arrangement.

[17] For a discussion of the Barmen Declaration of 1934 (and the Declaration itself) see Arthur C. Cochrane, *The Church's Confession Under Hitler* (Pittsburgh: Pickwick Press, 1962; rpt. 1976), On the use of 2 Thessalonians 2:7 by Jerome and Tertullian, see Jaroslav Pelikan, *The Excellent Empire: The Fall of Rome and the Triumph of the Church* (San Francisco: Harper & Row, 1987), 46-7.

[18] See Arthur C. Cochrane, "The Theology of Barmen," *The Church's Confession Under Hitler*, appendix xi, 284. For Luther's view of the two kingdoms, of which Bonhoeffer's doctrine of mandates is a modification, see W. D. J. Cargill Thompson, "The 'Two Kingdoms' and the 'Two Regiments': Some Problems of Luther's *Zwei-Reiche Lehre*," *Studies in the Reformation: Luther to Hooker*, ed. C. W. Dugmore (London: Athlone Press, 1980), 42-59. See also Hans Pfeifer, "Ethics for the Renewal of Life: A Reconstruction of Its Concept," *Bonhoeffer for a New Day*, 137.

[19] See footnote 3. I am aware of discussions that ground Bonhoeffer's resistance in his doctrine of responsibility. See, for example, Larry Rasmussen, *Dietrich Bonhoeffer: Reality and Resistance*. Recently, Jean Bethke Elshtain of the University of Chicago has written: "Bonhoeffer could never have made his peace with *any* regime (1) that promoted rabid nationalism with all its bitter fruits; (2) that eclipsed the space for the free exercise of human responsibility, for in a "world come of age" human beings are called to account; it follows that a system that leads us to surrender our identity to what Havel calls the "social-autotality" is an order whose claims on us are seriously compromised; (3) that served the ends of cynicism, collusion in evil deeds, human isolation, human desolation, and terror by contrast to trust, solidarity, and responsible freedom; (4) that worshipped history and power and accepted no brake by definition on its sovereign designs. Such a regime repudiates the sovereign God who holds the nations under judgment." "Caesar, Sovereignty, and Bonhoeffer," *Bonhoeffer for a New Day*, 223, 233-4. To the extent this passage is coherent, it is clearly wrong: it seriously misrepresents issues about which Bonhoeffer is perfectly clear in the *Ethics*.

[20] Concerning resistance theory, see W. D. J. Cargill Thompson, "Luther and the Right of Resistance to the Emperor," *Studies in the Reformation*, 3-41; and Myriam Yardeni, "French Calvinist Political Thought, 1534-1715," *International Calvinism (1541-1715)*, ed. Menna Prestwich (Oxford: Clarendon Press, 1985). See the discussion of resistance theory in John W. DeGruchy, *Bonhoeffer and South Africa: Theology in Dialogue* (Grand Rapids: Eerdmans, 1984), 91-122.

[21] In his criticism of Dilschneider's thesis Bonhoeffer writes: "It is precisely in the dispensation of strict justice and in the administration of the office of the sword, in maintaining the unmerciful character of the institutions of the state, that is to say their genuine worldliness, that the dominion of Christ, *i.e.*, the rule of mercy, is given its due" (328).

[22] In particular, Bonhoeffer cites the following: "She claims protection for the public Christian proclamation against violence and blasphemy; she claims protection for the institution of the Church against arbitrary interference, and she claims the protection for Christian life and obedience to Jesus Christ. The Church can never abandon these claims; and she must make them heard publicly so long as government itself maintains its claim to acknowledge the Church" (347-8).

[23] On the historical context of Bonhoeffer's discussion of the natural, see William J. Peck, "The Euthanasia Text," *New Studies in Bonhoeffer's Ethics*, 141. On Barth and the larger theological context, see Emil Brunner, *Natural Theology: Comprising "Nature and Grace" by Professor Dr. Emil Brunner and the Reply "No!" by Dr. Karl Barth*, trans. Peter Fraenkel (London: Centenary, 1946). Arthur Cochrane suggests that Brunner's tract in this famous debate amounted to a denial of the first thesis of the Barmen Declaration: "Barth was angered with Brunner because he had afforded comfort to the enemy at the very time the Church was fighting for its life" Cochrane, (72).

[24] See Eberhard Jungel, *Karl Barth: A Theological Legacy*, trans. Garrett E. Paul (Philadelphia: Westminster Press, 1986), 105-26.

[25] The point regarding the imitation of Christ is made by Larry Rasmussen, *Dietrich Bonhoeffer: Reality and Resistance*, 52. See Bonhoeffer, *Act and Being,* 138 ff.

[26] The roots of this view of conscience are to be found as early as *Act and Being* (177 ff.).

[27] I owe this insight to my friend and colleague, Professor Leonard V. Kaplan of the University of Wisconsin Law School.

[28] See Eberhard Bethge, "Christology and the First Commandment," *Holocaust and Genocide Studies* 4 (1989), 261-72. Bethge develops what he takes to be Bonhoeffer's thinking in the following passage: "Western history is, by God's will, indissolubly linked with the people of Israel, not only genetically but also in genuine uninterrupted encounter. The Jew keeps open the question of Christ" (89).

[29] Krister Stendahl, *Paul Among Jews and Gentiles and Other Essasys* (Philadelphia: Fortress Press, 1976; 1983), 37.

Reconciling with Injustice

Robert A. Burt[1]

There are two starkly opposed styles of responding to injustice. I will call one, somewhat tendentiously, the reconciliation model and the other, the elimination model. These are ideal types. It is not always possible either to eliminate injustice or to find reconciliation where injustice has occurred. But even if neither is attainable in practice, different consequences follow from choosing to pursue one rather than the other ideal. In the spirit of reconciliation, one might say that we should aim for both—elimination where possible, reconciliation where possible. But in the way I am invoking these two models, this is not possible. The two models are fundamentally inconsistent with one another; if you pursue one, you are disabled from pursuing the other. The inconsistency is this: where injustice has occurred, the elimination model rests on a premise either that there will be no future relationship between the wrongdoer and the victim or, if there is any future relationship, it will be based on a visible and permanent power differential between the victim and the wrongdoer. The reconciliation model rests on the opposite premise: that its goal is the restoration of an equal relationship between victim and wrongdoer.

The clearest expression of the severed relationship in the elimination model is the imposition of the death penalty on the wrongdoer. But imprisonment can also express this same implication of a permanent breach of relationship—not just life imprisonment without possibility of parole but imprisonment followed by a life-long regime of shunning and shame. The recently enacted so-called Megan's Laws for sexual predators rest on this premise: even after the aggressor's prison term has expired, he must register with the police wherever he lives and his neighbors will be informed of his past transgressions so that they may stay away from him and protect themselves and their children against him.[2] Megan's Laws illustrate another implication of this remedial perspective: that it is not only the victim who abandons any future relationship with the wrongdoer; the entire society extrudes the wrongdoer as an act of solidarity with the original victim.

Alternatively, the elimination model can rest on a premise that the only continuing relationship between victim and wrongdoer is based on a clear power differential between them—one might say, a reversal of the wrongful domination that the aggressor originally imposed on the victim, but now the victim (and the entire society on the victim's behalf) exercises controlling power over the wrongdoer. With a measure such as life imprisonment, or Megan's laws, this domination is permanent. We can glimpse the underlying impulse for the permanence of the elimination model in the Thirteenth Amendment to the U.S. Constitution. This was the Amendment that abolished slavery, but there was a significant exception to this abolition written into the text of the Thirteen Amendment, an exception that most people don't recall. The text reads as follows: "Neither slavery nor involuntary servitude shall exist within the United States, except as a punishment for crime whereof the party shall have been duly convicted." As the sociologist Orlando Patterson has observed, slavery is a species of social death, a kind of death while remaining alive.[3] It is striking then that the central abolitionist text in our culture retains the category of social death for those convicted of crimes. And it is not incidental that the way that this abolitionist text, the Thirteenth Amendment, came to be enshrined in our Constitution was through the medium of a civil war in which the underlying implication was that those people who had violated human rights, who had been slaveowners, deserved to die as a remedial consequence.

Invoking our Civil War and the American experience with abolishing slavery brings us to the second perspective on injustice, the question of reconciling with as opposed to eliminating injustice. Our Civil War demonstrates another way in which these two perspectives can be in opposition to one another. The terrible fact is that by 1876—just twelve years after the conclusion of the Civil War—Northern whites decided that it was more important to become reconciled with their Southern white brothers and sisters than to persist in protecting Southern blacks against re-imposition of their former enslaved status.[4] Twenty-five years later, when Jim Crow laws, involuntary peonage practices, and exclusion from political participation had been imposed on Southern blacks, it was clear that these former slaves were, if anything, more desperately vulnerable and oppressed than before abolition (when, at the least, they could depend on their white owners to value their physical lives and protect them against vigilante-style lynchings or other murderous assaults).[5]

I would not call this a genuine form of reconciliation with injustice, since it is clear that the wrongdoers and their victims were not reconciled. Instead, the broader society, which for a brief time had identified with and protected the victims, now had abandoned these victims and had become reconciled with the wrongdoers—thus not only leaving the victims both unreconciled and without remedy but even inflicting added injury on them. This is a common complaint made by victims of injustice in our own time. Those who speak on behalf of the victims of the massacres in the former Yugoslavia, for example, are understandably fearful that the wrongdoers will not be held accountable but will be accepted, if not welcomed, by the international community because of their brute power to foment new disruptions. Whether the U.N. International Tribunal currently convened at the Hague will stand firm against this impetus for false reconciliation, this abandonment of victims, remains to be seen.

Many victims of injustice contend, however, that any kind of reconciliation with their victimizing wrongdoers is itself an added injury, is itself an abandonment. These victims and those who identify with them reject the possibility of any reconciliation between them and their aggressors and by extension between the broader society and their aggressors. This is, I believe, the increasingly dominant response to the problem of injustice in our contemporary world—the position that the only conceivable remedy for injustice must be built on the premise either of no future social relations with wrongdoers or, at most, of a relationship based on the permanent future domination of past wrongdoers.

This position receives considerable impetus and salience in our time from the terrible example of the Nazi Holocaust. This was an infliction of evil almost unimaginable in its enormity, and it was correspondingly almost unimaginable that any kind of reconciliation— any kind of continuing or renewed relationship—might be justified between the perpetrators and their surviving victims or with a broader society of decent people. Nonetheless, after a brief post-War interlude of criminal prosecutions against a small number of highly visible Nazi officials, the international community backed away from the enterprise, the Western nations led by the United States ostentatiously reconciled with their new democratic German ally as the Soviet-dominated Eastern nations embraced their new German ally. And the surviving victims of the Holocaust became invisible—often even to themselves.

We are today in the midst of a virtual explosion of the renewed visibility of the Holocaust victims. With this renewed visibility—which in my judgment was long overdue in its own terms—has come a larger social claim that draws on the example of the Holocaust for its emotional and rhetorical force. The larger claim is that any form of reconciliation between wrongdoers and victims, or between "decent society" and wrongdoers, is itself wrongful, is an abandonment of the victims and an infliction of new injuries. I don't mean to trivialize this claim by overstatement. No one would make this claim without qualification, in this stark overstated way I have framed it. Proponents of this position would distinguish between serious and less serious wrongdoers, between purposefully evil inflictions and forgivable inflictions. But there is nonetheless an expansive impetus in the currently perceived categories of "serious" and "purposefully evil" wrongdoing that must be acknowledged, and that is why I have framed this position in this seemingly overstated way.

One clear instance of this stark, virtually complete rejection of the possibility of reconciliation is in the American domestic politics of crime control: the vast surge of support for the death penalty—from 1966 when, accordingly to opinion polls, more people opposed than favored capital punishment (47% opposed, 42% in favor, 11% undecided) to today (when almost 80% of Americans support it)[6]; the political popularity of "three strikes and you're out" laws; the huge expansion of our prison population, which is now on a per capita basis the largest in the world; and so on. The most telling instance of this trend is the new force behind the victims' rights movement, most recently epitomized by President Clinton's endorsement of a constitutional amendment to protect the rights of crime victims.[7] The usual argument for a constitutional amendment is to protect some vulnerable minority against future depredations from a hostile majority. This was the underlying justification for the entire Bill of Rights, as well as for the Civil War amendments abolishing slavery and protecting against future slave status. From this perspective, it might seem almost incredible to assert that crime victims need protection against a future hostile majority. But this is indeed an increasingly dominant sentiment in this country. We should not discount Bill Clinton's exquisitely tuned political sensitivities, his capacity to "feel ordinary people's pain" in endorsing this proposed constitutional amendment.

There is a widespread belief among crime victims and those who identify with them that the broader society has been too quick to become reconciled with the "criminal element," too quick to abandon victims—and that this, in particular, was the sinfulness of the 1960s-style "bleeding heart liberalism." I believe that the new visibility of Holocaust victims in America during the past fifteen years or so is, to a significant degree, a reflection of this widespread sense of victimization and abandonment in American society generally. I don't say this critically. I don't mean to diminish the injustice that was inflicted on Holocaust survivors by their social invisibility after World War II. And I don't mean to dismiss the legitimacy of grievances that large numbers of Americans now feel, grievances that lead them either to empathize in unaccustomed ways with Holocaust survivors or, like many African-Americans, to claim not just analogies between the Holocaust and their survivors but even to belittle the Nazi Holocaust by comparison. I want to approach this widespread sense of victimization sympathetically, not to recoil from it or condemn it out of hand. I want to understand it in its own terms, because I believe that this widespread sense is the impulse behind the dominant contemporary conviction in this country at least that reconciliation with injustice is neither possible nor desirable.

The watchword of, and on behalf of, Holocaust victims has become "never forget." In light of the enormity of the evil inflicted in the Holocaust, it is understandable that this credo of "never forget" has been extended to the proposition, "and never forgive." But it is also striking, and on its face not so easy to understand, that this conjunctive prescription—never forget and never forgive—has assumed such powerful force in contemporary American society. There are other countries today where this conjunction is being resisted. Contemporary South Africa is the most stunning example. This resistance is epitomized in the very name of the tribunal that the new black-majority South African government has established to deal with the terrible past injustices inflicted on black victims by the previous white-minority government. The tribunal is called the Commission on Truth and Reconciliation, which makes explicit the proposition that truth-telling about past evils (obeying the injunction "never forget") does not require "never forgive" as a corollary. Indeed, the basic underlying premise of the Commission's work is that insisting on remembrance is not only a possible but a necessary precondition for reconciliation.

But this South African endeavor—this experiment, if I may call it that—has not yet demonstrably succeeded. Already there has been much controversy about the abundant bestowals of amnesty by the Commission, of grants of immunity from criminal or civil punishment for wrongdoers in exchange for their willingness to admit, to publicly speak the truth about their transgressions.[8] The South African Commission is working against the background of recent similar efforts in Latin American countries, such as Argentina and Chile, which tried to strike some middle ground between punishing past transgressors and finding a way that the surviving victims and their aggressors could do more than come to a momentary truce in their persistent hostilities. The Chilean tribunal convened for this purpose by the newly restored democratic government was also called a Commission on Truth and Reconciliation. Amnesties for broad categories of wrongdoers was an important constituent element in the Chilean and Argentine endeavors.[9] In Eastern European countries just emerged from Communist dictatorships, similar admixtures of limited prosecutions, broad-brush amnesties and efforts at public truth-telling were also tried.[10] But it seems to many people that the newly constituted social arrangements in Latin America and Eastern Europe are based more on the dogma "forgive and forget" than on the more demanding injunction "remember but forgive" that South Africa, at least for the moment, is trying to accomplish.

The United States is not alone in struggling with this question. And, when we consider the contemporary urgency of this question in other countries or the almost overwhelming dimensions of destructive evil inflicted in the Nazi Holocaust, it is not clear why the sense of victimization and an accompanying rigidly unforgiving posture toward wrongdoers should be so strong in the United States today. But it has by now become, if I may resort to this overused phrase, clearly a part of our American *zeitgeist*. How, then, should we think about this issue? How should we evaluate the claims for remembering but forgiving, for reconciling with injustice?

Let me begin by posing this question methodologically rather than substantively. I will not ask, at the moment, what the correct answer is when choosing between the elimination and reconciliation models, but instead how we go about finding the proper substantive answer, and what sources of moral authority we consult to find our way toward an adequate resolution. Not so long ago the answer to this methodological question would have been obvious. The answer would have been to begin with biblical text. Invoking the Bible still has great salience in popular culture; we need only surf through the cable channels of television evangelism to recognize that citation of the Bible is accepted as self-evident authority without apparent question by many, perhaps even by most, people in our country today. But this is certainly not true, to use a somewhat discredited but nonetheless evocative phrase, in "high culture" such as academic intellectual circles.

Nonetheless, in the academic intellectual circle represented at least by the readers of this collection of essays, I want to rely on biblical text. To answer the question I have posed about choosing between the reconciliation and elimination models of responding to injustice, I propose to ask: what does the Bible tell us about the merits and demerits of reconciling with versus eliminating injustice? But this, in itself, is not a sufficient way of asking the question. There are two methodologically different ways of consulting biblical text. One is to see the Bible as a source of commandments, of abstract rules which must be obeyed. From this perspective, my task might seem simple: find a rule and apply it. If I relied on the Christian Bible, the relevant rule might seem to fall like an apple from the tree: "love your enemy as yourself and forgive your enemies"—and so we have our apparent answer, the text tells us that we must forgive those who trespass against us.

But there is another way to read the Bible—a richer and I think truer, or at least truer to life, way of reading. The Bible, after all, is not simply a list of abstract commandments. There are such lists that appear at various places in the text: the Ten Commandments from Mount Sinai, the Sermon on the Mount. But these various commandments are embedded in a rich, complicated narrative of the lives of people and their experiences in obeying, disobeying and struggling with these commandments. And it is also a rich narrative of the ways that God and His prophets—the recognized source of authority for these commandments—respond to obedience, disobedience and struggle among flesh-and-blood people. These narratives frame the abstract commandments, bring them into life, and serve as an implicit commentary on the commandments. This is the way that I propose to read the Bible to glean moral guidance about how we should approach those who commit injustice. I want to begin with the Hebrew Bible (the Tanakh, composed of the Torah, the Nevi'im (the prophetic writings), and the Kethuvim—what the Christian Bible calls the Old Testament), though my discussion will ultimately lead me to the Christian Bible and specifically to the parable of the prodigal son which is the most evocative narrative in the New Testament about reconciliation and injustice.[11]

I want to begin, however, with a narrative that seems to point emphatically in the opposite direction from the prodigal son parable and indeed from the entire thrust of Jesus' message about forgiveness of sinners. My starting-point is the first book of Samuel, which tells of how Saul lost God's mandate to rule as King of Israel. Saul's apparent offense was his failure to kill Agag, the king of the Amaleks. Many generations earlier, when the people of Israel were wandering in the wilderness during their flight from Egypt, the Amaleks attacked them but were soundly defeated by Joshua's forces. God then said to Moses: "Inscribe this in a document as a reminder, and read it aloud to Joshua: I will utterly blot out the memory of Amalek from under heaven!" (Exodus 17:14). Soon after the prophet Samuel had anointed Saul as king of Israel, he told him that God had commanded him to attack Amalek and destroy the tribe entirely, to kill all its "men and women, infants and sucklings, oxen and sheep, camels and asses" (I Samuel 15: 3). The rationale for this command was stunningly retributive, as Samuel reported, "Thus said the LORD of Hosts: I am exacting the penalty for what Amalek did to Israel, for the assault he made upon them on the road, on their way up from Egypt" (I Samuel 15:2). And, of course, the penalty was explicitly eliminative.

Saul did almost everything that was commanded. With a troop of 300,000 men, he slaughtered every man, woman and child among the Amaleks. But he captured Agag, the Amalek king, alive and did not kill him; nor did he or his troops slaughter the "best" of the Amalek's sheep, oxen and lambs. Immediately afterward, God told Samuel that He regretted having made Saul king because "he has turned away from Me and has not carried out My commands" (I Samuel 15:11). Samuel then confronted Saul, and Saul explained by way of justification that his troops had spared "the choicest of the sheep and oxen for sacrificing to the LORD" (I Samuel 15:15). Samuel scornfully dismissed this excuse, and Saul admitted that he had been wrong to disobey the Lord's command but now added, "I was afraid of the troops and I yielded to them" (I Samuel 15:24). But Samuel was adamant: "The Lord," he said to Saul, "has this day torn the kingship over Israel away from you" (I Samuel 15:29).

I begin with this episode because it is one of the strongest expressions of an unforgiving, elimination response to wrongdoing in the biblical text, both in God's attitude toward the Amaleks—whose sinful act was, after all, committed several generations earlier—and toward Saul for disobeying a specific injunction directed at him. I begin here too because this text is regularly invoked by ultra-right forces in Israel today to justify their relentless hostility toward the Palestinian Arabs who are, they claim, the modern embodiments of the Amaleks. I am quite sure that Yigal Amir, the assassin of Yitzhak Rabin, saw himself as doing battle against a modern-day Saul, a king of Israel who had disobeyed God's commandment to destroy the Amaleks.

To put it mildly, I do not agree with Yigal Amir's actions and the ultra-right's position or with this reading of the biblical text. This gives me two options. I can reject his actions and reject the text; or I can struggle with the text to take it away from Yigal Amir. Some might say that I have more options than this. For one, I might concede this text to Amir but point to other places in the Bible where there are clearly contradictory directives. But if I do this, then I am left with a problem: if some biblical texts speak of forgiveness and others demand nothing but punitive elimination for injustice, on what basis do we choose between them?

Let me list some possibilities, though I reject them. One possibility is what I will call the literalist Christian alternative: we might say that the Hebrew Bible gives conflicting instructions but this conflict is resolved in the New Testament in favor of forgiveness. I don't mind the substantive conclusion, but I do reject this way of getting there—and I should say, I reject this not only because I am a Jew. I reject it because I view the Christian gospel of forgiveness as quite complex, and the prodigal son parable specifically as consistent with the story of Saul and Amaleks, in all of its complexity. But I am getting ahead of the story here; and I have much to do before I get to the prodigal son.

Then there is another possibility—the rigorously secular possibility of turning away from biblical texts altogether. I may of course be following this course without acknowledgment. Where, after all, do I claim to find the source for my discomfort with the simple and obvious reading of the first book of Samuel, that God commands eternal warfare against and the complete destruction of the enemies of righteousness, be they the Amaleks who attacked His people, Israel, or Saul who disobeyed His commandment? Why do I struggle with this obvious meaning of the text? There may be extrinsic moral tenets that are guiding me in my discomfort. But I believe that close engagement with the details of the narrative, the kind of close engagement that each of us is drawn into in the rich texture of our social interactions with one another, reveals a complexity and even a purposeful subversion of the apparently obvious meaning that the literalist reading of this episode bleaches away. I may be driven by extrinsic considerations to find complexity beneath the apparently obvious meaning of this text, but I believe that the vision of those who see nothing beyond the surface of this text are at least equally blinkered by textually extrinsic forces.

There are two oddities in this narrative of Saul and the Amaleks that appear to me to be in some tension with its apparent endorsement of the elimination model. The first is the fact that Saul never attempts to justify his failure to kill King Agag. All of his justifications are directed at sparing the animals, and here Saul tries to shift blame away from himself to his troops—and he even claims to have been afraid of them. This is a weak and unworthy performance, I would say, by a king of Israel, much less by anyone who had disobeyed a clear divine commandment. Beyond this, there is a second and even more powerful oddity, a disturbing element, in the narrative. After Samuel rejects Saul's weak excuses about the animals, he turns to the disposition of Agag. Here is the entire text:

> Samuel said, "Bring forward to me King Agag of Amalek." Agag approached him with faltering steps; and Agag said, "Ah, bitter death is at hand!" Samuel said: "As your sword has bereaved women, So shall your mother be bereaved among women." And Samuel cut Agag down before the LORD at Gilgal.
>
> Samuel then departed for Ramah, and Saul went up to his home at Gibeah of Saul.
>
> Samuel never saw Saul again to the day of his death. But Samuel grieved over Saul, because the LORD regretted that He had made Saul king over Israel. (Samuel 15:32-5)

Reading this detailed narrative, I find it difficult to avoid feeling sorry for Agag, for Samuel, and for Saul—feeling sorry, that is, for the perpetrators of injustice and for the judge obliged to punish those perpetrators. My feelings were prompted by the emotional resonance of this narrative—by hearing Agag's last words, by learning of his faltering steps and his agonized recognition that "bitter death" was at hand for him, and by knowing that the last words Agag heard were about his mother and her bereavement. The text might have omitted these details; the narrator might have had Samuel kill Agag with swift economy.

It may be, of course, that this extended narrative was meant to prolong our awareness of Agag's agony so that he might suffer visibly and we might take pleasure in this and in his mother's grief. I can't definitively rule out this intensely retributive reading. But I do find it striking that the biblical text does at least imply—and I would say that it even directly conveys—that Samuel did not take pleasure in his execution of God's directive against Agag. It is not that Samuel felt pity for Agag—but it does seem clear that in killing Agag, he grieved for Saul. There is, moreover, at least a suggestive parallel in the text's portrayal of parental loss and grief. Samuel tells Agag that his mother will never see him again, kills him, and then—so we are immediately told—Samuel and Saul are separated, Samuel never sees him again alive, and Samuel mourns for him. The text could have offered a different parallel. Just as Agag had sinned against God and His people and deserved his harsh fate, so too Saul had disobeyed God's will and deserved his punishment; Samuel could have been content, if not joyful, in implementing God's will. But the only account of Samuel's mood offered by the text is grief: as his sword makes Agag's mother childless and bereaved, so too this execution ends Samuel's relationship with Saul and Samuel mourns.

The biblical text then continues: "And the LORD said to Samuel, 'How long will you grieve over Saul, since I have rejected him as king over Israel? Fill your horn with oil and set out'" (1 Samuel 16:1). Samuel did not disobey God's command as Saul had done, but he implemented this will with reluctance enough to attract God's notice and apparent annoyance. This passage, moreover, recalls that Samuel had not been happy with God's directive against Saul from its inception. At chapter 15, verse 11, God had told Samuel that He regretted Saul's anointment because of Saul's failure to kill Agag and all the Amalek livestock, and "Samuel was distressed and he entreated the LORD all night long." We don't know what Samuel said in this extended plea; we know only that it made no difference.

What might Samuel have said to God on Saul's behalf in that night-long pleading? The encounter is reminiscent of Abraham's appeal to justice and the imperative of saving innocent lives in response to God's revelation of His planned destruction of Sodom and Gomorrah

(Genesis 18:17-33). In the spirit of *Midrash*, we might imagine that Samuel considered the possibility of adapting Abraham's plea, perhaps claiming that Saul had spared Agag so as not to "sweep away the innocent along with the guilty" on the ground that Agag himself had not been party to the wrongs committed by his ancestors; or Samuel might simply have asked God to withhold judgment, as He had done by sending His angels to Sodom, to give Saul an opportunity to offer some mitigating explanation.

But there is good reason to think, as Samuel would have known, that these pleas would not have been convincing in Saul's case. The reason is that Saul had disabled himself from advancing any justification for disobeying the strictest letter of God's command. In an episode that is recounted immediately before Saul's disobedience regarding the slaughter of the Amaleks, Saul was prepared to kill his son Jonathan as punishment for violating his command against eating before battle. Jonathan was wholly innocent in this action since, as the biblical text pointedly observes, he "had not heard his father adjure the troops" (1 Samuel 14:27). But Saul was unbending in his insistence on strict liability; and, moreover, Saul showed no reluctance, no sign of internal struggle, about his impending execution of his own son. Indeed, when it was first apparent that someone had violated his command, Saul announced that the violator must be identified: "For as the LORD lives who brings victory to Israel, even if it was through my son Jonathan, he shall be put to death" (1 Samuel 14:39).

Jonathan was saved only because of a popular uprising on his behalf; after protesting, the "troops saved Jonathan and he did not die" (1 Samuel 14:45)—apparently by substituting an animal sacrifice for him. There is an echo here of the *Akidah* of Abraham and Isaac, but with stunning variations. In both cases, a father's execution of his innocent son is narrowly averted through the substitution of a sacrificial animal, but unlike Abraham, who stood ready to sacrifice Isaac because God had commanded it, Saul himself had ordered Jonathan's execution in order to enforce rigid adherence to his own overall authority. And whereas God was prepared to rescind his order, to hold back from demanding the last full measure of obedience from Abraham by Himself providing the substitute for sacrifice, Saul remained apparently unbending, apparently unmoved by any tension between the imperative of vindicating his authority and preserving his paternal relations with the putative wrongdoer.

Because this episode immediately precedes God's command that Saul slaughter all the Amaleks in strict retribution for their ancestors' wrongdoing, it offers a framing context that suggests something more, and even something different, than the conventional reading that God's command constitutes a flat endorsement of what I have called the elimination model for responding to injustice. This preceding episode makes clear that Saul followed this model in the exercise of his own authority: no excuses can mitigate wrongdoing, no personal bonds, no empathy with wrongdoers can inspire mercy or forgiveness. God's harsh judgment against the Amaleks exhibits these same traits, to be sure. But God's command to implement His judgment in this context, in immediate response to Saul's prior conduct, appears less an endorsement of retributive justice than as a test of Saul's willingness to subordinate his own judgment to God's will, as a test of the true significance of Saul's own personal willfulness and demand for absolute obedience from others. If this was God's test, Saul failed it miserably. He did not give God the unquestioning obedience that he demanded from his own son. Saul was accordingly disabled from offering any excuses on his own behalf—as demonstrated by the obviously insufficient, even pathetic excuses he did in fact offer—and Samuel could not provide any convincing mitigating circumstances for him.

This self-centered willfulness, this vindictiveness in response to personal injury, was even more evident in Saul's behavior after he definitively learned from Samuel that God had taken the kingship away from him. Rather than yielding to this clear judgment, he fought bitterly to retain his authority. Samuel himself understood this element in Saul's character; in response to God's impatient command that Samuel should stop grieving for Saul and go anoint someone else, Samuel responded, "How can I go? If Saul hears it, he will kill me" (1 Samuel 16:2). Saul's defensive vindictiveness is, of course, most clearly revealed in his repeated murderous attacks on David, in whom he glimpsed God's favor. His vengefulness, moreover, eclipsed all of his loving feelings toward David—an even more vivid demonstration of his inability or unwillingness to acknowledge empathic connections as a constraint on his self-absorbed and self-protective anger. In the initial episode of Saul's unbending retributionism toward Jonathan, we might say that God saw elements in Saul that raised doubts about his fitness as king, about his willfulness and self-absorption; that God tested these qualities in his command to Saul regarding the slaughter of the Amaleks and definitively determined that he had made a mistake in having Saul anointed; and that all of these disqualifying traits became even more visible—to the general public, as it were, or to readers of the biblical narrative—in Saul's subsequent conduct.

God's own vengefulness toward the Amaleks, His willingness to act on the basis of what I have called the elimination model, still remains in this account. But this vengefulness toward wrongdoers is, in the context of this reading, no longer the centerpiece. We do not know whether God might have relented in this harsh punitiveness if, for example, Saul had invoked his own empathic reluctance to kill Agag because he saw the fear in Agag's face and thought of Agag's grieving mother—if, that is, Saul had grasped the hints of empathic connection that the biblical account of Agag's death provides. We do know from the previous episode with Jonathan that this kind of empathic connection is outside Saul's own character; even after sparing Agag, it never occurs to Saul to offer this motive in justification. In this context, we might say that the lesson of Saul and the Amaleks is not endorsement of the elimination model for responding to injustice but rather an illustration of the principle, to jump forward to its explicit articulation in the New Testament, that "all they that take the sword shall perish with the sword" (Matthew 26:52).

Saul himself is led to an acknowledgment of precisely this principle in the extended events that follow his loss of God's favor. In the immediate aftermath of Saul's disobedience and Samuel's clear statement to him that God had rescinded his kingship, there might have been a more rapid dethronement of Saul than in fact occurred. God does dispatch Samuel immediately to find David and anoint him, and David is, of course, much too young and unseasoned to assume the throne at once. But in subsequent events, David repeatedly proves himself in battle and receives such widespread popular acclaim that he could readily have succeeded Saul long before he does so in fact. Saul, moreover, is hardly passive during these successive events; "Saul," we are told, "was David's enemy ever after" (1 Samuel 18:29). From early in his dealings with David, Saul suspected that this capable and much-loved young man was God's choice as his successor, and he worked relentlessly and repeatedly to kill him—moved to this self-serving vengefulness, the biblical narrative observes, by "an evil spirit of God"(1 Samuel 18:10).

David takes various measures to protect himself against Saul's murderous intent. But David rigorously limits himself to self-defense; he never takes retaliatory action. On two specific occasions, Saul is helplessly subject to David's power: once he is alone in a cave, relieving himself against a wall and not knowing that David is standing behind him (1 Samuel 24); on a second occasion, he and his entourage are asleep in an encampment as David and his men enter undetected (1 Samuel 26). The narrative repetition of these events—murderous attacks and plottings by Saul, strict forbearance by David—suggests that an edifying contrast is being drawn between the two men, that David's suitability for the kingship is being repeatedly demonstrated in his possession of one capacity clearly lacking in Saul, the capacity to forego vengeful retaliation on his enemies and, even more specifically, on enemies who clearly deserve punishment because they are wrong in injuring him.

David's restraint toward Saul might be explained only as deference toward God's anointed king, since David has not been explicitly told of his divinely sanctioned succession. But in an episode inserted directly between these two encounters with Saul (1 Samuel 25), David responds with similar restraint to an unprovoked and life-threatening offense from Nabal, a "Calebite . . . a hard man and an evildoer" (1 Samuel 25:3). In this case, however—as if to underscore the force of the lesson—David's restraint did not come easily to him. His immediate response to the offense was a command to his men, "Gird on your swords" (1 Samuel 25:13). But Nabal's wife, Abigail, immediately "made haste" to David's camp in order to appease him. She appealed to him in these words:

> Please, my lord, pay no attention to that wretched fellow, Nabal. . . . [W]hen the
> LORD . . . has appointed you ruler of Israel, do not let this be a cause of stumbling

> and of faltering courage to my lord that you have shed blood needlessly and that my lord sought redress with his own hand. (1 Samuel 25:25, 30-1)

David then responded,

> Praised be the LORD, the God of Israel, who sent you this day to meet me! And blessed be your prudence, and blessed be you yourself for restraining me from seeking redress in blood by my own hands. For as sure as the LORD, the God of Israel lives—who has kept me from harming you—had you not come quickly to meet me, not a single male of Nabal's line would have been left by morning. (1 Samuel 25:32-4)

Nabal did not go unpunished. We are immediately told that "about ten days later the LORD struck Nabal and he died" (1 Samuel 25:38). David rejoiced at this: "the LORD championed my cause against the insults of Nabal," but he pointedly observed that "the LORD has brought Nabal's wrongdoing down on his own head" and, at the same time, God "has held back His servant [David] from wrongdoing" (1 Samuel 25:39). It is possible to read this divine intervention as an endorsement of what I have called the elimination model of responding to injustice, with the proviso that this is God's exclusive province as opposed to human beings acting on their own judgment. This reading would, of course, still hold open the possibility that some people would claim the direct authorization of God Himself for carrying out His avenging purposes (what we might call the Yigal Amir reading of this passage).

My own view is that this brief passage noting God's reprisal against Nabal is not the central concern of the biblical narration in this episode. The extended narrative account and the true dramatic tension in this episode is focused on David's successful mastery of his retaliatory impulse. The direct thematic counterpoint to David's conduct is not God's action but Saul's failure in this self-mastery. The central role of God's action against Nabal is the same as the role of His directive to Saul against the Amaleks; both take place as part of God's test of character regarding the comparative fitness of Saul and David to rule over Israel.

Saul himself comes, for a brief moment, to understand the nature of this test and to acknowledge that he has failed it in the biblical passage immediately before the episode between David and Nabal. As Saul left the cave where he had unknowingly been vulnerable to David's retaliation, David revealed himself and showed that he had "cut off the skirt of [Saul's] robe" but nothing more as he had stood undetected behind Saul. Then Saul said,

> "Is that your voice, my son David?" And Saul broke down and wept. He said to David, "You are right, not I; for you have treated me generously, but I have treated you badly. Yes, you have just revealed how generously you treated me, for the LORD delivered me into your hands and you did not kill me. If a man meets his enemy, does he let him go his way unharmed? Surely the LORD will reward you generously for what you have done for me this day. I know now that you will become king, and that the kingship over Israel will remain in your hand." (1 Samuel 24:17-21)

Rather than retaliating in kind in response to Saul's wrongful assaults, David led Saul to this lesson that evil should be repaid by generosity. While protecting himself against Saul's wrongdoing, David nonetheless never abandoned his pursuit of reconciliation between them—a pursuit that Saul suddenly understood when he wept and called David "my son." But just as Saul had not been able to hold to this reconciliation goal when his son Jonathan had wronged him, he was not able to sustain his briefly restored relationship with David. After the interpolated episode between David and Nabal, we learn that Saul once again tries to kill David; once again David turns away from retaliation and vividly demonstrates his persistent forbearance to Saul; and once again Saul acknowledges his wrongdoing. The entire extended narrative of Saul's kingship repeatedly underscores the lesson of the moral superiority in human relationships of forbearance and restraint in response to wrongdoing. In its full narrative context, Saul's failure to learn and live by this lesson—much more than his failure to obey God's command to slaughter all of the Amaleks—seems to me to be the basic reason for his loss of God's favor and the kingship of Israel.

I suggested a moment ago that the most economical biblical expression of this lesson is in Jesus' observation, at Matthew 26:52, that those who "take the sword shall perish with the sword." Saul's death, it seems to me, is a vivid illustration of this proposition. Violent death is, of course, quite common in the Hebrew Bible. But Saul died by suicide—a self-inflicted violence that was at that point entirely without precedent in the biblical narrative.[12] Saul's violent nature is finally turned against himself. God withdraws His favor, but Saul destroys himself, and I would say that it was fundamentally because of this self-destructive flaw in Saul's character that God withdrew from him.

There is another way that David presents a contrast with Saul that offers instruction on the ways of responding to injustice, and the relationship specifically of punishment and reconciliation forgiveness. At a defining moment in his reign, David violated divine commandments against committing adultery and murder in a virtual orgy of self-aggrandizement: he had sexual intercourse with Bathsheba and then, to conceal this wrongdoing, arranged for the death of her husband, Uriah. God condemned David for these actions but did not withdraw the kingship or inflict direct retribution on him. David's wrongdoing was not, of course, in direct defiance of a specific instruction from God as Saul's had been. But this difference does not seem salient to me in explaining God's different response to their wrongdoing; the terms of God's condemnation seem almost identical toward both men: thus Samuel said to Saul, "Because you have rejected the word of the LORD, he has also rejected you from being king" (1 Samuel 15:22), while the prophet Nathan said to David, "why . . . you have flouted the command of the LORD, and done what displeases Him?" (2 Samuel 12:9).

The salient differences are in the responses of David and Saul to this condemnation. After Uriah's death and David's appropriation of Bathsheba as his wife, God sent Nathan to David with a parable about two men, one rich with many flocks and one poor with only one ewe lamb which "was like a daughter to him." When a hungry traveler came to the rich man, he refused any assistance from his own extensive flocks but instead took the poor man's lamb and killed it. David's instantaneous reaction was that the rich man "deserves to die . . . because . . . he showed no pity." Nathan then said to David, "That man is you." David's next utterance was "I stand guilty before the LORD," and Nathan replied, "The LORD has remitted your sin; you shall not die" (2 Samuel 12:1-13).

The parable and David's immediate talionic reaction point to a further similarity with Saul's wrongdoing. Just as he was prepared to exact remorseless retaliation against Jonathan for violating his command, David's instinctive response was to inflict death on this rich wrongdoer. Moreover, the parable itself echoes David's own prior encounter with Nabal, for Nabal was a "very rich" man, and his offense was his failure to give any of his three thousand sheep for sustenance to David and his men when they were needy travelers in his land (1 Samuel 25:2, 11). David's immediate response to the parable implied that he had forgotten the lesson of self-restraint that he had apparently learned regarding Nabal—a failure which amplified his self-aggrandizing appropriation of Bathsheba and suggested that he like Saul had substituted personal willfulness for obedience to God's commandments.

There were, however, two defining differences between the two men. Unlike Saul, David instantly acknowledged his wrongdoing, and, unlike Saul's persistent vengefulness toward Jonathan and David, David also instantly understood that his error was in a failure of "pity," of fellow-feeling and empathy for a person vulnerably subject to his authority. Even so, God underscored this lesson of failed empathy in the punishment he imposed on David—the death of the child that Bathsheba bore David from their adulterous union. It may seem odd to speak of this as a punishment for David; but David's response to the boy's dying revealed how deeply he suffered from it. He "sought God for the child"; he "fasted" and "wept for the seven days of the boy's illness" (2 Samuel 12:18, 21). He grieved with such intensity that, when the child finally died, his servants were afraid to tell him; they said, "We spoke to him while the child was still alive and he wouldn't listen to us; how can we tell him the child is dead? He might do something horrible" (2 Samuel 12: 18).

Here too there is an echo of Saul, of the possibility that David would kill himself; but there is also a difference, for David's motive would seem to be remorse for the innocent life lost on his behalf (as he had more directly forfeited Uriah's life on his behalf), while Saul's motive is more self-protective, to save himself from worse indignities at the hand of his enemies. David's seemingly abrupt transformation when he realized his child was dead—his setting aside of his deep anguish, thus confounding his servants' fears—itself suggests that David was grieving for the child, including the wrong he had done to the child, and not for his own paternal loss in the child's death.

The pain inflicted on David as punishment is characteristic of the Hebrew Bible's response to wrongdoing not only in those obvious instances which are at least arguably retributive (or eliminative, as I would call it), but, more interestingly, even in those instances that epitomize the reconciliation model. Reconciliation with injustice is not casually achieved in the Hebrew Bible. God's dealing with David is paradigmatic: the perpetrator must acknowledge his wrongdoing and must suffer punishment. The pain of punishment is not inflicted, however, for its own sake or as a simple retributive measure for measure; the punishment instead appears calculated to test the wrongdoer's remorse—that is, a demonstrated capacity to genuinely grieve for, to empathize with, the innocent victims who suffered as a consequence of the wrongdoing.

This paradigm, this required prelude to reconciliation, is even more clearly expressed in the Genesis account of Joseph's response to his brothers when they unknowingly encountered him as Vizier in Egypt. Joseph's tests were at once understood by his brothers as the "reckoning," punishment for what they had done to Joseph years before "because we looked on at his anguish, yet paid no heed as he pleaded with us" (Genesis 42:21). Notwithstanding their immediate expression of remorse—which Joseph heard, though his brothers did not realize that he understood their language—Joseph imposed increasingly severe tests, planting silver in their baggage in order to interrupt their homeward voyage to increase their sense of vulnerability and of their secret criminality "uncovered" (Genesis 44:16). He also demanded that they return with Benjamin, their younger half-brother (and Joseph's full brother) and then threatened to imprison Benjamin in order to test whether the brothers would resist or accept a re-enactment of the injury they had inflicted on him. Joseph revealed himself and "kissed all his brothers and wept upon them" (45:15) only after these extended, escalating tests, and only after his brother Judah pleaded that Joseph enslave him rather than Benjamin so as to spare their father the crushing loss of a second son. Judah, moreover, related that he had promised their father that if Benjamin did not return from Egypt, that he "shall stand guilty before my father forever" (Genesis 44:32)—an acceptance of personal responsibility that implicitly acknowledged his prior culpability for Joseph's disappearance. Thus, although God reconciles with David and Joseph reconciles with his brothers notwithstanding their guilt, the path toward this reconciliation is not made easy for the wrongdoers.

When we turn, however, to the Christian Bible and particularly to the parable of the prodigal son, these obstacles seem to melt away. In that parable, when the prodigal returns home after squandering his inheritance and disgracing himself through "riotous living" (Luke 15:13) his father offers him forgiveness before the son confesses to any wrongdoing—indeed, even before the son asks for forgiveness. Thus Luke recounts, "But when he was yet a great way off, his father saw him, and had compassion, and ran, and fell on his neck, and kissed him" (Luke 15:20). Thus on its face, this biblical account might seem to suggest that reconciliation with evildoers is an easier task in Christianity than in the Hebrew Bible. But this view, I believe, is as much an over-simplification of this parable as the single-minded version of unremitting punishment in the Hebrew Bible's account of divine vengeance against the Amaleks and against Saul.

In the Christian account, this oversimplification extends even to the title by which the parable is popularly and universally known. In fact the parable is not about the prodigal son; the phrase itself, "prodigal son," doesn't even appear in the biblical account. In Luke's gospel, Jesus begins the parable with these words, "A certain man had two sons" (Luke 15:11)—and this, properly speaking, is the true subject-matter of the parable. It is about a father and his two sons, not just about one, and the central drama of the parable is not about reconciliation

116

between the father and the younger son who had squandered his inheritance. The central dramatic tension in the parable is between the father and his elder son and, in turn, between the elder and younger son. The basic question posed by the parable is whether the elder son would forgive his father and whether the two brothers in turn would be reconciled with one another.

In a way, it is not surprising that this difficult and disturbing parable—difficult and disturbing, at least, in the way that I see it—should have been so simplified and bowdlerized in the common, popular understanding. If we restrict our attention to the interaction between the father and his younger son, then the message of the parable is both simple and readily reassuring: if you sin but return to the fold, you will be forgiven.[13] But if the central question posed by the parable is as I see it—whether the three actors (father, elder and younger son) will be reconciled to one another—then the parable poses this question without answering it; and that, in itself, is disturbing.

But this disturbance is on the very face of the telling of the parable. Let me quote the second half of the parable, after the younger son has been joyously welcomed by the father, adorned with the "best robe" in the house, and feasted with "the fatted calf" (Luke 15:22, 23). Jesus continues his recounting:

> Now his elder son was in the field: and as he came and drew nigh to the house, he heard music and dancing.

> And he called one of the servants, and asked what these things meant.

> And he said unto him, "Thy brother is come; and thy father hath killed the fatted calf, because he hath received him safe and sound."

> And he was angry, and would not go in: therefore came his father out, and entreated him.

> And he answering said to his father, "Lo, these many years do I serve thee, neither transgressed I at any time thy commandment: and yet thou never gavest me a kid, that I might make merry with my friends:

> But as soon as this thy son was come, which hath devoured thy living with harlots, thou hast killed for him the fatted calf."

> And he said unto him, "Son, thou art ever with me, and all that I have is thine.

> It was meet that we should make merry, and be glad: for this thy brother was dead, and is alive again; and was lost, and is found." (Luke 15:25-32)

This is the end of the parable. Thus we do not know whether the elder son was appeased by this appeal, whether he forgave his father or joined in the rejoicing at the return of his younger brother. The question, in a sense, is the same for the elder son as it was for the younger: that is, would the elder return to his father's house and, if so, on what terms would he return? But in answering this question, the stakes for the elder son were much higher than for the younger.

This does not seem apparent on the face of the narrative: the younger son, after all, had squandered his fortune and was living in poverty and disgrace before he decided to return home and seek forgiveness. But then, for what exactly did he need to be forgiven? He had disgraced himself and disappointed his father's expectations, but the principal harm he had inflicted had fallen on himself and he had already suffered considerably as a result. Even so, what more was at stake for the elder son? The answer is embedded in the parable. To discern it requires not only careful reading but a close familiarity with the Hebrew Bible. If we read carefully, we can see that the interaction between the father and two sons in this parable is a re-enactment of at least two earlier episodes recounted in Genesis—a re-enactment of the conflicts between Joseph and his brothers and between Cain and Abel. There are three small but powerful textual references in the parable that make this clear. Recall, first, that the father in the parable adorned his younger son with the "best robe" in his house; now listen to the account in Genesis of the origin of the conflict between Joseph and his brothers: "Now [Jacob] loved Joseph best of all his sons, for he was the child of his old age; and he [Jacob] had made him an ornamented tunic. And when his [elder] brothers saw that their father loved him more than any of his brothers, they hated him so that they could not speak a friendly word to him" (Genesis 37:3-4). Recall, too, that the father in the parable killed the fatted calf as a feast offering to his younger son, an act which echoes the origins of the conflict between Cain and Abel: Abel, the younger son, killed the "choicest of the firstlings of his flock" as an offering which God accepted while "He paid no heed" to Cain's offering of the fruit of the soil from his labor. At this inexplicable and unexplained rebuff, so Genesis says, "Cain was much distressed and his face fell" (Genesis 4:4,5).

Consider one other textual detail from the parable—here is the first appearance of the elder brother in the narrative: "Now his elder son was in the field: and as he came and drew nigh to the house, he heard music and dancing." The field is a fateful place in these Genesis accounts. Here is its significance for Cain and Abel: immediately after God accepted Abel's offering and rejected Cain's, Genesis recounts, "Cain said to his brother Abel, 'Come, let us go out into the field.' And when they were in the field, Cain set upon his brother Abel and killed him" (Genesis 4:8). So too for Joseph and his brothers. Their father, Jacob, sent Joseph to find his brothers and, so Genesis says, Joseph was "wandering in the fields" when his brothers "saw him from afar, and before he came close to them they conspired to kill him" (Genesis 37:15,18).

Now that we have located the parable and unearthed the identity of the two brothers, we can hear the full resonance of the offer that the father extends to his elder son, the full opportunity for reconciliation, for an undoing of a terrible injustice, that is presented to the elder son. The father says to him, "It was fitting to make merry and be glad, for this your brother [Abel] was dead, and is alive; [your brother Joseph] was lost, and is found." With this miraculous resurrection, the elder brother is given an opportunity that seems almost beyond imagination: he can be cleansed of guilt, he can undo the wrong he had committed years ago, he can—as Cain—end his punishing exile and return to his father's house. Why would he not, then, seize this chance, "make merry and be glad"? Why does the parable end with the elder son still uncertain, still standing outside?

With this question, I come to the most difficult place in this essay. I began with two models for responding to wrongdoing: one was a permanent severing of relationship between the victim and the wrongdoer (epitomized in the death penalty or life imprisonment without possibility of parole); the other model was a restoration of relationship. In using biblical narratives to find a guide for choosing between these two models, I have come thus far to the conclusion that even where these accounts appear to favor permanent severing, there is an implicit preference for restored relationship so long as the wrongdoer acknowledges guilt, atones for it, and even suffers some significant punishment (though a punishment calculated to instill empathy in him, that is, to reform or rehabilitate the character flaw that led him initially toward his unjust actions).

The so-called parable of the prodigal son presents the most difficult situation for those who would favor the model of restored relationship; it makes, on its face, a much stronger case for permanent severance. This is because, at the core of the parable, there is an injustice which was not acknowledged as such, which was not atoned for, and for which there was no prospect of punishment. The injustice was committed by the father and his victim was his elder son. The elder son's complaint was quite clear on this score; he explicitly said to his father, "Lo, these many years I have served you, and I never disobeyed your command; yet you never gave me a kid, that I might make merry with my friends." But for this less worthy, this disobedient and unworthy younger son of yours, you persist in showing favor. The father's response—"you are always with me, and all that is mine is yours"—is patently inadequate. That the elder son is "always with" the father is nothing more than a description of his faithful remaining in the father's house while his younger brother left for riotous living. And the supposed assurance "all that is mine is yours," is nothing more than a self-evident acknowledgment of the elder son's legal entitlement to all of the father's remaining estate, since the younger brother's portion had already been carved out.[14] Moreover, the father had already indicated his willingness to diminish this remainder; from whose share, after all, was subtracted the added gifts that the father lavished on the returning younger son after he had wasted his entitled portion? The father's reassurance to his elder son has a hollow ring, an injury dressed up as a gift.

The parable thus directly re-enacts the provocation of paternal disfavor that led Cain and Joseph's brothers to their murderous acts. And more than this, the provocation was clearly an unjust infliction committed by the father in favoring the younger son over the elder, in favoring Abel over Cain, in favoring Joseph over his brothers. If we return to the accounts in Genesis, it is apparent that God had no justification for preferring Abel's offering to Cain's, and He offered no justification even after he saw Cain's obvious distress. Without explaining why He had rejected Cain's offering, God only enjoined him to "master" the "sin couching at the door" (Genesis 4:7)—presumably Cain's vengeful impulse driven by displaced resentment at God's unexplained (and provocative) favoritism toward Abel. Jacob favored Joseph only because he was a child of his favored second wife Rachel—hardly an adequate reason from his elder half-brothers' perspective; as Genesis says, Joseph's elder brothers were so enraged at this favoritism that they "hated" him and "could not speak a friendly word to him."

As to Jesus' parable, even its popular name—the parable of the prodigal son—reiterates the injustice experienced by the elder son. The younger prodigal never suffers at his father's hand, he is never even rebuked, and he is not the centrally important actor in the parable. The elder brother holds its dramatic center and yet, even in the popular understanding of the parable, the younger brother is given an unjustified prominence. Some might think that this favoritism is too trivial to rank as an injustice. It certainly is too trivial to justify murder of the favored younger brother—but that, as I will develop in a moment, is precisely the point of all of these episodes. We can't get to that point, however, unless we first acknowledge the enormity—the unprovoked and unjustified enormity—of the initial injustice that the elder brothers experienced in all of these episodes.

But if this kind of sibling rivalry seems too trivial to support the charge of injustice, let me briefly refer to another biblical narrative that makes the same charge but even more clearly. Consider the Book of Job. Here God's injustice toward His servant Job could not be more clearly rendered. Indeed, as readers of the text, we know that the terrible injuries that fell on Job arose directly from God's inexplicable and even capricious wager with Satan. Job knows that he has done nothing to deserve his suffering, but if he knew what we know, that God was simply rolling dice at his expense, his sense of injustice would be even greater and even more justified than he knew. And like the father in the parable, like God toward Cain or Jacob toward Joseph's brothers, Job's God never apologizes, never explains, never justifies his wrongful inflictions.

Yet in the end, Job is reconciled not only to the injustice that has fallen on him but also with its perpetrator. The Book of Job is exceedingly complex. Job's reconciliation does not come easily: he protests, he demands an explanation and apology, he even threatens to sever all relationship with God by the one expedient within his power, that is, by killing himself. In the end he receives no satisfaction, and yet he becomes reconciled. If we read this text carefully, Job's reconciliation may not be complete; if not grudging, it seems to be more tentative and less trusting, less whole-hearted and joyous than the conventional accounts of the Book of Job admit. Nonetheless, even with all of these qualifications, Job does reconcile himself to the persistence of injustice.

Judah, one of Joseph's half-brothers, is even more forthright, less ambiguous, than Job in his ultimate acceptance of the unprovoked injustice that his father had visited on him. Even though Jacob emphatically reiterates his preference for Rachel's son Benjamin, as he had favored Rachel's son Joseph, Judah volunteers to accept enslavement himself in order to save his father from losing Benjamin as he had lost Joseph. Here is Judah's recounting of his father's admonition before releasing Benjamin for the required trip to Egypt: "my father said to us, 'As you know, my wife bore me two sons. But one is gone from me, and I said: Alas, he was torn by a beast! And I have not seen him since. If you take this one from me, too, and he meets with disaster, you will send my white head down to Sheol in sorrow'" (Genesis 44:28-9). Notwithstanding the patent insensitivity of Jacob's complaint—his dismissal of the ten sons of his other wife and his disregard for the threats to their safety in traveling to Egypt—Judah nonetheless spoke tenderly of his father's attachment to Benjamin: "Now, if I come to . . . my father and the boy is not with us—since his own life is so bound up with his—

when he sees that the boy is not with us, he will die. . . . For how can I go back to my father unless the boy is with me? Let me not be witness to the woe that would overtake my father" (Genesis 44:33-4).

For what reason, then, does Judah become reconciled to the unrecompensed injustice that he has suffered? Why does Job become reconciled? What is the underlying basis for the father's appeal to the elder son in Jesus' parable that he too should be reconciled to a continuing injustice? What is the meaning of God's injunction to Cain that in his anger at God's unexplained rejection of his offering, "sin crouches" at his door but he "can be its master" (Genesis 4:7)? As I read the basic teaching of all of these biblical episodes, it is that a victim's refusal to accept the stubborn persistence of injustice is likely to bring a terrible, further infliction on the victim himself. Joseph's half-brothers were victims; so were Job, and the elder son in the parable, and Cain. They all protested and struggled against their victimhood—none more strenuously and eloquently than Job. Only when Job directly encountered God and only at the very end of that encounter did he realize that he could not succeed in correcting the terrible wrong done to him. Only then did Job come to the realization that further struggle would have an even more terrible cost to him. He would—like Cain—become a permanent exile, a man locked in himself, isolated in his own deeply wounded grievance.

In the prodigal son parable, this is the same lesson urged on the elder son by his father, who is himself an unrepentant wrongdoer, like God in his final confrontation with Job. The offer that the father makes to his elder son is not attractive on its face: he is asked not only to forgive the injustice done to him, but even to accept its perpetuation. If he reconciles himself to this continuing injustice, then—says the father—he will be able to come in "out of the field," out of his current place of exile and murderous rage, and accept the comfort—the limited comfort—still available to him in his father's house.

From all of these biblical narratives I draw these lessons: first, that perfect justice is not available to us, that we will suffer unjust inflictions and though we are entitled to protest, to demand apology and compensation—indeed, we are expected to protest and demand—nonetheless, injustice cannot ultimately be eliminated. Second, that the impulse to sever all relationship with the perpetrator of injustice is understandable and strong but it should be understood as an inevitably futile effort to eliminate injustice from the world, to make this a place of perfect justice; and this elimination impulse is inherently excessive, it is violent, it is murderous at its core. I thus come to the conclusion, guided by these biblical narratives, that although it is exceedingly difficult to become reconciled with injustice, the alternative of giving rein to the perfectionist, elimination impulse is to live like Cain, in a state of permanent isolation and exile.

This kind of elimination impulse, this murderous enraged perfectionism, is epitomized in our country today by the perfervid support for the death penalty and for permanent banishment of criminals while holding no hope for rehabilitation and restored relationship. It is epitomized in our time by those who respond to the terrible injustice of the Holocaust by viewing all Germans or all Palestinians or all Arabs as Amalekites who are permanent enemies of righteousness and must somehow be expunged. It is epitomized by Yigal Amir, the assassin of Yitzhak Rabin. The moral guidance that I find in the Hebrew and Christian Bibles rejects this kind of perfectionism. But it is not a lesson that is categorically stated with the easy clarity of specific commandments. This lesson is too complex to be conveyed in this categorical format: it is a lesson not so much about particular measures—not about, for example, whether or when the new South African government should grant amnesty rather than pursuing criminal prosecutions for specific wrongdoers. The lesson is about the ultimate goal, about the underlying attitude, about the emotional tenor with which victims of injustice approach those who have wronged them.

Perhaps I can summarize the lesson as the need to temper justice with mercy, but, put this way, it may sound too trite, too simple, too easy to recognize the competing demands of justice and mercy. This is in fact a difficult prescription to put into practice. That is why the prescription only comes to life in the lived details of the biblical narratives that I have discussed. That is why the Book of Job is so puzzling and difficult on its face. That is why the question of the actual possibility of reconciliation between father and elder son, and between the two brothers, is left open at the end of Jesus' parable.

Let me give one more illustration of the difficulty of this lesson, a powerful if not overpowering illustration: I believe that God Himself succumbed to the temptations of perfectionism, to eliminate injustice from the world, at an early moment in the biblical history—at the moment, recounted in Genesis, when "the earth became corrupt before God; the earth was filled with lawlessness"(Genesis 6:11) and God resolved to destroy all living things except for Noah, the one righteous man. So the Flood came. But God immediately thereafter relented. Listen carefully to the biblical account of God's change of heart. After every living thing had been destroyed but for Noah and those with him in the ark, and after the Flood receded, Noah came onto land, built an altar to God and made a burnt offering. Genesis, chapter 8, tells us: "The Lord smelled the pleasing odor, and the Lord said to Himself: 'Never again will I doom the earth because of man, since the devisings of man's mind are evil from his youth; nor will I ever again destroy every living being, as I have done'" (Genesis 8:2). This assurance was not directed to any human being. God was speaking to Himself. He acknowledged the persistence of evil among humankind, though He did not excuse or belittle this fact. It is instead as if God were realizing, in His own mind, the excessive cost of expunging evil, the excessive cost of His own perfectionism, which would leave Him alone in the Universe, in a kind of exile deprived of the "pleasing odor" of human relationships, notwithstanding the evils that these humans inevitably would inflict on one another and on Him.

The Flood is not the last testimony to God's outrage at injustice and His readiness to inflict violent and relentless retribution on its perpetrators. When God revealed his elimination intentions toward the evildoers in Sodom and Gomorrah, Abraham diplomatically blended audacity with circumspection in challenging this plan. If we do not find comparably bold challenges to subsequent instances of God's apparent endorsement of elimination perfectionism, as in His command to slaughter the Amaleks, I believe nonetheless that these instances are not presented with unambiguous approbation. If we are looking for it, moreover, we can even find criticism—though carefully veiled and indirect—in the narrated presentations of God's vindictive anger. In the episodes that lead ultimately to Saul's self-destructive violence, I find it at least suggestive that he is prepared to treat Jonathan as God commands him to treat the Amaleks—to repay wrongdoing with elimination destruction—and that the vindictive rage that overtakes Saul toward David is three times described by the biblical narrator as an "evil spirit from the LORD" (1 Samuel 16:14, 18:10, 19:9).

In following the narrated course of Saul's escalating destructive vindictiveness, leading finally to his literal self-destruction, we can vividly see his downward spiral toward isolation and bitterness. Is it possible—I at least find it so—that the veiled parallels between God's vindictiveness and Saul's in these episodes suggest a similar critique of God? Is there a lesson from Saul's life in God's mind—about the isolating, self-punitive implications of elimination vengeance—when He chooses to respond differently to David's wrongdoing? Is God reluctant to reiterate the cycle of His experience with Saul—that is, a permanent estrangement between God and His anointed?

God does not "forgive and forget" David's sin. David carries a life-long burden of grief from his wrongdoing, not only in the loss of his infant son but in the violent deaths of his other children, most notably Absalom, who rebels against him. But David's persistent love for his sinful child Absalom, his (unsuccessful) effort to punish Absalom without losing him, may itself mirror God's attitude toward David's wrongdoing—as a terrible event that permanently alters and even afflicts, but nonetheless must not irrevocably sever, their relationship. For all its qualities of irreparable injury and grief, this persistent relationship appears preferable to the mirrored image that Saul's life offers in revealing the self-victimizing consequences of unrestrained vindictive rage. If after unleashing the Flood, God saw the hurtful consequences to Himself of enraged perfectionism and if He is periodically provoked to reiterate and then again to recant this elimination impulse, it is not surprising that we mortals would have a difficult time learning and holding to this lesson. But this is, I think, the underlying teaching of the Hebrew and Christian Bibles. And this, it seems to me, is a lesson worth observing.

Notes

[1] This essay is an extended version of the Bartlett Lecture delivered at Yale Divinity School on 9 October 1996.

[2] Constitutional challenges to these laws were recently rejected in E. B. v. Verniero, 119 F. 3d 1077 (3d Cir. 1997) and Doe v. Pataki, 120 F. 3d 1263 (2d Cir. 1997).

[3] Orlando Patterson, *Slavery and Social Death: A Comparative Study* (Cambridge: Harvard University Press, 1982).

[4] See Eric Foner, *Reconstruction, 1863-1877: America's Unfinished Revolution* (New York: Harper & Row, 1988), 564-612.

[5] See Joel Williamson, *A Rage for Order: Black/White Relations in the American South since Emancipation* (New York: Oxford University Press, 1986), 117-51.

[6] See Robert A. Burt, *The Constitution in Conflict* (Cambridge: Harvard University Press, 1992), 330.

[7] President Clinton put forward this proposal in his speech accepting the Democratic Party's nomination for re-election, see the *New York Times,* 30 August 1996, and reiterated it in his 1997 State of the Union Address, see the *New York Times,* 5 February 1997.

[8] See Timothy Garton Ash, *True Confessions*, New York Review, 17 July 1997, 33.

[9] See Carlos Santiago Nino, *Radical Evil on Trial* (New Haven: Yale University Press, 1996).

[10] See Bruce Ackerman, *The Future of Liberal Revolution* (New Haven: Yale University Press, 1992), 69-98.

[11] All citations to the Hebrew Bible are to the New Jewish Publication Society translation; all citations to the New Testament are to the King James version.

[12] There are only two subsequent suicides recounted in the entire corpus of the Hebrew Bible, and neither were such prominent figures: Ahithophel, a royal counselor who betrayed King David and killed himself when his plot with Absalom failed (2 Samuel 17:23), and Zimri, an army commander who succeeded to the throne of Israel by assassinating King Elah and who, after a bloody reign, was in turn overthrown (I Kings 16:18). In the New Testament of the Christian Bible, only Judas Iscariot commits suicide after betraying Jesus (Matthew 27:5).

[13] Jill Robins, *Prodigal Son / Elder Brother: Interpretation and Alterity in Augustine, Kafka, Levinas* (Chicago: University of Chicago Press, 1991), 38.

[14] For the source at Deuteronomy 21:17 of the elder son's entitlement, see Stephen Mitchell, *The Gospel According to Jesus* (New York: HarperCollins, 1991), 224-5.

Amnesty, Amnesia, and Remembrance:
Obligations Past and Present Duties to Future Generations
Heinz Klug

Each time we buried our friends and comrades who had been killed by the apartheid regime we made a commitment—singularly and collectively as a political movement—to pick up their fallen spear, to avenge their death and to achieve victory over apartheid in the name of the fallen. Today Apartheid is vanquished yet the killers are free, they receive amnesty, are guaranteed their government employment (where applicable) and are accepted as partners in the creation of a new South Africa. Viewing this new reality, in which Mandela's government stumbles forward daily against the legacies of apartheid strewn in its path, I am forced to recognize that we have always been trapped in an irreconcilable conflict between our past promises and our moral duty to the future. While we fought against evil and promised peace and justice, the needs of peace and the future generation required a forward looking vision, one in which justice is resolved without endangering the future. What place then for truth and reconciliation?

While we might point to international legal norms and instruments which might deny amnesty for such crimes, others decry South Africa's Truth and Reconciliation Commission (TRC) as a "witch hunt." These voices either demand collective amnesia in the form of a general amnesty for the past or continue to assert that their policies were merely misguided. The abuses of human rights which, they now acknowledge did occur, they characterize as infrequent aberrations and even equate with the actions of those who fought against apartheid. Yet as the hearings of the TRC have traversed the South African landscape, from cities to remote rural communities, the broad patterns of abuse and horrifying detail of each individual case has revealed to all that these atrocities were never isolated incidents but rather formed the very basis of the system. Are we to forgive this crime against humanity—as apartheid was defined in the International Convention on the Suppression and Punishment of the Crime of Apartheid—without even a decent demonstration of remorse or apology from the leaders and perpetrators of that system?

While democracy has not resolved the vast inequalities created by apartheid, there is no doubt in my mind that the compromises of a negotiated transition, even accepting the political participation of the creators of apartheid in South Africa's first post-apartheid government, was a moral and political necessity in which the demands of the "past" and even of many of the "present"—such as the generation of youth who gave up their chance for education to make apartheid ungovernable—were in part sacrificed in order to establish a viable future for the younger and future generations.

It is in this context and in the face of an ongoing conflict between the voices of victims and the strategies of denial, avoidance and justification by the perpetrators that we must try to evaluate the process of truth and reconciliation in South Africa. On the one hand are the victims, like the Biko and Mxenge families who, demanding justice, have challenged the TRC in court and continue to reject the amnesty it promises to the murderers of their loved ones. On the other hand, there are the former apartheid leaders and functionaries who either continue to justify their actions as a "natural and necessary result of revolutionary conflict . . . justifiable under international law"[1] or express no remorse. Take, for example, police agent and later apartheid police spokesman Craig Kotze, who told the TRC's hearing on the role of the media under Apartheid that he had "no regrets" for his role as "as a soldier/policeman," in which he infiltrated newsrooms and planted false information as part of the state's covert disinformation campaign.

And in the face of this I reflect back on the not so distant past—on the singing, speeches, and searing emotions of so many funerals—and I wonder about our commitments to the past

Transgression, Punishment, Responsibility, Forgiveness
Graven Images 4 (1998), 123-126.

and how they have been sustained in the complex interactions of South Africa's democratic transition. I recognize that peace and democracy was achieved—"a small miracle" to quote Nelson Mandela—with a promise of reconciliation and even a recognition of the dignity and rights of our nation's former oppressors. Yet, as I witness the continuing pain of the families of those who gave their lives and the many other victims bearing their souls before the TRC, I am returned to thoughts of those we left behind, thoughts that send my mind reeling and stumbling across so many memories:

> Of little Katryn as a precocious toddler, a child of hope born in exile to my comrades Marius and Jeanette Schoon, a political prisoner released after 12 years and a trade union activist banned from social contact and political activity, who met illegally and married before fleeing to Botswana.

> Of the cowardly parcel bomb that killed Katryn and her mother before she was old enough to go to school.

> Of Vernon "Rogers" Nkadimeng, the smiling young man whose shattered body was laid in its casket before the same altar where he had been married only two months before the bomb—wired to the ignition of his vehicle—ended his activities as an underground trade union organizer.

> Of Thami Mnyele the exquisite graphic artist who was machine-gunned to death amidst his art works as the Apartheid regime's commandos sowed death among refugees, activists and Motswana bystanders, killing twelve in a night of horror which the South African media boastfully headlined, "The Guns of Gaborone."

> Of the all-too-many, whose lives were destroyed or crippled by a system whose former leaders—political, social and economic—now wish to distinguish it from what they describe as the activities of "rogue elements" for whom they deny direct responsibility.

These memories and thoughts overwhelm me with the pain of survival and outrage against those who demand amnesia as an imperative for reconciliation. My sense of outrage is not focused on the horrors of torture and callous acts of killing that we have all been so aware of for so long, but rather on those more articulate perpetrators who would erase distinctions between oppressors and resisters and who still work so hard to suppress truth in order to elide history. I am also concerned about the focus on Christian forgiveness which has become such a marked feature of so many of the TRC's hearings, and of course I am troubled by my own ambivalent attitudes towards this process. I recognize that it is these tensions which motivate me to search for a position from which it will be possible to justify a forward looking vision without turning my back on my past commitments.

These concerns remind me of my attitudes towards Craig Williamson, the South African Police Major who was among the planners of the Botswana raid and who has publicly admitted, without remorse, to having sent the bomb that killed little Katryn and her mother, and who reluctantly applied for amnesty only after losing his motion to dismiss the civil law suit brought against him by Marius Schoon. I know I can never forgive him for the murders of Jeanette and Katryn, which can never be justified as a proportional response to Marius and Jeanette's resistance activities. Does this mean that I could not accept his receiving amnesty from the TRC? Not necessarily.

While I cannot accept the standard definition of amnesty as a "complete forgetfulness of the past,"[2] I do believe that pardons, based on a "full disclosure of all the relevant facts relating to acts associated with a political objective"[3] as required by the Promotion of National Unity and Reconciliation Act in South Africa, are one essential part of achieving the reconciliation required to rebuild community in the aftermath of violence and gross violations of human rights. The justification for pardon cannot however rest merely upon the assertion of political necessity—that South Africa's democratic transition was the product of a political compromise which required amnesty in order to avoid a military backlash and as the basis for agreement. In fact, the apartheid regime first insisted on a blanket amnesty and attempted, even in its final hours, to grant amnesty to some of its Ministers so as to avoid the need to account for their actions. It is this last element, the need to account, which for me, provides the essential link between our obligations to the past and the needs of the future.

It is only by requiring a full accounting of the events and circumstances surrounding these violations that it is possible to judge whether pardon may lead to acceptance and reconciliation, even if forgiveness is impossible. First, as in the case of Williamson, the statute requires a finding that the motives of perpetrators were political and not based on "personal malice, ill-will or spite." In the case of Katryn and Jeanette this will require a distinction between his decision to kill in order to curtail the family's political activities and the possible personal grudge that Williamson may have held as a result of the contribution Marius and Jeanette made in exposing him as an apartheid spy while he posed as an exiled anti-apartheid student activist and managed to become a senior official in the Geneva-based International University Exchange Fund. Second, it is only through a full accounting that it will be possible for the TRC to achieve its primary goal, which is to establish the truth about the gross violations of human rights which occurred. Third, it is only by establishing the truth of these events that it will be possible to ensure remembrance instead of amnesia, and thereby to work towards the goal of preventing "a repetition of such acts in future."

Remembrance then becomes both the justification for granting pardons to the perpetrators who have acted with a "political motive" and the basis for resolving the quandary posed by the need to reconcile our present and past commitments. By recording and elucidating the memory of those who suffered for their resistance to apartheid we are able to both fulfill our commitment to never forget their efforts and also to continue their mission by using them as an example to future generations of what should never be repeated. Thus it is neither amnesia nor forgiveness that is the basis of reconciliation but rather the recognition of past suffering as a lesson to the future and a symbol of what has been overcome.

Although I am able, in this way, to reconcile myself with the purpose and work of the TRC, my understanding of amnesty requires a clear rejection of the present attempts to shape the work of the TRC into an examination of human rights violations that refuses to make a moral distinction between the actions of those who fought apartheid and those who acted in its name. Instead of making a distinction between retributive justice and restorative justice as a way to justify amnesty over prosecutions, our understanding of truth and reconciliation should rather focus on the slow but steady process of accountability that the TRC is achieving. Not only have individual cases been resolved but the TRC has also refused to ignore the wider evils of the apartheid system, drawing heated criticism from even "liberal" white South Africans. Attempts to avoid the wider implications of apartheid policy has seen even Herman Giliomee, the noted Afrikaans political scientist and now President of the traditionally liberal Institute of Race Relations, argue that apartheid was not a crime against humanity, despite the revelations of the TRC hearings.

While the false arithmetic of moral equivalence is easily propagated, it is important that the TRC help reveal all gross violations of human rights, including those committed in the name of the liberation movements. However, the task of remembrance requires that there be accountability, not only of those who engaged in the countless acts of violation but also of those who enabled and sustained the system which provided the opportunities for such deeds. While the "justice" Archbishop Desmond Tutu promised in his eulogy at Griffith Mxenge's funeral in 1981 has not materialized to the satisfaction of the Mxenge family, the amnesty granted Mxenge's murderers may be sustained so long as the life and work of Griffith Mxenge is elevated in remembrance above the deeds of his killers and the continued denials of those who benefited from the system those killers upheld. It is only through direct public accountability and, hopefully, eventual remorse, that a collective memory can be created which will provide a fitting acknowledgment of those who suffered and will present a barrier against a repetition of the past.

Notes

[1] Dr. Niel Barnard, former head of the National Intelligence Service, before a special hearing of the Truth and Reconciliation Commission on the role of the former State Security Council (the highest decision-making body in the apartheid security apparatus which functioned as a subcommittee of the Cabinet) on December 4, 1997.

[2] See, Judgment of the Supreme Court of South Africa (Cape of Good Hope Provincial Division) on May 9, 1996 in *AZAPO v Truth and Reconciliation Commission* 1996 (4) SA 562 (C).

[3] Section 3(1)b of the Promotion of National Unity and Reconciliation Act 34 of 1995.

Forgiveness Disrupts Legal Order

Thomas L. Shaffer

Jesus told the story of two brothers who worked in their father's business. The younger brother said he wanted out of the business; he wanted his share of what he expected to get after his father died (Deuteronomy 21:17).[1] Their father agreed; the younger son took his share in cash and squandered the money. He was then destitute, far from home, feeding a herd of pigs, wishing he could return to the family business—not as an heir, but as a hired hand. He set out for home, toward his father's house, to try to work that out. His father greeted him with extravagant generosity, as if he were a guest deserving of unusual honor. "Quick, fetch a robe . . . and put it on him; put a ring on his finger and shoes on his feet. . . . [L]et us have a feast to celebrate the day" (Luke 15:22-4). The elder son, not consulted until the party was underway, found out about the reception given his brother and was resentful. "I slaved for you all these years," he said to his father. "[Y]ou never gave me . . . a feast for my friends." His father said, "Your brother here was dead and has come back to life, was lost and is found" (Luke 15:29-32).

In its traditional place as a New Testament forgiveness story, the Parable of the Prodigal Son parallels Reynolds Price's version of Jesus's healing of the crippled man who was let down through the roof. I remember the crippled-man story from images in Sunday school in the First Baptist Church, Fruita, Colorado, when I was a boy: Jesus is interested mostly in being a rabbi and is burdened by the fact that broken people come to him not to learn but to get over being sick. He takes refuge from the crowd in a house. Lawyers who hope to catch him breaking the law are also in the house. The crippled man has been kept out of the house. His brothers get him in by making a hole in the roof and lowering his pallet to "the spot where Jesus sat."[2] Jesus looks at him and says, "Son, your wrongs are forgiven." The crippled man is not impressed at being shriven. He nods. Jesus seems to have misunderstood. The crippled man is not worried about sin; he needs help for his ailment.

The lawyers are neither impressed nor amused. They say, "No one forgives real error but God." Jesus says, "So you know the Son of Man [meaning himself] has power to forgive all wrongs—" He raises his hand; the crippled man is now somewhat more impressed, perhaps hoping the hand in the air is a healing gesture. Then Jesus says, "Stand, take your cot and go." And the crippled man does. He is cured; he can walk. "But the lawyers were scandalized," Price writes. "By their lights this man [Jesus] was not only breaking the laws of God but was dangerously attracting mobs that might yet boil into one more round of the common bloody quarrels with Rome. From that day they and Herod's henchmen"—that is, lawyers, judges, and officers of the law—"all plotted to silence Jesus or end him." Told this way, and focused on forgiveness, both of these stories barely imply response from those who might have been serious about the Rule of Law. The lawyers in the crippled-man story are more concerned with politics than with jurisprudence, and the elder son in the parable gives no rationale for his resentment.

There is indication elsewhere in the New Testament of what legal concern might have looked like in these stories. For example, in the realistic argument made by high priest Caiaphas in St. John's Gospel: The Council (the government) have a meeting, to decide what to do about the wandering rabbi Jesus. "If we leave him alone like this the whole populace will believe in him. Then the Romans will come and sweep away our temple and our nation." Which, of course, the Romans did, and not much later. (The Council's small mistake as to timing was less a failure at realistic perception than the common ineptitude government shows in its practice of the ethics of consequences.[3])

There was nothing supposititious about the Council's concern for the common good. They were conscientious public officials. They needed a legal argument, though, and Caiaphas gave them one. He said, "It is . . . to your interest"—that is, in the interest of legal order—"that one man should die for the people, than that the whole nation should be destroyed" (John 11:47-50). In other words, legal order here makes it necessary to kill somebody—a familiar situation in the history of western law and, as to the high priest's point, a reasonable, sensible legal argument from a responsible public official: this man who goes around claiming to forgive people is dangerous. Capital punishment is justified; if we delay—disaster. If Caiaphas's argument is heard in reference to the parable and the story of the crippled man, the point is that forgiveness disrupts legal order. I want to see here if I can explore the jurisprudence that is in these three accounts. To introduce that, a modern story about forgiveness—and then back to the prodigal son (or, as modern preachers often have it, focusing on the father's forgiveness rather than the younger son's sinfulness, the prodigal *father*).

Joe Ross is a young priest in the Congregation of Holy Cross. He is a rector in one of the men's residence halls at the University of Notre Dame and, by his own appointment, friend and counselor to forty-three death-row prisoners in the death house at the Indiana State Prison. His purpose is to be a witness to and persuade those who are to be punished there for horrible crimes, who are waiting to be killed by the government. His agenda, he says, is that these forty-three men are forgiven by God, "completely and absolutely." An interviewer from the campus radio station asked Father Ross, as students in such settings always ask, what a student could do in aid of this death-house ministry. In response, he suggested that these young people become pen pals with condemned prisoners, get connected to them, but he also advised that they learn to confront lethal legal power. Read about death row, he said to the students, and dispel the "monster image" of the people who are imprisoned there.

I suspect that Father Ross's relatively gentle practice of forgiveness would disrupt legal order if it could—both in resistance to the death penalty (in general and in principle) and in asserting that the men in death row are forgiven, "completely and absolutely," by the Ruler of the Universe. There is no rational argument any longer to kill them—much less the common-good argument Caiaphas had for killing Jesus.[4] Legal power, it seems, has to kill them anyway, if only because it would not be legal power if it didn't.[5] Law here cannot take the *risk* of forgiveness. Forgiveness would remove the fear, the accountability, and the responsibility that law provides; thus, as law sees it, forgiveness would invite chaos.[6]

The interviewer for the campus radio station asked Father Ross what *he* had learned from the condemned prisoners. "The deep and transforming power of forgiveness," he said. "That and the fact that we're all connected." The prisoners teach him about connectedness, as well as about forgiveness. The prisoners, he said, try to connect their isolated repentance to those they have harmed; they keep pictures of their victims in their cells, Father Ross says, and they pray for their victims and the families of their victims. The prisoners are not allowed out of their cells for religious services, and Father Ross is not allowed to go into their cells, but he prays with them through the bars. One prisoner is—through the bars—studying religion with Father Ross in a formal Rite of Christian Initiation for Adults course. When Father Ross speaks about the "monster image" of the men he meets through the bars, he perhaps means that legal power has a larger political agenda than its interest in killing these men. It also has an interest in keeping them alien, and representing them to the community as alien,[7] as people so destitute of humanity, so completely removed from the community, that they cannot be allowed to go to church.

The Parable of the Prodigal Son ends without a response from the elder son. The prodigal father gets the last word. The elder son must have had a response, though; I doubt that he slunk away in silence. But to get a response from him one has to fashion a midrash; that is what I will do.[8] A midrash written by a lawyer might correct and amplify the jurisprudential perspective from which the scriptural account is conventionally read, in this case the perspective St. Luke's Gospel generally takes, which is not to rile the Roman authorities.[9] The lawyer's amplifying midrash might show—as it would if it were written by Caiaphas—how forgiveness disrupts legal order.

This is the midrashic response of the elder son:

The arrangement my brother and my father made here disrupted the legal order of property ownership and succession in our community and our culture. The law provided for division of the business at my father's death (Deuteronomy 21:17), but my father was not dead. My brother's demand for settlement was permitted, but it was unusual; it was the settlement a Jew made when he was leaving the Holy Land and going to some other place.[10] The legal maneuver removed my brother, as a matter of law, from the family and the community. He was not supposed to be allowed back in.[11] My brother then made things worse; he engaged in behavior that would put him out of the family and community, even if he had not taken his inheritance and left us. He lived with and fed pigs. Pigs are unclean (Leviticus 11:7). The Rabbis teach that the person who keeps pigs is cursed.[12] My father accepted my brother's claimed repentance, both for the squandering and for the pigs, and he kissed him, so that he would know he was forgiven.[13] But then my father upset sound social and familial order by treating my brother as he did:

Putting the ceremonial robe on him was as if my wretched brother were an *angel*.[14]

The ring and the shoes are symbols not so much of sonship as of personal freedom (shoes) and *authority*, as if my brother was not only restored to the bonds of family life but also was going to take over.[15]

Dinner with meat is a rare thing in our house, or any other house in our community. That, and the singing, the dancing, and the cordial speech—are all rare. They are extraordinary gestures. They do not fit the facts. My father asked me how I could help celebrating with this crowd. I *can* help celebrating; it is *unnatural* to celebrate; it is *wrong*.[16]

Finally, to all appearances, my father intends to restore ownership to my brother. He said that all he had (all that is left) is mine, but his extravagant treatment of my brother makes me wonder whether he will be able to deny my brother what I deserve, what the law provides for me, what I have labored faithfully to protect while my brother has been spending my father's wealth on whores.[17] I have learned to live with my brother's betrayal, and to shoulder the extra burden it put on me—only one son left to take care of business for an old man—but now my father will take what I have earned and give it to my wretched brother. I don't see why I should learn to live with that.

What my father really wants is for me to *forgive* my brother, as he did. I could do that, perhaps, if it meant learning to live with the proposal my brother made to my father—that he come back and become a hired hand. I am not vindictive. That arrangement would give me some relief, and would be consistent with the deal they made before he left. It might even be a *just* (if also merciful) resolution of the family situation—and, after all, it is what my brother says he wants. But my father has given every indication that he will not stop at accepting that arrangement. If it turns out that my brother is to regain his (my) wealth, I suppose my father will, as he does now, appeal to my conscience, to accept the arrangement. All I can say is that such a conscience would be as unfitting as this party is.[18]

If that is what is to happen, I could even say I will *try* to forgive my brother, and even try to mean it, but this will not work unless the forgiveness changes both my resentful heart and the relationships in our family and community. That is, forgiveness, given the way things seem to be, means that I would not only accept my brother back, as my brother, but accept his being given what belongs to me. Otherwise my forgiveness would be a vapid gesture, like what Voltaire and the McGuire Sisters claim God does when *He* forgives: "God forgives because that is God's business," Voltaire said (Jones, 19). Voltaire and I are not so sure it is *our* business. "Though it makes Him sad to see the way we live, He'll always say, 'I forgive,'" the McGuire Sisters sang. Easy for God to forgive; it doesn't *cost* him anything. Cost is the point. Dietrich Bonhoeffer, waiting in prison for the hangman, said that forgiveness was for him costly, painful, and burdensome. He did not say that it also disrupts legal order—but it does, and it did in his case: Hitler's regime was a *legal* order. The very *theory* of forgiveness, let alone the practice, was disruptive of that legal order—and so the Nazis killed Bonhoeffer, which is what they had to do.[19]

In addition to a sensible concern for what my forgiveness would do to our community, there is what it does to *me*. The conventional reading of the story of my father and my brother seems to endorse a kind of forgiveness that does not solve either the theological or the psychological mess my father put me in. The more natural course, and the healthier course, would be to hold on to my anger and my principles—not because it is a good thing to be angry, but because otherwise my anger will be suppressed and I will turn it on myself. The natural and healthy course would be to *be* angry, because my anger is *justified*. The sentimental Christian reading of the story either ignores my rights or writes me off as a wimp.[20] I know what Bonhoeffer meant by *costly* forgiveness. His was a case like mine, and, like me, he found that he could not comfortably follow the natural course. To forgive, I would not only have to say and believe that the value of this person, my brother, transcends custom and law but I would have to give more than my extravagant and unreasonable father did. But I cannot *not* forgive, either, because I love my father.

My brother told our father that he repents of what he has done. I must say that was convenient repentance. I doubt that he would tell *me* he repents—not and *mean* it. Suppose, as seems likely, he does not repent of what he has done to me. That, too, would be like Bonhoeffer's case. And it would be, perhaps, a case where even those who endorse sentimental Christian notions of forgiveness would permit me retribution. I guess I should hope that he does not repent. That might let me off the hook.

(End of midrash.)

Amplified to take account of what the elder brother has to say after his father tells him to rejoice at his brother's return, the story suggests that religion is fundamentally at odds with the law on this matter of forgiveness. That raises three problems. First, it puts a tension between forgiving in the community and order in the community. Its resolution of the tension depends on claiming membership in a community that is constituted by forgiveness rather than by force. The "addressing word," the mandate to forgive, as L. Gregory Jones puts it, "does not come to isolated individuals; it comes, rather, to the community" (11). The elder brother knows this; it is why he talks about order. "No longer is it necessary to live as if there is no alternative to the powers that feed on our fears, our lusts, our hopelessness," Stanley Hauerwas said in his Easter sermon in 1997. "There is an alternative kingdom to that rule of darkness— it is called forgiveness," rather than the community of law and order contemplated in the elder brother's midrash. "To be forgiven is not to be told that no matter what we may have done and did not do, it is all right with God. No, to be forgiven is to be made part of a community, a history." All of which is to say that the community, from a religious perspective, is expected to be or to become a community of forgiveness.

That curious answer to the problem of disorder raises the second problem: to make any sense, such a notion about community has to demonstrate an anthropology that is consistent with its politics. It has to show that such a thing as a community constituted by forgiveness is conceivable, given what we know and what the elder brother in the parable knew, about the way people are.[21] Jones's answer to the second problem, and thus to the first, is to appeal to the last days of Dietrich Bonhoeffer. Bonhoeffer, like the elder brother in the parable, was all alone. The believing community he had served, and which had served him, was gone. (Or maybe it was, in a sad sense, also at a party that didn't fit.) From Bonhoeffer's perspective, the church had disappeared; he seemed to have no community other than the one the Nazis had made in Germany. (The elder brother, in his appeal to his community's mores, thought he would have communal support—but he may have underestimated his father's influence on their neighbors, as resisting pastors in Hitler's Germany underestimated their influence on their congregations.[22])

Bonhoeffer's story nonetheless suggests the persistence of a community of memory, a believing community that was not like the community the Nazis made, and a *discipline* from that believing community. This was (from Bonhoeffer's perspective, waiting in prison to be killed) a community that *had been* and therefore *was*. Forgiveness, in the religious traditions

Bonhoeffer inherited, including Judaism,[23] contemplated a community in which, as Jones and Hauerwas say, forgiveness is a way of life. Bonhoeffer came to understand that he did not need to see the darkness all around him as determinative, did not need to see that violence had priority over peace. A community constituted by forgiveness was available to him. Bonhoeffer was thus able to fit his extreme situation into his religious heritage, and into his theology, which was a theology of costly discipleship. He wrote that his imprisonment and death were the cost of forgiveness, which seems to mean first a sharing of Jesus' passion, and then an acceptance of responsibility for what his Germany was doing—responsibility, in fact, for what he called "the apostasy of the western world" (quoted Jones 25). He also saw this acceptance of cost as the traditional discipline of the believing community—penance—performed alone in prison because there was no believing community physically with him to do penance with. Finally, he saw his forgiveness, in that extreme situation, as a *political* act—as disruptive of Hitler's legal order, even violently so.[24]

That anthropology and that theology have parallels in the history of the church. The practice of the skills of forgiveness among the Anabaptists of sixteenth-century Switzerland are an example. They took a stand, against the lethal, governmental force invoked by the Roman Catholic Church of Christendom and against what they called the "magisterial reformers" (Lutherans, Calvinists, and Zwinglians). They invited and suffered the sort of response Bonhoeffer invited and suffered, and they did it *communally*; they had in suffering fellowship what Bonhoeffer found in memory. They formed and practiced their discipline in a community constituted by forgiveness.[25] For example, they dealt in a communal way with the Reformation doctrine that justification comes through grace and not through works. The Protestant problem was this: if God forgives sin and enters into fellowship with people purely because He wills to do so, and without regard to what people do—then what reason is there for this redeemed people to behave themselves? The Anabaptist answer was that reconciliation with God (salvation, justification) is more a process than an event, and that the process is communal—that is, it is a dynamic process in a believers' church that is forgiven and that forgives. They "contended not for 'sinlessness' but for the possibility of living in victory over the inclination to evil." In their formulations of soteriology, they "preferred regeneration language to describe conversion."[26] They did not exclude the possibility that members might, as the Mormons of my boyhood used to put it, "backslide" from time to time. The important thing for and toward such people was to keep them in the community—membership, not perfection.

These practices disrupted legal order because the believers' church, a community constituted by forgiveness, sought to refrain from violence and practiced non-resistance. More important for jurisprudence, they saw themselves, so constituted, as ready for costly discipleship—ready for martyrdom as a real possibility, since discipleship was a noticeable and deviant way to live. To live as disciples was to invite the lethal suppression from both Catholic Christendom and the magisterial reformers. This, of course, meant that they answered this second problem, the problem of community, by realizing—slowly—that their believers' church would become separate from the society around them. They were killed for baptizing adults when the society around them baptized babies;[27] they were killed for teaching that capital punishment was wrong; they were killed for refusing to accept military service and for declining most other public offices. But through it all, and ever since among their spiritual descendants, they are an example of a community constituted by forgiveness—a separate community, finally, but separate more because the larger communities around them cast them out than because they sought to separate themselves.

This theological and anthropological response to the first two problems I posed for a community constituted by forgiveness has a negative historical argument to make, as well as these positive responses. The radical reformers did not concede that a civil community is *necessarily* constituted by force. A modern theologian in their tradition, John Howard Yoder, has argued that few political experiments in western history show that the non-violent alternative was attempted, and there is therefore little history of experimental failure of communities constituted by forgiveness[28] ; and that the rare attempt to form a political community without violence[29] had more success and more promise than conventional historians of church and state are willing to allow.

The notion that a civil community (everybody) might be constituted by forgiveness suggests, of course, a revolutionary anthropology—as revolutionary as Marx's and Engels's theory of primordial (in)justice. In that, though, it is closer to the anthropology of the Hebrew prophets than standard theology would allow, and, if revolutionary, nonetheless within what Catholics used to call "the deposit of the faith." (That is to say, of course, that Bonhoeffer and the Anabaptists found more in traditional Christianity than many Christians know to be there.) The anthropology of the prophets was revolutionary in this way in biblical Israel: the implicit "subversion (which means undermining and exposure to dismantling) is directed against a theology that knows too much, a God who is too strong, a church that is too allied with triumphalist culture, and a ministry that moves too much from strength," Walter Brueggemann says, as he surveys the modern situation in the United States from a biblical, prophetic perspective. Attention to the notion that God makes a covenant with a believing community constituted by forgiveness "exposes the failure of a remote God who has not triumphed, a church that has known too much, and a culture that has not kept its promises" (43).

In the midrash, the elder son understood that the critical boundary issue for such a community might be the biblical injunction to forgive enemies,[30] enemies who, by definition, are not repentant. The elder son in the midrash argued, at the end, that, if his brother did not repent of what he had done to the elder brother, the elder brother need not forgive. Sound Christian theology would support him in regarding his brother, his enemy, with "moral hatred," Dietrich Bonhoeffer notwithstanding (cf. Jones 241-78). He would, as he (anachronistically) said, find some support among modern theological writers. Jones, on this point, admits that the psychology of righteous indignation may be too strong—and justifiably so, as Nietzsche argued—to lead to re-established relationships with reprehensible people who refuse to repent. But, even there, Jones says, the community constituted by forgiveness practices the disciplines of forgiveness: such skills as refusing vengeance, wishing the wrongdoer well,[31] and refusing to join in the world's deviance systems (e.g., those practiced in Indiana toward death row in the Indiana State Prison). In all of these ways, Jones says, the believing community is able to recognize reality, to avoid the separation that divides "issues of forgiveness and justice into the spheres of the personal and private and of the political and public" (267), which is what the elder brother in the midrash is trying to do.

There is psychological wisdom, I think, in resisting the theology of "moral hatred." There is a sense—even a psychological sense—in which *forgiveness precedes repentance*: The elder brother in the midrash might consider that if he forgives his unrepentant brother, his brother will then repent. If this is so there is less moral comfort in deciding not to forgive him when he has failed to repent. The theological dimension here is another way forgiveness disrupts legal order: The believing community makes a mistake when it fastens too heavily on notions of pardon, which, as James McClendon—faithful to his own Anabaptist tradition—points out, is not based in forgiveness but in punishment, not in the anthropology of forgiving community but in an ecclesial analogue to the processes of the law. Presidents and governors pardon offenders; the church forgives them.

As much as one might hope for and describe a civil community (everybody) constituted by forgiveness, history describes confrontations (as in sixteenth-century Zurich) between the communities constituted by forgiveness and everybody else. There are historical examples of this confrontation, more mainline examples perhaps, some of them more quaint than the sixteenth-century radical reformers. One is the biblical and medieval practice of asylum, in which the community provided a place of refuge for people who were fleeing from the consequences of having committed crimes.[32] The Torah extends the required arrangements to include putting up signs to show offenders the way to the cities of refuge and maintaining roads that were straight and in good repair.[33] Robert E. Rodes, Jr., describes a medieval Christian practice, borrowed at least in part from Judaism, that had been maintained among Christians from the time of Constantine. In both biblical and medieval Christian manifestations, asylum kept the offender from the vengeance of the law as it offered methods of mediation by which, as Rodes puts it, "the unjust marauder was deterred from his wicked purpose by the awe of the Divine Presence, and the seeker of just vengeance was brought to exalt mercy over justice and to make peace with his adversary."[34]

Another example—and both of these are more symbols of hope than models—is the practice, in Jewish law, for loans to the poor. Lending to the poor, the Rabbis taught, is a *mitzvah*. If the loan involved pledged property the borrower needs, the lender cannot keep the pledge (cf. Exodus 22:24). Lenders are required to make "arrangements" for poor borrowers who are not to be left without the benefit of their furniture, tools, farm animals, etc., and of such food as they have on hand. A loan to a poor person for the repayment of a prior loan was prohibited—so that the prior lender would have an opportunity to forgive the prior loan.[35]

The third problem, given a theology of community constituted by forgiveness, and consequent on a distinction between the community of the faithful and the surrounding society (between the community and the state, perhaps, at least in some situations), asks what attitude the community of believers is to take toward the welfare of the surrounding community— toward the common good, if you like. As the prophet Jeremiah put it, the faithful are to "seek the peace of the city" (Jeremiah 29:7). Part of the answer is that the community of believers is *prophetic*, enjoying and practicing "a holiness that requires prophetic protest and action directed at any situation where people's lives are being diminished or destroyed" (Jones 4). "The most important and most subversive thing the church can now do," Walter Brueggemann says, in one of his pessimistic moods about the late twentieth century in America, is to "refuse to give up on the world and its promised transformation." It is a mistake for those who believe in a community constituted by forgiveness to "act as though the world gets to vote on its long-term future" (51).

Brueggemann suggests here, as he does in much of his scholarship, that the meaning of what Christians call the Old Testament is that there is a *reality* that is alternative to the "real world" that is first described and then ruled by legal order. The Hebrew prophets, he says, "have an alternative perception of social reality that they insist is true and for which they want to create working space and allow for social possibility to emerge. . . . The prophetic is not understood primarily as denunciation or rejection, unless it is clear that there is a positive alternative available that, in fact, is true, gives life, and really functions" (223-5). He continues, "The truth is that because of the enormous fear in our social context, our government and its allies have constructed for us a fanciful world of fear, threat, security, and well-being that has little contact with the data at hand." And, to us lawyers: "Because we are managers and benefactors of the system, we find it easy and natural to accept this imagined world as real. . . . The system . . . creates such disproportion. . .[and] a set of lenses so that we look and genuinely do not see" (223-5). Brueggemann proposes a political agenda, an agenda that would ponder the Parable of the Prodigal Son and conclude that Jesus there proposes a notion that is civilly controversial, particularly as it also proposes to forgive those who are not repentant. "Our cooperation in God's purposes," Robert E. Rodes, Jr., says, "is powerfully impeded by unjust economic and social structures"—particularly when God's purposes are the great commandment of Judaism and Jesus to love the neighbor.[36]

But there is a problem within the problem here, raised by reading scripture, particularly the scriptural teachings Jews and Christians preserve on the matter of forgiveness of unrepentant enemies. It is this: where are those who forgive to determine what to be prophetic about? The Anabaptist tradition (and, for the most part, the Baptist tradition) point to the community of believers, what the Anabaptists called the believers' church, both for the description of the reality of which Brueggemann speaks and for provisional answers on how and when to seek the peace of the city. "We can afford to begin with the gospel notions themselves and then work out from there," John Howard Yoder says, "rather than beginning with the 'real world' out there (someone else's definition of 'the nature of things') and then trying to place the call of God within it. . . . The fulcrum for change and *the forum of discernment is the moral independence of the believing community as a body*."[37]

Yoder and his tradition would excuse themselves from some political action. They do not buy into Reinhold Niebuhr's moral theology of necessary evil.[38] It is not quite clear in Brueggemann's more mainline Protestant scholarship that the believing community itself is such a forum. Nor is it clear in the scholarship of Robert E. Rodes, Jr., which is often similar to Brueggemann's in its prophetic clarity. Rodes speaks from the Catholic tradition, and counsels courage,[39] but he does not forswear violence. When they are clear on what they are doing, those in the believers' church pick and choose. They may, as the Anabaptists do, decline "the sword" of lethal government power—which probably means they will not seek most political offices in modern America, and, for those who are lawyers, will practice law selectively. Yoder says they can "serve the world but are not called to rule it" (*Body Politics* 74-6). Yoder emphasizes that this nonviolent stance does not counsel turning aside from those who serve (patriotically) the lethal power of the government. He makes the obvious distinction between the person who serves and the office in which he serves; he finds it compatible with prophetic witness to approach and deal with the person in public office *in that person's terms and from that person's frame of reference*:

> It may very well be, if this [person] is engaged in an activity . . . which a more sensitive or more informed Christian conscience would not permit, that in the process of responding to the gospel he might come to the conclusion that his office is incompatible with his faith. But it is improper to begin with this conclusion. It is impossible to impose this logic on him before beginning the conversation. . . . What we ask of him does not cease to be gospel by virtue of the fact that we relate it to his present available options.[40]

Wendell Berry's stories and essays about the farming communities of Northern Kentucky suggest a focus. Berry, whose politics is not obviously theological, finds no hope for large American political order unless its imposition on the citizen is mediated through the sort of local, familial communities he writes about. "The concerns of public and private, republic and citizen . . . are not adequate for the shaping of human life," he says. "Community alone, as principle and as fact, can raise the standards . . . without which the other two interests will destroy one another."[41] Community—local civil community, in that earthy sense—holds promise, I think, for the peaceful participation of the community within it that is constituted by forgiveness; at least, it holds more promise than larger governments which wage war and fashion the bureaucracies that oppress and exploit. There will be happy coincidences of purpose between the two kinds of local communities, even if, as I think, the coherence necessary for political action remains the agenda of the community of the faithful within the local civil community.

The discernment and coherence of selective politics, in communities constituted by forgiveness, is for the believing community itself. Its "constant inventive vision for the good of the larger society," its "witness reminding those in power of the continuing injustices of their regime," need only be consistent with the "general moral values to which [the wider society] has no spiritual or logical commitment."[42] The Christian, Yoder says, "*accepts* the powers that be and speaks to them in a corrective way" (emphasis added). And this, at the margins, without either practicing or counseling violence: "The choice between violence, which is always the easiest way, and justice, which is more difficult, more dangerous, and superficially less efficacious, is always a question of faith" (41-2; cf. Romans 13).

Notes

1 Citations are from the New English Bible, unless otherwise noted.

2 Reynolds Price, "An Honest Account of a Memorable Life," *Three Gospels* (New York: Scribner, 1996), 241-87; 251.

3 John Howard Yoder argues that such a political ethic makes the mistake of focusing all of its attention on power and then supposing it can predict what will happen. "Ethics and Eschatology," *Ex Auditu* 6 (1990), 119.

4 Father Ross here follows the most recent and most authoritative doctrine of his church on the subject: Pope John Paul II, *Evangelium Vitae: On the Value and Inviolability of Human Life* 56 (1995).

5 Professor William J. Stuntz argues that the modern American judiciary thus seizes and cherishes its power while it "thinks too poorly of its capacity for moral leadership" ("Pride and Pessimism in the Courts," *First Things* 70 [1997], 22, 27). Even as careful a scholar as Professor Paul D. Carrington notices the "judicial self-aggrandizement that characterizes law in the late twentieth century." "Law as 'The Common Thoughts of Men': Thomas McIntyre Cooley," *Stanford Law Review* 49 (1997), 495, 524.

6 Jose Porfirio Miranda, *Marx and the Bible: A Critique of the Philosophy of Oppression* (Maryknoll: Orbis Books, 1974) 182-3, 229-44, 253; L. Gregory Jones, *Embodying Forgiveness: A Theological Analysis* (Grand Rapids: Eerdmans, 1995), 113, 133, 271. For all of his messianic hope, Jones (272-5) envisions more involvement by Christians in the power of the coercive state than many other Christians would.

7 As in John Grisham's chilling novel *The Chamber* (New York: Dell, 1994).

8 A device that has become almost common among feminist theologians. For example: Judith Plaskow, "Standing Again at Sinai: Jewish Memory from a Feminist Perspective," *Tikkun* 1.2 (1986), 28; Rosemary Radford Ruether, "For Whom, With Whom, Do We Speak Our New Stories?" *Christianity and Crisis* 45.8 (1985), 183.

9 Walter Brueggemann, *A Social Reading of the Old Testament: Prophetic Approaches to Israel's Communal Life,* ed. Patrick D. Miller (Minneapolis: Fortress Press, 1994), 108. St. Luke was not worried about mere courtesy, of course. For that reason, this midrash, since it is modern and written by a lawyer, will need to keep in view challenges to the notion of forgiveness for slaughter in Bosnia and Rwanda—which is being turned into legal issues in international legal tribunals—as well as all of the slaughters carried out in the name of international law.

10 Joachim Jeremias, *The Parables of Jesus,* trans. S. H. Hooke, rev. ed. (New York: Scribner, 1963), 128-32. This was perhaps like the settlement a modern lawyer arranges for her clients to foreclose the claims of a surviving spouse, or to avoid death taxes.

11 Community was then and is now centrally important in the practices of Judaism. Rabbi Jacob Rothschild, after years of courageous witness for civil rights in Atlanta, found in 1968 that he was being excluded from further participation by the leaders of the black community there; he told his Protestant audience about Jews and their communities: "Reviled and persecuted, decimated by pogrom and holocaust, we have still maintained our visibility and sought to obey the rabbinic dictum: 'Separate not thyself from the community'" (Melissa Fay Greene, *The Temple Bombing* [Reading: Addison-Wesley, 1996], 429-30).

12 See Jeremias 129 n. 74.

13 Jeremias cites 2 Samuel 3:21 and 14:33 for the practice.

14 Jeremias says it was an apocalyptic symbol.

15 Jeremias cites 1 Maccabees 6:15: "Then he called Philip, one of his most trusted advisers, and put him in charge of his whole empire. He gave him his crown, robe, and official ring."

16 Judaism, then and now, announces forgiveness—with, perhaps, more attention to repentance than Christianity does ("Shabbath," *The Babylonian Talmud,* trans. Rabbi Dr. I. Epstein, vol. I [London: Socino, 1938], 264-5, 781, 146-7). The elder brother's argument here, once it settles down a bit, becomes an argument about repentance.

17 Jeremias likens this point to Matthew 21:28, where Jesus seems to have directed material gain to the brother who at first refuses to work for his father (131-2).

18 The elder brother's sense of the unfitness of such an appeal, as Judaism might teach, can be and should be expected. But Judaism also contrasts legal order with precisely what the elder brother cannot bear. Cf. David R. Blumenthal, *God at the Center: Meditations on Jewish Spirituality* (San Francisco: Harper and Row, 1988), 227: "When *halakhic* man approaches reality, he comes with his Torah, given to him from Sinai, in hand. He orients himself to the world by means of fixed statutes and firm principles. . . . The law with its sureness, with its very decisiveness, with its ability to encompass the holy, seduces even as it gives form, depth, and concreteness. The temptation is to submit totally to the authority of the law; to become God's judges and policemen, not His prophets and saints."

19 James William McClendon, Jr., *Systematic Theology* (Nashville: Abingdon, 1986), 186-208. These references are anachronisms, but since I have gone this far with a model from Judaism, I will claim the rabbinical perspective on chronological sequence and say that is permissible in midrashim.

20 Jones 244-6, discussing Nietzsche's *On the Genealogy of Morals.* There is a kind of refusal to forgive, which Nietzsche may have sometimes had in mind, that is an expression of love. Heathcliff, for example, says to Catherine Linton, "I forgive what you have done to me. I love my murderer—but yours! How can I?" Emily Bronte, *Wuthering Heights* (1847; Boston: Houghton Mifflin, 1976), 138.

21 Such a demonstration can overcome what Avivah Gottlieb Zornberg writes about as the experience of alilah—being caught up in a "plot" without knowing what the plot is. See *Genesis: The Beginning of Desire* (Philadelphia: Jewish Publication Society, 1995), 263-81.

[22] Helmut Thielicke's autobiography provides many examples, although it is the story of a Protestant pastor in Nazi Germany who did more than most of the others to confront the evils of that government. He wrote, in *Out of the Depths,* trans. G. W. Bromiley (Grand Rapids: Eerdmans, 1962), 278: "Whatever the truth of Goethe's saying that those who act are always right, there can be no doubt that those who observe, that is, who cross the boundary and take a bird's-eye view, are always wrong."

[23] Jones 49, citing Jeremiah 31:31-4, shows how the community contemplated by the Hebrew prophets, is a community that "knows about, experiences, and practices forgiveness."

[24] He referred, mysteriously, to "righteous action" and "the central events of life, which are not amenable to missionary demonstration" (Jones 24-33; McClendon 186-208). I sense a problem both Jones and McClendon have in coming to terms with Bonhoeffer's involvement in the plot to kill Hitler.

[25] My sources are: J. Lawrence Burkholder, "Non-Resistance, Nonviolent Resistance, and Power," *Kingdom, Cross, and Community,* ed. J. R. Burkholder and Calvin Redekop (Scottdale: Herald Press, 1976), 131; William R. Estep, *The Anabaptist Story,* 3rd ed. (Grand Rapids: Eerdmans, 1996); Ronald J. Sider, "Christian Ethics and the Good News of the Kingdom: Doing Christian Ethics in an Eschatalogical Key," *Within the Perfection of Christ,* ed. Terry L. Brensinger and E. Morris Sider (Grantham: Evangel Press, 1990), 13-32; J. Denny Weaver, *Becoming Anabaptist* (Scottdale: Herald Press, 1987); John Howard Yoder, "Gospel Renewal and the Roots of Nonviolence," *Faith and Freedom,* (December 1995), 5 and Yoder, *The Legacy of Michael Sattler* (Scottdale: Herald Press, 1973); the text and cover letter of the seminal Schleitheim confession of 1527 begin on p. 34.

[26] Luke L. Keefer, Jr., "Armenian Motifs in Anabaptist Heritage," Brensinger and Sider, 146, 150, 155.

[27] For doctrinal reasons, not social reasons. Melchior Rinck, in a letter written circa 1530, said, "[B]oth the work-saints [Roman Catholics] and the scribes [magisterial reformers] strive so mightily concerning infant baptism . . . not . . . out of love for the children, for they are precisely the ones who consume the bread that belongs to the children and to the poor orphans, and fatten themselves on it" (translated and quoted in Yoder, *Sattler* 136.

[28] John Howard Yoder, *The Priestly Kingdom* (Notre Dame: University of Notre Dame Press, 1984), 145-6: "If it is the case the God is providentially in charge of history, even though that has not hitherto been visible, would not divine sovereignty be able to bless the believing obedience of a Caesar who, taking the risk of faith like any other believer, from his position of relative power, would love his enemies and do justice? Does the argument need to grant that if a Caesar had done that, in the context of authentic faith . . . the results would have been bad? What would have counted as bad results in that case?"

[29] E.g. those of Waldo, Chelcicky, the Zurich radicals in 1523, George Fox in the 1640s, William Booth and Uchimura Kanza (Yoder, "Gospel Renewal," 5); also William Penn in the New World (187-8).

[30] An injunction in biblical Judaism as well as in the New Testament. "Even if the enemy come to your house to slay you, and he is hungry or thirsty," Rabbi Hanina bar Hama said, "give him food and drink; for thereby God will reconcile him to you" (quoted and discussed in my *Faith and the Professions* [Provo: Brigham Young University Press, 1987], 64-5).

[31] The Rabbis point to 2 Kings 6:21-3: "'Shall I kill them?' . . . 'No. . . . Give them something to eat and drink and let them return to their king.' So the king of Israel . . . sent them back to the king of Syria. From then on the Syrians stopped raiding the land of Israel."

[32] Exodus 21:14; Numbers 35:25; Deuteronomy 19:11.

[33] Menachem Elon, *The Principles of Jewish Law* (Brooklyn: Hamed Books, 1974), 475, 531. Jewish law came to distinguish between intentional homicide and accidental homicide—a distinction with warrant in the Torah. Rabbi Hertz claims that this distinction meant that the Jewish practice did not lead to the maintenance of "nurseries of criminals," as in ancient Greece and Rome, nor to refuges for "criminals of every description" as in the medieval church (*The Pentateuch and Haftorahs,* ed. J. H. Hertz [London: Soncino, 1987], 721 n.15).

[34] Robert E. Rodes, Jr., *Ecclesiastical Administration in Medieval England: The Anglo-Saxons to the Reformation* (Notre Dame: University of Notre Dame Press 1977), 52-4. The alternative in Reformation England became not reconciliation but a chance for the offender to "abjure the realm" (Robert E. Rodes, Jr., *Lay Authority and Reformation in the English Church* [Notre Dame: University of Notre Dame Press, 1982], 30-1; see also Jones 276). A feminine instance, within Islam, is described in Fatima Mernissi, "Women, Saints, and Sanctuaries," *Signs* 3 (1977), 101.

[35] Elon, 262, 628-30. The Rabbis pointed to Exodus 22:24, which is a prohibition on changing interest, "even to the poor with thee" [J. P. S. translation].

[36] Robert E. Rodes, Jr., *Law and Liberation* (Notre Dame: University of Notre Dame Press, 1986), 2, 4. Rodes teaches that liberation from oppression includes liberation of the oppressors—liberation of poor and rich alike from their unjust institutions—because the poor cannot love institutions that oppress them, and because the rich, "if the rich understood their true interests," would hate the institutions that make them rich. His perception depends on understanding that the prosperity of the prosperous is complementary to the suffering of the poor (52).

[37] John Howard Yoder, *Body Politics: Five Practices of the Christian Community Before the Watching World* (Nashville: Discipleship Resources, 1992), 76.

[38] This is the theme of what is probably Yoder's most influential book, *The Politics of Jesus* (Grand Rapids: Eerdmans, 1972; 2nd ed. 1994).

[39] Rodes, *Law and Liberation*, 213: "The will to impose standards of justice and morality on society without counting the cost is itself one of the facts of history. Even if we do not know what will come of it, we know that we would not care to be without it. Our faith is that it is not in vain."

[40] John Howard Yoder, *The Christian Witness to the State* (Newton: Faith and Life Press, 1964), 25.

[41] Wendell Berry, *Sex, Economy, Freedom and Community: Eight Essays* (San Francisco: Pantheon Books, 1993), 119.

[42] "The testimony that the risen Christ is Lord also over the world is to us the reason for speaking to the state," he says, "and the biblical witness concerning the reason for the state's continued existence enables us also to guide this testimony with definite standards." He summarizes these standards as faithfulness to "the church's clear conviction," consistent behavior in the church's management of its own affairs, and that "[t]he church should speak only when it has something to say" (19-21).

Losing Faith in the Secular:
Law, Religion, and the Culture of International Governance

David Kennedy

Thinking about what's happening on a really global scale, law is certainly back. After the Cold War gridlock and the Gulf War hype, the whole regime thing is hitting a crescendo. Now we see law in the slow knitting of interdependent markets where we once saw only economics and in the stable patterns of governmental consultation or the machinery of sanctions, enforcement, and compliance where we once saw only politics. Business at the International Court of Justice is up, if modestly, while the World Trade Organization has taken international economic relations from the mercantile world of bargaining to a smorgasbord of legal dispute settlement schemes. The neo-liberalism of institutional convergence, the rational discipline of mobile capital, the peace of ideological consensus and the civilizing market are upon us, and law is their handmaiden and their witness.

But so is religion. The Pope-mobile is everywhere, French youngsters lining up for a blessing, Russia as religious as Arkansas, a missionary energy in the third world rivaling the late nineteenth century, while here at home, Jesus on the Internet, alongside cults and chatroom confessionals. Children kneeling outside their schoolrooms, huddled like smokers on coffee break, begging just one quick nondenominational prayer. And then, of course, there is Islam, increasingly the modern figure for religion. Or, we should say, all the Islams, from the Million Man March to the Taliban, from sleek Gulf financiers to the butchery of an Algerian village, from the conventional liberal humanism of the mainstream Arab-American community to the anguished modernism of once secular politicians in Egypt, Iraq or Syria, learning new fealties and vocabularies. It is hard to get firm numbers from the religious sociologists—by last count it appeared there were 1,927,953,000 Christians—almost double the 1,099,634,000 Muslims and way ahead of the 225,137,000 "Chinese Folk Religionists."[1] In the United States, although Christianity is losing market share in a growing population to conversions—an annualized loss in the 1990s of 317,900 per year—there is some evidence that religious intensity of conviction has increased in many quarters. Time magazine tells us that 69% of Americans believe angels exist, for example.[2]

It is difficult to know how real either of these trends are on the ground—is Russia more or less governed by a rule of law today than in 1980? How many Americans believed in angels in 1950? And it is equally difficult to get much of a sense for what we mean by "law" or "religion" when we say they have returned. Which parts of the disaggregated regime of social regularity blossoming across cultures should we think of as "legal?" Or for that matter, "religious." At the O'Hare airport bookshop, under "religion" we find "The Bible," "Living Buddha," "The Living Christ," "A Life of Jesus," or "Jesus in Blue Jeans," along side "Foucault for Beginners," Aristotle and Machiavelli and Norman Vincent Peale. Right next to "Storming Heaven's Gate" we find "Snowboarding to Nirvana."

What interests me here is the return of law and religion to the consciousness of the secular establishment. For an intelligentsia always deferential to law and faith, but preferring the savvy of power politics and secular rationality, law and faith are all the rage. And it's not just Diana or Mother Theresa. Here is Hollywood mogul (and Harvard grad) Marty Kaplan:

> I'm the last guy you'd figure would go spiritual on you. . . . If Harvard had made
> me a more spiritual person, it would have failed in its promise to socialize me to
> the values of the educated élite. Those values are secular. . . . The educated person
> knows that love is really about libido, that power is really about class, that

> judgment is really about politics, that religion is really about fantasy. . . . The spirituality of [meditation] ambushed me. . . . To be awakened to the miracle of existence—to experience. . . . The God I have found is common to Moses and Muhammad, to Buddha and Jesus. . . . I used to think of psychic phenomena as New Age flimflam. . . . I used to think the soul was a metaphor. Now I know there is a God.[3]

If this was one giant leap for a man, how large a step for the secular establishment? And what links these uncanny returns of law and religion? If religion is no longer fantasy, is judgment also no longer politics? Love no longer libido? My responsive slogan, and also my title, is this: "Losing faith in the Secular: Law, Religion, and the Culture of International Governance."

II.

In the 1970s, when I studied international relations and political science, law was out; international law was a marginal and utopian wish to hard headed realists with their strategic models and multilevel games. Law was just a hypothesis—while we thought we knew what a prisoner would do in a dilemma. But now it's all different—the study of "regimes" and "institutions," and now "governance" has taken political scientists interested in the international on a great looping trek towards law. Their journey coincides with a post-Cold War outbreak of enthusiasm for international law in the foreign policy establishment—the law of a "New World Order," the law of liberal democracies, the law of a global market. Numbers are hard to find, but it appears spending on "rule of law" injection projects around the world now rivals food aid, refugee assistance, humanitarian aid of all sorts—dwarfed only by military assistance. And even the military is pitching in. I spent some time in Senegal a year ago with a training team of military lawyers instructing the local officer corp on rules of warfare—the need for good discipline and clear rules of engagement merging, in a post-CNN world, into compliance with international humanitarian norms. And it's a big program, operating in over 60 countries. Indeed, the U.S. military may now provide more training in international law and human rights than all the world's non-governmental organizations put together.

At the same time, when I studied international law, the point was to demonstrate our savvy about power. Nothing abstract or utopian about it. We were interested only in how nations behaved, in the regularities of coexistence, and the modalities of cooperation. International law was technical and hardboiled. Although as lawyers we held back from the apostasy of conflating law with politics, for a century international lawyers had castigated the idiolatry of naturalists and formalists in the name of reason and rationality and pragmatism, the law of international governance articulating its anticlerical cosmopolitanism with the convert's zeal, reducing concern about ethics and community and value to the periodic lamentations of crackpots and Catholics. Not so today. The study of human rights and democracy and the commonplaces of "liberal" societies has taken international law on a goose chase after the ethical. In the euphoria of post-1989 triumphalism, the discipline's focus on the ever receding horizon of pragmatism's contact with idealism has been radically foreshortened. Suddenly we are almost there—disaggregate the state, embrace the ragtag institutions of civil society, and reach for the good life.

III.

So the secular intelligentsia has a new sensibility about both political science and law. Political science takes a shine to law just as law embraces the worlds *both* of ethics, values, faith *and* of politics. And this new sensibility has an emotional tone, a tone of bravura and risk. Suddenly it's no longer suspect to stand for something, even if it is still feels scary—go ahead say it, I know it feels risky, but let's do something bold, now, here, all together—let's admit it, we're liberals.

I'm thinking of middle class men thronging the capital to affirm their faith in masculinity *and* family values, of loud-mouthed law professors bravely standing up for free speech, of internationalists loosed from the Cold War's coexistence constraints, standing together now for democracy and the peaceful tendencies of liberal states. As I read in all seriousness some time ago, and you may not know this, two nations with McDonald's arches have never gone to war with one another. Think about that.

There is a thrill here—not unlike Marty Kaplan's thrill in his new found faith. The thrill of return, of confession, of taking a little risk, a risk suddenly fashionable among all the multitudes gathered together to keep promises and affirm commitments. The little high of saying something together in a big crowd that still feels so unpopular—like that you support good government, think all men are created equal, believe in the spiritual, in humanism, in love, and why not, in the sacred, even in God. This is the thrill of coming out, and after all, why shouldn't straight people get to come out? Religion and law provide the titillation of identity for great mobs of identity wannabes whom deracination has left so haunted and empty and jealous. And it's also the cheap thrill of fashion—it's so cool now to have a close friend who's a practicing Catholic!

This thrill, this tiny rush of transgression, plays against the background of an ebbing faith, an ebbing faith in the secular. As religion has become a secular blasphemy, ethics has become a tempting little legal Lolita, at once fresh and formidable, while law plays Mrs. Robinson to the political scientist, all wet behind the ears with new fangled college talk about regimes and compliance loops. Like those first teenage rebellions—clunky boots or sagging bellbottoms— praying the common prayer pays homage to the secular parental authorities, who not only tolerate, but yearn, pray, for just *this* rebellion.

In all the clamor for God and law we can feel, faintly, the slight weightlessness of a pendulum reversing its course. And in the disequilibrium and equipoise of that moment, we can look briefly back at the secular, at the relations between religion and law, or law and politics, against which the blasphemous pendulum turns. It's elementary, after all, that you can't come out once everyone already knows—coming out must place you just ahead of the curve, be written on a denial, or at least on plausible deniability.

IV

The lawyer's denial that law is political *or* ethical, apology *or* utopia, the political scientist's denial that politics is legal, and the secularist's denial that humanism is religious have all been equivocal denials at best. Sure, we know law is a secular project, just as we are all, all secular men and women. However prone legal scholars have been to deny the politics of law, to charge only communists and other no-good-niks with having claimed that law is political, they have also developed a range of admissions to go with their denial, places for politics, exceptions, constitutional moments, moments of private cynicism. However sure political science has been that only utopians (and lawyers) dreamt of the normative, there were also regimes and stable expectations and feedback loops of legitimation and compliance. Law and politics have been disciplinarily divided by a smokey mirror, the lawyer claiming to see in politics only subjective arbitrariness and ideology, the political scientist in international law only hapless dreaming. In such a situation of willful blindness, when one comes out, transgresses to the other discipline from either direction, one will find only what one has already had—a liberal realism, hardboiled and hopeful.

But what about religion? What religion might read as "sacred" and "profane," the secular intelligentsia has read as "secular" and "religious," alternate domains, social configurations, spheres of influence, separate but (once) equal. The intelligentsia has said religion is private where the law is public. Religion is what we had before we had law. Religion is the domain of irrationality and charismatic authority, law the realm of reason and the bureaucratic. International law understands its birth as a flooding forth from the darkness of religious strife, antidote to the passions of faith, on guard against their re-emergence as ideology. Evil were not empires—we have much to learn from Rome—but imperial ambitions emboldened by religion, or ideology, straining against the leash of an agnostic territorial limit—that's evil. Religion, like cliterodectomy, was the sign of the inalienably different—which must be puzzled over and suppressed and tolerated and denied and accepted and outgrown. And religion marked not simply the crazy and the sane, passion and dispassion. As one international lawyer told me, "religion is about what happens after you die, and international law doesn't have anything to do with it"—read, "we are worried about life, not death, too busy lighting a single candle to contemplate the dark."

Still, even in the dark of the secular night, legal culture managed a relationship with religion. Religion was to be respected, even honored, in its own sphere—the domain of private commitment and spiritual meaning. Law could also honor its roots in religion, from which it inherited the "principles" and "values" of something as broad as the "Judeo-Christian" tradition. Religion begins as a social force, is then transcended and cabined by a new international plane of ecumenical insistence on the prince's prerogatives, is transformed into a "philosophy," the naturalist antidote to an emerging positivism, and survives in our pragmatic century as a set of "principles" guiding the practice of institutions.

Religion, reconfigured as a "tradition," would often rise to its new role in the secular establishment. I attended a conference in which the world's great ethical traditions Christianity, Judaism, Islam, Confucianism and (puzzlingly I thought) International Law were invited, alongside various strands of "liberalism," to contribute to thinking about an appropriate regime to govern territorial boundaries, personal mobility and citizenship. As we went around the room, it became clear that all the great traditions ended in consensus on a clear utopian vision, remarkably consonant with enlightened upper-west-side thinking—that utopia would roughly correspond to our current world, shifted perhaps two or three inches to the left. Suitably domesticated, churches might well take over civic responsibilities, act as arm of the law, provide social services. Religious organizations are prominent among the new NGOs whose "civil society" has been scripted to counteract both illiberal, if often elected, post-colonial governments and corrupt international bureaucracies.

And legal culture, in the old secular days, also knew a deeper truth about itself—that it had displaced religion, and would need to function as a religion—a civic religion, a secular faith. This could be high-minded—the Constitution pole star of a new covenant—or populist, even cynical—give the people courtroom spectacle, the savvy judge a strategic thinker, manager of a legitimation account always in danger of being overdrawn. If religion must be tamed to be deployed, law must also be careful to manage a faith which remains secular. And we find within law not only the narratives of religious redemption and delayed gratification—a substantive justice projected just in front of an interminable procedural present—but also a formidable machinery for purging the secular faith of the apostasy of sacrality. Chief Justice Bedjaoui of the World Court castigates us for "legal paganism."[4] "Formalism" has become an epithet. Our most dispassionate secular modernists denounce enduring faith in something called "sovereignty": Brierly notes "the confusion which the doctrine of sovereignty has introduced into international legal theory"[5]; Henkin insists that "[s]overeignty is a bad word . . . a substitute for thinking and precision"[6]; Lillich proclaims, "the concept of sovereignty . . . is an idea whose time has come and gone."[7] Indeed, washed clean of its idolatrous stain, the law of international governance sees the sacred only at the margins, in the three horsemen of terrorism, fundamentalism, and nationalism.

V

Against so equivocal a denial, what does it mean to come out, come out for the politics of law, the law of politics, the ethics of both—for the religious in secular society? The thrill in political science as the pendulum turns back to law is less the revenge of a liberal spirit against the perversions of an insistent, if largely imaginary, realism than the titillation of evading even for a moment the censor of pragmatism, finally enunciating the pluralist commitments which have hitherto dared not speak their name. For the secularly faithful, to speak of norms, still less of ethics, was to wash out the rocks of universalism, agnosticism and reason, upon which were built the latter-day edifice of political science and the priesthood of policy pragmatism. For a generation, it seemed that coming out as legal might disarm the liberal hegemon, just as coming out for the ethical would throw the game of cosmopolitan scientific neutrality, would make one just one more Cold Warrior. Only a studied ethical neutrality could steel the will of democratic hegemons to do what was necessary, could sustain the science of strategic studies, for fifty years the bulwark political science offered the West against the East. And now, if all the subtle communications of one hegemon to another across an ideological divide were normative all along, each assured about what the other's prisoner would do in just this dilemma, all that past could be redeemed as the work of a liberal spirit, which, we now know, makes commerce, not war. We were not playing with destroying the world, fiddling while Rome armed, we were hammering a new covenant, modeling a new language, enunciating a new law.

Meanwhile, an obverse story for law. For a generation international lawyers began their training by learning a thousand and one explanations why their discipline was "legal," why international law was "law," rather than politics or ethics, now that it had renounced both positivist form and naturalist value for an engaged pragmatic sensibility. Paradoxically, to have come out as politics would both throw the game to the totalitarians and sully one's neutral posture, the cosmopolitanism of coexistence. At the same time, to have come out as ethical would throw the race to the political scientists, foregoing a hard-fought realist savvy.

The thrill in contemporary returns to the ethical, in collective confessions of faith in the old liberal pieties, lies not in their surface rebellion against the devils of "political correctness," but in their escape from the censors of this secularism, from the high priests of antiformalist pragmatism and the anti-clerical routines of a committed cosmopolitan establishment. The thrill lies in their inversion of liberalism's own disciplines. Would it be too simple to observe that we can say law is politics now that politics has come out everywhere for the ethical, the normative, the liberal? Else who will be my role model, now that all the role models are gone? After 1989, flush with victory over an ideological foe onto whom all challenges to law's legality had been projected, we find international lawyers saying, chapter one, page one, that "law is politics" (Henkin et al. 1). Nothing else has changed, the thousand and one reasons for law's legality are still there, but now it can be said. And so also for political science—all the models and systems are still there, but now it can be said: the regime, my dear, is a legal one.

Ah, the new liberals: so brave, so risky, so risque. But how dramatic is it to come out for the politics of law, or the law of regimes, when one dreams only of ideal speech situations, infinite time behind veils of ignorance, the endless dialogic consensus of a liberal procedural regime? It seems such cant to come out as Kant.

The puzzling thing is that all these things would seem risky were we still living with faith in the secular, in pragmatism and political realism. In the church of policy pragmatism, there is a Satan, waiting to be loosed by a slip of the tongue, and that devil is ideology, first cousin of religion. Law is not political—because politics is the primitive stuff of ideology, passion, unreason. Political science is not law for the same reason—because law is the temple of norms, beliefs, ideological commitments. And little would have so triggered the pragmatist inquisition than the pious incantation of a universal liberalism. How satisfying, then, now to be able to come out for a global politics which eschews the ideological, for a cosmopolitan, global liberalism. Or for a global law purged of ideological commitment but committed to liberal virtue. After ideology, all the censors can relax. Including, it seems, the secular separation from religion. How bad can it be, after all, to come out as religious if one means simply that "family values" or "patriotism" or "ethics" are important? I mean, don't we all think that? Once the secular censors have relaxed, a little turn to religion provides a helpful divertissement.

VI

Today's turn to law and religion is thus more of a rotation, more an All-Saints'-Day role reversal than a transvaluation of values. Clausewitz said, "Is not War merely another kind of writing and language for political thoughts? It has certainly a grammar of its own, but its logic is not peculiar to itself."[8] Whether political scientists or lawyers, we are all Clausewitzians now, power a process of persuasion, the missile a missive. At the same time, our law has a religious sense and sensibility, a secret sentiment that powers are more than competencies, property more than a "bundle of rights," rights more than technically enforceable claims. Where there is law there is also mystery: judgment, doctrine, faith.

What work we ask of functionalism to say of this merely that law "functions" like a religion— why not say it, experience the thrill, law *is* a religion—and not just any religion. An islamo-judeo-christian faith in the secular, sustained by a complex movement, isolating religion, purifying itself in a catechism of anti-formalism, while returning over and over to the idols it has shattered. Of course, to come out strongly, publicly, proudly, when everyone has long known you're out as not out, is less risk than regression. When lawyers admit their faith in rights, politicians their faith in law, law its roots and reverence for religion, it may be a goodie, but it is certainly an oldie.

VII

Why do they do it? Because realism has been the Cerberus of the political savvy. Forswear law all who would enter here, law's door opens only for the realist. Once within, the routines and rationalities of lowest cost avoiders, profit maximizers and self interested sovereigns can be codified. Across the hall, liberal ecumenicalism stands guard at the door of law's empire, insisting on a penitent and persistent pluralism. All who pass murmur Yes, we have no religion. Once inside, secular cosmopolitans recognize one another in declarations of faith, in progress, in the international, in the pragmatic, and worship together in the routines of bureaucratic power. Everywhere there is culture but here, in the cosmopolis. Everywhere there is ideology, politics, passion, but not here, among the reasonable men and women of the enlightenment, graced with infinite time, reason, and the modesty of the truly powerful. But some days it's just not enough. Terror and nation and fundament, held firmly at bay, shame us, mock us—how long can we inhabit the high road of cultural denial when we know that we too stand for something dammit. It's not just the Sudanese and Chinese and Sinhalese who have roots and religion. My grandmother read the Bible whenever she was sad—she particularly liked Ecclesiastes and Psalms.

What is this wish for stronger stuff? Gay literary figure Mark Doty wraps his meditation on religion around this italicized sentence: *"My lover of twelve years died just last month."*[9] "It astonishes me to write that sentence," he continues. "It astonishes me that I am writing at all." Doty begins his meditation, "I grew up in two religions," a religion of "images," absorbed from his grandmother's songs and scents, and a "second religion, the codes of explanation and prohibition" learned after her death (13-4). "The prohibitions" he remembers "were worse than the explanations. They suggested that the divinity had constructed the earth as a kind of spiritual minefield, a Chutes and Ladders game of snares, traps and seductions, all of them fueled by the engines of our longing; the flames of hell were stoked by human heats" (17).

To be queer and literary and a figure, Doty rejected one religion and forgot another. And yet, the dead lover's introduction is preceded by this reflection:

> I cannot be queer in church, though I've tried, and though I live now in a place where this seems to be perfectly possible for a great many people. Here in Provincetown we have a wonderful Unitarian church, with a congregation largely gay and lesbian, and it pains me to admit that when I have gone to services there I have been utterly, hopelessly bored. There's something about the absence of imagery, an oddly flaccid quality of neutrality in the language of worship. I long for a kind of spiritual intensity, a passion, though I can certainly see all the errors and horrors spiritual passions have wrought. I don't know what I want in a church, finally; I think the truth is that I *don't* want a church.

> Perhaps my discomfort has to do, still, with issues of desire. Wind, glimmering watery horizon and sun, the watchful seals and shimmered flurries of snow seem to me to have far more to do with the life of my spirit. . . . There is something so *polite* about these Sunday gatherings of tolerant Unitarians that I feel like longing and need must be set aside.

Isn't the part of us that desires, that loves, that longs for encounter and connection—physical and psychic and every other way—also the part of us that knows something about God? The divine, in this world, is all dressed up in mortal clothes, and longing and mortality are so profoundly intertwined as to be, finally, entirely inseparable.

My lover of twelve years died just last month.

VIII

Maybe only gay people can come out. Maybe no one can come out anymore, maybe it's already too late. Perhaps everyone already knows. Or maybe there is more than one coming out, sometimes reassuring, sometimes transgressive. In the end, less significant than the coming out of religion or politics or law are the sectarian questions—what religion, what law, what politics? The emergence of religion in the secular intelligentsia today affirms the pieties of everyday life more than it risks secular martyrdom or blasphemy, is less Anabaptist than Episcopalian, less liberation theology than Unitarian. Now that Marty Kaplan knows there is a God—now what? Is judgment politics? Is love libido? Or has this new religion displaced his other knowledge, his confession replaced, come in the place of other action? You believe in God, very well, but also in Doty's desire? Law is politics, fine, but is it also ideology? A regime may well have ethics, but what are those ethics, what of choice and conflict? It is all well and good to know that the regime is a legal one, but what are its distributional consequences? Losing faith in the secular—yet how would we know, the secular at once so pious and pragmatic? The temptation, so familiar in millenarian times, is to wish, even pray, for law and religion to make a violent return. Liberalism at last triumphant, riding the white horse across the plain of collapsed states, fallen idols and empty ideologies. For I say you must first lose your faith to regain it.

But even these are easy pieties. These days, when lawyers tell me it's all really politics, when political scientists admit their interest in law, when secular humanists confess to the spiritual, I usually smile. But sometimes there is more. Sometimes this great turn, pendulums of commitment poised to crash back on the secular imagination, offers more than a routine ritual of reversal, a euphoric recollection of the everyday religion we left behind. I'm thinking of the white Houston mayor who came out for affirmative action by saying "don't let people like me get all the contracts." Coming out—here as white and male—can be a shock, an opening, a resistance—just as it can be a ritual, a repetition, nostalgia for the peace and quiet of the closet. As the secular prepares its fall back to the ethical, its shuttle weaving and unweaving the fabric of rulership, that was a gesture, a gesture of remembrance that we've been this way before, that ours is also an ambivalence without exit. Religion, law, politics—each can be reclaimed, invaded, embraced in registers of both routinization and resistance. But when we say they are "back," that law is back to politics, politics back to law, religion back to secular humanism, I'm afraid we usually mean only that the same pieties are being woven from the other side.

The gesture I'm after hints of new territory—new explorations across the boundaries of law and politics, and into a secular establishment's history of religious entanglements. And here we might find in international governance less a moment of tolerant generality, a culture above culture, than a practice of social exclusion, routinizing the exuberance of spiritual fervor as bureaucracy, cultural difference as tolerance. When we hear of religion's return, after all, we ordinarily do not think to upend the suppression of witchcraft, blasphemy, sorcery or ecstasy of so much millenarianism, unraveling centuries of inter-sovereign/religious collaboration. We normally return to religion less to question than to confirm our eclecticism, less as a displacement of secularism than as a continuation of its will to power. Like most interdisciplinary gestures, the move of law to politics, of politics to law, of both to religion, seeks across the border for reasons to celebrate the most central commitments of our own disciplinary domain. The interdiscipline comes not to confront, but to confirm, less to confound, than to comfort.

But while the pendulum pauses, we may have a moment to glimpse the transgressive, the innovative, before slipping into quiescent rotation among the pieties of a liberal politics, law or religion. For just a moment, we might think the realist adage that eggs must break to make an omelet in the language of sacrificial violence, we might read human rights violations in the register of pornographic desire, we might understand war "crimes" outside the usual list of quieting metaphors—"crime" joining "sin," "disease," "passion," the "unconscious" or the "primitive"—waiting to be routinized into the practices of global governance. If law and religion are indeed back, I pray we embrace this moment in all its delirium. Perhaps just for an instant we can glimpse together the pieties of power and the power of piety, the two sides of the liberal coin raised up against one another, a critical second of vertiginous equipoise, before one or the other is routinized as rebellion.

Notes

[1] "Religion," *Encyclopedia Britannica 1995 Book of the Year* (Chicago: Encyclopedia Britannica, 1995), 289, 298. Figures are as of mid 1995.

[2] Nancy Gibbs and Howard G. Chua-Eoan, "Angels Among Us," *Time,* 27 December 1993, at cover.

[3] "Ambushed by Spirituality," *Time Magazine*, 24 June 1996, 62.

[4] Mohammed Bedjaou, *Towards an International Economic Order* (New York: Holmes and Meier, 1979), 98.

[5] J. L. Brierly, *The Law of Nations* (6th edition, 1963), quoted Louis Henkin et al., *International Law: Cases and Materials*, 3rd edition (St Paul: West Publishing Co., 1993), 13.

[6] *International Law: Politics, Values, and Functions*, Rec. des Cours 24 (1989-IV), 216, quoted Louis Henkin et al, *International Law: Cases and Materials*, 3rd edition, 15.

[7] "Sovereignty and Humanity: Can They Converge?" *The Spirit of Uppsala*, ed. Grahl-Madsen & Toman (1984), 406, quoted Henkin et al., *International Law: Cases and Materials* (3rd edition, 1993), 19.

[8] Carl von Clausewitz, *On War*, ed. Anatol Rapoport (New York: Penguin, 1985), 402.

[9] *Heaven's Coast: A Memoir* (New York: HarperCollins, 1996), 18.

Three Excerpts from The Poem of Queen Esther

Joao Pinto Delgado (1585?-1653)
*Translated by David R. Slavitt**

I

On the court's turbulent ocean, Haman sails,
a proud vessel careening against the force
of buffeting winds that do not obstruct but serve
instead to hasten him further along his course.
If he hears moans and shrieks from high in the stays,
to his delighted ear they are hymns of praise.

He glows with the King's esteem, and the world, impressed,
caters to his every whim. Great men
hover about him, while lesser ones in need
turn to him as a magnetized needle when
you let it float will point to the pole star. He
is that fixed point in the skies of cupidity.

He comes to assume that such behavior is right
and proper and merely what he deserves. He grows
accustomed to hearing himself addressed in prayers
that he could grant in an instant if he chose —
or not, for either way his power seems
to have made the empire subject to his dreams.

The courtiers bow as low before him as
before their emperor or their god. In this
offense to heaven he takes outrageous pleasure.
That something in their behavior—or in his—
is blasphemous never crosses his mind at all
or that, given enough time, such pride must fall.

The only man who appears to have no fear
(or hopes of gain from Haman's fickle favor
that can produce the same servility)
is Mordecai, whose heart seems not to quaver
at Haman's scowls and frowns, however black.
In bland assurance, Mordecai stares back.

* Joao Pinto Delgado (1585?-1653) was a Marrano or "New Christian" poet. This translation from the Spanish is part of a longer work, "The Poem of Queen Esther," which retells the Book of Esther with obvious references to the Inquisition, of which the poet's family were victims first in Spain and then in France. They moved at last to the Netherlands, where it was safer for Jews.

What is this grandeur after all but a writ
signed with a bird's quill and light as a feather?
If Haman banks and soars in an updraft now,
the sky in which he flies is God's, and the weather
may change as shifting winds bring clouds that dim
the sun so that the heavens may frown at him.

He watches as the counselors strut and preen
to reassure one another how they are as great
and good as they are wise and deserve that wealth
by which the gods acknowledge and validate
what the emperor has decreed, the extravagant claims
implicit in all those titles before their names.

He is not blinded by this glitter whose eyes
are fixed on the much brighter eternal light
of the holiness of the law he trusts and loves
and, when called to account, the Israelite
is foolish enough—or brave enough—to declare
that the power and glory he worships are elsewhere.

"I am no ingrate," he says. "I am not disloyal,
but ever mindful and grateful for those rich
rewards I have received: my life, the world,
its wealth of wonders, and all the beauty which
my eyes behold are my creator's grand
gifts, more fine than man can understand.

I praise the Lord who made the universe
and is its master. In his hand is set down
on the slate of my heart his holy name that time
and change cannot erase. His is the crown
of glory I worship, honor, and revere
more than that of an emperor or vizier.

How can I, after contemplating such
heavenly splendors, see your poor displays
of pomp and ceremony and be impressed
or dazzled? How can they deserve my praise?
How should I fear your power, which is small
compared to that of the Lord who is master of all?

The vicissitudes of life on earth are merely
shadows that pass as the clouds fly by in the sky.
Above them, the sun still shines, and heaven reckons
rewards for our suffering here that, by and by
we'll have: for death, eternal life; for this
torture, an unimaginable bliss.

The kingdom of the Lord is good, and we
who know this are forgetful. Like the blind

147

we stumble along the road, confused, in flight
from what we cherish, leaving that behind.
We bubble up like fountains but then fall back
to seek the lowest level and make a track

of rivulets in the mud in which we settle.
How pitiable this is. Yet there are some
proud men who will congratulate themselves
and preen as if good fortune could not come
undone in an instant to be succeeded by
a wretchedness that lasts for eternity.

If I can glimpse, behind the billowing curtain
of the world's appearances, some indication
of what is worthy of worship, real, and true,
how can I bend my knee in subjugation
to mere shadows? Belief in fantasies
is childish or a symptom of disease."

Like a wounded lion, bellowing and roaring
from the spear that has struck his side and gives him pain
at every step, Haman groans and shouts,
which only distresses him further. Nearly insane,
that lion snaps at the spear shaft but it hurts
him all the worse as more and more blood spurts.

Having suffered this blow to his pride, his soul
snarls and snaps in rage and he aggravates
the wound that causes him further torment. He glares,
and plans his revenge against the man he hates,
to inflict that hurt a hundred, a thousand fold,
the thought of which will make the blood run cold.

Can his luck have deserted him? Is this a sign
of worse to come? How can he tolerate
such insolence? He has not changed, nor has
the world. He must somehow obliterate
this blemish to his honor and self-esteem.
Carefully, he formulates his scheme.

The death of a single man is not enough,
is hardly proportionate to the offense.
He broods, fanning the embers of his hatred
into a fire, blazing and intense:
nothing less than a holocaust will do:
let Mordecai die and all his people, too.

II

The Queen, meanwhile, has heard how Mordecai
sits in the antechamber where he wears
the paraphernalia of those who grieve the loss
of a loved one and recites a mourner's prayers.
She sends to know what hurt he has received—
to share it, if it cannot be relieved.

Her messenger returns with her cousin's words:
his wretchedness is not for himself but, worse,
for all the house of Jacob, Haman having
turned the King against them with his curse.
The edict has gone out, and everywhere
the Jews are terrified and in despair.

He explains the sad details, and Esther sees
what hurt Haman will cause her kinsmen—unless
she does as Mordecai asks and goes to the King
to appeal to his love, pity, and gentleness,
to retract his edict, for only he can give
the order that will let her people live.

But the King must send for her, as he has not
for thirty days now. Is his ardor cool?
Dare she go unbidden? Should she risk
her life that way by violating his rule?
It isn't fear for herself but, if she tries
and fails, what then? Will she not jeopardize

all Israel? She wrestles with this question.
Her desire is clear—to do what is right and good—
but how can her frail shoulders bear this burden?
Where can she find the strength and wit? Where should
she look for help and guidance? Has she a choice?
From deep in her soul, she hears an answering voice:

"Your life," it says, "is a part of your people's life.
You are not separate. Let the King know this—
that if he puts the rest of the Jews to death
he will, by that same order, execute his
own beloved Queen who shares that throne
on which he will remain to mourn alone.

Do not suppose a crown can keep you safe.
He cannot think so, either, who realizes
that to pardon one is to overturn the entire
edict: there can be no compromises.
There is either a law the soldiers are fulfilling
or else there is only so much random killing.

You could, of course, run away and save yourself,
but where would you go? And how could you bear the thought
of having failed your people? Bitter chagrin
would be your portion. Do as you know you ought,
whatever may be the outcome of your behavior,
as your father's child and, I hope, your people's savior.

You could perhaps do nothing, and try to pass
as a gentile, but it's a bitter life that awaits
those whose existence is fiction. At any moment
(which the impostor forever anticipates),
he may be unmasked. That self he has tried to deny
will return to life and betray him, and he will die.

Who can read the riddles of heaven? Why
were you picked out and promoted thus except
to serve God and your people? Can you refuse
your own fate? Heaven's hard bargains must be kept.
Trust in God, for He has entrusted you
with a sacred duty. What else can you do?"

Thus it says, and the Queen in her great anguish
has to accede to the force of its argument.
To prepare, she resolves not only to pray but also to fast
for three days and she makes known her intent
to Mordecai and asks that he invite
all Jews to pray with her, all day and night,

for her success, of course, but, failing that,
if she does not find favor with the King,
then for her soul's repose and the end of grief
which are the gifts that death is said to bring
to that narrow bed in which we all lie down,
the poor, the rich, and those who wear a crown.

III. Queen Esther's Prayer

She prays: "O Great and Eternal Being who
with a generous hand has bestowed upon us all
Your gifts and mercies, like the sun that supports
life here on earth, I pray to You now and call
on You for protection not for my life but for
that of Your people, who worship You and adore,

although for their faith in You they are facing death.
In pity, let Your holy name descend
to earth to show its power and in the hearts
of cruel men strike awe. Once more, defend
Your people from their blows and those that we
inflict upon ourselves in our misery.

We know only too well that we are unworthy,
having failed to keep Your laws, and yet our yearning
for truth and goodness must count for something. The spark
of faith is still alive in us and burning
however dimly. The tongues of its hot fire
dance in the gloom, the beacons of our desire

for heaven. We may be weak but You are strong
and on Your abundant patience we rely
and Your compassion as deep as the infinite sea.
The stoniest heart must yield itself, by and by,
to the battering on it of Your waves of grace
that offer redemption to even the hardest case.

If, from the scales of justice there is no
appeal, then which of us can doubt his fate?
For anyone here to rise, You must descend
and with a merciful thumb adjust, abate,
and mollify the findings of Your fury.
Be advocate as well as our judge and jury.

Those enemies of Israel who oppress us
are not Your servants; they are Your enemies too,
perverting Your righteous laws, but we imagine
there must be some explanation for what they do.
Is this perhaps a punishment we have earned—
to be imprisoned, tortured, and then burned?

It cannot be so, for You are a God of compassion,
and in loving-kindness will save us once again,
as You have done so many times before
from the cruel machinations of evil men.
Generations from now, we will tell the story
of how You preserved us and we will exalt Your glory.

Use me as You used Jaël, once, to smite
the mighty Sisera in her tent. I beg
to be Your instrument as that brave woman
was who took her hammer and tent peg
and drove it into his skull. By what she dared,
were the Canaanites subdued and Israel spared.

The hardest of Egyptian hearts was forced
to acknowledge at last Your majesty and might
as the wall of water that formed to let us pass
dissolved and drowned them all, and in the fright
of their final moments on earth, they understood
how evil's power is less than that of good.

To Pharaoh and then the Canaanites You displayed
a righteous wrath that surely You can repeat
in some impressive fashion, an intervention
by which You shall contrive again the defeat
of Israel's foe, for if You wished us ill,
I have no doubt that You would work your will

against us, Yourself, as a loving father should,
punish your errant children, but wield the rod
with Your own hand. Meanwhile, protect us from
those who have never acknowledged You as God
or prayed to You as our fathers did. Give aid
to Israel's children, suffering now and afraid."

She feels in her soul the calm of the ocean's depths
to which, nonetheless, a penetrating ray
of sunlight filters down. As if she were
a mermaid, she swims in grace. Fear floats away,
and she prepares for Haman and the King
with confidence of what the night will bring.

Fore/giveness On the Way:
Nesting in the Womb of Response

Elliot R. Wolfson

Seit menlich böser Geist sich
Bemächtiget des glüklichen Altertums, unendlich,
Langher währt Eines, gesangsfeind, klanglos, das
In Maasen vergeht, des Sinnes gewaltsames. Ungebundenes aber
Hasset Gott.
  Friedrich Hölderlin, *Der Einzige.*[1]

Time Of Forgiveness in the Giving Before Time

"To Err is *Humane*, to Forgive, *Divine*"[2]: in this relatively simple, albeit strikingly incisive, couplet, Alexander Pope offered the world one of the most memorable and oft-cited reflections on the constitutional difference between human and divine nature. But what does it mean to speak of forgiveness as a distinctive character trait of godliness in contrast to the all-too-human propensity to stray from the path of righteousness? To apprehend the signification of a forgiving God, indeed a God whose very way of being in relation to the world it is to forgive, we must chart three conditions contained analytically in the concept of forgiveness. We may call these conditions necessary, but not sufficient, that is, the saying of forgiveness implies that each of these conditions be met, but for there to be the forgiving of the other who is forgiven something more than these conditions must come to play. The conditions set the logical parameters of the experience, but the experience itself exceeds the parameters in which it allows itself to be present and verbally apprehended.

In the first instance, I note that forgiveness should be clearly demarcated from forgetfulness. Here I would take issue with a commonplace perception regarding the causal relationship between the two, which has been expressed by no less a figure than Shakespeare through the mouth of King Lear, "Pray you now, forget and forgive."[3] I do not think that forgiveness is consequent to forgetfulness; on the contrary, it seems reasonable to assume that the two are mutually exclusive, for if a matter is forgotten, there is no need for it to be forgiven. The consciousness we attribute to God does not forget, it forgives, it gives before there is forgetfulness. To give before, to fore/give, is precisely not to forget, for one who forgets cannot forgive. Forgiveness demands to come before forgetfulness.

The second condition is a correlate of the first: if forgiveness is predicated on the absence of forgetfulness, it presupposes the act of memory. For something to be forgiven, it must be remembered. Forgiveness demands. It entrusts the other by commissioning from the other, laying claim on one to respond to the other without an exchange of goods. Forgiveness bears within itself the limit of its own delimitation, by assuming the laying-at-hand of that which is remembered, that which proceeds (or slips) from the past into the present and thereby is anticipated in the future, the retrieval of that which is momentary, the return of that which is to come. Forgiveness happens in time, forgetfulness is the obfuscation of time. Forgiveness ensues from the mediated sense of time's immediacy, indeed from the experience of time as the immediate and irreducible possibility of there being something even if that something is nothing; forgetfulness holds sway when there is no more to become, when the light of there-being is veiled in the darkness of being-there. Forgiveness is the giving-before that grounds the fecundity of temporality in the *nunc stans*, forgetfulness the taking-away that extirpates the possibility of the present without which there is neither remembrance of the past nor expectation of the future. In the moment of forgiving, time endures, and no more turns into not yet, but in the standstill of forgetting, time withdraws, and not yet becomes no more.[4]

Transgression, Punishment, Responsibility, Forgiveness
Graven Images 4 (1998), 153-169

The third condition involves the axiological mechanism by means of which forgiveness is assured in God's relationship to human beings. Here the discourse turns to the culturally specific formulation, which may indeed have a more universalist application but which is nevertheless experienced as part of the foundation of the particular ethnic identity. The focus of my reflections henceforth refers to descriptions of God's unique relation to the Jewish people. In this case, forgiveness has been traditionally linked to the symbol of the covenant. Beyond the legalistic background of this ancient phenomenon, the covenant assumed semiological significance in the course of the religious history of Judaism: covenant is the sign that brings forth to memory, that which calls to mind, and thus breaks open the path to forgiveness. The resonance of what is unsaid in this saying can be heard best if we again contrast forgiveness and forgetfulness. Forgiveness is the presence of the sign, inscription, the cutting of the covenant upon the rock; forgetfulness the absence of the sign, erasure, the depositing of the trace beneath the rock. To erase that trace is the mark of humankind, to give before, to fore/give, that of transcendence. In forgiving one gives before, participating in the dialogue that releases the tension of the moment; by forgetting we remain submerged in the oblivion of the past, the silent speech of senseless chatter, the emptiness that is full.

Return of Daughter to Mother's Womb: Ontological Condition of the Turn

Having established some of the contours of forgiveness as it takes shape within a specific cultural matrix, I will set out to examine this phenomenon from the even more limited vantage point of the medieval kabbalistic tradition, and even here my scope is far more narrow as I will look at the symbolic depiction of forgiveness as this affectivity is refracted through the prism of the complex aggregate of textual units that we call *Sefer ha-Zohar*, the "zoharic literature,"[5] which in all likelihood assumed literary shape, more or less, in the thirteenth and fourteenth centuries in Castile. To lay out even more precisely the trajectory of my thinking, I will focus on the symbol of Yom Kippur, which is one of the standard names employed by kabbalists to delimit the third of the ten divine potencies, *Binah*, understanding, which is also referred to as the mother, the womb, the place of return, *teshuvah*, the retracing of the way to return to origin, the world of the masculine, the world that is coming, and a myriad of other poetic tropes. Yom Kippur, the day of atonement, is the day of amends, that is, the day on which there is the mending of that which is torn. The reparation (*tiqqun*) comes by way of the return of the lower seven emanations to the womb of the mother whence they emerged, a restoration that anticipates the state of union achieved in the eschaton.[6] By thinking philosophically about forgiveness and atonement, we set out to capture the mythic import of Yom Kippur, especially as it relates to the symbol of the mother in the esoteric tradition. In listening to the word communicated by the poetic utterance, we hear again that which has been uttered before, but never in the precise way that it is heard in this moment.[7] In that respect, we follow as we lead.

I begin with a zoharic text, an explication of the verse, *tiq'u va-ḥodesh shofar ba-keseh le-yom ḥaggenu*, "Blow the ram's horn on the new moon, on the full moon for our feast day" (Psalm 81:4), interpreted rabbinically as a reference to Rosh ha-Shanah, the new year festival celebrated on the first day of the seventh month, the festival that occurs when the moon is new, that is, when it is hidden, as opposed to the middle of the month, on the fifteenth, when the moon is full. The Hebrew rendered as the "full moon" is *keseh*, a term that is explicable (as medieval commentaries such as Abraham ibn Ezra and Rashi duly noted) from the occurrence of the expression *le-yom ha-kese'* in Proverbs 7:20, which seems to refer to the middle of the month, used there to signify the appointed time when the man returns home from his business trip. The rabbinic reading not only ignores the *peshaṭ*, the contextual sense, but turns the text against itself, for the term *ba-keseh* is understood as the time when the moon is hidden, that is at the beginning of the month when the moon is renewed rather than the middle of the month when it is full.[8] The mystical reading proffered in the following passage builds upon this interpretative foundation:

> R. Eleazar said: It is written, "on the full moon for our feast day" (Ps. 81:4) . . . [*ba-keseh*] with [the letter] *he'*, for the moon is concealed (*de-'itkasseya' sihara'*). . . . Come and see: On that day the moon is hidden, and she does not shine until the tenth of the month when Israel all repent in a perfect repentance,

and the supernal mother returns and illuminates her. On that day she takes the illumination of the mother, and joy is found in everything. Thus it is written, *yom ha-kippurim hu'* ("This is the day of Yom Kippur") (Lev. 23:27). It should have been *yom kippur* [in the singular]. Why is it *yom ha-kippurim* [in the plural]? To indicate that two lights are illumined as one, the upper radiance shining upon the lower radiance. On that day she shines from the supernal light and not from the light of the sun. Therefore it is written "on the full moon for our feast day." R. Abba sent [a question] to R. Simeon: What is the [appropriate] time for the copulation of the Community of Israel and the holy king? He responded to him [with the words of Abraham]: "And besides, she is in truth my sister, my father's daughter though not my mother's daughter; and she became my wife" (Gen. 20:12). . . . R. Hiyya said to R. Abba: What did he say in his response to you? He said that the coupling of the king and the queen is certainly only at the time that she is illumined from the supernal father, for when she is illumined from him they call her "holy" (*qodesh*), for she takes from the house of the father, and they are united as one, for the king is called "holy," as it is written, "Israel is holy unto the Lord" (Jer. 2:3), for he takes from the place that is called "holy."[9] Consequently, "she is my father's daughter though not my mother's daughter," for this name [*qodesh*] is from the house of the father and not from the house of the mother. And thus "she became my wife," to unite as one at that time and not another time, at the time she takes from the house of the father and not at the time she takes from the house of the mother. The day of Yom Kippur proves the point for sexual intercourse is forbidden, for the coupling does not take place since she takes from the house of the mother rather than from the house of the father. (*Zohar* 3:100b)

The secret unique to Yom Kippur is related to a theosophic process that unfolds therein, the ontological reality that yields the existential meaning associated with this particular moment in time. An analysis of the role of time in kabbalistic ontology obviously lies beyond the circumscribed boundaries of this study, but it is necessary to make a preliminary observation regarding the texture of time,[10] for without a working hypothesis with respect to this matter we cannot comprehend the theosophic mystery distinctive to the time of Yom Kippur. In general terms, we may say that for the medieval kabbalists time is not dependent on the motion of bodies in space nor is it conceived as the fleeting shadow of the eternal forms in the world of matter. Indeed, time is not dependent on physical existence at all, for it is of the very essence of the sefirotic potencies, which constitute the mystical shape of the Godhead. Time, therefore, is not extrinsic to God; on the contrary, it is the very pulsation of the divine energy.[11] To the degree that this energy is configured in the symbolic imagination of the kabbalists as consciousness, it follows that temporality is essentially indistinguishable from consciousness. Moreover, just as the consciousness of God is infinite in its extensionality, so too is the duration of time potentially infinite, an infinity that is expressed in the ceaseless cycle of renewal and regeneration of the moment.

The kabbalistic perspective is expressed succinctly by Moses Cordovero: "Time is the secret of the rotation of the emanations (*sod gilgul ha-sefirot*), during the day this particular emanation, during the night this particular emanation, and on Sabbath this particular emanation. The time that was from the day that the world was created and the emanations rotated is not the time that evolves from now and forward, but rather there are new aspects, for the succession of time (*seder zemanim*) that is before him has no boundary and no end."[12] Cordovero relates this ever-changing aspect of time to the phenomenon of new interpretations of Torah: there is always a novel explanation to be drawn forth from the text since the Torah is the manifestation of the divine essence that is infinite. Cordovero's linkage of innovative explications of Torah and the ever-changing nature of time is a fascinating idea worthy of further exploration, but what is most important for my purposes is his formulation that time is the secret of the rotation of the sefirotic emanations.[13] This underscores the point that time is the very essence of the divine nature and not something extrinsic to it. Moreover, inasmuch as the divine nature is limitless, it follows that each moment of time, which is the very expression of that nature, will be unlike that which has proceeded it. Indeed, from the perspective of kabbalistic theosophy, the element of time that is most real is the present, which is perhaps best captured by the Bergsonian idea of the *élan vital*, the ever-gushing stream of temporality that flows without pause, although never in the same manner. The present alone possesses ontic reality in the prehension of consciousness, for only the presence of the moment makes possible the remembrance of the past and the anticipation of the future.

With this brief introduction to the kabbalistic understanding of time, we may return to the specific example of Yom Kippur. This holiest day on the Jewish calendar assumes a particular theosophic significance, which in turn has an impact on the practitioner's liturgical experience of time. The mystery is laid bare by heeding the philological concealment unveiled in the utterance of its biblical name, *yom ha-kippurim*, literally, the "day of atonements." The plural form of this expression is decoded symbolically by the zoharic authorship as an allusion to the fact that on that day the supernal radiance, *Binah*, the third of the ten emanations, shines upon the lower radiance, *Malkhut*, the tenth emanation, an illumination that can be conveyed as well by the anthropomorphic image of the mother casting her light upon the daughter, which in another passage is depicted as the illumination of the lower mother by the supernal mother.[14]

The reunion of mother and daughter is also described as the time that the daughter takes from the house of the mother rather than from the house of the father. The incestuous relationship implied in the image of the daughter taking from the father is utilized by the author of the zoharic passage to depict symbolically the emanation of the lower wisdom, often referred to as the wisdom of Solomon (*hokhmat shelomo*), from the upper wisdom, or the wisdom of God (*hokhmat 'elohim*).[15] On the day that the daughter receives from the father, the daughter and the son unite in holy matrimony.[16] Interestingly enough, the incestuous mating of father and daughter facilitates the second incestuous relationship between sister and brother by means of which they adopt the personae of king and queen. Not only is there an astonishing use of incestuous relations on the part of kabbalists to characterize intradivine processes, but it is precisely the cohabitation of father and daughter, on the one hand, and that of son and daughter, on the other, that convey the notion of sacred sexuality, the theosophic symbol that underlies the pietistic ideal of spiritual eros.[17] The point is underscored in the afore-cited zoharic text by the claim that the word *qodesh*, "holy," applies to the father, the son, and the daughter, which correspond respectively to the second, sixth, and tenth emanations, *Hokhmah*, *Tif'eret*, and *Malkhut*. In this context, as elsewhere in the *Zohar*, the word *qodesh* is related specifically to the sacral dimension of sexual matters, for the operative notion is that holiness is attained not by sexual abstinence, but through the proper mental intentionality that purifies the act of intercourse.[18] In this particular setting, the point being made is that holiness consists of the son and the daughter, *Tif'eret* and *Malkhut*, the holy King and the Community of Israel, receiving the overflow from the father, *Hokhmah*, which facilitates the union of the king and the queen.[19]

By contrast, on Yom Kippur, when the daughter is illumined by the mother, the union between *Tif'eret* and *Malkhut* is forbidden. The theosophic secret is related sacramentally to the ritual prohibition of sex between a husband and his wife on that day. The temporary ascetic renunciation below symbolically reflects the ontological condition above, for the union of mother and daughter precludes the possibility of the union between daughter and son.[20] The reparation on the day of atonement, therefore, involves not the heterosexual image of the king cohabiting with the queen, but the presumably asexual image of the mother radiating upon the daughter, which is also portrayed as the return of the daughter to the mother's womb. It must be noted, however, that in some passages the zoharic authorship utilizes images of a decidedly erotic nature to depict the lower world of *Malkhut* receiving the blessing from the upper world of *Binah*. For instance, in one text, the relationship of these sefirotic gradations on Yom Kippur is described as the visitation of the mother to the palace of the daughter, which results in the radiation of the face (*nehiru de-'anpin*), a trope often used in zoharic texts to convey the sense of joy related to the overflow of the divine efflux, which on occasion is expressed in terms of the erotic union that binds together the different aspects of being.[21]

> Come and see: The lower world exists to receive constantly, and it is the precious
> stone, and the supernal world only gives her in the manner in which she exists. . . .
> In the manner in which the lower world is crowned she draws from that which is
> above. . . . When does she exist in the supernal light? I would say on Yom Kippur,

for on Yom Kippur that precious stone shines with the supernal light from the light of the world-to-come. . . . When the supernal mother, the world-to-come, comes to dwell in the palace of the lower world, so that there will be an illumination of the face . . . it emits all of the blessings and it shines on everything, and all that freedom is found and Israel takes from those blessings. When the world-to-come enters the palace of the lower world, the lower rejoices with her children in that supernal meal. The table is then blessed and all of the worlds are blessed, and all joy and all the illumination of the face are found there. (*Zohar* 2:184b-185a)

In the complex symbology embraced by the Castilian kabbalists who lie behind the fictional personae of the zoharic narrative, there are a variety of different unifications that characterize the intradivine processes. In general, most scholars have focused on the heterosexual motif of the *hieros gamos* that occurs between the sixth and the tenth emanations, *Tif'eret* and *Malkhut*, the holy King and his Matrona, as the central form of unity. There is certainly justification for this emphasis insofar as the kabbalists themselves often privilege heterosexual union as the most appropriate image to convey the ideal state of harmony and perfection that will be realized in the messianic age. Exile is marked by the separation of male and female, whereas redemption entails the reunification of the two. The eschatological goal of *tiqqun*, therefore, involves the repairing of male and female so that the primordial state of wholeness will be retrieved. In addition to the heterosexual image of union, however, there is incontrovertible evidence in kabbalistic writings for a paradigm of same-sex unions within the Godhead, either male-male or female-female. To be sure, these homosexual relationships are transmuted into heterosexual terms such that the active partner is portrayed as male vis-à-vis the passive partner who is female. In the specific case of the relationship between *Binah* and *Malkhut*, the former is depicted as the "world of the masculine" and the latter as the "world of the feminine," even though female images are clearly assigned to both of these gradations in the symbolic imagination of the kabbalists.[22] Thus the two *sefirot* are respectively imaged as mother and daughter, or alternatively as supernal mother and lower mother, as well as the two sisters, Leah and Rachel (see Tishby, *Wisdom of the Zohar*, 295.)

Moreover, not only is it the case that the upper female is valorized as male in relation to the lower female, but the latter is itself transformed into a male by virtue of its union with the former. This is precisely the import of the symbol of the mother as it emerges from the zoharic material and related kabbalistic sources: although we rightly assume that motherhood is a biological function of the female sex, from the perspective of gender as it is constructed in the relevant works of theosophic kabbalah the role of mothering is decidedly masculine, indeed phallic, in its nature.[23] Hence, in one passage, the zoharic authorship describes the transformation of the daughter into the mother in terms of the image of *Binah* bestowing her garments on *Malkhut* such that the latter is vested in the form of the Israelite males.[24] Yom Kippur itself is a symbolic embodiment of this transformation, which is portrayed either as the ascent of *Malkhut* to *Binah* or as the descent of *Binah* to *Malkhut*. In the final analysis, both processes signify the metamorphosis by means of which the lower female assumes the role of the upper female, which is to say, the lower female is masculinized and adopts the persona of the mother who bestows blessings of sustenance upon her offspring.[25] On Yom Kippur the *Shekhinah* is thus marked by a double movement: the ascent to the mother above and the overflowing to Israel below. The zoharic symbolism is well summarized by Moses de León:

> *Yom ha-kippurim*: All beginnings are difficult in their inception, but in the end they are well grounded [literally, "they stand in their property"]. The gradations revolve and rotate, each one according to its measure, one atop the other, and the higher one atop both of them [based on Ecclesiastes 5:7]. Indeed, her beginning is difficult in its inception, but in her end she dwells in the house of her mother, and her mother crowns her and adorns her, and she takes for her "seal and cord" (Gen. 38:25), "lighting oil and incense" (Num. 4:7), as her foundation, to illuminate the side of her face [based on Exodus 25:37]. She is called by the name of her mother in the splendor of her radiant face. *Yom ha-kippurim*, for the mother shines her face upon her, "and she said to her, 'I must seek a home for you, where you may be happy'" (Ruth 3:1). Israel, the holy nation, have repented from their ways . . . Forgive your nation, Israel . . . all the faces are illuminated in relation to them. . . . How good and pleasant is it when Israel are in their proper order, and "the mother sits over the fledglings" (Deut. 22:6). They are all holy, and the Lord

is in their midst, "they are the seed the Lord has blessed" (Isa. 61:9). For you must know that when Israel arouse the repentance, and they come before the Lord, blessed be he, in love, and they turn from their evil ways, they are called children of the blessed holy One, as it says, "You are children of the Lord your God" (Deut. 14:1). He placed his *Shekhinah* over them, to guide them, to discipline them, and to lead them, like a mother that disciplines her children, as it says, "the Lord your God disciplines you just as a man disciplines his son" (ibid. 8:5). Thus when the blessed One places his fear upon them, they return to him and they distance themselves from their evil ways. Consequently, the blessed One forgives them, and his *Shekhinah* returns to them, they are radiant and they are forgiven. (*Book of the Pomegranate*, 162-3.)

De León appropriates the rabbinic maxim that "all beginnings are difficult"[26] in order to characterize the nature of the *Shekhinah* at the beginning of the year, that is, on Rosh ha-Shanah, the day of judgment, *yom ha-din*. Kabbalistically understood, this implies that the attribute of judgment, which is the *Shekhinah*, has dominion on that day. By contrast, her end is related to Yom Kippur, for on that day the judgmental aspect of the *Shekhinah* is ameliorated and transformed by her ascent to and reintegration in the womb of *Binah*, which is metaphorically depicted as the stability that she achieves when she comes to dwell in the house of her mother. On Yom Kippur the *Shekhinah* is crowned and glorified by the illumination of *Binah*, and thus she assumes the name of her mother, for she is endowed with the properties of motherhood in relation to the people of Israel who have atoned for their sins and who have been forgiven by God. In her role of the mother sustaining her children in the hour that they have been forgiven, the *Shekhinah* is transformed from judgment to mercy, a transformation that implies as well the masculinization of her femininity. The point is underscored in the following zoharic passage wherein several interpretations of the verse "And Melchizedek, king of Shalem," *u-malki ṣedeq melekh shalem* (Genesis 14:18), are proffered:

> *Melekh shalem* precisely, the king that rules in perfection (*bi-shelemo*). When is he the perfect king (*melekh shalem*)? On Yom Kippur for all the faces are illuminated. . . . Another interpretation: "And Melchizedek," this is the final world, "king of Shalem," this is the supernal world, for the one is crowned in the other without separation, two worlds as one. (*Zohar* 1:87a.)

The cryptic biblical reference to Melchizedek is decoded as a symbolic allusion to the *Shekhinah* (cf. *Zohar* 3:193b) who is called by this name because this attribute is the "perfect king," *melekh shalem*, but she achieves this masculine status only on Yom Kippur when all of the sefirotic gradations radiate upon her as a result of her union with the supernal world of *Binah*. In the day of Yom Kippur, therefore, the heterosexual bonding of son and daughter, or king and queen, is transcended for the sake of the higher unification between the two female configurations, which is expressed in the above passage as the mutual crowning of the "final world," the *Shekhinah*, and the "supernal world," *Binah*. The unity of the two worlds entails the masculine transposition of the feminine character of the divine, which is depicted paradoxically by the convergence of the symbols of mother and king. As I noted above, this theosophic process is reflected in the traditional injunction to abstain from sexual intercourse on Yom Kippur. The ritual prohibition to engage in coitus reflects the ontological fact that above there is a union between the lower and the upper females, which results in the transformation of the daughter into the mother, a process that bestows upon the former the title of king, which is associated with the latter. The application of the symbol of the king to *Binah* and *Malkhut* denotes the quality of overflowing that is associated with both attributes in relation to what is beneath them. The point is disclosed in the following zoharic passage: "There is a king above, which is the mystery of the holy of holies . . . and there is a king below, which is in the likeness of that supernal king, and it is the king over everything that is below" (*Zohar* 2: 67b). When the female adopts the posture of that which emanates, the status of the masculine is conferred upon her.[27] On occasion the authorship of a particular zoharic text reflects an awareness of the complexity of the gender valence implied by the attribution of the title "king" to divine potencies that are ostensibly female. To cite one illustration of this phenomenon:

> "The house of the king" *(beit ha-melekh)* (1 Kings 9:1), this refers to the holy of
> holies, which is the inwardness of everything. "The king," this refers to the king
> in general *(setam melekh)*. Even though this is the supernal king, it is female in
> relation to the supernal point, the concealed of everything, but even though it is
> female, it is male in relation to the king below. *(Zohar 2:4a.)*

The fluidity of gender attribution is well captured in this passage: *Binah*, which is designated
the "supernal king," is female in relation to *Hokhmah*, the masculine potency depicted as the
"supernal point," but she is male in relation to the king below, which is *Malkhut*. Although it
is not stated explicitly in this context, it is not inaccurate to say (based on other zoharic
passages) that *Malkhut* itself is called "king" as well because she is masculine in relation to
the forces that exist beneath her insofar as they are sustained by the overflow of the divine
pleroma that emanates upon them through her channel.[28] The critical point for this analysis is
that the transposition of the female gender is actualized particularly on Yom Kippur for on that
day the daughter receives the illumination from the mother and thereby assumes the function
and the name of the latter.[29]

Concealment of Ascent : Forgiveness and the Eschatological Overcoming of Eros

The erotic texture of the merging of these two potencies, the revealed world (*'alma' de-
'itgalya'*) of the lower feminine and the concealed world (*'alma' de-'itkasseya'*) of the upper
feminine,[30] is disclosed in the fundamental paradox of veiling and unveiling, which is in fact
the basic structure of the symbol in kabbalistic lore in virtue of which one can justly speak of
the eros of language. In the context of describing the last of the seven holy palaces *(hekhalot)*,
which are chambers within the *Shekhinah* that parallel the lower seven emanations in the
sefirotic pleroma and thus serve as a bridge that links the divine and the mundane realms (see
Tishby, *Wisdom of the Zohar*, 591-4), the zoharic authorship offers an elaborate account of the
homosexual bonding of *Binah* and *Malkhut*, the upper and the lower *Shekhinah*, albeit
couched in heterosexual terms:

> The seventh palace: In this palace there is no actual image; everything is in
> concealment . . . . Thus this palace is called the holy of holies. The holy of holies
> is a place that is prepared for that supernal soul, the principle of everything, the
> world-to-come in relation to this world. When all the spirits are united one with
> the other, and they are perfected through one another, as is appropriate, then the
> supernal spirit, the soul of everything, is aroused in relation to that which is above,
> the concealed of all the concealed ones, so that it be aroused upon everything, to
> illuminate them from above to below, to perfect them, to kindle the lights. When
> all is perfected through the illumination of everything, and the supernal light
> descends, then this seventh palace is the concealed palace in the concealment of
> everything, to receive that holy of holies, the light that descends, and to be filled
> from there like a female that is impregnated from a male. It is filled only from that
> palace that is prepared to receive that supernal light. This mystery is: The seventh
> palace is the place of the union of the intercourse, to join together the seventh with
> the seventh, so that everything is one perfection, as is appropriate. Fortunate is the
> lot of the one who knows how to bind together this unity, he is beloved above and
> he is beloved below. *(Zohar 1:45a-b)*

It appears that in this passage the seventh palace is identified as the *Shekhinah* itself (see
Tishby, 613 n. 183), which is designated as the holy of holies.[31] The latter expression is
generally applied in the zoharic corpus to *Binah* (*Zohar 2:4b, 67b*. See above, n. 19), but it is
here associated with the *Shekhinah*, for she is the palace that is prepared to receive the
luminous overflow of *Binah*, which is referred to as well as the supernal soul and the world-
to-come. Indeed, from several other passages in the zoharic corpus the theosophic
significance of this title is related more specifically to the ascent and union of the *Shekhinah*
to *Binah*. Thus, for example, this mystery is linked exegetically (through the persona of R.
Eleazar) to the verse "Who is she who comes up from the desert?" (Song of Songs 3:6):
"'Who is she' *(mi zo't)*, the containment of the dual holiness of the two worlds in one unity
and in one bond. 'Who comes up' *('olah)*, verily, to constitute the holy of holies, for the holy
of holies consists of 'who' *(mi)* joined to 'she' *(zo't)*, so that she will be the burnt offering
('olah), which is the holy of holies." *(Zohar 1:10a.)* The holy of holies, therefore, denotes the

ascent of the *Shekhinah* (signified by the feminine demonstrative pronoun "this," *zo't*) to *Binah* (signified by the interrogative pronoun "who," *mi*). The ascending *Shekhinah* is also related to the mystery of the burnt offering, the *'olah*, whose lexical meaning denotes both the proper name of the sacrifice and more generically "she that rises."[32] The intricate weaving of the different symbolic threads is beautifully expressed in a second passage:

> He began his exposition, "This is the teaching regarding the burnt offering. This is the burnt offering" (Lev. 6:2). . . . The burnt offering (*'olah*) is the ascent and the binding of the Community of Israel above, and her conjunction within the world-to-come, so that everything will be one.[33] The burnt offering is called the holy of holies, and therefore she is called *'olah*, for she ascends and she is crowned, so that all will be unified in one joyous bond. On account of the fact that she ascends ever higher, it is written, "This is the teaching regarding the burnt offering," *zo't torat ha-'olah*, the secret of male and female as one, the written Torah and the oral Torah. The burnt offering (*ha-'olah*), for she ascends within the world-to-come, to be bound within that which is verily called the holy of holies, and the burnt offering, too, is the holy of holies. (*Zohar* 2:238b.)

The mystical significance of the burnt offering (*'olah*) is related symbolically to the ascent of the *Shekhinah* to her source in *Binah*, the world-to-come, which entails the masculinization of the feminine. The gender transformation is realized initially through the union of the female (*Malkhut*) and her masculine consort (*Tif'eret*), but it is ultimately and most fully achieved when the lower female (*Malkhut*) is restored to the upper female (*Binah*), a restoration that is conveyed in the symbol of the holy of holies (see *Zohar* 1:70a; 3:107b). This symbolic intent underlies the zoharic description of the seventh palace cited above. This palace assumes the name "holy of holies" on account of the fact that it receives the illumination of *Binah*, which is recurringly designated by this very term. In receiving the light of *Binah*, moreover, the seventh palace is described as the female who is impregnated by the male even though the union occurs between two females, *Binah* and *Malkhut*. The elusive remark that the "seventh palace is the place of the union of the intercourse, to join together the seventh with the seventh," must be decoded as a reference to the union of mother and daughter, for both *Binah* and *Malkhut* are referred to as the seventh, which relates as well to the application of the symbol of Sabbath to each of these gradations.[34] This pairing of the two female configurations can be depicted in heterosexual terms insofar as the former is masculine in relation to the latter.

The term "holy of holies" thus connotes the union of mother and daughter, a connotation that further illuminates something fundamental about the nature of secrecy. Indeed, the hermeneutical structure of the secret as that which is unveiled in its veiling and veiled in its unveiling is alluded to in the return of the daughter to the womb of the mother, which is also expressed as the entry of the mother into the palace of the daughter. In a parallel passage to the one cited above that describes the seventh palace, the zoharic authorship articulates this point more clearly by drawing a connection between three words, *'olam* ("world"), *'olim* ("ascending"), and *'ilum* ("concealment"),[35] in an effort to elucidate the nature of the *Shekhinah* in her ascent to *Binah*: "This palace is called the holy of holies, the place to receive the supernal souls that are called here in order to arouse the world-to-come in relation to her. This world is called *'olam*, for *'olam* refers to the ascent (*seliqa'*), for the lower world ascends to the supernal world, and it is hidden within her and concealed therein, revealed in the concealment (*'itgalya' vi-setirah*)" (*Zohar* 2:258b). The transformation of the daughter and her being uplifted to the status of the mother is predicated on her attaining the paradoxical posture of being revealed in the concealment. Precisely this form of union provides the model by which the kabbalists understood the symbolic import of the traditional notion of redemption. To be redeemed entails the theosophic process by means of which the feminine presence is restored to her source, the attribute of the divine that corresponds to the jubilee and to the world-to-come, two symbols that convey the idea of eschatological emancipation.

The symbolism posited in the main body of the *Zohar* is formulated succinctly by the Spanish kabbalist, Joseph Gikatilla, a likely member of the fraternity that produced the zoharic composition:

On occasion this emanation is called jubilee. I have already informed you that all types of freedom and redemption are dependent on this emanation. . . . When the lower emanations hold on to the emanation of the jubilee and draw down the efflux of her blessing below, then all types of freedom and redemption are found in all the emanations and in all things sustained by means of the emanation of *Malkhut* who receives the overflow of the blessing from them. Know that in a future time the righteous will ascend until they hold on to the emanation of *Binah*, which is the secret of the world-to-come. Then all types of destruction and all types of calamity will be liberated and redeemed. . . . The secret of *Binah* is called the jubilee because through it everything is liberated. The reason is that he who merits to be conjoined to her never sees any worry or any deficit . . . and he who is conjoined to the jubilee is redeemed, for there is nothing surrounding the jubilee that can be harmful . . . And this emanation is called in the language of our rabbis, blessed be their memory, repentance. The reason is that the souls (*neshamot*) emanate from this place, the spirits (*ruḥot*) from *Tif'eret*, and the souls (*nefashot*) from *Malkhut*, and they are all bound to one another to the point that they merit to be united in the emanation of *Binah* . . . and this is the secret of repentance. . . . Thus contemplate that repentance is the secret of the world-to-come. And after we have explained to you this great secret, we must again inform you of the order of the gradations of repentance. For everyone of Israel has a way of returning after he has been sold, "redemption shall be his and he will be released in the jubilee" (Lev. 25:31), and it says, "In the year of the jubilee, each man shall return to his holding" (ibid., 13). Through the secret of the emanation of *Binah* the soul can return and hold on to the place whence it was taken. This is [the meaning of] what is said, "each man shall return to his holding" (*tashuvu 'ish 'el 'aḥuzzato*)—the expression of holding (*'aḥizah*). (*Sha'arei 'Orah*, 2:59-61.)

Repentance is interpreted theosophically in light of the symbol of freedom, which in turn is equated with the mystical notion of conjunction with the world-to-come. The soul that repents, therefore, returns to the ontic source whence it derived. As Gikatilla notes, the secret of this ideal of conjunction is alluded to in the expression *'aḥizah*, literally, holding, utilized in the verse that describes the restoration of property to its original owner in the jubilee. Kabbalistically understood, redemption (*ge'ulah*) entails the return of the soul to its portion in the world-to-come. Just as no economic transaction can erase the memory of originary ownership, no barter of the soul can eliminate its sense of belonging to the womb of the mother whence it came into being. This belonging is the ultimate, and indeed the only genuine, sense of possession. *Teshuvah*, repentance, is the re/turn of the soul to its source, which occasions the sense of freedom bestowed on the one who is conjoined to the world-to-come. The esoteric significance of Yom Kippur is related to the fact that this day is marked essentially by the path of return of the repentant soul. The atonement granted this soul is explained theosophically in terms of the union of *Binah* and *Malkhut*, which results in the purification of the stains imparted to the latter as a consequence of the sins of Israel by means of the former. *Binah* draws her power of atonement from the fact that she is united to the world of mercy, i.e., the first emanation, *Keter*, which is entirely white (*lavan*),[36] and thus she is designated by the name Lebanon (*levanon*) and she is described as the one that "purifies the transgressions of Israel" (*melavenet 'avonotan shel yisra'el*). As a result of this purification, *Malkhut* is transformed, for she is restored from her displacement and exile brought about by the sinfulness of Israel to a state of adornment and reunification with the upper divine emanations. In Gikatilla's own words:

On account of his mercy and lovingkindness the Lord, blessed be he, instituted for Israel one day during the year to purify them from their impurities and to cleanse them, and he called it *yom ha-kippurim*. The reason it is called *yom ha-kippurim* in the plural is because these two emanations are united on that very day, the emanation of *Binah* and the emanation of *Malkhut*. Thus, the emanation of *Binah* purifies and cleanses every kind of filth and dirt that Israel bestowed on the emanation of *Malkhut*. When these two emanations are united to reverse [the judgments] to the merits of Israel and to purify their dirt, they are called accordingly *yom ha-kippurim*. Thus I will provide an allusion: "If your sins are like crimson, they will be whitened like snow" (Isa. 1:18). The supernal one is called Lebanon, and the lower one is garbed in a garment of crimson. Israel must transform the crimson garment into white, and therefore it is called *yom ha-kippurim*. . . . Since these two emanations, which correspond to one another in the secret of the supernal mother and the lower mother, are involved on this day in the purification of Israel, sexual intercourse is prohibited on Yom Kippur, even though it is permissible on Sabbaths and Festivals. The secret is known to those who know the esoteric lore. "And besides, she is in truth my sister, my father's daughter though not my mother's daughter; and she became my wife" (Gen. 20:12). This is the secret of its being called *yom ha-kippurim*. Understand this well. (*Sha'arei 'Orah*, 64-5)

Transgression creates a blemish above, which results in the separation of the male and the female aspects of the divine. It stands to reason, therefore, that the first phase in the rectification of this condition calls for the re/pairing of the King and his Matrona. This unification is facilitated, moreover, by righteous action below, especially by those who engage in conjugal sex with the right intention. For the kabbalists themselves intercourse was ideally limited to the Sabbaths, some of the Festivals, and other exceptional times that were endowed with the spiritual significance of holy days, such as the first night after a woman was cleansed from her menstrual cycle or the night after a man returned from a trip.[37] In spite of this rather austere lifestyle, which might strike the contemporary ear as severely constricting, it is correct to assert that kabbalists ascribed positive value to coitus as a redemptive act. Most scholars have affirmed this dimension of the kabbalistic attitude toward sexuality. This, however, is only part of the story. Beyond the fulfillment of sexual desire in the sacred coupling of husband and wife there is a return to ascetic denial, a refraining from engaging in physical sex, which mirrors an ontic state above whereby the divine forces are united in a manner that precludes the act of intercourse below. Yom Kippur is a ritual enactment of the alternative paradigm that needs to be considered carefully in an attempt to comprehend the soteriological teaching embraced by the kabbalists, particularly as it relates to the value assigned to sexual behavior. That is, the complete repair of the rupture in the Godhead exceeds the model of heterosexual bonding. The reunion of mother and daughter, or the upper and lower mothers, which occurs on Yom Kippur, the day of the great Sabbath, signifies the homoerotic mating that transcends male-female intercourse. The injunction to refrain from sex on Yom Kippur underscores the belief that ascetic renunciation provides the means by which the higher modality of union is achieved.

Heterosexuality serves as the intermediary step that leads from exile to redemption, from the state of separation to one of integration. In the redemptive process, the *Shekhinah* is transformed into *Binah* as a result of her union with the male *Tif'eret*. In a particularly poignant passage from one of the most recondite sections of the zoharic corpus, the *Sitrei 'Otiyyot* (*Zohar Ḥadash*, 5b-c), which deals with the mysteries of the letters of the Tetragrammaton, the transformation of the lower female feminine into the upper masculine feminine is expressed in terms of the metamorphosis of the letter *he'*, which is also identified as the *kaf*, into the final letter *mem*, the former represents the half-circle or the partially eclipsed moon and the latter the full circle or the moon in its complete illumination. The process by means of which the half-circle is completed is related more specifically to the image of the point that exists in the middle of the *kaf*. Utilizing the geometric conception that the circle is formed from its midpoint, the zoharic authorship asserts that the point in the middle of the lunar disk, which is gendered as feminine, receives the light of the masculine sun. As a result of this illumination, the open side of the *he'*, whose function is related to the reception of the male, is closed, and the letter itself is transformed into the final *mem*, which is sealed on all four sides. The midpoint, as is attested in other zoharic texts, corresponds to the vagina or the uterus, the part of the female that corresponds to the penis.[38] That the midpoint, which is also identified as the pupil of the eye, completes the circle by means of its receiving the light of the male signals the transmutation of the open vagina into the closed womb, a process that entails the masculinization of the feminine. The eschatological dimension of this transformation is highlighted by the fact that the final *mem* is associated orthographically with the words *le-marbeh ha-misrah*, "in token of abundant authority" (Isaiah 9:6), an expression that has obvious messianic implications.

Fore/Giveness and the Concealment of the Mother's Nakedness

In the coupling of mother and daughter, moreover, lies the secret of forgiveness, the giving before that engenders being in the concealment of its disclosure. The paradox is alluded to in the image of the holy of holies, the innermost secret whence all secrets are secreted in the fore/giving. In this space, memory is perfectly sealed, nothing is forgotten, only fore/given. When forgiveness is granted below the primordial act of fore/giveness is reenacted, an act that results in the opening of the path that leads to the holy of holies, the womb that holds the many in the diversity of its unity. This bond of mother and daughter, which is theurgically realized on Yom Kippur through the ritual acts of the community of Israel, signifies the ultimate oneness to which all things strive. It is a union that transcends heterosexual eros, an ideal unity that bespeaks the eschatological vision of the kabbalists. The union that is attained in the end is predicated on the sense of forgiveness, which is experienced as the liberation of the soul from the constraints of time and as the release from the chain of desire.

The giving before of fore/giveness is occasioned by the act of repentance, the turning back to the source, which is further characterized as the amelioration of the forces of judgment and the consequent dominion of the attribute of mercy such that each of the emanations is accorded its proper place. As a result of this realignment in the sefirotic realm, *Binah* is called the "complete repentance and the world is atoned, for the mother dwells in complete joy, as it is written, 'as a happy mother of children' (Psalm 113:9), and then it is called *yom ha-kippurim*, concerning which it is written, 'to purify you from all your sins' (Leviticus 16:30)" (*Zohar* 3:15b). Significantly, the return to origin is marked by the uncovering of that which is hidden. To the degree that the source whence all things return is characterized by the quality of hiddenness—indeed, as I have noted above, one of the designations of *Binah* in the zoharic corpus is the "concealed world"—the uncovering can never assume the form of revealing a reified and static essence. On the contrary, inasmuch as the disclosure is always of that which is concealed, the uncovered withholds its own presence in the moment of its uncovering. What is revealed, therefore, is an absence that is present only as that which shows itself as concealed. The union of mother and daughter, which is the symbolic import of Yom Kippur, embodies the paradox of the exposure of the withdrawal that is manifest as the withdrawal of the exposure. This paradox is conveyed philologically in the biblical expression *mi zo't*, which is not read by the zoharic authorship as a question but rather as an assertion. That is, *mi zo't* means not "who is she?" but "who is she," that is, the concealed world of *Binah* is the revealed world of *Malkhut*.

The day of atonement, therefore, is endowed with eschatological significance, for it is the time in which the supernal union of mother and daughter is realized. In that respect, Yom Kippur proleptically anticipates the utopian restoration of the lower female to the upper female, which entails the masculine transvaluation of the feminine. From one perspective the actualization of this union is predicated on the uncovering of that which is concealed, indeed the exposure of concealment as such. On the other hand, inasmuch as that which is revealed is hidden, and the presence is always a presence of an absence whose absence is only reinforced by the presencing of that which is present in its absence, disclosure itself is a form of concealment.[39] In the theosophic symbolism adopted in the zoharic texts discussed in this study, the mother re/presents the absence in the presence, which is the engendering dialectic of secrecy, that is, the veil that sets the limit of the ocular gaze and the contemplative vision just as the placenta and the amniotic fluid delimit the boundary of the first dwelling place to which the child perpetually seeks to return. The zoharic authorship artfully expresses this aspect of the concealed disclosure on Yom Kippur in the following passage:

> R. Isaac said: It is written, "as a happy mother of children, Hallelujah" (Ps. 113:9). The mother is known, but who are the children? R. Simeon said: It has been taught that the blessed holy One has two children, one male and the other female . . . and the mother hovers over them to nourish them. Thus it is written, "do not take the mother together with the children" (Deut. 22:6). It has been taught that people should not multiply their sins below for this results in the removal of the mother from her children. It is written, "She is your mother—do not uncover her nakedness" (Lev. 18:7). Woe to one who uncovers the nakedness!

> When people of the world repent and increase the merits before the blessed holy
> One, and the mother returns and covers her children, then she is called
> "repentance" (*teshuvah*). What is *teshuvah*? *Teshuvah* consists of the mother
> returning to her station, and then it is written, "as a happy mother of children," the
> mother of the children most certainly. Therefore a person is not exempt from the
> obligation to procreate until he begets a son and a daughter. (*Zohar* 1:219a)

In this context, Yom Kippur is depicted symbolically in terms of the union of the mother
with her two children, the son and daughter, which correspond respectively to *Tif'eret* and
Malkhut. The esoteric significance of *teshuvah*, therefore, is not simply the entry of the
daughter (or even the son and daughter) back into the womb, but it is related to the
repositioning of the mother as the one that hovers over her children in order to sustain them.
Sin severs the bond of the mother and her children, a bond predicated on the covering up of
her genitals in the moment that she nourishes them. Exposure of the genitals results in the
removal of the mother from the children, which is related to the biblical injunction of *shiluah
ha-qen*, driving away the mother bird from the nest (Deuteronomy 22:6-7). The kabbalistic
interpretation reverses the contextual meaning of the text, for the dislodging of the mother is
portrayed negatively as the uncovering of her genitals rather than as a positive act of mercy.
Through the act of repentance, by contrast, the nakedness is re/covered and the mother is
returned to her place.[40] To cite another zoharic passage where the matter is fully articulated:

> R. Yose said: It is written, "The nakedness of your father and the nakedness of
> your mother you shall not uncover" (Lev. 18:7), and it is written, "she is your
> mother—do not uncover her nakedness" (ibid.). It has been taught that she is
> certainly your mother. Thus if you uncover her nakedness, you must certainly
> restore her so that there will be repair. . . . It is written, "do not uncover," for when
> the matter is repaired, it is repaired corresponding to the one who uncovers, and
> this is called *teshuvah*. R. Isaac said: All the sins of the world are connected to
> this until the point that the mother is revealed on account of them. When she is
> revealed all the children are revealed, and it is written, "do not take the mother
> together with the children" (Deut. 22:6). When the world below is repaired all is
> repaired until the repair rises to the holy mother, and she is repaired and concealed
> from that which has been uncovered. Thus it is written, "Happy is he whose
> transgression is forgiven, whose sin is covered up" (Ps. 32:1). Then she is called
> *teshuvah*, *teshuvah* certainly, and then she is called *yom ha-kippurim*, as it is
> written, "from all your sins you will be purified before the Lord" (Lev. 16:30). R.
> Judah said: When is she called *teshuvah*? When the mother is concealed and she
> exists in joy over the children, as it is written, "as a happy mother of children" (Ps.
> 113:9), and she returns to her position. The one that is closed returns to its place.
> (*Zohar* 3:15b-16a)

The eschatological restoration, which is dramatized in the liturgical rites of Yom Kippur,
is linked to the setting of the proper boundaries established by returning the mother to her
children. This return entails the covering of the genitals of the mother that were uncovered as
a result of acts of transgression.[41] Repentance is identified theosophically with the attribute of
Binah, which is described as the "hidden place that is above, the depth of the well . . . the
depth of the depths" *(Zohar* 3:70a). The way to access that place is through fore/giving, the
giving before that occasions the fecundity of time as it materializes in the habitation of space.
Redemption, therefore, is characterized by the reversal of the erotic stimulus, the withholding
of the impulse to extend, the concealment of the projection in the inner sanctum where the
secrets are secreted. In the transition from the mundane to the sacred, from the weekday to
Sabbath, heterosexual eros is necessary to overcome the fragmentation. The will to bestow is
incited by the desire to receive.[42] But as the Sabbath progresses the erotic passion itself
dissipates as it gives way to a higher bond that relates more specifically to the elevation of the
Shekhinah and her restoration to *Binah*.[43] This dynamic typifies as well Yom Kippur, which is
indeed the great Sabbath. In the union of mother and daughter, the erotic yearning of the male
for the female and the female for the male yields to the bond that is beyond desire, the world-
to-come that comes beyond time in the giving before there is receiving. "The one who returns
in repentance is as one who restores the blessed holy One and the *Shekhinah* to their place,
and this is the secret of redemption" (*Zohar* 3:278a [Ra'aya' Meheimna']). In the end—not

the chronological terminus but the ontological purpose—heterosexual eros is overcome, for son and daughter, the King and the Matrona, are restored to their place of origin by the one who repents. The mystical efficacy of repentance is such that it is indistinguishable from redemption, for both terms signify the ultimate reintegration of the gender binary in the womb of the mother.

Notes

[1] Friedrich Hölderin, *Poems and Fragments*, trans. Michael Hamburger (Cambridge: 1980), 459:

> For since evil spirit
> Has taken possession of happy antiquity, unendingly
> Long now one power has prevailed, hostile to song, without resonance,
> That within measures transgresses, the violence of the mind. But God hates
> The unbound.

[2] Alexander Pope, *An Essay on Criticism*, 525, *The Poems of Alexander Pope*, ed. John Butt (New Haven: Yale University Press, 1963).

[3] William Shakespeare, *King Lear*, IV.vii.84, *The Complete Works*, gen. ed. Alfred Harbage (Baltimore: Penguin Books, 1969).

[4] My discussion of time here reflects the influence of Hannah Arendt's Heideggerian interpretation of the Augustinian notion of memory as the vast spaces of the inner life, which makes possible the recollection of the past as well as the anticipation of the future. See Hannaah Arendt, *Love and Saint Augustine*, ed. with an interpretative essay Joanna Vecchiarelli Scott and Judith Chelius Stark (Chicago: University of Chicago Press, 1996), 144-6.

[5] I borrow this term from Gershom Scholem, *Major Trends in Jewish Mysticism* (New York: Schoken Books, 1954), 159.

[6] See Elliot R. Wolfson, *Circle in the Square: Studies in the Use of Gender in Kabbalistic Symbolism* (Albany: State University of New York Press, 1995), 102-3.

[7] My thought in this matter has been influenced by Martin Heidegger. For instance, consider his formulation in *Parmenides*, trans. André Schuwer and Richard Rojcewicz (Bloomington: Indiana University Press, 1992), 12: "The poetry of the poet or the treatise of a thinker stands within its own proper unique word. It compels us to perceive this word again and again as if we were hearing it for the first time. These newborn words transpose us in every case to a new shore. . . . Only if we are already appropriated by this transporting are we in the care of the word."

[8] The rabbinic perspective is captured succinctly in the Targum, which renders the term *ba-keseh* as *be-yarha' de-mitkkasei*, "when the moon is hidden." See Babylonian Talmud, Beisah 16b.

[9] In a copy of the *Zohar* (Amsterdam, 1715) with variant readings supplied by R. Jacob Vilna, which was recently purchased by the Library at the Jewish Theological Seminary of America, there is here added the words, *we-'it'ahed qodesh be-qodesh*, "and holiness unites with holiness," a reading that underscores the erotic connotation of "holy" in this context.

[10] It is still my hope to write a comprehensive study of the ontology of time in kabbalistic sources. For preliminary reflections, which capture some of the drift of my thinking, see Elliot R. Wolfson, "From Sealed Book to Open Text: Time, Memory, and Narrativity in Kabbalistic Hermeneutics," *Interpreting Judaism in a Postmodern Age*, ed. Steven Kepnes (New York: New York University Press, 1995), 145-78; Wolfson, "The Face of Jacob in the Moon: Mystical Transformations of an Aggadic Myth," *The Seductiveness of Jewish Myth: Challenge and Response*, ed. S. Daniel Breslauer (Albany: State University of New York Press, 1997), 235-70, esp. 253-4 n. 4.

[11] In "From Sealed Book to Open Text," I argued that for the kabbalists, generally speaking, temporality is localized in *Yesod*, the phallic gradation of the divine. I suggested, moreover, that time is correlated with the masculine and space with the feminine. In a more extensive discussion of the phenomenology of time in kabbalistic symbolism, I hope to elucidate this point. I do want to note, however, that ostensibly there are exceptions to the paradigm I suggested. Consider, for example, the linkage of time, or more specifically the moment (*'et*), to the feminine potency of the *Shekhinah* in Joseph Gikatilla, *Sha'arei 'Orah*, ed. Joseph Ben-Shlomo, 2 vols. (Jerusalem: Bialik Institute, 1981), 1:135-6. According to Gikatilla, the attribute of Adonai, which is one of the designations of the *Shekhinah*, is called *'et*, and when she is conjoined to *Yesod*, she is called *'et tovah*, the "time of goodness," whereas when she is conjoined to the demonic force that lies outside the divine realm, she is called *'et ra'ah*, the "time of evil." The symbolic nexus between time and the *Shekhinah*, based on

a passage in *Sefer ha-Bahir*, is suggested by Gershom Scholem, *On the Mystical Shape of the Godhead: Basic Concepts in the Kabbalah* (New York: Schocken, 1991), 196. See, however, *Circle in the Square*, 86-7, where I argue that implicit in this bahiric text is the notion of time ensuing from the androgynous phallus. That is to say, time is marked by the duality of darkness and light, which corresponds respectively to the feminine and the masculine attributes of the divine. The ontological root for both of these elements is the phallic potency. See 201-2 n. 31, where I discuss this matter in more detail and provide some other texts to illustrate my thesis. In my opinion, the relevant discussion in Gikatilla is also predicated on a similar notion. That is, even though time is related to the feminine *Shekhinah*, the bestowal of temporality on her is due to the influence she receives from the male. If she receives from *Yesod*, then it is a time of goodness, and, conversely, if she receives from the demonic force, it is a time of evil. That time is ultimately related to the phallic potency is underscored in Gikatilla's comment, *Sha'arei 'Orah*, 1:134-5: "Know that when the attribute of *zakhor* [the masculine] is united with [that of] *shamor* [the feminine], all of the world is complete and perfect. The secret is [alluded to in the verse] 'All that he does is appropriate to its time' ['et ha-kol 'asah yafeh ve-'itto] (Eccles. 3:11), for the attribute of *zakhor* is called by the secret of 'all' (*kol*) and the attribute of *shamor* is called 'time' ('et). When *zakhor* and *shamor* are united as one, in the secret of *kol* and in the secret of 'et, then it says, 'et ha-kol 'asah yafeh ve-'itto. The secret [of the word 'itto] is 'et waw." The expression 'itto, "its time," can be decomposed into the word 'et together with the letter *waw*. The former stands symbolically for the feminine potency and the latter for the masculine. In the word 'itto, therefore, is an allusion to the mystery of the divine androgyne, the union of male and female in the Godhead. It is this union that underlies the kabbalistic understanding of time. Gikatilla also refers to this union as 'et rason, the "time of favor." The application of the word 'et to the feminine, therefore, is dependent on her union with the attribute that corresponds to the phallus, for the latter is the ultimate generative source of being/consciousness, which is the essence of time.

[12] *Zohar 'im Perush 'Or Yaqar* (Jerusalem: Achuzat Israel, 1987), 15: 89.

[13] This is not the context to provide a detailed account of the evolution of this idea in kabbalistic sources that may have influenced Cordovero. Let me simply state that kabbalists from an earlier period already identified the sefirotic emanations as the succession of time, *seder zemanim*. For instance, see Azriel of Gerona, *Perush 'Eser Sefirot*, printed in Meir ibn Gabbai, *Derekh 'Emunah* (Warsaw: Meir Yehiel Halter, 1890), 3d-4a.

[14] *Zohar* 3:102a: "On that day two lights shine as one, the supernal mother illumines the lower mother, and thus it is written *yom ha-kippurim* as has been said." See Isaiah Tishby, *The Wisdom of the Zohar*, trans. David Goldstein (Oxford: Oxford University Press, 1989), 1246-7. On the image of two mothers, which correspond respectively to *Binah* and *Malkhut*, see *Zohar* 2:22a.

[15] On the disproportionate love of the father for the daughter portrayed in the zoharic symbolism, which on occasion is described as provoking the jealousy of the mother, see Tishby, *Wisdom*, 299.

[16] According to other zoharic passages, the union of father and mother serves as a catalyst for the union of son and daughter or brother and sister. See *Zohar* 3:61b-62a; Tishby, *Wisdom*, 299.

[17] On the use of incestuous relations as the most appropriate means to convey the sacred coupling of divine potencies, see Elliot R. Wolfson, "Hebraic and Hellenistic Conceptions of Wisdom in *Sefer ha-Bahir*," *Poetics Today* 19 (1998), 147-78. On the ambiguous relationship of the son to the mother, see Zohar 3: 15b-16a, cited below. Interestingly enough, in the Indian esoteric tradition as well both brother-sister copulation and father-daughter incest are used as a symbolic means to convey processes amongst the deities. See Sadashiv Ambadas Dange, *Sexual Symbolism From the Vedic Ritual* (Delhi: Ajanta Publications, 1979), xvi-xvii, 117-59.

[18] See Elliot R. Wolfson, "Eunuchs Who Keep the Sabbath: Becoming Male and the Ascetic Ideal in Thirteenth-Century Jewish Mysticism," *Becoming Male in the Middle Ages*, ed. Jeremy J. Cohen and Bonnie Wheeler (New York: Garland Publications, 1997), 154.

[19] The point is particularly underscored according to the reading that I mentioned above in n. 9. In a similar vein, in the *Zohar* and related Hebrew theosophic works of Moses de León, *Binah* is called *heikhal ha-qodesh*, the "holy palace," or *qodesh qedashim*, the "holy of holies," inasmuch as it receives the seminal overflow from *Hokhmah*, which is identified as *qodesh*, "holiness." Regarding these symbolic images, see *R. Moses de Leon's Sefer Sheqel ha-Qodesh*, ed. Charles Mopsik (Los Angeles: Cherub Press, 1996), 24-5, and other references supplied in nn. 205-10.

[20] According to *Zohar* 2:185b, the prohibition of sexual intercourse on Yom Kippur corresponds to gradation of *Yesod*. See parallel to this text in *Sheqel ha-Qodesh*, 26.

[21] *Zohar* 1:70a, 71a; 2:135b, 259a, 271b. Another important connotation of the term *nehiru de-'anpin*

is the state of mystical ecstasy, which is applied more specifically to the priest who unifies the divine name by carrying out his sacrificial rites. See *Zohar* 3:39a, 89b, 241a. In one context, 3:146a, the zoharic author uses the expression *'anpin nehirin*, "illuminated face," to describe the ecstatic condition of the priest, which is based on the Hebrew phrase *panim me'irot* connected to the priestly blessing in *Numbers Rabbah* 11:6. See *The Book of the Pomegranate: Moses de León's Sefer ha-Rimmon*, ed. Elliot R. Wolfson (Atlanta: Scholars' Press, 1988), 254 (Hebrew section), where the zoharic expression is rendered as *panim me'irim*.

22 See Wolfson, *Circle in the Square*, 89, 99, 103, and reference to study of Scholem cited on 205 n. 47.

23 See Wolfson, *Circle in the Square*, 98-106. Arthur Green, "Kabbalistic Re-vision: A Review Article of Elliot Wolfson's Through a Speculum That Shines," *History of Religions* 36 (1997): 270, claims that my understanding of gender symbolism in the theosophic kabbalah has set aside "the truly important role occupied by the female, especially in the Zoharic sources." He then proceeds to offer a litany of images used to characterize the *Shekhinah*, including, queen of the lower worlds, hind of the dawn, mother that nourishes the universe, city, temple, holy of holies, kingship (*malkhut*, which Green perplexingly renders in the decidedly neutral term "realm") that exerts dominion, governance, and judgment over existence. After going through this list, Green concludes: "The Zohar is at least as fixed with the celebration of the female as it is with the male. . . . Wolfson's dismissal of this entire world of symbols through his single insight concerning *'atarah* . . . produces a significantly distorted picture of kabbalistic eros." The charge that I have dismissed the entire world of symbols characterizing the *Shekhinah* as feminine is simply inaccurate and unfair. The real contribution of my work, which is ignored by Green, is the recognition that the positive characteristics of the *Shekhinah* are predicated on an androcentric axiology that kabbalists shared with other medieval men, enhanced as well by biblical and rabbinic sources. Hence, as I have documented in detail, activities that clearly must be attributed to the female body, such as childbearing and lactation, are valenced as masculine in the symbology of the kabbalists. That is, when a woman gives birth or breast feeds, she assumes the gender value of a male. The masculine appropriation of female biological traits is the most revealing sign of the extent of the androcentrism that characterizes this tradition. I have not ignored the feminine depictions of the *Shekhinah*, as Green claims, but what I have done is contextualized them in a more nuanced gender analysis that is predicated on a clear distinction between gender as a cultural construct and biological sex. This is the point that is consistently missed by critics such as Green, but it is precisely with respect to this matter that the paradigm shifts as a result of my work. It is not sufficient to cite the presentation of the supposedly feminine traits of the *Shekhinah* in the work of a scholar like Tishby since the latter had no way of analyzing the use of gender in a sophisticated manner. To cite one of many possible examples, in *Wisdom of the Zohar*, 379-81, Tishby discusses the attribution of the symbol of the mother to the *Shekhinah*, but he nowhere notes that this very symbol involves the depiction of the feminine in terms that are clearly masculine according to the gender valuation accepted by medieval kabbalists like the author of the zoharic text. I fear that Green's reliance on Tishby as an authority to level a criticism against me is easily disposable.

24 *Zohar* 1:2a, translated and discussed in Wolfson, *Circle in the Square*, 104-5.

25 The masculinization of the lower female through her ascent to the upper female is connected in *Zohar* 2:182b-183a to the ritual practice of standing during the blessing and counting of the forty-nine days of the *'omer* between Passover and Pentecost: "When the house of the Matrona is sanctified, she ascends above to be bound to those supernal days above. Thus we stand when we count, for those are the supernal days, and whenever a person enters those supernal days, whether in prayer or in praise, he must stand on his feet . . . to stand as a male who stands in his strength and not as a female whose way it is to sit. . . . Since this is the mystery of the masculine, women are exempt from this computation . . . in the manner of 'all the males shall appear' (Exod. 23:17), men and not women, for the mystery of the covenant is in the masculine and not in the feminine." Cf. *Zohar* 3:97b: "Since those days are days of the world of the masculine, this enumeration is given only to men, and thus this enumeration is accomplished in a standing posture." See parallel in *Book of the Pomegranate*, 137-8.

26 *Mekhilta de-Rabbi Ishmael*, ed. H. S. Horovitz and I. A. Rabin (Jerusalem: Wahrmann Books, 1970), 208, and other references cited in n. 7.

27 The point is stated clearly in *Zohar* 1:163a: "Why is [*Binah*] called *ḥasidah* [derived from Psalm 104:17]? Even though this supernal world is female, she is called male when she emanates all beneficence and all light emerges from her. Therefore she is called *ḥasidah*, for mercy (*ḥesed*), which is the primordial light, emerges from her." The feminine *Binah* assumes the name *ḥasidah* when she functions as the male that overflows and the attribute of *ḥesed* issues forth from her.

[28] See *Zohar* 1:47b: "Who is the king? This is the Community of Israel, for he bestows upon her all the pleasures of the worlds, and all of the holy forces that issue from above go out from this place." The emanative capacity of *Shekhinah* is derived from the phallic potency of *Yesod* through which the supernal influx overflows to her. The procreative connotation of the term "king" when it is attributed to the *Shekhinah* is also made explicit in other zoharic passages. See, for instance, *Zohar* 1:122a, 235b, 246a.

[29] The zoharic interpretation of Yom Kippur is well summarized by Hayyim Vital, *Sha'ar ha-Kawwanot* (Jerusalem: Meqor Hayyim, 1963), 102b-c: "On this day *Malkhut*, which is the feminine of *Ze'eir 'Anpin*, receives all of these aspects from the supernal mother herself and not through her husband *Ze'eir 'Anpin*. It is called *yom ha-kippurim* in the plural, and this is the matter of Rachel, the feminine of *Ze'eir 'Anpin*, who ascends on this day until the supernal mother herself . . . and the two of them are united. . . . All of the prayers on Yom Kippur are for the sake of constructing Rachel, the main feminine of *Ze'eir 'Anpin*, so that she will be crowned and adorned by means of the supernal mother." Needless to say, many more examples could have been cited, but for the purposes of this study this one text will suffice to make the point.

[30] *Zohar* 1:152a (*Sitrei Torah*), 154a-b, 158a-b, 259a, 2:29b; Tishby, *Wisdom of the Zohar*, 295.

[31] On the use of the term "holy of holies" as a designation of the mystery of the womb related to the *Shekinah*, see Tishby, *Wisdom of the Zohar*, 381.

[32] See Tishby, *Wisdom of the Zohar*, 883, 923-4.

[33] Cf. *Zohar* 2:239b: "[The *Shekhinah* is called] the burnt offering (*'olah*), for she ascends and is crowned above, to be bound, as is fitting, until the place that is called the holy of holies."

[34] On the attribution of the term "seventh" to *Binah*, see *Zohar* 2:184a: "All mysteries and all of the precious holy ones are dependent on the seventh, and that seventh is the supernal world, which is called the world-to-come." See also *Zohar Hadash*, ed. Reuven Margaliot (Jerusalem: Mosad Rav Cook, 1978), 29a: "The great Sabbath is also called the seventh from below to above." Related to this symbol is the application of the image of the seven days (*Zohar* 3:89b) or that of the seven years (2:31a) to *Binah*. See Gikatilla, *Sha'arei 'Orah*, 2:46: "Know that in every place that you find in the Torah a sevenfold calculation, such as seven years, seven times, it refers to the secret of the *sefirot* from *Yesod* to *Binah*, and in some contexts from *Binah* to *Yesod*." The *Shekhinah* similarly is referred to throughout the zoharic corpus as the "seventh" insofar as this is the last of the lower seven emanations of the divine pleroma. See Tishby, *Wisdom of the Zohar*, p. 613 n. 183, interprets the zoharic remark that the seventh palace is the place of the union of the seventh with the seventh as a reference to the intercourse of *Yesod* and *Malkhut*. This interpretation privileges the heterosexual and obscures the female homoeroticism, which is related to the reunion of the mother and the daughter. Also relevant here is the attribution of the symbol of the seventh year, *shemittah*, to *Malkhut* and the seven cycles of seven, the jubilee, to *Binah*; see *Zohar* 1:22a, 50b, 95b, 147a, 147b, 153b, 154a, 183a, 240b, 251b; 2:22a, 85b, 114a, 121a; 3:97b, 108a, 110b, 115a, 180b). In that respect as well, we can meaningfully speak of the attribution of the term "seventh" to both *Binah* and *Malkhut*.

[35] The word *le-'olam* is vocalized as *le'alem* in several rabbinic texts, often associated with Exodus 3:15. See Palestinian Talmud, Yoma 3:7; Babylonian Talmud, Qiddushin 71a; *Kohelet Rabbah* 3:11; *Midrash Konen* in *Bet ha-Midrash*, ed. Adolph Jellinek (3rd edition; Jerusalem: Wahrmann Books, 1967), 2:24. See also the play on words between *ha-'olam* and *he'lem* in *The Book Bahir: An Edition Based on the Earliest Manuscripts*, ed. Daniel Abrams (Los Angeles: Cherub Press, 1994), § 8, p. 121. Most of the aforementioned rabbinic sources were previously noted by Gershom Scholem, *Das Buch Bahir* (Leipzig: Drugulin, 1923), § 8, p. 11 n. 1.

[36] See *Sha'arei 'Orah*, 126. In that context as well, Gikatilla enunciates the point that the power of forgiveness derives from the whiteness of *Keter*, the world that is complete mercy, which illuminates *Binah* on the day of Yom Kippur.

[37] See Wolfson, "Eunuchs Who Keep the Sabbath," 158-60. The comparison of the night of ritual immersion as well as the night that a man returns from a trip to that of the eve of Sabbath is implied in *Zohar* 1:50a, which influenced numerous subsequent kabbalists.

[38] See Elliot R. Wolfson, "Coronation of the Sabbath Bride: Kabbalistic Myth and the Ritual of Androgynisation," *Journal of Jewish Thought and Philosophy* 6 (1997), 316-24.

[39] Here my discourse is indebted to Luce Irigaray, *Sexes and Genealogies*, trans. Gillian C. Gill (New York: Columbia University Press, 1993), 30-3. The striking difference between Irigaray's discourse and the standard kabbalistic symbolism is that she posits the image of the womb as a counterpoint to

the phallic bias of the Freudian approach. To the degree that kabbalists interpret the womb in phallic terms, there may be a greater affinity between their symbolism and Freudian concepts. I have nevertheless availed myself of Irigaray for she has articulated in a profound way the convergence of absence and presence as it relates to the mother.

[40] This is the mystical rationale for the liturgical act of reading the laws pertaining to illicit sexual relations (Lev. 18) during the afternoon service of Yom Kippur. See Wolfson, *Circle in the Square*, 102-3, and sources cited on pp. 219-20 nn. 127-8.

[41] The sensitivity of the issue of the mother-son relationship, and the specific problem of uncovering the genitals of the mother, is emphasized in the interpretation of Gen. 29:31 in *Zohar* 1:154a-b. I will cite here only a portion of this psychologically-astonishing exegesis: "The jubilee is always the concealed world and all of its matters are not revealed. Therefore all of its actions are hidden from Jacob. Come and see: The lower world is revealed, and it is the beginning of everything to ascend in its gradations. Just as the supernal wisdom is the beginning of everything, so too the lower world is wisdom and it is the beginning of everything. Therefore it is called 'you' ('*atah*), for it is the sabbatical year, and it is revealed. The supernal world, which is the jubilee, is called 'he' (*hu'*), for all of its matters are concealed. The secret of the matter is related to Leah, as it is written, 'And he lay with her that night' (Gen. 30:16). . . . The supernal world is always concealed, and Jacob was conjoined through his will only to that which is revealed, and the secret of this is what is written, 'and he clings to his wife' (Gen. 2:24). 'The Lord saw that Leah was unloved' (ibid. 29:31): From here [it is deduced that] a man despises the nakedness of his mother, and thus one can unite with his mother in every place without any apprehension. Thus they said that a son joins with his mother [cf. Mishnah, Qiddushin 4:12]. All was hidden from Jacob for the supernal world was not revealed at all."

[42] That is, the female or the left side of judgment (or limitation) is considered to provide the stimulus for the male or the right side of mercy (or expansion) to project forward in the act of intercourse. See Tishby, *Wisdom of the Zohar*, 300-1.

[43] See Wolfson, "Coronation of the Sabbath Bride," 325-43.

Spare Time: Professional Responsibilities in Business Law and the Humanities

Jonathan Boyarin

This essay addresses certain responsibilities which, I claim, inhere in the situation of a scholar in the humanities now contemplating a career as a large-firm business lawyer. Parts of the essay will be cast in personal and anecdotal terms. Others are more analytic or programmatic. All grow immediately out of my own set of resources and obligations; still I am confident they pertain to the dilemmas of numerous colleagues. In sum, the essay aims to set out an alternative to the common view of the turn from scholarship in the humanities to the practice of business law as little more than desperate or opportunistic capitulation.

Although informed in part by the moral examination of contemporary business law in Anthony T. Kronman's recent *The Lost Lawyer: Failing Ideals of the Legal Profession*,[1] my considerations are not cast in the terms of recuperation of a lost ideal or searching for a new one. As my subtitle indicates, my presumption is rather that those who have had the ambiguous fortune of extended socialization into the humanities followed by the opportunity to enter the practicing legal profession are both constrained and enabled by that combination. The desire for a coherent "career"—a coherent narrative of developing personal action within a potentially fragmented series of institutional settings—is furthered by a better understanding of both the constraints and the abilities. As these are clarified, what once seemed a pragmatic compromise may well turn out to have unexpected potentials for the invigoration of responsible elites, whether in practice or in critical scholarship.

My impression is that this (I believe) more salutary approach toward the relation between criticism and practice is rare. Much more common are, on the one hand, laments for lost humanist commitment (on which more below), and on the other hand, laments for the loss of a sense of social responsibility on the part of the legal profession. A striking example of the latter is Robert W. Gordon's back-cover endorsement of Kronman's elegy for the lost lawyer-statesman ideal: "If lawyers could spare any time to read, *The Lost Lawyer* should really make them sit up and take notice of what has happened to them." Now, one might assume that an endorsement of a book about the lost ideals of the legal profession would be addressed first and foremost to lawyers. At first glance, that seems to be the case with Gordon's blurb. Yet the sentence bears close examination. On its own terms, it presumes in fact that lawyers cannot spare any time to read, and so presumably would not even be browsing. Certainly the conventional understanding in legal academia is that big-firm lawyers these days do little else but bill hours. So the judgment is made that lawyers cannot spare time for reading and do not read. Nevertheless the blurb soldiers on with a prescription: lawyers "should" sit up. They should be more upright, more *Aufrichtig*—leading to the further plausible inference that law professors, because they do have the time to read, may therefore be more upright.[2] Unfortunately, just as the lawyers imagined here don't have time to read, they have no time for the self-awareness required to "take notice of what has happened to them." They are slouching drones, obsessed with the bottom line. Actually, what the sentence most likely seeks to suggest, to any lawyer who does somehow manage to see it, is that she does indeed have time to read, and if only she will do so, she will be seized of self-awareness and will be stronger and more professionally responsible for doing so.

The implication in the preceding paragraph that law professors (or any professors) lead lives of leisurely contemplation itself seems to hark back to what could be called a lost ideal. The image and "reality" of contemporary academic schedules seems much more dominated by what the anthropologist Renato Rosaldo calls an academic culture of "busy-ness,"[3] in which the typical preliminary to any academic conversation is a mutual comparison of

Transgression, Punishment, Responsibility, Forgiveness
Graven Images 4 (1998), 170-180.

appointment books. In the academy as well as in law firms, not to be overburdened may be taken as a sign of not being sufficiently wanted. In the academy, in fact, the prominent discourse of "busyness" may be a kind of symbolic substitute for more direct participation in an economy of rewards dependent either on return on capital, or on time-access to expertise (billed hours). At the same time scholars, too, are subject to demands for increased productivity—a technologically-based "speedup" not unfamiliar to on-line legal researchers.

Time constraints governed a personal dilemma I faced as I began to draft this essay: whether, still in my last year of law school, to choose to work part time in the large firm where I had been a summer associate, or to concentrate this, perhaps my last chance for many years, on scholarship and on family. It is, of course, an extremely privileged dilemma. I could have chosen to take the time now, and to borrow more money instead, only because banks consider budding lawyers good credit risks. Banks don't worry about lost lawyers. Against that choice stood the specter of even more massive student debt further constraining the range of responsible choices I could make in the future.[4]

These quotidian considerations at the intersection of professional and personal life are not trivial.[5] Without taking them into consideration, it is impossible to sort out and articulate the welter of often-conflicting directions in which grander themes like "responsibility" are often sent flying. Thus, for example, it is only because the humanities somehow maintain a self-image of disinterested vocation that someone who knew me only by reputation could meet me in the halls at a literature convention and refer to my having "sold out." At the same time, the only reason I can think of for my wife to say that I have become more responsible is that law school and legal practice do somehow manage to instill a more sober attention to the needs of those with whom one is interdependent.

How could someone sell out and become more responsible at the same time? A pat answer about the inevitable tensions between professional demands and family demands is not really to the point here. At least part of a more satisfying explanation has to do with the signal contrast between the humanities and law: Whereas the fields that comprise the humanities for the most part find their exclusive professional structure within the academy, law is a socially and economically privileged profession fed by and supporting a relatively wealthy academic branch.

In turn, the interdependence of legal scholarship and the legal profession entails both constraints and freedoms somewhat different from those of humanities scholarship. Humanities scholars are shocked by the highly regularized editorial standards and tendency for overdocumentation of student-edited law journals, and even many law professors profess annoyance at these legal editorial practices, at least once they are past the professional need to publish in student-edited reviews. On the other hand, law schools are not as rigidly compartmentalized as are the various disciplines of the humanities.[6]

Styles of production in these different fields reflect in turn their contrasting economies. Work in the humanities is always torn between the approach of a meticulous *Wissenschaft* whose rudder is a concern for the preservation or recuperation of the past as it actually was, and a critical or speculative approach insisting on reshaping the *image* of how things are in the interests of reshaping how things *actually* are.[7] *Wissenschaft* tends to be answerable to a narrow range of fellow specialists; criticism is even more amorphously dependent on the contingencies of its reception. Criticism in particular seems vital in its interrogation of conventions and paradigms, but in a powerful sense "irresponsible" precisely because there is no independent measure of its validity or efficacy. Legal scholarship "answers," is responsible, differently, not necessarily because it is verifiable in some way that humanities scholarship is not. Legal writing, too, may be narrowly *Wissenschaftlich* or boldly speculative. A quick glance at Grant Gilmore's account of the "Holmesian revolution" by which the consideration theory of contract "promptly became the truth—the indisputable truth—of the matter" is enough to dispel any lingering notions that legal doctrines merely articulate common understandings.[8]

The main difference has more to do with the production of the law journals themselves. The student editors referred to above, derided and resented as they sometimes are, constitute an extraordinary, overabundant fund of free labor with at least some pertinent skills. The resulting tendency for overdocumentation is notorious, as in the rumored request for authority for the statement, "Japan is an island nation."[9]

What is more telling, in the context of professional economies, is the way in which such law journal service serves for the student editors as a socialization into equally painstaking (often equally tedious) legal drafting and "due diligence." Many or most of today's law review editors will tomorrow bear at least some junior responsibility to a group (a firm), working within the constraints of a set of conventions to structure an arrangement to the benefit of the client. The tension or challenge here is different from that of speculative criticism, which occupies an uneasy and ill-defined space defined by a generalized sense of humanist responsibility (criticism is in that sense "impartial," even when it is charged with being most identitarian) and the highly subjective standards according to which it is both produced and received; there is no law of critical malpractice. By contrast, the former law review editor turned big-firm associate is often carrying out, indirectly at least, the second of Karl Llewellyn's three "law jobs," that of counseling: "It is the counselor's job to help his clients plan for the future, more specifically, to help them identify and control the legal consequences of their actions" (Kronman, *The Lost Lawyer*, 121).

Anthony Kronman emphasizes, however, that the lawyer cannot take a merely partisan stance in identifying with her client. She is also engaged in a collaborative enterprise with those who "say what the law is;" Kronman speaks of judges, but these certainly include legislators and regulators. The point is that the "role of the counselor" cannot be narrowly technical or strategic, because the partisan counselor also depends upon and participates in the system of adjudication. Kronman insists on this cooperative enterprise between lawyer and judge, in opposition to what he supposes to be a radical epistemological gap between anthropologists and those whom they study:

> For if an anthropologist were unable to separate his own personal view of what is right and wrong, reasonable and unreasonable, from the view of those he is studying, he could not even aim to explain their behavior from an internal point of view—which is the only one that anthropologists with conflicting personal values can ever hope to have in common, hence the only perspective that is neutral between their different normative judgments. (136)

Now, the notions that anthropologists could or should neatly separate "their" notions of right and wrong from the moral beliefs of those whom they write about; that "internal" points of view can be adequately "explained" from a point outside; that anthropologists share the goal of producing an adequately "neutral" account which they can severally address—all these, it must be said, are regarded within anthropology today as at best lost ideals, and more commonly as colonial fictions of which the field is well ridded.[10] Indeed, to the extent that anthropology has lost a good deal of whatever academic ground it held earlier in this century, that effect may be traced to the peculiar ties of anthropology to colonialism.[11] Much as it has been linked to systems of domination; unlike law, anthropology is not central to the property relations that constitute the "core" of the capitalist framework. Its very existence as a discipline has thus been thrown into crisis by the decline of formal colonialism. That crisis has in turn entailed a discipline-wide project of self-criticism which is simultaneously salutary and debilitating.

My own turn to law school came after years of participation in the self-critical anthropological project, during which I both sought a safe professional place amidst the disciplinary crisis, and attempted to interject a Jewish voice into the debate. Law school for me is both a redemption and an interruption, and, where Kronman seeks to recuperate the lost figure of the "lawyer-statesman," I find myself struggling, as here, to articulate a possible alternative figure of the lawyer-critic. Whatever that figure might become may be indebted to Critical Legal Studies, but it will not quite recognize itself in Kronman's account of the CLS ethos:

> Seizing his opportunities where he finds them, a lawyer inspired by [Roberto] Unger's vision will seek to turn low-level disputes that arise against a familiar and unquestioned background into controversies about that background itself—to politicize the law by doing everything he can to ensure that 'focused disputes of legal doctrine repeatedly threaten to escalate into struggles over the basic imaginative structure of social existence.' (263-4)

Kronman's analysis suggests that this exhausting discipline of endless politicization is oddly complicit with a competing school in legal scholarship—law and economics. His account of both leads to a charge of a "pathological" division between the practical task of legal teaching and the discourse of legal scholarship (264 ff.). To them he contrasts a nexus of appeals—conservative in the noblest sense, perhaps, but certainly conservative: appeals to the old-fashioned, humane lawyerly common sense of "prudentialism" (especially at the end of Chapter 3) and "practical wisdom" (at the end of chapter 4). For Kronman, the last best hope for relinking professionalism to social, communal engagement is to aim at reproducing the lawyer-statesman on a smaller canvas, in a "small town or small-city practice" (300). What's striking in this prescription is not only its nostalgia, but also Kronman's implicitly Weberian account of the growth and rationalization of large law firms—an evolution whose effects, as his account (like Gordon's blurb) suggests, are virtually ineluctable. In any case Kronman, the dean of Yale Law School, certainly knows that few of his students will follow that prescription. Many more, if not a majority of his school's graduates, will join large, big-city firms. Yet for many of those who do enter large firms, associateships will only be stepping-stones toward further, much more diverse careers.

Would it not be possible, then, to train students to view large firm work as a continuing part of their education—as, if you will, a practicum in capitalism's possibilities and limitations? To do so would be consistent with an expanded account of "professional responsibility" that would not only be limited to ethical awareness (a zone of potential transgressions or temptations to be avoided) nor yet limited to "public-spiritedness" (the lawyer-statesman idea) but to a consistent invigoration of practice with a critical sensibility. Is it not *also* professionally responsible for a young practitioner to ask, "What does the work I'm doing teach me about the structures, the plumbing, of global economic organization? What is the universe of persons whose needs are addressed by this structure? Who is included, who is excluded, and what are the membranes for regulating inclusion and exclusion? What are the assumptions on which those structures are based? Where are those assumptions dangerously weak, so that they might mask predictable systemic crises? What other forms are imaginable, given what I know now about the weight of how things actually work?"

It should not be supposed, by critical scholars in the humanities or by law professors, that practice as it stands affords no opportunities for such critical reflection. Such chances as do exist must, however, be seized as they happen to come up, and the second part of this essay will close with examinations of two such chances. Yet it is plausible to suppose that such a critical infusion could also be urged upon the firms to some effect, such that they would be induced to provide institutional encouragement for such reflective discipline as part of their programs in professional development.[12] Firms that compete for top students try to provide what those students are looking for—at least as long as this doesn't cut into profits too deeply. Thus they tout their pro bono records in recruiting, and thus, if the demand were created, they could be induced to make space for professional reflection as well.

A case could even be made—though I cannot move beyond that bald claim here—that structured reflection as part of large-firm practice could address the increasing concern that professional boundaries no longer afford business lawyers anything like a monopoly on work which requires purely technical business-law knowledge.[13] One approach is to address the technical nature of this skill head on, and to insist that business lawyers maximize their skill as "transaction cost engineers:"

> Recent developments in two areas of economics—finance and transaction cost economics—now provide the tools necessary for serious inquiry into a theory of private ordering and for bringing that theory to bear not on criticizing public policy, or case law, or particular regulatory regimes, but, at last, on understanding how people order their relationships in the absence of regulatory interference, and on helping them improve their performance.[14]

Focusing, as Gilson suggests, on training prospective business lawyers more effectively to facilitate such regimes of "private ordering" (303) might in the short run produce more "value-productive" professionals. In the longer run, it provides no reason why law firms should endure as a distinctive professional institution, nor indeed why there should be a distinction between business lawyers and any other kind of financial workers. More troubling in the short run, it is astonishingly disingenuous in its assumption that "how people order their relationships in the absence of regulatory interference" is innocuous, really the best way for things to be ordered, assistance in the "performance" of which is a fit goal for responsible professionals. Arguably, what underlies Gilson's prescription is the financial equivalent of a natural-law theory of rights: what lawyers should do is to facilitate whatever their clients want to do, subject only to the resistance provided by the fact that they can't do it alone.

If this is unfair, it serves at least to illustrate the point that the most purportedly value-neutral analysis demands critical evaluation of the ends of practice. For again, what this essay is examining is the possible coexistence of legal practice with the exercise of critical sensibility. At least to a refugee from the humanities entering business-law practice, transaction engineering on Gilson's terms does not satisfy the sense, somehow engrained, that not to engage in such critical exercise is somehow irresponsible. In any case, it is a matter of years—longer, in fact, than a large number of young associates will stick it out at any of the large firms—before that recovering humanist will have the chance to engage in creative transaction engineering. When she starts out, her legal professional responsibility will be largely confined to what is known as due diligence: stolid thoroughness in checking, cross-checking, recording, and abstracting large masses of records. The work seems almost designed to limit the sense of contingent professional responsibilities, to foster the general notion that if everything is done properly, things will work out all right—a corporate version of jurisprudential proceduralism.

Had she stayed in the humanities, this hypothetical refugee would have had to confront different dilemmas of responsibility. In the humanities, there is a curious and probably necessary tension between professional discipline and critical responsibility. "Discipline" could be identified with the reasonable attempt to conform to the best of one's abilities to the standards of diligence, verifiability and shared method that in turn define the discipline. Discipline in the humanities, that is, represents the kind of schooling/socialization that makes one observe the norms of research and writing that are established by, and that constitute, the means by which the profession recognizes production within its limits and assures its own institutional reproduction. Yet there is a risk that, in expending all of one's care at this end of the spectrum, one could fail to attempt in some fashion to "wrest tradition away from a conformity that is about to overpower it."[15] More precisely perhaps, failure of critical engagement in the humanities bears a measure of irresponsibility, inasmuch as the costs of the academy are borne by society in exchange for its critical function.[16] Responsibility in the humanities entails, that is, a certain amount of speculative passion, the taking of considerable risk—a certain degree of resistance to discipline.

Whether law, as a social institution, bears the same critical responsibility is a question somewhat beyond the scope of this essay. The preceding paragraph, as I said, is more narrowly intended to explain the continuing sense of critical responsibility that will inform the earliest experience of legal practice of at least some who enter with a background in humanist scholarship. Beyond that, this first half of the essay has begun to sketch out some of the differences between the scope and character of professional responsibilities in law and the humanities. In the second and concluding part, I will suggest that the critical perspective of cultural studies can invigorate legal education in general, and I will give two fragmentary examples of applied criticism in a large-firm corporate practice setting.

What might happen if, rather than beginning professional legal education with an introductory set of courses generally understood to inculcate basic principles applicable to further study within the entire legal framework, we were to begin by attempting to inculcate a generalized understanding of law as a contingent cultural phenomenon? Without mapping out even a rudimentary program of this kind, I suggest that for some incoming students, it would greatly facilitate the learning of legal doctrine. For some people acquire structured bodies of normative knowledge better—more effectively and with less resistance—once they are seized with an awareness that these knowledges are contingent human products rather than externally-given phenomena.[17]

A strategy approaching legal education as a cultural study might, for example, begin by unpacking one of the central concepts underlying both Western law and ordinary life: the notion of "person." Fortunately, both the actual contingency of personal identity and at least some of the reasons why such identity is taken for granted in our culture have been well articulated in recent cultural criticism, notably by feminists such as Judith Butler and Donna Haraway.[18] Going through the labor of grasping this contingency of personal identity might, in turn, be an excellent preparation for a more supple and profound ability to conceive the notion of legal personhood. That is, once it's no longer taken for granted that an individual specimen of homo sapiens is ipso facto a "person," it may become much easier to think that any legal entity, such as a corporation, can be a person as well.

Another key concept in such a curriculum might be the presumption of continuous growth which underlies the logic of capitalism. Through the distinction made by capitalist economic rationality between "diversifiable risk" and "undiversifiable risk," it becomes possible to assume that, absent global catastrophe, there will be a certain rate of growth which can be reliably obtained as long as risk is sufficiently diversified. This presumption that growth is necessary, inevitable and desirable is generally unquestioned by theorists of law and economics. In the essay by Gilson discussed earlier, he disputes Derek Bok's assertion that "'engineers make the pie grow larger; lawyers only decide how to carve it up."[19] But Gilson is only taking issue with the claim that lawyers don't make the pie grow; he does not question the assumption that the appropriate goal is to bake as large a pie as possible, and to eat it. This limitation to think in terms of models other than continuous growth may be more important than sheer greed in explaining the extraordinary difficulty capitalism seems to have in anticipating the evident and growing need for sustainable life support systems on a limited resource base. It would seem, therefore, that a due concern for the professional responsibility of future corporate lawyers would require taking an initial step back, so that they are able to consider critically the assumptions of inevitable growth which will underlie all their training in business law.

Indeed, not to do so may leave these business lawyers-in-training liable to being blindsided by changes in investment patterns stemming from loss of future vision. Oddly, the capitalist assumption of limitless growth into an infinite future has begun to run up against a certain collapse of the imagined future—a collapse evident not only in the increased pressure on corporate directors to produce short-term economic gains (or leave themselves vulnerable to shareholder suits and to takeovers), but in the abandonment by that great image-maker, the Walt Disney company, of popular exhibitions about the future.[20]

Of course I have not randomly selected these two exemplary concepts—the individual organism as an ideally autonomous juridical person, and assumptions about inevitable growth into an indefinite future. It seems to me instead that the former depends on the latter. A (post)-Protestant liberal culture wants the individual to be autonomous, that is, self-ruling rather than determined by connections to ancestral authority, and hence developing only outward and forward from birth through maturity. Since in this culture, identity is not genealogically shared (as it is in most historical cultural systems), everything that is past is in a profound sense used up, unavailable. Hence without the continuous creation of new and more value, possibilities of development would inevitably be drastically limited. It is only possible to look forward, and the resources must therefore always be new. Liberty, capitalism and "development" are, in this system, indispensable concomitants of each other.

Arguing for a possible legal education which would deliberately work to bring to students' awareness the fact that our culture is dependent on such fundamental and problematic notions as the bounded individual and the inevitability of growth, I still find myself using those same notions when I worry about what "our" "future" will be. Furthermore, it seems that critical thinking has great difficulty finding languages for re-imagining possible futures. Intending to address this problem, or at least to articulate it better, I recently drafted the following call to a panel under the title "Law, Language and the Subject of the Future:"

> Is the critique of progress centered on the figure of Walter Benjamin actually the intellectual manifestation of a diminished capacity to imagine and work toward a better mid-range or long-range future? Perhaps, to the contrary, by clarifying the

relation between notions of progress and the fact of domination, that critique might contribute to a more effective future orientation. In order to explore that possibility, it becomes necessary to examine as well how the liberal notion of the subject, exhaustively situated and historicized in the work of contemporary criticism and especially in psychoanalytic notions of "law," is linked not only to individualized or masculinist notions of rights, but to conceptions of linear time and progressive cultural evolution. Bringing these somewhat disparate moments in millennial theory together might help us figure out how, as it were, finally to make the Angel of History turn around, or at least to situate better the problem of figuring the future without the comforting props of progress on one hand and the dignity of essential personhood on the other.

Admittedly, this is a bid for attention. It is a programmatic statement, a summons within a certain field. It is addressed to a certain audience that is not only composed of passive receptors but also of potential respondents, of co-respondents. That is indeed what it means to have a "field," to constitute or sustain a "field," defined more by the participants than by the objectively-delineated subject matter. It is at a few places laden with the codes by which members of the field might recognize each other (the cutesy pun on "millennial" theory, by which I simply mean the most up-to-date theory) and by the nod to the cult of Walter Benjamin (of which I carry card #156). Yet, perhaps because when I drafted it I had already had some short exposure to the demands of legal writing for transparency to a broader if still select readership, it is not quite as burdened with critical-theory jargon as I had feared upon coming back to it many months later.

The call is also a challenge. It insists that it is ultimately irresponsible to renounce the project of critically reimagining possible futures solely because we dread the disasters into which both utopian projects and quotidian progress have led us. It suggests, furthermore, that the more subtle understanding of our own notions of personal identity available to us now may provide new avenues for such critical re-imagination. As a challenge, I find myself hardly adequate to it, for I am still stymied when I try to think the future in terms other than those of progress. In my frustration, I want to shake the Angel: how can it continue to face backward, when in front of us looms the growing paradox of systemic limitation in a global order premised on indefinite growth of consumption. What that means, in turn, may become clearer when we remember that our fossil fuel, petroleum-based global system is actually a consumption of past life. In a sense it is not so much a storm but a conflagration, dare we say a holocaust with a lower-case "h," blowing from Paradise, causing global warming, threatening to suffocate us and end our collective story. But so far only threatening: some business leaders (including the head of British Petroleum) are at last beginning to acknowledge global warming.[21]

This, then—the link between our notions of bounded identity and perpetual systemic growth on the one hand, and the facts of interdependence and systemic limits on the other— is the subject of my two promised fragments of capitalist cultural criticism, arising as they do out of my summer-associate assignments in due diligence.

Due Diligence A: Annual Report

I came across this item when I was assigned to check the veracity of certain representations made in a private placement memorandum regarding a bank which was to serve as a liquidity provider, thus assuring timely payments on trust certificates. The paragraph appears at the end of the 1996 Annual Report of De Nationale Investeringsbank— the ninth-largest bank in The Netherlands, slightly more than half-owned by the Dutch government. It credits the artist and explains the bank's interpretation of several full-page illustrations interspersed through the text of the report:

> Kars Persoon (Eindhoeven, 1954) was commissioned by De Nationale Investeringsbank to paint a number of water-colors on the subject of risk. In Persoon's work, mankind is a floating, dancing *figure* on a journey through time. In these water-colors, it is above all the perils of banking that this *figure* encounters on its journey. The growing complexity and increasingly advanced virtuality of money transactions do not, it seems, leave the *figure* unmoved.

> Observations, lamentations, and old wise sayings succeed one another in dealing
> with the apparently unpredictable. But the *figure* triumphs: gently but firmly, it
> makes its way through a risky world.[22]

As the caption suggests, the format of the several images generally blends anonymous, vaguely outlined human figures facing "forward" (that is, to the right of the page), overlaid by fragments of text. The phrases appearing on one image are "in terminis possibilium" and "nasdaq," thus combining the imperial-universal aura of Latin, the message of possible infinite expanse, and a reminder of the practical means by which that growth is to be realized. On another page, a different image with similar figures bears the legend "our escape is almost a miracle."

On one hand, the figures are curiously anonymous, genderless and featureless, as far a cry from Rembrandt's group portrait of proud Dutch burghers as could be imagined. It is in fact striking to see such "figures" in the place of portraits of the bank's officers. The suggestion that the figure is not unmoved by the complexities of contemporary banking implies that the bankers, like the figure, can be trusted in part because of their very humanity. In its very anonymity, it is also a kind of Everyinvestor or Everybanker: the miraculous escape is cast in the plural. Nevertheless, the caption also suggests a clear dissociation between the figure and the world: it "floats" and "dances" on its journey through homogeneous time. Somehow, in its quiet and unobtrusive way, it is guaranteed of eventual triumph despite the need for near-miraculous rescue. Somewhat humbled and postmodern, it is all the same able to face the future (rather than turning back toward Paradise, like Benjamin's and Klee's Angelus Novus). Unlike the Angel of History, it has no wings. Still it is not quite human: perhaps the figure is actually a cipher.

By providing such ambivalent images and by venturing commentary on the images—even in a way that is meant ultimately to reassure readers of the bank's acumen and responsibility—those who produced Investeringsbank's Annual Report have offered a chance for reflection on the projections of risk and guarantee underlying capitalist imaginings of the future. These projections are usually cast only in technical financial terms; the Annual Report at least invites awareness that futures are existential projections as well. Whether this kind of invitation ends up being merely prophylactic—incorporating a measure of humble and sophisticated irony so that the institution may actually proceed on its smoothly dominant way—or whether it becomes the occasion for the hard work of engaged criticism, will depend largely on how many times those committed to critical engagement encounter such artifacts of esoteric global financial culture.

Due Diligence B: Compound Interest

I was assigned to determine whether it is legal under New York Law for a financial instrument to provide for the payment of compound interest. I learned that compound interest is indeed legal, but only by relatively recent statute.[23] The Practice Commentary accompanying that statute in McKinney's, the standard compendium of New York state law, explains that "compound interest has always been feared because it involves exponential growth:" that is, it seems at first glance to provide an oppressive engine whereby unmet payments of debt capital can accumulate infinite interest debt. The Practice Commentary goes on to explain that, nevertheless, compound interest is not necessarily oppressive, as long as the capital which it is meant to repay serves to fund growth in productivity. As Richard Givens, the author of the Commentary, puts it:

> The power of compound interest is only matched by the expanding power of
> human intelligence and its uses of technology for better or ill, provided less rather
> than more through-put of scarce resources is sought; otherwise, investment in pre-
> existing methodologies will eventually trigger what economists call the 'law of
> diminishing returns.[24]

Givens is concerned here with the relations among raw "scarce" resources, the innovative power of technology to increase productivity, and the rate of return on capital which can be supported by that increased productivity. If capital is loaned at compound interest and productivity does not grow apace, the results can be disastrous. In order not to be the ones who owe compound interest, we must be the ones who receive compound interest, "for better." More accurately perhaps, this logic leaves us in a sense always running away from ourselves, rushing to be ahead of ourselves.

Givens's Practice Commentary refers us to his treatise on Antitrust. A section of that treatise is devoted to the important link between antitrust enforcement and the facilitation of technological innovation.[25] Givens goes beyond the explanation above of the need for increased productivity, to point out some of the practical difficulties in encouraging research which will lead to such increased productivity: "It is difficult for the public or investors to visualize possibilities until they already exist (by which time they are likely to be left behind); the public is unaware of major possibilities for a better life or economic advantages which have not as yet been made practical." To his credit, Givens offers an outline proposal to overcome this persistent lag. In effect, he suggests that we re-nationalize the future through the creation of a scheme whereby "the Federal Reserve System . . . could repurchase any loans made by member banks to private enterprises undertaking research of the type determined to be vital to national goals." In this fashion, speculative basic research aimed at ultimate but unpredictable increases in productivity or better utilization of limited resources could be encouraged by what are in effect Federal guarantees, without the necessity for direct government budget outlays.

Givens offers a revealing list of benefits to be anticipated from such a scheme:

> Creating new jobs for new activities;
>
> Creating an atmosphere of thrilling advance on the part of the country;
>
> Creating exciting career-producing jobs, permitting the American Dream to be revived and surpassed, thereby also enabling society to compete effectively with criminal and drug syndicates for the allegiance of vulnerable young people;
>
> Strengthening the national defense industrial base;
>
> Producing substitutes for existing methods producing health, environmental or other problems;
>
> Permitting an active, high-wage and profitable economy to keep ahead of other advancing economies through new innovations making recently developed versions obsolete as fast as they can be copied.

What is appealing about this scheme is that it is, in the terms I am using here, an attempt to reinforce the institutional grounds for imaginable but unpredictable futures. Givens seeks new ways to sustain the modernist promise of better living through fruitful capitalist competition. Strikingly consistent both with the general proposal that funding for basic research "vital to national goals" be underwritten by the Federal Reserve, most of these benefits are cast at the level of the nation.

There is something curiously unfashionable about this kind of state-modernist proposal. There is a yawning discrepancy between Givens's evident devotion to an imaginable, social-technological future, and his unreflectively naive assumption that the "nation" remains the proper vehicle of determining what that future is to be. Who is to determine what interests are "vital?" To take just one example, it is highly debatable whether strengthening the industrial base with an eye toward military production has any overall positive effect on socially useful production.

In the age of global capitalism, with serious scholarly volumes proclaiming the imminent "end of the nation state,"[26] it is at least doubtful to what extent the nation-state could be the subject of the future. Any credible scheme for reintroducing a sense of responsibility for long-term social investment in the future must also consider what the boundaries of the investing "society" might be—and this, despite the failures of utopia, demands the consideration of alternatives. For me, this leads to the highly speculative (and, following the discussion in Part I above, to that degree potentially "irresponsible") project of embracing diaspora as an alternative to the nation-state. The broader point is that the possibility of a human future depends not only on new technology, but on the critical reinvention of polity as well.

Conclusion

The two examples just discussed—the "Annual Report" and "Compound Interest"—caught my attention because they raise, *within the context of business law*, critical questions about how the future is in fact (albeit usually implicitly) imagined in the dominant global socioeconomic structure, and what possible or necessary alternatives to such imaginings there might be. I explored the ambivalence of the *figure* in the Annual Report and Givens's proposed solution to a perceived crisis of investment in research aimed at greater productivity. Both examples suggest a degree of vaguely-sensed unease concerning the current state of the assumptions explored in the beginning of Part II, about autonomous individual identity and a reliably expansive future. I suggested further that cases like these are only likely to be noticed and examined by those with a developed critical sensibility and an exposure to the internal culture of capitalist elites. This supports my contention in Part I that, rather than mourning the loss of the lawyer-statesman, swallowed up in the utilitarianism of large firms, elite law schools whose students are for the most part headed toward such firms should both develop their critical sensibilities, and instill in them a belief that criticism is relevant outside the academy.

Finally, all that I have begun to say can only be a preamble to a reappraisal of the tension between the commitment to critical speculation and a world of practice that purports to take systems as they exist. As I indicated, the work of certain actors coincidentally located "across" professional boundaries will illuminate this tension, since it is one they in particular cannot avoid. No individual, of course, is or should be bound to criticism and to practice equally. Yet the tension remains, and it largely defines our joint and several responsibility for the maintenance of a possible lifeworld.

Notes

[1] Cambridge: Harvard University Press, 1993.

[2] Where possession of land was once the mark of a gentleman, perhaps distinction lies now more in the possession of time.

[3] My memory certainly attributes this quip to Rosaldo. In any case, a brief general discussion of time in academic culture may be found in his *Culture and Truth* (Boston: Beacon Press, 1989), 105.

[4] "[B]y inducing so many of our students to run up monumental debts to pay for their legal educations, law schools themselves are directly implicated in today's malaise." Aviam Soifer, "Who Took the Awe Out of Law?" *Madness, Melancholy, and the Limits of the Self: Studies in Culture, Law, and the Sacred, Graven Images* 3 (1996), 173, 174.

[5] I am reminded of the famous-and by now, generally anonymous-response of the husband of an earlier feminist scholar, on hearing the topic of her new paper: "My God, a paper on *housework*?"

[6] "If one added the law schools more systematically to the inquiry on the state of the universities, one would find that a generalist tradition still exists there in addition to a specialist tradition." Carol Weisbrod, book review of David Damrosch, *We Scholars: Changing the Culture of the University, Yale Journal of Law and the Humanities* 9 (1997), 443, 446.

[7] My own work has tended increasingly toward the latter approach, as in my collaborative writing on diaspora as an alternative logic to the nation-state for the organization of identities and polities. Some of this work has been received as missionizing: "In rather evangelical terms [Daniel Boyarin and Jonathan Boyarin] aver that if this message is understood it could help prevent the bloodshed produced by the ethno-nationalist struggles of recent years." Robin Cohen, *Global Diasporas* (Seattle: University of Washington Press, 1997), 123.

[8] Gilmore, *The Death of Contract,* 2d ed. (Columbus: Ohio State University Press, 1995), 23.

[9] I am indebted to my classmate Chris Kubiak for this anecdote.

[10] See James Clifford and George Marcus, eds., *Writing Culture* (Berkeley and Los Angeles: University of California Press, 1986).

[11] Talal Asad, *Anthropology and the Colonial Encounter* (Atlantic Highlands, NJ: Humanities Press, 1973).

12 Indeed a certain number of hours were spent working on this essay during my summer associateship, under the firm's policy of allowing summer associates necessary time to take care of law review responsibilities.

13 See Gilson, "The Devolution of the Legal Profession: A Demand Side Perspective," *Maryland Law Review* 49 (1990), 869.

14 Gilson, "Value Creation by Business Lawyers: Legal Skills and Asset Pricing," *Yale Law Journal* 94 (1984), 239, 305.

15 Walter Benjamin, "Theses on the Philosophy of History," in *Illuminations*, ed. Hannah Arendt, trans. Harry Zohn (New York: Schocken Books, 1969), 255.

16 See Louis Marin, "Frontiers of Utopia: Past and Present," *Critical Inquiry* 19 (1993), 397.

17 Thus in high school I became much more interested in Euclidean geometry when I was exposed, however briefly, to the possibility of there being a non-Euclidean geometry.

18 Judith Butler, *Gender Trouble: Feminism and the Subversion of Identity* (New York: Routledge, 1990); Judith Butler, *Bodies That Matter: On the Discursive Limits of "Sex"* (New York: Routledge, 1993): Donna Haraway, *Simians, Cyborgs and Women* (New York: Routledge, 1991).

19 Gilson, "Value Creation by Business Lawyers," 307.

20 Seth Schiesel, "New Disney Vision Making the Future a Thing of the Past," *New York Times*, February 23, 1997, A1.

21 William K. Stevens, "Industries Revisit Global Warming," *New York Times*, August 5, 1997, A1.

22 Emphasis in original. No better illustration, quite literally, could be found of Ulrich Beck's thesis that Western European capitalism is now dominated by the theme of risk management—unless, of course, this interpretation itself was directly inspired by Beck. See Beck, *Risk Society*, trans. Mark Ritter (Thousand Oaks, CA: Sage Publications, 1992).

23 New York General Obligations Law Section 5-527.

24 Givens, Practice Commentary to New York General Obligations Law Section 5-527. The long-standing opposition to compound interests is linked to the ban (still outstanding) on usurious rates of interest. In fact, under Delaware law compound interest is still strongly disfavored. *Weinberger v. OUP, Inc.*, 517 A. 2d 653, 657 (1986).

25 Givens, *Antitrust: An Economic Approach* (New York: New York Law Publishers, 1997), Section 29.03: Affirmative Promotion. Further citations are to this section.

26 Jean-Marie Guehenno, *End of the Nation-State,* trans. Victoria Elliot (Minneapolis; Unoversity of Minnesota Press, 1995); Kenichi Ohmae, *End of the Nation State* (New York: Free Press, 1995).

Three Poems

Lee Johnson

Ice-Fishing Over Christmas
(To My Brothers)

Somewhere above me in the windless cold,
Soft midnight clouds drift slowly back and forth:
I draw a circle on the plane of ice,
Cut and remove the frozen cylinder,
And stare into a darkness without depth,
A black intensity that gazes back
As if it were a mirror of the mind—
When suddenly within the void a glow
Takes shape, the arched flash of a graceful fish
Arising, or perhaps the gracious light
Of moon or star admitted through the clouds
To glance across the circle I have made.
Something beyond has caught the fisherman
Where three worlds meet: the time and space of ice,
Fractured in symbols breaking as we look,
The darkness of the mind's designs on light,
Circling an absent center, and the dark
Time of the year that circumscribes all time,
All darkness, and surprises us with light.

Meeting-Place

Three figures stand beside a lake:
The first, a child, with mystic glance
Blends all that waves and light can make
Of depths and surfaces that dance;

The second's older, earnest gaze
Searches reflections for their treasures
And finds a disconnected maze
Of motionless and abstract measures;

The third, with aging, ageless eyes,
Beholds all that the child could see,
And more, as thought and vision rise
Up to the glittering harmony
Of lakes and waves, of light and skies.

There have been Great and Extraordinary Lovers, My Dear,
But We are not among Them

Orpheus lost Eurydice
But once*; how therefore can it be
That lovers in an earthly way
Must lose and win their loves each day?

So rudely are the pansy's flowers
Plucked—yet restored through humble powers
That heal all by the morning dew
And bring sweet blossoms back to you.

Whatever rudeness I may speak
In losing all that I would seek,
Our daily love renews once more
What Orphic song could not restore.

* In Hades; on Earth, Orpheus was usually an ordinary lover.

Two Poems

Sonja Hansard-Weiner

In Memoriam*

Washing my hands, blood
draining down the sinkhole,
I stand waiting for the smell
to rise. Antigone also waited
until the full heat of the sun
burst upon the guards and sand
washed across the Theban plains.

Plunging her arms into his
thickening bile she filled
Polyneices' wounds with wine
muddying his body with her tears.
Did seeing *Antigone* as a child
in Macedonia teach Mother
to honor the dead, the dying?

Here beside newsphotos
of her coffin borne in state
among throngs of dignitaries,
untouchables, the stained faces
of the poor, the stench of her body
far away, I stand in my kitchen
readying myself to feed the hungry.

* Mother Theresa died September 25, 1997.

Transgression, Punishment, Responsibility, Forgiveness
Graven Images 4 (1998), 183-184.

A Reader Considers Ted Hughes' Destruction of
Sylvia Plath's Journals On the 35th Anniversary of
Her Suicide

I've stood aloof from her posthumous
sanctification but today reading "A Secret,"
seeing the big blue head of the illegitimate
baby breathing on the dresser (was it shredded
by the same trepanning tool that sliced her thumb?)

those other images ran through my memory:
her drugged and raped, a drowned girl, snares
like birth pangs, babies dangling from her cow-heavy
breasts, a goddam baby screaming—there's always
a bloody baby in the air— the bad smells.

I want to see her not avenged but understood.
Changing *Ariel* is crime enough to curse him
for— surely there are reasons a father might
spare his children details of a mother's daily
torments. What if instead of lamenting his infidelity

her journals were awash in infant gore—
the madly prating puling puking pestilence
of prams and post-partum depression
that can turn the most loving mother
into a Medea? What if the lioness

emerged, long past the doll-like need
of marriage marriage marriage, ready
to stand side split against the universe?
And if he spoke, what sacred trust might he revoke
if her secrets, not his, were what he kept?

The Lesson, Circa 1958

Roy Jacobstein

What transgression, Bobby Bordley,
what transgression made fat Mr. Hantler drop
his trowel, his gloves, everything
he was doing that hot May day to chase you from one end
of Fullerton to the other, trying to
wring your little neck?

The rest of our gang of ten-year olds
(the Sultans)
stood stupefied on the sidewalk
like livestock stunned before slaughter.
We held our breath,
running only in our minds,
but running with you still,
weaving a desperate curlicue
to evade that grown man—
someone's father, after all,
sport shirt riding up his ample belly.

Nothing about that day remains—not our Detroit
neighborhood of first- and second-generation Jews,
not the Dexter-Davison Kosher Market,
nor George V Drugs, nor the Avalon Theater.
Not Mr. Hantler—younger then, no doubt,
than any Sultan now.
Not the roses he trimmed so carefully
and watered with his green snake
of garden hose, nor the ball and curse
you must have hurled into his flower bed.

And Helen Hantler herself must be gray
and stout and only once or twice think back
to how her young loins twitched
behind the screen door
to see someone—anyone—
escape her father's meaty hands.

Transgression, Punishment, Responsibility, Forgiveness
Graven Images 4 (1998), 185.

Two Poems

Glori Simmons

Tidal Distortions
for D.M.

1.

He said: if you love me. I stood, half-dressed, in the woods behind the church.
The only time my father ever said cunt, we were in a strip mall parking lot.
The hollowed Music Hall reminded me of a gutted fish.

2.

He said, moving my hands away from my breasts: don't be so paranoid.
About cunt, my father said, "Don't mention it to your mother."
The pearled string of velvet seats had been beached along the sidewalk.

3.

He threw off his clothes and lay down in the snow, daring me to bury him.
My mother waded toward us under the aquatic glow of the K-Mart marquee.
You see, they knocked down the Music Hall for a parking lot.

4.

Shivering, we locked ourselves in the car and drank the last Old English.
My father liked to tease me by accelerating just as my mother reached to open the car door.
When the wrecking ball crashed through the last support, I caught it in my camera.

5.

Our heads banged against the Regal's back door. I closed my eyes to the cross.
From the rear window, I watched my mother sink into the asphalt.
Through the lens, a blue dust. Like snow in headlights.

6.

I gathered my clothes together, the sleeves reaching through the frozen layers.
The defroster's lines measured her distance in latitudes.
What is left is the brief impression of a shell in sand.

Transgression, Punishment, Responsibility, Forgiveness
Graven Images 4 (1998), 186-187.

The Virgins Of Murano

Gatherer, marver, cutter of necks, the artisans
burn with the chemistry of glass, chest hair singed
to flesh, wings melted back. November's
a busy month: ten haloed forms reflect

the furnace tongue. A mustached Gabriel, apron
smeared with soot, pours one more. In the kiln
her corsets flicker and glow, votive. Lost sailors
sifted the heat-hard beads from a campfire's cold bed

and brought the clear currency west. He's trapped
in the substance, like a flaw in glass, has seen what
they'll do to the glass makers who escape the islands:

returning with the nightly catch, bloated as wine jugs,
locked in fish net. So he forms each sheer shackle
into porthole lace, watching between the weathered slats

as Murano girls rush to meet the ships
at port. He molds, marvels and blows the virgin
from drop glob to skirted sphere. Pure, she is
a window that could frost or shatter, depending

on his tender precision. He'd throw the pretty thing—
milk bottle, flask—if she weren't filled with his exhale.
Part water, part sand, she is the island's unravel
as the sea's commerce rises to submerge them all.

He taps the hem free, melds the cullet in glory
hole. With pliers, swan-bill sharp, he pinches
a pedestal for her pearl head, composes her eyes closed.

Vitrified vessel, she'll export his breath, clear cut
and mournful. And he'll remain at the crucible,
repeating the secret he never chose to know.

Weaving a Transgressive Story:
Ekphrasis and Mimesis in Ovid's Arachne Episode

Ronald Harris

Ovid's Arachne episode spins around a central question explored throughout the *Metamorphoses:* what is the relation (proper or otherwise) between the gods and humans? This question is by its very nature one of boundaries, of establishing categories that define what is god and what is not, what is human, what is not, and what can be said of the gods by human poets.[1] In the Arachne story, Ovid employs figures of three weavers to establish—however provisionally—the boundaries that define the human, as opposed to the gods and the animals. Arachne's presumption in challenging Pallas Minerva, a goddess, to a weaving contest establishes the boundary that separates gods from humans, even as she transgresses that boundary through her expert weaving. The two tapestries that Pallas and Arachne work for their contest illustrate that only in Arachne's punishment, her transformation into a spider, does the boundary between human and animal become established.

Arachne's representation of the gods in her tapestry, with Ovid's voice concealed within the description of this ekphrasis, reveals a truth about the gods that subtly undermines Pallas's very different attempt to close down interpretation in her Humpty-Dumpty-like insistence that *res* and *verba* correspond, and correspond exactly as she sees them. Pallas presents the gods as atemporal, fixed, forever the same as their attributes, whereas in her weaving, Arachne pulls the gods into human time, using her skill to portray mimetically her world of random violence of the gods against humans. As her punishment for her transgressive aesthetic display, Arachne is pulled into Pallas's world to become fixed eternally as a spider, but ironically this happens only as Pallas enters into human time to act out the scenes depicted in Arachne's tapestry.

Ovid uses these descriptions of tapestries (visual art forms constructed from material substances by human hands) to discuss the nature and limits of something much less overtly material and more governed by time: poetry.[2] The Arachne episode becomes a story about how best to conceal the dissembling nature of gods, how best to conceal that it may be very human poets who through their art bring the gods into being. Ovid reveals this truth by exploiting the transgressive potential of ekphrasis, by disguising this inquiry within woven tapestries which conceal the transgressive nature of the inquiry itself. What becomes clear is that any inquiry into the nature of humans only engenders ever more stories. Yet it is the very telling of stories, what Plato called dissembling, that most precisely defines what is human.

Already at the very beginning of the *Metamorphoses*, Ovid offers, however provisionally, a set of fundamental boundaries that separate and thereby distinguish gods, humans, and animals.[3] Even so, these fixed categories exist in relationship to one another, with the effect that the human, occupying the middle place between gods and animals, can be defined only in relation to the other two.[4] The very origin of humans—in a book that is at least in part an aetiology—is less than clear, thus illustrating the problem of defining the human in fixed terms.

Ovid's aetiology of humans illustrates a narrative pattern that he seems to employ throughout the *Metamorphoses*. He first offers two opposed explanations of human origin, which are then supplanted by a third tangentially-related version. Initially, Ovid suggests that humans are either of divine inspiration or of the earth: "perhaps from divine seed formed by the great Creator . . . perhaps the new-made earth . . . that Prometheus moulded, mixed with water, in likeness of the gods."[5] Even from the start, then, transgression and representation are originally associated with humans, both in their creation and in the story about their creation.

While Ovid says that humans are from divine seed, he leaves unclear whether the creation was authorized ("formed by the great Creator") or transgressive ("moulded" by Prometheus). The paradox offers the possibility that humans are merely a watered-down representation, base matter formed in the likeness of the gods by a renegade Prometheus. Ovid seems to leave the answer to the question open only to offer a third possibility.

The humans, Ovid finally declares, come out of the blood of the giants, mixed with the earth. While the Gigantomachy supplements the earlier two versions of creation, it also returns to the original problem of human nature, since, after all, he tells us, the giants themselves were born of earth fertilized by the blood of Uranus.[6] What is needed is yet another story to explain the other stories, as inquiry engenders the narrative required to describe the inquiry.[7] Given the middle position of human, between the gods and the animals, however, any inquiry into the nature of humans immediately becomes transgressive, because it requires, as well, inquiry into the nature of the other two categories. Although the *Metamorphoses* seems to fix definitively the categories of god, human, and animal, the poem questions and undermines the boundaries of these categories through the relentless inquiry which propels ever and only more stories, disallowing any definitive closure.

Indeed, even while trying to define the category "god," Ovid, in his letters from exile, goes so far as to suggest that the gods themselves are creatures of narrative representation: "Even the gods, if it is permissible [*fas*] to say it, are created by poetry."[8] Here Ovid employs a passive construction to indicate that the gods themselves are not agents, but objects created by narrative. At the same time, Ovid qualifies his assertion, raising the issue of permissible speech—what one is permitted to say. By extension, Ovid addresses the issue of transgressive speech and raises the question, do the gods not exist if they are not narrated into being? Ovid's qualification to his assertion that the gods are created by poetry, "if it is permissible to say," carries a moral weight which speaks to issues of poetry's ability to reveal or conceal truths.

Ovid's qualification implies the issue is not whether the gods are indeed created by narrative—which the assertion carries as fact—but whether or not the poet is permitted to reveal this fact or is obliged to conceal it. This exploration of poetry's relationship to truth inevitably recalls Plato's objection to poetry in the *Republic*, when he argues that the poet conceals his own identity in his poem as he purports to speak as another (392c-395). Here, Plato distinguishes between "what is said (*logoi*)" and "its expression (*lexis*)." He addresses his objection not to the subject matter of poetry (roughly equivalent to plot), but to its manner of narration, as either *diegesis* or *mimesis*.[9] The mimetic poet, by presuming to speak as another, conceals himself and thereby commits a transgression, by misleading his audience.

Plato's discussion of mimetic poetry, in which the poet conceals himself in the narrative, suggests a promising approach to Ovid's ekphrases in the Arachne episode. The form of the ekphrasis itself permits Ovid to ascribe authorship of the tapestries to others, Arachne and Pallas. His role becomes that of translator of the verbal art the visual art of others. The narrator thereby distances himself from the contents of the tapestries. Furthermore, the choice of woven tapestry as the form of the visual art is hardly coincidental, since the language of weaving often serves as a metaphor for the art of poetry.

Indeed, Ovid's focus on weaving in this episode suggests that his discussion of the tapestries is as well a discussion of *mimesis* and transgression. One might argue that weaving serves as an art of concealment because the material woven might serve as a cover. For example, Sigmund Freud, in his essay on femininity, describes weaving as a feminine art of concealment, because it mimics nature's form of concealing the missing phallus—a web of pubic hair.[10] Besides gendering weaving as feminine, Freud's observation—however controversial it may be—makes the point that a function of textiles, be they window coverings, clothing, or carpets is to conceal things. Moreover, figuratively, weaving conveys the sense of a kind of literal covering that stands between the viewer and some other thing. Such a cover is all the more intriguing when one considers that the woven fabric itself might consist of a visual representation or design. Thereby the physical property (the textile—the form of discourse) comes to convey a visual image, the content of the message. The weaver becomes a poet, a person with a story to tell. While the Arachne episode's use of the language of spinning and weaving in relation to the aesthetics of the *Metamorphoses* is well established and well-documented, the relationship between weaving and poetry as mimetic arts of concealment may be pushed further in relation to this episode.[11]

When weaving is employed as a metaphor for poetry, the figuration conceals the verbal art by cloaking it in the language of visual art. In other words, the very nature of the weaving metaphor (metaphor used here in its strict sense of "to carry over") describes both the operation of revealing and concealing, and the movement from one category of artistic production to another. Ovid makes literal what is usually figurative; rather than only using weaving to describe the art of writing poems, Ovid also uses poetry to describe literal tapestries, products of the art of weaving. Moreover, Ovid's weaving metaphor extends the transgressive sense of translation inherent in ekphrasis.

For ekphrasis (a verbal representation of a visual representation) is by its nature a transgressive narrative strategy, both formally and ideologically.[12] In formal terms, ekphrasis serves as a kind of translation of visual signification into verbal signification. This represents, then, an inversion of what Roman Jakobson called "intersemiotic translation . . . an interpretation of verbal signs by means of non-verbal sign systems."[13] In its purest sense, translation (from the Latin *transferro*, to carry across) implies already a border between systems of signification that must be transgressed. The formal qualities of the ekphrasis, which join the literal sense of *transferro* to the figurative properties of language in an attempt to put into words the visual image, represent a kind of transgressive desire. For example, Murray Krieger argues that the ekphrasis represents "the ultimate translation"[14] of "the semiotic desire for the natural sign, the desire, that is, to have the world captured in the word, the word that belongs to it, or, better yet, the word to which it belongs."[15] Such strategies are one way verbal artists attempt to make sense of what at times seems to be an arbitrary and senseless world, by capturing this world in a word, to use Krieger's terms. Certainly, Ovid's *Metamorphoses* is, at some level, an attempt to make sense of his world by narrating its existence through a series of "just so" stories, which explain the relationships between gods, humans, animals, and what are normally thought of as inanimate objects. In the Arachne episode, Ovid employs the ekphrasis, a transgressive strategy, in order to tell stories which are themselves potentially transgressive.

Ekphrasis is also an ideologically transgressive strategy that serves well the poet attempting to define the relations between gods and humans. W. J. T. Mitchell argues that "word painting" is an ideal verbal strategy for a politically marginalized writer. While it might be unfair to describe Ovid as marginalized at the time he wrote the *Metamorphoses*, his telling of Arachne's story serves as a cautionary tale for humans who attempt to reveal the nature of the gods through art. Taking exception to the axiom that characterizes visual art as "spatial" representation and verbal art as "temporal," Mitchell asks, "What happens to our sense of 'the space of artistic representation' when we understand it not as a neutral field of inscription, but as a pre-inscribed site of ideological conflict?"[16] His question shifts discussion of ekphrasis away from the purely formal analysis of expression in terms of space and time into the political realm. As such, the ekphrasis offers to the artist the opportunity to transgress ideological boundaries while concealing his own voice within the formal constraints of the ekphrasis itself.

The Arachne episode, located at the beginning of the sixth book of Ovid's *Metamorphoses*, takes the form of a weaving contest in which the mortal Arachne dares to challenge the goddess Pallas. What characterizes Arachne's transgression, her sin, is her implicit denial that her weaving skills are a gift of the gods. Arachne's insistence that her art is hers alone is an act of pride, but in a very particular sense: she refuses to be bound by the tradition which has it that Pallas is the patron goddess of weaving. Arachne's presumption—that she is more skilled at weaving than the goddess of weaving herself—is encoded in her boast, "Let her contend with me."[17] Arachne's denial that her skills come from Pallas and her challenge to the goddess mark Arachne's refusal to acknowledge the superiority of gods to humans. Her denial of the traditional relationship of inter-dependency between gods and humans is in itself a transgression, because she refuses to be bound by any limit.[18] Her refusal to acknowledge that any boundary separates gods from humans at once establishes a boundary and constitutes a transgression for which she shall be punished.

Yet Arachne's crossing of that boundary does not lead her into any strange or new physical geography, but into a contest of contested representations—a weaving contest—where the political and the aesthetic are interwoven. The Arachne episode, a story about weaving tapestries at the literal level, becomes a metaphor for poetry—the weaving of stories—at the figurative level. The subsequent contest produces two narrative tapestries, ekphrases, that present, in radically different tellings, the relationship between the humans and the gods, the subject matter of the preceding five books of the *Metamorphoses*. Arachne, the human, perceives her art as the process of production, the act of weaving threads and spinning stories. Alternatively, Pallas Minerva, an immortal, sees art only in its perfected, completed state. She attempts to weave a seamless web, hiding the process of weaving and showing only the web.

The stories the two weavers tell and the aesthetics that guide them are as different as day and night. Ovid begins by describing Pallas's tapestry, which quite clearly emphasizes a well-ordered and hierarchal universe in her presentation of the gods gathered to award her the city of Athens. The twelve gods sit centrally in a fixed pose of "*augusta gravitate*," awful majesty (73). In his description, Ovid removes the gods from the temporal order and places them in a timeless frame, using the present tense to describe the action of the ekphrasis.[19] Pallas "paints"[20] both the physical space, the hills of Mars, and the scene of the "old dispute" [*antiquam litem*] between Neptune and herself. Doing so, Ovid gives the sense that, for the gods, time is all one, as the city of Athens is always and forever awarded to Pallas. Ovid reinforces the atemporality of the event by suggesting that the immortals inhabit a space removed from time. Commenting on this passage, D. C. Feeney observes that "appearance corresponds with actuality. When Pallas 'simulates' an event on her tapestry, it is no dissimulating lie, but the event itself" (191). That Pallas is able to present the event itself, instead of a representation of the event, suggests that, for the gods, words and things correspond because the moment of utterance is timeless. The gods, then, have no need for mimetic representation. Ovid describes Pallas's picture of the gods in these terms: "his own face inscribes each of the gods."[21] Yet it is not Pallas the goddess, but Ovid the human poet, who narrates the scene. Ovid combines the correspondence of signifier with the thing signified, the ideal sign, with the atemporality of event to create the illusion of "*augusta gravitate*" which dominates the tapestry.

Although the emphasis in Pallas's tapestry is precisely the centrality of the gods, humans are present, consigned to the margins. Pallas presents mortals off in a corner, in a state of timeless misery, being perpetually punished for their transgressions against the gods. While their transgressions are fixed in time, their punishments are captured visually, like the gods, in the present tense, and they signal a continually present state of punishment.[22] In Pallas's tapestry, to be human is to suffer punishment. Pallas's emphasis in her presentation of gods and humans alike is the ends, not the means. The gods are their attributes and mortals take the form of their perpetual punishment, depicting the end, not the process of their transformation, in the corners of an atemporal, always-present spatial frame.

Arachne's tapestry, naturally enough, emphasizes the process of divine transgression against humans—the representations of events, and not the events themselves. Ovid's description of her tapestry emphasizes the temporality of the event, but ignores place, as one transgression collides indiscriminately with another across the frame of her tapestry.[23] Through Ovid's combination of verb tense and word order, one event touches on another only by its placement within the ekphrasis. Arachne's tapestry is a world of time without any spatial orientation. In this ekphrasis, Ovid suggests an alternative system of signification, one which operates by tense and contiguity, an ordering of time without regard to any absolute sense of space. Instead, Arachne "rendered to all these both their own appearance and the appearance of the places."[24] Place exists only in relation to the crime, as one story dissolves into another and another, in an argument driven by accretion of examples.[25] What seems, in contrast to Pallas's tapestry, a world of endless and constant flux, whose only constant is the gods' mistreatment of humans is, in the end, a mimetic representation of the world Arachne inhabits.

In the Arachne ekphrasis, Ovid establishes temporality of event through verb tense and creates the illusion of space by his arrangement of the stories. Admittedly, it is the accumulation of the events that lends power to the narrative. Yet, since, as Pallas shows, the gods exist in an atemporal realm, and humans exist in time, Arachne can only represent the transgression of the gods by fixing the event in human time through use of verb tense. The first sentence of the ekphrasis serves as an example: "Arachne represents Europa cheated by the disguise of the bull."[26] Ovid describes Arachne's act of weaving in the poem's present tense, just as he describes Pallas. Yet the participle which describes Jupiter's enticement of Europa places the event itself in a nebulous past, very unlike the present tense used to describe Pallas's gods.[27] In this way, Ovid creates a mythic past in which the events Arachne represents do not depend on one another causally; rather, by being placed in proximity, the events attest by their sheer numbers to the crimes of the gods. The sense of accretion is created by touching, as one story overflows into another.

If Ovid's narrative descriptions of the two tapestries offer competing representations of the relationships between humans and gods, his descriptions of the outer edges of the tapestries comment on the aesthetic principles governing these political narratives. The final word in each ekphrasis describes the border or outer edge of the tapestry. Besides being a case of Ovid the weaver of stories mimicking these weavers of tapestries, the description of the frame says much about the aesthetic principles that underlie these competing narratives and about the power of representation.

The sense of *augusta gravitate* that Pallas's tapestry exudes is driven home by the solid and fixed olive leaf border that contains the scene. The closing word of Ovid's ekphrasis to describe Pallas's tapestry is consistent with the correspondence of image and thing within her tapestry, *"finem,"* the end (102). The word in this case does double duty, as Ovid's construction of the ekphrasis parallels Pallas's construction of her tapestry, imposing closure to the ekphrasis as Pallas does to her narrative. This description of the tapestry signals the limit of permissible interpretation: since Pallas presents things exactly as they are, any other interpretation would be a transgression of the line that separates permissible from impermissible speech, a line that roughly distinguishes between Plato's distinctions between diegesis and mimesis.

Both poet and weaver, both mimetic artists, are makers of texts.[28] Improvising on Simonides's dictum that "painting is inarticulate poetry and poetry is articulate painting,"[29] John Scheid and Jesper Svenbro suggest that Arachne's tapestry represents "a silent song," a poem.[30] To say this marks a return to the issue Ovid raised in his assertion that "the gods, if it is permitted [*fas*] to say, are created with poetry" (*Ex Ponto* 4.8.55).[31] The nature of the gods— that they are created with poetry and, thus, that they are subject to human making—is concealed in that making by the act of poetry. So, if it is speakable [*fas*], the gods are created. But what if it is unspeakable [*nefas*]? Can the gods then exist? *Nefas* exists in this sense to distinguish between the gods and humans and in this function conceals in unspeakability the true nature of this relationship. If the gods are narratable [*fas*], their true relationship to humans is non-narratable [*nefas*], as the respective tapestries of Pallas and Arachne demonstrate. Yet even in telling this story, Ovid would seem to overstep the bound. It is precisely by concealing his voice as that of Arachne via his description of her visual representation that he is able to pull this off.[32]

Arachne's portrait of disorder, of stories seeping from one into another, is accompanied by an equally fitting edging, which Ovid concludes with an equally fitting word. In contrast to Pallas's attempt to close off interpretation through her frame, Arachne's tapestry has no fixed border, but rather, a design of "flowers and clinging ivy intertwined [*intertextos*]."[33] Much as Arachne makes her tapestry one of flux, capturing the crimes of the gods in action, Ovid constructs the frame of her ekphrasis with a mixing of flowers and ivy, one growing into another.[34]

This clinging and intertwining suggests a kind of interpretation which transgresses the fixed bounds of the tapestry, as the crimes of the gods represented in Arachne's tapestry describe the intermingling of gods and humans in the world she inhabits. Yet the correspondence between crimes represented in her tapestry, the particular crimes fixed in time, do not correspond exactly with Arachne's own, on-going world. Rather, it is the pattern of random violence against humans, the pattern suggested by the seeping of one story and one crime into another, that describes her own world.

It is in the aftermath of the contest that Ovid offers a supplement to the two competing versions in the ekphrases, a narrative strategy similar to his explanation of the origins of humans in book one. Ovid reports, first, that "neither Pallas nor Envy himself was able to find fault in that work [opus]," Arachne's tapestry.[35] "Opus" here does double duty. The obvious meaning is in reference to Arachne's technical skill as a weaver, the original cause for the contest. In this respect, Arachne clearly is equal in skill to Pallas, the goddess of weaving, the one we would expect to be technically flawless. Yet "opus" also refers to the mimetic representations expressed by the tapestry, with the suggestion that they must be true, since Pallas is unable to find fault in them. It is upon this point that Arachne's transformation turns, and upon this point that Ovid the human poet reveals that the weaving contest was not about aesthetics, but politics concealed by the language of aesthetics. The weaving contest, which ostensibly ought to be ruled by aesthetic principles, is instead ruled by the political implications of Arachne's narrative, while Pallas's art transforming Arachne into a spider is one that should be governed by the principles of political power, but instead becomes purely aesthetic. As William S. Anderson notes, "Victory goes to the power of the goddess, not to her art."[36]

It is in Pallas's reaction to Arachne's tapestry, Ovid's narrative supplement to the two ekphrases, that the stories of the two tapestries begin to weave into one another.[37] Pallas, in her anger, steps into Arachne's narrated world of temporality.[38] Arachne, on the other hand, as a consequence of her punishment, is thrust into the atemporal, perpetual punishment described in Pallas's tapestry. In his narration of Arachne's transformation, Ovid employs the perfect tense to signal completed action: Pallas "tore" [rupit] (131) Arachne's tapestry, "struck" [percussit] (133) Arachne with the weaving shuttle, "lifted" [levavit] (134) the hanging girl from her noose, and "sprinkled" [sparsit] (140) her with magic herbs. Ovid's use of the preterite to describe Pallas's completed actions mimics the language he used earlier to describe Arachne's visual representations of the crimes of the gods. Ovid's description of Arachne's transformation into a spider, on the other hand, uses the present tense, after the manner of his description of Pallas's tapestry. Once Arachne is "touched [tactae]" by the magic potion, "All her hair falls off and with it goes her nose and ears [Defluxere comae, cum quis et naris et aures].[39] Her head shrinks [fit] tiny; her whole body is small [parva est]; instead of legs, slim fingers cling to [haerent] her sides. The rest is belly [venter habet]; yet from that she sends forth [remittit] a fine-spun thread and, as a spider, still weaving her web, pursues [exercet] her ancient skill."[40] Arachne's metamorphosis moves her from the realm of human temporality, the world she described in her own tapestry, into the atemporal, spatial world of the gods, the world of Pallas's tapestry. Ovid signals her removal from time by employing the present tense, mimicking Pallas's tapestry, and punctuates the transformation with the remark that as a newly-made spider, Arachne continues her ancient art. It is now as if she always has been a spider and, like the gods in Pallas's tapestry, always lives in an eternal present. The meanings of the two tapestries weave into one another in Arachne's transformation. As in Ovid's stories of human origin, the stories of spider origin lead only to other stories. Ovid's description emphasizes not Arachne's lifeless corpse, but the hideous transformation of girl into spider, not even Arachne's pain—what she feels—but the visual spectacle. Ovid maintains distance through the visual, "telling" in gruesome detail what Pallas sees.

What Pallas sees (and what Ovid describes for the reader) represents the weaving into one another of Pallas's and Arachne's versions of the relations between gods and humans. In this way, Pallas's and Arachne's versions become woven into the fabric of Ovid's text. Ovid describes a human punished for her crimes against the awful majesty of the gods—the subject of Pallas's own tapestry—yet the transformation itself recalls the expression of Arachne's tapestry, with its focus on the process of metamorphosis through which the gods abuse humans. In exercising her rite of pity, Pallas undermines her own story of order and implicitly affirms Arachne's portrait of disorder, of stories seeping from one into another. Ovid, by having Pallas carry the desire for order expressed in the tapestry into her interaction with Arachne, creates a scene in which the action of the ekphrasis, the god's punishment of mortals in the corners of the tapestry, seeps into the action of the tales' frame—Pallas's punishment of Arachne—in a way that resembles Arachne's tapestry. Pallas, punishing Arachne in this way, denies the closure she desires by affirming Arachne's version of the story.

Pallas's tapestry argues that the gods are their attributes, fixed and stony. From the perspective of a goddess describing the gods to a mortal, this seems a reasonable assertion, one that closes off the possibilities of any other, competing interpretations. Arachne's representation, on the other hand, not only offers another, adversarial assertion, but also argues that the fates of gods and humans are intertwined inextricably by the crimes of the gods, their transgressions against humans, much as the ivy and flowers at the edge of her tapestry intertwine. It is here that the politics and aesthetics of representation intertwine, much as in Arachne's edge. For the politics of representation, the true nature of the gods and their relationship to humans, is inseparable from narrative, the way each artist tells the story about the relationship between gods and humans. "Winning" the contest becomes not so much an issue of artistic skill, but of political power: Pallas can do things to Arachne by virtue of being a goddess, even if she isn't the better weaver.

The Arachne episode, then, shows that while the gods are dissemblers, it is best for the human artist to conceal this truth. Arachne's transgression is her refusal to conceal the true nature of the gods.[41] Her story becomes one about a young woman who transgresses the boundary between narrative representation and idealized correspondence, transgressing the boundary that separates the humans and the gods. Yet having done so, she shows that the gods are not just their attributes, but dissemblers as well. Again, since the power to narrate is the power to represent (which Plato called the power to dissemble) the gods themselves seem to take on human characteristics.

The nature of Arachne's punishment—she is turned into a spider, a creature of the animal world—suggests that the true nature of the gods is best concealed. Because, once revealed, the punishment is that one can no longer narrate. In this sense, Arachne's transformation into a spider is a punishment that fits not only the form of her art as a weaver, but the form of her narrative transgression, as well.

If it is true that spiders continually weave webs, an appropriate vocation for the transformed Arachne, it is also true that the nature of the weaving shifts from the creating of poetic texts to the mundane spinning of webs to snare insects. Feeney argues that Arachne's

> metamorphosis into a spider is a sickeningly appropriate punishment for Minerva to devise. The perpetual weaver of webs that are proverbially easy to destroy, her qualities of fine grace are exaggerated into parody as she becomes simply small, tiny, her fingers programmatically *exiles*, embodying the stylistic thinness which is the fate of a failed small-scale composition. The celebrator of beautiful disorder is now doomed to the spider's weaving of utter symmetry. Worst of all, as Seneca tells us in a fascinating disquisition on animal instinct, a spider's work is not art. All spiders produce the same, none is more skilled than the next. (193).

Indeed, Seneca observes "That art is innate, not learnt. And so no animal is more learned than the next: you'll see that spiders' webs are all equal. . . . Whatever art bestows is uncertain and uneven; what nature distributes issues from an even source."[42] Pallas's punishment is insidious precisely because, as a spider, Arachne's weaving is devoid of everything in which she took pride as a human. Arachne's weaving no longer creates art, but attracts flies. Her punishment is that she must weave in order to survive.[43]

It is also true that spiders do not possess the capacity or the need for mimetic narration, what distinguishes humans from gods. Unlike humans, spiders do not tell stories, do not reveal or conceal themselves through poetry, and do not make art. Rather, the transformed

Arachne "sends forth a fine-spun thread and, as a spider, still weaving her web, pursues her old [*antiquas*] skill" (144-5). Like the gods in Pallas's tapestry, the spider lives entirely in the present. Ovid's use of *antiqua* to describe Arachne's skill recalls his earlier use of the word to describe Pallas's quarrel with Neptune over possession of Athens (71). Like the naming of Athens, which will always and forever be decided in favor of Pallas, Arachne always and forever will practice what has always been and forever will be her skill, weaving.

While spiders exist in human time, they spin continuously and perpetually in the present. These are loaded words, recalling the programmatic language of the competing aesthetics in both the Arachne episode and in the *Metamorphoses* taken as a whole: the neoteric *carmen deductum* and the epic *carmen perpetuum*. Yet in the transformed Arachne, the programmatic words are themselves transformed, as well. They can no longer describe a poetic program, since spiders are incapable of art. Rather, by describing the spider's weaving in terms of a perpetual present, Ovid suggests that the very conflict over rival poetics and the debate about poetry's power to conceal or reveal define what it means to be human. This is, perhaps, another way of saying that "human" is defined in relation to "god" and "animal" by the act of asking what it means to be human. As Ovid's Arachne episode shows, that question is in itself transgressive, because to answer it requires one to inquire into and risk revealing the true nature of the gods. The revelation from such transgressive inquiry results in a punishment that distinguishes human from animal.

The place of the human, located between god and animal, seems now less certain, if only because the natures of god and animal are less certain. The boundary between humans and gods becomes blurred, because if it is the case that the gods created humans, it is also the case that the gods exist as a consequence of poetry. Further, it is through poetry that Ovid represents the god's creating humans. One might argue that the capacity to narrate is the distinguishing characteristic between humans and animals. Animals communicate, to be sure, but they don't tell stories. Humans tell stories. Nor, as Ovid's Arachne episode illustrates, do the gods narrate, because to narrate is to represent, which is to lie. No, the gods operate in a realm in which things correspond directly and exactly to words, and when they speak, they speak of the essential nature of things. In some sense, this idealized language of the gods represents a kind of logocentric desire on the part of humans. The gods, then, in their perfected state, offer to humans static ideals, and humans invent stories about the gods (thereby inventing and defining) the gods.[44] These stories, the stories that define the idealized gods, define the human. The ideal of one-to-one correspondence is a limit, something unavailable to human language.

Notes

[1] D. C. Feeney, *The Gods in Epic: Poets and Critics of the Classical Tradition* (Oxford: Clarendon Press, 1991, 1993), 198, argues that in the *Metamorphoses*, the category of "human" is defined by the conventions and norms that distinguish humans from *natura* (animal instinct) and *licentia* (the gods' power for self-indulgence). The basic problem Feeney identifies in Ovid's poem is the degree to which "divine and human are compatible," formulated in the question, "Are the gods like us or not, and what are the implications of asking, and attempting to answer, such a question?" As should be clear, my understanding of Ovid owes much to Denis Feeney, especially his discussion of the Arachne episode. Even so, I wish to put more pressure on this episode than Feeney does. Ovid's use of the ekphrasis in this particular episode provides a kind of answer in the very asking of what it means to be "human." Asking the question requires, as well, inquiry into the nature of gods and animals. Such inquiry requires a language to represent the world and in itself constitutes both the capacity and need for mimetic poetry as the thing which differentiates humans from gods and animals.

[2] I am not suggesting that Ovid describes any real tapestry. Rather, my point is that he uses the descriptions of fictional tapestries (which are created within the fiction of his own poem) to explore the limits of poetry and to discuss the nature of the gods. On the distinctions between descriptions of "real" pictures and those which are entirely "literary," see Andrew Laird, "Sounding out Ecphrasis: Art and Text in Catullus 64," *Journal of Roman Studies* 83 (1993), 18-9.

[3] *Metamorphoses* 1.69-78. Citations to the *Metamorphoses* are to the edition of Frank Justus Miller, as revised by G. P. Goold (Cambridge: Harvard University Press, 1977). I have also consulted the edition of William S. Anderson, *P. Ovidii Nasonis Metamorphoses* (Leipzig: Teubner, 1982).

4   Marcel Detienne explicates these relationships, with special reference to mythical treatment of cannibalism, in "Between Beasts and Gods," *Myth, religion, and society*, ed. R. L. Gordon (Cambridge: Cambridge University Press, 1981), 215-28, 270-1. I thank Denis Feeney for referring me to this item.

5   *Metamorphoses* 1.78-83: "sive hunc divino semine fecit / ille opifex rerum . . . sive recens tellus seductaque nuper . . . quam satus Iapeto, mixtam pluvialibus undis, / finixit in effigiem moderantum cuncta deorum." The translation is by A. D. Melville (Oxford: Oxford University Press, 1986).

6   *Metamorphoses* 1.151-62. My use of "supplement" to describe Ovid's narration follows the example of Tzvetan Todorov, *The Poetics of Prose*, trans. Richard Howard (Ithaca: Cornell University Press, 1977), 78. Todorov writes, "The narrating story always becomes a narrated story as well, in which the new story is reflected and finds its own image. Furthermore, every narrative must create new ones—within itself, in order that the characters can go on living, and outside itself, so that the supplement it inevitably produces may be consumed here." See the discussion of Todorov's narrative supplement by Susanne Lindgren Wofford, *The Choice of Achilles: The Ideology of Figure in the Epic* (Stanford: Stanford University Press, 1992), 13-4, 270.

7   Inquiry, as I use the term, takes on the double duty that the Greeks ascribed to *historia*, which refers to both that which is learned as a result of inquiring, as well as setting forth a narrative account of that which is learned.

8   Trans. Feeney, 224. *Ex Ponto* 4.8.55: "di quoque carminibus, si fas est dicere, fiunt."

9   *Diegesis* and *mimesis* are, respectively, the terms Plato uses in *The Republic* to distinguish between pure narrative, in which the author speaks without pretending to be a fictional character, and imitation, in which the author speaks as a fictional character (392c-395). Percy Lubbock, *The Craft of Fiction* (New York: Charles Scribner's Sons, 1921), 62, more bluntly describes them as showing and telling. Enlarging a line of argument similar to that which Wayne C. Booth, *The Rhetoric of Fiction* (Chicago: University of Chicago Press, 1961), 3-20, pursues, Gérard Genette, *Narrative Discourse: An Essay on Method*, trans. Jane E. Lewin (Ithaca: Cornell University Press, 1980), argues that it is impossible for narrative, in contrast to drama, to "'show' or 'imitate' the story it tells" (163-4); rather, narrative constructs "the *illusion of mimesis*" (164), a representation of words, as opposed to a representation of events. My understanding of the terms owes much to the distinctions that Susanne Wofford draws between allegorical and fictional modes in Edmund Spenser's *The Faerie Queene* (224-8).

10 *New Introductory Lectures on Psycho-Analysis*, trans. James Strachey (London: Hogarth Press, 1964), 132. In the ancient world, spinning and weaving were conventionally thought of as the work of women. Maria C. Pantelia, "Spinning and Weaving: Ideas of Domestic Order in Homer," *American Journal of Philology* 114 (1993), 494, further suggests that the art of weaving itself was one of concealment. She reckons that "since looms were situated in the inner palace [courtyard of a house], weavers could isolate themselves and perform their art away from the public eye." This is not to say that weaving was a solo art. As Elizabeth Wayland Barber, *Women's Work: The First 2000 Years: Women, Cloth, and Society in Early Times* (New York: Norton, 1992), 81-3, notes, the large size of the warp-weighted (upright) loom—the kind used in much of the Greco-Roman world—encouraged women to work cooperatively. While the collaboration between weavers no doubt served social as well as practical needs, the loom's location in a private part of the household suggests that weaving did not serve as a public function, but was itself concealed, along with many other routine domestic duties. For my understanding of textile production, I owe a great debt of gratitude to my colleague, Annabel Servat, herself an expert spinner and weaver. She not only lent me books, but also patiently explained and demonstrated her arts for me.

11 See, for example, the discussion and bibliography by D. C. Feeney, 191. On the centrality of the Arachne episode to understanding Ovid's poetics, see Heinz Hofmann, "Ovid's *Metamorphoses*: *Carmen Perpetuum, Carmen Deductum*," *Papers of the Liverpool Latin Seminar* 5 (1985), 223-41, who argues that the Arachne episode's "weaving contest . . . contains an implied discussion of the two poetic programs—*carmen perpetuum* and *carmen deductum*" (230), representing the aesthetics of epic and neoteric poetry.

12 My definition of ekphrasis is thoroughly modern, following the example of W. J. T. Mitchell, *Picture Theory: Essays on Verbal and Visual Representation* (Chicago: University of Chicago Press, 1994), 151-2, and James A. W. Heffernan, *Museum of Words: The Poetics of Ekphrasis from Homer to Ashbery* (Chicago: University of Chicago Press, 1993), 1-3. The ancients defined the term much more generally, as a rhetorical description of some thing or event. On the ancient sense of ekphrasis and its relationship to visual art, see Jas Elsner, *Art and the Roman Viewer: The Transformation of Art from*

the Pagan World to Christianity (Cambridge: Cambridge University Press, 1995), 23-8. In choosing to adopt a modern term to discuss an ancient text, I follow the example of Andrew Laird, 18, who argues, "The great benefit of considering 'ecphrasis' in the modern sense is that it forces us to confront both the nature of the visual artistic medium and that of the verbal medium describing it." Since my understanding of the Arachne episode depends on the relationship between poetry and a particular form of visual art, weaving, I chose to narrow my definition of ekphrasis to focus on these issues. This is not the only way to go. For example, D. P. Fowler, "Narrate and Describe: The Problem of Ekphrasis," *Journal of Roman Studies* 81 (1991), 25-35, addresses modern narratological issues raised by the "set-piece description" in ancient poetry.

[13] "On Linguistic Aspects of Translation." *On Translation*, ed. Reuben A. Brower (Cambridge: Harvard University Press, 1959), 233. Claus Clüver offers a discussion with illustrative examples of Jakobson's theory in "On Intersemiotic Transposition," *Poetics Today* 10 (1989), 55-90.

[14] *Ekphrasis: The Illusion of the Natural Sign* (Baltimore and London: The Johns Hopkins Press, 1992), 12.

[15] Krieger, 11, also says that "This desire to see the world in the word is what, after Derrida, we have come to term the logocentric desire." In this sense, Ovid's representation of Pallas's tapestry might by thought of as a displacement onto the gods of logocentric desire.

[16] W. J. T. Mitchell, "Space, Ideology, and Literary Representation," *Poetics Today* 10 (1989), 95. Here, Mitchell plays with what Frederic Jameson, *The Political Unconscious: Narrative as a Socially Symbolic Act* (Ithaca: Cornell University Press, 1981), 87, calls "ideologemes," allegories of power and value disguised as neutral metalanguage. See Mitchell's further discussion in *Picture Theory*, 157.

[17] *Metamorphoses* 6.25: "certet . . . mecum." Arachne repeats her boast in the form of a challenge in line 41: "cur non ipsa venit? cur haec certimina vitat?" [Why does she herself not come? Why does she avoid contending with me?]

[18] Romans were very conscious of boundaries. Indeed, the concept of *lex* (a word related to the verb *ligare*, to bind) signifies a binding agreement between contracting parties. In this sense, one's ability to defend a legal right depends upon knowing the boundary which defines that right and observing any transgressions of it. The need to be bound by limits was an idea central to Roman identity. Romulus killed Remus not out of hatred but because he crossed the wall, the border separating their properties: "So perish whoever else shall overleap my battlements" (Livy 1.6, trans. Aubrey de Selincourt, *The Early History of Rome* [Harmondsworth: Penguin, 1960]). Governance of home and state depended on each individual being subject to another, and humans being subject to the gods. While the subject of Roman boundary limit is too complex to discuss here in detail, Carlin A. Barton, *The Sorrows of the Ancient Romans: The Gladiator and the Monster* (Princeton: Princeton University Press, 1993), 65-6, esp., argues that the Romans were just as fascinated in enjoying forbidden pleasures as they were in erecting boundaries that set those pleasures apart. The *Metamorphoses'* persistent interest in issues of crime (transgression) and punishment suggests that Ovid is exploring their mythical origins and evolution. D. C. Feeney's reading of the Arachne episode leads him to conclude that "it becomes necessary to enquire into what the boundaries and transgressions are which constitute the *Metamorphoses'* disorderly order, and where the divine belongs in them, especially in relation to the human. How much is stable, how much in flux? What are the rules for the categories of perspective across these divisions?" (194).

[19] Michael Vincent, "Between Ovid and Barthes: *Ekphrasis*, Orality, Textuality in Ovid's 'Arachne,'" *Arethusa* 27 (1994), 371, also notes the different verb tenses Ovid uses to describe the two tapestries.

[20] *Metamorphoses* 6.71: *pingit*. William S. Anderson, *Ovid's Metamorphoses, Books 6-10* (Normal: University of Oklahoma Press, 1972), 154, notes that Ovid employs the painting metaphor to describe weaving. It is the case, then, that Ovid's poem uses the language of painting to describe the process of weaving in a passage about the nature of poetry.

[21] *Metamorphoses* 6.73-74: "sua quemque deorum / Inscribit facies."

[22] "One corner has" [*habet angulus unus*] Rhodope and Haemon, "who attributed to themselves" [*sibi qui tribuere*] "the names Jupiter and Juno," while the "other part has" [*altera pars habet*] the story of Oenoe. The fourth corner "has" [*habet*] Cinyras (6.87,89,90-91,98). *Pinxit* (line 93), in the perfect tense, does not fit at all into this scheme. While not in keeping with the rest of the passage, it is, however, very much in line with Ovid's earlier use of the word in the Arachne episode. The very first verb in the Pallas ekphrasis is *pingit* (71), establishing that Pallas "paints" her tapestry in the present. To follow with *pinxit* in line 93 of the same ekphrasis seems initially out of place. The perfect tense's

197

expression of completed action in line 93, does, however, lend a sense of finality to the depiction of Antigone, who is perpetually transformed into a stork. With these two verb tenses, Ovid describes Pallas as working simultaneously in the present and in the past. If this seems impossible, the impossibility only marks the distance between the gods, for whom time is all one, and humans, who, in order to represent reality, must resort to verb tenses in order to represent time. Hence, *pinxit* contrasts sharply with *pingebat* (23), the imperfect tense (denoting continued action) Ovid uses to describe Arachne's weaving. In this sense, the verb tenses Ovid employs to describe the two weavers correspond to their respective aesthetics: Pallas describes a world in terms of epic finality, while Arachne describes a continuing process of divine injustice, contradictory images of a perfect and imperfect universe.

[23] Eleanor Winsor Leach, "Ekphrasis and the Theme of Artistic Failure in Ovid's *Metamorphoses*," *Ramus* 3 (1974), 117, calls its effect "a cosmic panorama of shifting forms, natural objects set in natural backgrounds."

[24] 6.121-2: "omnibus his faciemque suam faciemque locorum reddidit."

[25] William S. Anderson, Review of Brooks Otis, *Ovid as an Epic Poet*, *American Journal of Philology* 89 (1968), 103, notes that the "cumulative effect" of the gods' crimes comes from Arachne's "swirl of divine figures in unedifying positions" and the juxtaposition of her tapestry to Pallas's vision of order.

[26] *Metamorphoses* 6.103-104: "Maeonis elusam designat imagine tauri Europam."

[27] Leach, quoting from 117, notes that the verbs Ovid used to describe the events in Arachne's tapestry [*elatus, luserit, visus, fallis,* and *deceperit*], words denoting deception, "underscore the insistent theme" of her tapestry. As well, these verbs describe actions which occurred in the past, descriptions that place the crimes of the gods within human time, unlike Ovid's description of a perpetual present tense in Pallas's tapestry.

[28] While *textum* refers literally to the product of the weaving process, a web, its figurative sense provides the word "text," used to describe the product of poetic art. On the intricate relationships between poetry and weaving, see the valuable discussion by John Scheid and Jesper Svenbo, *The Craft of Zeus: Myths of Weaving and Fabric* (Cambridge: Harvard University Press, 1996), 111-55.

[29] Plutarch, *Moralia* 346f. On the implications of Simonides' statement, see Wendy Steiner, *The Colors of Rhetoric: Problems in the Relation between Modern Poetry and Painting* (Chicago: University of Chicago Press, 1982), 5-7.

[30] "The song of the Pierid [from book five] becomes a weaving with voice, while Arachne's weaving seems . . . a silent song. In other words, the juxtaposition of the two stories seems to transform the song into a metaphorical weaving and the weaving into a metaphorical song" (135).

[31] Strictly, *fas* carried the sense of that which is right by divine law, the will of heaven, or that which is morally right. Yet, through its etymology, the word also offered the related sense of that which may be spoken or said. According to A. Ernout and A. Meillet, *Dictionnaire étymologique de la langue latine: historie des mots*, 4th ed. (Paris: Libraire C. Klincksieck, 1967), the etymology of *fas* is dubious, although the ancient authorities, Servius and Varro, attributed the word to *fari* (a form of the verb *for, faris, fatus sum, fari*), "to speak" in the sense of the French word *parler*. So, according to the ancient etymology, *fas* derived from the gerund of *for*, the root of *fandus*, that which may be spoken or said. In this sense, *fas* represents both what is permissible to do and what is permissible to say. Similarly, the negative form represents both an offense against divine law and that which cannot be spoken or said, with the sense of "unspeakable sin." Ovid plays on the dual meanings of *fas* and *nefas* in the Philomel episode. He describes the outrage of Procne upon discovering the rape and mutilation of her sister: "dolor ora repressit, / verbaque quaerenti satis indignantia linguae / defuerunt, nec flere vacat, sed fasque nefasque / confusura ruit poenaeque in imagine tota est" [Her tongue could find no speech to match her outraged anger; no room here for tears; she stormed ahead, confusing *fas* and *nefas*, her whole soul filled with visions of revenge] (*Metamorphoses* 6.583-6, trans. Melville). Though Procne retains her tongue (unlike Philomel) the unspeakable crime [*nefas*] leaves her both unable to distinguish what can and cannot be said and unable to distinguish right from wrong, a confusion of *fas* and *nefas*. Distinctions dissolve between what is permissible to say and what is permissible to do. Lacking the words that define civil behavior, what remains is Procne's visions of revenge, without any moral sensibilities to limit her visions of revenge.

[32] And, to boot, Ovid tells the story through Pallas's focalization, as a memory triggered by her moral indignation upon hearing the muses' story about their recent contest with the Pieredes, which concluded book five of the poem. On this point, see Heinz Hofmann, 230. Keith Cohen, "Unweaving

Puig's *Spider Woman:* Ecphrasis and Narration," *Narrative* 2 (1994), 17-28, discusses the narratological implications of interweaving ekphrasis and metadiegesis. As such, Ovid might be said to describe what Pallas sees. See Leach, 115, who argues that in the ekphrasis, "Ovid's voice now supercedes that of Minerva." Further, by narrating the episode in this way, Ovid invites his moral reader to step into Pallas's shoes and see Arachne through the eyes of a goddess. On focalization (the relation between the vision, the agent that sees, and that which is seen or perceived) and how it differs from point-of-view, see the discussion by Mieke Bal, *Narratology: Introduction to the Theory of Narrative*, trans. Christine van Boheemen (Toronto: University of Toronto Press, 1985), 100-6.

[33] Line 128. Michael Vincent, 369-70, argues credibly that this line itself mimics Arachne's weaving due to Ovid's chiasmatic patterning of the grammar.

[34] In short, Ovid in each ekphrasis aligns the expression with the content in such a way that one confirms the other: an orderly representation of an orderly universe and a disorderly representation of a universe in flux. See discussion of this point by Hans George Ruprecht, "The Reconstruction of Intertextuality," *Intertextuality*, ed. Heinrich F. Plett (Berlin: Walter de Gruyer, 1991), 61.

[35] *Metamorphoses* 6.129-130: "Non illud Pallas, non illud carpere Livor / possit opus."

[36] Review of Otis, 103.

[37] Leach, 118, calls the relationship between the two tapestries an "intricate interassociation," arguing that they offer a "momentary clarification" of "principles and perspectives" in the poem "that simultaneously complement and contradict one another, divine vengeance and divine comedy, visions of order and chaos intermingled." Arguing that "as the creator of the poem, Ovid maintains a vision embracing both points of view," Leach, 104, offers an interpretation that alters the terms of engagement with the poem's aesthetics. The issue is no longer whether Ovid's poetics are closer to Pallas's, as Brooks Otis, *Ovid as an Epic Poet* (Cambridge: Cambridge University Press, 1966), 146, argues, or closer to Arachne's, as William S. Anderson, in his review of Otis, 103, argues. Rather, by weaving both views into the fabric of the poem, Ovid creates a paradox that requires yet another story. While G. Karl Galinsky, *Ovid's Metamorphoses: An Introduction to the Basic Aspects of the Poem* (Berkeley and Los Angeles: University of California Press, 1975), 82-3, who follows Anderson's interpretation, rightly argues that the "Ovidian themes and fluidity of form" in Arachne's tapestries align her (not Pallas) with Ovid's own aesthetics, it is important to note that in his description of Arachne's transformation, Ovid interweaves the contradictions into a new image of order and disorder. On the competing aesthetics and criticisms of the Arachne episode, see the discussion by Feeney, 190-1.

[38] Leach, 117, makes a similar point, arguing that "by her violent reaction to the success of her rival the goddess betrays the very principle of just and rational triumph that she has illuminated in the center of her own tapestry." Indeed, Leach notes that it is Pallas's interpretation of Arachne's tapestry—not any moral judgment attributed to Arachne—that establishes the tapestry as a crime against the gods; but compare Donald Lateiner, "Myths and Non-Mythic Artists in Ovid's *Metamorphoses*," *Ramus* 13 (1984), 27 n. 69, and Michael Vincent, 377-8. Feeney, 203-4, argues that the disjunctive representations of Pallas, as an idealized form of divine justice in her own tapestry and as injustice incarnate in her passionate response to Arachne's tapestry, are part of Ovid's strategy of establishing an epic norm in the poem, only to destablize it with another, equally epic, norm. As when Ovid elsewhere, as in his stories of human origins (1.151-62), offers a contradiction, he answers the problems posed by the two tapestries with a description, Arachne's transformation, which muddies even as it clarifies. It is on this point that I question the assertion by Joseph B. Solodow, *The World of Ovid's Metamorphoses* (Chapel Hill: University of North Carolina Press, 1988), 197, that "metamorphosis introduces clarity of perception" by the process of making visible a character's inner qualities. In the case of Arachne, the nature of the metamorphosis itself seems to raise as many questions as it answers.

[39] *Defluxere* is, of course, an infinitive and, in this context, might just as easily be translated as "all her hair *fell away*." Either way, the falling of Arachne's hair is relative to her being touched by the magic potion. The sentence serves as a transition for Arachne, moving her out of time with the shedding of her human hair and into the eternal state of spiderhood, which Ovid describes in the present tense.

[40] *Metamorphoses* 6.140-5. Translation based on Melville's.

[41] But see Donald Lateiner, 17, who argues that Arachne's transgression is her failure "to recognize inspiration, the debt of the artist to something greater than himself. Technical excellence is not enough. . . . She has attained to [sic] truth, but not the meaning of it."

[42] Trans. Feeney, 194. Seneca, *Epistulae* 121.23, ed. Richard M. Gummere (Cambridge: Harvard University Press, 1925): "Nascitur ars ista, non discitur. Itaque nullum est animal altero doctius. Videbis araneorum pares telas. . . . Incertum est et inaequabile, quidquid ars tradit: ex aequo venit, quod natura distribuit."

[43] As an artist, Arachne survives only as the subject of other artists. On the afterlife of Arachne, see for example Leonard Barkan, *The Gods Made Flesh: Metamorphoses and the Pursuit of Paganism* (New Haven: Yale University Press, 1986), 1-8, and Marcia L. Welles, *Arachne's Tapestry: The Transformation of Myth in Seventeenth-Century Spain* (San Antonio: Trinity University Press, 1986). In the English tradition, the Arachne story is perhaps best known through Edmund Spenser's poem, *Muiopotmos: or the Fate of the Butterflie*, on which see Andrew D. Weiner, "Spenser's *Muiopotmos* and the Fates of Butterflies and Men," *Journal of English and German Philology* 84 (1985), 203-20.

[44] Paul Veyne, *Did the Greeks Believe in their Myths? An Essay on the Constitutive Imagination*, trans. Paula Wissing (Chicago: University of Chicago Press, 1988), 84, argues that "the [ancient] Greeks believe and do not believe in their myths. They believe in them, but they use them and cease believing at the point where their interest in believing ends." The problem Veyne addresses, one similar to the problems Ovid raises in the *Metamorphoses*, is how it is "possible to half-believe, or believe in contradictory things" (xi), as a means of investigating the historical quality of the human imagination: "I do not at all mean to say that the imagination will bring future truths to light and that it should reign; I mean, rather, that truths are already products of the imagination and that the imagination has always governed. It is imagination that rules, not reality, [or] reason" (xii). Indeed, whether or not the Greeks believed the events described by the myths really happened, the deeds of the gods and heroes contained in them the material for the stories that permitted them to define themselves as a people. Similarly, Ovid's inquiry into the nature of the gods generates the stories that permit him, in relative terms, to define the nature of the humans.

"I crave the law": Justice, Mercy, and the Law in *The Merchant of Venice*

Andrew D. Weiner

The law plays a major part in many of Shakespeare's comedies. In *The Comedy of Errors*, an old man is condemned to death by the Duke of Ephesus merely because he is from Syracuse and lacks the funds to pay a required fine; though the Duke pities the old man, he must let the law take its course:

> Now trust me, were it not against our laws—
> Which princes, would they, may not disannul—
> Against my crown, my oath, my dignity,
> My soul should sue as advocate for thee.
> But though thou art adjudgèd to the death,
> And passèd sentence may not be recalled
> But to our honour's great disparagement,
> Yet will I favour thee in what I can. (I.i.142-49)[1]

Similarly, *A Midsummer Night's Dream* begins with a father demanding that the Duke of Athens enforce the law that says his daughter must marry her father's choice of suitors or be put to death:

> I beg the ancient privilege of Athens:
> As she is mine, I may dispose of her,
> Which shall be either to this gentleman
> Or to her death, according to our law
> Immediately provided in that case.(I.i.41-45)

Somewhat reluctantly, the Duke acknowledges that the father has the law on his side:

> For you, fair Hermia, look you arm yourself
> To fit your fancies to your father's will,
> Or else the law of Athens yields you up—
> Which by no means we may extenuate—
> To death or to a vow of single life. (I.i.117-21)

By the end of each of these plays, the dukes have overruled the law and those demanding it be enforced, freeing the old man without payment of the fine and allowing the daughter to marry the suitor she loves.

In *The Merchant of Venice*, the same situation appears to hold: Antonio, the merchant, has entered into a "merry" bond (I.iii.143-50) with Shylock, a usurious Jewish money-lender who hates Antonio because Antonio is a Christian, because Antonio lends money without charging interest, and because Antonio is an anti-Semite:

> How like a fawning publican he looks.
> I hate him for he is a Christian;
> But more, for that in low simplicity
> He lends out money gratis, and brings down
> The rate of usance here with us in Venice.
> If I can catch him once upon the hip
> I will feed fat the ancient grudge I bear him.
> He hates our sacred nation, and he rails,
> Even there where merchants most do congregate,
> On me, my bargains, and my well-won thrift—
> Which he calls interest. Cursèd be my tribe
> If I forgive him. (I.iii.39-50)

In what appears to be the climactic scene in the play, Shylock's attempt to collect on his "merry bond" and cut from Antonio a pound of flesh nearest his heart in open court is frustrated by Portia, the newly-won wife of Antonio's friend, Bassanio, for whom Antonio had entered into his bond with Shylock. Although Portia, disguised as a judge, urges Shylock to be merciful, when he refuses she brings to bear upon him the full rigor of the law. By the end of the play, although Antonio is no longer in jeopardy from his bond with Shylock, he has entered into another bond with Portia:

> I once did lend my body for his wealth
> Which, but for him that had your husband's ring,
> Had quite miscarried. I dare be bound again,
> My soul upon the forfeit, that your lord
> Will never more break faith advisedly. (V.i.249-53)

The play ends with him bound again, this time in a spiritual bond that Bassanio will keep faith with his love, but now the stakes are higher: not merely a pound of his flesh but Antonio's very soul.

As this brief summary suggests, *The Merchant of Venice* both follows the pattern of Shakespeare's earlier plays in seeing the law as an obstacle to people's happiness and breaks it by presenting the "good" characters not as innocent victims of an arbitrary law but as complicit in their own jeopardy, a complicity that leads to Portia's famous speech urging mercy because no one can stand up to the rigor of the law:

> Therefore, Jew,
> Though justice be thy plea, consider this:
> That in the course of justice none of us
> Should see salvation. We do pray for mercy,
> And that same prayer doth teach us all to render
> The deeds of mercy. (IV.i.194-99)

However, as her words suggest, this play differs from most of the other comedies in that it has a character who does not share even nominally the values of the other characters. Shylock, the Jew, does not "pray for mercy" when he recites the Lord's prayer for Shylock does not recite the Lord's prayer. In recent years, Shylock has come to be seen as almost the major figure of the play, one who so dominates our post-Holocaust sympathies that the play is often seen as a failure because Shylock's murderous plot is foiled and he himself becomes the object of the law's not particularly tender ministrations. Although it is true that Antonio is an anti-Semite, Shylock is an anti-Christian; since Shakespeare was writing for a Christian audience, presumably Shylock's prejudices would render him far less attractive than Antonio to his audience. In this paper I will argue that Shakespeare did not intend us to see Shylock sympathetically because he is setting up a structure that will allow him to explore the Pauline debate between the law and mercy. To see this structure, however, we will have to look closely not simply at the moments when Bassanio wins Portia by choosing correctly in the casket test and when Portia frees Antonio from Shylock, but at the way in which Shakespeare presents the play as a whole to the audience, using structural repetition and juxtaposition to make us associate characters and ideas, often in surprising ways.

Knowing and Doing

The play begins with two characters lamenting their melancholic world-weariness in successive scenes and ends with a bawdy joke about procreation and the power of desire. In between, the audience is rarely allowed to forget the fallible human natures of the characters playing on the stage before them. Antonio's first speech sets forth one aspect of this condition:

> In sooth, I know not why I am so sad.
> It wearies me, you say it wearies you,
> But how I caught it, found it, or came by it,
> What stuff 'tis made of, whereof it is born,
> I am to learn;
> And such a want-wit sadness makes of me
> That I have much ado to know myself. (I.i.1-7)

Like Antipholus of Syracuse in *The Comedy of Errors* or Hamlet, Antonio has lost all his "mirth," and lacking it, lacks self knowledge as well. His companions, first Solanio and Salerio, and then Graziano all suggest that the cause of this melancholy must be in his fears about having his wealth at hazard with his argosies, searching for treasures elsewhere; although Solanio and Salerio sympathize with this presumed fear, Graziano takes it as the occasion for a warning:

> You look not well, Signor Antonio.
> You have too much respect upon the world.
> They lose it that do buy it with much care.
> Believe me, you are marvellously changed. (I.i.73-76)

Antonio's response—"I hold the world but as the world, Graziano— / A stage where every man must play a part, / And mine a sad one" (I.i.77-79)—draws another rebuke from Graziano, who accuses him of playing the melancholic for effect:

> I tell thee what, Antonio—
> I love thee, and 'tis my love that speaks—
> There are a sort of men whose visages
> Do cream and mantle like a standing pond,
> And do a wilful stillness entertain
> With purpose to be dressed in an opinion
> Of wisdom, gravity, profound conceit,
> As who should say "I am Sir Oracle,
> And when I ope my lips, let no dog bark."
> O my Antonio, I do know of these
> That therefore only are reputed wise
> For saying nothing, when I am very sure,
> If they should speak, would almost damn those ears
> Which, hearing them, would call their brothers fools. (I.i.86-99)

Antonio's unnatural sadness, Graziano suggests, is something counterfeited for the purpose of creating a false opinion of his wisdom, gravity, and deep thought, and masks the folly of one with nothing to say. Graziano's departure with Lorenzo (who is going about the business of preparing for his elopement with Jessica, Shylock's daughter) allows Bassanio to broach his business to Antonio. Where Antonio has put his argosies to sea in the hopes of a financial profit, Bassanio, who has "disabled" his estate with "showing a more swelling port / Than my faint means would grant continuance" (I.i.124-5), is trying to enlist Antonio's aid in a scheme to repay his debts by outfitting another argosy to travel to another Colchis to seek another "golden fleece":

> In Belmont is a lady richly left,
> And she is fair, and, fairer than that word,
> Of wondrous virtues. Sometimes from her eyes
> I did receive fair speechless messages.
> Her name is Portia, nothing undervalued
> To Cato's daughter, Brutus' Portia;
> Nor is the wide world ignorant of her worth,
> For the four winds blow in from every coast
> Renownèd suitors, and her sunny locks
> Hang on her temples like a golden fleece,
> Which makes her seat of Belmont Colchis' strand,
> And many Jasons come in quest of her.
> O my Antonio, had I but the means
> To hold a rival place with one of them,
> I have a mind presages me such thrift
> That I should questionless be fortunate. (I.i.161 76).

Portia, Bassanio's "richly left" lady, is "fair" and "virtuous," and Bassanio, who thinks he has read "speechless messages" in her eyes that presage success, believes that he will win the prize for which "many Jasons come in quest."[2]

Yet as we discover in the next scene, the lady is not to be won by wooing no matter what Bassanio thinks he read in her eyes and "thrift" is not a matter of having "means" to woo. Not only Portia's riches but her melancholy link her to Antonio as her opening speech suggests: "By my troth, Nerissa, my little body is aweary of this great world" (I.ii.1-2). Now, however, we are given a reason for this world-weariness: "this reasoning is not in the fashion to choose me a husband. O me, the word 'choose'! I may neither choose who I would nor refuse who I dislike; so is the will of a living daughter curbed by the will of a dead father. Is it not hard, Nerissa, that I cannot choose one nor refuse none?" (I.ii.20-6). Portia's complaint about the hardness of enduring her lack of choice is coupled with her recognition that knowing and doing have become divorced: "If to do were as easy as to know what were good to do, chapels had been churches, and poor men's cottages princes' palaces. It is a good divine that follows his own instructions. I can easier teach twenty what were good to be done than to be one of the twenty to follow mine own teaching. The brain may devise laws for the blood, but a hot temper leaps o'er a cold decree" (I.ii.12-8). Portia here finds herself witnessing to the truth of St. Paul's condemnation of the Jews who believe that because they know the law and glory in it that they are "a guide of the blinde, a light of them which *are* in darknesse," but who fail to do that which they teach others to do because they are sinners (Romans 2: 19-25).[3] Portia demonstrates the disconnect between knowing and doing in discussing one of her suitors: "In truth," she says, "I know it is a sin to be a mocker" (I.ii.55), but then proceeds to mock him, thus bringing herself within the bounds of Jesus' warning that "whosoeuer shall say, Foole, shalbe worthy to be punished with hell fire" (Matthew 5: 22) as Graziano reminded us in the preceding scene. Nor is this condemnation liable only to the Jews. As St. Paul argues, "What then? are wee more excellent? No, in no wise: for we haue already prooued that all, both Iewes and Gentiles are vnder sinne, As it is written, There is none righteous, no not one" (Romans 3: 9-10). Portia cannot choose to whom she will give her love and she cannot avoid doing the things she knows she must not do. Unlike Antonio, who is not able to give a cause to his sadness, Portia's profitless self-knowledge links the two of them in their melancholy and already begins to prepare us to accept her plea on his behalf in the trial scene to come.

The third scene establishes Shylock's hatred of Antonio and his intention to destroy him should the opportunity arise. Yet at the same time, Shakespeare shows us Antonio's contempt for Shylock and allows us to see that Antonio and Shylock are also linked by their mutual hatred not only of each other but also of their opposed religions. In what appears to be an attempt to justify his taking of interest, Shylock tells the story of Jacob's contract with Laban:

> When Laban and himself were compromised
> That all the eanlings which were streaked and pied
> Should fall as Jacob's hire, the ewes, being rank,
> In end of autumn turnèd to the rams,
> And when the work of generation was
> Between these woolly breeders in the act,
> The skilful shepherd peeled me certain wands,
> And in the doing of the deed of kind
> He stuck them up before the fulsome ewes
> Who, then conceiving, did in eaning time
> Fall parti-coloured lambs; and those were Jacob's.
> This was a way to thrive; and he was blest;
> And thrift is blessing, if men steal it not. (I.iii.77-89)

Jacob does not allow nature to take its course at random but intercedes, influencing the pregnant ewes by presenting them images of "parti-colored" wands while they were "doing . . . the deed of kind," but Shylock insists that this, since it did not violate the terms of his contract with Laban, was "a way to thrive," not theft.

Antonio's response, however, rejects the terms by which Shylock has tried to shape the question:

> This was a venture, sir, that Jacob served for—
> A thing not in his power to bring to pass,
> But swayed and fashioned by the hand of heaven.

> Was this inserted to make interest good,
> Or is your gold and silver ewes and rams? (I.iii.90-4)

Thrift"—ways of making money that do not break the law that commands "thou shalt not steal"—is not in itself a blessing; only what is "swayed and fashioned by the hand of heaven" can it be reckoned a sign of God's blessing, like, presumably, the safe return of one's argosies when one sends them out onto the perilous seas. Shylock turns Antonio's closing remark into a jest and tries to continue the argument, but Antonio cuts him off, ignoring him and turning instead to teach Bassanio:

> SHYLOCK: I cannot tell. I make it breed as fast.
> But note me, signor—
>
> ANTONIO: Mark you this, Bassanio?
> The devil can cite Scripture for his purpose.
> An evil soul producing holy witness
> Is like a villain with a smiling cheek,
> A goodly apple rotten at the heart.
> O, what a goodly outside falsehood hath! (I.iii.95-101)

Antonio's comment might have more force were he not seeking to borrow money from Shylock to make his friend Bassanio look more prosperous as a suitor than he actually is. Yet he is essentially correct: "one may smile and smile and be a villain" (*Hamlet*, I.v.109) in Venice as well as in Denmark, and Shylock too is playing the hypocrite: we have already heard of his hatred for Antonio and desire to "feed fat the ancient grudge I bear him" (I.iii.45).

For Antonio, Shylock is a devil; even when he tries to cite scripture to justify those practices for which Antonio has railed on him, Antonio rejects him out of hand. Yet when Shylock offers his "merry bond" to gain Antonio's love (I.iii.136-40), Antonio forgets the lesson he has just offered Bassanio and accepts despite Bassanio's warning, which in turn is based upon Antonio's earlier conclusions about Shylock:

> Why, fear not, man; I will not forfeit it.
> Within these two months—that's a month before
> This bond expires—I do expect return
> Of thrice three times the value of this bond. (I.iii.155-8)

Antonio does not fear for his pound of flesh because he takes God's blessing for granted—he does not consider his earlier reminder to Shylock that "returns" are "A thing not in . . . [man's] power to bring to pass, / But swayed and fashioned by the hand of heaven." Antonio is making God's blessing into a thing that can be counted upon, turning God's gifts into aging receivables. Nonetheless, though he ignores his own analysis of Shylock's nature, he is correct about Shylock's willingness to be a smiling villain. Like Portia, he seems to find it hard to follow his own teaching.

Hazarding

During the next few scenes, Shakespeare sandwiches Lancelot Gobbo's and Jessica's departures from Shylock's house between the arrival and departure of Morocco from Belmont after his failure to win Portia. In these scenes we move from characters risking everything for outcomes they cannot control to characters apparently risking nothing in order to achieve outcomes they have predetermined. Morocco, whom Portia had earlier described as having "the complexion of a devil" (I.ii.127), is worried that Portia will reject him for his "complexion" (II.i.1), but more worried about the terms of the choice of the caskets; he would rather win her by bravery in war rather than risk losing her, "blind Fortune leading him" (II.i.36), but agrees to take his "chance," to make his "hazard," and to let "Good fortune / . . . make . . . [him] blest or cursèd among men" (II.i. 38, 43, 45, 46); Lancelot, Jessica, and Lorenzo, however, are leaving little to chance; Lancelot has decided he can no longer stay at Shylock's house, even if that means following the counsel of the fiend:

> To be ruled by my conscience I should stay with the Jew my master who, God
> bless the mark, is a kind of devil; and to run away from the Jew I should be ruled
> by the fiend who, saving your reverence, is the devil himself. Certainly the Jew is

> the very devil incarnation; and in my conscience, my conscience is but a kind of hard conscience to offer to counsel me to stay with the Jew. The fiend gives the more friendly counsel. I will run, fiend. My heels are at your commandment. I will run. (II.ii.20-9)

Jessica, too, thinks of her father's house as hell (II.iii.2), and, though she regrets Lancelot's departure, prepares to use him to further her own escape by having him deliver a letter to Lorenzo:

> Alack, what heinous sin is it in me
> To be ashamed to be my father's child!
> But though I am a daughter to his blood,
> I am not to his manners. O Lorenzo,
> If thou keep promise I shall end this strife,
> Become a Christian and thy loving wife. (II.iii.16-21)

It may be sin to leave Shylock's house, but it is hell to stay; in both cases what seems like the lesser of two evils prevails; in both cases, moreover, it is Shylock's hatred of the "prodigal Christian" (II.v.15) that facilitates their departures. Shylock permits Lancelot to become Bassanio's servant in the hopes that Lancelot "will help to waste / His borrowed purse" (II.v.49-50). Jessica is enabled to escape when Shylock decides to "go in hate" to Bassanio's house "to feed upon" Bassanio's food and consume Bassanio's borrowed wealth by eating his dinner. (II.v.14). In the event, it is Shylock whose wealth is consumed. When Jessica flees with Lorenzo, she steals a casket of jewels from her father (II.vi.33) and gilds herself with more ducats taken from her father's house (II.vi.49-50). Lorenzo wins a golden Jessica and her casket without hazarding; one effect of their flight is that Shylock becomes even more incensed at the Christians generally and particularly Antonio than he already was.

In the following scene, Morocco fails to win at Portia's casket hazarding and goes away with only a death's head to show for his chance. Portia's portrait is immured in one of three caskets; to win her, the correct casket must be chosen. The only clues are their outsides and their inscriptions:

> This first of gold, who this inscription bears:
> "Who chooseth me shall gain what many men desire."
> The second silver, which this promise carries:
> "Who chooseth me shall get as much as he deserves."
> This third dull lead, with warning all as blunt:
> "Who chooseth me must give and hazard all he hath." (II.vii.4-9)

Like Lorenzo, he goes for the gold, first rejecting the lead as unworthy of the risk

> Must give, for what? For lead? Hazard for lead?
> This casket threatens. Men that hazard all
> Do it in hope of fair advantages.
> A golden mind stoops not to shows of dross.
> I'll then nor give nor hazard aught for lead. (II.vii.17-21)

Though tempted by the silver, he ultimately settles on the gold both because he reasons that Portia is what many men desire and because he worries that while he deserves much, "yet 'enough' / May not extend so far as to the lady" (II.vii.27-8). The scroll within the golden casket suggests a flaw in his reasoning:

> All that glisters is not gold;
> Often have you heard that told.
> Many a man his life hath sold
> But my outside to behold.
> Gilded tombs do worms infold. (II.vii.65-9).

Although everyone knows that "All that glisters is not gold," many are willing to hazard their lives in the hope of gain. Yet the death's head in the casket suggests that even those who win the gold will eventually have to yield it up in the grave. As Graziano had warned Antonio in the first scene, "You have too much respect upon the world. / They lose it that do buy it with much care" (I.i.75-6). Morocco's bravery on the battlefield has not served him in his quest for

Portia: if "faint heart n'er won fair lady," it seems brave heart didn't either. While it may be true that "All the world desires her" and that "From the four corners of the earth they come / To kiss this shrine, this mortal breathing saint (II.vii.38-40), what is universally desired may not be what all the world ought to desire.

For the next six scenes, Shakespeare alternates between Shylock's outraged response to his losses, which, it grows increasingly clear, will include the 3000 ducats he lent Antonio, thus putting Antonio's life at hazard, and the hazarding of the two remaining caskets in Belmont. Salerio and Solanio report upon the public response to Shylock's loss, characterizing him as "the villain Jew" and "the dog Jew" (II.viii.4, 14) and reporting how "all the boys in Venice follow him" (II.viii.23), mocking his cries of grief for his stolen ducats and his escaped daughter. Like one who does not know what he values most, Shylock's "passion" is characterized as "so confused, / So strange, outrageous, and so variable" that they have not heard its like (II.viii.12-3):

> My daughter! O, my ducats! O, my daughter!
> Fled with a Christian! O, my Christian ducats!
> Justice! The law! My ducats and my daughter!
> A sealèd bag, two sealèd bags of ducats,
> Of double ducats, stol'n from me by my daughter!
> And jewels, two stones, two rich and precious stones,
> Stol'n by my daughter! Justice! Find the girl!
> She hath the stones upon her, and the ducats!" (II.viii.15-22)

While Salerio and Solanio find this outcry amusing, they are clearly pleased that "Lorenzo and his amorous Jessica" (II.viii.9) have escaped, and their response to Antonio's distress is quite sympathetic as they describe his parting from Bassanio:

> And even there, his eye being big with tears,
> Turning his face, he put his hand behind him
> And, with affection wondrous sensible,
> He wrung Bassanio's hand; and so they parted. (II.viii.46-9)

They are likewise concerned and fearful for Antonio at the news that a vessel has been wrecked which might belong to Antonio: "You were best to tell Antonio what you hear—/ Yet do not suddenly, for it may grieve him" (II.viii.33-4), but unlike Shylock, Antonio has made it clear that he prefers those he loves to wealth, and Solanio notes at the end of the scene that "I think he only loves the world for him [i.e. Bassanio]" (II.viii.50).

The simple contrast between Antonio and Shylock is complicated by the next scene, which introduces another suitor who has come, as Portia puts it, "to hazard for my worthless self" (II.ix.17), for Aragon quite clearly loves only himself. He rejects the lead casket, saying, "You shall look fairer ere I give or hazard" (II.ix.21) and the gold, insisting

> I will not choose what many men desire,
> Because I will not jump with common spirits
> And rank me with the barbarous multitudes. (II.ix.30-2)

Aragon turns to the silver casket and meditates approvingly upon what he takes to be its message:

> "Who chooseth me shall get as much as he deserves"—
> And well said too, for who shall go about
> To cozen fortune, and be honourable
> Without the stamp of merit? Let none presume
> To wear an undeservèd dignity.
> O, that estates, degrees, and offices
> Were not derived corruptly, and that clear honour
> Were purchased by the merit of the wearer!
> How many then should cover that stand bare,
> How many be commanded that command?
> How much low peasantry would then be gleaned
> From the true seed of honour, and how much honour

> Picked from the chaff and ruin of the times
> To be new varnished? Well; but to my choice.
> "Who chooseth me shall get as much as he deserves."
> I will assume desert. (II.ix.35-50)

Believing in his own merit, Aragon confidently assumes that he deserves Portia, that she is a reward for his "deservèd dignity," his inherent worth. What he finds within the casket makes a quite explicit mockery of his pretensions:

> What's here? The portrait of a blinking idiot
> Presenting me a schedule. I will read it.
> How much unlike art thou to Portia!
> How much unlike my hopes and my deservings!
> "Who chooseth me shall have as much as he deserves."
> Did I deserve no more than a fool's head?
> Is that my prize? Are my deserts no better? (II.ix.53-9)

Obsessively repeating the inscription on the silver casket, Aragon cannot yet believe that he does not deserve Portia even while the fool's head is there to tell him that only fools can think they deserve love:

> The fire seven times tried this;
> Seven times tried that judgement is
> That did never choose amiss.
> Some there be that shadows kiss;
> Such have but a shadow's bliss. (II.ix.62-6)

To think that one can choose correctly every time is to be a fool; after all even Socrates, proclaimed by the oracle of Apollo to be the wisest man alive, deserved that honor only because he insisted that the only thing he knew was that he knew nothing.[4] Aragon's "desert" now appears to him as nothing but vanity and he acknowledges his folly: "With one fool's head I came to woo, / But I go away with two" (II.ix.74-5). Portia's comment on his parting lacks the slightest bit of sympathy: "O, these deliberate fools! When they do choose / They have the wisdom by their wit to lose" (II.ix.79-80). If, as Nerissa says, "Hanging and wiving goes by destiny" (II.ix.82), then success in "wiving" is like success in commerce: only by hazarding does one accept that like prosperity, winning a wife is not something one can accomplish on his own but is rather "A thing not in his power to bring to pass, / But swayed and fashioned by the hand of heaven" (I.iii.91-2). Deliberation does not bring success and human wisdom is not sufficient to bring one to the desired port. Human providence must give way to divine.

This notion appears to be holding true in Venice as well: Salerio and Solanio now have heard confirmation that Antonio has lost a ship and Shylock, on stage for the first time since Jessica fled with his treasure, is learning what it is to lose his own "flesh and blood" (III.i.32). But, as Salerio and Solanio hear him say, it is not just he who will lose his flesh and blood. Shylock has also heard of Antonio's loss, and gloats at his jeopardy:

> He hath disgraced me, and hindered me half a million; laughed at my losses, mocked at my gains, scorned my nation, thwarted my bargains, cooled my friends, heated mine enemies, and what's his reason?—I am a Jew. Hath not a Jew eyes? Hath not a Jew hands, organs, dimensions, senses, affections, passions; fed with the same food, hurt with the same weapons, subject to the same diseases, healed by the same means, warmed and cooled by the same winter and summer as a Christian is? If you prick us do we not bleed? If you tickle us do we not laugh? If you poison us do we not die? And if you wrong us shall we not revenge? If we are like you in the rest, we will resemble you in that. If a Jew wrong a Christian, what is his humility? Revenge. If a Christian wrong a Jew, what should his sufferance be by Christian example? Why, revenge. The villainy you teach me I will execute, and it shall go hard but I will better the instruction. (III.i.50-68)

Antonio's flesh may not be good for anything, but feeding it to fish would be a revenge for business losses and for religious slights to which Shylock looks forward eagerly. "He was wont to lend money for a Christian courtesy: let him look to his bond" (III.i.44-6). Shylock hates Christians and feels himself wiser than they, yet he will imitate them in the thing that they do in violation of divine law, for as St. Paul writes in Romans 12:19, "Dearely beloued, auenge not yourselues, but give place vnto wrath: for it is written, Vengeance is mine: I will repay, sayth the Lord."[5] What Shylock proposes is "villainy" to both Christians and Jews; and Shylock's desire to be a "better" villain is not an aspiration with which an audience is likely to sympathize. This passage, taken in part and quoted out of context has been used as a plea for tolerance, but in context it is an excuse for murder.

Having committed himself to murder Antonio, Shylock is stripped of whatever humanity he may have ever had. During the remainder of the scene, Shylock is torn back and forth between his two desires: to recover his money and to destroy Antonio. Tubal enters with the news that he could not find Jessica though he often came where she had been and that Antonio has lost another ship. Shylock's daughter now has value to him only as a means of recovering his lost valuables: "A diamond gone cost me two thousand ducats in Frankfurt. The curse never fell upon our nation till now—I never felt it till now. Two thousand ducats in that and other precious, precious jewels. I would my daughter were dead at my foot and the jewels in her ear! Would she were hearsed at my foot and the ducats in her coffin!" (III.i.78-84). Likewise Antonio is now only an object upon which Shylock can inflict pain: "I'll plague him, I'll torture him. I am glad of it" (III.i.108-9). Shylock's two desires come together in his final speech of the scene: "I will have the heart of him if he forfeit, for were he out of Venice I can make what merchandise I will. Go, Tubal, and meet me at our synagogue. Go, good Tubal; at our synagogue, Tubal" ((III.i.117-21). As Shylock is reduced to a personified desire for merchandise and revenge and as his plan to use the law for his revenge unfolds, the scene of his activities shifts from the public spaces of Venice where Jews and Christians meet to a private space from which Christians are excluded, the synagogue, symbolic opposite of the Church.

If III.i is the darkest scene in the play, III.ii is its opposite; where the one focuses on Shylock's murderous impulses and his greed, the other focuses on the freeing of love from its casket and upon wealth beyond counting. Bassanio, despite Portia's pleas that he wait a month or two before he "hazard" (III.ii.2), is ready to "venture" (III.ii.10) for Portia, because the not-knowing if he will win her is torture to him: "Let me choose, / For as I am, I live upon the rack" (III.ii.24-25). But his torture is something he shares with his torturer, for Portia also must wait and wonder if he will succeed:

> I am locked in one of them.
> If you do love me, you will find me out.
> Nerissa and the rest, stand all aloof.
> Let music sound while he doth make his choice.
> Then if he lose he makes a swanlike end,
> Fading in music. That the comparison
> May stand more proper, my eye shall be the stream
> And wat'ry deathbed for him. He may win,
> And what is music then? Then music is
> Even as the flourish when true subjects bow
> To a new-crownèd monarch. Such it is
> As are those dulcet sounds in break of day
> That creep into the dreaming bridegroom's ear
> And summon him to marriage. Now he goes,
> With no less presence but with much more love
> Than young Alcides when he did redeem
> The virgin tribute paid by howling Troy
> To the sea-monster. I stand for sacrifice.
> The rest aloof are the Dardanian wives,
> With blearèd visages come forth to view
> The issue of th' exploit. Go, Hercules.
> Live thou, I live. (III.ii.40-61)

It is not merely Portia who stands for sacrifice, here, but Bassanio and Antonio as well: all are at risk, in one way or another, and all are waiting to find out if their hazard will succeed or fail. But where Shylock merely wants money and revenge, they are hoping for life and love.

Bassanio's choice is a simple one: gold is dismissed because "The world is still deceived with ornament" (III.ii.74), silver because it is a "pale and common drudge / 'Tween man and man" (III.ii.103-4); instead, Bassanio chooses lead because he is "moved" by it:

> But thou, thou meagre lead,
> Which rather threaten'st than dost promise aught,
> Thy paleness moves me more than eloquence,
> And here choose I. Joy be the consequence! (III.ii.104-7)

Bassanio hazards all for joy and love, and it is given to him, though Portia is the first to feel it since she knows the consequences of his choice before he does:

> How all the other passions fleet to air,
> As doubtful thoughts, and rash-embraced despair,
> And shudd'ring fear, and green-eyed jealousy.
> O love, be moderate! Allay thy ecstasy.
> In measure rain thy joy; scant this excess.
> I feel too much thy blessing: make it less,
> For fear I surfeit. (III.ii.108-14)

In a play whose affective scale has so far ranged from melancholy, to scorn, to hatred, to guilt, these are strong new notes. Ecstasy, joy, blessing—love's train—drive out all other passions for Portia; Bassanio, opening the casket and finding Portia's portrait, first marvels that someone could come "so near creation" (III.ii.116), before turning to the scroll within, "The continent and summary of my fortune":

> You that choose not by the view
> Chance as fair and choose as true.
> Since this fortune falls to you,
> Be content, and seek no new.
> If you be well pleased with this,
> And hold your fortune for your bliss,
> Turn you where your lady is,
> And claim her with a loving kiss." (III.ii.130-8)

Shakespeare stresses the difficulty Bassanio, "Giddy in spirit, still gazing in a doubt" (III.ii.144), is having accepting the fortune that has fallen to him; he is, evidently, more comfortable with the language of contracts: "I come by note to give and to receive / . . . / As doubtful whether what I see be true / Until confirmed, signed, ratified by you." (III.ii.140, 47-48).

In her response, Portia takes Bassanio's contractual language and overgoes it much as Marc Antony will later do in his love talk with Cleopatra, "There's beggary in the love that can be reckoned" (I.i.15):

> You see me, Lord Bassanio, where I stand,
> Such as I am. Though for myself alone
> I would not be ambitious in my wish
> To wish myself much better, yet for you
> I would be trebled twenty times myself,
> A thousand times more fair, ten thousand times more rich,
> That only to stand high in your account
> I might in virtues, beauties, livings, friends,
> Exceed account. But the full sum of me
> Is sum of something which, to term in gross,
> Is an unlessoned girl, unschooled, unpractisèd,
> Happy in this, she is not yet so old
> But she may learn; happier than this,
> She is not bred so dull but she can learn;
> Happiest of all is that her gentle spirit
> Commits itself to yours to be directed
> As from her lord, her governor, her king.
> Myself and what is mine to you and yours
> Is now converted. But now I was the lord

> Of this fair mansion, master of my servants,
> Queen o'er myself; and even now, but now,
> This house, these servants, and this same myself
> Are yours, my lord's. I give them with this ring,
> Which when you part from, lose, or give away,
> Let it presage the ruin of your love,
> And be my vantage to exclaim on you. (III.ii.149-74)

Portia, the golden fleece, is now Portia, Bassanio's wife. What she is is what she is, though imagination magnify it ever so much. What she is is gift to Bassanio, and she both the giver and the thing given. The sign of that gift, the ring, is introduced in this moment of giving with the warning that it is not to be given away in turn, a condition Bassanio freely accepts.

Bassanio is moved by her speech to a dumbness that resolves itself into a few words of acknowledgment of the gift he has received and his reason

> Turns to a wild of nothing save of joy,
> Expressed and not expressed. But when this ring
> Parts from this finger, then parts life from hence.
> O, then be bold to say Bassanio's dead. (III.ii.182-5)

At this moment of joy, Nerissa and Graziano declare their love for each other and beg to be married with Portia and Bassanio, but the proceedings are interrupted by Salerio, Lorenzo, and Jessica bearing news from Venice that Antonio has failed to meet his bond and is to die at Shylock's hand. In this moment of joy, Shylock intervenes, apparently not to be bought off by the monies now available to pay him. As Jessica tells the others,

> When I was with him I have heard him swear
> To Tubal and to Cush, his countrymen,
> That he would rather have Antonio's flesh
> Than twenty times the value of the sum
> That he did owe him; and I know, my lord,
> If law, authority, and power deny not,
> It will go hard with poor Antonio. (III.ii.282-8)

While Jessica's flight with Shylock's ducats and diamonds has not increased his love for Christians, it has not had an effect on Shylock's hatred for Antonio, which as we saw earlier, long predated Jessica's flight and could hardly be increased by it.

Shylock himself, describing Antonio as "the fool that lent out money gratis" (III.iii.2), appears in the next scene, rejecting all talk of "mercy":

> I'll have my bond. Speak not against my bond.
> I have sworn an oath that I will have my bond.
> Thou called'st me dog before thou hadst a cause,
> But since I am a dog, beware my fangs.
> The Duke shall grant me justice. (III.iii.4-8)

Where Shylock professes two motives—to end the threat to his money lending to the fool that lent out money without charging interest and to revenge himself for Antonio's anti-Jewish slights, Antonio only sees one motive:

> He seeks my life. His reason well I know:
> I oft delivered from his forfeitures
> Many that have at times made moan to me.
> Therefore he hates me. (III.iii.21-4)

Moreover, Antonio acknowledges that the law is on Shylock's side and that "The Duke cannot deny the course of law" (III.iii.26) since Venice lives by trade and it is the law that protects those mercantile dealings. In this case, the law seems to demand Antonio's death and the state must enforce the law.

But when the law is at issue, what one needs is a lawyer. Portia, who has apparently decided that Antonio must be her wedding gift to Bassanio, sends a messenger to her cousin, Dr. Bellario, to receive his notes on the legal situation as well as the proper garments to allow her to appear a jurist so that she may take control of the case. Her motive, to the extent she expresses it, depends upon humanist conceptions of friendship:

> in companions
> That do converse and waste the time together,
> Whose souls do bear an equal yoke of love,
> There must be needs a like proportion
> Of lineaments, of manners, and of spirit,
> Which makes me think that this Antonio,
> Being the bosom lover of my lord,
> Must needs be like my lord. If it be so,
> How little is the cost I have bestowed
> In purchasing the semblance of my soul
> From out the state of hellish cruelty. (III.iv.11-21)

Her conclusion, perhaps not completely unexpected from one who had earlier stated, "I stand for sacrifice," puts her in a position analogous to that of Christ, whose sacrifice purchased the souls of mankind from hell. And yet, Portia is Portia, not Christ or even more than momentarily a figure who reminds us of Christ. Her "little body" cannot bear its own sins, let alone those of the world.

The theme of salvation is immediately picked up and burlesqued in the next scene in conversation between Lancelot, Jessica, and Lorenzo, to whom Portia left the charge of her house while she and Nerissa depart, supposedly to pray and contemplate in a nearby monastery until Bassanio and Graziano return (III.iv.26-31). Arguing that "the sins of the father are to be laid upon the children" (II.v.1-2), Lancelot argues that Jessica must be damned on account of her father's sins unless her mother was an adulteress and Shylock begat her not (III.v.9-10). When Jessica points out that by his logic that would damn her on account of the sins of her mother, he can only shrug at her apparently impossible situation: "Truly then, I fear you are damned both by father and mother. Thus, when I shun Scylla your father, I fall into Charybdis your mother. Well, you are gone both ways" (III.v.13-6). Jessica sees a way out of Lancelot's dilemma: "I shall be saved by my husband. He hath made me a Christian" (III.v.17-8). For Lancelot, however, this simply damns Lorenzo as well: "Truly, the more to blame he! We were Christians enough before, e'en as many as could well live one by another. This making of Christians will raise the price of hogs. If we grow all to be pork-eaters we shall not shortly have a rasher on the coals for money" (III.v.19-24). Lancelot, moral casuist extraordinaire, seems to be alone among the play's Christians in not welcoming Jessica into the Christian community, but in his inconsistency—we learn upon Lorenzo's entrance that Lancelot has welcomed the Moor more warmly and gotten her with child (III.v.35-7)—he is not atypical of the Christians in the opening scenes sinning the sins they know they ought not to sin. In a reversal of Graziano's opening speech to Antonio, Lorenzo urges silence as the only remedy against those who would misuse the word: "How every fool can play upon the word! I think the best grace of wit will shortly turn into silence, and discourse grow commendable in none only but parrots" (III.v.41-3) Evidently, the Christians cannot well live one by another any better than the Christians can live by the Jews. Jessica, overwhelmed by Portia's generosity, implies that the solution is that Christians must turn Jews and live an upright life according to the law if they are to "merit" heaven (III.v.68-73), yet, as we have seen, the idea of merit is undercut throughout the casket scenes.

"I crave the law"

Shakespeare's presentation of Shylock in the trial scene, however, reminds us why Jessica wanted to escape from the hell Shylock had made of their house to begin with. The Duke characterizes Shylock as "A stony adversary, an inhuman wretch / Uncapable of pity, void and empty / From any dram of mercy" (IV.i. 3-5). Shylock's response to the Duke when he asks Shylock to have pity on Antonio confirms this comment:

> You'll ask me why I rather choose to have
> A weight of carrion flesh than to receive
> Three thousand ducats. I'll not answer that,

But say it is my humour. Is it answered?
What if my house be troubled with a rat,
And I be pleased to give ten thousand ducats
To have it baned? What, are you answered yet?
Some men there are love not a gaping pig,
Some that are mad if they behold a cat,
And others when the bagpipe sings i' th' nose
Cannot contain their urine; for affection,
Mistress of passion, sways it to the mood
Of what it likes or loathes. Now for your answer:
As there is no firm reason to be rendered
Why he cannot abide a gaping pig,
Why he a harmless necessary cat,
Why he a woollen bagpipe, but of force
Must yield to such inevitable shame
As to offend himself being offended,
So can I give no reason, nor I will not,
More than a lodged hate and a certain loathing
I bear Antonio, that I follow thus
A losing suit against him. (IV.i.39-61)

For Shylock, emotion is supreme ruler in humans, and Shylock's innate hate and loathing are enough to justify his actions against Antonio. To Shylock, the idea that he should not kill a hated enemy when the law will let him is inconceivable: "Hates any man the thing he would not kill?" (IV.i.66). Shylock can do it so he will do it—for him it is a simple matter. When the Duke asks, "How shalt thou hope for mercy, rend'ring none?" (IV.i.87), Shylock immediately responds, "What judgement shall I dread, doing no wrong?" (IV.i.88). What Shylock is doing does not for him break the commandment against murder because he has a bond that permits him to do it:

The pound of flesh which I demand of him
Is dearly bought. 'Tis mine, and I will have it.
If you deny me, fie upon your law:
There is no force in the decrees of Venice.
I stand for judgement. Answer: shall I have it? (IV.i.98-102)

For Shylock, who would not hope for mercy from Christians if they were once to "catch him upon the hip," safety lies in following the letter of the law, and the bond says a pound of Antonio's flesh is his; the divine law ("thou shalt not kill") apparently does not concern him.

When Portia arrives at the court armed with her cousin's opinion and dressed as a young doctor, it becomes clear that her strategy is to encourage Shylock in his belief that his suit is within the law at the same time that she requires him to be merciful. Sigurd Burckhardt suggested in his influential essay on the play, "The Gentle Bond," that Portia comes with no "solution ready," that she "learns from Shylock himself the art of winning life from the deadly letter."[6] However, I think this demonstrably untrue. Portia comes with copies of the law that confiscates his land, goods and life if he breaks his bond by taking one drop of Christian blood along with his pound of flesh as well as the law that condemns Shylock to death and divides his fortune equally between the state and his intended victim, Antonio, for plotting to murder a citizen of Venice (IV.i.306-60).[7] Unless we are prepared to believe that Nerissa is capable of drawing up a legally-binding deed of gift of all Shylock's possessions at his death to Jessica and Lorenzo, Portia also seems to come prepared with that as well.

If Portia's speech about mercy is not aimed at Shylock, however, then it must rather be aimed at Antonio and the Duke, because, unless Shylock suddenly decides to be merciful, take the money Bassanio offers in lieu of his pound of flesh, and depart in safety, it is they who will have to deal with Shylock after he becomes caught up in the law. Hence Portia keeps reassuring Shylock that he may proceed to collect upon his bond until the moment she springs her trap:

> Of a strange nature is the suit you follow,
> Yet in such rule that the Venetian law
> Cannot impugn you as you do proceed. (IV.i.174-6)

>   I have spoke thus much
> To mitigate the justice of thy plea,
> Which if thou follow, this strict court of Venice
> Must needs give sentence 'gainst the merchant there. (IV.i.199-202)

>   Why, this bond is forfeit,
> And lawfully by this the Jew may claim
> A pound of flesh, to be by him cut off
> Nearest the merchant's heart. (IV.i.227-30)

> A pound of that same merchant's flesh is thine.
> The court awards it, and the law doth give it. (IV.1.296-7)

Portia does not want Shylock to be merciful; she wants him punished:

> For as thou urgest justice, be assured
> Thou shalt have justice more than thou desir'st. (IV.i.313-4)

> Soft, the Jew shall have all justice. Soft, no haste.
> He shall have nothing but the penalty. (IV.i.318-9)

> He shall have merely justice and his bond. (IV.i.336)

> Thou shalt have nothing but the forfeiture
> To be so taken at thy peril. (IV.1.340-1)

It is not until Shylock has given up his claim to the forfeiture ("Why then, the devil give him good of it. / I'll stay no longer question" [342-3]), that Portia springs her final trap:

>   Tarry, Jew.
> The law hath yet another hold on you.
> It is enacted in the laws of Venice,
> If it be proved against an alien
> That by direct or indirect attempts
> He seek the life of any citizen,
> The party 'gainst the which he doth contrive
> Shall seize one half his goods; the other half
> Comes to the privy coffer of the state,
> And the offender's life lies in the mercy
> Of the Duke only, 'gainst all other voice—
> In which predicament I say thou stand'st,
> For it appears by manifest proceeding
> That indirectly, and directly too,
> Thou hast contrived against the very life
> Of the defendant, and thou hast incurred
> The danger formerly by me rehearsed.
> Down, therefore, and beg mercy of the Duke. (IV.i.343-60)

Portia is not trying to make the Jew behave as a Christian, she is hoping to make the Christians—specifically the Duke and Antonio—behave as Christians, and as Christians it is they who must remember that unlike Shylock they cannot proclaim, "I stand here for law" (IV.i.141). It is their very fallibility, as Portia reminds them in her great speech on mercy that renders them dependent upon mercy:

>   It is twice blest:
> It blesseth him that gives, and him that takes.
> Tis mightiest in the mightiest. It becomes
> The thronèd monarch better than his crown.
> His sceptre shows the force of temporal power,
> The attribute to awe and majesty,
> Wherein doth sit the dread and fear of kings;
> But mercy is above this sceptred sway.
> It is enthronèd in the hearts of kings;

> It is an attribute to God himself,
> And earthly power doth then show likest God's
> When mercy seasons justice. Therefore, Jew,
> Though justice be thy plea, consider this:
> That in the course of justice none of us
> Should see salvation. We do pray for mercy,
> And that same prayer doth teach us all to render
> The deeds of mercy. (IV.i.183-199)

All humankind is vulnerable under the "course of justice." As Hamlet mordantly observes to Polonius, "Use every man after his desert, and who should scape whipping?" (II.ii.532-3). The Duke has learned Portia's lesson well. He forgives Shylock before Shylock even asks; Antonio's response is more complicated. Positioned by the ironically named Graziano, whose theme here is "A halter, gratis. Nothing else, for God's sake" (IV.i.376) and the gracious Duke, Antonio sets conditions:

> So please my lord the Duke and all the court
> To quit the fine for one half of his goods,
> I am content, so he will let me have
> The other half in use, to render it
> Upon his death unto the gentleman
> That lately stole his daughter.
> Two things provided more: that for this favour
> He presently become a Christian;
> The other, that he do record a gift
> Here in the court of all he dies possessed
> Unto his son, Lorenzo, and his daughter. (IV.i.378-87)

To critics, this has generally seemed unexceptional.[8] What, after all, could be wrong about requiring Shylock to become a Christian? To those minded like the inquisitors of the Elizabethan imagination, perhaps this could have been seen as appropriate behavior, but to both moderate Catholics and to Protestants, forced conversion is a violation of conscience and a thing of no use to the one being forced.

To Renaissance believers in free will like Erasmus or Bishop Bartolomó de Las Casas, entrance into the Church of Christ was a process that receipt of the gift of faith from God followed by a struggle within the new would-be believer to believe. As Erasmus put it, "Entrance into the Church is by faith, without which baptism is of no avail. But no one gives himself faith; it is a gift from God, by which God gives preliminary help to whom He wills and draws him to Christ."[9] Erasmus even goes so far as to suggest that if "we were truly merciful, we would show kindness even to the Turks, in the hope that they would be overcome by our goodness and want to share our religion."[10] Las Casas, a Dominican monk who became Bishop of Chiapas in Mexico, devoted most of his life to the cause of the inhabitants of the New World, subjects of the King of Spain by decree of the Pope, who were being tortured, enslaved, and forced to submit to conversion to Christianity. Las Casas appealed to Philip II to exercise his authority and to extend his protection to the Indians, to have them freed from slavery, taught, not tortured, and welcomed into the Church as full members. As J. H. Parry suggests, "The key to Las Casas's thought was his insistence upon liberty. . . . If the free exercise of reason was a right according to Natural Law, it belonged to infidels as to Christians, and not even the Vicar of Christ, in his zeal for the extension of the Faith, might lawfully invade such a right."[11] One of Las Casas best-known polemical writings, the *Brevíssima relacíon de la destruccíon de las Indias*, (1552) was translated by "M. M. S." into English and published in London in 1583 as *The Spanish Colonie, Or Briefe Chronicle of the Acts and Gests of the Spaniards in the West Indies, called the new World.* The epistle "To the Reader" offered the work as "a President [i.e. precedent] and warning to the xij. Prouinces of the lowe Countries," suggesting that what Spain had done in the New World it could do in the old as well, a suggestion that the English themselves would have to contemplate after the launching of the Armada in 1588.[12]

215

To Protestants as well, however, the suggestion that forced conversion could serve any useful purpose would be highly dubious. Article XI of the Thirty-Nine Articles of the Church of England, "Of the Justification of Man," insists that "We are accounted righteous before God, only for (1) the merit of our Lord and Saviour Jesus Christ (2) by faith, and (3) not for our own works or deservings. Wherefore that we are justified by faith only is a most wholesome doctrine, and very full of comfort, &c." Article XVII, "Of Predestination and Election," makes it clear that human actions are irrelevant in this process: "(1) Predestination to life is the everlasting purpose of God, whereby, (2) before the foundations of the world were laid, he hath (3) constantly decreed by his counsel secret to us, to deliver from curse and damnation (4) those whom he hath chosen (5) in Christ out of mankind, and to bring them by Christ to everlasting salvation, as vessels made to honour. Wherefore they which be endued with so excellent a benefit of God (6) be called according to God's purpose by his Spirit working in due season: (7) they through grace obey the calling: they be justified freely: they be made sons of God by adoption: they be made like the image of his only-begotten Son Jesus Christ." Shakespeare's "grace" on the scene, Graziano, however, offers quite a contrary sense to Shylock's forced conversion: "In christ'ning shalt thou have two godfathers. / Had I been judge thou shouldst have had ten more, / To bring thee to the gallows, not the font." (IV.i. 394-7). Unlike Jessica, who has chosen to seek a new life as a Christian wife,[13] Shylock is broken by Antonio's terms ("I am not well" [IV.i.393]) and is quite evidently not experiencing the "sweet, pleasant, and unspeakable comfort" that Article XVII promises to those who "feel in themselves the working of the Spirit of Christ, mortifying the works of the flesh, and their earthly members, and drawing up their minds to high and heavenly things, as well because it doth greatly establish and confirm their faith of eternal salvation to be enjoyed through Christ, as because it doth fervently kindle their love towards God." Shylock's choice was between literal death and figurative death, and he has chosen the figurative death: "you take my life / When you do take the means whereby I live" (IV.i.373-4); with the moiety left him by both the Duke and Antonio, he will live on, diminished, but without any sign that he will ever come to that fullness of life promised as one of the benefits of election.

In a very real sense, however, one might say that Antonio, as he showed at the beginning of the play and, indeed, at the beginning of this scene, finds himself in much the same position. In his world-weariness, his self-righteousness and his joylessness, he is demonstrating the same spiritual condition as the Redcrosse Knight, the hero of Book I of Spenser's *Faerie Queene* (first published 1590, reissued 1596) before he receives assurance of his election[14]:

> I am a tainted wether of the flock,
> Meetest for death. The weakest kind of fruit
> Drops earliest to the ground; and so let me. (IV.i.113-5)

Antonio's demand shows him, for at least some of Shakespeare's audience, no Christian; Shylock's acceptance of his terms, contrasting as it does with the heroes of the Old Testament who preferred martyrdom to apostasy, to be no Jew.[15] Shylock fears life in a world with diminished wealth less than he fears death in the name of fidelity to his God; if Solanio was correct that Antonio "only loves the world" (II.viii.50) for Bassanio's sake, the prospect of a Bassanio-less world may seem as bleak to him as a less-monied world does to Shylock.

With Shylock's exit, Portia is also ready to depart, her mission accomplished. Bassanio offers her the three thousand ducats owed Shylock, which she refuses:

> He is well paid that is well satisfied,
> And I, delivering you, am satisfied,
> And therein do account myself well paid.
> My mind was never yet more mercenary.
> I pray you know me when we meet again.
> I wish you well; and so I take my leave. (IV.i.412-7)

Her "pay" will come when she can twit her new husband for not knowing her when they met in Venice, perhaps by way of urging him to learn to know her better. But Bassanio pushes her into an improvisation when he insists that she choose to "Take some remembrance of us as a tribute, / Not as fee" (IV.i.419-20). Now she decides to test him by asking him for the ring that he has sworn never to remove as a sign of his love. Once armed with her cousin's legal opinions, freeing Antonio was pretty much a sure thing; now, however, the play swerves back into the realm of hazarding: in making this request, Portia cannot know what Bassanio will do. At first Bassanio refuses to give the disguised Portia the ring because it is "a trifle" and he will not "shame" himself to give something of so little worth, offering instead to find out "by proclamation" the "dearest ring in Venice" (IV.i.427-33), but when "Balthasar" takes offence, Bassanio confesses the truth:

> Good sir, this ring was given me by my wife,
> And when she put it on she made me vow
> That I should neither sell, nor give, nor lose it. (IV.i.438-40)

With this more frank explanation, Bassanio passes the test, "Balthasar" leaves, but Antonio then prevails upon Bassanio to break faith with Portia:

> My lord Bassanio, let him have the ring.
> Let his deservings and my love withal
> Be valued 'gainst your wife's commandement. (IV.i.446-8)

"Desert" and Bassanio's love for Antonio overrule Bassanio's pledge of faith and he sends Graziano off with the ring, setting the stage for the last scene's continuation of this scene's debate between law and mercy, a debate universalized when, in the brief following scene Nerissa vows to get Graziano's ring which he also swore to keep forever (IV.ii.13-4). That Graziano, who has no obligation to the clerk as Bassanio thinks he has to "Balthasar" and Antonio, evidently makes Portia a prophet when he yields Nerissa her ring upon no weighty cause, suggests that faith-breaking will be a universal problem, not a particular one, in the final scene.

The last scene begins with Lorenzo and Jessica bantering about woman betrayed by lovers or love:

> LORENZO: The moon shines bright. In such a night as this,
> When the sweet wind did gently kiss the trees
> And they did make no noise—in such a night
> Troilus, methinks, mounted the Trojan walls,
> And sighed his soul toward the Grecian tents
> Where Cressid lay that night.
>
> JESSICA: In such a night
> Did Thisbe fearfully o'ertrip the dew
> And saw the lion's shadow ere himself,
> And ran dismayed away.
>
> LORENZO: In such a night
> Stood Dido with a willow in her hand
> Upon the wild sea banks, and waft her love
> To come again to Carthage.
>
> JESSICA: In such a night
> Medea gathered the enchanted herbs
> That did renew old Aeson.
>
> LORENZO: In such a night
> Did Jessica steal from the wealthy Jew,
> And with an unthrift love did run from Venice
> As far as Belmont.
>
> JESSICA: In such a night
> Did young Lorenzo swear he loved her well,
> Stealing her soul with many vows of faith,
> And ne'er a true one.
>
> LORENZO: In such a night
> Did pretty Jessica, like a little shrew,
> Slander her love, and he forgave it her.

> JESSICA: I would outnight you, did nobody come.
> But hark, I hear the footing of a man.(V.i.1-24)

Love is not a sure thing, but something that must be hazarded, and where hazard exists, so does loss: Aeneas, with the best will in the world toward Dido, was commanded by the gods to leave her; Cressida was forced to leave Troilus, whom she loved, and quickly played him false; Thisbe loved Pyramus, but circumstances led each to kill themselves rather than live in the world without their love. Jessica can only hope that Lorenzo will not break the many "vows of faith" he made to steal her soul (and her father's money); Lorenzo can only hope that Jessica is only joking. When word comes that both Portia and Bassanio are about to return, their conversation shifts to the beauties of the moment:

> How sweet the moonlight sleeps upon this bank!
> Here will we sit, and let the sounds of music
> Creep in our ears. Soft stillness and the night
> Become the touches of sweet harmony.
> Look how the floor of heaven
> Is thick inlaid with patens of bright gold.
> There's not the smallest orb which thou behold'st
> But in his motion like an angel sings,
> Still choiring to the young-eyed cherubins.
> Such harmony is in immortal souls,
> But whilst this muddy vesture of decay
> Doth grossly close it in, we cannot hear it. (V.i.54-65)

Lorenzo's words conjure up a world in which harmony is not simply possible but present, in which the heavens themselves minister to our pleasures. But so long as we are enclosed in flesh, it is a harmony in which we cannot participate. Cut off by our bodies, the "muddy vesture of decay," from our immortal souls, we are cut off from the harmony that the angels experience; hence, as St. Paul argues in Romans 3: 10-20, we cannot avoid doing sin:

> As it is written, There is none righteous, no, not one: There is none that vnderstandeth: there is none that seeketh God. They haue all gone out of the way: they haue bene made altogether vnprofitable; there is none that doeth good, no, not one. Their throte is an open sepulchre: they have vsed their tongues to deceit: the poison of aspes *is* vnder their lips. Whose mouth is full of cursing and bitternesse. Their feete are swift to shed blood. Destruction and calamitie *are* in their wayes, And the way of peace they haue not knowen. The feare of God is not before their eyes. Now wee know that whatsoeuer the Lawe saith, it saith to them which are vnder the Lawe, that euery mouth may bee stopped, and all the world bee subiect to the iudgement of God. Therefore by the workes of the Lawe shal no flesh be iustified in his sight: for by the Law *commeth* the knowledge of sinne.

The remedy St. Paul urges for the law's inability to rescue us is faith:

> But now is the righteousnesse of God made manifest without the Law, hauing the witnesse of the Law and of the Prophets, *To wit,* the righteousnesse of God by faith of Iesus Christ, vnto all, and vpon all that beleeue. For there is no difference: for all haue sinned, and are depriued of the glory of God, And are iustified freely by his grace, through the redemption that is in Christ Iesus, Whom God hath set foorth *to be* a reconciliation through faith in his blood to declare his righteousnesse, by the forgiuenesse of the sinnes that are passed, Through the patience of God to shew at this time his righteousnesse, that hee might be iust, and a iustifier of him which is of the faith of Iesus. Where is then the reioycing? It is excluded. By what Law? of workes? Nay: but by the Law of faith. Therefore wee conclude, that a man is iustified by faith, without the workes of the Lawe. (Romans 3: 21-28)

Yet the world, by and large, is not a faithful world. As Portia observes when she and Jessica return to her house,

> That light we see is burning in my hall.
> How far that little candle throws his beams—
> So shines a good deed in a naughty world. (V.i.89-91)

In this naughty world, a good deed is like a warning beacon, yet it pales before the light of the universe in which it shines. As Nerissa observes, "When the moon shone we did not see the candle" (V.i.92). In a naughty world, even light itself can be suspect, as Portia's punning greeting to Bassanio suggests:

> Let me give light, but let me not be light;
> For a light wife doth make a heavy husband,
> And never be Bassanio so for me.
> But God sort all. (V.i.129-32)

Of course, before Bassanio does feel welcome in his home, Portia threatens precisely to make him heavy by being light as she accuses him of being light by giving away the ring he had sworn to keep.

When Portia intervenes in Nerissa's quarrel with Graziano about the fate of her ring, Portia makes clear the stakes involved in the game she is playing with Bassanio:

> You were to blame, I must be plain with you,
> To part so slightly with your wife's first gift,
> A thing stuck on with oaths upon your finger,
> And so riveted with faith unto your flesh.
> I gave my love a ring, and made him swear
> Never to part with it; and here he stands.
> I dare be sworn for him he would not leave it,
> Nor pluck it from his finger for the wealth
> That the world masters. Now, in faith, Graziano,
> You give your wife too unkind a cause of grief.
> An 'twere to me, I should be mad at it. (V.i.166-176)

What is put on with faith must be kept on in faith, and yet even the best of keepers will break faith. Bassanio, caught in Portia's trap, can only confess:

> If I could add a lie unto a fault
> I would deny it; but you see my finger
> Hath not the ring upon it. It is gone. (V.i.186-8)

Portia, however, claims not to be in a forgiving mood and threatens to take an action that could lead to the annulment of their as yet unconsummated marriage:

> Even so void is your false heart of truth.
> By heaven, I will ne'er come in your bed
> Until I see the ring. (V.i.189-91)

Depending upon how angry Portia is pretending to be, this could seem a very serious threat to both men. Antonio is apparently bankrupt and Bassanio, without Portia's fortune, is broke again.[16] Bassanio attempts to deflect this threat by promising to reveal information that would show her the necessity of his act:

> If you did know to whom I gave the ring,
> If you did know for whom I gave the ring,
> And would conceive for what I gave the ring,
> And how unwillingly I left the ring
> When naught would be accepted but the ring,
> You would abate the strength of your displeasure. (V.i.193-8)

Portia, seemingly anticipating Othello's insistence on the virtue of the handkerchief he gave Desdemona, appears to be unimpressed:

> If you had known the virtue of the ring,
> Or half her worthiness that gave the ring,
> Or your own honour to contain the ring,
> You would not then have parted with the ring.
> What man is there so much unreasonable,
> If you had pleased to have defended it
> With any terms of zeal, wanted the modesty
> To urge the thing held as a ceremony?

> Nerissa teaches me what to believe.
> I'll die for 't but some woman had the ring. (V.i.199-208)

Antonio, of course, was the man "so much unreasonable" when Bassanio did present the kind of explanation Portia here demands, though Portia had already left the stage when he did so. A better explanation is that she wants Bassanio to learn the lesson that Shylock tried to teach Antonio, that "merry bonds" can be converted to deadly bonds very quickly in a naughty world where words do not always mean what they seem to: Bassanio is certain that Portia's assurance is false ("No, by my honour, madam, by my soul, / No woman had it" [V.i.209-10]), yet her assertion is simple fact—Bassanio has forgotten that all that glitters is not gold, that appearances are not to be trusted.

Bassanio and Antonio both seek to win Portia's forgiveness by swearing by their souls (V.i.247, 252) that Bassanio "will never more break an oath with thee" (V.i.248), and Antonio even goes so far as to offer to enter into another bond for Bassanio:

> I once did lend my body for his wealth
> Which, but for him that had your husband's ring,
> Had quite miscarried. I dare be bound again,
> My soul upon the forfeit, that your lord
> Will never more break faith advisedly. (V.i.249-52)

Instead of accepting Bassanio's oath or drawing up a contract to enforce Antonio's bond, however, Portia reverts to character, giving not taking, reveals her role in saving Antonio, and further gifts Antonio with the news that three of his argosies have "richly come to harbour suddenly" (V.i.277) while Nerissa gives Lorenzo and Jessica the "special deed of gift, / After his death, of all he [Shylock] dies possessed of" (V.i.292-3). As Lorenzo exclaims, "Fair ladies, you drop manna in the way / Of starvèd people" (V.i.294-5).[17]

"Which is the merchant here, and which the Jew?" (IV.i.171)

Portia's query, asked in the persona of the young Roman judge, Dr. Balthasar, raises an interesting question. How do we distinguish a "royal" Venetian merchant from a gaberdine-clothed Jewish moneylender? The art of the Northern Renaissance, for instance, offers as a common composition a richly-clothed man sitting in front of a balance weighing gold coins while his wife looks up from an illustrated prayer book or book of hours to observe his counting.[18] Like Graziano's remark to Antonio at the beginning of the play—"You have too much respect upon the world./ They lose it that do buy it with much care" (I.i.74-5)—they remind us that there is a danger in getting too involved with worldly things, including the pursuit of wealth, even for Christians.[19] Antonio and Shylock seem equally dedicated to accumulating it, Shylock perhaps to show the Christians that he can out do them at their own game, Antonio apparently because he cannot think of what else to do except prosper in trade and give his wealth away to those who ask for his help, whether to woo rich beauties or to escape from the toils of Shylock's bonds and forfeits.

It has become almost compulsory in talking about the play to distinguish Belmont, where Portia lives in a green world in which quality of life is more important than anything else, from Venice, where men congregate on the Rialto to trade wealth and rumors of profit and loss.[20] Yet Belmont seems as much a center of wealth as Venice: people sail from all over Europe to try for the rich prize of the richly left Portia whose wealth is sufficient to pay Shylock what is due him twelve times over and not even notice the expenditure. Nor is money absent from consideration when the action moves back from Venice to Belmont in the last scene of the play when, as we have noted, Portia brings Antonio news of his trading successes and assures Lorenzo and Jessica's financial future.[21] Belmont, like Venice, is also a place where the rules must be strictly observed, whether in making contracts, winning wives, or observing ceremonies. The difference is that in Venice the penalty for forfeiture is death; in Belmont, there is forgiveness of what is owed.

In Portia, who gives herself twice to Bassanio, once when he has correctly hazarded, once when he has broken the faith he pledged, we find a spirit at odds with the rest of the characters of the play, a spirit that attempts obedience knowing that obedience will sometimes fail and that forgiveness will then become a necessity not a luxury. Recognizing that "in the course of justice none of us / Should see salvation" (IV.i.196-7), Portia forgives not to be forgiven but because she has been forgiven.[22] It is in this sense that Portia comes to embody the opposition to the Shylock who insists upon justice and who stands for the law. The logic of the play, based upon the logic of St. Paul's Epistles to the Romans and the Galatians, is that all who attempt to "stand . . . for law" are as "Jewish" as Shylock, whatever they call themselves.[23] In this play, one wins by surrendering control, by remembering what one is, and by trying to find the joys of love despite that knowledge.

In his 1996 study, *Shakespeare and the Jews*, James Shapiro argues for the centrality of Shylock as the "other" against whom all of the other characters in the play are defined just as "Englishness has in part defined itself by the wholesale rejection of that which is Jewish."[24] In response to the traditional objection that Shakespeare and his audience would not have had the opportunity to see any Jews since King Edward had banished the Jews in the late thirteenth century, Shapiro argues that there were Jews in late sixteenth-century: "There were Jews in Shakespeare's England, though probably never more than a couple of hundred at any given time in the whole country, a very small number in a population of roughly four million, and a small number even in relationship to the number of aliens residing in London. Their presence only seemed to disturb Catholic foreigners; in case after case the English show little surprise at the discovery of Jews living in their midst" (76).[25] Nonetheless, Shapiro finds the Elizabethans were obsessed about the Jews: "Ultimately, it is not the raw number of Jews in early modern England that is of interest as much as the kind of cultural preoccupation they became, that is, the way that Jews came to complicate a great range of social, economic, legal, political, and religious discourses, and turned other questions into Jewish questions as well" (88).

The chief problem I have with Shapiro's thesis is that the evidence to support it is almost entirely lacking. If Shapiro's thesis were valid, one would expect to find innumerable references in the *Calendar of State Papers, Domestic Series, of the Reigns of Edward VI, Mary, and Elizabeth*, yet a visit to the index to the volumes covering the years 1547–1601 reveals a total of four entries under "Jews," all for the year 1594 and all applied to Roberto Lopez, the Queen's physician, who was arrested for participating in a plot to poison the Queen in 1593 and executed in 1594.[26] Interestingly, the accounts of the affair calendared in the records make it very clear that so far as the government officials compiling the record were concerned, Lopez was involved in a Spanish, Catholic plot not a Jewish plot[27] and that the chief plotters included the King of Spain, Count Fuentes, Stephen Ferrera de Gama, Stephen de Ibarra, Gomes d'Avila, Emanuel Andrada, and Dr. Lopez, who was to be paid 50,000 crowns for poisoning the Queen. The records make it clear that Lopez was by no means the only one of the Queen's subjects who had agreed to kill her, and the names of several Irishmen (Patrick Collen, Hugh Cahill, born in Tipperary, John Daniell, an Irish gentleman, Father Holt, and Hugh Owen) figure prominently in the effort to find a soldier who would "kill her with a sword or a dagger at a gate or narrow passage, or as she walked in some of her galleries" (437). If Elizabethan England needed an "other" against which to define itself, it certainly had one near at hand, an enemy that had tried massive force in 1588 and private murder in 1593-94. In the alliance between the Papacy and the most Catholic King of Spain, England had an enemy in whom even the least paranoid of Elizabeth's subjects could believe.

Moreover, this enemy was an enemy of longstanding. From the 1560s, when the Pope first advanced the idea of excommunicating Elizabeth to the end of Elizabeth's reign, it was clear that her Protestant subjects feared her Catholic subjects and that her Catholic subjects could hardly find life under her Protestant government tolerable. In his "Letter... to Queen Elizabeth Touching Her Marriage with Monsieur" (1579), Sir Philip Sidney offered the Queen his analysis of the state of her kingdom. To Sidney, Elizabeth's "inward force," the "sinews of her crown... consisteth in your subjects... [who are] divided into two mighty factions, and factions bound upon the never ending knot of religion":

> The one is of them to whom your happy government hath granted the free exercise
> of the eternal truth. With these, by the continuance of time, by the multitude of

> them, by the principal offices and strengths they hold, and lastly, by your dealings at home and abroad against the adverse party, your state is so enwrapped, as it were impossible for you, without excessive trouble, to pull yourself out of the party so long maintained. . . . These, therefore, as their souls live by your happy government, so are they your chief, if not your sole, strength.[28]

Furthermore, Sidney argues, Elizabeth cannot expect to gain in support from Catholics what she loses by alienating the Protestants, because the Catholics are too desperate to accept any half measures:

> The other faction, most rightly indeed to be called a faction, is of the Papists: men whose spirits are full of anguish; some being forced to oaths they account damnable; some having their ambition stopped, because they are not in the way of advancement; some in prison and disgrace; some whose best friends are banished practisers; many thinking you an usurper; many thinking the right you had, disanulled by the Pope's excommunication; all burdened with the weight of their consciences; men of great number; of great riches (because the affairs of state have not lain on them); of united minds, as all men that deem themselves oppressed naturally are. (*MP* 48-9).

If the Catholics, not the Jews are the great Other, it makes far more sense to think of Shylock not simply as an alien "other" but also as a symbol of that other "other," the Catholics who would substitute their traditions for the Divine Word and good works for salvation as a gift of God's grace, and include in their ranks all who "crave the law." Although Shakespeare presents Shylock as one of his more unpleasant villains, it is not his Jewishness that makes him so—Jessica, after all, is presented quite sympathetically throughout—it is his humanness; his desire to glorify himself at the expense of his neighbors. The reason Shylock seeks to kill Antonio is because he hates him and he believes that the law permits him to do so; the reason why Portia forgives Bassanio at the end of the play for giving away the ring he had sworn to keep is because she loves him and she believes that having received mercy she must forgive him. By returning to him the ring whose absence, he had earlier said, would be the sign of his death, Portia is figuratively raising him from the grave.

Notes

[1] All citations of Shakespeare's works are to the Oxford Electronic text of *The Complete Works*, published under the General Editorship of Stanley Wells and Gary Taylor (Oxford: The Clarendon Press, 1988). All future citations will be parenthetically included in my text.

[2] Although the OED notes in its entry for "argosy" that "No reference to the ship Argo is traceable in the early use of the word" the cluster of allusions to Jason, Colchis, and the golden fleece makes it tempting to hear in the repetitions of argosies throughout the play a series of reminders of the Argonauts who sailed with Jason on his quest.

[3] Unless otherwise noted, all quotations from the New Testament are from the facsimile of the 1602 Geneva Bible New Testament, ed. Gerald T. Sheppard (New York: The Pilgrim Press, 1989).

[4] See, for example, Erasmus' discussion of Socrates in *The Praise of Folly*, *Literary and Educational Writings 5: Panegyricus, Moriae Encomium, Julius Exclusus, Institutio Principis Christiani, Querela Pacis*, Collected Works of Erasmus in English 27, ed. A. H. T. Levi (Toronto: University of Toronto Press, 1986), 100: "As an example of just how useless these philosophers are for any practice in life there is Socrates himself, the one and only wise man, according to the Delphic oracle. It showed little enough wisdom in its judgment, for once when he tried to do something in public he had to break off amid general laughter. Yet on one point the man was sensible enough—he refused to accept the epithet 'wise' but attributed it to the god."

[5] The passage to which St. Paul refers is Deuteronomy 12: 32, a passage that ought to be binding on Shylock; in the context of Romans, St. Paul is exhorting Christians to "Blesse them which persecute you: blesse, *I say*, and curse not. Reioyce with them that reioyce, and weepe with them that weepe. Be of like affection one towards another: bee not high minded: but make your selues equall to them of the lower sort: bee not wise in your selues. Recompense to no man euill for euill: procure things honest in the sight of all men. If it be possible, as much as in you is, haue peace with all men." (Romans 12: 14-8)

[6] *Shakespearean Meanings* (Princeton: Princeton University Press, 1968), 233.

[7] See IV.i. 311-2. Shylock asks, "Is that the law?" and Portia replies, "Thyself shalt see the act."

[8] The fullest justification of Shylock's forced conversion can be found in Barbara K. Lewalski, "Biblical Allusion and Allegory in *The Merchant of Venice, Shakespeare Quarterly* 13 (1962), 327-43. Roy Battenhouse, ed., *Shakespeare's Christian Dimension: An Anthology of Christian Commentary* (Bloomington: Indiana University Press, 1994), discusses criticism of the play and provides excerpts of essays on the plays illustrating their generic Christian thematics and a bibliography to which should be added James E. Siemon, *"The Merchant of Venice*: Act V as Ritual Reiteration," *Studies in Philology* 67 (1970), 201-9. Siemon suggests that Shylock's "conversion is certainly intended as a symbol of his integration into the social world of Venice, and as a thing good in itself" (206). To Battenhouse, Shylock's forced conversion "is a humane sentence that incorporates him into a community of reconcilement" (69).

[9] *On Mending the Peace of the Church* (1533), *The Essential Erasmus*, ed. and trans. John P. Dolan (New York: New American Library, 1964), 362.

[10] *Concerning the Immense Mercy of God* (1524), *Essential Erasmus* 268.

[11] *The Age of Reconnaissance* (1963; rpt. Berkeley: University of California Press, 1981), 308. Las Casas' *In Defense of the Indians*, a Latin manuscript read by Las Casas during a five-day oral presentation before Philip II, acting as Regent for his father Charles V, the Emperor and the King of Spain in 1550, has been Englished by Stafford Poole (DeKalb: Northern Illinois University Press, 1992).

[12] For a representation of Elizabethan concerns about the Inquisition's workings in the Netherlands, see Edmund Spenser, *The Faerie Queene*, ed. J. C. Smith (Oxford: The Clarendon Press, 1909), V.x.27-9. The literature on the Inquisition itself is vast, but see Henry Kamen, *The Spanish Inquisition: A Historical Revision* (New Haven: Yale University Press, 1997), B. Netanyahu, *The Origin of the Inquisition in Fifteenth Century Spain* (New York: Random House, 1995) and *Toward the Inquisition: Essays on Jewish and Converso History in Late Medieval Spain* (Ithaca: Cornell University Press, 1997). For a view of the Spanish activities in the Netherlands, see Pieter Geyl, *The Revolt in the Netherlands 1555-1609* (1935; London: Cassell, 1988). The memories of the Spanish terror were so strong that the publication in 1589 of Justus Lipsius's *Politica*, which argued that there could only be one official religion in a state, elicited a fervent attack by Dirck Volckertsz Coornhert charging Lipsius with being a forcer of conscience. Lipsius ultimately left Leiden and returned to Louvain and Catholicism. See Gerrit Voogt, "Primacy of Individual Conscience or Primacy of the State? The Clash between Dirck Volckerstz. Coornhert and Justus Lipsius," *Sixteenth Century Journal* 28 (1997), 1237-49. See also Brian Pullan, *The Jews of Europe and the Inquisition of Venice, 1550-1670* (1983; rpt. New York: Barnes & Noble, 1997).

[13]   Alack, what heinous sin is it in me
To be ashamed to be my father's child!
But though I am a daughter to his blood,
I am not to his manners. O Lorenzo,
If thou keep promise I shall end this strife,
Become a Christian and thy loving wife. (II.ii.16-21)

[14] See *The Faerie Queene*, I.ix.53, in which Una rebukes the Redcrosse Knight when she sees him, after hearing Despair's arguments that the divine justice punishes all sinners, begin to commit suicide and then hesitate:

    Come, come away, fraile, feeble, fleshly wight,
    Ne let vaine words bewitch thy manly hart,
    Ne diuelish thoughts dismay thy constant spright.
    In heauenly mercies hast thou not a part?
    Why shouldst thou then despeire, that chosen art?
    Where iustice growes, there grows eke greater grace,
    The which doth quench the brond of hellish smart,
    And that accurst hand-writing doth deface.

[15] In the introduction to his Oxford edition of the play (New York: Oxford University Press, 1993, 1994), Jay Halio notes that "If life is at risk, Jews may violate any of the 613 commandments in the Old Testament—except this one, which can require martyrdom (53 n. 4).

[16] All Antonio has is "the use" during Shylock's life of one quarter of his wealth (half of Antonio's half he already gave back to Shylock) during Shylock's life on Lorenzo and Jessica's part (IV.i.378-82).

This passage is often read as saying that Antonio will keep his entire half of Shylock's goods and let the Duke return the state's half to Shylock minus a fine as the Duke had earlier promised, yet it is not in his power to determine how the state will dispose of its half, only how he will dispose of the half the law gives to him.

[17] Is there an enactment of Matthew 13:10-13 in the play's denouement? "Why speakest thou to them in parables? And hee answered, and said vnto them, Because it is giuen vnto you to know the secrets of the kingdome of heauen, but to them it is not giuen. For whosoever hath, to him shalbe giuen, and he shall haue abundance: but whosoever hath not, from him shall bee taken away, euen that he hath. Therefore speake I to them in parables, because they seeing, do not see: and hearing, they heare not, neither vnderstand."

[18] Quentin Massys (1464/5–1530) is the painter of perhaps the best-known of these, *The Money-Lender and His Wife*, illustrated in Lawrence Gowing, *Paintings in the Louvre* (New York: Stewart, Tabori, & Chang, 1987), 228-31. Misers, of course, do not have to be Jewish (see Petrarch, *Rime 190*, "Una candida cerva sopra l'erba," *Petrarch's Songbook: Rerum Vulgarium Fragmenta*, trans. James Wyatt Cook [Binghamton: Medieval & Renaissance Texts & Studies, 1996)], 238-41) and Jews do not have to be misers, as the example of Jessica proves.

[19] Spenser's portrait of Mammon in *The Faerie Queene,* II.vii ("God of the world and worldlings I me call" [II.vii.8]) could just as well describe a Renaissance noble surrounded by his cabinet of possessions:

> And round about him lay on euery side
>> Great heapes of gold, that neuer could be spent:
>> Of which some were rude owre, not purifide
>> Of Mulcibers deuouring element;
>> Some others were new driuen, and distent
>> Into great Ingoes, and to wedges square;
>> Some in round plates withouten moniment;
>> But most were stampt, and in their metall bare
> The antique shapes of kings and kesars straunge & rare. (*The Faerie Queene,* II.vii.6)

[20] See especially C. L. Barber, *Shakespeare's Festive Comedy: A Study of Dramatic Form and its Relation to Social Custom* (1959; rpt. Cleveland: Meridian Books, 1963). Chapters 1-3 introduce Barber's concept of "festive" comedy; chapter 7 is devoted to *The Merchant of Venice,*

[21] It is apparently mere chance that brings Lorenzo and Jessica to Portia's attention. As Lorenzo tells Bassanio,

> For my part, my lord,
> My purpose was not to have seen you here,
> But meeting with Salerio by the way
> He did entreat me past all saying nay
> To come with him along. (III.ii. 224-8)

[22] Cf. Luke 7: 41-3: "There was a certain lender which had two debtors: the one ought five hundreth pence, and the other fifty: When they had nothing to pay, he forgaue them both: Which of them therefore, tell *me*, will loue him most? Simon answered, and said, I suppose that he, to whom he forgaue most. And he said vnto him, Thou hast truely judged."

[23] It is common in Humanist and Reformation polemic to call one's opponents Jewish should they attempt to argue against faith by standing upon their laws. Hence Folly, after presenting the rules of the monks, brings in Christ to rebuke them: "But Christ would interrupt the unending flow of these self-glorifications to ask: 'Where has this new race of Jews sprung from? l recognize only one commandment as truly mine, but it is the only one not mentioned. Long ago in the sight of all, without wrapping up my words in parables, I promised my father's kingdom, not for wearing a cowl or chanting petty prayers or practising abstinence, but for performing the duties of faith and charity. I do not acknowledge men who acknowledge their own deeds so noisily. Those who also want to appear holier than I am can go off and live in the heavens of the Abraxasians, if they like, or give orders for a new heaven to be built for them by the men whose foolish teaching they have set above my own commands'" (CWE 27, 132).

[24] New York: Columbia University Press, 1996, 4.

[25] Shapiro's numbers are not firm. Later in his book he observes that "By the early seventeenth century a handful of Jewish merchants had availed themselves of the opportunity of becoming denizens"

(189). From his own statements, one can hypothesize that a relatively small number of Jews lived in England in the late sixteenth-century without causing much concern to many people besides Catholics. Where those Jews lived is not at all clear. Whether Shakespeare knew any Jews is not known.

[26] (London: HMSO, 1856). Volume 1 covers the years 1547-1580, Volume 2, 1581-1590, Volume 3, 1591-1594, Volume 4, 1595-1597, and Volume 5, 1598-1601. Only the index to Volume 4 contains entries listed under "Jews." Interestingly, Lopez' trial and execution do not seem to have created any official interest in the Jews, for succeeding volumes revert to the absences of entries to be seen in earlier volumes. Interest in "Catholics," "Papists," and "Jesuits" is intense. There are 51 items in vol. 1, 149 in vol. 2, 382 in vol. 3, 111 in vol. 4, and 87 in vol. 4. These items include lists of Catholics, priests, seminarians studying abroad, harborers of priests, and proceedings against recusants.

[27] See *Calendar of State Papers, Domestic Series, of the Reign of Elizabeth,* 1591-1594 (London: HMSO, 1867), 436-476, for abstracts of the examinations of various of the Spanish, Irish, Portuguese, and English plotters, including Dr. Lopez, whose indictment is included at 445. None of the documents abstracted express any doubt about Lopez' guilt; neither to two early histories. See George Carleton. *A Thankfvll Remembrance of Gods Mercy In an Historicall Collection of the great and mercifull Deliverances of theChurch and State of England, since the Gospel beganne here to flourish, from the beginning of Queene Elizabeth* (1624; rpt. London, 1627), 163-214. Carleton was Bishop of Chichester; see also William Camden, *Tomus Alter, & Idem: Or The Historie of the Life and Reigne of that Famous Princesse, Elizabeth,* trans, Thomas Browne (London: 1629), 103-6. The first Latin edition of the *Annales* was published in 1615.

[28] *Miscellaneous Prose of Sir Philip Sidney,* ed. Katherine Duncan-Jones and Jan Van Dorsten (Oxford : The Clarendon Press, 1973), 47. Future references will be given parenthetically in my text.

"Why do the heathen rage?":
Psalm 2 as Comfort and Instruction in
Paradise Lost, Books 1-3

Robert J. De Smith

Paradise Lost begins by proclaiming "Disobedience," "Death," and "all our woe" (1.1, 3), the pronoun "our" jarring readers by including them inexorably in a cause-effect pattern of transgression and its consequences (or "Fruit"[1.1]).[1] The following lines hold out the promise of salvation and forgiveness, though the phrase "till one greater Man" (1.4) seems to push that promise off toward some future time, placing readers in a medial space between promise and fulfillment. In fact, the distance implied in such space—a distance played out in the structure of *Paradise Lost* as well as in the space created within Milton's cosmos between heaven and hell—becomes a metaphor for the consequences of transgression as well as suggesting the urgent need for divine forgiveness. Thus when at the beginning of Book 9 Milton's narrator takes up the narrative of the fall, he links human disobedience with alienation:

> I now must change
> Those Notes to Tragic; foul distrust, and breach
> Disloyal on the part of Man, revolt,
> And disobedience: On the part of Heav'n
> Now alienated, distance and distaste,
> Anger and just rebuke, and judgment giv'n,
> That brought into this World a world of woe. (9.5-11)

The consequences of the fall are summarized here as "breach" and "distance": seen from the perspective of fallen humans, their transgression has resulted in God's absence. God is far from human beings and humans far from God.

In this essay I explore how Milton in the first three books of *Paradise Lost* uses God's apparent absence to raise for readers serious questions about the consequences of their transgression. But Milton also offers consolation—the assurance of God's overarching presence—in these books, at least in part by means of a pattern of allusions to Psalm 2, where the question "Why do the heathen rage?" (verse 1) is answered with a vision of the establishing of God's Son as king. Within a narrative that emphasizes the consequences of fallenness for Satan and his cohorts, Milton directs his readers toward another perspective, one governed by God's power, goodness, and grace.

Reading the first two books of *Paradise Lost* means experiencing the absence of God. Such absence, of course, is a definition of hell,[2] which is exactly what Satan and "those bad Angels" (1.344) who have fallen with him are experiencing. Absence from God terrorizes Satan, motivates him, and pressures him into his self-justifications and accommodations. Thus when Satan calls himself (and, as part of his argument, his fellows),

> Irreconcilable to our grand Foe,
> Who now triumphs, and in th' excess of joy
> Sole reigning holds the Tyranny of Heav'n (1.122-4)

he is not just creating an image of God as a distant, tyrannous enemy. He is also expressing his own distance from that God—a distance as much moral as physical. If that absence is not completely apparent in Satan's words, the comment by Milton's narrator which follows in the next two lines makes it clear: "So spake th' Apostate Angel, though in pain, / Vaunting aloud, but rackt with deep despair" (1.125-6). Satan's "pain" and "despair," the effects of his apostasy, are expressions of his absence from God. Indeed, absence from God now characterizes his existence.

But in as much as Stanley Fish is right that "the poem's centre of reference is its reader who is also its subject,"[3] the reader also experiences a hellish absence from God in these two books. Though the opening lines of the work hold out the promise that "one greater Man" will

Transgression, Punishment, Responsibility, Forgiveness
Graven Images 4 (1998), 226-232.

"Restore us, and regain the blissful Seat" (1.4-5), the process of reading these two books largely buries that opening perspective, as under the weight of hell itself (or under the weight of Satan, called "in bulk as huge" as a Titan or Leviathan [1.195-201]). We are not without reminders along the way—many of them coming by means of the narrator's intrusive comments—of God's goodness. For instance, Satan's perversion of the ethic of Romans 8:28, "And out of good still to find means of evil" *(1.165)*, is answered a few lines later with the narrator's reminder that "all his [Satan's] malice serv'd but to bring forth / Infinite goodness, grace and mercy" (1.217-8). Still, the experience of absence from God in these books is real. It is effected simply by the extended time spent in hell. This is "that obscure sojourn" which "long detain'd" (3.14-5) the narrator and which he connects with his own blindness in the opening lines of Book 3. More specifically, it is effected by a great deal of malicious name calling on the part of Satan and his army of fallen angels. We have already noted Satan's calling God his "grand Foe," and his description of God as he who "holds the Tyranny of Heav'n" (1.122-4). In addition, Satan calls God "Thunderer" (2.28), "Conqueror," and "angry Victor" (1.143, 169). Moloch calls God "the Torturer" (2.64), and Beëlzebub, snidely, "Heav'n's perpetual King" (1.131). We are presented with God in the devil's image: distant, inscrutable, and characterized by mere power and the will to rule.

For readers, God's persistent absence raises questions about God's role in the events we are witnessing and his attitude toward those events. Indeed, these questions are all reflections—or deflections—of deeper questions centered on the issues of our transgression and the possibility of God's forgiveness. We are led to worry about God's attitude toward us as sinners and, ultimately, about his goodness and providence. All of these questions can be summarized in a single, urgent query: "Where is God?" The force of this question increases in Books 1 and 2 as we witness Satan taking action, for instance when he breaks free from the burning lake. "Why did you let that happen, God?" we may ask—a response that is scarcely allayed by the narrator's assurance that

> the will
> And high permission of all-ruling Heaven
> Left him at large to his own dark designs,
> That with reiterated crimes he might
> Heap on himself damnation. (1.211-5)

The question's force increases when Satan talks his way through the gates of Hell and when he seemingly by chance is not lost forever in Chaos (1.934-35). The intensity of this question climaxes at the end of Book 2, as we observe Satan perch himself on the edge of the created realm and then approach our world even nearer: "Thither full fraught with mischievous revenge, / Accurst, and in a cursed hour he hies" (2.1054-5). Here the bombastic language of the lines broadcasts the impending evil and the powerful impetus of the bringer of evil. Given for a moment a God-like perspective on Satan, and feeling the full force of the poem's dramatic irony (we know not only Satan's intent but that he will succeed), we are led to ask, with desperate urgency, "Where are you, God? Why are you absent? Don't you know what's happening? Don't you care?"

The shift to God's perspective, presaged at the end of Book 2, is completed at the beginning of Book 3. In his invocation, Milton's narrator emphasizes the difficulty of such a shift, embodying it particularly in the radical disparity between the biblical truth that "God is light" (I John 1:5) and his own blindness. But for readers this piles difficulty upon difficulty: Milton suggests that we may have trouble adjusting, like someone coming from a dark room into bright sunlight. That problem of adjustment, in turn, is located in the celestial dialogue between the Father and the Son in Book 3. We are likely to carry our insistent questioning— "Where is God?"—over to the conversation we witness. To what extent are the Father's opening words comforting or disconcerting? God may seem, at least to our perspective, too calm, too unperturbed. We may even remember Belial's description of God's potential reaction to a devilish assault on heaven: "yet our great Enemy / All incorruptible would on his Throne / Sit unpolluted" (2.137-9). Belial's God is too pure to get his hands dirty.

Fish comments on the Father's first words, "He sees what we see, but his reaction differs from ours and the difference is corrective" (78). Ultimately, the Father's eternal perspective offers us reassurance that he is in control, and there is relief in the Son's subsequent expressions of love mediated from the Father through him to us. Nonetheless, the Father's voice is unsettling, for it is convicting as well as comforting. Humankind is declared "ingrate" (3.97), an appellation the believer resists but knows is apt. Indeed, much of the Father's speech here seems designed to leave readers "without excuse"[4]—caught in a pattern of transgression and retribution. But if our proper response to God at the beginning of Book 3 is comfort, not despair, how does Milton prepare us for such a correcting answer to the question, "Where are you, God?" Fish calls Milton's rhetoric a "programme of reader harassment" (4): we are more or less beaten into submission by the disconcerting experience of getting things wrong so often. But Milton is also careful to see that we get it right, and one way he does so involves his use of Psalm 2. Alluded to in significant ways in the first two books of *Paradise Lost*, Psalm 2 offers readers a means to the correcting, biblical vision that is announced in the beginning of Book 3. God has been present all along: we just have to know where to look.

Psalm 2 is a coronation Psalm, celebrating the advent of David's kingship. It is also, typologically speaking, a Messianic Psalm, linking the earthly king to his offspring who will sit on David's throne forever (see Isaiah 9 and Psalm 89) and linking the nation of Israel to the kingdom of God. These links probably explain why this Psalm is the one most often quoted in the New Testament, notably in Revelation, where references to it are used to describe the final consummation of God's kingdom. Moreover, this is a Psalm of comfort: it moves from images of rebellious nations to images of God's Anointed One who rules with holy power to the injunction "Kiss the Son" and the declaration "Blessed are all they that put their trust in him" (verse 12). In the context that I have been suggesting, one of unsettling disturbance and discomfort, the consolation of the entire Psalm is relevant to Milton's purposes.[5]

In addition, the Psalm's most dramatic moment, in which God the Father declares, "Thou art my Son; this day have I begotten thee" (verse 7), is central to Milton's structural design in *Paradise Lost*. Borrowing the Psalm's language, Milton enacts this exaltation of the Son before the angels in Book 5:

> This day I have begot whom I declare
> My only Son, and on this holy Hill
> Him have anointed, whom ye now behold
> At my right hand; your Head I him appoint;
> And by my Self have sworn to him shall bow
> All knees in Heav'n, and shall confess him Lord. (5.603-8)

This is the earliest event in the chronology of *Paradise Lost* and the inciting impulse for Satan's rebellion.[6] It is also a central image of the work—focusing attention on the preeminence of the Son. This theme is first alluded to in the proem to Book I with the "one greater Man" who will "regain the blissful Seat" (1.4-5). And as W. B. Hunter demonstrates, it recurs in a set of complementary scenes describing the Son's exaltation: in Book 3, when the Son assumes the role of Savior, in Book 6 when he ascends following his victory in the War in Heaven, and in Book 12 when Michael prophesies concerning Christ's death and resurrection in a way which evokes not only the Gospels but the Revelation account (in chapter 12) of the birth of a child which gives rise to the war in heaven where Satan, the great dragon, is defeated.[7] In a variety of ways, then, Psalm 2 is an important and resonant one for Milton.

How does Milton use Psalm 2 as a kind of stabilizing influence as we read the first books of *Paradise Lost*? Fundamentally, he draws an analogy between the "kings of the earth" (verse 2), who are portrayed in the beginning of the Psalm, and the rebellious angels in hell—an analogy which suggests not just what the devils are like but how futile their efforts will be. Here is how the first section of Psalm 2 describes the enemies of God:

> Why do the heathen rage, and the people imagine a vain thing? The kings of the earth set themselves, and the rulers take counsel together, against the Lord, and against his anointed, saying, Let us break their bands asunder, and cast away their cords from us. (verses 1-3)

Milton's description of the "great consult" (1.798) in hell mimics this scene in a number of ways. First, Satan at the beginning of Book 2 is described as a king—he sits "High on a

Throne of Royal State" (2.1)—and he addresses his companions as "Powers and Dominions" (2.11). They meet, like the rulers in the Psalm, in an atmosphere of conspiracy and rebellion.[8] During the "great consult," Moloch blurts out, "My sentence is for open War" (2.51), voicing blatant rebellion. A bit later, Beëlzebub summarizes the purpose not just of their meeting but of their existence in a rhetorical question: Should we not be, he asks, "Yet ever plotting how the Conqueror least / May reap his conquest" (2.338-9). "'Yet ever plotting'" is an apt summary of the attitude of God's enemies in both the Psalm and Milton's work.[9]

The Psalm's image of chains ("bands" and "cords" in the King James Version; "fetters" and "chains" in other versions) from which the earthly kings wish to rebel, are echoed by Milton in various places. Satan's opening statement at the "consult"—"For since no deep within her gulf can hold / Immortal vigor" (2.12-3)—evokes the image of breaking bonds. We have earlier seen Satan at least seem to enact this statement when, though "Chain'd on the burning Lake," he "rears from off the Pool / His mighty Stature" (1.210, 221-2). And later, Beëlzebub calls hell his "dungeon" (2.317). In summary, Milton's devils voice the words of the Psalm, "Let us break their bands asunder, and cast away their cords from us" (verse 3).

Even God the Father, describing in his first speech Satan's approach to the world, uses the images of breaking chains:

> Only begotten Son, seest thou what rage
> Transports our adversary, whom no bounds
> Prescrib'd, no bars of Hell, nor all the chains
> Heapt on him there, nor yet the main Abyss
> Wide interrupt can hold. (3.80-4)

But as this passage from Book 3 suggests, the comparison between the devil's situation and the gathering of earthly kings in Psalm 2 is not without irony—irony which helps us gain some perspective on their activity. In the Psalm, the first verse poses ungodly rebellion as a bemused question: "Why do the heathen rage," as if to say, "What's the point?" This is precisely the idea of the Father's first words when he asks, "seest thou what rage / Transports our adversary?" (3.80-1). John Calvin, commenting on the early verses of the Psalm, says we know that the enemies of Christ "are making war against God over whom they shall not prevail" (12).

But this correcting—and comforting—perspective is available to readers before we get to Book 3 within the dynamics of Milton's allusions to Psalm 2, even when those allusions come from the mouths of devils. As we've just noticed, the Psalm holds up the "heathen" declarations of rebellion for ridicule as so much "rage" and "vain" imagination (where "imagine," colored by "vain," suggests fruitless fantasy: Milton in his versification of the Psalm says they "Muse a vain thing" [Hughes 162]). Milton suggests both rage and futility in his description of Satan presiding over that "great consult":

> Satan exalted sat, by merit rais'd
> To that bad eminence; and from despair
> Thus high uplifted beyond hope, aspires
> Beyond thus high, insatiate to pursue
> Vain War with Heav'n, and by success untaught
> His proud imaginations thus display'd. (2.5-10)

The tenor of this passage is the irony of hope based on despair and of a rising which is a falling. Specifically, Satan's "proud imaginations" are glossed by Psalm 2, as is his "Vain War." Thus if as readers we hear, "Why do the heathen rage, and the people imagine a vain thing?" as an echo to this description of Satan, we receive the comfort of understanding the ultimate futility of all the ungodly—earthly or devilish.

The irony of Satan and his cohorts mouthing the words of a Psalm which undercuts their voice and their actions occurs elsewhere in Book 2. Beëlzebub recognizes the futility of devilish plotting when he disparages Belial's counsel to "sit in darkness here / Hatching vain Empires" (2.377-8).[10] It is as if Beëlzebub has picked up the tone of Psalm 2. Two other inhabitants of hell allude directly to verse 4 of the Psalm: "He that sitteth in the heavens shall laugh: the Lord shall have them in derision." In the Psalm, this verse introduces a response to the gathering of God's enemies; just as the beginning of Book 3 does in *Paradise Lost*, this verse shifts to God's perspective on these rebellious words and plots. Belial seems to sense this heavenly response, for when he argues against Moloch's call to direct action, he says he fears the one who "from Heav'n's highth / All these our motions vain, sees and derides" (2.190-1). Later in the book, when Satan and Death are about to fight, Sin interrupts, reminding them of

> him who sits above and laughs the while
> At thee ordain'd his drudge, to execute
> Whate'er his wrath, which he calls Justice, bids,
> His wrath which one day will destroy ye both. (2.731-4)

Sin has turned prophet here, referring both to God's laughter at the petty actions of the wicked and to the ultimate end of God's enemies, which the Psalm puts this way: "Thou shalt break them with a rod of iron; thou shalt dash them in pieces like a potter's vessel" (verse 9). That Satan's final defeat is implied in these lines is suggested by the Psalm's "rod of iron," which in Revelation 12 is the instrument by which the child rules and, by implication, defeats the dragon named Satan. And here is the crowning irony of Milton's use of Psalm 2 in Book 2: the devils, despite themselves, speak the good news of the gospel! Just as, following Satan's return to hell after his successful tempting of Adam and Eve, the devils are humbled into serpents which utter nothing more than "A dismal universal hiss" (10.508), in this early book they speak against themselves and in praise of him who "sitteth in the heavens" (verse 4).

Belial, Sin, and (we infer) Satan himself, see only despair and mockery in God's laughter. They see it (to compare small things with large) a bit as I did when, as a young boy in church, I heard Psalm 2 read and wondered if God's laughter were not inappropriate, and perhaps even scary. After all, every kindergartner knows you're not supposed to laugh at people, especially if they are in a bad situation. But both Calvin and Luther find comfort—not unsettling distance—in heavenly laughter. Calvin says God's laughter teaches us "that he does not stand in need of great armies to repress the rebellion of wicked men, as if this were an arduous and difficult matter" (14). And Luther writes,

> In order to strengthen the assurance of the afflicted he says emphatically: "He will laugh and scorn," as if he were saying: So certain it is that they struggle in vain, however solid their cause may be in the opinion of others, that the Lord does not consider it worthwhile to resist them seriously or as if it were a great thing. He laughs at and scorns them as being absolutely nothing. (321)

Comparing believing and non-believing responses to God's laughter in Psalm 2 is instructive: Milton's devils can only hear the laughter as convicting, derisive scorn, while believers find comfort in God's control, certainty, justice, and power. Milton elsewhere expresses the idea that a vision of God's power is comforting when, in his Sonnet 19, "his State / Is Kingly" fills out Patience's declaration that "'God doth not need / Either man's work or his own gifts'" (lines 11-2, 9-10). The speaker's consternation at being disabled from the very task to which God has called him is resolved in a comforting picture of God's self-sufficiency and power. And in *Paradise Lost*, Milton wants us to apply this lesson, gleaned from the Psalm, to the Father as he speaks in the beginning of Book 3. Allusions to Psalm 2 should remind us that God's laughter is our comfort.

If Milton's God the Father is not literally laughing in his first speech in Book 3, the early Reformers can provide a link between the laughter of the Psalm and the Father's tone here. Luther and Calvin both find in God's laughter an evocation of his calmness and serene, benevolent control. Commenting on Psalm 2, Luther observes,

> He who concerns Himself about us dwells there secure and calm; and if we are disturbed, He who cares for us is not disturbed. We are tossed about, but He is calm; He will not let the righteous be eternally restless. (321-2)

Calvin responds to the vaunting of the heathen in the Psalm this way:

> Let them exalt themselves as they may, they shall never be able to reach to heaven; yea, while they think to confound heaven and earth together, they resemble so many grasshoppers, and the Lord, meanwhile, undisturbed beholds from on high their infatuated evolutions. (14)

Seeing the enemies of God as grasshoppers is an apt metaphor for God's perspective in *Paradise Lost*: he observes Satan "from his prospect high, / Wherein past, present, future he beholds" (3.77-9) and is, to cite the Reformers, "undisturbed." For Milton, our implicit response to Psalm 2 becomes a model for our response to the Father in Book 3.

A final connection between the Psalm and Milton's work is worth exploring. The climax of Psalm 2 is this heavenly declaration: "Thou art my Son; this day have I begotten thee" (verse 7). In the Psalm, the declaration confers on David, Israel's king, God's divine authority; from the New Testament perspective, it evokes the exaltation of Christ in his resurrection and ascension (see Acts 13:33, where Paul explicitly connects Christ's resurrection with Psalm 2:7, and compare with Acts 2:34). We have already noticed that Milton uses this declaration in Book 5 as a central metaphor and as the inciting impulse of his work. But in Book 3, after the Son has assumed the role of Savior, there occurs an enactment of this declaration which brings closure to the set of allusions we have been examining. God declares the Son to be "By Merit more than Birthright Son of God" (3.309), a paraphrase of Psalm 2:7 by which Milton extends the Psalm's frame of reference, establishing the Son's preeminence based on what he has done ("Merit"), not just on who he is ("Birthright"). A few lines later, God the Father adds:

> Therefore thy Humiliation shall exalt
> With thee thy Manhood also to this Throne;
> Here shalt thou sit incarnate, here shalt Reign
> Both God and Man, Son both of God and Man,
> Anointed universal King; all Power
> I give thee, reign for ever, and assume
> Thy Merits; under thee as Head Supreme
> Thrones, Princedoms, Powers, Dominions I reduce:
> All knees to thee shall bow, of them that bide
> In Heaven, or Earth, or under Earth in Hell. (3.313-22)

This passage offers a prophetic look at the consummation of all things in the Son—the ultimate expression of his preeminence. Its vision of the Son's reign is rooted in (among other places) Psalm 2, particularly verses 6-9 which assert the universal rule of God's King which will extend to "the uttermost parts of the earth" (verse 8). Even Satan's "Powers and Dominions" (2.11) from his address at the "great consult" are encompassed by the Son's rule. As such, this passage follows Psalm 2 in answering its opening question "Why do the heathen rage?" with the overwhelmingly benevolent power and preeminence of the Son.

Here then is a striking answer to the question we found lurking in the first two books of *Paradise Lost*: "Where is God?" Among the answers that Psalm 2, and this vision of the Son's exaltation, suggests is that God is present in his Son, ultimately the central figure of *Paradise Lost*. These words of comfort and instruction, evoked in the context of *Paradise Lost* Books 1–3, provide—I have been suggesting—a stablizing perspective on the events of these early books, allowing readers to mediate between the vision of an absent God, which is the fruit of their transgression, and the forgiveness which is implicit in his comforting presence and explicit as the Son takes on the role of Savior in Book 3. Milton would, I think, find the final verses of Psalm 2 a fitting doxology to this movement in his work: "Kiss the Son, lest he be angry" and "Blessed are all they that put their trust in him."

Notes

[1] Citations to Milton's works are from John Milton, *The Complete Poems and Major Prose*, ed. Merritt Y. Hughes (New York: Odyssey Press, 1957). An earlier version of this essay was presented at the Fifth Dakotas-Nebraska Conference on Earlier British Literature, held 24-25 April 1997 at Jamestown College in Jamestown, ND.

2 The Larger Catechism, based on the Westminster Confession, defines hell in this way: "The punishments of sin in the world to come are, *everlasting separation from the comfortable presence of God,* and most grievous torment in soul and body, without intermission, in hell-fire forever" (my emphasis). Cited from Arthur C. Cochrane, *Reformed Confessions of the 16th Century* (Philadelphia: Westminster Press, 1966), 158.

3 Stanley Fish, *Surprised by Sin: The Reader in* Paradise Lost (1967; Berkeley: University of California Press, 1971), 1.

4 Romans 1, from which I quote this phrase, suggests what Milton has in mind as he presents us with the Father: "For the invisible things of him from the creation of the world are clearly seen, being understood by the things that are made, even his eternal power and Godhead; so that they are without excuse: Because that, when they knew God, they glorified him not as God, neither were thankful; but became vain in their imaginations, and their foolish heart was darkened" (1:20-1, my emphasis; I quote from the KJV). In the context of Milton's poem, the passage stands as a warning: God is clearly portrayed—do not miss it in your vanity or foolishness.

5 A. S. P. Woodhouse and Douglas Bush, in *A Variorum Commentary on the Poems of John Milton*, vol. 2.3 (New York: Columbia University Press, 1972) remind us that "Milton had a lifelong devotion to the Psalms," and they quote Helen Darbishire: "they 'were in esteem with him above all Poetry'" (1000). Milton versified the first eight psalms—including Psalm 2—in 1653.

6 John Calvin, in his *Commentary on the Book of Psalms*, 1563, trans. James Anderson, 5 vols. (Grand Rapids: Eerdmans, 1949), makes this observation on the first section of the Psalm, verses 1-3: "Nor is it at all wonderful, or unusual, if the world begin to rage as soon as a throne is erected for Christ" (12). Milton seems to have reached a similar insight, applying it to angelic rebellion in Heaven.

7 W. B. Hunter, "The War in Heaven: The Exaltation of the Son," *Bright Essence: Studies in Milton's Theology*, ed. W. B. Hunter, C. A. Patrides, and J. H. Adamson (Salt Lake City: University of Utah Press, 1971), 128-9. Significantly for our discussion, Revelation 12 alludes to Psalm 2: the child who is born "was to rule all the nations with a rod of iron" (verse 5); compare Psalm 2, verse 9: "Thou shalt break them with a rod of iron." Hunter uses the links between these passages in Milton, various Scriptural references (especially Hebrews 1:3-5 and 5:5), and Psalm 2 to suggest that the repeated enactments of Christ's exaltation form "a theme which in both its literal and metaphorical sense dominates the poem" (129), becoming, as he says of the Son's exaltation in Book 5, "one enormous metaphor" (124).

8 Calvin says the earthly kings in the Psalm are "making war against God" (12); Milton, in his versification of Psalm 2, interpolates the clause "though ye rebel" in line twelve (Hughes 162), strengthening the suggestion that rebellion characterizes the heathen.

9 Luther, in his commentary on this Psalm, links the earthly with the devilish when he writes that all believers "will suffer his Herods, Pilates, rulers, kings, Gentiles, and other people who rage against him, meditate vain things, set themselves against him, and take counsel together. And if this does not happen through men, it will surely happen through devils and finally at all events through conscience itself in death." I cite Luther from Martin Luther, *Luther's Works*, ed. Jaroslav Pelikan, et al., 55 vols. (St. Louis: Concordia Publishing House, 1955-86), 14:321.

10 The Revised English Bible, a twentieth-century version, translates Psalm 2:1b "Why do these peoples hatch their futile plots?"

Crime, Insanity, and Responsibility:

The Dostoevskian Dialectic of Redemption in *Crime and Punishment*, the Kornilova Case, and *The Brothers Karamazov*

Gary Rosenshield

During the years of the great novels (1865-1881), Dostoevsky continually contemplated and planned what he believed to be his crowning achievement, his magnum opus, a long novel about the life of a great sinner, the first half of which would relate the deeds of the sinner, the second half the transformation of the sinner into saint.[1] Although only once did he actually make extensive plans for such a work—the first drafts for what eventually became *The Possessed*—each of his major works can be seen, in retrospect, as a variant beginning of that life-long novelistic endeavor. Dostoevsky writes over and over again the first half of the life, only to leave the second half to the next novel, the novel, of course, that never gets written. The first novel is about sin, the second about redemption.

Dostoevsky's own life, or at least the semi-autobiographical novel he wrote about his prison experiences (*Notes from the House of the Dead* [1860-62]), served as a partial blueprint for this hagiographical plot. Dostoevsky served eight years in Siberia (1850-58) for subversive activities: four years of hard labor and then another four years in the ranks. In the late 1840s, he belonged to a small group that was planning to set up a secret printing press for the dissemination of radical political literature. He was originally condemned to death, but the tsar commuted this sentence to imprisonment and service in the ranks (Dostoevsky was a retired army officer). By 1860 Dostoevsky had imaginatively transformed his prison experience into a semi-autobiographical novel, presenting his incarceration and suffering not only as just, but as essential to his resurrection from the dead, a sentiment underscored by the ecstatic optimism of the last lines of *Notes from the House of the Dead*.

> The fetters fell off. I picked them up. I wanted to hold them in my hand, to look at them for the last time. It was as though I were surprised that they could have been on my legs a minute before.
>
> "Well, with God's blessing, with God's blessing!" said the convicts in coarse, abrupt voices, in which, however, there was a note of pleasure.
>
> Yes, with God's blessing! Freedom, new life, resurrection from the dead. . . . What a glorious moment![2]

From *Notes from the House of the Dead* on, Dostoevsky would often link crime to the possibility of redemption, predicated on the criminal's taking responsibility for his criminal acts. But by the middle 1860s no serious moral and social Russian novelist could take the "old" ideas about responsibility for granted. Russian radical thinkers like Chernyshevsky and Pisarev had waged a concerted attack against conventional notions of responsibility, arguing a social and economic determinism whose implications, at least for Dostoevsky, entailed the elimination of free will and therefore the all-important category of responsibility. In the newly established courts, lawyers began to make increased use of one of the more fashionable extenuating circumstances defenses: temporary insanity. Since it could be argued that all criminals were temporarily insane or acting under diminished mental capacity when they committed their crimes, Dostoevsky saw the insanity defense, especially the temporary insanity defense, as an assault against the idea of responsibility, and thus a clear and present danger for Russian society, a danger against which he soon began to take up arms both in his novels and his journalism.

Dostoevsky, in part, used *Crime and Punishment*, the Kornilova case, and *The Brothers Karamazov*, to conduct moral experiments, in which he could dramatize the real relationships

Transgression, Punishment, Responsibility, Forgiveness
Graven Images 4 (1998), 233-248.

among crime, insanity, responsibility, and redemption. In each succeeding work, he takes the experimental conditions bearing on responsibility to greater extremes, all the time insisting on responsibility as a precondition for redemption and utilizing temporary insanity as a way of defining the meaning and limits of individual responsibility. In the present study, I will attempt to analyze in *Crime and Punishment*, the Kornilova case, and *The Brothers Karamazov* the interrelation of crime, insanity, and responsibility and the significance of that interrelation for Dostoevsky's implied vision of redemption: resurrection from the dead.

I.

In part one of *Crime and Punishment*, Raskolnikov, a twenty-six-year-old former university student, carries out a plan, which he has mulled over for many months, to kill an old pawnbroker and steal her money. The novel emphasizes Raskolnikov's premeditation: long before the novel begins, Raskolnikov has worked out a theory for the justification of murder; a month before the murder he actually makes a trial run, coming with a pledge in order to case the pawnbroker's apartment. In order to demonstrate that murder is inexcusable under any circumstances, Dostoevsky provides Raskolnikov with what the social determinists would call extenuating if not exculpatory circumstances. Raskolnikov has not eaten for days; he lives on the top floor of an apartment house in the St. Petersburg slums: it is ninety-eight degrees; he is suffering from severe depression; after his trial run he receives infuriating news from his family: his sister has decided to sell herself in marriage to a man (Luzhin) she despises in order to further her brother's career. It seems to Raskolnikov that he must do something drastic—and immediately—to save himself, his family, and all the others being oppressed by the Luzhins and the pawnbrokers of the world. But not only does Dostoevsky discredit these circumstances as extenuating factors in the crime, he has Raskolnikov himself deny their relevance in his famous confession to Sonia Marmeladov.

> I longed to kill without casuistry, to kill for my own benefit, and for that alone! I would not lie about it even to myself! I did not commit the murder to help my mother—that's rubbish! I did not even commit murder in order to use the profit and the power I gained to make myself a benefactor to humanity. Rubbish! I simply murdered; I murdered for myself, for myself alone, and whether I became a benefactor to anybody else, or, like a spider, spent the rest of my life catching everybody in my web and sucking the life-blood out of them, should have been a matter of complete indifference to me at that moment! [3]

Dostoevsky introduces the last extenuating red herring in the insanity defense used by Raskolnikov's lawyers in the epilogue, who argue that since Raskolnikov did not count the stolen money, he must have committed the murder in a state of temporary insanity.

> They spent a long time trying to discover why the accused should be lying in this one particular [of course Raskolnikov was telling the truth], when he so freely and accurately acknowledged his guilt in every other respect. In the end, some of them (especially some who were psychologists) even admitted the possibility that he really did not know what was in the purse because he had hidden it under the stone without looking inside it, but from this they concluded that the crime itself could have been committed only in a state of temporary mental derangement, so to speak, as the result of homicidal mania expressed in murder and robbery for their own sakes, *without motive and calculation*. This conclusion coincided happily with the latest fashionable theory of temporary insanity, which our contemporaries so often try to apply to various criminals. (452; 6: 410-11; italics mine)

Whereas the lawyers argue that Raskolnikov committed the murder without calculation and motive, the novel not only reveals Raskolnikov's calculation, it devotes hundreds of pages to his motivation. Dostoevsky brings up the argument of temporary insanity at the end to ridicule it.[4] We know that Raskolnikov was not temporarily insane. Moreover, what Raskolnikov needs least is an explanation of his behavior that relieves him of the responsibility for what he has done, especially since he cannot achieve redemption without acknowledging his complete responsibility for his crime. Throughout the novel, and through a large section of the epilogue, Raskolnikov, completely unrepentant, continues to dissociate himself from the murder.

> But although he judged himself severely, his lively conscience could find no particularly terrible guilt in his past, except a simple *blunder*, that might have happened to anybody. He was ashamed precisely because he, Raskolnikov, had perished so blindly and hopelessly, with such dumb stupidity, by some decree of blind fate, and must humble himself and submit to the "absurdity" of that decree, if he wished to find any degree of peace. (458; 6: 417).

Raskolnikov thinks that he can find peace if he submits to a senseless decree, but Dostoevsky shows that Raskolnikov's resentful submission to blind fate is the very antithesis of what he must do in order to achieve spiritual renewal. Only when he begins to understand—through his frequent nightmares—the logical implications of his actions and his own responsibility for these actions, does Dostoevsky imply that Raskolnikov has turned the corner, that he has entered upon that slow path toward spiritual rebirth. We learn in the last paragraph of the novel that Raskolnikov's resurrection from the dead, however miraculous, will nevertheless be a slow and gradual process; every step of the way entails great suffering. This is the story that Dostoevsky promises to tell but never does.

> But that is the beginning of a new story, the story of the gradual renewal of a man, of his gradual regeneration, of his slow progress from one world to another, of how he learned to know a hitherto undreamed-of reality. All that might be the subject of a new tale, but our present one is ended. (465; 6:422)

II.

After Dostoevsky completed *Crime and Punishment* in 1866, he did not deal again in depth with the question of redemption—and especially its relationship to crime, insanity, and responsibility—until the Kornilova case, which was tried in 1876. Right before the Kornilova case, Dostoevsky had waxed indignant in the pages of *The Diary of a Writer* over two court trials (the Kroneberg and Kairova cases) in which he believed the jury, by acquitting obviously guilty defendants, not only failed to do its legal duty, but contributed to undermining the moral foundations of Russian society.[5] When he read about the upcoming trial of Ekaterina Kornilova, a recently married twenty-year-old woman who threw her six-year-old step-daughter out of a fourth-story window (the child miraculously sustained no physical injuries), he immediately anticipated an even greater judicial outrage: Kornilova's acquittal.

Dostoevsky imagines that the defense of Kornilova will closely resemble those of Kroneberg and Kairova. The lawyer will undoubtedly show that Kornilova committed no crime; even worse, that she was justified in defenestrating the child, for it was in fact the child who was at fault. Dostoevsky admits that he is drawing a caricature, but given the example of the Kroneberg and Kairova cases, the caricature cannot, he implies, be far from the truth.

> By the way, I imagine how advocates will be defending that stepmother: we shall hear about the helplessness of her situation, and about the fact that she is a recent bride of a widower whom she married under compulsion or force, or by mistake. We shall have pictures drawn portraying the miserable existence of destitute people, their never-ending work. She, the naive, the innocent, believed when she married, an inexperienced little girl (particularly under our system of upbringing!) that married life brings nothing but joys—and here instead of them—washing of dirty linen, cooking, bathing the child: "Gentlemen of the jury, it is only natural that she started hating the child (who knows, maybe there will appear a 'defense lawyer' who will begin to smear the child and will find in a six-year-old girl some bad and hideous qualities!)—in a moment of despair, in a state of madness, almost without remembering herself, seized the girl, and. . . . Gentlemen of the jury, who among you wouldn't have done the same thing? Who among you wouldn't have thrown the child out of the window?"[6]

But while imagining the possible grotesque rationalizations of Kornilova's defense lawyer (the child was at fault!), Dostoevsky senses something "fantastic" about the case and postulates that there might, indeed, have been extenuating circumstances, circumstances that should bear on the sentence, if not on the crime itself. In fact, not long after her conviction (Kornilova was sentenced to two years and eight months of hard labor in Siberia), Dostoevsky wrote an article in *The Diary of a Writer* contesting the court's decision. The article played an important role in the nullification of Kornilova's conviction and in her later acquittal at a second trial.[7]

Since Dostoevsky had taken a very strong stand against child abuse in the Kroneberg case, he was acutely aware of the risk he was taking in defending Kornilova. Would he not be fostering in the minds of his readers the same confusion about crime—that is, about good and evil—that he himself had so recently denounced in the pages of the *Diary*? But once Dostoevsky sees that Kornilova is sincerely contrite, that she abhors her act, and that she accepts full responsibility before God and the community for her crime, Dostoevsky immediately changes gears. The focus of attention shifts from the castigation of the legal system and its tolerance of crime to the possibility of redemption, or in Dostoevskian maximalist terms, of resurrection from the dead.

The first of the four pieces Dostoevsky wrote about the Kornilova trial was so successful that it resulted in the rescinding of Kornilova's conviction and a retrial. The prosecutor and the presiding justice announced publicly at the retrial that, as Dostoevsky states, "the first verdict was quashed precisely because of my suggestion in the *Diary* that 'the act of the criminal woman may have been prompted by her pregnant state'" (914; 26: 92). Further, Dostoevsky started to visit Kornilova in prison about once a month after the conviction, and he visited Kornilova and her husband at their home after the acquittal at her second trial.

To justify his call for acquittal by reason of pregnancy—or "insanity without insanity"—Dostoevsky briefly outlines Kornilova's situation at home and her actions directly after the crime. Her relationship with her husband right before the crime had become especially strained. He had beaten her in front of her relatives two days earlier for not having returned one night from a family gathering. They had not talked for two days. When her husband went out to work on the third day, she fed and dressed her stepdaughter. Then, in a sudden vindictive impulse, she told the child to go to the window to look for something and then pushed her out. Kornilova did not even look out the window to see what happened to the girl, but immediately went to the police station to confess the crime. She told the police that she had contemplated committing the crime the night before because of malice towards her husband. She pleaded guilty, making no attempt to defend herself.

As Dostoevsky emphasizes, Kornilova could easily have gotten away with the crime had she wanted to. She was conscious of what she was doing, but she was herself amazed by what she had done. As she later explained to Dostoevsky during one of his visits, it was as if she were two women: "I wanted to do that evil thing, but it was as though it were not my will to do so, but someone else's," and "I didn't want to go to the police station at all, but somehow I arrived there, I don't know why, and then I confessed to everything" (531; 24: 39). Dostoevsky's explanation of Kornilova's strange behavior was that Kornilova, who was in the fourth month of her pregnancy, was subject to an admittedly rare pathological compulsion, "an insanity without insanity" (*sumasshestvie bez sumasshestviia*) (534; 24: 43) caused by her pregnancy.[8] Even had she not experienced these pathological inclinations, she might, to be sure, have thought about doing harm to the child to get back at her husband, but she certainly would not have thrown the child from the window. Dostoevsky does not insist that Kornilova experienced this pregnancy-induced pathological state when she committed the crime, but that she *may* have; and that if she may have, then the jury should give her the benefit of the doubt and—despite her crime—acquit her, this time, out of mercy.

> It is well known that during pregnancy a woman (especially with her first child) is subject to strange influences and impressions which strangely and fantastically affect her mind and spirit. The influences, at times—however, in rare cases only—assume extraordinary, abnormal, almost absurd, forms. But what does it matter if this occurs rarely (i.e., as exceptional phenomena)? In the present case, to those who had to decide upon the fate of a human being, it should have been sufficient that such phenomena do occur, and even only that they may occur. (461; 23: 138)

Dostoevsky visited Kornilova in prison, partly on the request of the official from the Ministry of Justice who had interceded for her, but also to find out whether Kornilova was the woman he imagined her to be, for only if she was could he justify his advocacy of her cause. In other words, he needed to know if Kornilova's condition when she committed the crime really was an aberration of pregnancy. Dostoevsky was pleased with his first impressions of Kornilova. She turned out to be a simple woman (*prostodushnaia*) with an intelligent face. Although during the first visit she was still enervated by her recent childbirth and shaken by the guilty verdict, she answered all of Dostoevsky's questions about the crime forthrightly. "She fully confessed that she was a criminal guilty of everything of which she had been accused" (531; 24: 39) and showed no bitterness towards her husband. But Dostoevsky was equally impressed by the testimony of the prison guards and the assistant warden. The assistant warden, in whom Kornilova had aroused considerable sympathy, confided to Dostoevsky that a dramatic change had taken place in Kornilova after she had been in prison for two weeks: she had become an altogether different creature. Whereas on arrival she had been coarse, rude, spiteful and wicked-tongued, she soon became kind-hearted, open, and meek. Kornilova's dramatic change played an important role in her acquittal at the second trial. The prison guards, who had been with Kornilova every day for a long time, confirmed the warden's testimony. They had come to know the real Kornilova, the real self who returned after the temporary aberration induced by pregnancy. The real Kornilova, as Dostoevsky had hoped, proved worthy of vindication because she demonstrated the potential for moral and spiritual regeneration; the real Kornilova was not the malicious woman who had entered prison, but a good, kindhearted, and meek woman who merited a second chance.

At first, Dostoevsky's use of the insanity defense would seem in flagrant contradiction to his views on crime and responsibility. It is surprising to see Dostoevsky defending a woman accused of child abuse, but even more surprising to see him resorting to temporary insanity as a major part of his argument for acquittal. Dostoevsky interceded for Kornilova not only because he thought her to be temporarily insane and because he believed that she was basically a good person, but because she recognized what she had done was a crime, accepted her punishment, and showed true contrition. She went immediately to the police and made a complete confession; she never tried to defend her action. In addition she understood that she alone had to take complete responsibility for her sins before God and her fellow man and that the community had every right to punish her severely. After her conviction, she had accepted her punishment as just. For Dostoevsky, then, Kornilova turns out to be worthy of compassion and forgiveness, and therefore, of acquittal; she seems to be the good soil on which the proverbial seed needs to fall, a woman whose acknowledged crime and repentance make her ripe for spiritual rebirth, for resurrection from the dead. If she is such a one, a conviction can only be the antithesis of Christian justice, for it will deprive her of the chance radically to change her life, to be reborn for herself and her family. Once the social issue has been satisfactorily resolved by Kornilova's confession, it is the duty of the court to deal with the equally important religious duty of sowing the seeds of mercy essential to the salvation of an errant soul. As Dostoevsky says: "Of two possible errors, it is far better to err on the side of mercy" (462-3; 23: 139).

Kornilova seems at times to dissociate herself from the crime, to look upon the person who committed the crime as not herself, as another being, even an alien being, who took possession of her soul against her will, a being against whom, at that crucial moment, she was absolutely helpless. Dostoevsky himself occasionally gives the impression that the Kornilova who committed the crime was, as it were, not the real Kornilova, but another Kornilova, a temporary aberration, an aberration that would probably never return. He cites the testimony of the prison warden and guards about Kornilova's radical transformation after childbirth in order to show that the real Kornilova in no way resembles the woman who threw her step-daughter out of the window. But Dostoevsky maintains this dissociation between the actions and character of the two Kornilovas only metaphorically and rhetorically, as a way of emphasizing the radical disjunction in Kornilova's behavior and the improbability that Kornilova will commit another crime if acquitted. Dostoevsky obviously cannot at one and the same time maintain that she who committed the crime is not the real Kornilova and maintain that the real Kornilova must take responsibility for the crime that was committed. If, in effect, another person committed the crime, if Kornilova merely provided the physical container for an alien presence, she could not be responsible for committing the crime.[9]

Dostoevsky ultimately argues that the self that committed the crime and the self that dissociated itself from the crime both belong to Kornilova. She is no less responsible in the end for the actions of her "temporary evil self" than for the actions of her more regular good self. The bad self is no less Kornilova's true self than her good self; it is the self that came out as a result of conditions that Dostoevsky argues were beyond her control. Though Dostoevsky maintains that Kornilova cannot be held as responsible in the same way—at least in terms of punishment—as she would and should have been had she not been pregnant, he also implies that only he and the court can and should look at her crime in this fashion: on the contrary, Kornilova must see herself as completely responsible for what she did. In fact, the court must make this distinction between the two Kornilovas only on the condition that Kornilova herself does not, that she continues to consider herself a criminal, to take responsibility for her actions, and to ask forgiveness publicly of the community against which she has sinned. She must accept the self that committed the crime as her self, as a self for all of whose actions she personally must take responsibility. For only when Kornilova takes responsibility for her actions can the court have any confidence that the good Kornilova is the truer—or less aberrant—self, and that there will be no recurrence of the crime. To reason otherwise would mean that temporary insanity could be used to explain and extenuate all crimes, since all crimes could obviously be ascribed to a bad self that was temporarily overcome by a superior force. Paradoxically, the only way that the court can permit the temporary insanity defense is if the perpetrator refuses to accept temporary insanity as an explanation of her behavior, if she assumes responsibility for the action committed when she was temporarily insane.

But if criminals refuse to acknowledge that what they have done is really a crime, and thus remain unrepentant, then it becomes the duty of the court to proclaim officially that a crime has indeed been committed and to make the perpetrator accountable for it. In such a case, if the temporary insanity defense is used successfully to acquit a guilty defendant—in contrast to its use in the Kornilova case—it leads to both a personal and social miscarriage of justice. First, it sends the wrong message to society about responsibility for wrongdoing, blurring the distinction between right and wrong. Secondly, since it does not encourage those who have committed crimes to acknowledge their culpability, it makes spiritual regeneration virtually impossible. In fact, Dostoevsky implies, the court can only make judicious use of the temporary insanity defense, as in the Kornilova case, in inverse proportion to defendants' acknowledgment of their personal responsibility for their crimes and their desire to ask forgiveness of the community against which they have sinned.

Thus, the Kornilova case shows Dostoevsky taking his dialectic of responsibility and redemption to a much more extreme conclusion than he did in *Crime and Punishment*. In *Crime and Punishment*, the narrator carefully constructs "extenuating circumstances," and he notes that the temporary insanity defense had something to do with the amelioration of Raskolnikov's sentence. But the novel undermines these excuses. It is not the author, or narrator, who argues for extenuating circumstances—and therefore diminished responsibility—but Raskolnikov, the determinists (Dostoevsky's ideological enemies), and the shallow psychologist-lawyers at Raskolnikov's trial. The Kornilova case, however, presents a very different situation, because now Dostoevsky himself argues for the possibility of diminished capacity—therefore diminished responsibility—for his "client." He not only does not scoff at temporary insanity but employs temporary insanity as the grounds for acquittal. At the same time, he paradoxically predicates Kornilova's acquittal and redemption on her taking responsibility for an action for which she was not completely responsible.

Though Dostoevsky takes a hard line on responsibility in *Crime and Punishment*, the category itself is not logically problematic. The main obstacle to Raskolnikov's moral regeneration is his refusal to take responsibility for a murder for which he was entirely responsible. In contrast to Raskolnikov, Kornilova is less responsible for what she had done, but, as we have seen, this does not relieve her of the necessity of taking full responsibility for her acts if she wishes to achieve redemption. By diminishing Kornilova's responsibility and then insisting on her taking full responsibility for her actions, Dostoevsky underscores the irrational nature of the categories of responsibility and redemption. Thus, if in *Crime and Punishment*, Dostoevsky created a convincing case of extenuating circumstances in order to show the indefensibility of murder under any conditions, in the Kornilova case he argued for diminished capacity in order to show that there are no conditions under which responsibility can be dismissed or denied without sacrificing the possibility of redemption. Dostoevsky does not see responsibility as a logical category, but rather as a mystical one—though no less existential for that—one which demands faith not logical consistency. Our assertion of responsibility in the teeth of the evidence to the contrary is an absolute necessity for moral being, human intercourse, even for self-definition.

Critics have often seen Raskolnikov as a personality split in two: he has a more spontaneous, emotional side (his better self) and a more rational, calculating, intellectual side (his lesser self). Raskolnikov, whose name suggests not an equal split but a division into many different—too many—selves, is threatened throughout the novel with complete dissolution of self.[10] As Dostoevsky showed in *The Double*, the projection of responsibility onto an alien self leads to the dissolution of personality, madness, and damnation. The only way that Raskolnikov can prevent this dissolution is by assuming responsibility for his criminal actions. Dostoevsky implicitly presents responsibility as the major power that we possess for self-integration, for reconstituting the self as an agent, and for overcoming the view of the self as a loosely integrated complex of memories and states of consciousness determined primarily by social forces beyond our control. An integrated self, a self to which we can attribute agency, is not a natural phenomenon, but a free and active creation of the individual, a voluntary assumption of responsibility for all one's actions past and present. For Dostoevsky, at least, the self comes to be a true self only through the assumption of responsibility.[11]

3.

Dostoevsky's portrayal of Dmitry Karamazov in *The Brothers Karamazov* represents the final stage in his mystical expansion of the category of responsibility. But he not only gives responsibility an even more explicitly mystical grounding, he transforms it into the moral counterpoint to Ivan Karamazov's extreme relativism, expressed in his formula of "all is permitted." Dmitry Karamazov does not even commit the crime, the murder of his father, Fedor Karamazov, but nonetheless he is supposed to assume the responsibility for the deed.

Engaged in a bitter rivalry with his father over the woman he loved (Grushenka), Dmitry had often threatened to kill his father in the presence of witnesses. On one occasion, he even violently assaulted him; had his brothers, Ivan and Alesha, not interceded, Dmitry would have beaten him to death. There is no question that Dmitry had murder in his heart. On the night of the murder, Dmitry admits that he was within a hair's breadth of actually killing his father and that it was a miracle that he did not kill him: something held him back at the very last moment, something that permitted him to overcome an almost overwhelming hatred of his father: "'God was watching over me then,'" and "'whether it was someone's tears, or my mother prayed to God, or a good angel kissed me at that instant, I don't know. But the devil was conquered. I rushed from the window and ran to the fence.'"[12] Given his well-known rivalry with his father, his oft stated intentions to kill him, his physical assaults, and the extremely incriminating evidence fabricated against Dmitry by the real killer, his half brother Smerdiakov, we should hardly be surprised by the guilty verdict. The jury, obviously, does not know and has no way of ascertaining the facts. Dmitry's lawyer, Fetiukovich, gives a fairly accurate description of what really happened, but it is only one of the scenarios he presents; besides the jurors profoundly mistrust him. Dmitry, to be sure, knows much of what happened, but for obvious reasons he is an unreliable witness. Though Dostoevsky hardly views the jury trial as a satisfactory means of ascertaining truth, he presents the jury's verdict as probably the best decision it could have made under the circumstances—especially when it is seen in light of some of the negatively portrayed courtroom sentiment for Dmitry's acquittal.

The Brothers Karamazov is not real life; it is a novel, in which, as in all his other novels, Dostoevsky imposes extreme conditions in order to carry out his moral experiments: for Dostoevsky, in contrast to Chekhov (any fool can be a hero), character and truth are revealed only *in extremis*. He sets up Dmitry's trial in a way that does not admit of a compromise or middle position. In the Kornilova case, Dostoevsky had to deal with the material that was given to him, and in effect he worked out a compromise in the middle ground; he even argued against a relatively light sentence of two and a half years for attempted homicide. Even Raskolnikov faced only seven years of prison for two brutal murders, one of which was a text-book case of premeditation. But in *The Brothers Karamazov*, Dostoevsky can more easily mold the moral issue by presenting us with an either/or at the extremes: Dmitry must be acquitted, that is set free as innocent of all charges, or be sent to the mines in Siberia for a period of not less than twenty years: in reality for a crime that he did not commit. One can blame Dostoevsky for setting up such stark alternatives or the Russian legal system for not permitting a lesser sentence for the crime with which Dmitry is charged. We cannot know how Dostoevsky would have argued for or against Dmitry were he a journalist writing an article on an actual case. But it seems that in *The Brothers Karamazov*, Dostoevsky was determined not to be bound by the facts of an already existing case, as he was in Kornilova. Kornilova was the incentive to revisit the issues of responsibility and redemption, *The Brothers Karamazov* to take the Kornilova case to its extreme conclusions.

Many aspects of Dmitry's trial, the concluding and longest section of *The Brothers Karamazov*, are the quintessence of farce, especially the section dealing with temporary insanity. Dostoevsky goes over the same ground as he had with Raskolnikov, and in far greater detail, but with, of course, one very important difference: Dmitry is not the murderer. In contrast to the Kornilova case where all the experts agreed in their assessment of temporary insanity—and were lavishly praised by Dostoevsky for, in effect, concurring with his opinion—in *The Brothers Karamazov*, the three medical experts called to assess Dmitry's psychological state at the time of the crime, radically disagree, and disagree in the most ridiculous manner. They largely base their assessment of Dmitry's mental health on the direction of his glance as he first entered the court room.

The famous Moscow doctor whom Katerina Ivanovna calls in to take care of the severely depressed and hallucinative Ivan Karamazov maintains, in effect, that Dmitry was temporarily insane when the murder was committed.

> The Moscow doctor, being questioned in his turn, definitely and emphatically repeated that he considered the defendant's mental condition abnormal "in the highest degree." He talked at length and with erudition of "aberration" and "mania," and argued that, from all the facts collected, the defendant had undoubtedly been in a condition of aberration for several days before his arrest, and, if the crime had been committed by him, it must, even if he were conscious of it, have been almost involuntary, as he had not the power to control the morbid impulse that possessed him. (638; 15: 104)

Dostoevsky makes the Moscow doctor's testimony look even more ridiculous by having him argue that Dmitry's inability to speak of the three thousand rubles (that he believed his father owed him) constituted the main indication of this mania and that Dmitry's looking ahead rather than to the right at his attorney, "on whose help all his hopes rest and on whose defense all his future depends" indicated his "abnormal mental condition" (639; 15: 104-5). The local doctor, Herzenstube, who also maintains that the "abnormality of the defendant's mental faculties was self-evident" (637-38; 15: 103), bases his argument on Dmitry's looking forward instead of to the left "where, among the public, the ladies were sitting, seeing that he was a great admirer of the fair sex and must be thinking much of what the ladies are saying about him now" (638; 15: 103-04). The third doctor, Dr. Varvinsky, predictably argues not only for Dmitry's sanity, but partly bases his argument on Dmitry's looking straight ahead. "So that it was just by looking straight before him that he showed his perfectly normal state of mind at the present" (639; 15: 105). Dostoevsky takes the ridiculous to the absurd by trotting out psychological theories that attempt to explain a murder that the defendant did not commit.

If the arguments on temporary insanity are absurd because Dmitry did not commit the murder, so are the arguments for extenuating circumstances, although Dostoevsky presents them much more seriously.[13] Dmitry's own attorney, Fetiukovich, makes the argument for extenuating circumstances (he also takes a brief half-hearted stab at the temporary insanity defense as well)[14] not because he believes his client is guilty—though he actually does—but because he fears that the evidence, however much it cuts both ways, will not favor his client in the end. In his closing argument, Fetiukovich denies that Dmitry killed his father, but presents the jury with a hypothetical situation in which Dmitry actually wielded the weapon that resulted in his father's death but still could not be held responsible for murder, especially parricide. We have seen this argument before—in the Kornilova case—but, of course, in a radically different, and more positive, guise: responsibility without responsibility. Fetiukovich, in effect, argues that Fedor Karamazov was responsible for his own death. He maintains that the law of "Provoke not your children to wrath" is a higher law than thou shalt not kill thy father. Moreover, since Fedor Karamazov was not a real father, but a monster, even an enemy to his children, then Dmitry not only did not kill his father, but the man that he did kill, if he indeed did kill him, was responsible for provoking his own murder. What could one expect a son to do in a moment of rage when confronted by such a father? One can't, after all, throw nature out of the window.

> "Let the son stand before his father and ask him, 'Father, tell me, why must I love you? Father, show me that I must love you,' and if that father is able to answer him and show him good reason, we have a real, normal, parental relation, not resting on mystical prejudice, but on a rational, responsible and strictly humanitarian basis. But if he does not, there's an end to the family tie. He is not a father to him, and the son has a right to look upon him as a stranger, and even an enemy. Our tribune, gentlemen of the jury, ought to be a school of true and sound ideas. . . . Such a murder is not a parricide. No, the murder of such a father cannot be called parricide. Such a murder can only be reckoned parricide by prejudice." (708-10; 15: 171-72)

By creating such a speech for Dmitry's defense attorney, Dostoevsky drives the experimental conditions to even greater extremes. For an acquittal now has tremendous social as well as personal ramifications. To acquit Dmitry, on Fetiukovich's terms, is tantamount to proclaiming publicly that parricide is not parricide under certain conditions; that crime is not crime; and that in the end everything is permissible because a way can be found to justify it in terms of circumstance and context. Since Dostoevsky presents Dmitry's trial almost as though it were the major Russian trial of the century (it is being covered by all the major newspapers and viewed by the lawyers as vehicles to advance their political agendas—the Simpson trial in America would be the closest analogue), the fate of Russia herself seems at stake. Dostoevsky, too, who shows the personal fate of Dmitry unfortunately overshadowed by all the other political, social, and judicial aspects of the trial, cannot ignore the tremendous implications of Dmitry's acquittal for Russian society.

The Brothers Karamazov presents universal responsibility (that everyone is guilty—and thus responsible—before everyone else for everyone and for everything; *vsiakii pred vsemi za vsekh za vse vinovat*, 14:262) as the antithesis to Fetiukovich's (and Ivan Karamazov's) moral relativism. Universal responsibility is not a rationally deducible idea or doctrine in *The Brothers Karamazov*, it can be learned only through traumatic life-changing experiences, often of a clearly mystical nature. Father Zosima, Father Zosima's brother, Alesha Karamazov, Dmitry Karamazov, and Ivan Karamazov all undergo such experiences, of which the most paradigmatic is Alesha Karamazov's mystical vision of universal harmony, which he experiences during the vigil over Father Zosima's body. Alesha does not understand rationally why we must love each other, but knows and feels that it must be so: his religious ecstasy and rapture provide a validation higher than reason.

> The silence of earth seemed to melt into the silence of the heavens. The mystery of earth was one with the mystery of the stars. . . . Alesha stood, gazed, and as though mown down, fell to the ground.
>
> He did not know why he embraced it. He could not have told why he longed so irresistibly to kiss it, to kiss it all. But he kissed it weeping, sobbing and watering it with his tears, and vowed passionately to love it, to love it forever and ever. "Water the earth with the tears of your joy and love those tears," echoed in his soul. What was he weeping over? Oh! in his rapture he was weeping even over those stars, which were shining to him from the abyss of space, and "he was not ashamed of that ecstasy." There seemed to be threads from all those innumerable worlds of God, linking his soul to them, and it was trembling all over "in contact with other worlds." He longed to forgive everyone and for everything, and to beg forgiveness. Oh, not for himself, but for all men, for all and for everything. "And others are praying for me too," echoed again in his soul. But with every instant he felt clearly and, as it were, tangibly, that something firm and unshakable as that vault of heaven had entered into his soul. It was as though some idea had seized the sovereignty of his mind—and it was for all his life and forever and ever. He had fallen on the earth a weak youth, but he rose up a resolute champion, and he knew and felt it suddenly at the very moment of his ecstasy. And never, never, all his life long, could Alesha forget that minute. "Someone visited my soul in that hour," he used to say afterwards, with implicit faith in his words.

> Within three days he left the monastery in accordance with the words of his elder, who had bidden him to "sojourn in the world." (340-1; 14: 328. Alyosha, the transliteration used in this translation, has been silently changed to Alesha in all quotations to conform to my practice in my text.)

Dmitry's imminent indictment on charges of parricide motivates his dreams of the starving babes (Richard Peace calls the dream the expression of Dmitry's parricidal guilt)[15] in which Dmitry implicitly acknowledges his responsibility not only for the death of his father, which he wished and willed, and for which he prepared the ground, but for all suffering, in particular for starving peasant mothers and their innocent children. In the notebooks, Dostoevsky links Dmitry's dream with Alesha's mystical vision (Mochulsky 593-4):

> "Why are they so dark from black misery? Why don't they feed the babe?"

> And he felt that, though his questions were unreasonable and senseless, yet he wanted to ask just that, and he had to ask it just in that way. And he felt also that a passion of pity, such as he had never known before, was rising in his heart, and he wanted to cry, that he wanted to do something for them all, so that the babe should weep no more, so that the dark-faced, dried-up mother should not weep, that no one should shed tears again from that moment, and he wanted to do it at once, at once, regardless of all obstacles, with all the Karamazov recklessness. (479; 14: 456-7)

Dmitry explicates the meaning of this dream to Alesha on the day before the trial:

> Why was it I dreamed of that "babe" at such a moment? "Why is the babe so poor?" That was a sign to me at that moment. It's for the babe I'm going. Because we are all responsible for all. For all the "babes." . . . I go for all, because someone must go for all. I didn't kill father, but I've got to go. I accept it. It's all come to me here, here, within these peeling walls [that is, in prison]. (560; 15: 31)

As we have seen with Raskolnikov, a character must heed his visions and dreams (especially nightmares) if he hopes to achieve salvation. This romantic view undergirds Dmitry's stark choices at the end of *The Brothers Karamazov*: freedom in America or suffering and incarceration in Russia. In *Crime and Punishment*, Raskolnikov was offered the choice between two diametrically opposite paths—again no middle ground was available—the amoral path of Svidrigailov and the path of suffering and redemption offered by Sonia—which of course involved confession and incarceration in Siberia. In *The Brothers Karamazov*, Dostoevsky presents Dmitry with, at least in this one respect, a very similar choice: there is the path of the moral relativism of Fetiukovich (and thus the path of the Grand Inquisitor) or the path of Father Zosima (an obvious analogue of Dmitry), who propounds a philosophy of mutual and universal responsibility.

Just as in the Kornilova case, in *The Brothers Karamazov*, Dostoevsky differentiates between the social and the personal. It was the responsibility for the Kornilova jury first to make sure that crime was proclaimed as crime. Acquittal could be contemplated only when the criminal took upon herself full responsibility for what she had done, when she confessed before the whole community that what she had done was a crime. In *The Brothers Karamazov*, the jury, if it believes that Dmitry committed the crime, has the duty to proclaim that crime as crime, that parricide is more than an unfortunate prejudice. To do otherwise would be to commit a crime equal to the one they thought Dmitry had committed in murdering his father.

But does the social justice of the conviction coincide with personal justice? Is a conviction really the best outcome for Dmitry? Could a twenty-year sentence for a crime he did not commit really be in Dmitry's best interest? Neither of his brothers, Ivan and Alesha, thinks so. Nor do the women he loves, Katerina Ivanovna and Grushenka. Hingley blithely comments that "Dmitry is not afraid of twenty years in the mines,"[16] but in reality Dmitry himself is deeply divided about what would be in his best interest. Some critics formulaically emphasize that Dmitry must suffer for his sins and the sins of others and leave the matter at that.[17] But neither Dmitry nor Dostoevsky leaves it there. To be sure, as we have seen above, Dmitry feels that he must act upon his dream and go to Siberia in order to suffer and thereby atone for sin—his sins and the sins of others. And he understands that going to America is an escape not only from suffering but also from the possibility of salvation.

> But on the other hand, my conscience? I would have run away from suffering. A
> sign has come, I reject the sign. I have a way of salvation and I turn my back on
> it. Ivan says that in America, "with good inclinations" I can be of more use than
> underground [that is, forced labor in the mines of Siberia]. But what becomes of
> our hymn from underground? What's America? America is vanity again! And
> there's a lot of swindling in America, too, I expect. I would have run away from
> crucifixion! (564; 15: 34)[18]

But in the very same passage Dmitry tells Alesha that he definitely plans to go to America with
Grushenka and that if he would be sent to Siberia without Grushenka, he would not be able to
survive. (Dostoevsky unambiguously shows in the epilogue of *Crime and Punishment* that
without Sonia's presence in Siberia, Raskolnikov would have had little chance of any moral or
spiritual regeneration.) "And without Grusha what would I do there underground with a
hammer? I would only smash my skull with the hammer!" (564) Something of course that he
had intended to do to his father because of Grushenka. Of course, he did not smash his father's
head, and he may not smash his own head in Siberia without Grushenka; but we are speaking
here not about what may or may not happen, but Dmitry's own view of both what he is capable
of doing and what he ought to do. Moreover, In Dmitry's last scene, Dmitry dwells on his plans
of escaping to America with Grushenka: it will be hard for him there, but being without
Grushenka in Siberia is completely unimaginable and he knows that the authorities will not
permit Grushenka to travel to Siberia with him. He also confesses that there are other things
about Siberia which make him believe that "I have not the strength to bear it" (723; 15: 185).

The idea that Dmitry is incapable of bearing his suffering in Siberia derives directly from
the Grand Inquisitor's view of the weakness of the common man, and Ivan, the main engineer
of the escape, had Dmitry specifically in mind in the Grand Inquisitor's contemptuous portrait
of common humanity. In other words, in acceding to Ivan's plans for escape to America,
Dmitry would implicitly accept Ivan's depreciative definition of Dmitry's abilities and
potential. Indeed, a good many critics, although a minority, have viewed Dmitry's resolve to
suffer in Siberia with some skepticism. R. P. Blackmur emphasizes the ephemerality of
Dmitry's dreams and intentions, comparing Dmitry's dream of the babe unfavorably ("a lower
version") with Alesha's dream of Christ at Cana. "Dmitri is one of those for whom rebirth is
not permanent, but only a deeper form of a New Year's resolution . . . an onion for the
moment."[19] Ronald Hingley implies that for Dmitry to suffer twenty years in prison so defies
common sense that not only will Dmitry have to escape to America but that Dostoevsky is wise
to give Dmitry that way out (213). And Nathan Rosen, despite his relatively favorable
presentation of Dmitry's moral ideal, states that Dmitry "may instead accept the unheroic
destiny urged by Alesha of escaping with Grushen'ka to America. Dostoevskii leaves this
deliberately open as if he could not come to a decision himself."[20]

Dostoevsky does not unequivocally say it would be in Dmitry's interest to bear his cross
in Siberia, but he strongly suggests it in the way he shapes Dmitry's alternatives. Although
Dmitry does not think that he can bear his cross, Dmitry understands that America really
represents escape from his responsibility and the loss of salvation.[21] And Dostoevsky compels
Dmitry to confront the casuistry of the argument for escape when he has, of all people, Alesha
play the role of the Grand Inquisitor, arguing that Dmitry must escape to America because he
is not yet ready for "such a cross." Dmitry immediately senses Alesha playing the role of the
Jesuit, and when confronted by Dmitry on this point, Alesha must confess: "'That's how the
Jesuits talk, isn't it? Just as we are doing?' 'Yes,' Alesha smiled gently" (723-4).[22] Dostoevsky
is implying that Dmitry will begin to understand existentially the justness of his punishment
only after years of initial bitterness and despair. But eventually, as the notes to the novel imply,
"he will get used to it." Dostoevsky provides Dmitry a choice without a real choice. He can
escape to America, but he cannot escape to America and save his soul; that he can do only in
Siberia, in Russia. Can Dmitry, who is of the earth, the Russian earth, Dostoevsky's
quintessential prototype of Russianness, save himself in America?

Raskolnikov's crime was premeditated. Kornilova committed a crime possibly when
mentally incapacitated. Dmitry did not even commit the crime.[23] But until Dmitry
acknowledges his responsibility for the crime and accepts it as his own and suffers for it, he,
too, can never achieve spiritual redemption. To a Fetiukovich—and to most of us—this would

be a mystical understanding of responsibility that should be left not only out of court but out of real life. Though Dostoevsky probably doubts whether the mystical could ever become a part of the secular court, he tries to show that it can be eliminated from real life only with dehumanizing consequences for all of us.[24] What the court must do and what is best for the individual may not coincide, for what is truth and justice in the social realm is not necessarily truth and justice for the individual. A decision of the court may be justice or a miscarriage of justice (a judicial error) at one and the same time. That is why Dostoevsky presents the concordance of these two realms in the Kornilova case as a miracle, no less great than the unharmed child. Dostoevsky withheld that possibility, probably purposely, for the court in Dmitry's case. He needed to take the category of responsibility to its absolute—mystical— limit. The fate of Dmitry Karamazov provided him with that opportunity.

That Dostoevsky had probably projected this fate for Dmitry from the very beginning is revealed in the following notebook excerpt from 13 September 1874, which describes the time spent in prison by the older brother, the prototype for Dmitry. There are only two brothers in this scenario: the younger (who more resembles the "the mysterious visitor" from Father Zosima's reminiscences than either Alesha, Ivan, or Smerdiakov) falsifies evidence against the older brother, which results in the judicial error of the older brother's conviction.

> *Scene* in prison. They want to kill *him* [*ego khotiat ubit'*].
>
> Administration. He doesn't betray. The convicts swear fraternity to him. The Administrator reproves him for killing his father.
>
> Twelve years later the brother comes to see him. Scene, where *silently* they understand each other.
>
> Another seven years later, the younger brother has attained rank and station, but is tormented, splenetic, discloses to his wife that he killed him. "Why did you tell me?" He goes to his brother. The wife also runs to him.
>
> On her knees the wife asks the convict to remain silent, to save her husband. The convict says: "I've gotten used to it [*Ia privyk*]." They are reconciled. "You're punished even without that," the older says.
>
> The younger brother's birthday. Guests are gathered. He comes in: "I killed him." They think he has had a stroke.
>
> Ending: the other returns. The first at a transport point. He is being sent away. The younger asks the older to be a father to his children.
>
> "You have gone on the right path." (749: 15: 405)

Of course, we do not have to place this notebook plan on the same level as the novel, especially given its conflation of the younger brother and the mysterious stranger; but the older brother here is clearly Dmitry, who bears the same relationship to his father that he has in the final version: that is why it is possible for the younger brother to have evidence falsified against the older brother. But here Dostoevsky takes the story twenty years beyond that of *The Brothers Karamazov*. The older brother (Dmitry) has spent twenty years in prison for a murder he did not commit. He has forgiven his younger brother. He has taken the responsibility for the murder of his father upon himself, for himself, for his brother, for all those responsible for his father's death. Rather than being destroyed by his imprisonment and suffering, he has become purified by his experiences—although at the beginning, like Raskolnikov before him, and Dostoevsky himself in Siberia, he was extremely bitter. This is what the first two lines of the above passage signify: "*Scene* in prison. They want to kill *him*."[25] But *eventually*, he gets used to it (Dmitry's doubts about his strength to bear his cross do not determine the outcome of his imprisonment); he is able to bear his punishment and even forgive his brother.

We also need to remember that in *The Brothers Karamazov*, Dmitry Karamazov is more than an individual: he plays important social, symbolic, and even allegorical functions. The suffering that he must take upon himself derives as much from these larger suprapersonal roles that Dostoevsky imposes on him as his personal need to suffer for his past and take responsibility for it. As we have seen, Dostoevsky sees the court as the school from which the Russian people, recently liberated from serfdom, will derive their moral and spiritual education. There can be nothing worse for Russia at this time than for the court to send the message that "all is permitted." In addition, Dmitry becomes the son who must suffer for the sins of his class, the Russian nobility, and the sins of the past. He becomes a sacrificial offering—and here it important that he is not guilty of shedding his father's blood—taking the sins of others upon himself. By assuming responsibility for these sins and suffering for them, he gives not only himself but Russia the possibility of redemption—and salvation.[26] In *The Brothers Karamazov*, Dostoevsky obviously views the mystical realization of universal responsibility as an absolutely essential step toward spiritual regeneration, but it is only the initial stage in the process toward redemption: it is the turning point that the narrator proclaims at the end of *Crime and Punishment*. True responsibility is something that is achieved through the active process of suffering: its result is atonement, self-realization, being at one with oneself.[27]

Fetiukovich would look upon this "ancient" view of suffering and its relation to redemption as irrational and mystical, something that again belongs neither in the court nor in real life, but to Dostoevsky the mystery of redemptive suffering through the assumption of responsibility for one's fellow man lies at the heart of what it means to be human. It preserves for human beings a view of agency—no less, in the end, a mystical concept than responsibility—that makes possible the only moral world in which human beings, according to Dostoevsky, will consent to live. *The Brothers Karamazov*, therefore, quite consciously takes Dostoevsky's mystical view of responsibility and redemption, which we saw him working out in *Crime and Punishment* and the Kornilova case, to its extreme conclusions.

In *The Brothers Karamazov*, Dostoevsky anticipates the postmodern debate on the self and the possibilities of human agency. As usual, he is not arguing from ignorance of the existing and potential arguments on the other side. He, of course, may himself have had doubts about the mystical doctrine of responsibility and redemption—and they, too, find expression in *The Brothers Karamazov*—but when he examines the alternatives, Dmitry's choices—and Ivan's—he finds no other possibility for preserving man's moral universe. Given that all the empirical and rational choices, in his view, lead to the abyss, the antirational (or irrational) and metaphysical alternatives become our last hope.[28] Yet he also presents a practical as well as an idealistic argument about responsibility. On one hand it is a mystical category to which the only appropriate epistemological response is belief—or rather faith; on the other hand, if we want to preserve human agency and to give meaning to human action, it is practically, even logically, necessary: it is a truth that even the Grand Inquisitor, the agent of the devil, must concede.[29]

> In bread there was offered Thee an invincible banner; give bread, and man will worship Thee, for nothing is more certain than bread. But if someone else gains possession of his conscience—oh! then he will cast away Thy bread and follow after him who has ensnared his conscience. In that Thou wast right. For the secret of man's being is not only to live but to have something to live for. Without a stable conception of the object of life, man would not consent to go on living, and would rather destroy himself than remain on earth, though he had bread in abundance. (235; 14: 232).

Dostoevsky, *pace* his many disciples, wisely provides no real answers, only problematic alternatives. But all those who deal and struggle with the ideas of responsibility and redemption may find it worthwhile to visit—or revisit—perhaps the most brilliant, albeit mystical and antirational, dramatization of these problems in Western literature and culture. Dostoevsky can be a dangerous writer, a creator of utopian alternatives for redemption, but we ignore his deconstruction of the empirical and utilitarian ethics of responsibility at our own peril.

Notes

[1] In the earliest stages of thinking about *The Life of a Great Sinner*, Dostoevsky contemplated three to five independent short novels, whose combined length would equal that of *War and Peace*. See F. M. Dostoevskii, *Polnoe sobranie sochinenii*, ed. V. G. Bazanov et al., 30 vols. (Leningrad: Nauka, 1972-91), 29.1: 117-8. Hereafter this edition will be cited as *PSS*.

[2] Fyodor Dostoyevsky, *The House of the Dead*, trans. Constance Garnett (New York: Dell, 1959), 352; 4:32 All translations from Dostoevsky's works have been checked against the original texts in *PSS*. Russian pagination from the above edition will directly follow the English paginations. Other translations from the Russian are my own, unless otherwise indicated.

[3] Feodor Dostoevsky, *Crime and Punishment*, trans. Jessie Coulson (New York: Norton, 1975), 354; 6: 321-2.

[4] For a recent attempt to show that Raskolnikov was actually insane when he committed the crime and therefore should not have been convicted at all, see Dennis Whelan, "*Crime and Punishment*: The Missing Insanity Defense," in *O Rus!: Studia Litteraria Slavica in Honorem Hugh McLean*, ed. Simon Karlinsky, James L. Rice, and Barry P. Scherr (Oakland: Berkeley Slavic Specialties, 1995), 270-80.

[5] For an examination of Dostoevsky's use of the Kroneberg and Kornilova trials as means of excoriating the Western jury trial just introduced into Russia, see Gary Rosenshield, "The Imprisonment of the Law: Dostoevskij and the Kroneberg Case," *The Slavic and East European Journal* 36 (1992), 415-34; and "Western Law vs. Russian Justice: Dostoevsky and the Jury Trial, Round One," *Graven Images* 1 (1994), 117-35.

[6] All translations of passages from *The Diary of a Writer* are from F. M. Dostoievsky, *The Diary of a Writer*, trans. Boris Brasol (Santa Barbara: Peregrine Smith, 1979), 329; 23: 19.

[7] Dostoevsky eventually wrote four articles on Kornilova. For the English translations, see Dostoievsky, *The Diary of a Writer*, 459-65, 527-35, 691-92, 913-35. The pagination of the articles in the Academy edition is as follows: 23: 136-41, 24: 36-43, 25: 119-21, 26: 92-110.

[8] What is of most importance here is not the accuracy of Dostoevsky's analysis of Kornilova's "diminished capacity"—Dostoevsky himself admits that he may be wrong about that—but his moral reasoning.

[9] If we creatively interpret the fourth edition of *The Diagnostic and Statistical Manual of Mental Disorders* (Washington, D. C.: American Psychiatric Association, 1994), Kornilova could probably be said to have experienced an episode of autoscopic depersonalization disorder, a psychological condition in which subjects feel that they are watching their own physical and mental behavior as though it were the behavior of another person. In her book on criminal responsibility and multiple personality disorder (MPD)—or what is now called dissociative identity disorder—Elyn R. Saks (*Jekyll on Trial: Multiple Personality Disorder and Criminal Law* [New York: New York University Press, 1997]) argues that those suffering from depersonalization disorder should almost always be held accountable for their criminal actions; she maintains that multiples, in contrast, are almost always nonresponsible.

[10] Philip Rahv ("Dostoevsky in Crime and Punishment," *Partisan Review* 27.3 [1960], 393-425), among others, saw that in *Crime and Punishment* "we are dealing not with one but with several Raskolnikovs" (424), and that through Raskolnikov we see revealed "Dostoevsky's acute awareness (self-awareness at bottom) of the problematical nature of the modern personality and of its tortuous efforts to stem the disintegration threatening it" (401).

[11] One of Ian Hacking's (*Rewriting the Soul: Multiple Personality and the Sciences of Memory* [Princeton: Princeton University Press, 1995]) greatest fears—shared by some feminists—about the multiple personality disorder movement is its implicitly demeaning view of its subjects as victims, who are sometimes more encouraged to revisit past traumas and live a type of false consciousness rather than to seek integration and selfhood, "our best vision of what it is to be a human being" (267). "That we are responsible for constructing our own moral selves . . . is perhaps the most enduring aspect of Kant's ethics" (264).

[12] Fyodor Dostoevsky, *The Brothers Karamazov*, trans. Constance Garnett, Norton Critical Edition, ed. Ralph E. Matlaw (New York: Norton: 1976), 370; 14: 355 and 446; 14: 425-26.

[13] Dostoevsky also takes another jab at the environmental determinism of his ideological opponents in his satiric portrait of the former seminarian and now progressive journalist Rakitin, who, according to Dmitry, wishes, in the interests of his career, to show that Dmitry "couldn't help murdering his father, he was corrupted by his environment" (557; 15: 28).

[14] Towards the end of his concluding remarks, Fetiukovich says: "A feeling of hatred came over him [Dmitry] involuntarily, irresistibly, clouding his reason. It all surged up in one moment! It was an impulse of madness and insanity" (709; 15: 172).

[15] Richard Peace, *Dostoyevsky: An Examination of the Major Novels* (Cambridge: Cambridge UP, 1971), 284.

[16] Ronald Hingley, *The Undiscovered Dostoyevsky* (London: Hamilton, 1962), 212.

[17] "Dmitri is willing, indeed anxious, to go to Siberia for 'the little child.'" He must do something for him, "and the only way to do this is to suffer, and, although innocent, go to Siberia. Suffering from this perspective, is the only way to redeem the suffering of the child, to heal the pain of all since 'we

are all guilty and must answer for the sufferings of others.'" Luigi Pareyson, "Pointless Suffering in The Brothers Karamazov," *Cross-Currents* 37 (1987), 271-86; 280.

[18] Dmitry makes other statements about his desire to suffer for his sins. He is by far the most garrulous of the brothers: "I accept the torment of accusation, and my public shame, I want to suffer and by suffering I shall be purified. . . . I accept my punishment not because I killed him, but because I meant to kill him and perhaps I really might actually have killed him" (481; 14: 458).

[19] R. P. Blackmur, *Eleven Essays in the European Novel* (New York: Harcourt, 1964), 223.

[20] Nathan Rosen, "Why Dmitrii Karamazov Did Not Kill His Father," *Canadian-American Slavic Studies* 6 (1972), 209-24; 224. Another doubter about Dmitry's ability to bear his cross, Maurice Friedman, ("Martin Buber's *For the Sake of Heaven* and F. M. Dostoevsky's *The Brothers Karamazov*," *Comparative Literature Studies* 3 [1966], 155-67; 164), states that Dmitry opts for America because, although he has great breadth, he does not have the requisite depth. Robert Louis Jackson, "Dmitrij Karamazov and the 'Legend,'" *Slavic And East European Journal* 9 (1965), 257-67, does not preclude the possibility of Dmitry's salvation through suffering in Siberia, and therefore offers "a hope of no small consequence for mankind" (266), but he remarks that Dmitry's "desire to suffer, his yearning to bear the cross and to sing a 'tragic hymn' to God, turns out to be more symbolic than real" (264). Soviet criticism, as one might imagine, has not looked favorably on the American alternative. See especially Ia. E. Golosovker, *Dostoevskii* (Moscow: 1963), 29-30: "The secret of escape to America, that is, the decision to renounce suffering, purification, the hymn, immortality, God—turns out to be the invention of the devil, 'the devil's secret'" (30; author's translation).

[21] The earliest prototype of Dmitry, a character based on a young parricide that Dostoevsky met in prison, was eventually vindicated. Dostoevsky received this news while still at work on *Notes from the House of the Dead*. The editor prefaces the seventh chapter of the novel with the following remarks: "The criminal was really innocent, and had suffered in penal servitude for ten years in vain (*naprasno*); his innocence has been officially revealed by the court; the real criminals were found and confessed; the unfortunate man has already been released from prison . . . There is no reason to go into the profound tragedy of these facts, into the life, which, under such a terrible sentence, was ruined at such a young age" (*PSS* 4: 195). Written in 1862, before Dostoevsky's religious views had taken shape, these lines show not so much that Dostoevsky may also have been ambiguous about Dmitry's punishment in Siberia, but that he radically reimagined both the character of the parricide (Dmitry Karamazov is not Dmitry Il'inskii) and the significance of his suffering in Siberia, a fact attested by the reworked version of the parricide's story from the 1877 notebook, to be discussed later. Dostoevsky always radically transforms the real-life prototypes for his novels. For the tragic details surrounding the Il'inskii case— including Tsar Nicholas the First's unfortunate intervention—see Boris Fedorenko and Irina Yakubovich, "Ilyinsky—Karamazov: A Key to a Character," *Soviet Literature* 6, issue 339 (1976): 131-47; *PSS* 4: 284-5. Robert L. Belknap (*The Genesis of The Brothers Karamazov: The Aesthetics, Ideology and Psychology of Text Making* [Evanston: Northwestern University Press, 1990], 57-71) nicely outlines the transformations from Il'inskii to Dmitry.

[22] In *Crime and Punishment*, Svidrigailov, who knows that Raskolnikov committed the murder, offers to save him—as Ivan does Dmitry—by engineering his escape to America. But later Svidrigailov uses the expression of going to America as a synonym for committing suicide.

[23] In fact, most critics view Ivan Karamazov, who also did not commit the crime, as far more guilty of his father's murder than Dmitry. Ivan is the "mentor" and "creator" of the murderer, Smerdiakov, whom he infected with his doctrine of "all is permitted." Though he was staying with his father to protect him from his brother Dmitry, Ivan abandoned the house on Smerdiakov's suggestion, leaving the field open for Smerdiakov to commit the murder. Ivan's mental breakdown at the end indicates the extent to which he believes himself more responsible for his father's death than his brother Dmitry, perhaps even more than his other half-brother, Smerdiakov. See, for example. Ernest J. Simmons, *Dostoevsky: The Making of a Novelist* (New York: Vintage, 1940), 354; Edward Wasiolek, *Dostoevsky: The Major Fiction* (Cambridge: M. I .T Press, 1964), 175-7; Peace 239-42, 279-80; Hingley 200; Konstantin Mochulsky, *Dostoevsky: His Life and Work*, trans. Michael A. Minihan (Princeton: Princeton UP, 1967), 598. But as Peace points out, Smerdiakov is as much Dmitry's instrument as Ivan's (260-1).

[24] Father Zosima suggests religious courts as a better alternative to secular courts: see book 2, chapter 5, "So Be It! So Be It!" Dostoevsky argues similarly about responsibility whenever environment and responsibility—determinism and free will—are at issue. In *Notes from the Underground*, the Underground Man, the quintessential proponent of free will, argues that the only thing that a human being can do to guarantee his humanity, to prove that he is a human being and not a piano stop, is to

assert his free will against all the deterministic (environmental) evidence. Here free will becomes an article of faith, something that must be believed in—for without that belief, life becomes unlivable. In a typically maximalist move, the Underground Man takes responsibility for the laws of nature, the very laws to which he ascribes all his ills and misfortunes. It is a masochistic solution, for he becomes responsible for all that afflicts him, but he would rather assume responsibility, and thereby preserve his freedom—and humanity—than to be the innocent victim of forces beyond his control, to be a piano stop and not a human being.

[25] Dostoevsky depicts the same scenario in the epilogue of *Crime and Punishment*. "'You're an atheist! You don't believe in God!' they shouted. 'We must kill you.' He had never spoken to them about God or religious beliefs, but they wanted to kill him (oni khoteli ubit' ego)" (460; 6: 410).

[26] In "Dostoevsky and Parricide," *Dostoevsky: A Collection of Critical Essays,* ed. René Wellek (Englewood Cliffs: Prentice-Hall, 1962), 98-111, Freud writes: "A criminal to him is almost a Redeemer, who has taken on himself the guilt which must else have been borne by others" (108). For an interpretation of Freud's comments, see Joyce Carol Oates "The Double Vision of *The Brothers Karamazov*," *Journal of Aesthetics and Art Criticism* 27 (1968), 203-13; 206. For the more standard religious interpretation, see W. J. Leatherbarrow (*The Brothers Karamazov* [Cambridge: Cambridge University Press], 52), who writes that "as he takes on the sins of humanity and embarks upon the road to Calvary, Dmitry assumes the appearance of Christ . . . whose role is to restore the world of man to the world of God."

[27] For an excellent analysis of the relationship between suffering and redemption in *The Brothers Karamazov*, see Edward Hallett Carr, *Dostoevsky: 1821-1881* (London: George Allen & Unwin, 1962), 222-31. Carr argues that the main theme of the novel is "the redemption of Dmitri through sin and suffering" (220). For an attempt to summarize the various interpretations of redemptive suffering in the novel, see Geir Kjetsaa, *Fyodor Dostoyevsky: A Writer's Life,* trans. Siri Hustvedt and David McDuff (New York: Viking, 1987), 344-9. Whereas Carr treats Dostoevsky's mystical view of suffering in *The Brothers Karamazov* with considerable sympathy, Ronald Hingley, obviously more at home in Chekhov than in Dostoevsky, adopts a far more skeptical, western view: "Dmitry is thus the embodiment of one central message of the novel, that man should cultivate and distend to its ultimate limit the feeling of guilt inside him and find relief in purification and suffering. As Dostoyevsky knew himself, this doctrine runs contrary to common sense. The logic on which this is based is 'not of this world.' It operates as interpreters have explained, on a 'heavenly' or 'metaphysical' level and it is not susceptible of discussion in everyday terms. . . . It is possible to be a sincere admirer of Dostoyevsky's art without being at all a disciple of Dostoyevskianism. To enjoy *The Brothers Karamazov* one does not have to be obsessed with a desire to purify oneself by suffering. One does not even need to feel that this is a serious concept" (212). Dostoevsky obviously goes beyond Paul ("The evil that I would not, that I do"). He sees suffering not only as a *consequence* of sin (thoughts and actions that separate us from God), but as a positive force that we voluntarily must take upon ourselves for our own sake as well as for the sake of others. For another fervent apology for the novel's view of suffering, see Pareyson, "Pointless Suffering."

[28] For one of the best discussions of Dostoevsky's psychological and metaphysical attack against rationalism and utilitarian empiricism, see Eliseo Vivas, "Two Dimensions of Reality in *The Brothers Karamazov*," from *Creation and Discovery* (New York: Noonday, 1955), 47-70. For a Russian Orthodox eulogy of Dostoevsky's mystical ethics, see V. V. Zenkovsky, "Dostoevsky's Religious and Philosophical Views," in Wellek, 130-45; 138-41.

[29] Mochulsky has argued that the ruthless arguments of the Grand Inquisitor revealed that "freedom is an act of faith" (621).

Starvation Camp Near Jaslo

Wysława Szymborska
Translated by Clare Cavanagh

Write it down. Write it. With ordinary ink
on ordinary paper: they weren't given food,
they all died of hunger. *All. How many?*
It's a large meadow. How much grass
per head? Write down: I don't know.
History rounds off skeletons to zero.
A thousand and one is still only a thousand.
That *one* seems never to have existed:
a fictitious fetus, an empty cradle,
a primer opened for no one,
air that laughs, cries, and grows,
stairs for a void bounding out to the garden,
no one's spot in the ranks.

It became flesh right here, on this meadow.
But the meadow's silent, like a witness who's been bought.
Sunny. Green. A forest close at hand,
with wood to chew on, drops beneath the bark to drink—
a view served round the clock,
until you go blind. Above, a bird
whose shadow flicked its nourishing wing
across their lips. Jaws dropped,
teeth clattered.

At night a sickle glistened in the sky
and reaped the dark for dreamed-of loaves.
Hands came flying from blackened icons,
each holding an empty chalice.
A man swayed
on a grill of barbed wire.
Some sang, with dirt in their mouths. *That lovely song*
about war hitting you straight in the heart.
Write how quiet it is. Yes.

Transgression, Punishment, Responsibility, Forgiveness
Graven Images 4 (1998), 249.

Of Transgression and Forgiveness

Leonard V. Kaplan

Three years ago I was invited to give a paper addressing, among other issues, questions of difference and social justice at an international conference sponsored by and attended predominantly by members of the United Church of Christ. After presenting a paper on prophecy, law, and revelation, I was approached by a German theologian who asked me if, as a Jew, I could ever forgive her, or Germany? The question was asked in earnest, and left me confused and inarticulate. I finally told her that I did not think it up to me to forgive, and, in any case, that it was not in my power to do so. I saw that she was disappointed. Although I do not regret my response, I am left with a series of questions that are far from academic and theoretical. Should I have said more to my interrogator? If so, what would have made me say more than I did? Why could I not say, "I forgive you"? So far as I know, I lost no immediate family in the concentration camps. Yet I fully identify with the Jews, Gypsies, and Catholics who died under the Nazis. I was not in a unique situation. Many of my family, friends, and students also carry ethnic and/or religious identifications that have deep historic roots and in some important but mysterious manner ground their respective identities, bequeathing them friends and enemies that they did not personally choose. Yet many of us have close friends and commitments unmarked by and sometimes antithetical otherwise to family history or to the history of the people with whom we enjoy primary or more attenuated identifications. If I felt fellow feeling toward her, a sympathy about some great guilt that might have prompted the question, could I have assuaged her by saying that any German guilt was not hers personally since she was of a much later generation or that, had she been able, she might have been, like Bonhoeffer, heroic in her resistance?

How could I seriously answer such a question for myself, her, or others. Who was I to answer for 6,000,000 people. Could even a survivor do so for more than himself or herself? Was there some authority that could warrant an answer that I would find ethically and psychologically binding or even persuasive? Did I even wish to confront my bewilderment? Who after all was she to confront me so? How could I tell if her question was genuine, if she really felt some sense of communal guilt for past historical atrocity of "her" people toward "mine." Why should it make a difference to me if the question was genuine or authentic? What was the continuity of each set of people, of each set of identifications? Do individuals have a responsibility to forgive an offending other? If so under what circumstances? Do peoples share the same responsibility for forgiveness for offenses against them? The questions of forgiveness are at once deeply theological and pragmatic.

Judaism and Christianity prescribe an ethos of forgiveness towards both former friends and current enemies. These revelatory theologies, on their own terms, are not merely functional for communal effective operation but mandate an attitude toward self and God that commands concern for even the hated other. Forgiveness is a question of spiritual commitment. The righteous forgive. In 2 Samuel 21, King David turns over innocent Hebrew princes to atone for Saul's slaughter of Gibeonite priests, setting the scales in balance. Who is forgiven by this act of justice and what kind of reconciliation is effected are both open questions. But David thinks he and the Hebrews owe no less so as to gain God's forgiveness for the people's crimes. Similarly, "Turn the other cheek" and "love your enemies" is not counsel only for helpless peoples, but the admonition of revelation that Christ brings to all who accept his incarnation. For Christians, Christ died for the sins of others, forestalling both judgment and the vengeful human impulse to even the score against aggression. In this light, the wars subsequent to Christ's assumption of mankind's sinful burden continue to defeat the purpose of the crucifixion. Private cruelties seem as little abated.

Philosophers, theologians, and lawyers concern themselves with the ethics of conflict resolution and the pragmatics of forgiveness. So do writers of literature. Ariel Dorfman's *Death and the Maiden,* a play set in the context of post-Pinochet Chile about the reaction of a woman to a chance encounter with the man whom she believes tortured her during the period of the army's rule, explores the ethics of revenge by dramatizing the struggle between the woman and her husband, a member of the national reconciliation board.[1] It raises the question what is the proper response to one who has intentionally harmed you before plunging us into the psyche of the torturer, a doctor whose participation in the torture sessions transforms him from healer to sadistic torturer and rapist who acts because he finds himself in a situation in which he is free to cast aside all the restraints that civilization has constructed to keep us from that terrible freedom. The play forces us to confront not merely the question of what a "proper" response to having been tortured might be but also to consider how being tortured changes one. The central figure's husband repeatedly is forced to acknowledge the gap between his wife and himself—he escaped torture and remains a "liberal" desiring to achieve a peaceful reconciliation between the tortured and the torturers; she is filled with rage and desires vengeance (23-6, 33-42). To what extent is the individual psychological response shaped both by cultural expectations and by individual experiences? What kinds of psychologies are constituted by particular cultures and economic configurations? The larger movement that contains questions about the possibilities for individual and communal forgiveness is the quest for justice, in the course of which we will also touch on questions of transgression, punishment and responsibility.

This essay will start with an analysis of *Lone Star.* The movie combines several cinematic genres: it is a western, a police procedural, and partakes of some of the conventions of film noir. In the second section of the essay, I examine an essay by Emmanuel Levinas on the Talmudic responsibility to forgive.[2] Levinas, who died recently, was a Lithuanian Jewish philosopher engaged in the centuries long attempt to join the rigor of Athens with the ethical concerns of Jerusalem. Here I will interrogate Levinas' struggle to forgive Heidegger his Nazi politics as he feels Talmudically bound to do so. The last part of the essay returns to fiction and looks at *The Reader,* a German attempt to consider German responsibility for the Holocaust.

Lone Star: Forgiveness Simulated

Set in a contemporary Texas border town, *Lone Star* explores issues that are of concern for an analysis of responsibility and forgiveness. The movie opens on Texas desert that has functioned in the past as a rifle training ground for a military post that the U.S. government is about to close down. Two sergeants are walking through the desert: Mickey is using a metal detector to look for the spent shells that he uses in creating sculptures and Cliff, an amateur botanist, is looking at various types of cactus. Mickey finds a human skull. Later, after Sam Deeds, the local sheriff arrives, Mickey finds a sheriff's star. This discovery initiates a quest to unravel what turns out to be a series of mysteries. The Texas ranger who is called into the case tells Sam that Sam has to investigate because apparently a lawman has been killed, and that death calls the laws of the genre into play. The ranger begins to reminisce about the bad old days, introducing us to both Charlie Wade, a despotic sheriff who disappeared years ago, and Buddy Deeds, a deputy sheriff who succeeded him.

The story is the stuff of local myth. As a deputy, Buddy refused to cooperate with Charlie Wade, whom we see offer Buddy a share of the weekly protection money from a local bar with the understanding that part of his job would entail acting as the sheriff's bagman. Buddy rejects the offer in a classic western standoff: were Buddy not holding his drawn gun under the table, Wade might have shot him on the spot, for Wade, as we come to learn, was a remorseless killer who effectively backed up his threats to those who opposed him, notably vulnerable business people, illegal Mexicans coming over the very loosely patrolled border for job opportunities, and resident African-Americans. Turning the tables on Wade, Buddy warns Wade to get out of town or be arrested for corruption. The legend continues that Wade disappeared after the confrontation. Sam, Buddy's son, suspects that the skull and the star belong to Charlie Wade. He further suspects that his heroic father, beloved by everyone but Sam, killed him and stole $10,000 that disappeared at the same time.

In *Lone Star,* the quest for the killer is also Sam's quest for his personal identity, which turns out to turn around his broken relationship with his teenage love. Sam has come back to

Rio County after years away. His relationship with Buddy was soured when Buddy and a deputy separate Sam and his girlfriend Pilar while the two are making-out in a car at the local drive-in movie theater. Sam's rage at his father turns any early ambivalence he might have had toward his father into complete hostility and the unexplained loss of his true love leaves him distant, ironic, and bitter. As he later tells Pilar, he spent the first fifteen years of his life trying to be like his father and the next fifteen trying to give him a heart attack. Sam is called back home after his father's death when Hollis and the local establishment need someone named Deeds to run for sheriff. Sam has rejected his heroic father, and the movie presents his investigation into his father's past as an enforced coming to terms with Buddy. A contemporary Oedipus, he is now motivated to confront his dead father and the legend that he left behind. The narrative line opens on father-son and mother-daughter relationships, in their various states of conflict, love, and deception. It also explicitly points to the public power relations in the county, to the Mexican side of the border and, more allusively, to the wealthier part of the state. The powerful maintain their control by controlling the institutions of power, but other perspectives are available within the movie. Sayles uses history—personal, local, and, political—and its relevance to responsibility to present the film's deeper question. As we watch the movie it becomes clear that Sayles is using the individual story lines to ask us to consider whether individuals can avoid history and start life fresh and free. With tradition dispelled, are all responsibilities also annulled? In the movie, the border functions as both place and figure. Set on the border between two countries, *Lone Star* also depicts the borders of friendship, responsibility, transgression, potential forgiveness, and reconciliation. The border is a place of limits, of transformations, and of danger. It marks the antipathy between privilege and poverty, ethnic and racial divisions, conflict between love and rage, commitment and despair.

In the course of Sam's homicide investigation, taking place amidst the details of the town's daily life, the story flashes back to the love story of two adolescents, one a fourteen-year old Chicana and the other the fifteen-year old son of an Anglo sheriff. The girl is Pilar, now a school teacher involved in trying to find a way to teach the equivocal and multivocal history of the region to the Mexican-Americans, African-Americans and Whites in her classes despite great pressure from the parents of the Whites, who are enraged by the history she is teaching. She is also pushed by a more radical Mexican-American contingent who demand that their story be told less diplomatically. Pilar is a gentle, firm, caring teacher. She has two children, a teen-aged boy and girl. Her daughter, an excellent student, is appropriately disdainful of those who do not share her mother's values, but her son is resentful because he does poorly in school and feels no sympathy with Pilar's faith in intellectual values. He, like his dead father Nando, is a good mechanic, but unlike his father, his skills do not make him happy. His father has died young, leaving a young, unprepared Pilar with a sense of an arrested life and his son without a father. Pilar has been without a man since Nando's death and misses both the physicality and the spiritual qualities of a mate. Pilar has a difficult but loving relationship with her mother, Mercedes Cruz; her father, she has been told, died before she was born.

Mercedes is hard working and successful. She owns a restaurant, a fine house on the river which marks the border between the U.S. and Mexico, and a place on the town council. She has evidently assimilated well into Anglo society: she demands that her Mexican-American employees speak English at the restaurant, she calls the border patrol when she spots "wet backs" crossing the river, and she claims that she is Spanish in origin, not Mexican. However, we learn through flashbacks that, in fact, she had been a wet back herself and had been rescued by Eladio Cruz, whom she subsequently married. Her animus against other Mexicans is the animus of remembrance of a past and difficult history that pulls her back toward identification with the degraded and painful experience and those who are still suffering in similar ways. Pilar wants to know from her mother why she has not remarried and how she copes without masculine companionship. Her mother's answer is that one copes through work. Mercedes had to work and she still feels that she has to work even though she is now accepted in the local power establishment. But her acceptance is predicated on her identification with the ruling class. She has, for example, voted to name the new court house after Buddy Deeds. Without her vote, we are told, the courthouse would have borne an Hispanic name and been dedicated to an Hispanic figure.

During the course of Sam's investigation we also learn that Eladio Cruz was cold-bloodedly executed by Charlie Wade because Wade believed that Cruz had been bragging about smuggling in illegals without making payoffs to Wade. The past is revealed when Sam crosses the border to speak to an eyewitness to the killing. The witness presents a cynical view of borders and governments: "A bird flying south, a rattlesnake, you think they see this line? You think half way across that line they start to think different? Why should a man?" An arbitrary line spells the difference between having human dignity and being at the mercy of homicidal sheriffs. After making clear that since they are on the Mexican side he doesn't have to oblige Sam, he nonetheless tells Sam the story of Eladio's murder, and the movie flashes back to allow us to see the events from his perspective. We see Wade asking for Eladio's gun and we see him shoot Eladio as he reaches to give the gun to the sheriff. We also learn that Hollis Pogue, now mayor of the town, was at the scene of Eladio's execution as Wade's deputy. Though he was horrified by Wade's actions, he did nothing about the murder. The question of various degrees of complicity for various unjust acts begins to run through the narrative proper.

In another scene, Sam stops at the road side shopping stand set up by an old Indian friend of his father's. The stand is on a road that has no traffic, between no place and nowhere. The goods for sale include both Indian artifacts and tourist junk. The Indian provides some outside perspective on Sam's parents: we learn that Buddy was a war hero—they don't give medals unless you've killed someone, he says—but that after the war Buddy could as easily have become an outlaw as a lawman. On the other hand, Sam's mom was a saint so Buddy became a lawman. But this wry Indian who is living and working on this road not traveled by anyone cautions Sam about investigating his father's path too deeply. He shows Sam the skin of a dead rattlesnake that tried to strike him while he was exploring the place where it was coiled. Instinctively protecting himself, he shot and killed the rattler, which was just protecting itself. But the parable, while signifying the danger of Sam's quest, also suggests the equivocalness of the triumph of self defense: like Oedipus, he preserves himself from danger, but at what cost?

In the course of the movie, Sam finally comes to see his father and the role that Buddy has played in the community. Charlie Wade had represented an old, powerful, corrupt judge who was boss of the county. Wade killed both for fun and as a deterrent to anyone who wanted to break his rule; Buddy's ascendance marked a sea change in the local police and political regime. He was fair to everyone no matter what their race or religion. Yet he represented a rationalized, not a rational, form of governance. Unlike Charlie Wade, Buddy was not personally enriching himself, yet he profited by helping to assure the hegemony of the new establishment, including ousting a Mexican-American community from a lake area that then was redeveloped and subdivided to the establishment's interests—and his own. The picture that comes across is of Buddy's relative fairness, lack of bias, and predictability: he is part of a pluralistic local government dominated by interests from the various communities, Otis from the African-American community, Mercedes and others from the Hispanic, and Hollis from the dominant White community.

Sayles traces a trajectory similar to that traced in the Godfather trilogy but from the policing side. Charlie Wade represented a renegade, evil regime, Sam a pluralistic order able to rationalize its actions for the good of all. Everyone at the personal level trusted Buddy and knew he was honorable and reliable. Even those arrested by him felt fairly treated. An old Mexican-American prisoner sweeping the office for Sam told him how he enjoyed working on Buddy's patio and being served good food by Sam's mother. He saw nothing corrupt in this. Better to be out in the air working on the patio than locked away. In an ironic contrast, we learn that in the past he had been busted for keeping a still that Buddy feared might poison people; now he has been jailed by Sam for growing marijuana—an acre's worth—for his health. The legend of Buddy's deeds is the legend of a certain rough justice, respected and understood by those under its control. Of course, there were losers. Any African-American who tried to open a bar to compete with Otis (who could be counted on to deliver the African-American vote in the county) was discouraged. Mexican-Americans were forced to move from property in the name of redevelopment (though Mercedes gets her river-front house). The audience learns that after Sam politics will continue as usual though middle-class Mexican-Americans will get a more proportionate share of the pie since their voting numbers have gone up. There will be a new jailhouse whose construction will serve the profit needs of the establishment even though Sam thinks it is not needed. This may not be a just utopia, but it is hardly the evil of the transgressive Charlie Wade. At the level of politics, Sayles conveys the ease with which the system accommodates the every day needs of those who control it. Sam, a decent man, but apparently committed to nothing, sees without liking but accepts the realpolitik of the movie's microcosm.

Inevitably, Sam solves the mystery of the murder and of his childhood. Not Buddy but Hollis killed Charlie Wade. Wade was going to shoot Otis Payne, who as a young man was carrying on a gambling operation in the African-American bar he later purchased. Otis's bar and the African-American church together were the public spaces for the African-American community. In the present, Otis, the unofficial mayor of Darktown, has become a benevolent patriarch to the town's African-Americans. But in the past, Otis had been warned by Wade against unsanctioned illegal activities, and the prejudiced Wade, having caught him running gambling, was about to shoot him in the back just as he had killed Eladio Cruz. Hollis, whose motives we are not shown, shoots Wade. Buddy, who was just entering the bar saw the scene. Since the old judge was still in power, Buddy and Otis, who were strangers until that point took over, and, with Hollis looking on, faked Wade's disappearance by burying his corpse in the desert. Otis explains to Sam that he and Buddy just decided to trust each other. Sam has his answer: Buddy did not commit murder. When Hollis suggests that people will now believe that Buddy killed Wade if the story is not reported, Sam retorts that Buddy is a legend and he can take it.

Through the investigation Sam solves a more personal mystery. If Buddy was not a racist why did he break up Sam's relationship with Pilar and humiliate Sam in the process? Sitting with Pilar at the broken down old drive-in, Sam asks her who her father was. "Eladio Cruz," she replies. But Sam has learned that Eladio was dead months before she was conceived. Sam tells her that Buddy was her father. This is the reason for Mercedes' vehemence against their relationship and Buddy's intervention: Sam and Pilar are half-brother and sister. Pilar responds that she always felt connected to him from the first time she saw him in the schoolyard. Pilar looks at him expressing the unfairness of this revelation. She cannot have children anymore she assures him. He assures her if he saw her for the first time he would want to be with her, though it is clear that initially part of her attraction for him was that he saw her as a thing apart from Buddy. The implication is that they will remain together. Forget the Alamo.

What can one make of this, about transgression, about forgiveness? Sayles is interested in community and he hates borders, whether racial, ethnic, or otherwise. If this much were not obvious from the movie, he tells us so in an interview about the movie.[3] But this is hardly enough. Further what does he say through the interwoven, intergenerational narratives of Sam and Buddy, Pilar and Mercedes, and the subplot concerning Otis, his son and his grandson? I can offer two possible readings; one reading, the one I find most persuasive is an ironic Brechtean reading that assumes that Sayles is showing us ideal states—states that are exemplary in the flawed world of liberal capitalism, but implausible in their respective resolutions. An alternative reading, a more Stoic reading, would suggest a certain optimistic view of will and radical freedom implausible in the network of relationships that Sayles spins. But even Brechtean irony is based on a fundamental optimism about the possibility of individual and institutional transformation. What terms does Sayles provide for understanding the historically-tangled border mess he presents? Is he preaching freedom from history, from even the taboo of incest? Should we forget all histories of transgression to get on with flawed human life? Without memory, personal or collective, forgiveness presents no issue. We must remember before we can decide whether to forgive.

Even if Sayles does not intend to, *Lone Star* evokes only to reject the endings of Greek tragedy. Narrative themes intimate the shadows of Oedipus and Electra. Buddy and Sam, and their doubles, Otis, his son Delmore, and Delmore's son Chip, each play psychoanalytic father-son variations. Mercedes and Pilar seem less conflicted but no less central. *The Libation Bearers* and the theme of brother-sister incest are no less evoked. Mickey and his African-American female sergeant fiancée are also set up as exemplary of the radical freedom that love and good will can bring to unknotting the ancient and modern taboos that confound mating and relating. When asked by his friend Cliff whether her family will accept this white man as their son-in-law, he replies that they will be so relieved that she is bringing a man home and not a woman that he will be acceptable. Cliff's reply, funny and dark, "it's always nice when one prejudice trumps another," makes clear that Sayles is no Pollyanna. Why then the resolutions for all the private relational conflicts? Why does Sayles suggest no political solutions for the border problems, for the corruption problems? Do the individual resolutions suggest that leading a Stoic life is necessary, that individual freedom is possible and worthwhile but only by negating the political as well as abandoning historical memory and any obligation that continues with that memory? Is he suggesting that individual freedom is possible, that Pilar and Sam can continue as lovers despite their newly-discovered identities, that Otis and Delmore can resolve Otis's betrayal of his obligations as a father because Otis kept a record of his son's development even though there was no contact between them? How can Pilar so easily accept without rage her mother's duplicity in misidentifying and otherwise hiding her father's identity?

Freud's Oedipus Complex, his attempt to universalize human psychology, negating history in his ontology of myths, puts the transgressive at the heart of early twentieth-century notions of human development. The little boy must love the mother, challenge, and hate the father, fear retaliation to the point of fearing castration, let go of the mother, accept the father, and separate from parental imagoes in the process of individuation toward autonomous genital consciousness.[4] This is the classic simplified psychoanalytic narrative. More recently, the model has awakened to the primary identification that the male child has with the maternal force and the difficult struggle that the male must make in separating from the mother to even consider the battle with the father for the mother's affection.[5] The primary identification with the maternal for each gender is now a psychoanalytic commonplace and a function of "empirical" observation by psychologists of human development. If this empiricism is justified, it necessitates the reordering of the psychoanalytic paradigm.[6]

But I want to offer another suggestion here and use it to challenge the ease with which Sayles ironically charms us into accepting, however uneasily, his fable of resolutions of acts of transgression and betrayal. What is at stake is whether the transgressive can be forgiven at all? Are human beings so opaque to themselves as to make forgiveness in the face of transgression anything but verbal rationalization or bad faith? Does Pilar's desire to maintain her relationship with Sam represent a psychological and ethical letting go of internal strictures? Is this desire free in the sense that Pilar or anyone in the audience can will an acceptance and forgiveness for self and others from ancient and not-so-ancient intended and consequential harms? Does Pilar forgive herself her unintended past incest and her fully-intended future incest as well? Does her plea to Sam to "Forget the Alamo" mean that her view expressed in the earlier confrontation between the teachers and the parents—especially the Anglo parents—that history is more complex than who won is cancelled out or does it mean that the fact that they have just discovered that they are brother and sister does not cancel out their love and sexual attraction for each other, that taboos are less important than personal realities? As a committed teacher is she no longer to teach historical truth, truth that enrages some, makes others defensive, and yet others melancholy or bored? Or is this new complexity in her personal relationship with Sam a proof of her position that history is more complicated than "propaganda" and partial views? As the movie ends, we see Sam and Pilar sitting on the hood of his car, holding hands, and staring at the blank screen of an abandoned drive-in movie theater. Is history no more than this? Is transgression an outmoded concept?

To the extent that we accept Sam and Pilar's decision to continue as lovers, we must move towards seeing the transgressive as only a social construction, serving to differentiate "us" from all of the other "thems," be they Pharonic rulers, pagans, Jews, gentiles, cannibals, or those who open their eggs at the big end and not the little. However, another way to define transgression is as behavior that threatens social order. Many believe that the taboo against incest keeps societies from reproducing themselves in an ever-downward spiral of genetic inbreeding. But Pilar points out to Sam that she cannot have any more children. Does that mean their incest is acceptable because it presents no threat to society. To what extent can we decide that old taboos no longer apply? To those who went along with Charley Wade's behavior because it was easier than risking his psychopathic and homicidal response, taboos yield place to "getting along." One could assume that neither Hollis nor Otis, who surely knew that Pilar is Sam's daughter, would have any public objections to a relationship between Sam and Pilar. While Mercedes most certainly would object—she still refuses even to say hello to Sam at the dedication of the courthouse—it is easier to imagine that she would keep her objections to herself than that she would risk losing her position within the town power structure by making a public denunciation of Pilar's brotherly lover.

Is transgression absolute or relative? For Freud, for whom God was the projection of the father onto self and history, culture or civilization necessitated the recognition of tabooed or transgressive acts. Denial and frustration of innate narcissistic tendencies and the relinquishment of socially-defined and denied objects of desire were each necessary for any semblance of separation into autonomous personhood. Where Paul held that the law made for sin and destroyed the possibility of a belief in our own righteousness throughout consciousness of our omnipresent guilt, Freud saw the law as necessary in order to teach us that we must renounce our instincts in order to participate in the civilizing processes. Paul, of course, held that even though all were guilty under the law, love nevertheless obtained and that love trumped the law. For Freud, society defines what must be repressed as a condition of its own civilization; for Paul, love forgives all faults. Freud, we presume, would not be sympathetic to Pilar and Sam's dilemma; Paul, we presume, would pray for them in love. For Freud, history is important; for Paul, only Christ's role in history counts.

Jean-Joseph Goux, in his *Oedipus, Philosopher*, critiques Freud's interpretation of Oedipus. Freud, says Goux, misunderstood and universalized an anomalous case, that presented by Sophocles, in his *Oedipus*.[7] Goux's reading, undertaken in the light of recent analyses of Greek myths and tragedy, is persuasive and suggestive to me.[8] Freud claimed that his interpretation of the story of Oedipus in itself allowed him (and us) to answer the riddle of the sphinx, to understand the mystery of human self-deception. For Freud, the boy does want to replace his father with his mother and assume the power of the law, but that is not what Goux's *Oedipus* is about (5-24). Oedipus wanted to solve—and thought he did—the Sphinx's riddle, but he ultimately discovered that the naming of man did not penetrate man's mystery in relationship to self, other, or the sacred. Goux points out that Oedipus of all the heroic Greeks alone uses only his intellect to defeat the feminine monster (see chapter 1, especially 19). He does not even kill the Sphinx, herself a Fury guarding Apollo's temple. She flings herself to death in spite and rage at his puzzle solving. All the other heroes must pass through more elaborate initiation, calling on physical, mental and sacred assistance in slaying their Medusas and Chimeras. For Goux, the "correct" form of initiation requires the hero to discharge an impossible set of obligations, intrinsically fatal and unreasonable, culminating in destroying a female monster and thereby gaining the innocent female as mate (23).

Oedipus alone truncates the process and uses reason for triumph, but his reward is his mother and not an innocent, appropriate female. For Goux, Oedipus' tragedy lies in his confidence and rivalry with Apollo himself, the God of disinterested wisdom and intellect (97). Sophocles' Oedipus is convinced he can and should get to the bottom of things; he discovers horrible personal transgression, and his reward is a life time of not-so-clarifying suffering. Man would be better off not to be born. Goux speculates that *Oedipus at Colonus* represents the only realization available to Oedipus through a lifetime of disgrace, abject horror, and banishment (196). The prototypic philosopher, Oedipus at the doors of Athens in Colonus finds himself in the sacred space where the Eumenides safeguard the city, as Aeschylus would have it, as part of their agreement with Athena in allowing forgiveness to Orestes for slaying his mother at Apollo's dictate. Oedipus at first does not know where he is, but finally recognizes, sightless as he is, that this is the place destined for the next step of the mystery that engulfs him and his house. In this play Oedipus makes no rash claim concerning his intellectual prowess to get to the bottom of pollution or anything else. In fact, he is reverent. He asks what the appropriate rituals and prayers of the space are and fulfills them.[9] Oedipus is no longer in a contest with Apollo or any other god. Yet he has not transformed so much either. He does not forgive his sons, Creon, or Thebes. He rails at those he feels have betrayed him, including Polyneices, the son for whom Antigone expresses compassion to no avail. Before he begins his mysterious ascent from the sacred grove at Colonus, Oedipus has tempered his will to accept the mystery and the power of the gods and their sacred spaces, but he insists that he does not deserve the destiny accorded him (ll. 1104-53), a point the gods do not contradict.

Like Oedipus and Jocasta, Sam and Pilar are completely ignorant of their relationship, have intercourse when they are both adolescents. Through his father's intervention, he loses his love, leaves her, enters into a marriage that fails, and lives miserably until he divorces his wife, and returns home to become sheriff and to see Pilar again. Along the way, he, like Oedipus, must discover the dirty secrets of his youth and the guilt of his mythical father. He discovers a father who is neither the perfect hero the town remembers nor the complete villain Sam has created but a man whose character is more gray than black or white. As politically corrupt as Buddy may have been, he was both heroic and admirable: a quantum advance on Charlie Wade in administering individual justice. He looked out for people, he loved, and he was loved. Sam discovers a father less flawed than he has spent his adulthood believing; in fact, he discovers a father who is a bit of a hero. He also discovers why Buddy (and Mercedes) destroyed his affair with Pilar. (Sayles, no doubt to Goux's distress, never makes Sam come to terms with his mother.)

Bound by Oedipal hate, Sam must work through his past. At the end, though, Sayles allows Sam understanding of his father, but never has him express forgiveness of him. When Otis and the mayor worry that by closing the investigation of Charley Wade's death by issuing a public conclusion, he will leave the impression that it was Buddy, not Hollis, who really killed him, Sam merely says that Buddy's myth can withstand this false conclusion. Sometimes life should go on, sometimes justice dictates forgetting if not forgiving, Sayles is telling the audience. Sam has given much energy to his Oedipal search for justice. He has his woman, but she is his sister. He may stay with her, but their bond will yield no children. Sayles makes this concession to allow his apparent happy ending. We know that Sam has already decided not to run for sheriff again and that he will not reveal the identity of Charley Wade's killer nor of the conspiracy that hid the facts of Wade's death from the town. The mystery has yielded its secrets but little joy seems to follow. Sam's victory over his Oedipal feelings may be merely a Pyrrhic one. Sam's story is not tragic, however. He does not put his eyes out. He does not wander through the world led by a self-sacrificing daughter to come to a mythic resting place. Buddy may be the subject of local myth, but Sam will not be. Rio County is not Colonus. None of the Eumenides there reside to protect the sacred grove from contamination. His search has been for his father and he has found him. He has not begun to discover his mother, frequently proclaimed a "saint" by others in the movie.

Sam is no great advertisement for enablement through human will and effort, a freedom more transparent than that open either to Sophocles or Freud's Oedipus. Even if his quest has opened to human love of Pilar, the public space of action seems foreclosed in any satisfying way. He cannot be the sheriff his father was either in myth or reality. Sayles provides a social space too complicated for anything but the individual self forgiveness and private life. "Forget the Alamo" indeed! How about Pilar? She had no satisfactory private life before her reconnection to Sam. She was a good if frustrated parent, particularly to her son. She had love for her mother, but certainly not an open and honest, undisturbed dialogue. She seems more accepting than Sam, not even angry with Mercedes before or after she learns of her relationship to Buddy and Sam. She is loving and accepting and committed. I've always been intrigued by Jocasta when she warns Oedipus to abandon his quest. She understands the mystery before he does and warns him off. Could she have continued in the marriage if he heeded her? Pilar has always sensed a connection to Sam. His explanation fills in her experience without harming her. Her only response is a fear that Sam will insist they end their newly-restarted relationship. Sayles allows neither Pilar nor Sam any histrionics. She has no need to forgive in her private relationships, it seems, as long as she can keep the relationship. Is incest no longer transgressive? Is incest something that bothers men more than women? Phaedra fears the loss of her reputation in her lust for Hippolytus more than horror of the act, but he is only her stepson. Jocasta's attitude remains problematic. Perhaps the scene of instruction must go to Jerusalem here. Sarah is both Abraham's wife and half sister. As Regina Schwartz argues in *The Curse of Cain*, the boundaries of incest and all other boundaries are not so certain.[10] Sarah remains the exemplary wife and sister. Perhaps brother-sister incest did not become transgressive until it was forbidden by the Torah in Leviticus 18:9. Does this suggest that all transgression is socially constructed?

Pilar may have found Sam again but will this sustain her? If she forgets the Alamo, will she opt out of her self-chosen professional commitments? She may be reaching few students and changing few historical perceptions, but she is an exemplary teacher, fair-minded, loving, and nuanced in her detailing and balancing of very unattractive history at the border. If she chooses to forget her own private Alamo, must she necessarily forget the public one as well? Can she not keep Sam without losing her own identity? Is that identity merely a social construction? Is to forget to be free? Alternatively, can she still remember the Alamo and have her relationship with Sam? Can we select our battles, forget, if not forgive some past harm, and still engage other harms with enough commitment to remain vital? Where is her responsibility?

Sayles tempts us by juxtaposing attitudes that we prefer, liberal, life-affirming and tolerant values with tight, privatized attitudes that would close his characters off from one another. The public world can be approached only through the private, and there only in ineffectual ways. The border is still there. The new sheriff will call for a new, unneeded jail house. The poor will stay poor and the border, finally, is only the border, removed from the heart of significant power. As Goux says, Oedipus must remain merely philosopher. He has no easy access to the gods until they are ready to show themselves (3 and passim). Sam investigates both as lawman and as son. What he finds is more than he had before the investigation. *Lone Star* indicates some directions toward responsible action, some forgiveness, some reconciliation. But forgiveness and reconciliation may only be what we would like, not what happens in the real world. As in Brecht's *Caucasian Chalk Circle* or *The Three-Penny Opera*, the fable unravels upon reflection. After viewing the movie, we may well conclude that forgiveness and responsibility are more difficult than shown, yet still within human possibility. Transgression remains present, however, hard it is to explain what it is.

Levinas and the Frustration of Forgiveness

Emmanuel Levinas, a philosopher and teacher of adult Jewish education, has attracted significant attention in the United States in recent years for his unique critique of Heidegger's analysis of being. [11] Levinas was born into an orthodox Jewish household in Lithuania where he was trained in Hebrew, studied the Talmud, and the greats of Russian and world literature, particularly Dostoevsky, Pushkin, Tolstoy and Shakespeare. He went on to training in Germany, attending a class offered by Husserl and becoming familiar with the work of Heidegger. He moved to France where he directed an adult Jewish education institute. He is also credited with translating Heidegger into French, thus bringing him to the notice of those like Sartre who became the leaders of French existentialism. His family died in the Holocaust and he himself was a prisoner in a war camp. His work is much informed by the Holocaust experience. He argues for the necessity of recognizing and responding to the limitless call the other has on us. [12] His work ultimately can best be seen as another attempt to bring the rigors of Athens to Jerusalem. As a philosopher, Levinas wrestles with sacred texts in the service of extending philosophic understanding. For Levinas the term "God" is an unknowable pointer towards an alterity beyond being, a pointer against the totalizing tendencies he sees in western philosophy. [13]

Levinas opposes Heidegger's definition of philosophy as a critique of being. [14] For Levinas ethics precede ontology; philosophical concepts arise from preconscious human experience. For Levinas, philosophical concepts grow out of individual humans confronting everyday experience. Ethical response to experience, for him, is necessarily a response to the face of the other. Hence responsibility also precedes ontology. Levinas specifically engaged the relationship between transgression and forgiveness in "Toward the Other," his contribution to a symposium concerning whether and how Jews are to forgive Germans and Germany in the face of the horrific transgressions of the Holocaust. Levinas seeks instruction on the obligation for forgiveness from both the Hebrew Scriptures and the Talmud. [15] He also draws from philosophy and adverts to psychoanalysis in his speculative searching. The Talmud teaches that God will forgive transgression toward him on the Day of Atonement (when properly approached) but that transgression toward others can only be excused by gaining forgiveness from the one offended (20). Levinas stresses that mere verbal action, the "I am sorry," is insufficient for expiation. Judaism is very much a theology of this life and the interpersonal everyday nature of human interchange, and the Talmud makes explicit that a substantial cash payment is a necessary but not sufficient sign of a true apology. But even an honest attempt at apology may prove difficult if the other can not be satisfied.

As a prelude to his consideration of the Jews' German problem, Levinas considers the question of transgression in general. Levinas makes clear that in his understanding, Judaism concerns itself with how to lead a responsible life (14). Following Maimonides, Levinas views Judaism as a rational theology (14). God is approachable only through everyday interaction. Transgressions against God's law may involve breaches of ritual obligation, but the spirit of that obligation is to believe in and to live the good life. The Law tells us to forswear idolatry, to live for something beyond material gain, to be responsible to the other. The existence of an annual Day of Atonement signifies the concrete nature of Jewish theology: it is a time when God can forgive the ritual transgressions of those seeking forgiveness. Levinas points out that transgression against God requires a return to God through self-searching and actions that manifest a soul-healing that is much more than ritual adherence (15-6). In this sense being Jewish is a marker for being "a light unto the nations," standing for justice and believing in the ultimate realization and necessity of the good. For Levinas, the Day of Atonement calls forth the community whose objective presence facilitates the internal struggle expiate transgressions (17).

But expiation requires that the other must forgive transgressions. Since the way to God for Levinas is through the other, responsibility toward the other is an imperative (20). In Levinas's understanding, transgression includes criminal action, civil harms, or even intentional verbal infliction of pain. Transgression at this level is more inclusive than what is covered by contemporary secular law (20-1). Moreover the obligations toward forgiveness are not symmetrical. A confused set of hurts (who did what to whom first) does not relieve the other of making a necessary reparative act. Levinas explicitly realizes the danger that the other will not pardon (20). Unresolved transgression is dangerous for the individual soul and implicitly for the world. Perhaps there is a key here toward remembrance of past historical harm as essential for human existence. There is no metaphysical break between this reality and fundamental mystery. Reality is of a piece. Justice itself is costly and harsh, as Levinas makes clear at the finish of his commentary (29).

Levinas draws on two stories from the Gemara to exemplify the problem of seeking forgiveness from a recalcitrant other. In the first, Rab, a noted rabbi, is blamelessly involved in a fight with a local butcher. On the night preceding the Day of Atonement, Rab determines to visit the butcher to allow the butcher an opportunity to apologize. A student warns Rab not to undertake the visit because "Abba is going to commit a murder" (23). Rab goes nevertheless. The butcher angrily tells him to leave. While he is distracted with Rab, a bone fragment splits off and kills the butcher. Rab's visit fulfilled his student's prediction, without achieving the reconciliation that he felt obliged to offer and seek. Rab is at the center of the second Talmudic parable as well. He is reading from the Torah when he is interrupted by two other rabbis. Each time Rab goes back to the beginning and starts the reading anew so that they will hear the entire reading. His teacher Rab Hanina then enters, but Rab continues to read without restarting, and thus offends his mentor. For thirteen years Rab seeks to apologize to Rab Hanina but is always rebuffed (23). What conclusions does Levinas draw from these two incidents involving Rab, who went on to become the founder of his own academy in Babylon? Further on what does Levinas base his interpretations?

Levinas cautions that the appeal to Biblical or Talmudic texts is not an appeal to authority but rather a baseline for struggle toward meaning (14). New contexts make for new struggles against past examples. Why was Rab wrong in pursuing the butcher, despite the warning, to allow him an opportunity to apologize. Levinas bases his interpretation on one line in the text: "Go away, Abba. I have nothing in common with you"(Levinas 23). Levinas argues that the story shows that "Mankind is spread out on different levels. It is made up of multiple worlds that are closed to one another because of their unequal heights. Men do not yet form one humanity. And the slaughter keeps strictly to his level" (23). The butcher knows it and so should Rab. Rab is a sage, but even a sage must be cautious and thoughtful about the capacities of another. Nor is this a moral elitism. The principle that everyone must be offered the opportunity to ask for forgiveness does not relieve an individual from assessing context and the capacity of others. Forced reconciliation achieves nothing. Brilliance is no warrant of wisdom or depth of ethical consciousness. Rab was a sage and as such his ethical sense and intellectual achievements were or should have been integrated. If a sage can be presumptive, how much less likely that the butchers of the world will measure up to normative demands that they be responsive to others. For Levinas, this is an empirical, not a normative point (18). Normative demands are worthless where compliance is unlikely.

What does Levinas make of the second story in which Rab hurts his teacher by not respectfully restarting his reading from the Torah because he is exasperated at having had to restart his reading by the arrival of latecomers? Rab was obliged by the law to seek forgiveness three times (22), but far exceeded what the law required by doing so for thirteen years in a row in the face of constant resistance from Rab Hanina. According to the story, after the thirteenth rejection, Rab left for Babylon and became a great teacher himself. Certainly one should be respectful to sages, but should not Rab Hanina himself have reached out to his student, particularly after so much effort? Levinas wonders whether hurt between intellectuals is more difficult to cure than quarrels between people on lower levels and requires great care and sensitivity. He also observes that though repentance is possible for sinners, it is more righteous never to have transgressed. Otherwise all manner of perversion can ultimately be thought excusable (24). Levinas is disturbed by one Talmudic explanation that because Rab was so elevated more was expected from him (24). Instead, he suggests that Rab Hanina condemned his pupil precisely because of Rab's brilliance. His offence, in this reading, is not that he was exasperated but that he was arrogant (24). Rab Hanina, he argues, was of impeccable character and would not have been motivated by fear or envy.[16] Levinas instead sees Rab Hanina's dream as informing him of Rab's destiny and his ambition. The interpretation turns the situation around. Rab, the brilliant, is denied because his teacher is aware of Rab's unconscious hostility toward him. Whereas Rab Hanina might have accepted the apology of a lesser spirit despite his unconscious hostility, the brilliant Rab must be held to a higher standard. Levinas draws a contemporary application (25). Where lesser Germans may be excused, the brilliant Heidegger may not because he should have known better.

Heidegger held himself out as a philosopher, a teacher of wisdom who averred he was going to the pre-Socratic root of Being. His chosen politics was a politics of hatred and exclusion, whatever his alleged naivete. His teaching pretended the universality of its vision. I can understand why Levinas would reject his apology if it had ever been offered. But Rab Hanina was Rab's teacher. Why does Hanina not instruct Rab about his secret ambition that his lack of self-knowledge hid from him (25)? Does not the teacher have a higher responsibility, than the unconscious, if brilliant student? If such is the case, why has Rab Hanina failed his higher obligation. These two personalities must have created significant distress for the community over the thirteen years of unforgiveness. Do the two tales of Rab juxtaposed as they are reveal something about Rab's character at that stage of his life?

The Rab of the two tales can be viewed as mechanically motivated by principle. He goes off to the butcher when a student warns him not to do so. He offends his teacher and doesn't know why his teacher will not be reconciled by all of his apologies. His brilliance is theoretical but he lacks psychological acuity into himself and others. In contemporary psychoanalytic discourse he is a bit of a narcissist.[17] But he is Rab, who ultimately becomes a sage. Change is possible, yet premature forgiveness would signify nothing. Until he achieves self-knowledge, Rab cannot understand the true nature of his transgression and consequently cannot atone for it. Rab, it seems, must leave and himself become a teacher before he can come to Rab Hanina's understanding of Rab's transgression and understand the response of the other. It is Levinas' purpose to warn us that Rab's path to God is illusory; the only way to get there is by encountering others in all their inadequacies (25).

As for individuals, so for communities. Levinas engages the Torah itself to apprehend the limits of collective responsibility. Levinas here invokes 2 Samuel 21: "There was a famine in the days of David three years, year after year; and David sought the face of the Lord. And the Lord said: 'It is for Saul, and for his bloody house, because he put to death the Gibeonites.'"[18] David summons the Gibeonites to hear their complaints. Their rage is against the House of Saul and not against Israel. What and why Saul struck at them is not clear here or elsewhere in the Torah. But David granted their demand for redress against seven princes of the House of Saul, reasoning that either the cause "lay in the corruption of men" (26) or there "must be a political wrong here, an injustice which is not caused by private individuals" (27). Because his analysis of the state of affairs in Israel convinces him that it is indeed the latter situation that holds, David accedes to the Gibeonite demand and has them all executed: seven princes of Israel are executed because seven Gibeonites were unjustly executed by Saul. Levinas wants us to see a parallel with the Holocaust in Saul's actions:

> The Midrash affirms that the crime of extermination begins before the murder takes place, that oppression and economic uprooting already indicate its beginnings, that the laws of Nuremberg already contain the seeds of the horrors of the extermination camps and the "final solution." But the Midrash also affirms that there is no fault that takes away the merit: there is simultaneously a complaint against Saul and the recalling of his rights. Merits and faults do not enter into an anonymous bookkeeping, either to annul each other or to increase one another. They exist individually. That is, they are incommensurable, and each requires its own settlement. (27)

If each good or bad act must be dealt with separately, interpersonally, then how can any punishment be meted out? Despite law, despite innocence the debt to the stranger must be paid. Levinas does not comment on the resentment that must have followed from the sacrifice of the princes among the people. Nor does he object that David, the one chosen to be king for Israel, makes the judgment to kill Saul's innocent grandchildren. Levinas argues that David as king must punish the innocent in order to make a political statement (27). Levinas here repeats his theme that responsibility is not symmetrical (27). Though Talmudically only the victim can forgive, the Gibeonites instead demand punishment. By doing so they exclude themselves from Judaism (28). To be Jewish is not to demand punishment, Levinas asserts. But he doesn't forgive and he doesn't condemn David for the harshness of his punishment (28).

But this creates a problem for us because Deuteronomy 24.16 states, "the fathers shall not be put to death for the children, neither shall the children be put to death for the fathers; every man shall be put to death for his own sin" (Chumash, 322). Levinas does not try to unpack the tension between the Deuteronomic proscription on punishing the father for the sins of the child or the child for that of the father. Instead, he finds a higher principle to justify God's demand that David act:

> It is better that a letter of the Torah be damaged than that the name of the Eternal be profaned. To punish children for the faults of their parents is less dreadful than to tolerate impunity when the stranger is injured. Let passersby know this: In Israel princes die a horrible death because strangers were injured by the sovereign. The respect for the stranger and the sanctification of the name of the Eternal are strangely equivalent. And all the rest is a dead letter. All the rest is literature. The search for the spirit beyond the letter, that is Judaism itself. We did not wait until the Gospels to know that. (27-8)

David's act exemplifies the terrible truth of the human necessity for blood retribution. Punishing the innocent children is less intolerable than permitting harm to a stranger to be left unredressed. The spirit of the law trumps the letter. [19]

Levinas's commentary ends unsatisfactorily. To be Jewish is not to demand punishment, but Levinas cannot get beyond his unwillingness to forgive Heidegger, and he can only forgive the German people, it seems to me, by holding Heidegger and his ilk to a standard higher than that by which we measure those on a lower intellectual plane. Levinas's followers also have trouble with his position. Alain Finkielkraut, though influenced by Levinas, argues that being unexceptional, Klaus Barbie's crimes against humanity are worth prosecuting. Barbie, the butcher of Lyon, was responsible for exporting French Jews from Germany to their death; he also tortured, killed, and exported French resistance fighters.[20] Finkielkraut laments the fact that the French, not the world community, tried Barbie, because such a trial confounds war crimes with crimes against humanity. By trying Barbie for local crimes in a local court, genocide loses its unique status and becomes just another horrible transgression in much the same way that the term Nazi has been appropriated for anyone who commits any political act that the speaker finds repugnant. Finkielkraut wants to universalize and institutionalize certain aspects of the administration of international justice (10, 12). He wants a world tribunal and a rigorous definition of crimes against humanity (12). He is appalled by the lead prosecutor's comment that the Barbie case taught him and the world something about muticulturalism and the vicissitudes of achieving justice (44). For Finkielkraut, the Barbie trial confused genocide with any other transgression, thereby trivializing what happened to the Jews, the Gypsies, the Cambodians, the Bosnians, the Kurds, and so on and on (13).

Finkielkraut makes a powerful and sad case that the Barbie trial allowed immediate political rhetorical opportunities to reduce the significance of the Holocaust and to divide humanity into local tribes in a way that would have been unthinkable at the time of the Nuremberg trials. The Barbie defense team, composed of non-Europeans, took the trial as an occasion to make a political case that for Europeans, in order for a crime to be worthy of being called a Holocaust, white Europeans must be engaged in killing their own (25-6). They further argued that crimes against non-Europeans, for example Algerians, were perpetuated by the French, who thus lacked moral standing to judge their client, and that they were ignored by the rest of Europe, who also lost any moral stature they might otherwise have had through their complicity (31-6). Their strategy was quite deliberately to trivialize their client's acts by trivializing a merely local (i.e., European) Holocaust, by attempting to politicize the attempt to exterminate whole peoples because of who they are, not because of what they have done (73). To Barbie's defense team, Barbie's victims are merely white Europeans whose fates do not participate in any universal principle of justice. Their own sense of the injustice done by Europeans in Algeria prevents them from recognizing that egregious harm can be done to any national or ethnic group (31-6).

Forgiveness is frustrated for even Levinas who knows that the failure to give forgiveness is spiritually costly in that even intimations of God come only through the other (Levinas 17). As Chet, the colonel's son, says when he is caught making animated cartoons instead of attending to the lessons he is being taught in Pilar's history class in *Lone Star*, all history is the same: everyone is busy killing everyone else. If even Holocausts can be trivialized, can we do anything more than "forget the Alamo?" Levinas leaves us with the responsible struggle of adults to remember, to punish and where possible to forgive; Finkielkraut shows us how in the name of local politics transgression can be trivialized or reduced to the status of everyday bad faith (69-71).

Forgiveness Problematized

If Levinas is correct that each transgressive act must be answered for and in itself, and if, further, only the victim can excuse the act, we are left to wonder if it will ever be possible for states to excuse transgressions if the individuals under the regimes of those states would resist forgiveness if presented the opportunity. Can we ever end the endless cycle of violence unless, as in the *Orestia*, the gods directly intervene and start a new cycle of justice?[21] Finkielkraut's desire to constitute an international court seems frustrated by his own analysis that local politics will always undercut ethical principle. The perpetrators of crimes against humanity today will officially pay only if they have the bad luck to get caught. Given the Judeo-Christian preference for forgiveness, why is forgiveness so difficult for individuals and states to achieve? My intuition is that interpersonal forgiveness in contemporary culture is more frequently than not merely a verbal act. Those to whom we are closest say they forgive us our transgressions only to recall them when it is convenient. The moral "edge" is banked for moral capital despite the verbal formality of forgiveness and acceptance. Nor does the new dereliction have to bear too much resemblance to the "forgiven" misdeed to reinvoke it. In some cases the very obligation to seek forgiveness calls forth guilt and resentment that may lead to even more animosity toward the one against whom one has already transgressed and can exacerbate the already-inflicted wound rather than helping to heal it. Nor is the position of the one from whom forgiveness is sought any easier. Everyday experiences teaches us that forgiveness is not easily given even by those who feel obliged to offer it.

Popular literature offers numerous examples of works that revolve around situations in which a transgression raises the possibility of forgiveness as a means of resolving the narrative's plot dilemmas. Bernhard Schlink's *The Reader* presents a reflection on the Holocaust from an unusual angle.[22] At the start of the novel the narrator, a fifteen-year-old German school boy, is home from school recovering from an illness when he meets Hannah, an older woman who becomes his lover. He reads to her from his books after he returns to school and they talk about the stories. He thrives in this relationship until one day Hannah disappears without a word to him. Several years later, he reencounters Hannah. A professor assigns his law class to attend and analyze a trial of people accused of criminal activities under the Nazi regime. Several women, one of whom is Hannah, are on trial. They had been guards watching over female concentration camp prisoners who were left in charge of a group of variously aged women incarcerated in a barn when everyone else fled at the approach of American troops. The barn caught fire but neither the townspeople nor the guards released the prisoners, all but one of whom died. At the time of the trial several years after the war, the sole survivor has emigrated to Israel. At the trial, Hannah voluntarily tries to explain why the guards failed to act, telling the court that they were confused by suddenly finding themselves in charge, that they feared retribution from the Nazis, and that they did not know what to do when the fire began (108-12).

At a key point in the trial, Hannah is asked to read a document, but she refuses. The other defendants and their lawyers seize upon this refusal to imply that she was the leader and the one most responsible for the horrible end of the victims (132). Ultimately, she receives the harshest sentence. Hannah and the narrator are each aware of the other in the courtroom, but they do not speak to one another (109-17). The narrator realizes that Hannah cannot read and is so ashamed of her illiteracy that she prefers to be punished rather than admit she can not read (132-7). While she is in prison, the narrator regularly makes and sends her tapes of books. He finds that she looks forward to the tapes and finally learns how to read. When, after many years, she is about to be released, a compassionate warden contacts him since he is the only person outside the prison with whom she communicates. Although the narrator does not particularly want to have any personal contact with her, he finds her a place to stay and gets her a job (193). He feels an obligation towards her, but, rejecting the ethic Levinas insists upon, he does not feel comfortable in any face-to-face involvement with her. When he visits her shortly before she is to be freed, she laments that now that she is to be released, he will no longer read to her, that her personal contact with him will cease (197). Although he says that he will continue to be her friend, the reader senses that she is correct. In his irritation with her, he asks her whether, while they were lovers, she had ever thought about the acts that she had committed during the war (198).

Hannah responds: "I always had the feeling that no one understood me anyway, that no one knew who I was and what made me do this or that. And you know when no one understands you, then no one can call you to account. Not even the court could call me to account. But the dead can. They understand. They don't even have to have been there, but if they were, they understand even better. Here in prison they were with me a lot. They came every night, whether I wanted them or not. Before the trial I could still chase them away when they wanted to come" (Schlink 198-9). Hannah here comes as close as she can to expressing her sense that she can only have communion with the dead, whether the ones for whose deaths she was responsible or others with whom she had no connection, that only the dead can understand that humans cannot live with their transgressive acts. The narrator finds himself angered by her response, which implies that all of life is transgressive and all of the living are transgressors, that only through death can we find an understanding of our transgressions (190). In some way he feels polluted by his sexual intercourse with her as if it has involved him in her crimes. He seems to need her to make some act of expiation for her crimes both to the dead and to him; for him, it is not enough to leave her to the silent company of the dead.

Like Finkielkraut, he wants the guilty to be punished, but he does not want to see himself among their number. In this light, Finkielkraut's desire to precisely name the guilty and their precise acts may be seen as a desire not to universalize guilt, to separate humanity into guilty wolves and innocent sheep who need to be protected from the predators who would prey upon them. Unable to live amongst the living, Hannah hangs herself before her release. The warden who had grown fond of her and who had admired the dignity she had developed in prison is angry at Hannah and "the reader" because no letter is left, no explanation given (208-9). All that Hannah leaves is a request that the money she had saved while she was in prison be given to the sole survivor of the fire. The narrator flies to New York and meets with the daughter of the survivor. She refuses either to take Hannah's money or to forgive her. The novel ends with the narrator, who tells us that he has written this account ten years after Hannah's death to work through his own confusion and guilt (215-8). All he can do within the novel is to give the money Hannah had left to the "Jewish League Against Illiteracy," and to visit Hannah's grave, neither of which give him any sense of closure. In this novel written in German for a German audience, Schlink offers little guidance to readers on how to deal with their sense of the inadequacy of their response to all of the novel's depicted injustices. We are left only with the narrator's guilt, suffering, and the diminished consciousness that time brings to all transgression. Finally what the novel offers its reader is sense of melancholy, but a consciousness that no true forgiveness occurs.

Forgiveness is such a complex psychological and ontological problem and no literary example can be more than suggestive. If we accept fiction as capable of pointing to human truths it can only be because we find fictional representations plausible, but even actual claims of forgiveness, if accepted as true, face questions of plausibility. One who forgives may, after all, be self deceived or lying. Plausibility involves the judgment of the other as well as the self. Forgiveness is possible but in history, that is, in ethics, life, and various kinds of fictions, it seems necessarily destined to be unstable.

Notes

[1] Ariel Dorfman, *Death and the Maiden* (New York: Penguin, 1991).

[2] Emmanuel Levinas, *Nine Talmudic Readings,* trans. Annette Aronowicz (Bloomington: Indiana University Press, 1994).

[3] *The Houston Chronicle*, Sunday, 30 June 1996), 8.

[4] The Oedipus Complex and its vicissitudes undergirds Freud's theory of the formation of neurosis. The relationship between castration anxiety and the Oedipus Complex is classically represented in light of his clinical and theoretical presentations. See Sigmund Freud, *Analysis of a Phobia in a Five-Year-Old Boy*, The Standard Edition of the Complete Psychological Works of Sigmund Freud, trans. James Strachey (London: The Hogarth Press, 1909). XXIV: 337-8. Note various discussions of the complex throughout the Collected Works including overidentification and the Oedipus Complex XVIII: 105-6, 108, on neuroses, XX: 55, 86, 113-115, 122, and 223 *inter alia*. On the legend itself, see VI: 178, XIV: 62, XXIII: 11, 13, 187, 190n, 191, 205. For an influential essay on the working of the Oedipus Complex in clinical practice and the reasons for the phenomenon, see Hans W. Loewald, "The Waning of the Oedipus Complex," *Papers on Psychoanalysis* (New Haven & London: Yale University Press, 1980), 384.

[5] For early theorists of the primary role of the maternal who cast doubt on Freud's original identification of male children with fathers and argue that both males and females initially identify with the female, see Robert J. Stoller, *Sex and Gender, On the Development of Masculinity and Femininity* (New York: Science House, 1968) and Nancy Chodorow, *The Reproduction of Mothering, Psychoanalysis and the Sociology of Gender* (Berkeley: University of California Press, 1978).

[6] Psychoanalytic theory has been in flux from its inception. For examples of paradigm shift, see Jay R. Greenberg & Stephen A. Mitchell, *Object Relations in Psychoanalytic Theory* (Cambridge: Harvard University Press, 1983). For two influential theoretical directions, see Heinz Kohut, *The Restoration of the Self* (New York: International University Press, 1977) and Roy Schafer, *The Analytic Attitude* (New York: Basic Books, 1983). See also Jonathan Lear's recent philosophic defenses of Freudian psychoanalysis against contemporary attack, *Love and Its Place in Nature, A Philosophic Interpretation of Freudian Psychoanalysis* (New York: Farrar, Straus & Giroux, 1990); and *Open minded Working on the Logic of the Soul* (Cambridge: Harvard University Press, 1998).

[7] See Jean-Joseph Goux, *Oedipus, Philosopher* (Stanford: Stanford University Press, 1993), 25-39.

[8] For a compilation of some of the standard criticism about the play, see Sophocles, *Oedipus Tyrannus*, trans. & ed. Luci Benkowitz & Theodore F. Brunner (New York: W. W. Norton & Co., 1970). See also Jean-Pierre Vernant & Pierre Vidal-Naquet, *Myth and Tragedy in Ancient Greece*, trans. Janet Lloyd (New York: Cone Books, 1990). For a recent consideration of Nietzsche's work on tragedy and its influence, see M. S. Silk & J.P. Stern, *Nietzsche on Tragedy* (Cambridge: Cambridge University Press, 1981). See also Charles Segal, *Interpreting Greek Tragedy, Myth, Poetry, Text* (Ithaca: Cornell University Press, 1986). See also George Steiner, *Antigones: How the Antigone Legend Has Endured* (New Haven: Yale University Press, 1996) for analysis of the response history to the stories of Antigone and Oedipus.

[9] See *Oedipus at Colonus*, trans. David Grene, *The Complete Greek Tragedies, Vol. II: Sophocles*, ed. David Grene and Richmond Lattimore (Chicago: University of Chicago Press, 1992).

[10] See Regina Schwartz, *The Curse of Cain, The Violent Legacy of Monotheism* (Chicago: The University of Chicago, 1997).

[11] The most important studies of Levinas include Colin Davis, *Levinas, An Introduction* (Notre Dame: University of Notre Dame Press, 1996); Adrian T. Peperzak ed. *Ethics as First Philosophy, The significance of Emmanuel Levinas For Philosophy*, Literature and Religion, (London: Routledge, 1995); John Llewelyn, *The Genealogy of Ethics, Emmanuel Levinas* (Evanston: Northwestern University Press, 1997); Richard A. Cohen, *Elevations, The Height of the Good in Rosenzweig and Levinas* (Chicago: University of Chicago Press, 1994); Adrian Peperzak, *To the Other, An Introduction to the Philosophy of Emmanuel Levinas* (West Lafayette: Purdue University Press, 1993); Robert Bernasconi & Simon Critchley, eds., *Re-Reading Levinas* (Bloomington: Indiana University Press, 1991).

[12] See Levinas, "The Temptation of Temptation," 50, *Nine Talmudic Readings*.

[13] For "alterity" as a key term in Levinas' writing, see Ira F. Stone, *Reading Levinas/ Reading Talmud*, An Introduction (Philadelphia: The Jewish Publication Society, 1998) where Stone talks of the "Other" as central to Levinas: "This is Levinas' goal: to explain the presence of another for whom I am responsible and who breaks my solitude and thereby breaks the solitude of being as mistakenly described by western philosophy (13). Mark C. Taylor, *Alterity* (Chicago: University of Chicago Press, 1987) 204, more specifically defines "alterity" in Levinas' usage: "To suggest the nonthematizable source of the subject, Levinas uses the term *ille*, which is both a Latin word and includes the third person singular, it. 'Alterity' links up with 'Other,' 'Infinite,' and 'Alterity' to form a metonymic chain of signifiers intended to evoke what cannot be designated." Taylor differentiates various uses of "alterity" in Levinas from the usages of others like Kierkegaard and Hegel (205).

[14] See Emmanuel Levinas, *Ethics and Infinity, Conversations with Phillipe Nemo*, trans. Richard A. Cohen (Pittsburgh: 1985).

[15] Levinas' lecture is reprinted in *Nine Talmudic Readings*, trans. Annette Aronowicz (Bloomington,: Indiana University Press, 1990, 1994). "Toward the Other" was delivered in October 1963 as part of The Colloquia of Jewish Intellectuals organized by the French section of the World Jewish Conference. In an introduction to the original 1968 French publication of *Quatre lectures talmudique*, Levinas said that "the program of the Colloquia of Jewish Intellectuals always envisaged a Talmudic commentary, next to a biblical commentary, to be related to the general theme suggested to its members" (3). The Talmud, consisting of two parts, the Mishnah, which includes the Rabbinic commentary on the Hebrew Scriptures, and the Gemara, a collection of later rabbinic commentaries on the Mishnah, preserves the original Rabbinic commentaries of the first four centuries of the common era, itself reflects tension as the preserved voices of the rabbis try to come to terms with the indeterminacy of the revealed texts.

[16] As is his wont, Levinas brings forward a young woman poet who, he claims, helped him in his interpretation and whom he calls Diotima. The name, of course, recalls Plato's seer in the *Symposium*, who instructs Socrates, and the allusion suggests that traditional sources of wisdom are not always adequate.

[17] Opening a brilliant narcissist to ideas is a simple thing. He can get lost in his brilliance and his assumed relationship to deep mysteries.

[18] *The Soncino Books of the Bible* (London: The Soncino Press, 1978), 319.

[19] As would be expected much commentary attempts to work through the tension. I do not find any of those attempts satisfactory. To me this problem remains unresolved in Levinas's commentary as well as in the Rabbinic texts. See Chumash, 459 for their attempts to soften the harshness of the cost of the "sins of the fathers."

[20] Alain Finkielkraut, *Remembering in Vain: The Klaus Barbie Trial and Crimes Against Humanity*, trans. Roxanne Lapidus with Sidney Godfrey (New York: Columbia University Press, 1989), 8.

[21] For an instance of the intervention of the gods to start a new cycle of justice, see Aeschylus, *The Oresteian Trilogy*, trans. Philip Vellacott (London: Penguin, 1959). Athena establishes a court to try Orestes and thereby breaks the cycle of generative violence. (170-1).

[22] Bernhard Schlink, trans. Carol Brown Janeway, *The Reader* (New York: Pantheon Books, (1997).

A Dissenter's Life

Stephen Toulmin

I

My story today begins in Washington nearly 200 years ago.[1] Thomas Jefferson was inaugurated as President on March 4, 1801. Less than three weeks later, he wrote to a friend who had come to the United States as a political refugee from England in 1794. The friend had built up his reputation here as a natural scientist and as a writer on philosophy and religion, and Jefferson wrote:

> Yours is one of the few lives precious to mankind, and for the continuance of which every thinking man is solicitous. Bigots may be an exception. What an effort, my dear sir, of bigotry in politics and religion have we gone through! The barbarians flattered themselves they should be able to bring back the times of the Vandals, when ignorance put everything into the hands of power and priestcraft. All advances in science were proscribed as innovations. They pretended to praise and encourage education, but it was to be the education of our ancestors. We were to look backwards, not forwards, for improvement. . . . This was the real ground of all the attacks on you. Those who live by mystery and *charlatanerie*, fearing you would render them useless by simplifying the Christian philosophy,—the most sublime and benevolent, but most perverted, system that ever shone on man,—endeavored to crush your well-earned and well-deserved fame.[2]

Jefferson was writing to a man whom we know today for books on electricity, oxygen, and other scientific subjects, but who was known at the time as the Unitarian Minister in Birmingham, England, and who had his church and home burnt down for defending the French Revolution. Joseph Priestley was now settled in Northumberland, Pennsylvania, and he had three years to live.

Why was Priestley's fame of such concern to Jefferson? What made a scientist of Unitarian persuasion the target of politically contrived resentment and violence? The alliance of these two distinguished figures throws light on British and American attitudes 200 years ago that had a wider historical significance and still survive among us today. Priestley was a Freethinker and Nonconformist—a "dissenter," the term then was. He reached his own opinions on any subject he took up in religion or philosophy, in science or politics. He wrote on a dozen other subjects as well as science: not just the nature of factitious airs (what we call *gases*) but also rhetoric, free will, and the origin of language. Jefferson and he had corresponded since the early 1780s. As Minister of the Unitarian New Meeting in Birmingham, he had taught a common sense Christianity that avoided all doctrinal technicalities. The Trinity and Transubstantiation were for him "ideas at which the common sense of mankind will ever revolt."[3] Jesus' teachings were (he said) intelligible today to the kinds of men and women who were the first disciples: this was what Jefferson meant by *simplifying* Christianity and defending the laity from *power and priestcraft*.

What then got Priestley into trouble: his theology, science, or politics? Nowadays in the United States, Unitarian Universalism is hardly a matter for scandal, but in 1794 it was still a cutting edge system: in Philadelphia, Priestley gave the series of lectures that firmly linked Unitarian theology to Universalist natural philosophy. Nor need we assume that Unitarianism no longer has political overtones. The religion of Bosnia, for instance, originated in the theological debates of eleventh-century Constantinople. The Bogomils of the Balkans, skirting around the mystery of how Jesus could be both God and Man, saw him as the best of human teachers. In a word, they were not Trinitarians, but Monophysites, the nearest thing in the year 1100 to Unitarians. Only later, coming under criticism from the Roman Church to the West and from the Orthodox Church to the East, both of which are Trinitarian churches, did the Bosnian Bogomils join Islam; and they did so for theological as much as political reasons: if Jesus had been a human "messenger" from God, after all, his standing was like that of Muhammad. (At a time when people in this country are tempted to *demonize* Islam, we need to recall just how much theological history Islam and Christianity share.)

Still, a Birmingham mob in the 1790s would not have rioted about theology alone, so what about Priestley's scientific ideas? There too he took a solitary road, which led him to conclusions that sound more innocent in the 1990s than they did in the 1790s. Though widely respected, he was an idiosyncratic scientist who walked a cusp between the respectable and the unorthodox. From the seventeenth century on, European discussions of Mind and Body had been (as we say) *dualistic*: they treated Mind and Matter as distinct and separate realms, so that the question was, "How do the two interact?" A minority of writers argued that mental activity needs bodies or brains to support it, not a *separate* mind or soul, but they were denounced as materialists and Epicureans—wrong-headed, immoral, or worse. When the liveliest of these writers, Julien de la Mettrie, died of food poisoning at the Court in Berlin, the reaction was that he had met his just reward. Priestley also belonged to this despised minority, and he put up a plausible defense of his beliefs. The point of the Resurrection, he said, is not that we survive death as immaterial souls, but rather that, at the Last Day, God restores our Material Bodies, so that we can resume our interrupted lives in the flesh.

Priestley could afford to take such eccentric positions because *socially* he did not belong to the English Establishment. He was always a religious Nonconformist, and this—looking back—was an advantage: as such he was barred, not just from joining Parliament and the professions, but from attending Oxford and Cambridge Universities, where he would have learned only Ancient Literature and the mathematics of Newton. Instead, he went to the Dissenters' Academy at Daventry in the Midlands, where the students had a richer curriculum. With this as background, he could read La Mettrie's polemic against the narrowness of seventeenth-century physical theory and speculate about the spiritual potentialities of the material world.

Yet the Mind-Body Problem was scarcely a reason for riot. What got Priestley into trouble was his support for the French Revolution. He was a colleague of Richard Price, whom Edmund Burke pilloried in his *Reflections on the Revolution in France*—and he himself wrote a reply to Burke. Why was it so shocking to applaud the French Revolution? At first, many English people saw 1789 as continuing the 1688 English Revolution, when the Dutch Protestant Prince William of Orange replaced the Catholic James II, and the Revolution of the 1580s, in which the Dutch reacted to Spanish religious persecution by abjuring their earlier loyalty to Philip of Spain. After the Terror of 1791, however, Anglican preachers attacked dissenters as enemies of the British Monarchy, and for thirty years events in France traumatized respectable England, as the Russian Revolution of 1917 traumatized mid-twentieth-century America.

Calling Priestley a dissenter was thus only to call him a religious nonconformist who did not accept the teaching of the Anglican Church. Yet feeling against dissenters cut deep. The Revolution in France convinced many people in England that religious conformity was needed in order to defend the State from *sedition*. (The word keeps cropping up in sermons and pamphlets in the 1790s.) After the American War of Independence, the British monarchy had been frail, but the execution of Louis XVI was the last straw: from then on, anyone with a good word to say for the French was suspected of plotting against George III and damned as a "regicide" or King-killer.

How wonderful is the power of denial! In his *History of the Peloponnesian War*, Thucydides tells us how, flushed with pride at their victories over Persia, the Athenians would not let the colony of Melos declare its neutrality between Sparta and Athens, but "put to death all who were of military age, and made slaves of the women and children."[4] This barbarism was not acceptable in the city of Pericles and Phidias, and the name of Melos—like My Lai for us—was one the Athenians preferred to forget. Likewise, when they executed Charles I in 1649, the English had set an example of the very "regicide" they now chose to condemn, yet by 1790 most people in England found the memory of that event unacceptable. Priestley might insist that Unitarians had nothing against the Royalty—indeed, had no *political* agenda at all—but by this time blood was stirred, and a riot was easily whipped up.

The bigotry that burnt Priestley's home and church was just the pigheadedness that led the Founding Fathers to reject any *establishment* of religion. Before independence, the history of Europe taught them that, for the sake of civil peace, no country could risk religious war. Priestley's last public act in England was the sermon *On the Present State of Europe,* which forecast a replacement of feudal monarchies by more egalitarian régimes. He spoke in the measured tones of Vaclav Havel today, but, after his own misfortunes, he feared changes as violent as those in France and looked to America as a laboratory of toleration in which the contrast of establishment and dissenters finally lost sense. For, in America, there *were* no established doctrines for dissenters to dissent *from.*

Priestley's arrival in Philadelphia did not end his troubles: once here, he was still open to attack. Jefferson hoped to attract him to Monticello, where they might jointly pursue their shared interest in natural science together. As it was, Priestley was active in the American Philosophical Society to which Jefferson (the Society's President from 1797 to 1815) gave papers on paleontology—e.g., on the large fossils from Paraguay of a clawed animal known to scientists today as the Giant Sloth, *Megalonyx Jeffersoni.* Still, despite Jefferson's support for education, his scientific interests did him no good politically—as is evident from when he put the bones of ancient vertebrates on show in the East Room of the White House.

Even in religion, Jefferson was an ambiguous ally, for his views made him plenty of enemies among the Churchmen of his time:

> The Christian priesthood finding the doctrines of Christ leveled to every understanding, and too plain to need explanation, saw in Plato materials with which they might build up an artificial system which might give employment for their order and introduce it to profit, power and preeminence. The doctrines which flowed from the lips of Jesus himself are within the comprehension of a child; but thousands of volumes have not yet explained the Platonisms grafted on them. . . . For this obvious reason, that nonsense can never be explained.[5]

But, in saying this, Jefferson based his views on ideas set out in Priestley's own book, *A History of the Corruption's of Christianity.* So, as a refugee from England, Priestley did not set up a new home in Pennsylvania expecting his life to be one of pure peace. It was not obvious that the U.S. he actually came to was exactly the U.S. he idealistically foresaw: a place where religious toleration was the rule in fact, not just an article in the Constitution. But that did not matter to him; he had never shirked a good argument.

To sum up this story, I am not arguing that Priestley was *right* in all he believed and everybody else was *wrong.* I am not saying that he was right to be a Republican not Monarchist in politics, a Materialist not an Idealist in philosophy, or a Unitarian not a Trinitarian in religion. None of his dissenting opinions *taken alone* explains why he was attacked quite as violently as he was. As we shall see, the explosive mixture was made up of all his opinions *taken together.* But again, even that is not the point. The point is that he was entitled to hold and argue for his opinions, and many of his English contemporaries were too intolerant to respect this right. The first question to ask is, "Why?"

II

Let me now step aside, and look at the backdrop to this episode. Neither Priestley nor Jefferson was *just* a scientist or a *mere* essayist. Neither of them may have been a William Shakespeare or an Isaac Newton, but both combined literary sensibility with scientific talent. Ask my old friend, the late C. P. Snow, which of his "Two Cultures" they belonged to—Natural Sciences or Humanities—and he could not put either of them on one side only: their minds transcended that division, so he would have had to reply, *Both.* So let me now take a wider angle lens, and set the present episode at a point half way between the Gutenberg revolution of the late fifteenth century and the new revolution in communication in which we are living today. Snow's Two Cultures—I will suggest—separated as a result of two different innovations that followed Gutenberg's invention, each of which carried its own distinct philosophical preoccupations.

Around 1500, it was at last economic to distribute knowledge in printed form, not as manuscripts. Along with this came a revival of the old tradition of Humane Letters: what we now know as the humanities. The worlds of learning and public service were opened to a lay public, who could now study texts that had been closed to them before. Print taught readers to recognize the complexity and diversity of our human experience: instead of abstract theories of Sin and Grace, it gave them rich narratives about concrete human circumstances. Aquinas had been all very well, but figures like Don Quixote or Gargantua were irresistible. You did not have to approve of or condemn such figures: rather, they were mirrors in which to reflect your own life.

Like today's film makers, sixteenth-century writers in the humanities from Erasmus and Thomas More to Montaigne and Shakespeare present readers with the *kaleidoscope* of life. We get from them a feeling for the *individuality* of characters: no one can mistake Hamlet for Sancho Panza, or Pantagruel for Othello. What count are the differences among people, not the generalities they share. As Eudora Welty said in appreciation of V. S. Pritchett, who died just recently at the age of 96:

> The characters that fill [his stories]—erratic, unsure, unsafe, devious, stubborn, restless and desirous, absurd and passionate, all peculiar unto themselves—hold a claim on us that cannot be denied. They demand and get our rapt attention, for in the revelation of their lives, the secrets of our own lives come into view. How much the eccentric has to tell us of what is central![6]

What an "unscientific" thought Eudora Welty here offers us—that the eccentric explains the central, rather than the other way around! No wonder the humanities contributed as little as it did to the creation of the exact sciences. As late as 1580, Montaigne questioned whether any *universal* theories about Nature were possible at all, let alone mathematical ones like Newton's were to be. Given the uncertainties, ambiguities, and disagreements in our experience, that ambition struck him as presumptuous.

The creation of the exact sciences was, thus, a separate, seventeenth-century story, which I turn to now. In 1618, the final and most brutal of Europe's religious wars broke out. Henri IV of France set an example of toleration by treating his Protestant and Catholic subjects as equal citizens: this led a fanatic to murder him in 1610. From then on, things went only downhill. From 1618 to 1648 Central Europe was laid waste: during thirty years of war, one third of the population of Germany was killed, half of its cities destroyed. (From Grimmelshausen to Brecht, playwrights have written of this horror.) One event was especially ironic. To commemorate the slaughter of a Protestant army outside Prague, in 1620, a pearl among Rome's smaller churches was built. Dedicated to the Holy Mother of the Prince of Peace, it was called *Santa Maria della Vittoria*—or Saint Mary of the Victory.

With Europe split by war, the sixteenth-century humanists' modesty about the human intellect and their taste for diversity came to look like luxuries. Instead, new and more systematic ways of handling problems were devised, what we call disciplines, whose standardized procedures could be taught as a drill, which students learned to perform step by step, in one-and-only-one right way. Devised by the Flemish scholar Lipsius, this method was put to practical use by Maurits van Nassau, the Dutch Prince whose military academy at Breda in Holland was a Mecca for students from all across Europe. Maurits was struck by the consensus achievable in mathematics. If religion had been discussed with the same kind of neutrality, what miseries Europe might have escaped! Even while dying, he was no partisan. A Protestant Minister asked him to declare his beliefs: he replied, "I believe that 2 + 2 are 4, and 4 + 4 are 8. This gentleman here [pointing to a mathematician at his side] will tell you the details of our other beliefs."[7] Soon, this mathematical ideal took a more general hold. In theory and practice alike—in jurisprudence and philosophy, as much as in the training of infantry— skill gave way to technique, artistry to artisanship.

The young Descartes himself visited Maurits's academy after dropping out of law school in 1618 and before he joined the Duke of Bavaria's staff. Caught up in the prevailing religious war, he looked for a rational alternative to those rival theological systems that had lost their credibility: ideally, for a *mathematical* system, free of the uncertainties, ambiguities and disagreements that Montaigne had seen as unavoidable. Following Galileo's example, Descartes adopted as goal a universal system of physics in mathematical form. So began both those philosophical inquiries that John Dewey was much later to call *The Quest for Certainty*, and also the scientific investigations that would lead, in 1687, to Newton's *Mathematical Principles of Natural Philosophy*.

The two independent products of the new print culture—first the humanities, later the exact sciences—embodied different conceptions of philosophy and different ideals of human reason. On the one hand, the humanists saw arguments as expressing human disagreements, in whose resolution rhetoric had a legitimate role; on the other, exact scientists saw arguments as formal inferences, which appeals to rhetoric could only distort. In the humanities, the term *reason* thus referred to reasonable practices; in the exact sciences, it referred to rational theories. The humanities recalled the variety in our experiences: in real life, generalizations are hazardous and certitude too much to ask. The exact sciences sought to put everything in theoretical order: formal certainty was their goal. So, a tension between the claims of rationality and reasonableness—the demand for demonstrably right answers to questions of theory and respect for honest disagreements about matters of Practice—posed a challenge which (as we shall see) has lasted to our own time.

III

The Thirty Years War ended in 1648 with the Peace of Westphalia, from which emerged the forms of the world in which we live today—forms so familiar we forget they were then brand new. The Peace introduced three novel elements: a new system of states, a new policy in church/state relations, a new concept of rational thought. Political power was vested absolutely in individual sovereign states: within each state power was exercised from the top by a sovereign, and states did not meddle in each other's affairs. Religious conflict was overcome by compromise: reviving an old formula from the 1555 Treaty of Augsburg—*cuius regio eius religio*—every sovereign was free to choose the church for his or her particular country. So the Westphalian system created, for the first time, established churches— Anglican in England, Calvinist in Holland, Catholic in Austria. Finally, the new idea of reason took as starting point Descartes' claim that true knowledge must have the certainty of a geometrical system: opinions unsupported by theory were just that—unsupported opinions.

On the face of it, the three parts of the Westphalian system—absolute sovereignty, established religion, and logical demonstration—were distinct and separable. As a matter of practical politics, however, they were closely related: all of them operated top down and gave power to oligarchies—political, ecclesiastical and academic—that supported one another, and they formed a single package. As Voltaire commented, "One leaves Paris, where Space is Full, and everything happens through Vortices, and reaches London, where Space is Empty, and everything happens through Attraction."[8] In a word, the three elements of the Westphalian scheme formed, not just a package, but an *ideological* package. Challenging any one of the three axioms was thus viewed as attacking them all.

This was what got Priestley finally into trouble. For late eighteenth-century Englishmen, Newton's physics was part of a larger ideological scheme. As it mapped God's plan for the Creation and proved the stability of the solar system, its success was *political* as much as astronomical: bolstering the English self-image of Hanoverian Monarchy, Anglican Church and all. By rejecting the odd blend of Newtonianism, Anglicanism, and Monarchism that passed as "respectable opinion"—talking at the same time as a nonconformist in religion, a Republican in politics, and a materialist in philosophy—Priestley was throwing himself into hot water. From then on, he was regarded less as a man of unusual beliefs than as a trouble-maker, less a *dissenter* than a *dissident*.

It was and remains the fundamental defect of any public ideology that it does not allow people to put forward unorthodox or even unfamiliar views without being accused of promoting hostility to the Powers that Be. The Birmingham Mob was not ready to let Priestley explain his opinions, let alone listen to him and see if they might learn anything from his views. For them, Priestley was a source of trouble, and they preferred to drive him out of town. Nor was this habit merely English. After 1650, states required that people's loyalties be *exclusive*: no citizen could be a subject of more than one sovereign. Established religions, similarly, expected their adherents to avoid churches of other faiths: the English were as harsh to Papists in their midst as the French and Austrians were to Protestants. As for rational knowledge, from Leibniz on most philosophers relied on formal deductions, rejected appeals to rhetoric as irrational, and so on. The Westphalian settlement thus imposed exclusive attitudes on religious, political, and intellectual life equally.

Things had not always been that way. Medieval rulers never exerted the exclusive sovereignty that nation states later claimed: after Thomas à Becket's murder, Henry II of England found that the church's criticisms could shame him into changing policies. Nor was sovereignty necessarily linked to nationhood: the Hapsburgs' subjects spoke not just German, but Polish, Portuguese, Magyar, and Dutch. Nor was religion always and everywhere exclusive. It is our custom to practice one-and-only-one religion, and other people's open-mindedness can be a surprise. Friends from Tokyo who joined us in Chicago for Christmas sang carols at the Fourth Presbyterian Church on Michigan Avenue *from memory*. As they told us, many people in Japan build their lives around ceremonies from several religions. Baptized in Shinto, married in a Christian service, buried as Buddhists: for them, the three religions peaceably coexist.

Nor have philosophers always been exclusive in demanding formal proofs. When things go well, they have no objection to humane arguments: Diderot's *Encyclopedia* shows his passion for the activities and instruments of practical crafts, and his concern for physical theory was purely pragmatic. When things go badly, on the other hand—in the Thirty Years War, the French Revolution, or the First World War—they are again tempted to insist on rigorous geometrical proofs. So, the history of philosophy has been an intellectual see-saw. The Westphalian settlement was, thus, a poisoned chalice—a mixture of intellectual dogmatism, political chauvinism, and sectarian religion whose effect endured into our century. Priestley was right to decline it: the establishment of religion was, indeed, a policy of temporary necessity for countries that had lost their earlier habits of toleration. In 1794, the American Constitution enshrined the values of toleration, and Priestley seized on the opportunities it provided. To be more exact: the Westphalian system *ended* as a poisoned chalice. Initially, all its terms met needs of the time. Sovereign states, established religions, and formal rationality: at the time, all of these served as ways of ordering life and thought and tempering the conflicts among countries and religions. (Again, a parallel with Bosnia and Dayton is to the point.)

From 1650 to 1950, then, the states of Europe lived in an international anarchy: each went its own way, without fear of outside criticism. Established churches were emasculated churches: state and church were tied at the ankles, in a three-legged race that spared any state the indignity of moral reproof. Even in philosophy, the charms of rationalism were reinforced by the needs of the day. Leibniz had hoped that his formal arguments might succeed where diplomacy and war had failed, by ensuring agreement between the rival religions that had devastated his native Germany. But in time, these devices outgrew their initial efficacy, and, at the end of our terrible twentieth century, they need to be reconsidered as new ideas or institutions come on the stage. Above all, the facts of global interdependence are no longer reconcilable with claims to unfettered national sovereignty: especially as such claims are expressed most stridently nowadays by such palpable villains as the military régime in Burma.

For his image of the seventeenth-century sovereign state, Thomas Hobbes chose the sea monster he called the *Leviathan*—a natural image for a theorist from the British Isles: nowadays, a nuclear superpower calls to mind rather a 900-pound gorilla who sleeps wherever he pleases. The general interest lies in *moderating* the force of nation states, not *increasing* it, so we find states joining together in larger units, such as the European Union, which limit their sovereignty. Meanwhile, on a global level, *non*-governmental organizations are becoming more influential, "voluntary associations" of the kind that—as George Abdo points out—

Hobbes himself, sounding for once like the government of Nigeria, called "worms in the intestines of Leviathan" that need to be "purged."[9]

These transnational NGOs remind us of an earlier stage when sovereigns were still subject to reproof. NGOs like Amnesty International are not *emasculated*: as the voice for the conscience of humanity, they keep a distance from national states, which are agents of force. NGOs cannot *force* governments to act as they would please, but in suitable cases they can *shame* them into changing policies: they thus recall that the *politics of shame* which the church used to reprove Henry II is sometimes as effective as the *politics of force*. Here again, the Westphalian system has outlived its efficacy, and the older tension between the church and the state is reemerging on a new level. From now on, the governments of states need to retune their ears and listen to those unofficial institutions that speak not for the special interests of any particular nation or party but for "the decent opinion of humankind."

IV

In closing this discussion, I have three chief points to make: first, we must not unthinkingly assume that dissenters, as such, are dissidents. We too easily conclude that we need not listen to those groups that "cause trouble"—Islamic militants, maybe—instead of recognizing that they may end by causing trouble *just because* we refuse to listen to them. Having begun as "dissenters," they become "dissidents" in despair that their views will not otherwise be heard. For those who learned from the Thirty Years War, it is no longer permissible to make religious or ideological differences a *casus belli;* and for serious politicians in the United States to speak of this country as involved in a religious war is a mark either of ignorance or of irresponsibility.

Second, we cannot safely leave the building of what is now known as "civil society" to the governments of separate existing states that serve as (e.g.) member states of the United Nations, for that would perpetuate the top-down relations of the Westphalian system. States and the power they wield will not, of course, disappear overnight, nor is it wholly desirable that they should do. But increasingly, their powers will be qualified and criticized by other rival global or transnational organizations that link together people in different countries, as subscribers to Amnesty International or whatever. As time goes on, indeed, it becomes ever harder for states to control the activities of the transnational organizations: Leviathan can no longer "purge the worms" from its intestines. Here, the renewed revolution in communications has a part to play in overcoming the international anarchy of the Westphalian system. The Soviet government's monopoly of power was undermined by e-mail, and the Beijing government has given up trying to stop the transmission of faxes to China from other countries: so, too, the Internet—particularly the World Wide Web—is becoming a main locus of transnational communication and institution-building. Ever since the 1992 United Nations meeting on Environment and Development at Rio de Janeiro, the Association for Progressive Communication has provided a channel of communication and exchange of views to non-governmental agencies and individuals on a transnational basis, and these channels serve as foundations for a civil society that has a power to bind together peoples and groups that were kept apart by the exclusivity of the Westphalian tradition. (In this we hear echoes of Schiller and Beethoven's "Ode to Joy": *deine Zauber binden wieder / was der Mode Schwert geteilt.*[10])

Finally, for Joseph Priestley, what made the country we call the United States extraordinary in 1794 is the chance it had to escape horrors to which more ordinary countries were exposed. But it had this chance *only* to the extent that it understood the inevitable failure of any established religion, maintained its policy of religious toleration, and held at bay all the temptations of religious and cultural particularism. The rhetoric of "Americanism"—all attempts to impose ideological conditions on the opinions and activities of America's citizens—thus undermines the central ideals on which the country was built by Thomas Jefferson and his colleagues.

America's poets have captured these truths. Listen, for one, to Wallace Stevens. Writing early in World War II, near the end of his *Notes toward a Supreme Fiction*, he refers to the contrast between reasonableness and rationality I have emphasized here. For him, too, reasonableness is more important than rationality, and its importance is itself more than an intellectual one. It is the expression—as he puts it—of a "more than rational distortion, / the fiction that results from feeling."[11] I recall one of my Chicago colleagues lecturing on the theme, "Is it *rational* to act *reasonably*?" Unless reasonable actions could be proved to fit his abstract moral theory with geometrical precision, respect for human frailty was for him intellectually suspect. Yet, rather than ask, "Is it rational to be reasonable?", we might instead ask, "Is it *reasonable* to argue in *rational* terms alone? In what situations can we reasonably rely on formal theories?" Since 1960, we have seen a turn of the tide, which at last lets us overcome this tension. As technological skills in engineering and medicine meet the limits of practical wisdom, we are learning to match the virtuosity of the exact sciences with the reasonable claims of human need. These days we are *not*—as some will argue—confronting the *end* of Modernity so much as its *fulfillment*. Rationality did not fail us. It was just that, in a technological age, we did not always ask when or how far formal calculations alone can give us humanly relevant answers, and when or how far practical circumstances leave room to pursue or balance legitimate interests in their human detail.

We too easily forget how recent this change is. Forty years ago, you could read the *Washington Post* or the *Chicago Tribune* a whole month without finding any articles about moral issues in medical practice: nowadays, such issues are raised every week. It is not that clinical medicine is now less ethical, but that medicine can no longer be—as we used to say— "clinically detached." We now understand the part that lay people have to play in helping to resolve moral problems in medicine. Increasingly, clinical practice requires a moral analysis of particular cases; and, as the old maxim has it, the Devil lies in the details. So, when physicians today face moral problems, they cannot fasten their eyes on a disciplinary high road and plug straight ahead. More and more, they have to recognize that other parties to any case— a patient's parents, or life partner, or spiritual adviser—need to be *listened to*, since the stakes they have in these issues are not merely legitimate, but crucial.

The key word here is, once again, *listen*. Rachel Carson's *Silent Spring* appeared thirty-five years ago, in 1962, at a time when the role of ecology in politics was near to zero. By now, the environmental effect of technological projects can raise problems of global concern, and no self-respecting government lacks an agency to deal with these issues. Figuring how to build a dam at this or that location calls for *rational* virtuosity, but the decision to build such a dam at all—asking if we can *reasonably* accept its side effects—does not call for calculations alone. As in medicine, the Devil lies in the details, and the voices we must listen to most carefully are those of all the other human beings who will be on the receiving end of those side effects.

To sum up, like the uniqueness of names, the individuality or particularity of cases and characters divides the world of practice, in its actuality, from the world of theory, with its abstractions. Behind the contrast of the reasonable and the rational, behind the rival attractions of nation state and global future, underlying the survival in a time of general toleration of the things Jefferson called *bigotry* and *priestcraft*, lie abstractions that may still tempt us back into the dogmatism, chauvinism, and sectarianism our needs have outgrown. To this extent, the conflict between Joseph Priestley and his English enemies is alive today, even on American soil. Nor is this conflict likely to be resolved *permanently*. It is another of those conflicts that demand eternal vigilance. So listen again to Wallace Stevens, writing in 1942:

> They will get it straight one day at the Sorbonne.
> We shall return at twilight from the lecture
> Pleased that the irrational is rational. . . .

> ———

> Soldier, there is a war between the mind
> And sky, between thought and day and night. It is
> For that the poet is always in the sun,

> Patches the moon together in his room
> To his Virgilian cadences, up down,
> Up down. It is a war that never ends.[12]

Notes

[1] This essay was delivered on 24 March 1997, at the Kennedy Center, Washington, D.C., as the National Endowment for the Humanities Thomas Jefferson Lecture.

[2] Letter from Thomas Jefferson to Joseph Priestley, March 21, 1801. See Thomas Jefferson, *Works*, ed. Paul Leicester Ford (New York: G. P. Putnam's sons, 1904-5), iv: 373.

[3] Joseph Priestley, *A History of the Corruptions of Christianity* (London, 1782). See also Daniel Boorstin, *The Lost World of Thomas Jefferson* (Boston: Henry Holt, 1948), 151-66, esp. 158.

[4] Thucydides, *History of the Peloponnesian War*, *The Greek Historians*, trans. Benjamin Jowett, 2 vols. (New York: Random House, 1942), I.850 (Book V: chapters 84-114, quotation from 116).

[5] Thomas Jefferson, *Writings*, ed. Andrew A. Lipscomb (Washington, D.C.: Thomas Jefferson Memorial Association, 1907), xiv: 149.

[6] The English writer V.S. Pritchett died on 20 March 1997; Eudora Welty's comment is quoted in the *New York Times* obituary, 22 March 1997, p. 14, col. 1.

[7] Richard Watson, "On the Zeedijk," *The Georgia Review*, XLIII: 1 (Spring 1989), 24. This essay describes Descartes' stay at Franeker in Northern Holland, to which he retreated in late 1628 to escape growing religious intolerance in France.

[8] For Voltaire's full wording, see *Letters concerning the English Nation*, Letter XIV, "On Des Cartes and Sir Isaac Newton." The first paragraph begins, "A FRENCHMAN who arrives in London, will find Philosophy, like every Thing else, very much chang'd there. He had left the World a *plenum*, and he now finds it a *vacuum*."

[9] Cf. Thomas Hobbes, *Leviathan*, ed. Richard E. Flathman and David Johnston (New York: Norton, 1997), chap. XXIX, "Of those things that Weaken, or tend to the DISSOLUTION of a Commonwealth": "Corporations [as he calls 'voluntary associations'] are as it were many lesser Commonwealths in the bowels of a greater, like wormes in the entrayles of a naturall man" (169), and should be treated accordingly.

[10] Friedrich Schiller, "An die Freude," *Sämtliche Werke* (München, 1962), vol. 1, "Gedichte 1782-1788," 133-6.

[11] Wallace Stevens, *Notes toward a Supreme Fiction*, Pt. III ("It must give pleasure"), sec. x, ll. 14-5, *Collected Poetry and Prose*, ed. Frank Kermode and Joan Richardson (New York: Library of America, 1997).

[12] III.x.16-8, and Conclusion, 1-6.

Transgression, Punishment, Responsibility, Forgiveness

Joan Gardy Artigas

JOAN GARDY ARTIGAS (b. 1938) is a living embodiment of the modernist art movement. The son of Josep Llorens Artigas, Picasso's and Miró's favorite ceramicist, Artigas grew up surrounded by both the art and the artists who revolutionized twentieth-century art. Impressed into service as Miró's assistant as a teenager, he left Spain several years later both to escape the oppressive Franco regime and to try and establish an independent artistic identity. After a period as a student at the Ecole des Beaux Arts in Paris, he became friends with the sculptor Alberto Glacometti in Paris and, opening a ceramics atelier in Paris, worked with Georges Braques and Marc Chagall. When his father became too frail to work, Miró called him back to Spain and a twenty-year partnership—broken only by Miró's declining health in 1981—ensued. The fruits of this partnership can be seen in large ceramic murals and sculptures all over the world including ceramic murals for Harvard University, UNESCO (Paris), Fondation Maeght (St. Paul), the 1970 World's Fair in Osaka, the Barcelona airport, the Kunsthaus in Zurich, the Haack Museum (Ludwigshafen), IBM Headquarters (Barcelona), and a 60-meter ceramic mural for the Palais des Expositions et des Congres de Madrid, He and Miró also collaborated on a 22-meter ceramic sculpture for a fountain in Barcelona.

In addition to his work with Miró, he has made a number of monumental public sculptures including a monumental work in Zurich, a large fountain for Vitry-sur-Seine, *La Porta Blanca*, an 8.5-meter cement and bronze sculpture for Chamonix, *Forma de dona* for Plateau d'Assy, *Porta per una ciutat*, an 11-meter scupture outside Barcelona, *La porta de Franca,* a 15-meter sculpture on the French side of the tunnel at Mont-Blanc, *Terra I foc*, a 15-meter work for "la Caixa," Barcelona, and works for Dallas, Atlanta, Miami, London, the Fonda Europa de Granollers, Barcelona, and the Fundació Pilar I Joan Miró in Palma de Mallorca, and sculpture gardens in London and Tokyo. He also participated in several architectural projects with the firm of Skidmore Owings, and Merrill, making ceramic floors and fountains in Atlanta, Chicago, Cairo, Egypt. Artigas began exhibiting his own smaller ceramic and bronze sculptures in France and Spain during the mid-1960s and began making lithographs and etchings in 1968. He has had a number of commissions for large public sculptures (in bronze, ceramics, and concrete) in Europe, Japan, and the U.S. and has had shows in many European, Japanese, and American galleries and museums, including The Meadows Museum of Spanish Art at Southern Methodist University in Dallas, the Hispanic Institute in New York, and Galerie Lelong in Paris. A major retrospective of his works in all media was held at the Tecla Sala Centre Cultural in Barcelona in 1996 and a large exhibition documenting Miró's collaborations with Josep Llorens Artigas and Joan Gardy Artigas was held at the Fundació Pilar I Joan Miró in Palma de Mallorca in 1998.

He has been a visting artist at the UW–Madison, and the University of Nebraska–Lincoln. In 1989 he created the Fundació Tallers Josep Llorens Artigas in Gallifa, Spain in memory of his father and to provide a place where artists from all parts of the world come together to work for a period of up to six months.

Of this year's featured print, Artigas says he made a work in four parts to convey the quadripartite topic of the issue. (When it comes to transgression, Artigas knows whereof he speaks: at a party celebrating his twenty-first birthday, he accepted a dare to assassinate one of Salvador Dalí's trademark mustaches and unrepentently dispatched the offending extravagance of waxed hair.)

Joan Gardy Artigas and John Himmelfarb
(1994)

Composition
Drawing (1996)
Image size 148x100mm

Homage to Brancusi
Ceramic Sculpture (1983)
280x100x110cm

Angel of Death
Original etching (1974)
Image size 393x297mm

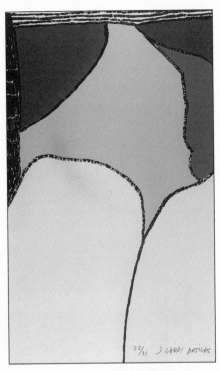

Geography of Desire
Original lithograph (1979)
Image size 501x322mm

Composition I
Drawing (1982)
Image size 320x408mm

Tryptique
Acrylic on board (1994)
3 pieces, Image size 180x120mm

Element for a Police Dossier
Original lithograph (1977)
Image size 385x545mm

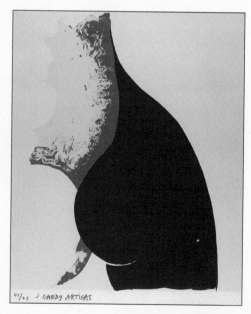

Porta per a una ciutat
Autopista A-17, km 78,5
Concrete: height 11 meters

Black Thigh
Original lithograph (1968)
Image size 400x365mm

Eroticizing the World[1]

Joan Gardy Artigas

First, I believe that a person is an artist not necessarily by the grace of God—but, well yes . . . by genetics . . . by force of character. Then . . . given that anything is possible and that everything has already been done, that we have had a total liberty to create since Dada and Duchamp (there's nothing left to destroy), that the academy and academics are totally outdated . . . Then (given all this) . . . the artist has to choose [what] (a subject) and [how] (a technique).

It is rare to find great works in the history of art that do not have at their origin a profound motivation, be it religious, nationalistic, social, or even personal. In my case, the choice was made almost "automatically." Not being a believer, God could not help me. Not having any particular political sympathies because I am too critical of all of them, I could not be nationalistic. The creative adventure, then, became for me one of *eroticizing the world:* this desire, nonetheless, attenuated by something I have inherited from my father and from Miró, a taste for work and the pleasure of the raw materials of my work.

For me, it is evident that you cannot do the game work, create the same piece twice with earth, stone, and bronze. Each materia, having its own characteristics, must be respected for its individuality. If you sculpt the same piece twice with different materials, one of these will undoubtedly be bad and it will also be the one that did not take into consideration the possibilities of the material chosen. (In other words, you cannot play the same music on any kind of instrument.)

So—for any beginning artist, especially a sculptor, the fundamental problem is that of choosing the kind of medium in which to work. This might not be the essential problem, but it is the one which will determine all his or her future creations. He might therefore say that it *is*, indeed, the essential problem.

Now—why eroticize the world? If I were not Spanish, educated during the reign of Franco, in a Catholic environment in a state of extreme decadence, with institutionalized intolerance all around me, perhaps I would not be the artist I am with the concerns I have. But it *was* like that and I *am* who I am.

I eroticize the world to de-dramatize the subject, to strike down taboos, to prove that what "they" told us was ugly is, in fact, beautiful. I eroticize the world—especially—to take on a dangerous subject. There is no "beauty" without ulterior motives. There is no longer ugliness *or* beauty, good or evil; THERE IS, that is all. And sex (and sexuality) exist—they are approached differently according to different countries, different cultures—but everywhere sex is immense, the source of the future, of beauty, of passion.

And as for the "subject": if the artist has a personality the subject must disappear in the work (otherwise the result is decoration, "decorative art"). When Giacometti sculpts a woman, the result is a sculpture by Giacometti, not a woman. We learn more about Giacometti from that sculpture than about the woman sculpted by him. The subject must serve only as a support, a point of reference: that is why almost all artists willingly limit their choice of subject matter—to give them more strength. The goal, then, is not the beautiful but the true and not truth in the eyes of others but truth in regard to oneself.

For a plastic artist, it is not a matter of speaking but of doing. The work only exists when *it exists,* because if it is only spoken about, it remains literary, which in my opinion is a serious error. To speak or to do, the ephemeral or the concrete: there is not much to say but so much to do. I think that every work which has ever been *created* takes much greater effort to be destroyed. That is, after creation the work has its own life which totally escapes the artist, and . . . that is good because that is what permits him or her to advance, to progress. Using as a

Transgression, Punishment, Responsibility, Forgiveness
Graven Images 4 (1998), 279-280.

base a definite knowledge, a definite mastery of the métier, every creator must subvert the subject. It's a matter of breaking the structure—but this is based on " . . . ." When the surrealists speak about assassinating painting, it's obvious that the " . . . " is the basis or point of departure for the assassination because their means of expression *is* painting or literature.

Just as the choice of subject presents itself so does the choice of techniques. One must ask: "For this project, should I transform it into a sculpture, a drawing, an engraving, or a lithograph?" At this point one's mastery of techniques comes into play. If I want power, impact, a startling image, I use lithography. With the technique of printing directly off the stone, it is possible to get a maximum of ink on the paper. This direct impression from stone or zinc allows the kind of powerful color that is impossible to get with an off-set process. (Think, for example, of the strength of Toulouse Lautrec's posters.)

If, on the other hand, I want a secret image with a magic quality, I turn to etching. The pressure of the damp paper will insure that the intensity of the black, the relief of the features etched on the copper will remain on the paper, giving it a richness and a finesse that forces us to look closely at it, making us wish to hold the etching in our hands, to feel the quality of the paper. The result is a work more secret, more intimate—more precious.

When the concern is creating a sculpture for a specific location, it is obvious that the first thing to do is to study the site. An urban landscape, the open-air environment of the country, a highway, a huge space or a small one sets the conditions for the sculpture—both its dimensions and its form, even its color. The sculpture can be implanted by opposition to the environment as well as through integration with it. In fact, the location, the site, dictates at least 50% of what the work will be; but it is always, in the end, based on that " . . . ." A " . . ." that, little by little, bit by bit, because of the work undertaken, grows and becomes richness itself.

To conclude, if there were a magic key to open doors and explain everything I do, it would be the one opening onto hard work and the pleasure of doing and of choosing an ambitious project. And a sense of humor, too—because, after all, we should not forget that none of this is very serious.

Notes

[1] This is the translated text of a speech delivered by Joan Gardy Artigas at the Elvehjem Museum of Art of the University of Wisconsin–Madison on 3 May 1982. It is reprinted here by the permission of the artist and the translator, Judith G. Miller.

The Fires of the Spirit

Joan Gardy Artigas[1]

From the deep, gloomy cavern black smoke issues forth. It is the dark, greasy soot of the paintings of early times. It is the black of Joan Miró.

From the still, stinking, putrid waters, a clay-like mud is spawned: flat molecules which enable the earth we tread to conserve its malleable shape, the first medium to be modelled, a creative act even earlier than the first drawings.

Crossing millions of years, from before time could be calculated, the dawn rays of the first lights reach us.

The whites are chalk, lime, milk and paper.

Red is blood, lava in fusion, the cockerel's comb, the energy and uncontrolled force which, with its creative power will transform this putrid clay into a stone harder than steel: a chemical transformation accompanied by huge, barely understood, cataclysmic phemonena. This is nothing frivolous. The mediocre, please salute!

Blue is the colour of the ocean, of cobalt, of endless skies. That blue ocean inhibited by cartilaginous monsters, foul reptiles and nameless animals. The cradle of life. Ulysses sailing along, the huge, ever-vigilant eye of Polyphemus.

Green is the colour of our fields, the almond trees in spring, cypresses, olive and carob trees, copper and bile.

Yellow is the colour of sunlight, gold, urine and uranium: the latter needed to make yellows for earthenware ceramics . . . and also needed for bombs.

This is the world of the Miró-Artigas ceramics. I would not actually dare to say that they are pretty, but I can assure you they contain all of the magic and mystery that their creative process involved, all the enigmas that the making of artisanal ceramics entails, all the necessary mess and motivation required to make the work of art actually exist, that mysterious, convulsive force that makes art so difficult to define and so clear when we find ourselves faced with a genuine work of art. What are the rules? Where does the truth lie?

Once again, this is nothing frivolous.

The mediocre, please salute one more time!

When the sun heats the earth enough to make us forget our wretched condition, our problems, our daily to-ing and fro-ing, when the light is strong enough to make us close our eyes, the possibility of creation rears its head, glazes fuse together, ceramicists burn. When the mediocrity of man can be overcome by the spirit, the artist emerges.

Let us then take our hats off to these exceptional moments that lead to the creation of a work of art, with their powers to subvert, with their power of truth which broaden our horizons and open our eyes to poetry, to the spirit and to the possibility of overcoming which, in the end, makes this grotesque human adventure worth living.

Gallifa 1998

---

[1] First published in *Miró-Artigas Cerámiques* (Mallorca: Fundació Pilar i Joan Miró, 1998), 104. Reprinted with permission of the author.

Juan Gardy Llorens Artigas

John Himmelfarb

As a young person, I was greatly pained to find that authors, composers or other artists whose work I greatly admired, and whose artistic voice spoke with warmth, wisdom, and charm, were, in their day-to-day dealings, difficult and possibly very unpleasant people. As I became an artist myself, I came to accept that one's work might be better than one's temperament or character. I would like to point out that in the case of Juan Gardy Llorens Artigas (Joan Gardy Artigas), the person and the person's work are one. I don't know who is responsible for this, but his artistic point of view matches well his own character. If this issue of *Graven Images* is your first experience with the works of Juan Gardy Llorens Artigas, I wish you many more. If, by some accident of time and space, you later find yourself face to face in dialog with the artist rather than his work, you will at once recognize him.

JGLA grew up in the glow of European Modernism, helping his father and his father's friends in their studios. No doubt you have read elsewhere how he was raised on the knee of Joan Miró, his parents' close friend, and how he met and worked with many other fine artists of international repute, not the least of whom was his father Josep.[1] In the last forty years, Juan Gardy Llorens Artigas has energetically and without hesitation built his own realms of imagery and abstraction. These do not rebel against the patriarchs, nor do they imitate them.

While Artigas pays sufficient homage to European art history to have his place in its successions, his extensive knowledge of Asian, African and Western Hemispheric traditions is delightfully evident in his work. The Isms and Schisms since Modernism he knows all about. Although he is a little vague about conceptualism, he was post-modern before the first post was put in the ground. He puts these resources together with direct and elegant formalism. The result is idiosyncratic works whose grace and nuance catch me by surprise and make me smile.

What I find *missing* from his work, and I say this with the authority of one who has seen his mid-career retrospective at Barcelona's *Tecla*, is didactic politics. Neither Marxism nor capitalism—not even rugged individualism *über alles*. No promises, no threats. Instead, you will be moved by a combination of empathy and horror, joy and romance in his unsentimental depiction of us and our world. Humanism without apology. I guess that *is* politics. And it is not a pose.

When his father died, Artigas decided to create a place to honor his father's memory where artists from around the world could come to work together, much as they had come to his father's studio during his lifetime. JGLA has devoted years of his time and energy to this project. The resulting Josep Llorens Artigas Workshop and Foundation is now ten years old.[2] Artists from all over the world have come to work there and have derived great benefit from the opportunity. I am happy to say that I am one of those artists. Many people devote themselves to self-promotion, thanking no one for their support and in turn lending none to others. For these, if they were ever aware of others, JGLA's example would be a prick on the conscience. His reward is not only in his many friends and admirers, but also in the beauty of his work. This beauty is not to be confused with the word "pretty." While restless with all that remains to be done, the art of Juan Gardy Llorens Artigas radiates the inner satisfaction gained from his work to honor the past and share the future. Thanks, Artigas!

---

[1] For an introduction to the works of Josep Llorens Artigas, see Francesc Miralles: *Artigas: Catalogue de l'oeuvre personnel et créations avec Dufy, Marquet, Miró* (Paris: Editions Cercle d'Art, 1993).

[2] For plans, models, and photographs of the Josep Llorens Artigas Foundation Studio, see Bruce Graham, *Bruce Graham of SOM* (NY: Rizzoli, 1989), 112-5.

Contributors

Joan Gardy Artigas, creator of *Transgression, Punishment, Responsibility, Forgiveness* (an original color lithograph included in the deluxe version of this issue and reproduced on our back cover), is founder of the Fondació Tallers J. Llorens Artigas in Gallifa, Spain..

Jonathan Boyarin is an associate in the tax department at the law firm of Debevoise & Plimpton. New York, NY.

Rachel Feldhay Brenner is Associate Professor of Hebrew and Semitic Studies at the University of Wisconsin, Madison.

Robert A. Burt is Alexander M. Bickel Professor of Law, Yale University.

Clare Cavanagh is Associate Professor of Slavic Languages at Northwestern University.

Robert J. De Smith is Associate Professor of English at Dordt College.

Michal Govrin an Israeli novelisit; her novel, *The Name*, has just been published in an English translation.

Sonja Hansard-Weiner is Instructor of English and Women's Studies at Madison Area Technical College.

Ronald Harris is Assistant Professor of English, Southeastern Louisiana University.

John Himmelfarb, creator of the work reproduced on our front cover, is represented by the Steinbaum-Krauss Gallery in New York and numerous other galleries in the U.S.

Roy Jacobstein is a physician; his poems have appeared in a number of journals.

Lee Johnson is Professor of English at the University of British Columbia, Vancouver, Canada.

Leonard V. Kaplan is Professor of Law and Jewish Studies at the University of Wisconsin, Madison.

David Kennedy is Professor of Law at Harvard University.

Heinz Klug is Assistant Professor of Law at the University of Wisconsin, Madison.

Judith G. Miller is Director, New York University in Paris.

Stephen J. Morse is Professor of Law at the University of Pennsylvania.

Carl Rasmussen is a partner in the law firm of Boardman Suhr Curry & Field, Madison WI.

Gary Rosenshield is Professor of Slavic Languages and Literatures and Jewish Studies at the University of Wisconsin, Madison.

Eric Rothstein is Edgar W. Lacy Professor of English at the University of Wisconsin–Madison.

Thomas L. Shaffer is Professor of Law at Notre Dame University.

Andrew W. Siegel is Staff Philosopher, National Bioethics Advisory Commission.

Glori Simmons teaches writing at the University of San Francisco; her poems have appeared in a number of journals.

David R. Slavitt is Lecturer in English at the University of Pennsylvania; Oxford University Press just published his translation, *61Psalms of David*.

Wisława Szymborska was awarded the Nobel Prize in Literature in 1996.

Leonard L. Thompson is Professor Emeritus of Religious Studies, Lawrence University.

Stephen Toulmin is Henry R. Luce Professor at the Center for Multiethnic and Transnational Studies, University of Southern California.

Andrew D. Weiner is Professor of English at the University of Wisconsin–Madison.

Brenda Wineapple is Washington Irving Professor of Modern Literary and Historical Studies at Union College and Co-Director of the New York University Biography Seminar.

Elliot R. Wolfson is Professor of Hebrew and Semitic Studies at New York University.